NINTH CANADIAN EDITION

VOLUME II

Fundamental Accounting Principles

NINTH CANADIAN EDITION

VOLUME II

Fundamental Accounting Principles

Kermit D. Larson
University of Texas—Austin

John J. Wild
University of Wisconsin at Madison

Barbara Chiappetta
Nassau Community College

Morton Nelson
Wilfrid Laurier University

Ray F. Carroll
Dalhousie University

Michael Zin
Professor Emeritus
University of Windsor

McGraw-Hill Ryerson

Toronto Montreal New York Burr Ridge Bangkok Bogotá
Caracas Lisbon London Madrid Mexico City Milan New Delhi
Seoul Singapore Sydney Taipei

McGraw-Hill
Ryerson Limited

A Subsidiary of The ***McGraw-Hill*** *Companies*

FUNDAMENTAL ACCOUNTING PRINCIPLES
Volume II
Ninth Canadian Edition

ISBN: 0-07-560478-7

1 2 3 4 5 6 7 8 9 10 GTC 8 7 6 5 4 3 2 1 0 9

Printed and bound in Canada

Sponsoring Editor: *Jennifer Dewey/Lisa Feil*
Developmental Editor: *Denise McGuinness*
Senior Supervising Editor: *Margaret Henderson*
Production Editor: *Shirley Corriveau*
Production Co-ordinator: *Nicla Dattolico*
Interior Design: *Ellen Pentengell*
Cover Design: *Liz Harasymczuk*
Cover Illustration: *Dave Cutler/SIS©*
Page Make-up: *Valerie Bateman/ArtPlus Limited*
Typeface: *Times Roman*
Printer: *Transcontinental*

Canadian Cataloguing in Publication Data

Main entry under title:

Fundamental accounting principles

9th Canadian ed.
Fourth Canadian ed. written by W.W. Pyle, K.D. Larson and M. Zin.
Includes index.

ISBN 0-07-560477-9 (v.I) ISBN 0-07-560478-7 (v.II)
ISBN 0-07-560479-5 (v.III)

1. Accounting. I. Larson, Kermit D.

HF5635.P975 1998 657 C98-932756-6

Contents in Brief

Preface

Part I *Financial Reporting and the Accounting Cycle*

Chapter 1 Accounting in the Information Age 2
Chapter 2 Financial Statements and Accounting Transactions 42
Chapter 3 Analyzing and Recording Transactions 96
Chapter 4 Adjusting Accounts for Financial Statements 150
Chapter 5 Completing the Accounting Cycle and Classifying Accounts 204

Part II *Accounting for Operating Activities*

Chapter 6 Accounting for Merchandising Activities 257
Chapter 7 Merchandise Inventories and Cost of Sales 316
Chapter 8 Accounting Information Systems 364

Part III *Accounting for Investing and Financing Activities*

Chapter 9 Internal Control and Cash 422
Chapter 10 Receivables and Temporary Investments 472
Chapter 11 Payroll Liabilities 520
Chapter 12 Capital Assets: Plant and Equipment, Natural Resources, and Intangible Assets 556
Chapter 13 Current and Long-Term Liabilities 614

Part IV *Accounting for Partnerships and Corporations*

Chapter 14 Partnerships 660
Chapter 15 Corporations 692
Chapter 16 Corporate Reporting: Dividends, Shares, and Income 730
Chapter 17 Bonds and Long-Term Notes Payable 778
Chapter 18 Long-Term Investments and International Accounting 830

Part V *Analysis of Accounting Information*

Chapter 19 Reporting and Analyzing Cash Flows 874
Chapter 20 Analyzing Financial Statements 938

Part VI *Managerial Accounting and Product Costing*

Chapter 21 Managerial Accounting Concepts and Principles 990
Chapter 22 Manufacturing and Job Order Costing 1034
Chapter 23 Process Cost Accounting 1104
Chapter 24 Cost Allocation and Performance 1154

Part VII *Cost Planning and Control*

Chapter 25 Cost-Volume-Profit Analysis 1204
Chapter 26 Master Budgets and Planning 1244
Chapter 27 Flexible Budgets and Standard Costs 1292

Part VIII *Strategic Analysis in Managerial and Cost Accounting*

Chapter 28 Capital Budgeting and Managerial Decisions 1342

Appendix I Financial Statements I-1
Alliance I-1
Atlantis I-34

Appendix II Present and Future Values II-1

Appendix III Accounting Concepts and Alternative Valuations III-1

Codes of Professional Conduct CPC-1

Chart of Accounts CH-1

Credits CR-1

Index IND-1

Contents

Preface ix

Chapter 12 Capital Assets: Plant and Equipment, Natural Resources, and Intangible Assets 556

Section 1—Capital Assets: Property, Plant, and Equipment 558
Cost of Capital Assets 559
Land 560
Land Improvements 560
Buildings 560
Machinery and Equipment 561
Lump-Sum Asset Purchase 561
Amortization 562
Factors in Computing Amortization 562
Amortization Methods 563
Partial Year Amortization 569
Revising Amortization Rates 569
Reporting Amortization on Assets 570
Mid-Chapter Demonstration Problem 572
Solution to Mid-Chapter Demonstration Problem 572
Revenue and Capital Expenditures 572
Repairs 573
Betterments 573
Low-Cost Asset Purchases 574
Disposals of Capital Assets 574
Discarding Capital Assets 575
Selling Capital Assets 576
Exchanging Capital Assets 577
Section 2—Natural Resources 582
Acquisition Cost and Depletion 582
Capital Assets Used in Extracting Resources 583
Section 3—Intangible Assets 583
Accounting for Intangible Assets 583
Patents 584
Copyrights 585
Leaseholds 585
Leasehold Improvements 586
Goodwill 586
Trademarks and Trade Names 587
Cash Flow Impacts of Capital Assets 588
Using the Information—Total Asset Turnover 588
Summary 590
Demonstration Problem 592
Planning the Solution 593
Solution to Demonstration Problem 594
Glossary 596
Questions 597
Quick Study 597
Exercises 599
Problems 602
Alternate Problems 606
Analytical and Review Problems 610
Beyond the Numbers 611

Chapter 13 Current and Long-Term Liabilities 614

Characteristics of Liabilities 616
Defining Liabilities 616
Classifying Liabilities as Current or Long-Term 616
Uncertainty in Liabilities 617
Known (Determinable) Liabilities 618
Accounts Payable 618
Goods and Services Tax and Sales Taxes Payable 618
Unearned Revenues 619
Short-Term Notes Payable 619
Estimated Liabilities 624
Warranty Liabilities 624
Income Tax Liabilities for Corporations 625
Deferred (Future) Income Tax Liabilities for Corporations 626
Contingent Liabilities 627
Accounting for Contingent Liabilities 627
Examples of Contingent Liability Disclosures 628
Mid-Chapter Demonstration Problem 630

Solution to Mid-Chapter Demonstration Problem 630
Long-Term Liabilities 630
Present Value Concepts 630
Applying Present Value Concepts to Long-Term Notes 634
Known (Determinable) Long-Term Liabilities 637
Estimated Long-Term Liabilities 638
Contingent Long-Term Liabilities 638
Using the Information—Times Interest Earned 638
Summary 640
Demonstration Problem 642
Planning the Solution 643
Solution to Demonstration Problem 643
Glossary 645
Questions 645
Quick Study 646
Exercises 647
Problems 649
Alternate Problems 652
Analytical and Review Problems 654
Comprehensive Problem 655
Beyond the Numbers 657

Chapter 14 Partnerships 660

Partnership Form of Organization 662
Characteristics of General Partnerships 662
Basic Partnership Accounting 664
Organizing a Partnership 665
Dividing Income or Loss 665
Partnership Financial Statements 668
Mid-Chapter Demonstration Problem 669
Solution to Mid-Chapter Demonstration Problem 669
Admission and Withdrawal of Partners 669
Admission of a Partner 669
Withdrawal of a Partner 671
Death of a Partner 672
Liquidation of a Partnership 673
No Capital Deficiency 673
Capital Deficiency 674
Summary 675
Demonstration Problem 677
Planning the Solution 677
Solution to Demonstration Problem 678
Glossary 679
Questions 680
Quick Study 680
Exercises 681
Problems 683
Alternate Problems 686
Analytical and Review Problems 689
Beyond the Numbers 690

Chapter 15 Corporations 692

Corporate Form of Organization 694
Characteristics of Corporations 694
Organizing a Corporation 696
Management of a Corporation 698
Rights of Shareholders 699
Shares of a Corporation 699
Basics of Capital Stock 700
Shareholders' Equity 702
Common Shares 702
Issuing Shares 702
Mid-Chapter Demonstration Problem 704
Solution to Mid-Chapter Demonstration Problem 704
Issuing Shares through Subscriptions 704
Preferred Shares 704
Issuing Preferred Shares 705
Dividend Preference 705
Convertible Preferred Shares 707
Callable Preferred Shares 708
Motivation for Preferred Shares 708
Using the Information—Book Value per Share 710
Summary 712
Demonstration Problem 713
Planning the Solution 713
Solution to Demonstration Problem 714
Glossary 715
Questions 716
Quick Study 716
Exercises 717
Problems 719
Alternate Problems 723
Analytical and Review Problem 727
Beyond the Numbers 728

Chapter 16 Corporate Reporting: Dividends, Shares, and Income 730

Dividends 732
Cash Dividends 732
Stock Dividends 734

Stock Splits 738
Reacquisition of Shares 739
Purchasing Treasury Shares 740
Reissuing Treasury Shares 741
Mid-Chapter Demonstration Problem 743
Solution to Mid-Chapter Demonstration Problem 743
Reporting Income Information 744
Continuing Operations 744
Discontinued Segments 744
Extraordinary Items 745
Changes in Accounting Principles 746
Earnings Per Share 748
Stock Options 751
Retained Earnings 751
Restricted Retained Earnings 752
Appropriated Retained Earnings 752
Prior Period Adjustments 752
Changes in Accounting Estimates 753
Statement of Changes in Shareholders' Equity 753
Using the Information—Dividend Yield and the Price-Earnings Ratio 754
Dividend Yield 754
Price-Earnings 754
Summary 756
Demonstration Problem 758
Planning the Solution 759
Solution to Demonstration Problem 759
Glossary 760
Questions 761
Quick Study 761
Exercises 762
Problems 765
Alternate Problems 770
Analytical and Review Problems 775
Beyond the Numbers 776

Chapter 17 Bonds and Long-Term Notes Payable 778

Basics of Bonds 780
Bond Financing 780
Types of Bonds 781
Bond Trading 783
Bond Issuing Procedures 783
Bond Issuances 784
Issuing Bonds at Par 784
Determining Bond Discount or Premium 785
Issuing Bonds at a Discount 786
Amortizing a Bond Discount 787
Issuing Bonds at a Premium 790
Amortizing a Bond Premium 791
Mid-Chapter Demonstration Problem 793
Solution to Mid-Chapter Demonstration Problem 793
Issuing Bonds between Interest Dates 793
Accruing Bond Interest Expense 794
Bond Pricing 795
Bond Retirements 797
Bond Retirement at Maturity 797
Bond Retirement before Maturity 797
Bond Retirement by Conversion of Shares 798
Long-Term Notes Payable 798
Interest-Bearing Notes 799
Non-interest-Bearing Notes 799
Installment Notes 801
Mortgage Notes 805
Using the Information—Pledged Assets to Secured Liabilities 806
Collateral Agreements for Bonds and Notes 806
Ratio of Pledged Assets to Secured Liabilities 807
Summary 808
Demonstration Problem 810
Planning the Solution 810
Solution to Demonstration Problem 810

Appendix 17A—Present Values of Bonds and Notes 812

Glossary 816
Questions 817
Quick Study 817
Exercises 819
Problems 822
Alternate Problems 825
Analytical and Review Problem 827
Beyond the Numbers 827

Chapter 18 Long-Term Investments and International Accounting 830

Classifying Investments 832
Temporary versus Long-Term 832
Classes of Long-Term Investments 832
Long-Term Investments in Securities 833
Investments in Debt Securities Held to Maturity 833
Investment in Equity Securities with Significant

Influence 836
Investment in Equity Securities with Controlling Influence 838
Mid-Chapter Demonstration Problem 839
Planning the Solution 840
Solution to Mid-Chapter Demonstration Problem 840
Investments in International Operations 842
Exchange Rates between Currencies 842
Sales or Purchases Listed in a Foreign Currency 843
Consolidated Statements with International Subsidiaries 844
Using the Information—Components of Return on Total Assets 845
Summary 846
Demonstration Problem 848
Planning the Solution 849
Solution to Demonstration Problem 849

Appendix 18A—Parent and Subsidiary Corporations 851

Glossary 858
Questions 858
Quick Study 859
Exercises 860
Problems 862
Alternate Problems 866
Analytical and Review Problems 870
Beyond the Numbers 871

Chapter 19 Reporting and Analyzing Cash Flows 874

Basics of Cash Flow Reporting 876
Purpose of the Statement of Cash Flows (SCF) 876
Importance of Cash Flows 876
Measuring Cash Flows 877
Classifying Cash Flows 878
Classification Issues 880
Noncash Investing and Financing Activities 880
Format of the Statement of Cash Flows 882
Preparing the Statement of Cash Flows 882
Cash Flows from Operating Activities 885
Methods of Reporting Operating Cash Flows 885
Direct Method of Reporting Operating Cash Flows 888
Mid-Chapter Demonstration Problem 894
Solution to Mid-Chapter Demonstration Problem 895
Indirect Method of Reporting Operating Cash Flows 895
Cash Flows from Investing Activities 901
Capital Asset Transactions 902
Cash Flows from Financing Activities 904
Bonds Payable Transactions 904
Common Shares Transactions 905
Retained Earnings Transactions 905
Proving Cash Balances 906
Using the Information—Cash Flow Analysis 907
Analyzing Cash Sources and Uses 907
Cash Flow on Total Assets 908
Summary 910
Demonstration Problem 912
Planning the Solution 913
Solution to Demonstration Problem 913

Appendix 19A—Using a Spreadsheet to Prepare the Statement of Cash Flows 916

Glossary 919
Questions 920
Quick Study 920
Exercises 923
Problems 928
Alternate Problems 931
Analytical and Review Problems 934
Beyond the Numbers 935

Chapter 20 Analyzing Financial Statements 938

Basics of Analysis 940
Purpose of Analysis 940
Building Blocks of Analysis 941
Information for Analysis 941
Standards for Comparisons 942
Tools of Analysis 943
Horizontal Analysis 943
Comparative Statements 943
Trend analysis 947
Vertical Analysis 949
Common-Size Statements 949
Common-Size Graphics 950
Mid-Chapter Demonstration Problem 952
Planning the Solution 953
Solution to Mid-Chapter Demonstration Problem 954
Ratio Analysis 955
Liquidity and Efficiency 956
Solvency 961
Profitability 962

Market 964
Summary of Ratios 965
Analysis Reporting 966
Summary 967
Demonstration Problem 969
Planning the Solution 970
Solution to Demonstration Problem 970
Glossary 971
Questions 971
Quick Study 972
Exercises 973
Problems 976
Alternate Problems 980
Analytical and Review Problems 984
Beyond the Numbers 986

Appendix I—Financial Statement Information I-1

Appendix II—Present and Future Values II-1

Appendix III—Accounting Concepts and Alternative Valuations III-1

Code of Professional Conduct CPC-1

Chart of Accounts CH-1

Credits CR-1

Index IND-1

Preface

Let's Talk

Through extensive market-based surveys, focus groups, and reviews, we discovered several interests and needs in accounting education today. In a nutshell, these desires can be grouped into eight pedagogical areas: (1) motivation, (2) organization, (3) preparation, analysis, and use, (4) ethics, (5) technology, (6) real world, (7) active learning, and (8) flexibility. Our main goal in this edition of *Fundamental Accounting Principles* (F.A.P.) is to address these needs and create the most contemporary, exciting, relevant, and flexible principles book in the market. A quick summary of these areas follows.

Motivation. Motivation drives learning. From the chapter's opening article and its focus on young entrepreneurs to the decision-making prompted by You Make the Call, **F.A.P.** motivates readers. It brings accounting and business to life and demonstrates that this material can make a difference in your life.

Organization. Organization serves the learning process, and **F.A.P.'s** outstanding organization aids that process. From "Chapter Linkages" and learning objectives to chapter outlines and Flashbacks, **F.A.P.** is the leader in lending readers a helping hand in learning about accounting and business.

Preparation, Analysis, and Use. Accounting involves preparing, analyzing, and using information. **F.A.P.** balances each of these important roles in explaining and illustrating topics. From the unique Using the Information section to the creative Hitting the Road projects, **F.A.P.** shows all aspects of accounting.

Ethics. Ethics is fundamental to accounting. **F.A.P.** highlights the roles of ethics and social responsibility in modern businesses. From the Judgment and Ethics decision-making feature to its Ethics Challenge assignments, **F.A.P.** alerts readers to relevant and important ethical concerns.

Technology. Technology continues to change business and accounting, creating new and exciting accounting opportunities. **F.A.P.** is the leader in applying and showing technology in accounting. From the innovative Taking It to the Net projects to its Web-based assignments, **F.A.P.** pushes the accounting frontiers.

Real World. Accounting is important to the information age. From features and assignments that highlight companies like Alliance Communications Corporation, and Atlantis Communications Inc. to the Teamwork in Action and Communication in Practice activities, **F.A.P**. shows accounting in a modern, global context. It also engages both accountants and nonaccountants. From the exciting Did You Know? features to its Business Break, **F.A.P.** shows accounting is relevant to everyone.

Active Learning. Active learning implies active inquiry and interaction. The Teamwork in Action and Communicating in Practice are excellent starting points in developing an active learning environment.

Flexibility. **F.A.P.** is the undisputed leader in offering a strong pedagogical support package. Also, the *MHLA* service is a new, special addition to our support package.

This is just a sneak preview of **F.A.P.'s** new and exciting features. From communication, interpersonal, and critical thinking skills to the development of ethical and global awareness. **F.A.P.** is the leader. We invite you to take a complete look at these and other special features in the remainder of this preface to see why **F.A.P.** is the *first choice* in accounting principles books.

To Instructor

F.A.P. gives Web addresses for current follows-ups to articles, excerpts, and financial statements, and for a real world flavour.

To Student

The chapter's opening article and its *You Make the Call* features drive home the relevance of accounting and business.

Motivation

Motivation is a main goal of **F.A.P.** We know information retention is selective—if it does not apply to the lives of readers, they typically are not motivated to learn. **F.A.P**. explains and illustrates how accounting applies to the reader. Here is a sampling of materials that motivate the reader.

The **Chapter Opening Article** sets the stage and shows how the chapter's contents are relevant to the reader. Articles often focus on young entrepreneurs in business who benefit from preparing, analyzing, and using accounting information. These articles bring the material to life in concrete terms.

Fizzling Inventory

Toronto, ON—By June 1997, 27-year-old Rob Stavos was living his dream. He'd just opened **Liquid Nectar,** a small retail outlet devoted to serving the quirky tastes of young and old alike. But within months, this young entrepreneur's dream had become a nightmare.

Liquid Nectar started out with a bang. Customers raved about its stock of exotic and unique beverage products. Profit margins on successful drinks far outweighed the costs of unsold products. "We were ready to take on the large producers," boasts Rob. Within two months, however, Rob lost control of inventory and margins were being squeezed. What happened? Was Liquid Nectar soon to be another flash-in-the-pan?

You Make the Call features develop critical thinking and decision-making skills by requiring decisions using accounting information. Each chapter contains two to four of these features. They are purposely chosen to reflect different kinds of users. Examples are investors, consultants, programmers, financial planners, engineers, appraisers, and political and community activists. Guidance answers are provided.

Entrepreneur
You are the owner of a small retail store. You are considering allowing customers to purchase merchandise using credit cards. Until now, your store only accepted cash and cheques. What form of analysis do you use to make this decision?

You Make the Call

Company Excerpts call attention to well-known organizations to illustrate accounting topics. These excerpts are often accompanied by text describing the nature of the business and its relevance to readers.

...the Company announced it was proceeding with the construction of a 375,000-tonne smelter at Alma, Quebec. Total cost is estimated at $1,600 [million], most of which will be incurred over the next three years. Approximately $220 [million] is expected to be spent in 1998.

ALCAN

CONSOLIDATED STATEMENTS OF EARNINGS AND RETAINED EARNINGS
ALLIANCE COMMUNICATIONS CORPORATION

For the years ended March 31, 1997, March 31, 1996 and March 31, 1995
(In thousands of Canadian dollars, except per share data)

	1997	1996	1995
REVENUES	$ 282,599	$ 268,945	$ 233,811
DIRECT OPERATING EXPENSES	213,816	209,789	183,685
GROSS PROFIT	68,783	59,156	50,126
OTHER EXPENSES			
Other operating expenses	42,037	40,363	28,643
Amortization	5,160	5,038	5,164
Interest (note 10)	1,296	8[illegible]	[illegible]

Financial Statements of familiar companies are used to acquaint readers with the format, content, and use of accounting information. The financial statements for Alliance, and Atlantis are reproduced in an appendix at the end of the book and referenced often.

Organization

Organization is crucial to effective learning. If it is not well-organized or linked with previous knowledge, learning is less effective. **F.A.P.** helps readers organize and link accounting concepts, procedures, and analyses. A **Preview** kicks off each chapter. It introduces the importance and relevance of the materials. It also links these materials to the opening article to further motivate the reader. Here are some additional materials to enhance learning effectiveness.

To Instructor

Use the learning objectives to help structure the course and assignment material to your instructional style.

To Student

Study each of these helpful organizational aids to increase your understanding and learning of accounting and business.

A Look Back

Chapter 1 began our study of accounting by considering its role in the information age. We described accounting for different organizations and identified users and uses of accounting. We saw that ethics and social responsibility are crucial to accounting.

A Look at This Chapter

In this chapter we describe financial statements and the accounting principles guiding their preparation. An important part of this chapter is transaction analysis using the accounting equation. We prepare and analyze financial statements based on transaction analysis.

A Look Forward

Chapter 3 explains the recording of transactions. We introduce the double-entry accounting system and show how T-accounts are helpful in analyzing transactions. Journals and trial balances are also identified and explained.

Chapter linkages launch a chapter and establish bridges between prior, current, and upcoming chapters. Linkages greatly assist readers in effectively learning the materials and help them link concepts across topics.

Learning Objectives

LO 1 Identify and explain the content and reporting aims of financial statements.

LO 2 Describe differences in financial statements across forms of business organization.

LO 3 Explain the roles of preparers, auditors and users of financial statements.

LO 4 Identify those responsible for setting accounting and auditing principles.

LO 5 Identify, explain and apply accounting principles.

LO 6 Analyze business transactions using the accounting equation.

Learning Objectives are shown at the beginning of the chapter to help focus and organize the materials. Each objective is repeated in the chapter at the point it is described and illustrated. Self-contained summaries for learning objectives are provided at the end of the chapter.

Flashback

10. Identify seven internal operating functions in organizations.
11. Why are internal controls important?

A series of **Flashbacks** in the chapter reinforce the immediately preceding materials. Flashbacks allow the reader to momentarily stop and reflect on the topics described. They give immediate feedback on the reader's comprehension before going on to new topics. Answers are provided.

Chapter Outline

- **Communicating with Financial Statements**
  - Previewing Financial Statements
  - Financial Statements and Forms of Organization
- **Transactions and the Accounting Equation**
  - Transaction Analysis—Part I
  - Transaction Analysis—Part II
  - Summary of Transactions

A colour-coded **Chapter Outline** is provided for the chapter. This gives a mental and visual framework to help readers learn the material.

To Instructor

A focus on Using the Information section is a great way to develop analytical thinking.

To Student

Learning accounting principles greatly increases your understanding of articles such as those in *Canadian Business* and other business magazines.

Preparation, Analysis, and Use

Accounting is a service focused on preparing, analyzing, and using information. **F.A.P.** presents a balanced approach to those three crucial aspects of accounting. The preparation aspect of **F.A.P.** is well established and highly regarded. A new progressive emphasis and use continues to put **F.A.P.** in the frontier of practice. Here's a sampling of new or revised textual materials on analysis and use:

The **Accounting Equation** (Assets = Liabilities + Equity) is used as a tool to evaluate a journal entry. The accounting equation is especially useful in learning and understanding the impacts of business transactions and events on financial statements. **F.A.P.** is a pioneer in showing this additional analysis tool.

Aug. 31	Cash	6,300	
	Sales		6,000
	Sales Taxes Payable ($6,000 × 0.05)		300
	To record cash sales and 5% sales tax.		

Assets	= Liabilities	+ Equity
+6,300	+300	+6,000

The **Using the Information** section wraps up each chapter and emphasizes critical-thinking and decision-making skills. Each section introduces one or more tools of analysis. It applies these tools to actual companies and interprets the results. The section often focuses on use of ratio analyses to study and compare the performance and financial condition of competitors.

Return on Investment — USING THE INFORMATION

LO 10 Compute and interpret return on investment.

We introduced return on investment in assessing return and risk earlier in the chapter. Return on investment is also useful in evaluating management, analyzing and forecasting profits, and planning future activities. **Dell Computer** has its marketing department compute return on investment for *every* mailing. "We spent 15 months educating people about return on invested capital," says Dell's Chief Financial Offi-

Hitting the Road is a unique addition to the chapter's assignment material. This activity requires readers to work outside the book and often requires application of interpersonal and communication skills. Tasks range from visits to local merchandisers and government offices to conducting phone interviews and Web searches. These activities help readers understand and appreciate the relevance of accounting.

Hitting the Road LO 5

Select a company in your community which you may visit in person or interview on the telephone. Call ahead to the company to arrange a time when you can interview a member of the accounting department who helps in the preparation of the annual financial statements for the company. During the interview inquire about the following aspects of the company's accounting cycle:

Business Break requires the reader to apply the chapter's material to read and interpret a business article. It also aids in developing reading comprehension skills and gives exposure to business happenings.

Business Break LO 11

Read the article, "Car and Strive," in the September 1996 issue of *Canadian Business.*

Required

1. Contrast the profitability of **Magna** in the early 1990s to 1996.
2. What is the amount of revenue for Magna in the 1996 fiscal year?
3. What is the reason for Magna's success?
4. Despite its recent profitability what does the article identify as a possible problem for Magna?

Ethics

Ethics is the most fundamental accounting principle. Without ethics, information and accounting cease to be useful. **F.A.P.** is the leader in bringing ethics into accounting and demonstrating its importance. From the first chapter's article to the ethics codes at the end of the book, **F.A.P**. sets the standard in emphasizing ethical behaviour and its consequences. Here's a sampling of how we sensitize readers to ethical concerns and decision making:

The **Judgment and Ethics** feature requires readers to make accounting and business decisions with ethical consequences. It uses role-playing to show the interaction of judgment and ethics, the need for ethical awareness, and the impact of ethics. Guidance answers are provided.

Judgment and Ethics

Accountant
You are a public accountant consulting with a client. This client's business has grown to the point where its accounting system must be updated to handle both the volume of transactions and management's needs for information. Your client requests your advice in purchasing new software for its accounting system. You have been offered a 10% commission by a software company for each purchase of its system by one of your clients. Do you think your evaluation of software is affected by this commission arrangement? Do you think this commission arrangement is appropriate? Do you tell your client about the commission arrangement before making a recommendation?

A new **Ethics Challenge** is provided in the *Beyond the Numbers* section. It confronts ethical concerns based on material from the chapter. Many of these challenges involve actions where the ethical path is blurred.

Ethics Challenge
LO 2, 3

Randy Meyer is the chief executive officer of a medium-sized company in Regina, Saskatchewan. Several years ago Randy persuaded the board of directors of his company to base a percent of his compensation on the net income the company earns each year. Each December Randy estimates year-end financial figures in anticipation of the bonus he will receive. If the bonus is not as high as he would like he offers several accounting recommendations to his controller for year-end adjustments. One of his favourite recommendations is for the controller to reduce the estimate of doubtful accounts. Randy has used this

Social Responsibility is a major emphasis of progressive organizations. **F.A.P.** is unique in introducing this important topic in Chapter 1. We describe social responsibility and accounting's role in both reporting on and assessing its impact. **F.A.P.** also introduces social audits and reports on social responsibility.

Did You Know?

In Pursuit of Profit
How far can companies go in pursuing profit? Converse proposed to name a new footwear product Run N' Gun. This sparked debate on ethics, social responsibility and profits. Converse said Run N' Gun was a basketball and football term. Critics claimed it invited youth violence and links with the gun culture. To the credit of Converse, it changed the name from Run N' Gun to Run N' Slam prior to its sale to consumers.

To Instructor

The Judgment and Ethics feature raises the role of ethics in accounting and develops critical thinking skills.

To Student

Use these features and book materials to remind us that accounting and business decisions affect peoples' lives.

To Instructor

PowerPoint presentation slides can be customized for your instructional style and are great visual aids to lecture materials.

To Student

Use **F.A.P.**'s Home Page for current updates, hot links to important sites, and much more . . .

Student Software provides several technology-assisted educational activities. These include (1) *Tutorial*—interactive review of topics, and (2) *SPATS*—instructional software to solve problems.

Technology

Technology and innovation can be exciting and fun. **F.A.P.** makes the transition to new technologies easy. It is the leader in demonstrating the relevance of technology and showing readers how to use it. To ensure easy access, all technology offerings are linked to the Larson booksite. The address is **www.mcgrawhill.ca/college/larson**. Here's a sampling of items pushing the technology frontier:

Accounting Web Community

The Financial Accounting Web Community is a place on the Internet designed and built with our adopters in mind. It is a place where instructors can quickly access teaching resources directly related to the text they are using. It is also a place where instructors can share ideas and information with each other.

The Financial Accounting Web Community is the starting point for accessing accounting and business resources on the Web. The book's Web site harnesses technology resources to provide the most up-to-date and powerful Web services available.

Taking It to the Net requires accessing a Web site and obtaining information relevant to the chapter. It aims to make readers comfortable with Web technology, familiar with information available, and aware of the power of Web technology.

Taking It to the Net
LO 1, 7

There is extensive accounting and business information available on the Internet. This includes the **TSE's** on-line address at **http://www.tse.com** and the Depository for Canadian Securities' database referred to as **SEDAR** (**http://www.sedar.com**) and numerous other Web sites offering access to financial statement information or related data.

Required

Access at least one of the Web sites selected by either you or your instructor and answer the following:

a. Write a brief report describing the types of relevant information available at this Web site.

b. How would you rate the importance of the information available at this Web site for accounting and business?

PowerPoint® Presentations and Supplements augment each chapter with colorful graphics, interesting charts, innovative presentations, and interactive activities. The PowerPoint® materials are flexible and can be customized for any use.

Real World

Showing readers that accounting matters is part of an effective learning package. **F.A.P.** is the leader in real world instructional materials. It offers unique assignments challenging the reader to apply knowledge learned in practical and diverse ways. These challenges include analytical problems, research requirements, comparative analysis, teamwork assignments, and communication exercises. They also allow greater emphasis on conceptual, analytical, communication, and interpersonal skills. Here's a sampling of these materials:

Questions

13. Refer to Alliance's financial statements in Appendix I. On March 31, what percentage of Alliance's assets was represented by what would be Alliance's inventory?

14. Refer to Atlantis' financial statements in Appendix I. Is it possible to determine a cost of sales figure for Atlantis?

15. Refer to the Wired scenario at the beginning of the chapter. What does Russo need to know about Wired to be able to calculate gross margin and inventory turnover?

To Instructor and Student

The **glossary** gives complete and accurate definitions of key terms. A key term is set in bold in the chapter, and the glossary references this page number. It also gives synonyms for key terms.

A **summary** describes the chapter in terms of its learning objectives. It assists in assessing one's understanding of key concepts, procedures, and analyses.

Questions give readers quick feedback on their understanding of key chapter topics.

Quick studies are effective checks on concepts, procedures, and analyses. They help build the reader's confidence with the material. Each are keyed to usually one learning objective.

Exercises focus on one or more learning objectives. They are mildly challenging and are an effective way to launch into more challenging problems.

Check Figures serve as an aid to readers.

Reporting in Action requires analysis and use of Alliance's annual report information.

Reporting in Action

LO 2, 6, 10

Alliance Communication produces, markets and sells movies and television programs. Key financial figures for Alliance Communication's fiscal year ended March 31, 1997, are:

Key Figure	$ millions
Financing (liabilities + equity)	$353.7
Profit	18.2
Sales	282.6

Required

1. What is the total amount of assets invested in Alliance Communication?
2. What is Alliance Communication's return on investment? Alliance Communication's assets at March 31, 1996, equal $238.9 (in millions).
3. How much are total expenses for Alliance Communication?

Analysis component:

4. Does Alliance Communication's return on investment seem satisfactory if competitors average a 5% return?

Comparative Analysis compares the performance and financial condition of Alliance and Atlantis using the accounting knowledge obtained from the chapter. These activities help develop analytical skills.

Comparative Analysis

LO 2, 6, 10

Both **Alliance Communications** and **Atlantis Communications** produce, market and sell movies and television programs. Key comparative figures ($ millions) for these two organizations follow:

	Alliance	Atlantis
Financing (liabilities + equity)	$353.7	$333.5
Profit	18.2	5.6
Sales	282.6	178.0

Source: Alliance figures are from its annual report for fiscal year-end March 31, 1997. Atlantis figures are from its annual report for fiscal year-end December 31, 1997.

Note: In September 1998 shareholders of Alliance Communications Corp. and Atlantis Communications Inc. approved a merger of the two companies. The new company will be known as Alliance Atlantis Communications Inc. and will "be far more effective around the world and. . . will be positioned for further growth" according to Michael MacMillan, the newly appointed chairman and chief executive officer. Although it will not be possible to compare the Alliance and Atlantis results past 1997, it will be interesting to compare the new company's results to the previous individual entities. Here is an opportunity to see if expected synergies are realized.

Comprehensive and Serial Problems are included in several chapters and focus on multiple learning objectives from multiple chapters. They help integrate and summarize key principles.

Comprehensive Problem

Alpine Company

LO 1

(If the Working Papers that accompany this text are not available, omit this comprehensive problem.)

Assume it is Monday, May 1, the first business day of the month, and you have just been hired as the accountant for Alpine Company, which operates with monthly accounting periods. All of the company's accounting work has been completed through the end of April and its ledgers show April 30 balances. During your first month on the job, you record the following transactions:

May 1 Issued Cheque No. 3410 to S&M Management Co. in payment of the May rent, $3,710. (Use two lines to record the transaction. Charge 80% of the rent to Rent Expense, Selling Space and the balance to Rent Expense, Office Space.)

2 Sold merchandise on credit to Essex Company, Invoice No. 8785, $6,100. (The terms of all credit sales are 2/10, n/30.)

2 Issued a $175 credit memorandum to Nabors, Inc., for defective merchandise sold on April 28 and returned for credit. The total selling price (gross) was $4,725.

Problems often cover multiple learning objectives and usually require preparing, analyzing, and using information. They are paired with **Alternate Problems** for further review of the same topics. Problems are supported with software and other technology options. Many include an **Analytical Component** focusing on financial statement consequences and interpretations.

Problem 7-3A

Income statement comparisons and cost flow assumptions

LO 4, 9

The Denney Company sold 2,500 units of its product at $98 per unit during 19X1. Incurring operating expenses of $14 per unit in selling the units, it began the year with, and made successive purchases of, units of the product as follows:

January 1 beginning inventory . .	740 units costing $58 per unit
Purchases:	
April 2	700 units @ $59 per unit
June 14	600 units @ $61 per unit
August 29	500 units @ $64 per unit
November 18	800 units @ $65 per unit
	3,340 units

Required

Preparation component:

1. Prepare a comparative income statement for the company, showing in adjacent columns the net incomes earned from the sale of the product, assuming the company uses a periodic inventory system and prices its ending inventory on the basis of (a) FIFO, (b) LIFO, and (c) weighted-average cost.

Check Figure Net income (LIFO), $69,020

A **Demonstration Problem** is at the end of the chapter. It illustrates important topics and shows how to apply concepts in preparing, analyzing, and using information. A problem-solving strategy helps guide the reader. Most chapters also have a **Mid-Chapter Demonstration Problem** with solution.

Demonstration Problem

On July 14, 19X1, Truro Company paid $600,000 to acquire a fully equipped factory. The purchase included the following:

Asset	Appraised Value	Estimated Salvage Value	Estimated Useful Life	Amortization Method
Land	$160,000			Not amortized
Land improvements .	80,000	$ -0-	10 years	Straight line
Building	320,000	100,000	10 years	Double-declining balance
Machinery	240,000	20,000	10,000 units	Units of production*
Total	$800,000			

*The machinery is used to produce 700 units in 19X1 and 1,800 units in 19X2.

Required

1. Allocate the total $600,000 cost among the separate assets.

Infographics and Artwork aid in visual learning of key accounting and business topics. Photos, colour, highlighting, and authentic documents all help with visual learning.

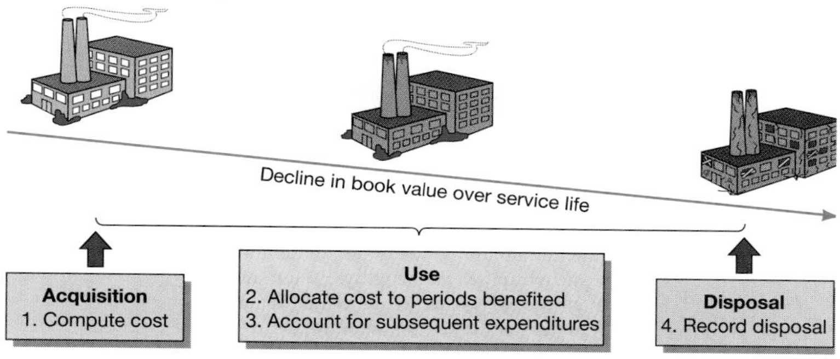

Exhibit 12.2

Issues in Accounting for Capital Assets

This chapter focuses on the decisions and factors surrounding these four important issues.

To Instructor

Teamwork in Action and Communicating in Practice are excellent starting points in developing an active learning environment. Both develop communication and interpersonal skills.

To Student

Team-building, collaborative effort skills are usually crucial to career success.

Active Learning

Active learning requires effective assignments. **F.A.P.** is the student-proven and instructor-tested leader in assignment materials. Proven and thoughtful assignments not only facilitate but motivate effective and active learning. many assignments include writing components. Here's a sampling of relevant assignment materials:

Teamwork in Action assignments require preparing, analyzing, and using information in teams. They can be completed in or outside of class. These active learning activities reinforce understanding of key topics and develop interpersonal skills.

Teamwork in Action

LO 5

A team will be called upon to personify the operation of a voucher system. Yet all teams must prepare for the potential to be selected by doing the following:

1. Each team is to identify the documents in a voucher system. The team leader will play the voucher, and each team member is to assume "the role" of one or more documents.
2. To prepare for your individual role you are to:
   a. Find an illustration for the document within the chapter.
   b. Write down your document function, where you originate, and how you flow through the voucher system.
3. Rehearse the role playing of operating the system. You may use text illustrations as props, and for visual effort you may wear a nametag identifying the part you play.

Communicating in Practice exercises aim at applying accounting knowledge to develop written and verbal communication skills.

Communicating in Practice

LO 12

The classroom should be divided into teams. Teams are to select an industry, and each team member is to select a different company in that industry. Each team member is to acquire the annual report of the company selected. Annual reports can be obtained in many ways including accessing this book's Web page or **http://www.sedar.com**. Use the annual report to compute total asset turnover. Communicate with teammates via a meeting, e-mail or telephone to discuss the meaning of this ratio, how different companies compare to each other, and the industry norm. The team must prepare a single memo reporting the ratios for each company and identify the conclusions or consensus of opinion reached during the team's discussion. The memo is to be duplicated and distributed to the instructor and all classmates.

Flexibility

Learning and instructing requires flexibility **F.A.P.** offers flexibility in meeting the unique demands of individual students and teachers. From the conventional classroom to the active learning environment, **F.A.P.'s** new edition and its pedagogical package give more flexibility and options for innovation in learning and instruction. It does this while maintaining the rich content that has made it the market-leading book in accounting principles.

Packaging Options

Unique **packaging options** support **F.A.P.** flexibility. Nobody matches McGraw-Hill Ryerson when it comes to packaging options for accounting principles. Discuss the flexible packaging options with your McGraw-Hill Ryerson sales representative.

To Instructor

F.A.P. supports all instructional and learning styles.

Additional Supporting Materials

Instructor's Resource Manual

Solutions Manual

Test Bank

Solutions Acetates

Teaching Acetates

PowerPoint Slides

Tutorial Software

SPATs

Videos (U.S.)

To Student

F.A.P. provides learning aids.

Additional materials that may be helpful in your accounting course include

Working Papers

Study Guide

GLAS (General Ledger Applications Software)

Essentials of Financial Accounting: A Multimedia Approach

Innovations and Enhancements

In preparing this edition, we asked questions of instructors and students. We asked what topics to add, or change in emphasis. We asked what pedagogical aids would help in teaching and learning. We wanted to know what innovations and enhancements would help them and maintain **F.A.P.** leadership in accounting principles. From these questions came several requests. We listened, and this edition is the result. We have already described major content and pedagogical changes. This section identifies many other chapter-by-chapter innovations and enhancements:

Chapter 1

- New focus on the information age and the relevance of accounting.
- Early introduction to income, revenues, and expenses using Alliance Communications.
- New discussion of return and risk as part of all business decisions.
- New descriptions of business activities: financing, investing, and operating.
- New and unique presentation of ethics and social responsibility.

Chapter 2

- ***FASTForward,*** an athletic service company, introduced as the new focus company for Chapters 2–5.
- New company transactions to add realism and interest.
- Revised discussion and presentation of accounting principles.
- Added analysis of each transaction using the accounting equation.
- New presentation and integration of cash flow statement with other financial statements.
- New description of reporting differences between proprietorships, partnerships, and corporations.

Chapter 3

- Revised presentation of transactions and source documents.
- New exhibits on the accounting equation and double-entry accounting.
- New exhibits and discussion linking transactions to financial statements, including the statement of cash flows.
- Revised discussion and exhibits for recording transactions.
- Expanded discussion of debt ratio with new comparative analysis.

Chapter 4

- New discussion of the accounting period and the motivation for adjusting accounts.
- New framework for preparing and analyzing adjustments.
- Several new exhibits and graphics illustrating adjusting accounts.
- New presentation linking adjustments to financial statements.
- Several new features highlighting current happenings in revenue recognition and the role of technology.
- Revised discussion of profit margin using Loblaw along with comparative analysis.

Chapter 5

- Revised presentation and new exhibits for the closing process.
- Revised presentation and discussion of the statement of cash flow as an integral part of the full set of financial statements.
- New exhibits presenting the accounting cycle.
- New presentation of the classified balance sheet.
- Revised current ratio discussion using Canadian Tire and industry analyses.

Chapter 6

- New discussion comparing a service company and a merchandiser.
- New presentation of the operating cycle of a merchandiser with credit or cash sales.
- New design of source documents including an invoice and debit and credit memoranda.
- Revised presentation of merchandising sales and purchases using the perpetual inventory system.
- Revised discussion on the transfer of ownership for inventory.
- New discussion and presentation of merchandising cost flows across periods.
- New comparison of cash and accrual measures of sales and costs.
- Revised acid-test ratio and gross margin discussion using Mitel and industry analyses.
- New appendix on accounting for merchandise sales and purchases under both the periodic and perpetual inventory systems.

Chapter 7

- Revised presentation of assigning costs to inventory using the perpetual inventory system.
- Revised discussion of inventoriable items and costs.
- New exhibits illustrating statements effects of inventory errors.
- Revised presentation of alternative inventory valuation methods.
- New appendix presentation assigning costs to inventory using the periodic system.
- Expanded merchandise turnover and days' sales in inventory ratio discussion and industry analyses.

Chapter 8

- New section on fundamental system principles.
- Contemporary and streamlined presentation on components of accounting systems.
- Revised discussion of hardware and software for systems.
- Contemporary presentation of Special Journals.
- Revised discussion of technology-based accounting systems.
- Revised layout for Special Journals reflecting current practice.
- New discussion of *enterprise-application software*, including SAP and Oracle.
- New analysis of business segments using a contribution matrix and Bombardier data.

Chapter 9

- New sections on the purpose of internal control and its limitations.
- Revised discussion on the principles of internal control.
- New feature boxes involving current technological developments.
- Revised discussion on control of cash.
- New presentation and exhibits on the voucher system of control.
- New depictions of important source documents.
- New presentation on using banking activities as controls, including the bank reconciliation.
- Revised discussion of days' sales uncollected using comparative analyses of Oshawa Group and George Weston.

Chapter 10

- New organization focuses on receivables first and short-term investments second.
- Revised discussion of credit sales, including use of credit cards.
- New presentation on accounting for accounts receivables.
- New ordering of (simpler) write-off method before (more complex) allowance method.
- New presentation and exhibits for estimating bad debts.
- Revised presentation and exhibits for notes receivable.
- Streamline accounting for investments including unrealized lower of cost and market.
- Revised discussion of accounts receivable turnover using comparative analyses of Imperial Oil and Ocelot Energy.

Chapter 11

- New exhibits including introducing computerized payroll systems.
- Excerpts from Revenue Canada forms.

Chapter 12

- New introduction and motivation on accounting for capital assets.
- New discussion to describe and illustrate amortization.
- Revised presentation and exhibits for disposals of capital assets.
- New discussion on natural resources and intangible assets.
- New discussion on the cash flow impacts of long-term assets.
- Revised total asset turnover illustration using George Weston and Oshawa Group.

Chapter 13

- New introduction on accounting for liabilities.
- Revised presentation of known (determinable) liabilities.
- New exhibits and discussion on promissory notes.
- Revised discussion of accounting for long-term liabilities.
- Transfer of present value discussion of liabilities to Chapter 16.
- Revised presentation of times interest earned with application to Best Buy.

Chapter 14

- New discussion of partnerships, including financial statements, admission/withdrawal, and liquidation.

Chapter 15

- Revised corporation coverage to focus on its characteristics and both common and preferred shares.
- New summary exhibit highlighting differences across alternative forms of organization.

- New exhibits including share certificate.
- Streamlined coverage of share subscriptions.
- Transfer of cash dividends discussions to Chapter 16.
- Revised book value per share discussion with references to Royal Bank.

Chapter 16

- Reorganization into four main sections: dividends; treasury shares; reporting income; and retained earnings.
- New dividends presentation with new exhibits.
- Revised and streamlined discussion on treasury shares.
- Streamlined presentation on reporting income information.
- Revised earnings per share discussion.
- New section on accounting for share options.
- Revised presentation of reporting retained earnings.
- New presentation of dividends yield and price-earnings ratios using Viceroy Homes, Nova Scotia Power, Noranda and CIBC.

Chapter 17

- New introduction to bond (long-term debt) financing.
- Revised bond presentation with new exhibits.
- New layout for effective interest amortization tables.
- Revised presentation of accounting for bond retirements.
- Revised presentation for notes payable.
- New explanation of present value concepts.
- New discussion of present values using interest tables.
- New discussion of collateral agreements for bonds and notes.
- Revised presentation of pledged assets to secured liabilities.

Chapter 18

- Streamlined coverage of investments and international accounting.
- Reorganized into three sections: Classification of investments; long-term investments in securities; and international investments.
- New presentation on the components of return on total assets with real company application.

Chapter 19

- New presentation on the motivation for cash flow reporting.
- New exhibits on the format of the statement of cash flows replacing the statement of changes in financial position.
- Revised discussion on cash from operating activities—both direct and indirect methods.
- New flexible presentation allows coverage of either or both direct or indirect methods.
- New exhibits summarize adjustments for both the direct and indirect methods.
- Revised discussion of cash flows from investing activities.
- Revised discussion of cash flows from financing activities.
- Revised presentation of analysis of cash sources and uses.

Chapter 20

- New discussion on the basics of financial statement analysis.
- New explanation of the building blocks of analysis.
- Revised discussion on analysis tools and standards for comparisons.
- Revised presentation of horizontal and vertical analysis.
- Revised summary exhibit of financial statement analysis ratios.
- New section on analysis reporting.

Chapter 21

- New introduction to managerial accounting.
- New section and exhibit on the purpose of managerial accounting.
- Revised presentation of reporting manufacturing activities.
- New section on cost accounting concepts emphasizing cost identification and classification.
- New discussion of manufacturing management principles.
- New introduction to important managerial topics including prime, conversion, product, and period costs.
- New infographics augment many new and revised topics.
- Transfer of discussion of a manufacturing statement and a general accounting system to Chapter 22.
- New presentation on unit contribution margin with illustrations using a bike manufacturer.

Chapter 22

- New focus on manufacturing and job order cost accounting.
- Revised presentation of manufacturing activities and reporting.

- Revised discussion of the job order cost accounting system.
- Streamlined discussion of underapplied and overapplied overhead.
- New presentation on multiple overhead allocation rates.
- Revised discussion of general accounting system (periodic) in a new appendix.

Chapter 23

- Revised introduction with discussion of motivation for a process manufacturing system.
- New exhibit and discussion comparing job order and process manufacturing systems.
- New exhibit to explain process manufacturing operations.
- Revised discussion of computing and using equivalent units.
- New discussion on the physical flow of units and preparation of a cost reconciliation.
- New presentation on spoilage in process costing and its effects on costs per equivalent unit.

Chapter 24

- New section and exhibits on two-stage allocation.
- New presentation and exhibits for activity-based costing.
- Transfer of activity-based costing upfront to link with Chapter 23.
- Revised discussion of decision-making relevance of cost allocation and performance measurement.
- Revised discussion of department expense allocation.
- New exhibit and presentation of joint costs.
- New presentation of return on assets by investment centres.
- Transfer of discussion of "eliminating an unprofitable department" to Chapter 28.

Chapter 25

- Revised discussion on describing and identifying cost behaviour.
- Revised presentation and comparison of the high-low, scatter diagram, and regression methods.
- Revised presentation on applying cost-volume-profit analysis.
- New presentation of operating leverage and its role in determining income.

Chapter 26

- New presentation of the budget calendar.
- New exhibit showing the master budget sequence.
- Expanded discussion and new exhibits of production and manufacturing budgets.
- Revised discussion motivated by new material on planning objectives.
- New presentation on zero-based budgeting.

Chapter 27

- New discussion and exhibit on the process of budgetary control.
- Revised emphasis on a decision making role for budgets and standard costs.
- New presentation of standard costs and the standard cost card.
- Revised organization of variance analysis.
- New presentation of and visual orientation to variance analysis.
- New separate analysis of variable and fixed overhead variances.
- New presentation on sales variances with illustrations.

Chapter 28

- Revised presentation of capital budgeting.
- New exhibits illustrating capital budgeting and its computations.
- New presentation of the internal rate of return for capital budgeting.
- New section comparing methods of analyzing investments using capital budgeting.
- New section on managerial decision making, information, and relevant costs.
- Revised presentation of short-term managerial decision tools.
- New section on qualitative factors in managerial decisions.
- New presentation of break-even time with illustrations.

Supplements

Instructor's Resource Manual
This manual contains materials for managing an active learning environment and provides new instructional visuals. Each chapter provides a Lecture Outline, a chart linking Learning Objectives to end-of-chapter material, and transparency masters. For instructor's convenience, student copies of these visuals are provided in the *Study Guide*. If students do not acquire the study guide, adopters are permitted to duplicate these visuals for distribution.

Solutions Manual
The manuals contain solutions for all assignment materials. Transparencies in large, boldface type are also available.

Test Bank
The Test Bank contains a wide variety of questions, including true-false, multiple-choice, matching, short essay, quantitative problems, and completion problems of varying levels of difficulty. All Test Bank materials are grouped according to learning objective. A computerized version is also available in Windows.

PowerPoint Slides
This is a package of multimedia lecture enhancement aids that uses PowerPoint® software to illustrate chapter concepts. It includes a viewer so that they can be shown with or without Microsoft PowerPoint® software.

McGraw-Hill Learning Architecture
This Web-based Class Management System distributes product course materials for viewing with any standard Web Browser. This online learning centre is packed with dynamically generated pages of text, graphics, PowerPoint® slides, exercises, and more. Customization possibilities are easily implemented.

PageOut
PageOut is a McGraw-Hill online tool that enables instructors to create and post class-specfic Web pages simply and easily. No knowledge of HTML is required.

Online Learning Centre
A body of online content to augment the text and provide students with interactive quizzing features.

Videos (U.S.)
Lecture Enhancement Video Series. These short, action-oriented videos provide the impetus for lively classroom discussion. There are separate *Financial Accounting and Managerial Accounting* libraries. Available upon adoption.

SPATS (Spreadsheet Applications Template Software).
Excel templates for selected problems and exercises from the text. The templates gradually become more complex, requiring students to build a variety of formulas. What-if questions are added to show the power of spreadsheets and a simple tutorial is included. Instructors may request a free master template for students to use or copy, or students can buy shrinkwrapped versions at a nominal fee.

Tutorial Software
Windows version of multiple-choice, true-false, journal entry review and glossary review questions are randomly assessed by students. Explanations of right and wrong answers are provided and scores are tallied. Instructors may request a free master template for students to use or copy, or students can buy shrinkwrapped versions for a nominal fee.

Solutions Manual to accompany the practice sets.

Student

Working Papers
These new volumes match end-of-chapter assignment material. They include papers that can be used to solve all quick studies, exercises, serial problems, comprehensive problems, and Beyond the Numbers activities. Each chapter contains one set of papers that can be used for either the problems or the alternate problems.

Study Guide
For each chapter and appendix, these guides review the learning objectives and summaries, outline the chapter, and provide a variety of practice problems and solutions. Several chapters also contain visuals to illustrate key chapter concepts.

Additional Software (U.S.)
Essentials of Financial Accounting: A Multimedia Approach
GLAS (General Ledger Applications Software) by Jack E. Terry, ComSource Associates, Inc.

Practice Sets
Student's Name CD Centre, by Harvey C. Freedman of Humber College of Applied Arts and Technology. A manual, single proprietorship practice set covering a one-month accounting cycle. The set includes business papers and can be completed manually and/or using computer data files for use with *Simply Accounting for Windows*. The problem set can be assigned after Chapter 8.

Adders 'N Keyes, Fourth Edition by Brenda Mallouk. *Adders 'N Keyes* is a sole proprietorship practice set that gives students exposure to a real life business setting.

Barns Bluff Equipment, by Barrie Yackness of British Columbia Institute of Technology and Terrie Kroshus. A manual, single proprietorship practice set with business papers that may be assigned after Chapter 9.

Computerized Practice Set
Interactive Financial Accounting Lab by Ralph Smith, Rick Birney and Alison Wiseman.

Acknowledgments

We are thankful for the encouragement, suggestions, and counsel provided by the many instructors, professionals, and students in preparing the 9th Canadian edition. This new edition reflects the pedagogical needs and innovative ideas of both instructors and students of accounting principles. If has been a team effort and we recognize the contributions of many individuals. We especially thank and recognize individuals who provided valuable comments and suggestions to further improve this edition, including:

Reviewers:

John Glendinning — Centennial College
Allen McQueen — Grant MacEwan Community College
Peter Woolley — BCIT
Ann Paterson — Humber College
Bob Holland — Kingstec Community College
David Bopara — Toronto School of Business
Donna Grace — Sheridan College Brampton
Aziz Rajwani — Langara College
Margaret Tough — Seneca College
Neill Nedohin — Red River Community College
Peter Norwood — Langara College
Tony McGowan — Lambton College
Jim Chambers — St. Clair College
Jack Castle — SIAST—Palliser
Cecile Ashman — Algonquin College
Shawn P. Thompson — Algonquin College
Micheal S. Sirtonski — Assiniboine Community College
George Duquette — Canadore College
Denis Woods — Centennial College—Progress Campus
Robin Hemmingsen — Centennial College
Harold J. Keller — College of the Rockies
Joe Pidutti — Durham College
Robert Bryant — Durham College
Ralph Sweet — Durham College
Paul Hurley — Durham College
Bill Rice — Fairview College
Elaine Hales — Georgian College
Don Smith — Georgian College
G. D. McLeod — Humber College—Lakeshore Campus
Gordon Holyer — Malaspina University College
Jeffery Rudolph — Marianopolis College
Wayne Larson — Northern Alberta Institute of Technology
John Daye — New Brunswick Community College
Brad MacDonald — Nova Scotia Community College—Annapolis Campus
Heather Martin — Nova Scotia Community College—I.W. Akerley Campus
Louise Conners — Nova Scotia Community College—I.W. Akerley Campus
Carol Derksen — Red River Community College
Randy Ross — Ridgetown College, University of Guelph
Greg Fagan — Seneca College
Michael A. Perretta — Sheridan College—Brampton Campus
Don Thibert — Toronto School of Business—Windsor
Pamela Hamm — New Brunswick Community College—Saint John

Problem checkers:

Connie Hahn — Southern Alberta Institute of Technology
Albert Ferris — UPEI
Dirk VanVoorst — Sheridan College—Oakville
Richard Wright — Fanshawe College
Elaine Hales — Georgian College
Maria Belanger — Algonquin College
Karen Matthews — SIAST—Palliser
Neill Nedohin — Red River Community College
Bonnie Martel — Niagara College

Students input plays an important role in the new edition. Over 300 students from the schools below contributed to Student Focus Groups and Student Surveys.

Acadia University
Algonquin College
British Columbia Institute of Technology
Kwantlen College
Northern Alberta Institute of Technology
Nova Scotia Community College
Saskatchewan Institute of Applied Science and Technology (Palliser Campus)
Simon Fraser University
Souther Alberta Institute of Technology

We also want to recognize the contribution of Dennis Wilson of Centennial College who prepared the updates of the payroll liabilities chapter and solutions for this edition and also our final accuracy checker, Elaine Hales of Georgian College. Special thanks also go to Matthew Carroll and Marife Abella for their research assistance.

Morton Nelson *Ray Carroll* *Michael Zin*
Kermit D. Larson *Barbara Chiappetta* *John J. Wild*

NINTH CANADIAN EDITION

VOLUME II

Fundamental Accounting Principles

12

Capital Assets: Plant and Equipment, Natural Resources, and Intangible Assets

CHAPTER

A Look Back

Chapters 9 and 10 focused on short-term assets: cash, cash equivalents, receivables and temporary investments. We explained why they are known as liquid assets and described how companies account and report for them. Chapter 11 dealt with accounting for payroll and the payroll liability.

A Look at This Chapter

This chapter introduces us to capital (long-term) assets including property, plant and equipment, natural resources, and intangible assets. We explain how to record a capital asset's cost, the allocation of an asset's cost to periods benefiting from it, the recording of additional asset costs after an asset is purchased, and the disposing of an asset.

A Look Forward

Chapter 13 emphasizes both current and long-term liabilities. We explain how they are computed, recorded, and reported in financial statements. We also describe and apply present value concepts.

Chapter Outline

Section 1—Capital Assets: Property, Plant and Equipment

- **Cost of Capital Assets**
  - Land
  - Land Improvements
  - Buildings
  - Machinery and Equipment
  - Lump-Sum Asset Purchase
- **Amortization**
  - Factors in Computing Amortization
  - Amortization Methods
  - Partial Year Amortization
  - Revising Amortization Rates
  - Reporting Amortization on Assets
- **Revenue and Capital Expenditures**
  - Repairs
  - Betterments
  - Low-Cost Asset Purchases
- **Disposals of Capital Assets**
  - Discarding Capital Assets
  - Selling Capital Assets
  - Exchanging Capital Assets

Section 2—Natural Resources

- **Natural Resources**
  - Acquisition Cost and Depletion
  - Capital Assets Used in Extracting Resources

Section 3—Intangible Assets

- **Intangible Assets**
  - Accounting for Intangible Assets
  - Patents
  - Copyrights
  - Leaseholds
  - Leasehold Improvements
  - Goodwill
  - Trademarks and Trade Names
- **Cash Flow Impacts of capital Assets**
- **Using the Information—Total Asset Turnover**

Bug Killer

Calgary, AB—Jenna Lee doesn't fancy herself a consumer crusader. "I'm no Ralph Nader," she says bluntly. But when the 19-year-old Calgary student stumbled upon a serious glitch in the amortization calculation in *PCaccount*, an accounting package for PCs, she complained to the program' s developer, **Intech.** When the company rudely brushed her off, she got angry enough to take her story to the *Alberta Chronicle*—a phone call that helped ignite a national firestorm of controversy.

Shortly after the *Chronicle's* August 1 exposé, a "deeply distressed" Samuel Carter, Intech's president, confessed that his company's line of accounting software contained a "few bugs" in its amortization schedules producing inaccurate calculations. With customers already surly over problems with Intech's customer-service lines, Carter moved quickly. He offered to replace disks on request for Intech' s one million customers.

The errors are no small problem—particularly to consumers who already used these amortization programs to prepare their financial or tax reports. Management experts say Intech's aggressive response to the problems helped defuse a potential disaster. "The public loves a confessed sinner," notes Sherry Williams of **Consumer Research.** Along with the replacement offer, Carter penned an apology in a letter to the product's registered users: "We really let our customers down," he wrote. So far, Carter's willingness to publicly swallow a serving of humble pie appears to be working.

Not everyone is content, though. Even an apologetic telephone call from Intech's president and the offer of a replacement disk haven't managed to mollify Ms. Lee. "It shakes my faith in the whole industry," she says. "Next time, I'm doing my own amortization calculations!"

Learning Objectives

LO 1 Describe capital assets and issues in accounting for them.

LO 2 Apply the cost principle to compute the cost of capital assets.

LO 3 Explain amortization and the factors affecting its computation.

LO 4 Compute and record amortization using the methods of straight-line, units-of-production, and declining-balance.

LO 5 Compare and analyze amortization for different methods.

LO 6 Explain amortization for partial years and when estimates change.

LO 7 Distinguish between revenue and capital expenditures, and account for these expenditures.

LO 8 Account for asset disposal through discarding, selling, or exchanging an asset.

LO 9 Account for natural resources and their depletion.

LO 10 Account for intangible assets and their amortization.

LO 11 Identify cash flow impacts of capital asset transactions.

LO 12 Compute total asset turnover and apply it to analyze a company's use of assets.

CHAPTER PREVIEW

This chapter focuses on capital (long-term) assets used in the operation of a company. These assets can be grouped into property, plant and equipment, natural resources, and intangible assets. Capital assets are a major investment for most companies. They make up a major part of assets on the balance sheet and often represent one of the largest expenses on the income statement. They also affect the statement of cash flows when cash is spent to acquire capital assets or received from the sale of them. When companies acquire or build capital assets, it is often referred to as a "capital expenditure." Capital expenditures are important news because they impact both the short- and long-term success of a company. Both natural resources and intangible assets have similar impacts. Because of this and other reasons it is important we understand accounting for long-term assets. This chapter will describe the financial impact of these asset purchases. We also explain what distinguishes these assets from other types of assets, how to determine their cost, how to allocate their costs to periods benefiting from their use, and how we dispose of long-term assets. This knowledge can help us avoid blind reliance on software that might yield errors as evidenced in the opening article.

SECTION 1—CAPITAL ASSETS: PROPERTY, PLANT, AND EQUIPMENT

Capital assets are tangible assets used in the operations of a company and have a useful life of more than one accounting period. Capital assets, or *fixed assets*, include *plant and equipment*, or *property, plant and equipment*, *natural resources*, and *intangible assets*. For many companies, capital assets make up the single largest asset it owns. Exhibit 12.1 shows capital assets as a percent of total assets for several companies. Not only do they make up a large percent of these companies' assets but their dollar values are huge. **Imperial Oil's** capital assets, for instance, are reported at more than \$8 billion. Also, **Bombardier** and **Alcan Aluminium** report capital assets of more than \$1 billion and \$5 billion, respectively.

Capital assets are set apart from other assets by two important features. First, they are used in operations. This makes them different, for instance, from *inventory* that is held for sale and not used in operations. The distinctive feature here is use and not type of asset. A company that purchases a computer for the purpose of selling it, reports it on the balance sheet as inventory. But if the same company purchases the same computer for use in operations, it is a capital asset. Another case

Exhibit 12.1

Capital Assets as Percent of Total Assets

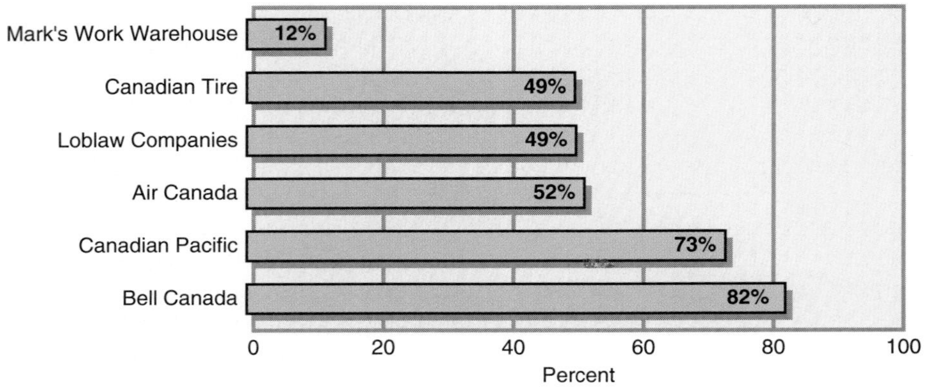

is that of *long-term investments* such as land held for future expansion. If this same land holds a factory used in operations, the land is part of capital assets. Still another case is *equipment* held for use in event of a breakdown or for use in peak periods of production. This equipment is reported in capital assets. But if this same equipment is removed from use and held for sale it is not reported in capital assets.

LO1 Describe capital assets and issues in accounting for them.

A second important feature is that capital assets have useful lives extending over more than one accounting period. This makes capital assets different from *current assets* such as *supplies* that are usually consumed in a short time after they are placed in use. The cost of current assets is assigned to the single period when they are used. Many *prepaid expenses* are distinguished from capital assets based on the length of their useful lives.

The accounting for capital assets reflects these two important features. Since capital assets are used in operations, we try to match their costs against the revenue they generate. Also, since capital assets' useful lives extend over more than one period, our matching of costs and revenues must extend over several periods. We must measure capital assets (balance sheet focus) and allocate their cost to periods benefiting from their use (income statement focus).

Exhibit 12.2 shows the four main accounting issues with capital assets. They are:

1. Compute the costs of capital assets.
2. Allocate costs of capital assets against revenues for the periods they benefit.
3. Account for expenditures such as repairs and improvements to capital assets.
4. Record the disposal of capital assets.

Exhibit 12.2

Issues in Accounting for Capital Assets

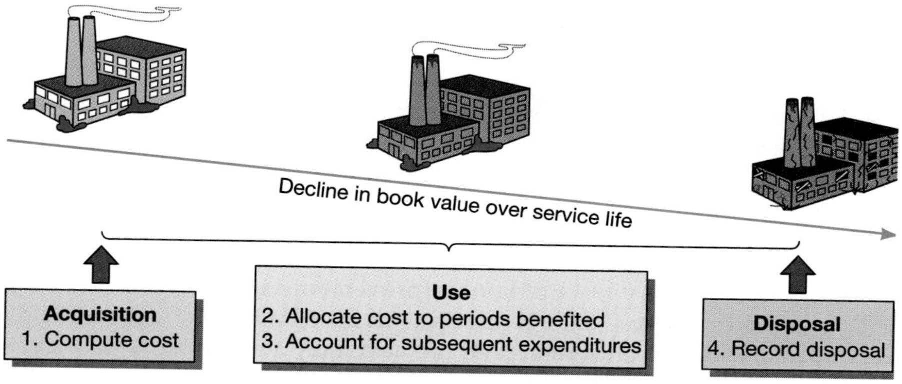

This chapter focuses on the decisions and factors surrounding these four important issues.

Cost of Capital Assets

LO2 Apply the cost principle to compute the cost of capital assets.

Capital assets are recorded at cost when purchased. This is consistent with the *cost principle.* **Cost** includes all normal and reasonable expenditures necessary to get the asset in place and ready for its intended use. The cost of a factory machine, for instance, includes its invoice price, less any cash discount for early payment, plus freight, unpacking, and assembling costs. The cost of a capital asset also includes the necessary costs of installing and testing a machine before placing it in use. Examples are the costs of building a base or foundation for a machine, of providing electrical hook-ups, and of adjusting the machine before using it in operations.

An expenditure must be normal, reasonable, and necessary in preparing an asset for its intended use to be charged to and reported as part of the cost of a capital asset. If a machine is damaged during unpacking, the repairs are not added to its cost. Instead, they are charged to an expense account. Also, a traffic fine paid for moving heavy machinery on city streets without a proper permit is not part of the machinery's cost. But payment for a proper permit is included in the cost of machinery. Charges in addition to the purchase price are sometimes incurred to modify or customize a new capital asset or to bring a used asset up to specifications. These charges are added to the asset's cost. We explain how to determine the cost of capital assets in the remainder of this section for each of the four major classes of capital assets.

Land

When land is purchased for a building site, its cost includes the total amount paid for the land, including any real estate commissions. Its cost also includes fees for insuring the title, legal fees, and any accrued property taxes paid by the purchaser. Payments for surveying, clearing, grading, draining and landscaping also are included in the cost of land. Other costs of land include assessments by the local government, whether incurred at the time of purchase or later, for items such as roadways, sewers and sidewalks. These assessments are included because they "permanently" add to the land's value.

Land purchased as a building site sometimes includes a building that must be removed. In such cases, the total purchase price is charged to the Land account. But the cost of removing the building, less any amounts recovered through sale of salvaged materials, is also added to the Land account. To illustrate, assume a company bought land for a retail store for cash of $167,000. This land contains an old service garage that is removed at a net cost of $13,000 ($15,000 in costs less $2,000 proceeds from salvaged materials). Additional closing costs totalled $10,000, consisting of brokerage fees ($8,000), legal fees ($1,500), and title costs ($500). The cost of this land is $190,000 and is computed as shown in Exhibit 12.3.

Exhibit 12.3

Computing Cost of Land

Net cash price of land	$167,000
Net cost of garage removal	13,000
Closing costs	10,000
Cost of Land	**$190,000**

Land Improvements

Because land has an unlimited life and is not consumed when it is used, it is not subject to amortization. But **land improvements** such as parking lot surfaces, driveways, fences, and lighting systems have limited useful lives. While these costs increase the usefulness of the land, they are charged to a separate Land Improvement account so their costs can be allocated to the periods they benefit.

Buildings

A Building account is charged for the costs of purchasing or constructing a building when it is used in operations. When purchased, the costs of a building usually include its purchase price, brokerage fees, taxes, title fees, and attorney costs. Its costs also include all expenditures to make it ready for its intended use. This includes any necessary repairs or renovations to prepare the building for use such as wiring, lighting, flooring and wall coverings.

When a building, or any capital asset, is constructed by a company for its own use, its cost includes materials and labour plus a reasonable amount of indirect overhead cost. Overhead includes the costs of heat, lighting, power, and amortization on machinery used to construct the asset. Cost of construction also includes design fees, building permits, and insurance during construction. But insurance costs for coverage after the asset is placed in use are an operating expense. **Alcan Aluminium,** for instance, recently reported plans in its 1997 annual report to construct capital assets for its own use.

...the Company announced it was proceeding with the construction of a 375,000-tonne smelter at Alma, Quebec. Total cost is estimated at $1,600 [million], most of which will be incurred over the next three years. Approximately $220 [million] is expected to be spent in 1998.

Machinery and Equipment

The cost of machinery and equipment consists of all costs normal and necessary to purchase them and prepare them for their intended use. It includes the purchase price, less discounts, and plus taxes, transportation charges, insurance while in transit, and the installing, assembling and testing of machinery and equipment. **Sony**, for instance, disclosed in a recent annual report that:

capital expenditures [much of this machinery and equipment] during the year under review increased 27.9% to ... $2,817 million ... Sony intends to further increase its capital expenditures.

Lump-Sum Asset Purchase

Capital assets often are purchased in a group with a single transaction for a lump-sum price. This transaction is called a *lump-sum purchase*, also called group or basket purchase. When this occurs, we allocate the cost of the purchase among the different types of assets acquired based on their *relative market values*. Their market values can be estimated by appraisal or by using the tax-assessed valuations of the assets. To illustrate, Cola Company, paid $90,000 cash to acquire land appraised at $30,000, land improvements appraised at $10,000, and a building appraised at $60,000. The $90,000 cost was allocated on the basis of appraised values as shown in Exhibit 12.4.

Exhibit 12.4

Computing Costs in a Lump-Sum Purchase

	Appraised Value	Percent of Total	Apportioned Cost
Land	$ 30,000	30% ($30,000/$100,000)	**$27,000** ($90,000×30%)
Land improvements	10,000	10 ($10,000/$100,000)	**9,000** ($90,000×10%)
Building	60,000	60 ($60,000/$100,000)	**54,000** ($90,000×60%)
Totals	$100,000	100%	$90,000

Flash back

1. Identify the asset category for each of the following: (a) office supplies, (b) office equipment, (c) merchandise, (d) land held for future expansion, (e) trucks used in operations.
2. Identify the account charged for each of the following expenditures: (a) purchase price of a vacant lot, (b) cost of paving that vacant lot.
3. What amount is recorded as the cost of a new machine given the following items related to its purchase: gross purchase price, $700,000; sales tax, $49,000; purchase discount taken, $21,000; freight to move machine to plant, $3,500; assembly costs, $3,000; cost of foundation for machine, $2,500; cost of spare parts used in maintaining the machine, $4,200?

Answers—p. 592

Amortization

LO3 Explain amortization and the factors affecting its computation.

We explained in the prior section how capital assets are purchased for use in operations for more than one period. It is helpful to think of a capital asset as an amount of "usefulness" contributing to the operations of a company throughout the asset's useful life. Because the lives of all capital assets other than land are limited, the amount of usefulness expires as an asset is used. This expiration of a capital asset's amount of usefulness is called amortization. **Amortization** is the process of allocating the cost of a capital asset to expense in the accounting period benefiting from its use, which is required by the matching principle. That is, a portion of the cost of the asset is matched against the revenue it helps to generate.

The term *amortization* is the general term used for many situations where amounts are allocated to different accounts over varying lengths of time. When the Accounting Standards Board revised and reissued the standard on capital assets (Section 3060),[1] they said that the cost of capital assets should be amortized over their useful lives in a rational and systematic manner. In practice, the term **depreciation** still tends to be used for plant assets such as machinery and buildings, and the term *depletion* still tends to be used for natural resources. Amortization continues to be used for intangible assets and other items such as premium or discount on long-term debt. *We will continue to use the terms depreciation and depletion from time to time. Remember that they are terms that are specialized names for amortization.*

When a company buys a delivery truck for use as a capital asset, for instance, it acquires an amount of usefulness in the sense that it obtains a quantity of transportation. The total cost of this transportation is the cost of the truck less the expected proceeds to be received when the truck is sold or traded in at the end of its useful life. This net cost is allocated to the accounting periods that benefit from the truck's use. This allocation of the truck's cost is amortization.

Note that amortization does not measure the decline in the truck's market value each period. Nor does it measure the physical deterioration of the truck each period. Amortization is a process of allocating a capital asset's cost to expense over its useful life, nothing more. Because amortization reflects the cost of using a capital asset, we do not begin recording amortization charges until the asset is actually put into use providing services or producing products. This section describes the factors we need in computing amortization, the amortization methods used, revisions in amortization, and amortization for partial periods.

Factors in Computing Amortization

Three factors are relevant in determining amortization. They are (1) cost, (2) salvage value, and (3) useful life.

Cost

The cost of a capital asset consists of all necessary and reasonable expenditures to acquire it and to prepare the asset for its intended use. We described the computation of cost earlier in this chapter.

Salvage Value

The total amount of amortization charged off over an asset's benefit period equals the asset's cost minus its estimated salvage value. **Salvage value**, also called *residual value* or *scrap value*, is an estimate of the asset's value at the end of its benefit period. This is often viewed as the amount we expect to receive from selling the asset at the end of its benefit period. If we expect an asset to be traded in on a new asset, its salvage value is the expected trade-in value.

[1] *CICA Handbook*, section 3060, "Capital Assets," par. .31.

Useful (Service) Life

The **useful life** of a capital asset is the length of time it is productively used in a company's operations. Useful life, also called *service life*, is not necessarily as long as the asset's total productive life. As an example, the productive life of a computer is often four to eight years or more. Yet some companies trade in old computers for new ones every two years. In this case, these computers have a two-year useful life. This means the cost of these computers (less their expected trade-in value) is charged to amortization expense over a two-year period.

Several variables often make the useful life of a capital asset hard to predict. A major variable is the wear and tear from use in operations. But two other variables, inadequacy and obsolescence, also demand consideration. When a company grows more rapidly than expected, its assets sometimes do not meet the company's productive demands. **Inadequacy** refers to the condition where the capacity of a company's capital assets is too small to meet the company's productive demands. Obsolescence, like inadequacy, is hard to predict because the timing of new inventions and improvements normally can't be predicted. **Obsolescence** refers to a condition where, because of new inventions and improvements, a capital asset is no longer useful in producing goods or services. A company usually disposes of an obsolete asset before it wears out.

A company is often able to better predict the useful life of a new asset based on its past experience with a similar asset. When it has no experience with a type of asset, a company relies on the experience of others or on engineering studies and judgment. In note 1 of its 1996 annual report, **Call-Net Enterprises** reported the following useful lives:

Depreciation and amortization are being provided based on the estimated useful lives of the assets on a straight-line basis as follows:

Buildings	40 years
Fibre optic cable and equipment	20 years
Multiplex and telephone switch equipment	10 years
Computer equipment and software	3 to 5 years
Furniture and fixtures	5 years
Leasehold improvements	term of the lease
Equipment under capital lease	term of lease, not exceeding estimated useful life

Life Expectancy

The life expectancy of capital assets is often in the eye of the beholder. Take **Imperial Oil** and **Suncor Energy,** for instance. Both compete in the oil industry, yet their refineries' life expectancies are quite different. Imperial amortizes its refineries over 25 years, but Suncor amortizes its refineries over an average of 32 years. Such differences can dramatically impact their financial statement numbers. [Source: *Imperial Oil Annual Report,* 1997; *Suncor Energy Annual Report,* 1997.]

Did You Know?

Amortization Methods

LO 4 Compute and record amortization using the methods of straight-line, units-of-production, and declining-balance.

There are many *amortization methods* for allocating a capital asset's cost over the accounting periods in its useful life. The most frequently used method of amortization is the straight-line method. Another common amortization method is the units-of-production method. We explain these two methods in this section.

We also describe accelerated amortization methods, with an emphasis on the declining-balance method.

The computations in this section use information from an athletic shoe manufacturer. In particular, we look at a machine used for inspecting athletic shoes before packaging. This machine is used by manufacturers such as **Converse, Reebok, Adidas** and **L.A.Gear,** and its data for amortization are shown in Exhibit 12.5.

Exhibit 12.5

Data for Athletic Shoe Testing Machine

Cost	$10,000
Salvage value	1,000
Amortizable cost	$ 9,000
Useful life:	
Accounting periods	5 years
Units inspected	36,000 shoes

Straight-Line Method

Straight-line amortization (or depreciation) charges the same amount to expense for each period of the asset's useful life. A two-step process is used to compute expense. We first compute the *amortizable cost* over the asset's life; this amount is also called the *cost to be amortized (or depreciated).* It is computed by subtracting the asset's salvage value from its total cost. Second, amortizable cost is divided by the number of accounting periods in the asset's useful life.

The formula and computation for straight-line amortization of the inspection equipment described above is shown in Exhibit 12.6.

Exhibit 12.6

Straight-Line Amortization Formula

$$\frac{\textbf{Cost} - \textbf{Salvage value}}{\textbf{Useful life in years}} = \frac{\$10{,}000 - \$1{,}000}{5 \text{ years}} = \$1{,}800 \text{ per year}$$

If this equipment is purchased on December 31, 1998, and used throughout its predicted useful life of five years, the straight-line method allocates an equal amount of amortization to each of the years 1999 through 2003. We make the following adjusting entry at the end of each of these five years to record straight-line amortization of this equipment:

Dec. 31	Amortization Expense	1,800	
	Accumulated Amortization, Equipment		1,800
	To record annual amortization over its five-year useful life.		

Assets = Liabilities + Equity
− 1,800 − 1,800

The $1,800 Amortization Expense appears on the income statement in operating expenses. This entry uses the common practice of crediting Accumulated Amortization, a contra account, to the Equipment account in the balance sheet.

The graph on the left in Exhibit 12.7 shows the $1,800 per year expense amount reported each of these five years. The graph on the right shows the amounts reported on each of the six December 31 balance sheets while the company owns the asset. The net balance sheet amount is the asset's **book value** for each of those years and is computed as the asset's original cost less its accumulated amortization. At the end of year two, its book value is $6,400 and is reported in the balance sheet as:

Equipment	$10,000	
Less accumulated amortization	3,600	$6,400

Note the book value declines by $1,800 of amortization each year. From these graphs we can see why this method is called straight-line.

We can also compute a straight-line amortization rate, computed as 100% divided by the number of periods in the asset's useful life. In the case of our machine, this rate is 20% (100% ÷ 5 years). We use this rate and other information on this machine to compute its *straight-line amortization schedule* shown in Exhibit 12.8.

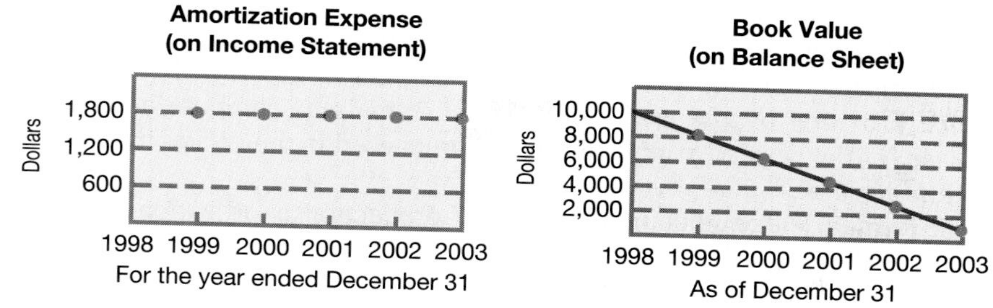

Exhibit 12.7

Financial Statement Effects of Straight-Line Amortization

Exhibit 12.8

Straight-Line Amortization Schedule

	Amortization for the Period			End of Period	
Period	Amortizable Cost	Amortization Rate	Amortization Expense	Accumulated Amortization	Book Value
1998	—	—	—	—	$10,000
1999	$9,000*	20%	$1,800	$1,800	8,200
2000	9,000	20	1,800	3,600	6,400
2001	9,000	20	1,800	5,400	4,600
2002	9,000	20	1,800	7,200	2,800
2003	9,000	20	1,800	9,000	1,000

*$10,000 − $1,000.

Note three items in this schedule. First, amortization expense is the same each period. Second, accumulated amortization is the sum of current and prior periods' amortization expense. Third, book value declines each period until it equals salvage value at the end of its useful life.

Straight-line is by far the most frequently applied amortization method in financial reporting. **Bombardier,** for instance, discloses its amortization method in its 1997 annual report as follows:

> Depreciation is computed under the straight-line method over the...estimated useful lives.

Units-of-Production Method

While many companies use straight-line amortization, other methods are common in certain industries. The main purpose of recording amortization is to provide relevant information about the cost of consuming an asset's usefulness. This means that in each accounting period an asset is used it is charged with a share of its cost. The straight-line method charges an equal share to each period. If capital assets are used about the same amount in each accounting period, this method produces a reasonable matching of expenses with revenues. Yet the use of some capital assets varies greatly from one accounting period to the next. A builder, for instance, may use a piece of construction equipment for a month and then not use it again for several months.

When use of equipment varies from period to period, the units-of-production amortization method can provide a better matching of expenses with revenues than straight-line amortization. **Units-of-production amortization** charges a varying amount to expense for each period of an asset's useful life depending on its usage.

A two-step process is used to compute units-of-production amortization. We first compute the *amortization per unit*. It is computed by subtracting the asset's salvage value from its total cost, and dividing by the total number of units expected to be produced during its useful life. Units of production can be expressed in units of product or in any other unit of measure such as hours used or distance driven. This gives us the amount of amortization per unit of service provided by the asset. The second step is to compute amortization expense for the period by multiplying the units used in the period by the amortization per unit.

The formula and computation for units-of-production amortization for the testing machine described above (note, we expect 7,000 shoes inspected in its first year) are shown in Exhibit 12.9.

Exhibit 12.9

Units-of-Production Amortization Formula

Step 1:

$$\textbf{Amortization per unit} = \frac{\textbf{Cost} - \textbf{Salvage value}}{\textbf{Total units of production}} = \frac{\$10{,}000 - \$1{,}000}{36{,}000 \text{ units}} = \$0.25 \text{ per shoe}$$

Step 2:

$$\textbf{Amortization expense} = \textbf{Amortization per unit} \times \textbf{Units used in period}$$

$$0.25 \text{ per shoe} \times 7{,}000 \text{ shoes} = \$1{,}750$$

Using the production estimates for the machine we compute the *units-of-production amortization schedule* shown in Exhibit 12.10. If the machine inspects 7,000 shoes in its first year, amortization for that first year is $1,750 (7,000 shoes at $0.25 per shoe). If the machine inspects 8,000 shoes in the second year, amortization for the second year is 8,000 shoes times $0.25 per shoe, or $2,000.

Exhibit 12.10

Units-of-Production Amortization Schedule

	Amortization for the Period			End of Period	
Period	**Number of Units**	**Amortization per Unit**	**Amortization Expense**	**Accumulated Amortization**	**Book Value**
1998	—	—	—	—	$10,000
1999	7,000	$0.25	$1,750	$1,750	8,250
2000	8,000	0.25	2,000	3,750	6,250
2001	9,000	0.25	2,250	6,000	4,000
2002	7,000	0.25	1,750	7,750	2,250
2003	5,000	0.25	1,250	9,000	1,000

Note that amortization expense depends on unit output, accumulated amortization is the sum of current and prior periods' amortization expense, and book value declines each period until it equals salvage value at the end of its useful life.

Units-of-production amortization method is not as frequently applied as straight-line. **Imperial Oil,** for instance, is one company using it and reports the following in its 1996 annual report:

> Depreciation and depletion are calculated using the unit-of-production method for producing properties.

Declining-Balance Method

This section describes an accelerated amortization method. An **accelerated amortization method** yields larger amortization expenses in the early years of an asset's life and smaller charges in later years. While there are several accelerated methods used in financial reporting, the most common is the declining-balance method. The **declining-balance** method of amortization uses an amortization rate of up to twice the straight-line rate and applies it to the asset's beginning-of-period book value. Because book value *declines* each period, the amount of amortization also declines each period.

A common amortization rate is twice the straight-line rate. This method is called *double-declining-balance* method. The double-declining-balance method is applied as follows: (1) compute the asset's straight-line amortization rate; (2) double it; and (3) compute amortization expense by applying this rate to the asset's beginning-of-period book value. Note salvage value is *not* used in these computations.

Let's return to the athletic shoe testing machine and apply the double-declining-balance method to compute its amortization expense. Exhibit 12.11 shows this formula and its first year computation for the testing machine. The three-step process is: (1) divide 100% by five years to determine the straight-line annual amortization rate of 20% per year, (2) double this 20% rate to get a declining-balance rate of 40% per year, and (3) compute annual amortization expense as shown in Exhibit 12.11.

Exhibit 12.11

Double-Declining-Balance Amortization Formula

Step 1:

Straight-line amortization rate = 100% ÷ Useful life in periods = 100% ÷ 5 years = 20%

Step 2:

Double-declining-balance rate = 2 × Straight-line rate = 2 × 20% = 40%

Step 3:

Amortization expense = Double-declining-balance rate × Beginning period book value

40% × $10,000 = $4,000

The *double-declining-balance amortization schedule* is shown in Exhibit 12.12. Note in year 2003, amortization expense is $296. This is not equal to 40% × $1,296, or $518.40. Instead, the $296 is computed by subtracting the $1,000 salvage value from the $1,296 book value at the beginning of the fifth year. This is done because an asset should not be amortized below its salvage value. If we had used the $518.40 for amortization expense in 2003, then ending book value would equal $777.60, which is less than the $1,000 salvage value.

Exhibit 12.12

Double-Declining-Balance Amortization Schedule

	Amortization for the Period			End of Period	
Period	Beginning-of-Period Book Value	Amortization Rate	Amortization Expense	Accumulated Amortization	Book Value
1998	—	—	—	—	$10,000
1999	$10,000*	40%	$4,000	$4,000	6,000
2000	6,000	40	2,400	6,400	3,600
2001	3,600	40	1,440	7,840	2,160
2002	2,160	40	864	8,704	1,296
2003	1,296	40	296*	9,000	1,000

*Year 2003 amortization is $1,296 − $1,000 = $296. This is because book value can't be less than salvage value.

Comparing Amortization Methods

LO 5 Compare and analyze amortization for different methods.

Exhibit 12.13 shows the amortization expense for the athletic shoe testing machine under each of the three amortization methods.

Exhibit 12.13

Amortization Methods Compared

Period	Straight-Line	Units-of-Production	Double-Declining Balance
1999	$1,800	$1,750	$4,000
2000	1,800	2,000	2,400
2001	1,800	2,250	1,440
2002	1,800	1,750	864
2003	1,800	1,250	296
	$9,000	$9,000	$9,000

Note that while the amount of amortization expense per period is different for different methods, total amortization expense is the same for the machine's useful life. This is to say each method starts with a total cost of $10,000 and ends with a salvage value of $1,000. The difference is the pattern in amortization expense over the useful life. In this regard, note the book value of the asset when using straight-line is always greater than when using double-declining-balance, except at the beginning and end of an asset's useful life. Also, note the straight-line method yields a steady pattern of amortization expense, while the units-of-production does not because it depends on the number of units produced. But each of these methods is acceptable as they allocate cost in a rational and systematic manner.[2] The method chosen should be the one which provides the best matching of expenses to revenue.

Did You Know?

What's Hot in Amortization

A recent survey suggests 90% of companies use straight-line amortization for their capital assets, 7% use declining-balance, and 2% use units-of-production. [Source: *Financial Reporting in Canada*, 1997.]

Amortization for Income Tax Reporting

The rules a company follows for financial accounting purposes are usually different from the rules it follows for tax accounting purposes. Remember that financial accounting aims to report useful information on financial performance and position. Tax accounting reflects government objectives in raising revenues. Differences between these two accounting systems are normal and expected. Amortization is a common example.

The Income Tax Act requires that companies use a declining-balance method for calculating the maximum **capital cost allowance** (amortization or depreciation for tax purposes) that may be claimed in any period. This is because it reduces taxable income with higher amortization expense in the early years of an asset's life. But taxable income is higher in the later years. The government's goal here is to decrease taxes in the early years to encourage capital investment. This means a company can use these resources now to earn additional profit through lower taxes. The act specifies the rates for various classes of assets. For example, a rate of 20% would be used for general machinery and equipment, and a rate of 4% for most buildings. Further discussion of the details of tax accounting for capital assets is deferred to a more advanced course.

---

[2] Ibid.

Did You Know?

AmortizationTech

Computer technology greatly simplifies amortization computations and revisions. There are many inexpensive, off-the-shelf software packages and business calculators that allow a user to choose from a variety of amortization methods for each asset entered. Detailed amortization schedules for both financial reporting and income tax reporting are quickly and accurately generated.

Partial Year Amortization

LO 6 Explain amortization for partial years and when estimates change.

Capital assets are purchased and disposed of at various times during a period. When an asset is purchased (or disposed of) at a time other than the beginning or end of an accounting period, amortization is recorded for part of a year. This is so the year of purchase or the year of disposal is charged with its share of the asset's amortization.

To illustrate let's return to the athletic shoe testing machine. *Assume this machine is purchased and placed in service on October 8, 1999*, and the annual accounting period ends on December 31. Recall this machine costs $10,000, has a useful life of five years, and a salvage value of $1,000. Because this machine is purchased and used for nearly three months in 1999, the annual income statement should report amortization expense on the machine for that part of the year. The amount of amortization reported usually is based on the assumption that an asset is purchased on the first of the month nearest the actual date of purchase. In this case, since the purchase occurred on October 8, we assume an October 1 purchase date. This means three months' amortization is recorded in 1999. If the purchase occurred anytime between October 16 through November 15, amortization is computed as if the purchase is on November 1. Using straight-line amortization, we compute three months' amortization of $450 as follows:

$$\frac{\$10{,}000 - \$1{,}000}{5 \text{ years}} = \$1{,}800 \times \frac{3}{12} = \$450$$

A similar computation is necessary when disposal of an asset occurs during a year. As an example, let's suppose the machine described above is sold on June 24, 2004. Amortization is recorded for the period January 1 through June 24 when it is disposed of. This partial year's amortization, computed to the nearest whole month, is:

$$\frac{\$10{,}000 - \$1{,}000}{5 \text{ years}} = \$1{,}800 \times \frac{6}{12} = \$900$$

Revising Amortization Rates

Because amortization is based on predictions of salvage value and useful life, amortization expense is an estimate. During the useful life of an asset, new information may indicate the original predictions are inaccurate. If our estimate of an asset's useful life and/or salvage value changes, what should we do? The answer is to use the new estimate of the remaining useful life to compute amortization for current and future periods. This means we revise amortization expense computation by spreading the remaining cost to be amortized over the revised useful life remaining. This approach is used for all amortization methods.

Let's return to our athletic shoe testing machine using straight-line amortization. At the beginning of this asset's third year, its book value is $6,400, computed as:

Cost	$10,000
Less two year's accumulated amortization	3,600
Book value	$ 6,400

At the beginning of its third year, we suppose the predicted number of years remaining in its useful life changes from three to four years *and* its estimate of salvage value changes to $400. Amortization for each of the machine's four remaining years is computed as shown in Exhibit 12.14.

Exhibit 12.14

Computing Revised Amortization Rates

$$\frac{\textbf{Book value} - \textbf{Revised salvage value}}{\textbf{Revised remaining useful life}} = \frac{\$6,400 - \$400}{4 \text{ years}} = \$1,500 \text{ per year}$$

This means $1,500 of amortization expense is recorded for the machine at the end of the third through sixth years of its remaining useful life.

Note this asset was amortized at the rate of $1,800 per year for the first two years. It is tempting to conclude that amortization expense is overstated in these first two years. But these expenses reflected the best information available at that time. Therefore we do not go back and restate past years' financial statements in light of this new information. Instead we adjust the current and future periods' statements to reflect this new information.

Revising estimates of the useful life or salvage value of a capital asset is referred to as a **change in an accounting estimate**. A change in an accounting estimate results from "the exercise of judgement and reappraisal as new events occur, as more experience is acquired, or as additional information is obtained."[3] Such a change in an accounting estimate is reflected in future financial statements, and does not result in changes in past statements.[4]

Flash back

4. On January 1, 1999, a company pays $77,000 to purchase office furniture with a zero salvage value. The furniture's useful life is somewhere between 7 to 10 years. What is the 1999 straight-line amortization on the furniture using a (a) 7-year useful life and (b) 10-year useful life?

Answer—p. 592

Reporting Amortization on Assets

Both the cost and accumulated amortization of capital assets are reported on the balance sheet. **Semi-Tech Corporation,** for instance, reports the following in its balance sheet:

($ in millions)	1997	1996
Property, plant and equipment:		
Land	$217	$172
Buildings	208	200
Machinery	333	309
Construction in Progress	6	9
	$764	$690
Less accumulated amortization	(280)	(251)
Total	$484	$439

[3] *CICA Handbook*, section 1506, "Accounting Changes," par. .22

[4] Ibid. par. .25

Many companies show capital assets on one line with the net amount of cost less accumulated amortization. When this is done the amount of accumulated amortization is disclosed in a note. Note that Alliance reports only the net amount of its property and equipment in its balance sheet in Appendix I. To satisfy the *full-disclosure principle*,[5] Alliance also describes its amortization methods in note 1 and the individual amounts comprising capital assets in note 3.

Reporting both the cost and accumulated amortization of capital assets helps balance sheet readers compare the assets of different companies. For example, a company holding assets costing $50,000 and accumulated amortization of $40,000 is likely in a different situation from a company with new assets costing $10,000. While the net unamortized cost is the same in both cases, the first company may have more productive capacity available but likely is facing the need to replace older assets. These insights are not provided if the two balance sheets report only the $10,000 book values.

We emphasize that amortization is a process of cost allocation. Capital assets are reported on a balance sheet at their remaining unamortized costs (book value), not at market values. This emphasis on costs rather than market values is based on the *going-concern principle* described in Chapter 2. This principle states that, unless there is evidence to the contrary, we assume a company continues in business. This implies that capital assets are held and used long enough to recover their cost through the sale of products and services. Since capital assets are not intended to be sold until they are no longer useful, their market values are not reported in the financial statements. Instead, assets are reported on a balance sheet at cost less accumulated amortization. This is the remaining portion of the cost that is expected to be recovered in future periods.

Accumulated amortization on a balance sheet does not reflect funds accumulated to buy new assets when the assets currently owned are replaced. Accumulated amortization is a contra account with a credit balance that can not buy anything. If a company has funds available to buy assets, the funds are shown on the balance sheet in liquid assets such as *Cash*.

Flash back

5. What is the meaning of the term *amortization* in accounting?
6. A company purchases a new machine for $96,000 on January 1, 1999. Its predicted useful life is five years or 100,000 units of product, and its salvage value is $8,000. During 1999, 10,000 units of product are produced. Compute the book value of this machine on December 31, 1999, assuming (a) straight-line amortization and (b) units-of-production amortization.
7. In early January 1999, a company acquires equipment at a cost of $3,800. The company estimates this equipment to have a useful life of three years and a salvage value of $200. Early in 2001, the company changes its estimate to a total four-year useful life and zero salvage value. Using straight-line amortization, what is amortization expense on this equipment for the year ended 2001?

Answers—p. 592

[5] *CICA Handbook*, section 3060, "Capital Assets," par. .58.

Judgment and Ethics

Controller

You are the controller for Fascar Company. Fascar has struggled financially for more than two years, and there are no signs of improvement. Fascar's operations require major investments in equipment, and amortization is a large item in computing income. Fascar's industry normally requires frequent replacements of equipment, and equipment is typically amortized over three years. Your company's president recently instructed you to revise estimated useful lives of equipment from three to six years and to use a six-year life on all new equipment. You suspect this instruction is motivated by a desire to improve reported income. What actions do you take?

Answer—p. 591

Mid-Chapter Demonstration Problem

Gemini Fitness Club used straight-line amortization for a machine that cost $43,500, under the assumption it would have a four-year life and a $4,500 trade-in value. After two years, Gemini determined that the machine still had three more years of remaining useful life, after which it would have an estimated $3,600 trade-in value. (a) Calculate the machine's book value at the end of its second year. (b) Calculate the amount of amortization to be charged during each of the remaining years in the machine's revised useful life.

Solution to Mid-Chapter Demonstration Problem

a.	Original cost of machine	$ 43,500
	Less two years' accumulated amortization	
	[($43,500 − $4,500)/4] × 2	(19,500)
	Book value at end of second year	$ 24,000

b.	Book value at end of second year	$ 24,000
	Less revised salvage value	(3,600)
	Remaining amortizable cost	$ 20,400
	Revised annual amortization to be charged = $20,400/3 =	$6,800

Revenue and Capital Expenditures

LO7 Distinguish between revenue and capital expenditures, and account for these expenditures.

When a capital asset is acquired and put into service, additional expenditures often are incurred after the acquisition to operate, maintain, repair and improve it. In recording these added expenditures, we must decide whether they are capitalized or expensed. To capitalize an expenditure is to debit the asset account. A main issue is whether more useful information is provided by reporting these expenditures as current expenses or by adding them to the capital asset's cost and amortizing them over its remaining useful life.

Revenue expenditures are additional costs of capital assets that do not materially increase the asset's life or productive capabilities. They are recorded as expenses and deducted from revenues in the current period's income statement. Examples of revenue expenditures, also called *income statement expenditures*, are supplies, fuel, lubricants and electric power. **Capital expenditures**, also called *balance sheet expenditures*, are additional costs of capital assets that provide material benefits extending beyond the current period. They are debited to asset accounts and reported on the balance sheet. Capital expenditures increase or improve the type or amount of service an asset provides. Examples are roofing replacement, plant expansion, and major overhauls of machinery and equipment.

Financial statements are affected for several years by the choice between recording costs as revenue expenditures or as capital expenditures. Managers must be careful in classifying them. This classification decision is helped by identifying costs as repairs, betterments, or low-cost asset purchases.

Repairs

Repairs are expenditures to keep the asset in normal, good operating condition. They are necessary if an asset is to perform to expectations over its useful life. Repairs do not extend an asset's useful life beyond its original estimate and do not increase its productivity beyond original expectations. Examples are costs of cleaning, lubricating, adjusting, and replacing (small) parts of a machine. Repairs are treated as *revenue expenditures*. This means their costs are reported as expenses on the current income statements. Consistent with this rule, **Air Canada** reports:

> Maintenance and repair costs are charged to operating expenses as incurred. Significant modification costs are capitalized and amortized over the remaining service lives of the assets.

Betterments

Betterments, also called *improvements*, are expenditures making a capital asset more efficient or productive. A betterment might increase the physical output or service capacity, lower operating costs, extend the useful life, or improve the quality of output. A betterment often involves adding a component to an asset or replacing one of its old components with a better component. However, a betterment does not always increase an asset's useful life. An example is replacing manual controls on a machine with automatic controls to reduce labour costs. This machine will still wear out just as fast as it would with manual controls.[6]

Because a betterment benefits future periods it is debited to the asset account as a capital expenditure. The new book value (less salvage) is amortized over the asset's remaining useful life. As an example, suppose a company pays $8,000 for a machine with an eight-year useful life and no salvage value. On January 2, after three years and $3,000 of amortization, it adds an automated system to the machine at a cost of $1,800. This results in reduced labour cost in operating the machine in future periods. The cost of this betterment is added to the Machinery account with this entry:

Jan. 2	Machinery	1,800	
	Cash		1,800
	To record installation of automated control system.		

Assets = Liabilities + Equity
+ 1,800
− 1,800

After the betterment is added, the remaining cost to be amortized is $6,800, computed as $8,000 + $1,800 − $3,000. Amortization expense for the remaining five years is $1,360 per year, computed as $6,800/5 years as shown in Exhibit 12.15.

[6] One special type of betterment is an *addition*. Examples include a new wing to a factory or a new dock to a warehouse. All additions are capitalized.

Exhibit 12.15

Revised Amortization Schedule from Betterments

	Before	Betterment	After
Original cost	$8,000	$1,800	$9,800
Accumulated amortization	(3,000)		(3,000)
Book value	$5,000		$6,800
Amortization in remaining years ($6,800/5 years)			$1,360

You Make the Call

Mechanic

You are a mechanic who recently opened your own auto service centre. Because of a cash shortage, you are preparing financial statements in the hope of getting a short-term loan from the bank. A friend of yours suggests you treat as many expenses as possible like capital expenditures. What are the impacts on financial statements of treating expenses as capital expenditures? What do you think is the aim of your friend's proposal?

Answer—p. 591

Low-Cost Asset Purchases

Maintaining individual capital asset records can be expensive, even in the most advanced system. For that reason many companies do not keep detailed records for assets costing less than some minimum amount such as $100. Instead, these low-cost capital assets are treated as a revenue expenditure. This means their costs are directly charged to an expense account at the time of purchase. This practice is acceptable under the *materiality principle*. Treating immaterial capital expenditures as revenue expenditures is unlikely to mislead users of financial statements. As an example, in its 1996 annual report **Coca-Cola** discloses that it only capitalizes *major* or material betterments:

> Additions and major replacements or betterments are added to the assets at cost. Maintenance and repair costs and minor replacements are charged to expense when incurred.

Flash back

8. At the beginning of the fifth year of a machine's estimated six-year useful life, the machine is overhauled and its estimated useful life is extended to nine years in total. This machine originally cost $108,000 and the overhaul cost is $12,000. Prepare the entry recording the cost of this overhaul.
9. Explain the difference between revenue expenditures and capital expenditures and how they are recorded.
10. What is a betterment? How is a betterment recorded?

Answers—p. 592

Disposals of Capital Assets

Capital assets are disposed of for several reasons. Many assets eventually wear out or become obsolete. Other assets are sold because of changing business plans. Sometimes an asset is discarded or sold because it is damaged by fire or accident. Regardless of the cause, disposals of capital assets occur in one of three ways: discarding, sale, or exchange. The accounting for each of these three types of disposals of capital assets is described in Exhibit 12.16.

LO 8 Account for asset disposal through discarding, selling, or exchanging an asset.

Exhibit 12.16

Accounting for Disposals of Capital Assets

1. Record amortization expense up to the date of disposal. This updates the accumulated amortization account.
2. Remove the balances of the disposed asset and related accumulated amortization accounts.
3. Record any cash (and other assets) received or paid in the disposal.
4. Record any gain or loss resulting from comparing the asset's book value with the net amount received or paid at disposal.*

*There is one exception to step 4 in the case of asset exchanges that we will describe later in this section.

Discarding Capital Assets

A capital asset is *discarded* when it is no longer useful to the company and it has no market value. To illustrate, assume a machine costing $9,000 with accumulated amortization of $9,000 is discarded on June 5. When accumulated amortization equals the asset's cost it is said to be fully amortized (zero book value). A *fully amortized* (or depreciated) asset does not usually yield a gain or loss on disposal. The entry to record the discarding of this asset is:

June 5	Accumulated Amortization, Machinery	9,000	
	Machinery		9,000
	To record the discarding of fully amortized machinery.		

Assets	= Liabilities	+ Equity
+9,000		
−9,000		

Note this entry reflects all four steps of Exhibit 12.16. Step 1 is not needed since the machine is fully amortized. Step 2 is shown in the debit to Accumulated Amortization and credit to Machinery. Since no cash is involved, step 3 is irrelevant. Also, since book value is zero and no cash is involved, no gain or loss is recorded in step 4.

How do we account for discarding an asset that is not fully amortized? Or one whose amortization is not up to date? To answer this, consider equipment costing $8,000 with accumulated amortization of $6,000 on December 31 of the prior fiscal year-end. This equipment is being amortized using the straight-line method over eight years with zero salvage value. On July 1 it is discarded. Step 1 is to bring amortization expense up to date:

July 1	Amortization Expense	500	
	Accumulated Amortization, Equipment		500
	To record the first six months amortization ($1,000 × 6/12).		

Assets	= Liabilities	+ Equity
−500		−500

The second and final entry reflects steps 2–4 of Exhibit 12.16.

July 1	Accumulated Amortization, Equipment	6,500	
	Loss on Disposal of Equipment	1,500	
	Equipment		8,000
	To record the discarding of machinery having a $1,500 book value.		

Assets	= Liabilities	+ Equity
+6,500		−1,500
−8,000		

The loss is computed by comparing the equipment's $1,500 ($8,000 − $6,000 − $500) book value with the zero net cash proceeds. The loss on disposal is reported in the Other Expenses and Losses section of the income statement. In some circumstances, an asset disposal might also yield a cash payment, such as a removal cost, instead of a receipt. Entries like those shown above are made in this case so that the income statement shows any gain or loss from disposal and the balance sheet reflects changes in the asset and accumulated amortization accounts.

Selling Capital Assets

To illustrate the accounting for selling capital assets we consider SportsWorld's April 1 sale of its delivery equipment costing $16,000 with accumulated amortization of $12,000 on December 31 of the prior fiscal year-end. Annual amortization on this equipment is $4,000 computed using straight-line amortization. The entry (step 1) to record amortization expense and update accumulated amortization to April 1 is:

Assets	= Liabilities	+ Equity
−1,000		−1,000

April 1	Amortization Expense	1,000	
	Accumulated Amortization, Equipment		1,000
	To record the first three months amortization ($4,000 × 3/12).		

The second entry to reflect steps 2–4 of Exhibit 12.16 depends on the amount received in the sale. We consider three different possibilities.

Sale at Book Value

If SportsWorld receives $3,000 cash, an amount equal to the equipment's book value, there is no gain or loss on disposal. The entry is:

Assets	= Liabilities	+ Equity
+3,000		
+13,000		
−16,000		

April 1	Cash	3,000	
	Accumulated Amortization, Equipment	13,000	
	Equipment		16,000
	To record the sale of equipment for no gain or loss.		

Sale above Book Value

If SportsWorld receives $7,000 cash, an amount $4,000 above the equipment's book value, there is a gain on disposal. The entry is:

Assets	= Liabilities	+ Equity
+7,000		+4,000
+13,000		
−16,000		

April 1	Cash	7,000	
	Accumulated Amortization, Equipment	13,000	
	Gain on Disposal of Equipment		4,000
	Equipment		16,000
	To record the sale of equipment for a $4,000 gain.		

Sale below Book Value

If SportsWorld receives $2,500 cash, an amount $500 below the equipment's book value, there is a loss on disposal. The entry is:

Assets	= Liabilities	+ Equity
+2,500		−500
+13,000		
−16,000		

April 1	Cash	2,500	
	Loss on Disposal of Equipment	500	
	Accumulated Amortization, Equipment	13,000	
	Equipment		16,000
	To record the sale of equipment for a $500 loss.		

Companies at times restructure or downsize operations, which often involves selling capital assets. As part of its restructuring, **Woolworth** sold approximately 120 of its Woolco discount stores to Wal-Mart. Sale of its Woolco stores yielded a $168 million loss charged against revenues.

Exchanging Capital Assets

Many capital assets such as machinery, automobiles and office equipment are disposed of by exchanging them for new assets. In a typical exchange of capital assets, a trade-in allowance is received on the old asset and the balance is paid in cash. Accounting for the exchange of assets is similar to any other disposal with one exception depending on whether the old and the new assets are similar in the functions they perform. Trading an old truck for a new truck is an exchange of similar assets, whereas trading a truck for a machine is an exchange of dissimilar assets. The recognition of gains and losses on exchanging capital assets is shown in Exhibit 12.17.

Exhibit 12.17

Gains and Losses on Capital Asset Exchanges

Assets Exchanged	Losses Recognized	Gains Recognized
Dissimilar	Yes	Yes
Similar—Monetary	Yes	Yes
Similar—Nonmonetary	No	No

Note that gains and losses on dissimilar and monetary asset exchanges are recognized, but gains and losses are not generally recognized for similar, nonmonetary asset exchanges. The reason gains and losses from a similar asset exchange is not recognized is because the exchanged asset's earnings process is not considered complete. The decision to recognize a loss from a similar asset exchange is an application of *accounting conservatism*. This section explains the accounting for these cases.

Exchanging Dissimilar Assets

If a company exchanges a capital asset for another asset that is dissimilar in use or purpose, any gain or loss on the exchange is recorded. Any gain or loss is computed by comparing the book value of the asset given up with the fair market value of the asset received.

Receiving More in Exchange: A Gain

Let's assume a company exchanges both an old machine and $16,500 in cash for land. The old machine originally cost $18,000 and has accumulated amortization of $15,000 at the time of exchange. The land received has a fair market value of $21,000. Using the four steps outlined in Exhibit 12.16, the entry to record this exchange is:

Jan. 2	Land	21,000	
	Accumulated Amortization, Machinery	15,000	
	Machinery		18,000
	Cash		16,500
	Gain on Exchange of Assets		1,500
	To record exchange of old machine and cash for land.		

Assets	= Liabilities	+ Equity
+21,000		+1,500
+15,000		
−18,000		
−16,500		

We compute the gain on this transaction in the second column of Exhibit 12.18. Note the book value of the assets given totals $19,500. This includes the $16,500 cash and the $3,000 ($18,000 − $15,000) book value of the machine. This $19,500 book value of assets given is compared to the fair market value of the land received ($21,000). This yields a gain of $1,500 ($21,000 − $19,500).[7]

Exhibit 12.18

Computing Gain or Loss on Dissimilar Asset Exchanges

Dissimilar Plant Asset Exchange	Gain		Loss	
Fair Market Value of Asset(s) Received		$21,000		$16,000
Book Value of Asset(s) Given:				
Machine	$ 3,000		$ 3,000	
Cash	16,500		16,500	
		19,500		19,500
Gain (Loss) on Exchange		$ 1,500		($ 3,500)

Receiving Less in Exchange: A Loss

Let's assume the same facts as in the exchange above except the land received has a fair market value of $16,000, not the $21,000 noted previously. The entry to record this exchange is:

Jan. 2	Land	16,000	
	Loss on Exchange of Assets	3,500	
	Accumulated Amortization, Machinery	15,000	
	Machinery		18,000
	Cash		16,500
	To record exchange of old machine and cash for land.		

Assets	=	Liabilities	+	Equity
+16,000				−3,500
+15,000				
−18,000				
−16,500				

We compute the loss on this transaction in the third column of Exhibit 12.18. The $19,500 book value of assets given is compared to the fair market value of the land received ($16,000). This yields a loss of $3,500 ($16,000 − $19,500).

Exchanging Similar Assets—Monetary

In general, accounting for exchanges of similar assets depends on whether the amount of cash involved is more or less than 10% of the total consideration given up or received. If the amount of cash is more than 10%, the transaction is a monetary transaction and a gain or loss on the exchange is recorded in the same manner as for exchanges of dissimilar assets.

Receiving Less in Exchange: A Loss

Let's assume a company exchanges both old equipment and $33,000 in cash for new equipment. The old equipment originally cost $36,000 and has accumulated amortization of $20,000 at the time of exchange. The new equipment received has a fair market value of $42,000. This would be considered a monetary exchange because the cash involved is more than 10% of the value of the total consideration. These details are reflected in the middle column of Exhibit 12.19.

[7] We can also compute a gain or loss by comparing the machine's book value with the trade-in allowance for the machine. Since the fair market value of the land is $21,000 and the cash paid is $16,500, the trade-in allowance for the machine is $4,500. The difference between the machine's $3,000 book value and its $4,500 trade-in allowance gives us the $1,500 gain on exchange.

Exhibit 12.19

Computing Gain or Loss on Similar Asset Exchanges

Similar Capital Asset Exchange	Loss		Gain	
Fair Market Value of Asset(s) Received		$42,000		$52,000
Book Value of Asset(s) Given:				
Equipment	$16,000		$16,000	
Cash	33,000		33,000	
		49,000		49,000
Gain (Loss) on Exchange		($ 7,000)		$ 3,000

The entry to record this similar, monetary, asset exchange is:

Jan. 3	Equipment (**new**)	42,000	
	Loss on Exchange of Similar Assets	7,000	
	Accumulated Amortization, Equipment	20,000	
	Equipment (**old**)		36,000
	Cash		33,000
	To record exchange of old equipment and cash for new equipment.		

Assets	= Liabilities	+ Equity
+42,000		−7,000
+20,000		
−36,000		
−33,000		

Note the book value of the assets given totals $49,000. This includes the $33,000 cash and the $16,000 ($36,000 − $20,000) book value of the old equipment. This $49,000 book value of assets given is compared to the fair market value of the new equipment received ($42,000). This yields a loss of $7,000 ($42,000 − $49,000).

Receiving More in Exchange: A Gain

Let's assume the same facts as in the similar asset exchange above *except* the new equipment received has a fair market value of $52,000, not the $42,000 noted previously. The entry to record this exchange is:

Jan. 3	Equipment (**new**)	52,000	
	Accumulated Amortization, Equipment	20,000	
	Equipment (**old**)		36,000
	Cash		33,000
	Gain on Exchange of Similar Assets . .		3,000
	To record exchange of old equipment and cash for new equipment.		

Assets	= Liabilities	+ Equity
+52,000		+3,000
+20,000		
−36,000		
−33,000		

We compute a gain on this transaction shown in the third column of Exhibit 12.19.

Exchanging Similar Assets—Nonmonetary

There are three possibilities when similar assets are exchanged and the amount of cash involved is less than 10% of the total consideration. First, no cash is paid or received and the assets are simply traded for each other. Second, a small amount of cash is paid. And third, a small amount of cash is received. In all three cases the asset received may not be recorded at an amount which is greater than its fair market value.

Case 1: No Cash Paid or Received

Let's assume a company exchanges its old equipment for new equipment and no cash is paid or received. This would be considered a nonmonetary exchange because the cash involved is less than 10% of the value of the total consideration. The old equipment originally cost $36,000 and has accumulated amortization of $20,000 at the time of exchange. The new equipment received has a fair market value of $19,000. In this case the new equipment is recorded at the net book value of the old equipment which is $16,000 ($36,000 − $20,000). These details are reflected in the second column of Exhibit 12.20.

The entry to record this exchange is:

Assets = Liabilities + Equity
+16,000
+20,000
−36,000

Jan. 3	Equipment (**new**)	16,000	
	Accumulated Amortization, Equipment	20,000	
	Equipment (**old**)		36,000
	To record exchange of old equipment for new equipment.		

Exhibit 12.20

Computing Gain or Loss on Similar Nonmonetary Asset Exchanges

Similar Capital Asset Exchange		Case 1		Case 2		Case 3
Cash Paid/Received		None		Cash Received		Cash Paid
Fair Market Value of Asset(s) Received		$19,000		$19,000		$19,000
Book Value of Asset(s) Given:						
Equipment	$16,000		$16,000		$16,000	
Cash	Nil		(1,000)		1,000	
		16,000		15,000		17,000
Gain (Loss) on Exchange		$ 3,000		$ 4,000		$ 2,000
Gain (Loss) Recorded		Nil		Nil		Nil

Case 2: $1,000 Cash Received

Let's assume the same company exchanges its same old equipment for new equipment and receives $1,000 in cash. This would be considered a nonmonetary exchange because the cash involved is less than 10% of the value of the total consideration. In this case the new equipment is recorded at the net book value of the old equipment less the cash received or $15,000 ($36,000 − $20,000 − $1,000). These details are reflected in the third column of Exhibit 12.20.

The entry to record this exchange is:

Assets = Liabilities + Equity
+1,000
+15,000
+20,000
−36,000

Jan. 3	Cash	1,000	
	Equipment (**new**)	15,000	
	Accumulated Amortization, Equipment	20,000	
	Equipment (**old**)		36,000
	To record exchange of old equipment for new equipment plus cash.		

Case 3: $1,000 Cash Paid

In this case the company exchanges its old equipment for new equipment and pays $1,000 in cash. This would still be considered a nonmonetary exchange because the cash involved is less than 10% of the value of the total consideration. The new equipment is recorded at the net book value of the old equipment plus the cash paid or $17,000 ($36,000 − $20,000 + $1,000). These details are reflected in the fourth column of Exhibit 12.20.

The entry to record this exchange is:

Assets = Liabilities + Equity
+17,000
+20,000
−36,000
−1,000

Jan. 3	Equipment (**new**)	17,000	
	Accumulated Amortization, Equipment	20,000	
	Equipment (**old**)		36,000
	Cash		1,000
	To record exchange of old equipment for new equipment and payment of cash.		

	Case 1	Case 2	Case 3
Cost of old equipment	$36,000	$36,000	$36,000
Less accumulated amortization	20,000	20,000	20,000
Book value of old equipment	16,000	16,000	16,000
Cash (received) paid	Nil	(1,000)	1,000
Cost recorded for new equipment	**$16,000**	**$15,000**	**$17,000**

Exhibit 12.21

Cost Basis of New Asset When Gain Is Not Recognized

The historical cost principle requires an asset be recorded at the cash or cash equivalent amount given in exchange. Referring to Exhibit 12.21, we see that the amounts recorded for the new equipment equal the historical cost book value of the old equipment ($16,000) plus the cash paid or less the cash received in the exchange. We carry over the old equipment's book value because its earnings process is not considered complete in these cases.

Although the general rule is that no gains or losses should be recorded on nonmonetary exchanges of similar assets, the maximum amount at which we may record the new asset is its market value. In Case 3 the value of the assets delivered is $17,000 ($1,000 cash plus equipment with a $16,000 book value). However, assume instead that the market value of the equipment received is only $14,000. The cost of the equipment received must not be recorded at more than $14,000. Therefore, we must record a $3,000 loss as follows:

Jan. 3	Equipment (**new**)	14,000	
	Accumulated Amortization, Equipment	20,000	
	Loss on exchange of equipment	3,000	
	Equipment (**old**)		36,000
	Cash		1,000
	To record exchange of old equipment for new equipment and payment of cash.		

Assets =
+14,000
+20,000
−36,000
−1,000

In nonmonetary exchanges of similar assets, the cost of the asset received is ecorded at the book value of the asset given up, minus any cash received or plus ny cash paid, as long as this amount is not greater than the market value of the set being received.[8] A loss might need to be recorded but it is unlikely that a in would arise.

ash back

. A company acquires equipment on January 10, 1999, at a cost of $42,000. Straight-line amortization is used assuming a five-year life and $7,000 salvage value. On June 27, 2000, the company sells this equipment for $32,000. Prepare the entry or entries for June 27, 2000.

A company trades an old truck for a new truck. The original cost of the old ruck is $30,000, and its accumulated amortization at the time of the trade is 23,400. The new truck has a cash price of $45,000. Prepare entries to record e trade under two different assumptions where the company receives (a) a 000 trade-in allowance or (b) a $7,000 trade-in allowance.

Answers—p. 592

n

ok, section 3830, "Non-Monetary Transactions," par. .10

SECTION 2—NATURAL RESOURCES

Natural Resources

LO 9 Account for natural resources and depletion.

Natural resources are assets that include standing timber, mineral deposits, and oil and gas fields. Because they are physically consumed when used, they are often called *wasting assets*. The natural state of these assets represent "inventories" of raw materials that will be converted into a product by cutting, mining, or pumping. But until that conversion takes place, they are non-current assets and reported in a balance sheet using titles such as Timberlands, Mineral deposits, or Oil reserves. These natural resources are reported under either capital assets or a separate category. **Barrick Gold Corporation,** for instance, reports its natural resources under the balance sheet title *Property, plant and equipment*. In a note to the financial statements, **Barrick** reports separate amounts for *Property acquisition* and *Deferred mine costs and mineral properties in development*. **Abitibi Consolidated** reports its timber holdings as part of its Fixed assets.

Acquisition Cost and Depletion

Natural resources are initially recorded at cost. Cost includes all expenditures necessary to acquire the resource and prepare it for its intended use. **Depletion** (or amortization) is the process of allocating the cost of natural resources to periods when they are consumed, known as the resource's useful life. Natural resources are reported on the balance sheet at cost less *accumulated depletion*. The amount these assets are depleted each year by cutting, mining or pumping is usually based on units extracted or depleted. This is similar to units-of-production amortization. **Imperial Oil** uses this approach to amortize the costs of discovering and operating its oil wells.

To illustrate depletion of natural resources, let's consider a mineral deposit with an estimated 500,000 tonnes of available ore. It is purchased for $500,000 and we expect zero salvage value. The depletion charge per tonne of ore mined is $1, computed as $500,000 ÷ 500,000 tonnes. If 85,000 tonnes are mined and sold in the first year, the depletion charge for that year is $85,000. These computations are detailed in Exhibit 12.22.

Exhibit 12.22

Depletion Formula and Computations

Step 1:

$$\textbf{Depletion per unit} = \frac{\textbf{Cost} - \textbf{Salvage value}}{\textbf{Total units of capacity}} = \frac{\$500{,}000 - \$0}{500{,}000 \text{ tonnes}} = \$1 \text{ per tonne}$$

Step 2:

$$\textbf{Depletion expense} = \textbf{Depletion per unit} \times \textbf{Units extracted in period}$$

$$= \$1 \times 85{,}000 = \$85{,}000$$

Depletion expense is recorded as:

Assets = Liabilities + Equity
−85,000 −85,000

Dec. 31	Depletion Expense, Mineral Deposit	85,000	
	Accumulated Depletion, Mineral Deposit		85,000
	To record depletion of the mineral deposit.		

The balance sheet at the end of this first year reports the deposit as shown Exhibit 12.23.

Mineral Deposit	$500,000	
Less Accumulated Depletion	85,000	$415,000

Exhibit 12.23

Balance Sheet Presentation of Natural Resources

Because the 85,000 tonnes of mined ore are sold in the year, the entire $85,000 depletion charge is reported on the income statement. But if some of the ore remains unsold at year-end, the depletion cost related to the unsold ore is carried forward on the balance sheet and reported as Unsold Ore Inventory, which is a current asset.

Capital Assets Used in Extracting Resources

The conversion of natural resources by mining, cutting, or pumping usually requires machinery, equipment and buildings. When the usefulness of these assets is directly related to the depletion of the natural resource, their costs are amortized over the life of the natural resource in proportion to the depletion charges. This means amortization is computed using the units-of-production method. For example, if a machine is permanently installed in a mine and one-eighth of the mine's ore is mined and sold in the year, then one-eighth of the machine's cost (less salvage value) is charged to amortization expense. If the machine is abandoned because the resources are fully extracted, any unamortized balance is written off. But if this machine will be moved to another site when extraction is complete, then it is amortized over its useful life.

SECTION 3—INTANGIBLE ASSETS

Intangible Assets

LO 10 Account for intangible assets and their amortization.

Intangible assets are rights, privileges, and competitive advantages to the owner of capital assets used in operations that have no physical substance. Examples are patents, copyrights, leaseholds, leasehold improvements, goodwill, and trademarks. Lack of physical substance is not sufficient for an asset to be an intangible. Notes and accounts receivable, for instance, lack physical substance but are not used in operations to produce products or services. Assets without physical substance that are not used in operations are reported as either current assets or investments. This section explains accounting for intangible assets and describes the more common types of intangible assets.

Accounting for Intangible Assets

Accounting for intangible assets is similar to that for all other capital assets. An intangible asset is recorded at cost when purchased. Its cost must be systematically allocated to expense over its estimated useful life through the process of amortization. The amortization period for an intangible asset must be 40 years or less.[9] Disposal of an intangible asset involves removing its book value, recording any asset received, and recognizing any gain or loss for the difference.

Amortization of intangible assets is similar to amortization of capital assets and depletion of natural resources in that it is a process of cost allocation. But only the straight-line method is used for amortizing intangibles *unless* the company can show another method is preferred. Another difference is the effects of

[9] *CICA Handbook*, section 3060, "Capital Assets," par. .32

amortization and depletion are recorded in a contra account (Accumulated Amortization or Accumulated Depletion), but amortization of intangible assets is usually credited directly to the intangible asset account. This means the original cost of intangible assets is rarely reported on the balance sheet. Instead, only the net amount of unamortized cost is reported.

Some intangibles have limited useful lives due to laws, contracts, or other characteristics of the asset. Examples are patents, copyrights and leaseholds. Other intangibles such as goodwill, trademarks and trade names have useful lives that can not be easily determined. The cost of intangible assets is amortized over the periods expected to benefit by their use (economic life). But in no case can this be longer than their legal existence. Also, the amortization period of intangible assets must never be longer than 40 years even when the life of an asset (for example, goodwill) can continue indefinitely into the future.

Intangible assets are often shown in a separate section of the balance sheet immediately after capital assets. **Bombardier,** for instance, follows this approach in reporting $229.6 million of *Other assets* in its January 31, 1997, balance sheet. Companies also usually disclose the amortization periods they apply to intangibles. **Rogers Communications'** 1997 annual report, for instance, says it amortizes the cost of subscribers and licences on an increasing charge basis over a 40-year period. Goodwill is amortized over periods of from 5 to 40 years on a straight-line basis.

Patents

The federal government grants patents to encourage the invention of new machines, mechanical devices, and production processes. A **patent** is an exclusive right granted to its owner to manufacture and sell a patented machine or device, or to use a process, for 17 years. When patent rights are purchased, the cost of acquiring the rights is debited to an account called *Patents*. If the owner engages in lawsuits to effectively defend a patent, the cost of lawsuits is debited to the Patents account. The costs of research and development leading to a new patent are expensed when incurred.[10]

Did You Know?

Drug War
Mention "drug war" and most people think of fighting cocaine or heroin use. But there's another drug war under way: Brand-name drugmakers' fight to stop generic copies of their products from hitting the market once their patents expire. Successfully delaying a generic rival means hundreds of millions of dollars in extra sales. [Source: *Canadian Business*, April 24, 1998.]

While a patent gives its owner exclusive rights to it for 17 years, the cost of the patent is amortized over its estimated useful life but not to exceed 17 years. If we purchase a patent costing $25,000 with a useful life of 10 years, we make the following adjusting entry at the end of each of the 10 years to amortize one-tenth of its cost:

Assets = Liabilities + Equity
−2,500 −2,500

Dec. 31	Amortization Expense, Patents	2,500	
	Patents		2,500
	To write off patent costs over its 10-year useful life.		

[10] *CICA Handbook*, section 3450, "Research and Development," par. .16 and .18

The debit of $2,500 to Amortization Expense appears on the income statement as a cost of the product or service provided under the protection of the patent. This entry uses the common practice of crediting the Patents account rather than using a contra account.

Copyrights

A copyright is granted by the federal government or by international agreement. A **copyright** gives its owner the exclusive right to publish and sell a musical, literary, or artistic work during the life of the creator plus 50 years. Yet the useful life of most copyrights is much shorter. The costs of a copyright are amortized over its useful life. The only identifiable cost of many copyrights is the fee paid to the Copyright Office. If this fee is immaterial, it is charged directly to an expense account. But if the identifiable costs of a copyright are material, they are capitalized (recorded in an asset account) and periodically amortized by debiting an account called *Amortization Expense, Copyrights*.

Go PHISH

PHISH, a popular band, refused to give up copyrights to their first two independently produced CDs when signing with a recording company. This was unique for the recording industry. These two CDs generate more money for PHISH than some of their more recent recordings that sold more copies.

Did You Know?

Leaseholds

Property is rented under a contract called a **lease.** The property's owner grants the lease and is called the **lessor.** The one who secures the right to possess and use the property is called the **lessee.** A **leasehold** refers to the rights granted to the lessee by the lessor in the lease. A leasehold is an intangible asset for the lessee.

Certain leases require no advance payment from the lessee but do require monthly rent payments. In this case we do not need a Leasehold account. Instead, the monthly payments are debited to a Rent Expense account. But if a long-term lease requires the lessee to pay the final period's rent in advance when the lease is signed, the lessee records this advance payment with a debit to a Leasehold account. Because the usefulness of the advance payment is not used until the final period, the Leasehold account balance remains intact until that time. Then, its balance is transferred to Rent Expense.[11]

A long-term lease can increase in value when current rental rates for similar property increase while the required payments under the lease remain constant. This increase in the value of a lease is not reported on the lessee's balance sheet since no extra cost is incurred to acquire it. But if the property is subleased and the new tenant makes a cash payment to the original lessee for the rights under the old lease, the new tenant debits this payment to a Leasehold account. The balance of this Leasehold account is amortized to Rent Expense over the remaining life of the lease.

---

[11] Some long-term leases give the lessee essentially the same rights as a purchaser and result in tangible assets and liabilities reported by the lessee. Chapter 13 describes these leases.

Leasehold Improvements

Long-term leases sometimes require the lessee to pay for alterations or improvements to the leased property, such as partitions, painting and storefronts. These alterations and improvements are called **leasehold improvements,** and their costs are debited to a *Leasehold Improvements* account. Since leasehold improvements become part of the property and revert to the lessor at the end of the lease, the lessee amortizes these costs over the life of the lease or the life of the improvements, whichever is shorter. The amortization entry debits Rent Expense and credits Leasehold Improvements.

Goodwill

Goodwill has a special meaning in accounting. **Goodwill** is the amount by which the value of a company exceeds the fair market value of this company's net assets if purchased separately. This usually implies the company has certain valuable attributes not measured among its net assets. These can include superior management, skilled workforce, good supplier and customer relations, quality products or services, good location, or other competitive advantages.

Goodwill Illustration

Conceptually, a company has goodwill when its rate of expected future earnings is greater than the rate of normal earnings for its industry. To illustrate this concept, consider the information in Exhibit 12.24 for two competing companies (Winter Gear and Wild Sports) of roughly equal size in the snowboard industry.

Exhibit 12.24

Data for Goodwill Illustration

	Wild Sports	Winter Gear
Net assets (excluding goodwill)	$190,000	$190,000
Normal rate of return in this industry . .	10%	10%
Normal return on net assets	$ 19,000	$ 19,000
Expected net income	24,000	19,000
Expected net income above normal . .	**$ 5,000**	**$ -0-**

The expected income for Wild Sports is $24,000. This is $5,000 higher than the norm (10%) for this industry. This implies Wild Sports has goodwill that yields above normal net income. But Winter Gear's net income of $19,000 is the norm for this industry. This suggests zero goodwill for Winter Gear. What this means is we are willing to pay more for Wild Sports than for Winter Gear because goodwill is a valued asset.

Goodwill is usually recorded only when an entire company or a business segment is purchased. In determining the purchase price of a company, the buyer and seller can estimate the amount of goodwill in more than one way. For instance, how do we value Wild Sports' $5,000 per year above normal net income? One way is to value goodwill at some *multiple* of above normal net income. If we choose a multiple of four, our goodwill estimate for Wild Sports is four times $5,000 (or $20,000). Another method is to assume the $5,000 above normal net income continues indefinitely. This is like an *annuity*. If we assume a 16% discount rate, our estimate of goodwill is $5,000/16%, or $31,250. We describe this computation in a later chapter. But whatever method we choose, the value of goodwill is confirmed only by the price the seller is willing to accept and the buyer is willing to pay.

Accounting for Goodwill

To keep financial statement information from being too subjective, goodwill is not recorded unless it is purchased. Goodwill is measured by subtracting the fair

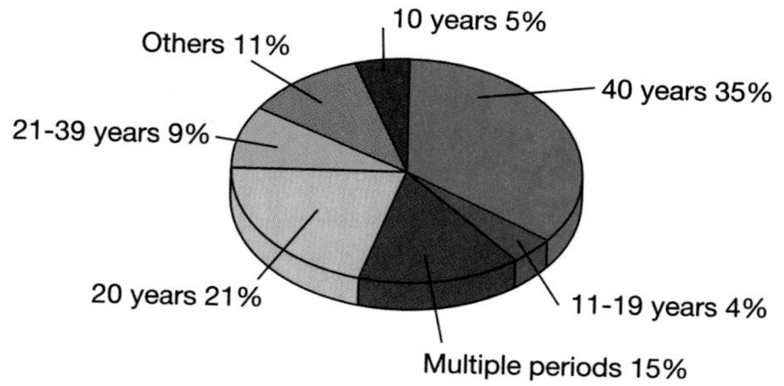

Exhibit 12.25

Goodwill Amortization Period

market value of the purchased company's net assets (excluding goodwill) from the purchase price. Goodwill is a major part of many company purchases. For instance, **Bombardier's** purchase of all the shares of **Waggonfabrik,** a German manufacturer of transportation equipment, included goodwill of $40.1 million.

Goodwill is amortized on a straight-line basis over its estimated useful life just like other intangible assets. Since estimating the useful life of goodwill is difficult, there is a wide range of estimates. Exhibit 12.25 shows us results from a recent survey on the goodwill amortization period. Note the most common amortization period is 40 years. This is not surprising because it allows companies to spread goodwill costs over more years.

Trademarks and Trade Names

Companies often adopt unique symbols or select unique names and brands in marketing their products. A **trademark** or **trade name** is a symbol, name, phrase, or jingle identified with a company, product or service. Examples are **Speedy Muffler, NIKE's** swoosh, **Tim Hortons, Second Cup, Coca-Cola** and **Honda.** Ownership and exclusive right to use a trademark or trade name is often established by showing that one company used it before another. But ownership is best established by registering a trademark or trade name with the government's Patent Office. The cost of developing, maintaining or enhancing the value of a trademark or trade name by means such as advertising is charged to expense when incurred. But if a trademark or trade name is purchased, its cost is debited to an asset account and amortized.

What's in a Name?
When it comes to brand building, nobody does it better than NIKE. Its swoosh is one of the best-known trademarks on the globe. It has helped **NIKE** pump out sales and earnings growth of nearly 40% for three years straight. Equally impressive in brand identity is the **"Intel Inside"** campaign created with a product consumers never see and few understand. [Source: *Business Week*, March 24, 1997.]

Did You Know?

Flashback

13. Give an example of both a natural resource and an intangible asset.
14. A mining company pays $650,000 for an ore deposit. The deposit is estimated to have 325,000 tonnes of ore that will be fully mined over the next 10 years. During the current year, 91,000 tonnes are mined, processed and sold. What is current year's depletion expense?
15. On January 6, 1999, a company pays $120,000 for a patent with a 17-year legal life to produce a toy that is expected to be marketable for about three years. Prepare entries to record its acquisition and the December 31, 1999, adjustment.

Answers—p. 592

Cash Flow Impacts of Capital Assets

LO 11 Identify cash flow impacts of capital asset transactions.

Acquisition and disposal transactions involving capital assets impact the statement of cash flows. Acquisitions of long-term assets are investing activities and are reported in the investing section of the statement of cash flows. Most acquisitions are an immediate *use* of cash and the amount paid at acquisition is deducted in the statement. **Alliance,** for instance, reports these as follows in its statement of cash flows:

Cash provided (used) by investing activities ($ thousands):	
1997 Net additions to property and equipment	($5,237)

Disposals of long-term assets usually create an immediate receipt of cash. When they do yield cash they are reported as a *source* of cash (an addition) in the investing section of the statement of cash flows or, as the case of Alliance, as a net figure. Gain or loss from disposal is the difference between an asset's book value and the value received. A gain or loss does not reflect any cash flow from investing activities (we explain this in Chapter 17).[12]

Total Asset Turnover

USING THE INFORMATION

LO 12 Compute total asset turnover and apply it to analyze a company's use of assets.

A company's assets are important in determining its ability to generate sales and earn profits. Managers devote a lot of attention to deciding what assets a company acquires, how much is invested in assets, and how assets can be used most efficiently and effectively. Decision makers and other users of financial statements are especially interested in evaluating a company's ability to use its assets in generating sales.

One measure of a company's ability in using its assets is **total asset turnover.** The formula for computing total asset turnover is shown in Exhibit 12.26.

Exhibit 12.26

Total Asset Turnover Formula

$$\textbf{Total asset turnover} = \frac{\textbf{Net sales}}{\textbf{Average total assets}}$$

Total asset turnover can be computed regardless of the type of company being evaluated. It can be applied to manufacturing and merchandising companies, and even to service companies. The numerator, net sales, reflects all operating revenues generated by the company. The denominator, average total assets, is usually measured by averaging total assets at the beginning of the period with total assets at the end of the period.

To illustrate, let's look at a company with total assets of $96,500 at the beginning of the year and $108,500 at the end of the year. Net sales for this company is $440,000 for the year. The company's total asset turnover for the current year is computed as:

$$\text{Total asset turnover} = \frac{\$440{,}000}{(\$96{,}500 + \$108{,}500)/2} = 4.3$$

We describe this company's use of assets in generating net sales by saying "it turned its assets over 4.3 times during the year." This means each $1.00 of assets produced $4.30 of net sales for the year.

12 Also, amortization of capital assets do *not* impact cash (see Chapter 17).

Is a total asset turnover of 4.3 good or bad? It is safe to say all companies desire a high total asset turnover. But like many ratio analyses, a company's total asset turnover must be interpreted in comparison with prior years and with similar companies. Interpreting the total asset turnover also requires we understand the company's operations. Some operations are capital intensive, meaning a relatively large amount is invested in assets to generate sales. This suggests a relatively lower total asset turnover. Some other companies' operations are labour intensive, meaning sales are generated more by the efforts of people than the use of assets. In this case we expect a higher total asset turnover.[13]

To show how we analyze companies using total asset turnover, we use data from the annual reports of two competing companies: **George Weston** and the **Oshawa Group.** Exhibit 12.27 shows results from computing total asset turnover for these two companies.

Exhibit 12.27

Analysis using total asset turnover

Company	Figure ($ millions)	1996	1995
Weston	Net sales	$12,709	$12,966
	Average total assets	$5,282	$4,955
	Total asset turnover	**2.41**	**2.62**
Oshawa	Net sales	$6,384	$6,161
	Average total assets	$1,428	$1,344
	Total asset turnover	**4.47**	**4.58**

To show how we compute and use total asset turnover, let's look at the numbers for Weston in 1995–1996 as reported in Exhibit 12.27. We compute Weston's1996 turnover as:

$$\text{Total asset turnover} = \frac{\$12{,}709}{\$5{,}282} = 2.41$$

This means Weston's average total asset balance is converted into sales 2.41 times in 1996. Another way to say this is that Weston generated $2.41 of net sales for each $1 of assets. We also see Weston's turnover is steady over the period 1995–1996, and is less than Oshawa's turnover. Is Weston's turnover high enough? Total asset turnover for Weston's other competitors, available in industry publications such as Dun & Bradstreet, is generally in the range of 2.0 to 2.5 over this same period. It appears Weston is competitive and possibly doing slightly better than its competitors on total asset turnover.

Environmentalist

You are an environmentalist battling a paper manufacturer on environmental concerns. The company claims it cannot afford any additional controls. It points to its low total asset turnover of 1.9 and argues it cannot compete with other companies where total asset turnover is much higher. Examples mentioned are food stores (5.5), wholesalers (4.0) and builders (3.5). The company suggests it might need to lay off workers to pay for any added costs. How do you respond?

You Make the Call

Answer—p. 591

[13] There is a relation between total asset turnover and net profit margin. Companies with low total asset turnover require higher profit margins (examples are hotels and real estate), whereas companies with high total asset turnover can succeed with lower profit margins (examples are food stores and merchandisers).

Summary

LO1 Describe capital assets and issues in accounting for them. Capital assets are tangible assets used in the operations of a company and have a useful life of more than one accounting period. Capital assets are set apart from other assets by two important features: use in operations and useful lives longer than one period. There are four main accounting issues with capital assets: (1) computing their costs, (2) allocating their costs to the periods they benefit, (3) accounting for their subsequent expenditures, and (4) recording their disposal.

LO2 Apply the cost principle to compute the cost of capital assets. Capital assets are recorded at cost when purchased. Cost includes all normal and reasonable expenditures necessary to get the asset in place and ready for its intended use. The cost of a lump-sum purchase is allocated among its individual assets based on their relative market values.

LO3 Explain amortization and the factors affecting its computation. Amortization is the process of allocating to expense the cost of a capital asset over the accounting periods benefiting from use of the capital asset. Amortization does not measure the decline in a capital asset's market value, nor does it measure the asset's physical deterioration. Amortization occurs when an asset is being used to produce products or services. Three factors determine amortization: cost, salvage value, and useful life. Salvage value is an estimate of the asset's value at the end of its benefit period. Useful (service) life is the length of time an asset is productively used in operations.

LO4 Compute and record amortization using the methods of straight-line, units-of-production, and declining-balance. The straight-line method of amortization divides the cost less salvage value by the number of periods in the asset's useful life to determine amortization expense for each period. The units-of-production method divides the cost less salvage value by the estimated number of units the asset will produce to determine the amortization per unit. The declining-balance method multiplies the asset's book value by a rate that is usually double the straight-line rate.

LO5 Compare and analyze amortization for different methods. The amount of amortization expense per period is usually different for different methods. Yet total amortization expense is the same for all methods. Each method starts with the same total cost and ends with the same salvage value. The difference is in the pattern in amortization expense over the asset's useful life. The book value of an asset when using straight-line is always greater than when using double-declining-balance, except at the beginning and end. The straight-line method yields a steady pattern of amortization expense, while the units-of-production does not because it depends on the number of units produced. Amortization methods are acceptable if they allocate cost in a rational and systematic manner.

LO6 Explain amortization for partial years and when estimates change. Partial years' amortization is often required because assets are bought and sold throughout the year. Amortization is revised when changes in estimates such as salvage value and useful life occur. If the useful life of a capital asset changes, for instance, the remaining cost to be amortized is spread over the remaining (revised) useful life of the asset.

LO7 Distinguish between revenue and capital expenditures, and account for these expenditures. Revenue expenditures expire in the current period. They are debited to expense accounts and matched with current revenues. Repairs are an example of revenue expenditures. Capital expenditures benefit future periods and are debited to asset accounts. Betterments are a capital expenditure. Immaterial expenditures on capital assets are treated as revenue expenditures.

LO8 Account for asset disposal through discarding, selling, or exchanging an asset. When a capital asset is discarded, sold or exchanged, its cost and accumulated amortization are removed from the accounts. Any cash proceeds from discarding or selling an asset are recorded and compared to the asset's book value to determine gain or loss. When dissimilar assets are exchanged, the new asset is recorded at its fair value, and any gain or loss on disposal is recognized. When similar assets are exchanged, neither gains nor losses are normally recognized. The new asset account is debited for the book value of the old asset plus any cash paid and less any cash received.

LO9 Account for natural resources and their depletion. The cost of a natural resource is recorded in an asset account. Depletion of a natural resource is recorded by allocating its cost to expense normally using the units-of-production method. Depletion is credited to an Accumulated Depletion account.

LO10 Account for intangible assets and their amortization. An intangible asset is recorded at the cost incurred to purchase the asset. Allocation of the cost of an intangible asset to expense is normally done using the straight-line method and is called amortization. Amortization is recorded with a credit made directly to the asset account instead of a contra account. Intangible assets include patents, copyrights, leaseholds, goodwill, and trademarks.

LO 11 **Identify cash flow impacts of capital asset transactions.** Acquisition and disposal of capital assets impact the investing section of the statement of cash flows. Acquisitions are a use of cash, while disposals are a source of cash.

LO 12 **Compute total asset turnover and apply it to analyze a company's use of assets.** Total asset turnover measures a company's ability to use its assets to generate sales. Total asset turnover is defined as net sales divided by average total assets. The turnover measure is interpreted as the dollars of net sales generated for each dollar of assets. While all companies desire a high total asset turnover, it must be interpreted in comparison with prior years and with similar companies.

Guidance Answers to **You Make the Call**

Mechanic

Treating an expense as a capital expenditure means expenses will be lower and income higher. This is because unlike an expense, a capital expenditure is not expensed immediately. Instead, the cost of a capital expenditure is spread out over the asset's useful life. Treating an expense as a capital expenditure also means asset and equity totals are reported at a larger amount. This continues until the asset is fully amortized. Your friend is probably trying to help, but the suggestion hints at unethical behaviour. You must remember that only an expenditure benefiting future periods is a capital expenditure. If an item is truly an "expense" not benefiting future periods, then it must not be treated as a capital expenditure.

Environmentalist

You need to point out the company's comparison of its total asset turnover with food stores, wholesalers and builders is misdirected. You must explain these other industries' turnovers are higher because their profit margins are lower (about 2%). Profit margins for the paper industry are usually 3% to 3.5%. You also need to collect data from competitors in the paper industry to show that a 1.9 total asset turnover is about right for this industry. You might even go further and collect data on this company's revenues and expenses, along with compensation data for this company's high-ranking officers and employees.

Guidance Answer to **Judgment and Ethics**

Controller

Before you conclude this instruction is unethical, you might tell the president of your concern that the longer estimate does not seem realistic in light of past experience with three-year replacements. You might ask if the change implies a new replacement plan. Depending on the president's response, such a conversation might eliminate your concern. It is possible the president's decision to change estimated useful life reflects an honest and reasonable prediction of the future. Since the company is struggling financially, the president may have concluded the normal pattern of replacing assets every three years cannot continue. Perhaps the strategy is to avoid costs of frequent replacements and stretch use of the equipment a few years longer until financial conditions improve. Even if you doubt the company will be able to use the equipment six years, you should consider the possibility the president has a more complete understanding of the situation and honestly believes a six-year life is a good estimate.

On the downside, you may be correct in suspecting the president is acting unethically. If you conclude the president's decision is unethical, you might confront the president with your opinion that it is unethical to change the prediction just to increase income. This is a personally risky course of action and you may want to remind the president of her own ethical responsibility. Another possibility is to wait and see if the auditor will insist on not changing the estimate. You should always insist the statements be based on reasonable estimates.

Guidance Answers to Flashbacks

1. (a) Office supplies—current assets
   (b) Office equipment—capital assets
   (c) Merchandise—current assets
   (d) Land held for future expansion—long-term investments
   (e) Trucks used in operations—capital assets
2. (a) Land
   (b) Land Improvements
3. \$700,000 + \$49,000 − \$21,000 + \$3,500 + \$3,000 + \$2,500 = \$737,000
4. Straight-line with 7-year life: (\$77,000/7) = \$11,000
   Straight-line with 10-year life: (\$77,000/10) = \$7,700
5. Amortization is a process of allocating and charging the cost of capital assets to the accounting periods that benefit from the assets' use.
6. (a) Book value using straight-line amortization:
   \$96,000 − [(\$96,000 - \$8,000)/5] = \$78,400
   (b) Book value using units of production:
   \$96,000 − [(\$96,000 − \$8,000) × (10,000/100,000)] = \$87,200
7. (\$3,800 − \$200)/3 = \$1,200
   \$1,200 × 2 = \$2,400
   (\$3,800 − \$2,400)/2 = \$700
8.

Machinery	12,000	
Cash		12,000

9. A revenue expenditure benefits only the current period and should be charged to expense of the current period. A capital expenditure has a benefit that extends beyond the end of the current period and should be charged to an asset.
10. A betterment involves modifying an existing capital asset to make it more efficient, usually by replacing part of the asset with an improved or superior part. A betterment should be debited to the improved machine's account.
11.

Amortization Expense	3,500	
Accumulated Amortization		3,500
Cash	32,000	
Accumulated Amortization	10,500	
Gain on Sale of Equipment		500
Equipment		42,000

12.

(a) Truck	45,000	
Loss on Trade-In	3,600	
Accumulated Amortization	23,400	
Truck		30,000
Cash		42,000

(b) Truck	45,000	
Accumulated Amortization	23,400	
Truck		30,000
Cash		38,000
Gain on Trade-In		400

13. Examples of intangible assets are: Patents; Copyrights; Leaseholds; Leasehold improvements; Goodwill; Trademarks; Exclusive licences.
    Examples of natural resources are: Timberlands; Mineral deposits; Oil reserves.
14. \$650,000 × (91,000/325,000) = \$182,000
15.

Jan. 6	Patents	120,000	
	Cash		120,000
Dec. 31	Amortization Expense	40,000*	
	Patents		40,000
	*Amortization computation: \$120,000/3 = \$40,000		

Demonstration Problem

On July 14, 19X1, Truro Company paid \$600,000 to acquire a fully equipped factory. The purchase included the following:

Asset	Appraised Value	Estimated Salvage Value	Estimated Useful Life	Amortization Method
Land	\$160,000			Not amortized
Land improvements	80,000	\$ -0-	10 years	Straight line
Building	320,000	100,000	10 years	Double-declining balance
Machinery	240,000	20,000	10,000 units	Units of production*
Total	\$800,000			

*The machinery is used to produce 700 units in 19X1 and 1,800 units in 19X2.

Required

1. Allocate the total \$600,000 cost among the separate assets.

2. Compute the 19X1 (six months) and 19X2 amortization expense for each type of asset and compute the total amortization expense each year for all assets.
3. On the first day of 19X3 the machinery and $5,000 cash is exchanged for similar equipment with a fair value of $210,000. Journalize the exchange of assets.
4. Assume the exchange in part 3 was for dissimilar, not similar, equipment. Journalize the dissimilar exchange.

Additional company transactions to account for dealing with long-term assets:

5. On the last day of the fiscal year the company discards equipment that has been on the books for five years. The original cost of the equipment was $12,000 (estimated life of five years) and the salvage value is $2,000. No amortization has been recorded for the fifth year before the disposal occurs. Journalize the fifth year of amortization (straight-line method) and the asset disposal.
6. At the beginning of the year the company purchases with cash a patent right for $100,000. The company estimates the useful life of the patent to be 10 years. Journalize the patent acquisition and amortization for the year.
7. Late in the year the company makes its final addition to property and equipment with the acquisition for cash of an ore deposit for $600,000. Access roads and shafts are added for an additional cost of $80,000. Salvage value of the mine is estimated to be $20,000. The company estimates 330,000 tonnes of available ore. Only 10,000 tonnes of ore are mined and sold before the end of the year. Journalize the mine's acquisition and first year's depletion.

Planning the Solution

- Complete a three-column worksheet showing these amounts for each asset: appraised value, percentage of total value, and allocated cost.
- Using the allocated costs, compute the amount of amortization for 19X1 (only one-half year) and 19X2 for each asset. Then, summarize those computations in a table showing the total amortization for each year.
- Remember that gains on nonmonetary exchanges of similar assets are not recognized. Make a journal entry to add the acquired machinery to the books, remove the machinery given in the Exchange along with its accumulated amortization, and the cash given in the exchange.
- Remember that gains on exchanges of dissimilar assets are recognized. Make a journal entry to add the acquired machinery to the books, remove the machinery given in the exchange along with its accumulated amortization, and the cash given in the exchange. Also record the gain on the exchange in a separate account titled "Gain on Exchange of Dissimilar Assets."
- Remember that all amortization must be recorded before removing a disposed asset from the books. Calculate and record the amortization expense for the fifth year using the straight-line method. Since salvage value has not been received at the end of the asset's life the amount of the salvage value becomes a loss on disposal. Record the loss on the disposal as well as the removal of the asset and its related accumulated amortization from the books.
- Record the patent as an intangible asset for its purchase price. Use straight-line amortization over the years of useful life to calculate amortization expense. Remember that no accumulated amortization account is used in recording amortization expense. Rather the intangible asset account is credited directly.
- Record the ore deposit as a natural resource asset including all additional costs to ready the mine for use. Calculate depletion per tonne using the depletion formula. Multiply the depletion amount per tonne by the amount of tonnes mined since the acquisition to calculate the appropriate depletion expense for the current year.

Solution to Demonstration Problem

1. Allocation of total cost among the assets:

Asset	Appraised Value	Percentage of Total Value	Allocated Cost
Land	$160,000	20%	$120,000
Land improvements	80,000	10	60,000
Building	320,000	40	240,000
Machinery	240,000	30	180,000
Total	$800,000	100%	$600,000

2. Amortization for each asset:

Land Improvements:	
Cost	$ 60,000
Salvage value	-0-
Net cost	$ 60,000
Useful life	10 years
Annual expense ($60,000/10)	$ 6,000
19X1 amortization ($6,000 × 6/12)	$ 3,000
19X2 amortization	$ 6,000
Building:	
Straight-line rate = 100%/10 = 10%	
Double-declining-balance rate = 10% × 2 = 20%	
19X1 amortization ($240,000 × 20% × 6/12)	$ 24,000
19X2 amortization [($240,000 − $24,000) × 20%]	$ 43,200
Machinery:	
Cost	$180,000
Salvage value	20,000
Net cost	$160,000
Total expected units	10,000
Expected cost per unit ($160,000/10,000)	$ 16

Year	Units	×	Unit Cost	Amortization
19X1	700	×	$16	$11,200
19X2	1,800	×	$16	28,800

Total amortization expense:

	19X2	19X1
Land improvements	$ 6,000	$ 3,000
Building	43,200	24,000
Machinery	28,800	11,200
Total	$78,000	$38,200

3. Recording the exchange of similar assets with a gain on the exchange:
The book value on the date of exchange is $180,000 (allocated cost) − $40,000 (accumulated amortization). The cash involved is less than 10% of the value of the assets involved; therefore, this is a nonmonetary exchange of similar assets. The book value of the machinery given in the exchange of $140,000 plus the $5,000 cash paid thus becomes the recorded cost of the new asset.

Machinery (new) [$140,000 + $5,000]	145,000	
Accumulated Amortization, Old Machinery	40,000	
Old Machinery		180,000
Cash		5,000

4. Recording the exchange of dissimilar assets with a gain on the exchange:

Machinery (new)	210,000	
Accumulated Amortization, Old Machinery	40,000	
Old Machinery		180,000
Cash		5,000
Gain on exchange of dissimilar assets		65,000

5. Recording the amortization on the discarded asset:

Amortization Expense, Equipment	2,000	
Accumulated Amortization, Equipment		2,000
To record amortization to date of disposal:		
($12,000 − $2,000/5 = $2,000)		

Recording the loss on disposal and asset removal:

Accumulated Amortization, Equipment	10,000	
Loss on Disposal of Equipment	2,000	
Equipment		12,000
To record the discarding of machinery with a $2,000 book value.		

6.

Patent	100,000	
Cash		100,000
To record patent acquisition.		

Amortization Expense, Patent	10,000	
Patent		10,000
To record amortization expense:		
($100,000/10 years = $10,000)		

7.

Ore Deposit	680,000	
Cash		680,000
To record ore deposit acquisition and related costs.		

Depletion Expense, Ore Deposit	20,000	
Accumulated Depletion		20,000
To record depletion expense:		
[($680,000 − $20,000)/330,000 tonnes available] = $2.00 per tonne		
10,000 tonnes mined and sold × $2.00 = $20,000 depletion		

Glossary

Accelerated amortization method Amortization methods that produce larger amortization charges during the early years of an asset's life and smaller charges in the later years. (p. 566)

Amortization A process of systematically allocating the cost of a capital asset to expense over its estimated useful life. (p. 562)

Betterment An expenditure to make a capital asset more efficient or productive and/or extend the useful life of a capital asset beyond original expectations; also called *improvements*. (p. 573)

Book value The original cost of a capital asset less its accumulated amortization. (p. 564)

Capital assets Assets used in the operations of a company that have a useful life of more than one accounting period; also known as *fixed assets*, or *property, plant and equipment*. (p. 558)

Capital Cost Allowance (CCA) The system of amortization required by federal income tax law. (p. 568)

Capital expenditures Additional costs of capital assets that provide material benefits extending beyond the current period. (p. 572)

Change in an accounting estimate A change in a computed amount used in the financial statements that results from new information or subsequent developments and from better insight or improved judgment. (p. 570)

Copyright A right granted by the federal government or by international agreement giving the owner the exclusive privilege to publish and sell musical, literary, or artistic work during the life of the creator plus 50 years. (p. 585)

Cost Includes all normal and reasonable expenditures necessary to get a capital asset in place and ready for its intended use. (p. 559)

Declining-balance amortization An amortization method in which a capital asset's amortization charge for the period is determined by applying a constant amortization rate (up to twice the straight-line rate) each year to the asset's book value at the beginning of the year. (p. 567)

Depletion The process of allocating the cost of natural resources to the periods in which they are consumed. Another term for *amortization*. (p. 582)

Depreciation The process of allocating to expense the cost of a capital asset to the accounting periods benefiting from its use. Another term for *amortization*. (p. 562)

Goodwill The amount by which the value of a company exceeds the fair market value of the company's net assets if purchased separately. (p. 586)

Inadequacy A condition in which the capacity of the company's capital assets is too small to meet the company's productive demands. (p. 563)

Intangible assets Rights, privileges, and competitive advantages to the owner of capital assets used in operations that have no physical substance; examples include patents, copyrights, leaseholds, leasehold improvements, goodwill, and trademarks. (p. 583)

Land improvements Assets that increase the usefulness of land but that have a limited useful life and are subject to amortization. (p. 560)

Lease A contract allowing property rental. (p. 585)

Lessee The party to a lease that secures the right to possess and use the property. (p. 585)

Leasehold A name for the rights granted to the lessee by the lessor by a lease. (p. 585)

Leasehold improvements Alterations or improvements to leased property, such as partitions, painting, and store fronts. (p. 586)

Lessor The party to a lease that grants the right to possess and use property to another. (p. 585)

Natural resources Assets that are physically consumed when used; examples include timber, mineral deposits, and oil and gas fields; also called *wasting assets*. (p. 582)

Obsolescence A condition in which, because of new inventions and improvements, a capital asset can no longer be used to produce goods or services with a competitive advantage. (p. 563)

Patent An exclusive right granted to its owner by the federal government to manufacture and sell a machine or device, or to use a process, for 17 years. (p. 584)

Repairs Expenditures made to keep a capital asset in normal, good operating condition; treated as a revenue expenditure. (p. 573)

Revenue expenditure An expenditure that should appear on the current income statement as an expense and be deducted from the period's revenues because it does not provide a material benefit in future periods. (p. 572)

Salvage value Management's estimate of the amount that will be recovered at the end of a capital asset's useful life through a sale or as a trade-in allowance on the purchase of a new asset; also called *residual or scrap value*. (p. 562)

Straight-line amortization A method that allocates an equal portion of the total amortization for a capital asset (cost minus salvage) to each accounting period in its useful life. (p. 564)

Total asset turnover A measure of the ability of a company to use its assets to generate sales; computed by dividing net sales by average total assets. (p. 588)

Trademark or **trade name** Symbol, name, phrase, or jingle identified with a company or service. (p. 587)

Units-of-production amortization A method that charges a varying amount to expense for each period of an asset's useful life depending on its usage; expense is computed by taking the cost of the asset less its salvage value and dividing by the total number of units expected to be produced during its useful life. (p. 565)

Useful life The length of time in which a capital asset will be productively used in the operations of the business; also called *service life*. (p. 563)

Questions

1. What characteristics of a capital asset make it different from other assets?
2. What is the balance sheet classification of land held for future expansion? Why is the land not classified as a capital asset?
3. In general, what is included in the cost of a capital asset?
4. What is the difference between land and land improvements?
5. Does the balance of the account, Accumulated Amortization, Machinery, represent funds accumulated to replace the machinery when it wears out? What does the balance of Accumulated Amortization represent?
6. Why is capital cost allowance not generally accepted for financial accounting purposes?
7. What is the difference between repairs and betterments and how should they be recorded?
8. What accounting principle justifies charging the $75 cost of a capital asset immediately to an expense account?
9. What are some of the events that might lead to the disposal of a capital asset?
10. Should a gain on an exchange of capital assets be recorded?
11. How does accounting for long-term property and equipment impact the statement of cash flows?
12. How is total asset turnover computed? Why would a financial statement user be interested in computing total asset turnover?
13. What is the name for the process of allocating the cost of natural resources to expense as the natural resources are used?
14. What are the characteristics of an intangible asset?
15. Is the declining-balance method an acceptable means of computing depletion of natural resources?
16. What general procedures are followed in accounting for intangible assets?
17. When does a business have goodwill? Under what conditions can goodwill appear in a company's balance sheet?
18. X Company bought an established business and paid for goodwill. If X Company plans to incur substantial advertising and promotional costs each year to maintain the value of the goodwill, must the company also amortize the goodwill?
19. Refer to the consolidated balance sheets for **Alliance** in Appendix I. What phrase does Alliance use to describe its capital assets? What is the book value of capital assets as of March 31, 1997, and March 31, 1996?
20. Refer to the consolidated balance sheet of **Atlantis** in Appendix I. How are the property and equipment and intangibles of Atlantis presented on the balance sheet?

Quick Study

QS 12-1
Defining capital assets
LO 1

Explain the difference between (a) capital assets and current assets; (b) capital assets and inventory; and (c) capital assets and temporary investments.

QS 12-2
Cost of capital assets
LO 2

Starbuck Lanes installed automatic score-keeping equipment. The electrical work required to prepare for the installation was $18,000. The invoice price of the equipment was $180,000. Additional costs were $3,000 for delivery and $12,600, sales tax. During the installation, a component of the equipment was damaged because it was carelessly left on a lane and hit by the automatic lane cleaning machine during a daily maintenance run. The cost of repairing the component was $2,250. What is the cost of the automatic score-keeping equipment?

QS 12-3
Alternate amortization methods
LO 4

On January 2, 19X1, Crossfire acquired sound equipment for concert performances at a cost of $55,900. The rock band estimated they would use this equipment for four years, during which time they anticipated performing about 12 concerts. They estimated that at that point they could sell the equipment for $1,900. During 19X1, the band performed four concerts. Compute the 19X1 amortization using (a) the straight-line method and (b) the units-of-production method.

QS 12-4
Computing revised amortization
LO 6

Refer to the facts in QS 12-3. Assume that Crossfire chose straight-line amortization but recognized during the second year that due to concert bookings beyond expectations, this equipment would only last a total of three years. The salvage value would remain unchanged. Compute the revised amortization for the second year and the third year.

QS 12-5
Double-declining balance method
LO 4

A fleet of refrigerated delivery trucks acquired on January 5, 19X1, at a cost of $930,000 had an estimated useful life of eight years and an estimated salvage value of $150,000. Compute the amortization expense for the first three years under the double-declining-balance method for financial accounting purposes.

QS 12-6
Revenue and capital expenditures
LO 7

a. Classify the following expenditures as revenue or capital expenditures:
(1) The cost of annual tune-ups for delivery trucks.
(2) The cost of replacing a compressor for a meat-packing firm's refrigeration system that extends the estimated life of the system four years, $30,000.
(3) The cost of $220,000 for an addition of a new wing on an office building.
(4) The monthly replacement cost of filters on an air-conditioning system, $175.

b. Prepare the journal entry to record each of the above.

QS 12-7
Dissimilar asset exchanges
LO 8

Spectrum Flooring owned an automobile with a $15,000 cost and $13,500 accumulated amortization. In a transaction with a neighbouring computer retailer, Spectrum exchanged this auto for a computer with a fair market value of $4,500. Spectrum was required to pay an additional $3,750 cash. Prepare the entry to record this transaction for Spectrum.

QS 12-8
Similar asset exchange
LO 8

Mayes Co. owns an industrial machine that cost $38,400 and has been amortized $20,400. Mayes exchanged the machine for a newer model that has a fair market value of $17,000. Record the exchange assuming that Mayes (a) paid $1,500 and (b) received $1,000.

QS 12-9
Cash impacts from acquisitions and disposals
LO 11

Identify the section in the cash flow statement where the following transactions are reported along with whether it is a source or use of cash.

Key: **A.** Source of cash from investing activities
B. Use of cash for investing activities

_____ **1.** Cash purchase of machinery
_____ **2.** Sale of patents for cash
_____ **3.** Purchase of productive timberland for cash
_____ **4.** Cash sale of factory warehouse

QS 12-10
Computing total asset turnover
LO 12

Photo Film Company reported the following facts in its 19X2 annual report: net sales of $13,557 million for 19X2 and $12,670 million for 19X1; total end-of-year assets of $14,968 million for 19X2 and $18,810 million for 19X1. Compute the total asset turnover for 19X2.

QS 12-11
Natural resources and depletion
LO 9

Sudbury Industries acquired an ore mine at a cost of $1,300,000. It was necessary to incur $200,000 to access the mine. The mine is estimated to hold 500,000 tonnes of ore and the estimated value of the land after the ore is removed is $150,000.

a. Prepare the entry to record the acquisition.

b. Prepare the year-end adjusting entry assuming that 90,000 tonnes of ore were removed from the mine this year.

QS 12-12
Intangible assets and natural resources
LO 9, 10

Which of the following assets should be reported on the balance sheet as intangible assets? Which should be reported as natural resources? (a) leasehold, (b) salt mine, (c) building, (d) oil well, (e) trademark.

QS 12-13
Intangible assets and amortization
LO 10

On January 4 of the current year, Amber's Boutique incurred a $95,000 cost to modernize its store. The improvements included new floors, lighting, and shelving for the merchandise. It was estimated that these improvements would last for 10 years. Amber's leases its retail space and has eight years remaining on the lease. Prepare the entry to record the modernization and the adjusting entry at the end of the current year.

Exercises

Exercise 12-1
Cost of a capital asset
LO 2

Santiago Co. purchased a machine for $11,500, terms 2/10, n/60, FOB shipping point. The seller prepaid the freight charges, $260, adding the amount to the invoice and bringing its total to $11,760. The machine required a special steel mounting and power connections costing $795, and another $375 was paid to assemble the machine and get it into operation. In moving the machine onto its steel mounting, it was dropped and damaged. The repairs cost $190. Later, $30 of raw materials were consumed in adjusting the machine so that it would produce a satisfactory product. The adjustments were normal for this type of machine and were not the result of the damage. However, the items produced while the adjustments were being made were not saleable. Prepare a computation to show the cost of this machine for accounting purposes. (Assume Santiago pays for the purchase within the discount period.)

Exercise 12-2
Lump-sum purchase of capital assets
LO 2

Horizon Company paid $368,250 for real estate plus $19,600 in closing costs. The real estate included land appraised at $166,320; land improvements appraised at $55,440; and a building appraised at $174,240. Prepare a computation showing the allocation of the total cost among the three purchased assets and present the journal entry to record the purchase.

Exercise 12-3
Recording costs of real estate
LO 2

After planning to build a new plant, Monarch Manufacturing purchased a large lot on which a small building was located. The negotiated purchase price for this real estate was $225,000 for the lot plus $120,000 for the building. The company paid $34,500 to have the old building torn down and $51,000 for landscaping the lot. Finally, it paid $1,440,000 in construction costs, which included the cost of a new building plus $85,500 for lighting and paving a parking lot next to the building. Present a single journal entry to record the costs incurred by Monarch, all of which were paid in cash.

Exercise 12-4
Alternative amortization methods
LO 4

On the first day of the year Barrow Company installed a computerized machine in its factory at a cost of $42,300. The machine's useful life was estimated at 10 years, or 363,000 units of product, with a $6,000 trade-in value. During its second year, the machine produced 35,000 units of product. Determine the machine's second-year amortization under the (a) straight-line, (b) units-of-production, and (c) double-declining-balance methods.

Exercise 12-5
Alternative amortization methods; partial year's amortization
LO 6

On April 1, 19X1, Rodgers Backhoe Co. purchased a trencher for $250,000. The machine was expected to last five years and have a salvage value of $25,000. Compute amortization expense for 19X2, using (a) the straight-line method and (b) the double-declining-balance method. Rodgers Backhoe has a December 31 year-end.

Exercise 12-6
Revising amortization rates
LO 6

BodySmart Fitness Club used straight-line amortization for a machine that cost $21,750, under the assumption it would have a four-year life and a $2,250 trade-in value. After two years, BodySmart determined that the machine still had three more years of remaining useful life, after which it would have an estimated $1,800 trade-in value. (a) Compute the machine's book value at the end of its second year. (b) Compute the amount of amortization to be charged during each of the remaining years in the machine's revised useful life.

Exercise 12-7
Income statement effects of alternative amortization methods
LO 5

Shamrock Enterprises recently paid $235,200 for equipment that will last five years and have a salvage value of $52,500. By using the machine in its operations for five years, the company expects to earn $85,500 annually, after deducting all expenses except amortization. Present a schedule showing income before amortization, amortization expense, and net income for each year and the total amounts for the five-year period, assuming (a) straight-line amortization and (b) double-declining-balance amortization.

Exercise 12-8
Alternate amortization methods
LO 5

In January 19X1, Labtech purchased computer equipment for $147,000. The equipment will be used in research and development activities for four years and then sold at an estimated salvage value of $30,000. Prepare schedules showing the amortization and book values for the four years assuming (a) straight-line amortization and (b) double-declining balance.

Exercise 12-9
Repairs and betterments
LO 7

Archer Company paid $262,500 for equipment that was expected to last four years and have a salvage value of $30,000. Prepare journal entries to record the following costs related to the equipment:

a. During the second year of the equipment's life, $21,000 cash was paid for a new component that was expected to increase the equipment's productivity by 10% each year.

b. During the third year, $5,250 cash was paid for repairs necessary to keep the equipment in good working order.

c. During the fourth year, $13,950 was paid for repairs that were expected to increase the useful life of the equipment from four to six years.

Exercise 12-10
Betterments
LO 7

Flemming Company owns a building that appeared on its balance sheet at the end of last year at its original $561,000 cost less $420,750 accumulated amortization. The building has been amortized on a straight-line basis under the assumption that it would have a 20-year life and no salvage value. During the first week in January of the current year, major structural repairs were completed on the building at a cost of $67,200. The repairs did not increase the building's capacity, but they did extend its expected life for 7 years beyond the 20 years originally estimated.

a. Determine the building's age as of the end of last year.

b. Give the entry to record the repairs, which were paid with cash.

c. Determine the book value of the building after the repairs were recorded.

d. Give the entry to record the current year's amortization.

Exercise 12-11
Partial year's amortization; disposal of capital asset
LO 8

Levy Co. purchased and installed a machine on January 1, 19X1, at a total cost of $92,750. Straight-line amortization was taken each year for four years, based on the assumption of a seven-year life and no salvage value. The machine was disposed of on July 1, 19X5, during its fifth year of service. Present the entries to record the partial year's amortization on July 1, 19X5, and to record the disposal under each of the following unrelated assumptions: (a) the machine was sold for $35,000 cash; and (b) Levy received an insurance settlement of $30,000 resulting from the total destruction of the machine in a fire.

Exercise 12-12
Exchanging capital assets
LO 8

Greenbelt Construction traded in an old tractor for a new tractor, receiving a $28,000 trade-in allowance and paying the remaining $82,000 in cash. The old tractor cost $95,000, and straight-line amortization of $52,500 had been recorded under the assumption that it would last eight years and have an $11,000 salvage value. Answer the following questions:

a. What was the book value of the old tractor?

b. What is the loss on the exchange?

c. What amount should be debited to the new Tractor account?

Exercise 12-13
Recording capital asset disposal or exchange
LO 8

On January 2, 19X1, Hammond Service Co. disposed of a machine that cost $42,000 and had been amortized $22,625. Present the journal entries to record the disposal under each of the following unrelated assumptions:

a. The machine was sold for $16,250 cash.

b. The machine was traded in on a new machine of like purpose having a $58,500 cash price. A $20,000 trade-in allowance was received, and the balance was paid in cash.

c. The machine plus $1,500 was exchanged for a new machine of like purpose having a fair value $9,000.

d. The machine was traded for vacant land adjacent to the shop to be used as a parking lot. The land had a fair value of $37,500, and Hammond paid $12,500 cash in addition to giving the seller the machine.

Exercise 12-14
Cash flows related to capital assets
LO 11

Refer to the statement of cash flows for **Atlantis** in Appendix I for the year-ended December 31, 1997, to answer the following:

a. What amount of cash is used to purchase fixed assets?

b. What amount of cash is received from sales of fixed assets?

c. How much amortization and depreciation is recorded?

d. What is the total amount of net cash used in investing activities?

e. Are there any gains or losses from sale of fixed assets?

Exercise 12-15
Evaluating efficient use of assets
LO 12

Atherton Co. reported net sales of $4,862,000 for 19X2 and $7,542,000 for 19X3. End-of-year balances for total assets were: 19X1, $1,586,000; 19X2, $1,700,000; and 19X3, $1,882,000. Compute Atherton's total asset turnover for 19X2 and 19X3 and comment on the corporation's efficiency in the use of its assets.

Exercise 12-16
Depletion of natural resources
LO 9

On April 2, 19X1, Cascade Mining Co. paid $3,633,750 for an ore deposit containing 1,425,000 tonnes. The company also installed machinery in the mine that cost $171,000, had an estimated seven-year life with no salvage value, and was capable of removing all the ore in six years. The machine will be abandoned when the ore is completely mined. Cascade began operations on May 1, 19X1, and mined and sold 156,200 tonnes of ore during the remaining eight months of the year. Give the December 31, 19X1, entries to record the depletion of the ore deposit and the amortization of the mining machinery.

Exercise 12-17
Amortization of intangible assets
LO 10

The Falstaff Gallery purchased the copyright on an oil painting for $236,700 on January 1, 19X1. The copyright legally protects its owner for 19 more years. However, the company plans to market and sell prints of the original for only 12 years. Prepare journal entries to record the purchase of the copyright and the annual amortization of the copyright on December 31, 19X1.

Exercise 12-18
Estimating goodwill
LO 10

Corey Boyd has devoted years to developing a profitable business that earns an attractive return. Boyd is now considering the possibility of selling the business and is attempting to estimate the value of the goodwill in the business. The fair value of the net assets of the business (excluding goodwill) is $437,000, and in a typical year net income is about $85,000. Most businesses of this type are expected to earn a return of about 10% on net assets. Estimate the value of the goodwill assuming (a) the value is equal to 10 times the excess earnings above average, and (b) the value can be found by capitalizing the excess earnings above average at a rate of 8%.

Problems

Problem 12-1
Real estate costs; partial year's amortization
LO 2, 3, 6

In 19X1, Lightscapes paid $2,800,000 for a tract of land and two buildings on it. The plan was to demolish Building One and build a new store in its place. Building Two was to be used as a company office and was appraised at a value of $641,300, with a useful life of 20 years and an $80,000 salvage value. A lighted parking lot near Building One had improvements (Land Improvements One) valued at $408,100 that were expected to last another 14 years and have no salvage value. Without considering the buildings or improvements, the tract of land was estimated to have a value of $1,865,600. Lightscapes incurred the following additional costs:

Cost to demolish Building One	$422,600
Cost of additional landscaping	167,200
Cost to construct new building (Building Three), having a useful life of 25 years and a $390,100 salvage value	2,019,000
Cost of new land improvements near Building Two (Land Improvements Two) which have a 20-year useful life and no salvage value	158,000

Required

1. Prepare a schedule having the following column headings: Land, Building Two, Building Three, Land Improvements One, and Land Improvements Two. Allocate the costs incurred by Lightscapes to the appropriate columns and total each column.
2. Prepare a single journal entry dated March 31 to record all the incurred costs, assuming they were paid in cash on that date.
3. Using the straight-line method, prepare December 31 adjusting entries to record amortization for the nine months of 19X1 during which the assets were in use.

Check Figure Accumulated Amortization, Land Improvements Two, $5,925

Problem 12-2
Capital asset costs; partial year's amortization; alternative methods
LO 2, 3, 6

Gunner Construction recently negotiated a lump-sum purchase of several assets from a company that was going out of business. The purchase was completed on March 1, 19X1, at a total cash price of $787,500 and included a building, land, certain land improvements, and 12 vehicles. The estimated market values of the assets were: building, $408,000; land, $289,000; land improvements, $42,500; and vehicles, $110,500. The company's fiscal year ends on December 31.

Required

Preparation component:

1. Prepare a schedule to allocate the lump-sum purchase price to the separate assets that were purchased. Also present the journal entry to record the purchase.
2. Compute the 19X1 amortization expense on the building using the straight-line method, assuming a 15-year life and a $25,650 salvage value.
3. Compute the 19X1 amortization expense on the land improvements assuming a five-year life and double-declining-balance amortization.

Check Figure 19X1, amortization expense on land improvements, $13,125

Analysis component:

4. Defend or refute this statement: Accelerated amortization results in lower taxes over the life of the asset.

Problem 12-3
Alternative amortization methods; partial year's amortization; disposal of capital asset
LO 4, 6, 8

Part 1. A machine that cost $210,000, with a four-year life and an estimated $20,000 salvage value, was installed in Casablanca Company's factory on January 1. The factory manager estimated that the machine would produce 475,000 units of product during its life. It actually produced the following units: year 1, 121,400; year 2, 122,400; year 3, 119,600; and year 4, 118,200. Note the total number of units produced by the end of year 4 exceeded the original estimate. Nevertheless, the machine should not be amortized below the estimated salvage value.

Required

Prepare a form with the following column headings:

Year	Straight-Line	Units-of-Production	Double-Declining-Balance

Then show the amortization for each year and the total amortization for the machine under each amortization method.

Check Figure Year 4, units-of-production amortization expense, $44,640

Part 2. Casablanca purchased a used machine for $167,000 on January 2. It was repaired the next day at a cost of $3,420 and installed on a new platform that cost $1,080. The company predicted that the machine would be used for six years and would then have a $14,600 salvage value. Amortization was to be charged on a straight-line basis. A full year's amortization was charged on December 31, the end of the first year of the machine's use. On September 30 of its sixth year in service, it was retired.

Required

1. Prepare journal entries to record the purchase of the machine, the cost of repairing it, and the installation. Assume that cash was paid.
2. Prepare entries to record amortization on the machine on December 31 of its first year and on September 30 in the year of its disposal.
3. Prepare entries to record the retirement of the machine under each of the following unrelated assumptions: (a) it was sold for $13,500; (b) it was sold for $36,000; and (c) it was destroyed in a fire and the insurance company paid $24,000 in full settlement of the loss claim.

Problem 12-4
Partial year's amortization; revising amortization rates; revenue and capital expenditures
LO 6, 7

Crenshaw Contractors completed these transactions involving the purchase and operation of heavy equipment:

19X1

July 1 Paid $255,440 cash for a new front-end loader, plus $15,200 in sales tax and $2,500 for transportation charges. The loader was estimated to have a four-year life and a $34,740 salvage value.

Oct. 2 Paid $3,660 to enclose the cab and install air conditioning in the loader. This increased the estimated salvage value of the loader by $1,110.

Dec. 31 Recorded straight-line amortization on the loader.

19X2

Feb. 17 Paid $920 to repair the loader after the operator backed it into a tree.

June 30 Paid $4,500 to overhaul the loader's engine. As a result, the estimated useful life of the loader was increased by two years.

Dec. 31 Recorded straight-line amortization on the loader.

Required

Prepare journal entries to record the transactions.

Check Figure Dec 31, 19X2, Accumulated Amortization, Heavy Equipment, $48,674

Problem 12-5
Partial year's amortization; revising amortization rates; exchanging capital assets

LO 6, 8

ACT, Inc., completed the following transactions involving delivery trucks:

19X1

Mar. 26 Paid cash for a new delivery truck, $19,415 plus $1,165 sales tax. The truck was estimated to have a five-year life and a $3,000 trade-in value.

Dec. 31 Recorded straight-line amortization on the truck.

19X2

Dec. 31 Recorded straight-line amortization on the truck. However, due to new information obtained earlier in the year, the original estimated useful life of the truck was changed from five years to four years, and the original estimated trade-in value was increased to $3,500.

19X3

July 7 Traded in the old truck and paid $13,565 in cash for a new truck. The new truck was estimated to have a six-year life and a $3,125 trade-in value. The invoice for the exchange showed these items:

Price of the new truck	$22,550
Trade-in allowance granted on the old truck	(9,750)
Balance of purchase price	$12,800
Sales tax	765
Total paid in cash	$13,565

Dec. 31 Recorded straight-line amortization on the new truck.

Check Figure July 7, 19X3, Loss on Exchange of Delivery Trucks, $1,527

Required

Prepare journal entries to record the transactions.

Problem 12-6
Partial year's amortization; alternative methods; disposal of capital assets

LO 6, 4, 8

Wallingford Co. completed the following transactions involving machinery:

Machine No. 15-50 was purchased for cash on May 4, 19X1, at an installed cost of $158,700. Its useful life was estimated to be six years with a $12,900 trade-in value. Straight-line amortization was recorded for the machine at the end of 19X1, 19X2, and 19X3. On April 27, 19X4, it was traded for Machine No. 17-95, a similar asset with an installed cash price of $185,700. A trade-in allowance of $90,330 was received for Machine No. 15-50, and the balance was paid in cash.

Machine No. 17-95's life was predicted to be four years with a $24,600 trade-in value. Double-declining-balance amortization on this machine was recorded each December 31. On November 5, 19X5, it was traded for Machine No. BT-311, which was a dissimilar asset with an installed cash price of $537,000. A trade-in allowance of $81,000 was received for Machine No. 17-95, and the balance was paid in cash.

It was estimated that Machine No. BT-311 would produce 600,000 units of product during its five-year useful life, after which it would have a $105,000 trade-in value. Units-of-production amortization was recorded for the machine for 19X5, a period in which it produced 93,000 units of product. Between January 1, 19X6, and August 24, 19X8, the machine produced 324,000 more units. On the latter date, it was sold for $243,600.

Check Figure Nov 5/X5 Gain on Sale of Machinery, $8,783.

Required

Prepare journal entries to record: (a) the purchase of each machine, (b) the amortization expense recorded on the first December 31 of each machine's life, and (c) the disposal of each machine. (Only one entry is needed to record the exchange of one machine for another.)

Problem 12-7
Intangible assets and natural resources

LO 9, 10

Part 1. In 19X1, The Pullman Company leased space in a building for 15 years. The lease contract calls for annual rental payments of $70,000 to be made on each July 1 throughout the life of the lease and also provides that the lessee must pay for all additions and improvements to the leased property. In 19X6, Pullman decided to sublease the space to Kidman & Associates for the remaining 10 years of the lease. On June 20, 19X6, Kidman paid $185,000 to Pullman for the right to sublease the space and agreed to assume the obligation to pay the $70,000 annual rent to the building owner beginning July 1, 19X6. After taking possession of the leased space, Kidman paid for improving the office portion of the leased space at a cost of $129,840. The improvements were paid for on July 5, 19X6, and are estimated to have a life equal to the 16 years remaining in the life of the building.

Required

Prepare entries for Kidman to record (a) its payment to Pullman for the right to sublease the building space, (b) its payment of the 19X6 annual rent to the building owner, and (c) its payment for the office improvements. Also, prepare the adjusting entries required at the end of 19X6 to amortize (d) a proper share of the $185,000 cost of the sublease, (e) a proper share of the office improvements and (f) a proper share of the rent expense applicable to 19X6.

Part 2. On July 3 of the current year, Jackson Mining Co. paid $4,836,000 for land estimated to contain 7.8 million tonnes of recoverable ore of a valuable mineral. It installed machinery costing $390,000, which had a 10-year life and no salvage value, and was capable of exhausting the ore deposit in eight years. The machinery was paid for on July 25, nine days before mining operations began. The company removed 400,000 tonnes of ore during the first five months of operations.

Required

Preparation component:

Prepare entries to record (a) the purchase of the land, (b) the installation of the machinery, (c) the first five months' depletion under the assumption that the land will be valueless after the ore is mined, and (d) the first five months' amortization on the machinery, which will be abandoned after the ore is fully mined.

Check Figure Depletion Expense, $248,000

Analysis component:

Describe the similarities and differences in depletion, and amortization.

Problem 12-8
Goodwill

LO 10

Canadian Rental Co. an equipment rental business, has the following balance sheet on December 31, 19X1:

Cash	$ 93,930
Equipment	678,800
Accumulated amortization, equipment	(271,500)
Buildings	340,000
Accumulated amortization, buildings	(182,400)
Land	93,000
Total assets	$751,830
Accounts payable	$ 18,650
Long-term note payable	337,250
J. Reynolds, capital	395,930
Total liabilities and owner's equity	$751,830

In this industry, earnings average 20% of owner's equity. Canadian Rental, however, is expected to earn $100,000 annually. The balance sheet amounts are reasonable estimates of fair market values for all assets except goodwill, which does not appear on the financial statement. In negotiations to sell the business, Canadian Rental has proposed that goodwill should be measured by capitalizing the amount of above-average earnings at a rate of 15%. On the other hand, the potential buyer thinks that goodwill should be valued at five times the amount of earnings above the average for the industry.

Required

Check Figure Goodwill, $138,760 or $104,070

1. Compute the amount of goodwill proposed by Canadian Rental.
2. Compute the amount of goodwill according to the potential buyer.
3. Suppose that the buyer purchases the business for the amount of the net assets reported on the December 31, 19X1, balance sheet plus the amount proposed by Canadian Rental for the goodwill. If the amount of expected earnings (before amortization of goodwill) is obtained the first year, and the goodwill is amortized over the longest permissible time period, what amount of net income will be reported for the first year after the business is purchased?
4. What rate of return on the buyer's investment does the first year's net income represent?

Alternate Problems

Problem 12-1A

Real estate costs; partial year's amortization

LO 2, 3, 6

In 19X1, Spicewood Technologies paid $1,350,000 for a tract of land on which two buildings were located. The plan was to demolish Building A and build a new shop in its place. Building B was to be used as a company office and was appraised at a value of $472,770, with a useful life of 15 years and a $90,000 salvage value. A lighted parking lot near Building B had improvements valued at $125,145 that were expected to last another six years and have no salvage value. Without considering the buildings or improvements, the tract of land was estimated to have a value of $792,585.

Spicewood incurred the following additional costs:

Cost to demolish Building A	$ 117,000
Cost of additional landscaping	172,500
Cost to construct new building (Building C), having a useful life of 20 years and a $295,500 salvage value	1,356,000
Cost of new land improvements near Building C, which have a 10-year useful life and no salvage value	101,250

Required

1. Prepare a schedule having the following column headings: Land, Building B, Building C, Land Improvements B, and Land Improvements C. Allocate the costs incurred by Spicewood to the appropriate columns and total each column.
2. Prepare a single journal entry dated October 1 to record all the incurred costs, assuming they were paid in cash on that date.
3. Using the straight-line method, prepare December 31 adjusting entries to record amortization for the three months of 19X1 during which the assets were in use.

Problem 12-2A
Capital asset costs; partial year's amortization; alternative methods
LO 2, 3, 6

The Timberline Company recently negotiated a lump-sum purchase of several assets from a contractor who was planning to change locations. The purchase was completed on September 30, 19X1, at a total cash price of $1,610,000, and included a building, land, certain land improvements, and six trucks. The estimated market values of the assets were: building, $784,800; land, $540,640; land improvements, $226,720; and trucks, $191,840. The company's fiscal year ends on December 31.

Required

Preparation component:

1. Prepare a schedule to allocate the lump-sum purchase price to the separate assets that were purchased. Also present the journal entry to record the purchase.
2. Compute the 19X1 amortization expense on the building using the straight-line method, assuming a 12-year life and a $100,500 trade-in value.
3. Compute the 19X1 amortization expense on the land improvements assuming a 10-year life and double-declining-balance amortization.

Analysis component:

4. Defend or refute this statement: Accelerated amortization results in higher taxes over the life of the asset.

Problem 12-3A
Alternative amortization methods; partial year's amortization; disposal of capital assets
LO 4, 6, 8

Part 1. On January 2, Brodie Co. purchased and installed a new machine that cost $312,000, with a five-year life and an estimated $28,000 salvage value. Management estimated that the machine would produce 1,136,000 units of product during its life. Actual production of units was as follows: Year 1, 245,600; Year 2, 230,400; Year 3, 227,000; Year 4, 232,600; and Year 5, 211,200. Note that the total number of units produced by the end of Year 5 exceeded the original estimate. Nevertheless, the machine should not be amortized below the estimated salvage value.

Required

Prepare a schedule with the following column headings:

Year	Straight-Line	Units-of-Production	Double-Declining-Balance

Then show the amortization for each year and the total amortization for the machine under each amortization method.

Part 2. On January 1, Brodie purchased a used machine for $130,000. The next day, it was repaired at a cost of $3,390 and was mounted on a new platform that cost $4,800. Management estimated that the machine would be used for seven years and would then have a $18,000 salvage value. Amortization was to be charged on a straight-line basis. A full year's amortization was charged on December 31 of the first through the fifth years of the machine's use; and on April 1 of its sixth year of use, the machine was retired from service.

Required

1. Prepare journal entries to record the purchase of the machine, the cost of repairing it, and the installation. Assume that cash was paid.
2. Prepare entries to record amortization on the machine on December 31 of its first year and on April 1 in the year of its disposal.
3. Prepare entries to record the retirement of the machine under each of the following unrelated assumptions: (a) it was sold for $30,000; (b) it was sold for $50,000; and (c) it was destroyed in a fire and the insurance company paid $20,000 in full settlement of the loss claim.

Problem 12-4A
Partial year's amortization; revising amortization rates; revenue and capital expenditures
LO 6,7

Rush Delivery Service completed these transactions involving the purchase and operation of delivery equipment:

19X1

Mar. 25 Paid cash for a new delivery van, $24,950 plus $1,950 sales tax. The van was estimated to have a five-year life and a $3,400 salvage value.

Sept. 30 Paid $1,550 to replace the manual transmission in the van with an automatic transmission. This increased the estimated salvage value of the van by $200.

Dec. 31 Recorded straight-line amortization on the van.

19X2

May 10 Paid $600 to repair the van after the driver backed it into a loading dock.

Oct. 1 Paid $1,970 to overhaul the van's engine. As a result, the estimated useful life of the van was increased by two years.

Dec. 31 Recorded straight-line amortization on the van.

Required

Prepare journal entries to record the transactions.

Problem 12-5A
Partial year's amortization; revising amortization rates; exchanging capital assets
LO 6,8

Precision Machine Shop completed the following transactions involving machinery:

19X1

June 24 Paid cash for a new machine, $106,600 plus $6,400 sales tax. The machine was estimated to have a six-year life and a $9,800 trade-in value.

Dec. 31 Recorded straight-line amortization on the machine.

19X2

Dec. 31 Recorded straight-line amortization on the machine. However, due to new information obtained earlier in the year, the original estimated useful life of the lathe was changed from six years to four years, and the original estimated trade-in value was increased to $13,050.

19X3

Nov. 4 Traded in the old machine and paid $89,500 in cash for a new, similar machine. The new machine was estimated to have an eight-year life and a $10,380 trade-in value. The invoice for the exchange showed these items:

Price of the new machine	$123,000
Trade-in allowance granted on the old machine	(38,000)
Balance of purchase price	$ 85,000
Sales tax	4,500
Total paid in cash	$ 89,500

Dec. 31 Recorded straight-line amortization on the new machine.

Required

Prepare journal entries to record the transactions.

Problem 12-6A
Partial year's amortization; alternative methods; disposal of capital assets
LO 6,4,8

Central Printing Co. completed the following transactions involving printing equipment:

Printing press A was purchased for cash on April 3, 19X1, at an installed cost of $169,400. Its useful life was estimated to be seven years with a $25,200 trade-in value. Straight-line amortization was recorded for the press at the end of 19X1, 19X2, and 19X3, and on July 2, 19X4, it was traded for printing press B, a similar asset with an installed cash price of $206,400. A trade-in allowance of $112,000 was received for printing press A, and the balance was paid in cash.

Printing press B's life was predicted to be ten years with an $22,000 trade-in value. Double-declining-balance amortization was recorded on each December 31 of its life. On March 31, 19X6, it was traded for a colour laser copier, which was a dissimilar asset with an installed cash price of $153,000. A trade-in allowance of $138,000 was received for printing press B, and the balance was paid in cash.

It was estimated that the copier would produce 1,000,000 copies during its four-year useful life, after which it would have a $13,000 trade-in value. Units-of-production amortization was recorded for the copier for 19X6, a period in which it produced 190,000 copies. Between January 1, 19X7, and February 10, 19X9, the copier produced 640,000 more copies. On the latter date, it was sold for $40,000.

Required

For each piece of equipment, prepare journal entries to record: (a) its purchase, (b) the amortization expense recorded on the first December 31 of its life, and (c) its disposal. (Only one entry is needed to record the exchange of one piece of equipment for another.)

Problem 12-7A
Intangible assets and natural resources

LO 9, 10

Part 1. In 19X1, Granite Co. leased space in a building for 12 years. The lease contract requires: (1) $26,400 annual rental payments to be made each May 1 throughout the life of the lease, and (2) the lessee to pay for all additions and improvements to the leased property. In 19X8, Granite decided to sublease the space to Magnolia Service Co. for the remaining five years of the lease. On April 25, 19X8, Magnolia paid $30,000 to Granite for the right to sublease the space, and agreed to assume the obligation to pay the $26,400 annual rent to the building owner beginning May 1, 19X8. After taking possession of the leased space, Magnolia paid for improving the office portion of the leased space at a cost of $18,000. The improvements were paid for on May 6, 19X8, and are estimated to have a life equal to the 13 years remaining in the life of the building.

Required

Prepare entries for Magnolia to record (a) its payment to Granite for the right to sublease the building space, (b) its payment of the 19X8 annual rent to the building owner, and (c) its payment for the office improvements. Also, prepare the adjusting entries required on December 31, 19X8, to amortize (d) a proper share of the $30,000 cost of the sublease, (e) a proper share of the office improvements and (f) a proper share of the rent expense applicable to 19X8.

Part 2. On February 19 of the current year, Wayman Industries paid $4,450,000 for land estimated to contain five million tonnes of recoverable ore of a valuable mineral. It installed machinery costing $200,000, which had a 16-year life and no salvage value, and was capable of exhausting the ore deposit in 12 years. The machinery was paid for on March 21, eleven days before mining operations began. The company removed 352,000 tonnes of ore during the first nine months of operations.

Required

Preparation component:

Prepare entries to record (a) the purchase of the land, (b) the installation of the machinery, (c) the first nine months' depletion under the assumption that the land will be valueless after the ore is mined, and (d) the first nine months' amortization on the machinery, which will be abandoned after the ore is fully mined.

Analysis component:

Describe the similarities and differences in depletion and amortization.

Problem 12-8A
Goodwill
LO 10

Kudos Casual Wear has the following balance sheet on December 31, 19X1:

Cash	$ 138,700
Merchandise inventory	607,950
Buildings	451,500
Accumulated amortization	(210,800)
Land	192,400
Total assets	$1,179,750
Accounts payable	$ 98,325
Long-term note payable	414,050
N. Pursley, capital	667,375
Total liabilities and owner's equity	$1,179,750

In this industry, earnings average 32% of owner's equity. Kudos, however, is expected to earn $230,000 annually. The balance sheet amounts are reasonable estimates of fair market values for all assets except goodwill, which does not appear on the financial statements. In negotiations to sell the business, Kudos has proposed that goodwill should be measured by capitalizing the amount of above-average earnings at a rate of 10%. On the other hand, the potential buyer thinks that goodwill should be valued at eight times the amount of earnings above the average for the industry.

Required

1. Compute the amount of goodwill proposed by Kudos.
2. Compute the amount of goodwill according to the potential buyer.
3. Suppose that the buyer purchases the business for the amount of the net assets reported on the December 31, 19X1, balance sheet, plus the amount proposed by Kudos for the goodwill. If the amount of expected earnings (before amortization of goodwill) is obtained the first year, and the goodwill is amortized over the longest permissible time period, what amount of net income will be reported for the first year after the business is purchased?
4. What rate of return on the buyer's investment does the first year's net income represent?

Analytical and Review Problems

A & R Problem 12-1

At the last meeting of the executive committee of Kearins, Ltd., Milton Vacon, controller, was severely criticized by both President Kearins and Kate Ryan, vice president of production. The subject of criticism was the recognition of periodic amortization. President Kearins was unhappy with the fact that what he referred to as "a fictitious item" was deducted, resulting in depressed net income. In his words, "Depreciation is a fiction when the assets being depreciated are worth far more than we paid for them. What the controller is doing is unduly understating our net income. This in turn is detrimental to our shareholders because it results in the undervaluation of our shares on the market."

Vice President Ryan was equally adamant about the periodic amortization charges; however, she came on from another side. She said, "Our maintenance people tell me that the level of maintenance is such that our plant and equipment will last virtually forever." She further stated that charging amortization on top of maintenance expenses is double-counting—it seems reasonable to charge either maintenance or amortization but not both.

The time taken by other pressing matters did not permit Vacon to answer; instead, the controller was asked to prepare a report to the executive committee to deal with the issues raised by the president and vice president.

Required

The controller asks you, his assistant, to prepare the required report.

A & R Problem 12-2

The Shape Company purchased a large earth-mover four years ago at a cost of $750,000. At that time it was estimated that the economic life of the equipment would be 12 years and that its ultimate salvage value would be $140,000.

Assuming the company uses straight-line amortization, state whether each of the following events requires a revision of the original amortization rate, with reasons for your answer:

a. Due to persistent inflation, the present replacement cost of the same type of equipment is $975,000.

b. Because of the higher replacement cost, as described in (a) above, the ultimate salvage value is now estimated at $95,000.

c. The company, in connection with having its line of credit increased, was required by the bank to have the assets appraised. The earth-mover was estimated to have a current value of $450,000.

d. At the time the appraisal was made in (c) above, it was determined that technological change was progressing more slowly than originally estimated and that the earth-mover would probably remain in service for 15 years with the ultimate salvage value as originally estimated at the end of 12 years.

BEYOND THE NUMBERS

Reporting in Action

LO1

Refer to the financial statements and related information for **Alliance** in Appendix I. Answer the following questions by analyzing the information in its annual report:

1. What percent of the original cost of Alliance's property and equipment remains to be amortized as of March 31, 1997 and 1996? Assume these assets have no salvage value.

2. Over what periods of time is Alliance amortizing intangible assets and goodwill?

3. What is the net change in total property and equipment (before amortization) for the year ended March 31, 1997? What is the amount of cash generated by (or used for) investment in property and equipment during the year ended March 31, 1997? What is one possible explanation for the difference between these two amounts?

4. Compute Alliance's total asset turnover for the year ended March 31, 1997.

Comparative Analysis

LO12

Both **Alliance** and **Atlantis** produce and distribute movies and television programs. Key comparative figures ($thousands) for these two companies follow:

	Alliance		Atlantis	
Key Figures	**1997**	**1996**	**1997**	**1996**
Total Assets	$353,722	$238,898	$333,547	$334,826
Net Sales	$282,599	$268,945	$177,960	$137,984

* Alliance figures are from the annual reports for the fiscal years ended March 31, 1997 and 1996. Atlantis figures are from the annual reports for the fiscal years ended December 31, 1997 and 1996.

Required

1. Compute Alliance's total asset turnover as of March 31, 1997. Compute Atlantis' total asset turnover as of December 31, 1997.

Analysis Component:

2. Which company is more efficient in generating net sales given the total assets employed?

Ethics Challenge

LO 3

Marcia Diamond is a small business owner and handles all the books for her business. Her company just finished a year when a large amount of borrowed funds were invested into a new building addition as well as numerous equipment and fixture additions. Marcia's banker requires that she submit semiannual financial statements for his file so he can monitor the financial health of her business. He has warned her that if profit margins erode he might raise the interest rate on the borrowed funds since this means the loan is riskier from the bank's point of view. Marcia knows profit margin is likely to decline in this current year. As she posts year-end adjusting entries she decides to apply the following amortization rule: All capital additions for the current year are considered put into service the first day of the following month.

Required

1. Identify the decisions managers like Ms. Diamond must make in applying amortization methods.
2. Is Marcia's decision an ethical violation or is it a legitimate decision that managers make in computing amortization?
3. How will Marcia's amortization rule affect the profit margin of her business?

Communicating in Practice

LO 12

The classroom should be divided into teams. Teams are to select an industry, and each team member is to select a different company in that industry. Each team member is to acquire the annual report of the company selected. Annual reports can be obtained in many ways including accessing this book's Web page or **http://www.sedar.com**. Use the annual report to compute total asset turnover. Communicate with teammates via a meeting, e-mail or telephone to discuss the meaning of this ratio, how different companies compare to each other, and the industry norm. The team must prepare a single memo reporting the ratios for each company and identify the conclusions or consensus of opinion reached during the team's discussion. The memo is to be duplicated and distributed to the instructor and all classmates.

Taking It to the Net

LO 1

Visit the Web site of the Canadian Intellectual Property Office at **http://strategis.ic.gc.ca**. Use the search function to look for any existing patents protecting some of your favourite products. For example, if you search "hockey skates" you will find a patent protecting a Blade for Ice Hockey Skates. Search three different products and note the range of patents protecting the product. (Note: If you have an idea for a new product you might also want to search the database to see if there are any preexisting patents on your idea.)

Teamwork in Action

LO 3, 5, 4

Each member of the team has a responsibility to become a resident expert on a specific amortization method. This expertise is used to facilitate their teammates understanding of the concepts relevant to the method they have chosen. Follow the procedure outlined below:

1. Each team member is to select their area for expertise by choosing one of the following amortization methods: straight-line, units-of-production, and declining-balance. You have one minute to make your choice.
2. Learning teams are to disburse and expert teams are to be formed. Expert teams are made up of students who have all selected the same area of expertise. The instructor will identify the location where each expert team meets.
3. Using data below, the expert teams are to collaborate and develop a presentation illustrating each of the relevant procedures and concepts required below. Each expert team member must write-up the presentation in a format they can show to their learning teams in the next step in the activity.
4. **Data:**

   On January 8, 1998, Whitewater Riders purchased a van to transport rafters back to the point of departure at the conclusion of the rafting adventure tours they run. The cost of the van is $44,000. It has an estimated salvage value of $2,000 and is expected to be used for four years and to be driven 100,000 kilometres. The van is expected to be driven 20,000 kilometres in 1998, 30,000 kilometres in 1999, 34,000 in 2000, and 16,000 in 2001.

Procedures and concepts to illustrate in expert presentation:

a. Compute annual amortization expense for each year of the asset's estimated useful life.

b. Explain when and how annual amortization is recorded.

c. Explain the impact of this method versus other methods on net income over the life of the asset.

d. Identify the book value of the asset over each year of the asset's life and illustrate the reporting of this amount for any one year.

4. Re-form learning teams. In rotation, each expert is to present to their teams the results from part 3. Experts are to encourage and respond to questions.

Hitting the Road

LO1

Team up with one or more classmates for this activity. You are to brainstorm and do any necessary research to identify companies in your community or your area of the country that have and must account for the following assets: natural resource; patent; lease; leasehold improvement; copyright; trademark; and goodwill.

You might need to identify seven different companies given there are seven assets or you might find a company having more than one type of asset. Once you have matched a company with the asset, then identify the accounting this company must use for that asset to allocate its cost to the periods benefited from its use.

Business Break

LO1

Read the article "Guardian of the Famous and the Dead" in the May 8, 1995, issue of *Business Week*.

1. What is the purpose of the **Curtis Management Group** run by CEO Mark A. Roesler?
2. What is the difference between a "trademark" and "rights of publicity"?
3. Identify one famous person in each of the following categories represented by the Curtis Management Group: movies, music, sports and historical.

13

Current and Long-Term Liabilities

CHAPTER

A Look Back

Chapter 12 focused on capital assets including plant assets, natural resources, and intangible assets. We showed how to record their costs, allocate their costs to periods benefiting from them, and disposing of them.

A Look at This Chapter

This chapter emphasizes current liabilities, and also introduces long-term liabilities. We explain how these liabilities are identified, computed, recorded, and reported in financial statements.

A Look Forward

Chapter 14 focuses on the partnership form of organization. Important characteristics of partnerships are described along with some of their initial transactions.

Chapter Outline

- **Characteristics of Liabilities**
  - Defining Liabilities
  - Classifying Liabilities as Current or Long-Term
  - Uncertainty in Liabilities
- **Known (Determinable) Liabilities**
  - Accounts Payable
  - Goods and Services Tax and Sales Taxes Payable
  - Unearned Revenues
  - Short-Term Notes Payable
- **Estimated Liabilities**
  - Warranty Liabilities
  - Income Tax Liabilities for Corporations
  - Deferred (Future) Income Tax Liabilities for Corporations
- **Contingent Liabilities**
  - Accounting for Contingent Liabilities
  - Examples of Contingent Liability Disclosures
- **Long-Term Liabilities**
  - Present Value Concepts
  - Applying Present Value Concepts to Long-Term Notes
  - Known (Determinable) Long-Term Liabilities
  - Estimated *Long-Term* Liabilities
  - Contingent *Long-Term* Liabilities
- **Using the Information —Times Interest Earned**

Tax Cop

Ottawa, ON—Carmen Benish and her two comrades jump out of their battered Zhiguli and walk briskly to the door of a bicycle sales and services shop in the Moscow suburb of Podolsk. Ducking under bicycle frames and wheels hanging from the ceiling, they approach a salesclerk and flash their badges. A few days earlier, an undercover colleague made a purchase that wasn't rung up on the register. Now, Benish, Mikail Nikolas and Val Yaroslav are investigating whether the business is underreporting sales to avoid paying taxes. Two burly policemen in bulletproof vests stand guard as Benish and her fellow investigators confiscate Vladimir Zolov's records. "We pay our taxes on time. We are law-abiding citizens," he protests.

Benish is unique. She grew up in a tough Halifax environment. But Benish was determined to stay out of trouble. "I went to community college and took accounting and criminal justice," says Benish. "I also joined an international group. Loved the cultural differences." When she graduated with her degree this past June, she faced a dilemma. "I really liked both accounting and criminal justice," says Benish. "I didn't know which way to go."

Fortunately for Benish, her counsellor heard that sometimes people with exactly the type of background Benish has are hired by a unique program for international tax investigators. "It is a match made in heaven! I get to use my accounting and criminal justice background to help track down people who are underreporting international income to avoid taxes." Given the huge growth in international sales, this is a high priority.

Benish is presently assigned to a one-month internship in Moscow. "Russia's environment is a nightmare for us," says Peter Eastwood, Benish's supervisor. "But our job is to ensure that companies and their affiliates doing business here, pay their required taxes." These investigators also have considerable power. They can levy fines up to three times taxes owed, and can seize taxpayers' property and freeze bank accounts during investigations.

But the job is dangerous. Last year in Russia alone, 26 tax officials were killed and 74 wounded, while 18 tax offices were bombed or sprayed with gunfire. "Sure I'm scared sometimes." says Benish. "But I'm really having fun, and the odds of something bad happening are pretty low." Adds Benish, "No green eyeshades and cushy desk job for me!"

Learning Objectives

LO 1 Describe current and long-term liabilities and their characteristics.

LO 2 Identify and describe known current liabilities.

LO 3 Prepare entries to account for short-term notes payable.

LO 4 Account for estimated liabilities including warranties and income taxes.

LO 5 Explain how to account for contingent liabilities.

LO 6 Describe accounting for long-term liabilities.

LO 7 Explain and calculate the present value of an amount to be paid at a future date.

LO 8 Describe how present value concepts are used in accounting for long-term notes.

LO 9 Compute times interest earned ratio and use it to analyze liabilities.

CHAPTER PREVIEW

Previous chapters introduced us to liabilities for accounts payable, notes payable, wages, and unearned revenues. In this chapter, we learn more about these liabilities and additional ones such as warranties, taxes, vacation pay, and leases. We also describe contingent liabilities and look at some long-term liabilities. This includes how we define, classify, and measure liabilities for the purpose of reporting useful information about them to decision makers. Understanding tax liabilities is especially important for Carmen Benish and people like her as described in the opening article.

Characteristics of Liabilities

LO1 Describe current and long-term liabilities and their characteristics.

This section discusses important characteristics of liabilities, how they are classified, and how they are reported when there are questions about them.

Defining Liabilities

A liability is a probable future payment of assets or services that a company is presently obligated to make as a result of past transactions or events.[1] This definition includes three crucial factors:

- Due to past transaction or event
- Present obligation
- Future payment of assets or services

These elements are portrayed visually in Exhibit 13.1.

Exhibit 13.1

Characteristics of a Liability

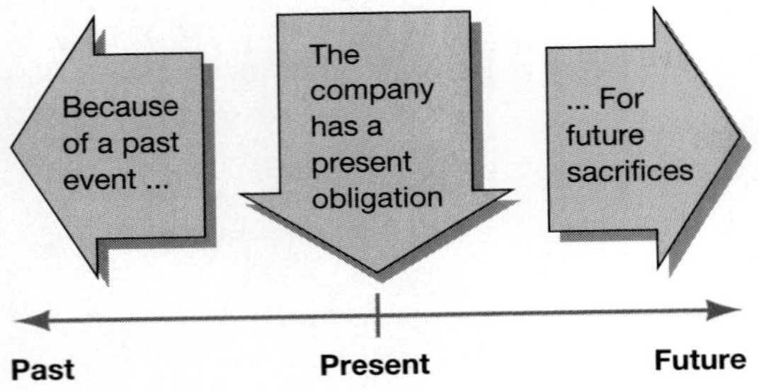

Liabilities do not include all expected future payments. For example, most companies expect to pay wages to their employees in upcoming months and years. But these future payments are not liabilities because the company is not presently obligated to pay them until employees earn their future wages. In this case, there is no past event such as employee work resulting in a present obligation. Future liabilities will arise when employees perform their work.

Classifying Liabilities as Current or Long-Term

Information about liabilities is more useful when the balance sheet identifies them as either current or long-term. Decision makers need to know when obligations are due so they can plan for them and take appropriate action. Others use financial statements to predict future cash flows and knowing when obligations are due aids this process.

Current Liabilities

Current liabilities, also called *short-term liabilities*, are obligations expected to be paid using current assets or by creating other current liabilities (e.g., replacing an account payable with a note payable).[2] Current liabilities are due within one year or the company's operating cycle, whichever is longer. Examples of current liabilities are accounts payable, short-term notes payable, wages payable, warranty liabilities, lease liabilities, payroll and other taxes payable, and unearned revenues.

[1] *CICA Handbook*, section 1000, "Financial Statement Concepts," par. 32.

[2] *CICA Handbook*, section 1510, "Current Assets and Current Liabilities," par. .03

Long-Term Liabilities

A company's obligations not expected to be paid within one year (or a longer operating cycle) are reported as **long-term liabilities.** Long-term liabilities include long-term notes payable, warranty liabilities, lease liabilities, and bonds payable. They are sometimes reported on the balance sheet in a single long-term liabilities total. But many companies show them as two or more items such as *long-term debt* and *other liabilities*. **Barrick Gold Corporation,** for instance, reports long-term liabilities in its fiscal 1997 balance sheet of ($ millions): long-term debt, $500; reclamation and closure liabilities, $144; deferred income taxes, $145. These are reported after current liabilities.

Liabilities can be either current or long-term depending on their characteristics. A single liability also can be divided between these two sections if a company expects to make payments toward it in both the short- and long-term. **Alcan Aluminium,** for instance, reports in its 1997 balance sheet ($ millions): debt not maturing within one year, $1,241; debt maturing within one year, $36. The second item is reported in current liabilities. We sometimes see liabilities not having a fixed due date, but payable on the creditor's demand. They are reported as current liabilities because of the possibility of payment within the year or its longer operating cycle. Exhibit 13.2 shows amounts of current and long-term liabilities for selected companies.

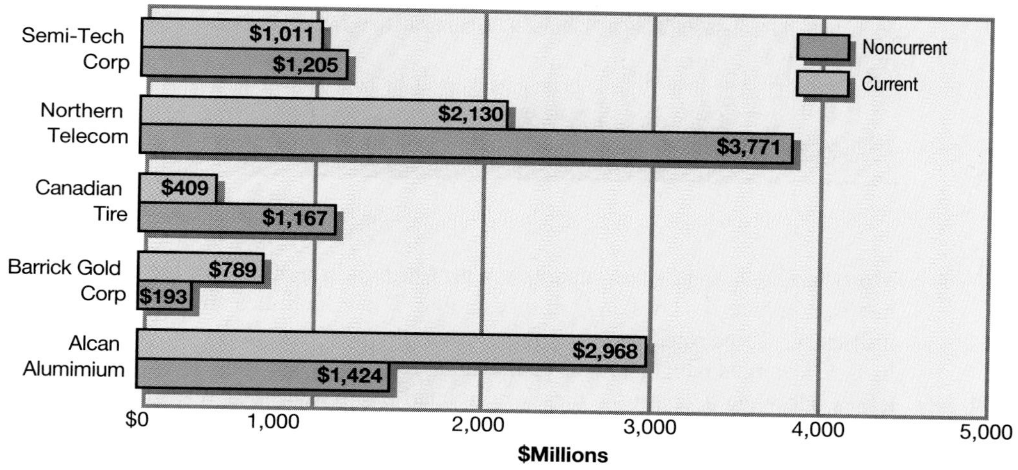

Exhibit 13.2

Current and Long-Term Liabilities

Uncertainty in Liabilities

Liabilities involve three important questions: Whom to pay? When to pay? How much to pay? Answers to these questions often are decided when a liability is incurred. For example, if a company has an account payable to a specific individual for $100, payable on August 15, 1999, there is no uncertainty about the answers. The company knows whom to pay, when to pay, and how much to pay. But we do see liabilities with uncertainty in one or more of the answers to these three questions.

Uncertainty in Whom to Pay

Certain liabilities involve uncertainty as to whom is to be paid. For instance, a company creates a liability with a known amount when issuing a note that is payable to its holder. This type of note is negotiable and can be sold by the holder to another party. Although a specific amount is payable to the note's holder at a specified date, the company does not know who the holder is until that date. Despite this uncertainty, the corporation reports this liability on its balance sheet.

Uncertainty in When to Pay

A company can have an obligation of a known amount to a known creditor but not know when it must be paid. For example, a legal services firm can accept fees in advance from a client who expects to use its services in the future. This means the legal services firm has a liability that is settled by providing services at an unknown future date. Even though this uncertainty exists, the firm's balance sheet must report this liability. These types of obligations are reported as current liabilities because they may be settled in the short term.

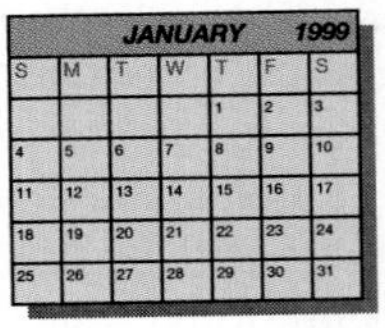

Uncertainty in How Much to Pay

A company can know it has an obligation but not know how much will be required to settle it. For example, a company using electrical power is billed only after the meter is read. This cost is incurred and the liability created before a bill is received. A liability to the electric company is reported as an estimated amount if the balance sheet is prepared before a bill arrives.

Flash back

1. What is a liability?
2. Is every expected future payment a liability?
3. If a liability is payable in 15 months, is it classified as current or long-term?

Answers—p. 642

Known (Determinable) Liabilities

LO 2 Identify and describe known current liabilities.

Most liabilities arise from situations with little uncertainty. They are set by agreements, contracts, or laws and are measurable. These liabilities are called **known liabilities**, or sometimes called *definitely determinable liabilities*. Known liabilities include accounts payable, notes payable, payroll, sales taxes, unearned revenues, and leases. How we account for these and related liabilities is described in this section.

Accounts Payable

Accounts payable, or trade accounts payable, are amounts owed to suppliers for products or services purchased on credit. Accounting for accounts payable is explained and illustrated in several prior chapters. Much of our discussion of merchandising activities in Chapters 6 and 7, for instance, dealt with accounts payable.

Goods and Services Tax and Sales Taxes Payable

Sales tax liabilities arise because the federal government and most provincial governments require businesses to act as collection agencies for the Goods and Services Tax (GST) and provincial sales taxes (PSTs). When a business makes a sale, the customer is charged for the sales tax on top of the selling price, in most cases, and the tax is later paid to the government(s).

Chapter 6 illustrated how the sales taxes would be accumulated in the sales journal. Assume that Superior Clothing Store collected $8,750 of GST and $7,500 of PST[3] during September. At the end of September these amounts would appear

[3] In some jurisdictions the GST and PST are combined into the harmonized sales tax (HST).

on the balance sheet as current liabilities. The entry to pay these taxes during October would be as follows:

Oct. 25	GST Payable	8,750	
	Cash		8,750
	To pay GST for September.		

Assets = Liabilities + Equity
−8,750 −8,750

Oct. 25	PST Payable	7,500	
	Cash		7,500
	To pay PST for September.		

Assets = Liabilities + Equity
−7,500 −7,500

Note that the sales taxes are neither a revenue nor an expense for the enterprise. However, when a business purchases goods and services for its own use, the sales taxes (GST and PST) paid become part of the cost of these items. In the case of goods purchased for resale, either the business would be exempt from paying the sales taxes on the purchase or the sales taxes paid could be deducted from the sales taxes collected when determining the amount to be remitted to the government(s).

Unearned Revenues

Unearned revenues (also called deferred revenues, collections in advance, and prepayments) are amounts received in advance from customers for future products or services. Advance ticket sales for sporting events or music concerts are examples of unearned revenues. **Orca Bay Hockey Holdings Inc.**, owners of the Vancouver Canucks, reported "Deferred revenue on advance sale of tickets" of nearly $6 million at June 30, 1997. When Orca sells $6 million of advanced tickets, its entry is:

July 30	Cash	6,000,000	
	Deferred Revenue		6,000,000
	To record sale of Canuck season tickets		

Assets = Liabilities + Equity
+6,000,000 +6,000,000

As the hockey season progresses Orca records the portion of revenue earned:

Oct. 30	Deferred Revenue	40,000	
	Season Ticket Revenue		40,000
	To record season ticket revenues earned.		

Assets = Liabilities + Equity
−40,000 +40,000

Deferred Revenue is an unearned revenue account and is reported as a current liability. Beyond sporting and music events, unearned revenues arise with airline ticket sales, magazine publishers, construction projects, hotel reservations, and custom orders.

Short-Term Notes Payable

LO 3 Prepare entries to account for short-term notes payable.

A **short-term note payable** is a written promise to pay a specified amount on a specified future date within one year or the company's operating cycle, whichever is longer. These promissory notes are negotiable (as are cheques). This means they can be transferred from party to party by endorsement. Written documentation is helpful in resolving disputes and for pursuing legal actions involving liabilities. Most notes payable are interest bearing to compensate for the time until payment is made. Short-term notes payable arise from many transactions. A company purchases merchandise on credit and sometimes extends the credit period by signing a note to replace an account payable. They also arise when money is borrowed from a bank. We describe both these cases in this section.

Note Given to Extend Credit Period

A company can create a note payable to replace an account payable. Most often, the creditor asks that an interest-bearing note be substituted for an overdue account payable that does not bear interest. A less common situation is where a debtor's weak financial condition encourages the creditor to obtain a note, sometimes for a lesser amount, and then close the account to ensure no additional credit sales are made to this customer.

Illustration of Note to Extend Credit Period

To illustrate, let's assume on August 23 that Wiley asks to extend its past-due $600 account payable to McGraw. After some negotiations, McGraw agrees to accept $100 cash and a 60-day, 12%, $500 note payable to replace the account payable. Wiley records this transaction with this entry:

Assets	= Liabilities	+ Equity
−100	−600	
	+500	

Aug. 23	Accounts Payable—McGraw Company	600	
	Cash		100
	Notes Payable		500
	Gave $100 cash and a 60-day, 12% note to extend due date on account.		

Signing the note does not pay off Wiley's debt. Instead, the form of debt is changed from an account to a note payable. McGraw prefers the note over the account payable because it earns interest and also because it is documentation of the debt's existence, term and amount.

When the note comes due, Wiley pays the note and interest by giving McGraw a cheque for $509.86. This payment is recorded with this entry:

Assets	= Liabilities	+ Equity
−509.86	−500	−9.86

Oct. 22	Notes Payable	500.00	
	Interest Expense	9.86	
	Cash		509.86
	Paid note with interest ($500 × 12% × 60/365).		

The interest expense is computed by multiplying the principal of the note ($500) by the annual interest rate (12%) for the fraction of the year the note is outstanding (60 days/365 days).

Note Given to Borrow from Bank

A bank nearly always requires a borrower to sign a promissory note when making a loan. The borrower then repays the note with a larger amount than received when the note matures. The difference between the amount received and the amount repaid is *interest*. A note often states the signer of the note promises to pay *principal* (the amount borrowed) plus interest. In this case the *face value* of the note equals principal. Face value is the value shown on the face of the note.

A bank sometimes has a borrower sign a note with a face value that includes both principal and interest. In this case the signer of the note receives *less* than the note's face value. The difference between the borrowed amount and the note's face value is interest. Since the borrowed amount is less than the note's face value, the difference is sometimes called **discount on note payable.**

To illustrate these two different loans, let's assume a company needs $2,000 for a specific project and borrows this money from a bank at 12% annual interest. The loan is made on September 30, 1999, and is due in 60 days.

Face Value Equals Amount Borrowed

The bank in this case requires the company to sign a note with a face value equal to the $2,000 borrowed. The note includes a statement similar to: "I promise to pay $2,000 plus interest at 12% within 60 days after September 30." This note is shown in Exhibit 13.3. The borrowing company records its receipt of cash and the new liability with this entry:

Sept.30	Cash	2,000.00	
	Notes Payable		2,000.00
	Borrowed $2,000 cash with a 60-day, 12%, $2,000 note.		

Assets	=	Liabilities	+	Equity
+2,000		+2,000		

When the note and interest are paid 60 days later, the company records payment with this entry:

Nov. 29	Notes Payable	2,000.00	
	Interest Expense	39.45	
	Cash		2,039.45
	Paid note with interest ($2,000 × 12% × 60/365).		

Assets	=	Liabilities	+	Equity
−2,039.45		−2,000		−39.45

Promissory Note

$2,000 — **Face Value** *Sept. 30, 1999* — **Date**

Sixty days **after date** *I* **promise to pay to the order of**

National Bank
Regina, SK

Two thousand and no/100 ---------------------------- **Dollars**

plus interest at the annual rate of *12%*.

Janet Lee

Exhibit 13.3

Note Where Face Value Equals Amount Borrowed

Face Value Equals Amount Borrowed Plus Interest

The bank in this case writes a note with the 12% interest in its face value. This type of note includes a promise similar to: "I promise to pay $2,039.45 within 60 days after September 30." This note is shown in Exhibit 13.4. The note does not refer to the rate used to compute the $39.45 of interest included in the $2,039.45 face value. In other respects, this note is identical to the one above. Because this note lacks a stated interest rate it is sometimes called a **non-interest-bearing note.** This term can be misleading since the note does bear interest, but interest is included in the face value.

Promissory Note

$2,039.45 — **Face Value** *Sept. 30, 1999* — **Date**

Sixty days **after date** *I* **promise to pay to the order of**

National Bank
Regina, SK

Two thousand thirty-nine and 45/100 ---------------------- **Dollars**

Janet Lee

Exhibit 13.4

Note Where Face Value Equals Amount Borrowed plus Interest

When the face value of the note includes principal and interest, the borrowing company can record this note with an entry exactly like the previous September 30 entry. But it is more common to credit Notes Payable for the face value of the note and record the discount in a *contra-liability* account. This more common entry is:[4]

Assets	=	Liabilities	+	Equity
+2,000		+2,039.45		
		−39.45		

Sept.30	Cash	2,000.00	
	Discount on Notes Payable	39.45	
	Notes Payable		2,039.45
	Borrowed $2,000 cash with a 60-day, 12%, $2,039.45 note.		

Discount on Notes Payable is a contra-liability account to the Notes Payable account. If a balance sheet is prepared on September 30, the $39.45 discount is subtracted from the $2,039.45 balance in the Notes Payable account to reflect the $2,000 net amount borrowed as follows:[5]

Note payable	$2,039.45	
Less discount on note payable	39.45	$2,000

When this note matures 60 days later on November 29, the entry to record the company's $2,039.45 payment to the bank is:

Assets	=	Liabilities	+	Equity
−2,039.45		−2,039.45		−39.45
		+39.45		

Nov. 29	Notes Payable	2,039.45	
	Interest Expense	39.45	
	Cash		2,039.45
	Discount on Notes Payable		39.45
	Paid note with interest.		

You Make the Call

Rock Band

You are a member of a rock band. Your band needs $15,000 to upgrade equipment. You receive loan approvals for $15,000 at two banks. One bank's proposed loan contract reads: "Band promises to pay $15,000 plus interest at 14% in six months." The competing bank's contract reads: "Band promises to pay $16,000 in six months." Which loan do you prefer?

Answer—p. 641

End-of-Period Adjustments to Notes

When the end of an accounting period falls between the signing of a note payable and its maturity date, the *matching principle* requires us to record the accrued but unpaid interest on the note.

To illustrate these end-of-period adjustments, let's return to the short-term note above and assume the company borrowed the $2,000 on December 16, 1999, instead of September 30. This 60-day note then matures on February 14, 2000. Because the company's fiscal year ends on December 31, we need to record interest expense for the 15 days in December. The entries depend on the form of the note.

---

[4] The discount is computed as $2,000 × 12% × 60/365.

[5] We approximate the annual interest rate on a short-term loan as: ($interest paid ÷ $amount received) × (365 days ÷ loan period in days).

Face Value Equals Amount Borrowed

When the note's face value equals the amount borrowed, the accrued interest is charged to expense and credited to an Interest Payable account. To illustrate, we know 15 out of the 60-day loan period for the $2,000, 12% note have elapsed by December 31. This means one-fourth (15 days/60 days) of the $39.45 total interest is an expense of 1999. The borrowing company records this expense with the following adjusting entry at the end of 1999:

1999			
Dec. 31	Interest Expense	9.86	
	Interest Payable		9.86
	To record accrued interest on note ($2,000 × 12% × 15/365).		

Assets = Liabilities + Equity
+9.86 −9.86

When this note matures on February 14, the company records this entry:

2000			
Feb. 14	Interest Expense ($2,000 × 12% × 45/365)	29.59	
	Interest Payable	9.86	
	Notes Payable	2,000.00	
	Cash		2,039.45
	Paid note with interest.		

Assets = Liabilities + Equity
−2039.45 −9.86 −29.59
−2,000

This entry recognizes 45 days of interest expense for year 2000 and removes the balances of the two liability accounts.

Face Value Equals Amount Borrowed plus Interest

We now assume the face value of the note *includes* interest. To illustrate, we assume the borrowing company signs a $2,039.45 non-interest-bearing note on December 15. When recording this note on December 15, the company credits the $2,039.45 face value to Notes Payable and debits the $39.45 discount to a contra-liability account. At year-end, an adjusting entry is needed to record the accrual of 15 days of interest for 1999:

Dec. 31	Interest Expense	9.86	
	Discount on Notes Payable		9.86
	To record accrued interest on note ($2,000 × 12% × 15/365).		

Assets = Liabilities + Equity
+9.86 −9.86

Note accrued interest is not credited to Interest Payable. Instead, this entry reduces the balance of the contra-liability account from $39.45 to $29.59. This increases the net note liability to $2,009.86 ($2,039.45 note less $29.59 discount).

When the note matures, we need an entry both to accrue interest expense for the last 45 days of the note and to record its payment:

2000			
Feb. 14	Interest Expense	29.59	
	Notes Payable	2,039.45	
	Discount on Notes Payable		29.59
	Cash		2,039.45
	Paid note with interest ($2,000 × 12% × 45/365).		

Assets = Liabilities + Equity
−2039.45 −2039.45 −29.59
+29.59

Did You Know?

IHOP notes
Many franchisers use notes to help entrepreneurs acquire one of its franchises. **International House of Pancakes (IHOP)** often allows about 80% of the franchise fee to be covered with a note payable. Payments on these notes are usually collected weekly.

Flash back

4. Why does a creditor want a past-due account replaced by a note?
5. A company borrows money by signing a note payable promising to pay $1,050 in six months. In recording the transaction, the company correctly debits $50 to Discount on Notes Payable. How much is borrowed? What annual rate of interest is charged?

Answers—p.642

Estimated Liabilities

LO 4 Account for estimated liabilities including warranties and income taxes.

An **estimated liability** is a known obligation of an uncertain amount, but one that can be reasonably estimated. Three common examples are warranties offered by a seller, income taxes, and employee benefits such as vacation pay, pensions, and health care. We discuss each of these in this section. Other examples of estimated liabilities include property taxes and certain contracts to provide future services.

Warranty Liabilities

A warranty is an estimated liability of the seller. A **warranty** obligates a seller to pay for replacing or repairing the product (or service) when it fails to perform as expected within a specified period. Most cars, for instance, are sold with a warranty covering parts for a specified period of time. Ford reported nearly $6 billion in "dealer and customer allowances and claims" in 1996.

To comply with the *full disclosure* and *matching principles*, the seller reports the expected expense of providing the warranty in the period when revenue from the sale of the product is reported. The seller reports this warranty obligation as a liability, even though there is uncertainty about existence, amount, payee, and date of future sacrifices. The seller's warranty obligation does not require payments unless products fail and are returned for repairs. But future payments are probable and the amount of this liability can be estimated using, for instance, past experience with warranties.

Illustration of Warranty Liabilities

To illustrate, let's consider a dealer who sells a used car for $8,000 on December 1, 1999, with a one-year or 15,000-kilometre warranty covering parts. This dealer's experience shows warranty expense averages about 4% of a car's selling price. This means expense is expected to be $320 ($8,000 × 4%). The dealer records this estimated expense and liability with this entry:

Assets	= Liabilities	+ Equity
	+320	−320

1999			
Dec. 1	Warranty Expense	320	
	Estimated Warranty Liability		320
	To record warranty expense and liability at 4% of selling price.		

This entry alternatively could have been made as part of end-of-period adjustments. Either way, it causes the estimated warranty expense to be reported on the 1999 income statement. Also, it results in a warranty liability on the balance sheet for December 31, 1999.

Suppose the customer returns the car for warranty repairs on January 9, 2000. The dealer performs this work by replacing parts costing $200. The entry to record partial settlement of the estimated warranty liability is:

2000			
Jan. 9	Estimated Warranty Liability	200	
	Auto Parts Inventory		200
	To record costs of warranty repairs.		

Assets = Liabilities + Equity
−200 −200

This entry does not record any additional expense in year 2000. Instead, this entry reduces the balance of the estimated warranty liability. Warranty expense was already recorded in 1999, the year the car was sold with the warranty and reported in the income statement.

What happens if total warranty costs turn out to be more or less than the estimated 4% or $320? The answer is that management should monitor actual warranty costs to see whether the 4% rate is accurate. If experience reveals a large difference from estimates, the rate should be changed for future sales. This means while differences are expected, they should be small.

Income Tax Liabilities for Corporations

Financial statements of both proprietorships and partnerships do not include income taxes because these organizations do not directly pay income taxes. Instead, taxable income for these organizations is carried to the owners' personal tax return and taxed at that level. But corporations are subject to income taxes and must estimate their income tax liability when preparing financial statements. We explain this process in this section. Then, in the next section, we discuss deferred (future) income tax liabilities arising from temporary differences[6] between GAAP and income tax rules.

Income tax expense for a corporation creates a liability until payment is made to the government. Because this tax is created through earning income, a liability is incurred when income is earned. This tax must usually be paid monthly under federal regulations. The monthly installment is equal to one-twelfth of the corporation's estimated income tax liability for the year.

Illustration of Income Tax Liabilities

To illustrate, let's consider a corporation who prepares monthly financial statements. Based on its income earned in 1998, this corporation estimates it will owe income taxes of $145,200 for 1999 or $12,100 per month. The following adjusting entry records this estimate:

Jan. 31	Income Tax Expense	12,100	
	Income Tax Payable		12,100
	Accrued income tax expense and liability based on income for January.		

Assets = Liabilities + Equity
+12,100 −12,100

[6] Section 3465 "Income Taxes" of the *CICA Handbook* was released in December 1997. As of January 2000, the tax effect of temporary differences will be referred to as "Future income tax assets" or "Future income tax liabilities."

The tax installment is paid in the next month and the entry to record its payment is:

Assets = Liabilities + Equity
−12,100 −12,100

Feb. 10	Income Tax Payable	12,100	
	Cash		12,100
	Paid income tax installment for January 1999.		

This process of accruing and then paying taxes continues through the year. By the time annual financial statements are prepared at year-end, the corporation knows its total earned income and the actual amount of income taxes it must pay. This information allows it to update the expense and liability accounts.

Suppose this corporation determines that its income tax liability for 1999 is $156,700. The entry to record the additional income tax for 1999 is as follows:

Assets = Liabilities + Equity
+11,500 −11,500

Dec. 31	Income Tax Expense	11,500	
	Income Tax Payable		11,500
	To record additional tax expense and liability.		

This liability is settled when the corporation makes its final payment early in year 2000.

Deferred (Future) Income Tax Liabilities for Corporations

An income tax liability also can arise when the amount of income before taxes that is reported on a corporation's income statement is not the same as the amount of income reported on its income tax return. This difference occurs because income tax laws measure income differently than GAAP.[7]

Some differences between tax laws and GAAP are temporary. *Temporary differences* arise when the tax return and the income statement report a revenue or expense in different years. As an example, companies are often able to deduct higher amounts of amortization in the early years of an asset's life and smaller amounts in the later years for tax reporting. But for their income statements, they often report an equal amount of amortization expense each year. This means in the early years, amortization expense for tax reporting is more than amortization expense on the income statement. But in later years, amortization for tax reporting is less than amortization on the income statement.

When there are temporary differences between taxable income on the tax return and income before taxes on the income statement, corporations are required to compute income tax expense based on the income reported on the income statement. In the above example involving amortization, the result is income tax expense reported in the early years is more than the amount of income tax payable. This difference is called a **(deferred) future income tax liability.**

Illustration of Deferred Income Tax Liabilities

To illustrate, let's assume that after making and recording its monthly income tax payments, a corporation finds at the end of the year that an additional $25,000 of income tax expense should be recorded. But it also determines only $21,000

---

7 Differences between tax laws and GAAP arise because Revenue Canada uses tax laws to generate receipts, stimulate the economy, and influence behaviour, whereas GAAP are intended to provide financial information useful for decision making.

is currently due and $4,000 is deferred to future years (a timing difference). The entry to record the required end-of-year adjustment is:

Dec. 31	Income Tax Expense	25,000	
	Income Tax Payable		21,000
	Future Income Tax Liability		4,000
	To record tax expense and deferred tax liability.		

Assets	=	Liabilities	+	Equity
		+21,000		−25,000
		+4,000		

The credit to Income Taxes Payable reflects the amount currently due to be paid. The credit to Future Income Tax Liability reflects tax payments deferred until future years when the timing difference reverses.

Many corporations have deferred income tax liabilities. **Imperial Oil Limited,** for instance, reports deferred income taxes of $1 billion in its December 29, 1997, balance sheet.

Timing differences also can cause a company to pay income taxes before they are reported on the income statement as expense. If so, the company often reports a *future (deferred) income tax asset* on its balance sheet. This is similar to a prepaid expense. **Bombardier Inc.,** for instance, reports a deferred income tax balance of $13.8 million as part of other assets in its 1998 balance sheet.

Flashback

6. Estimated liabilities include an obligation to pay:
   a. An uncertain but reasonably estimated amount to a specific entity on a specific date.
   b. A known amount to a specific entity on an uncertain due date.
   c. A known amount to an uncertain entity on a known due date.
   d. All of the above.
7. A car is sold for $15,000 on June 1, 1999, with a one-year warranty covering parts and labour. Warranty expense is estimated at 1.5% of selling price. On March 1, 2000, the car is returned for warranty repairs for parts costing $75 and labour costing $60. The amount recorded as warranty expense at the time of the March 1 repairs is (a) $0, (b) $60, (c) $75, (d) $135, or (e) $225.
8. Why does a corporation accrue an income tax liability for quarterly reports?

Answers—p. 642

Contingent Liabilities

LO 5 Explain how to account for contingent liabilities.

A **contingent liability** is a potential obligation that depends on a future event arising out of a past transaction or event. A typical example is a lawsuit pending in the court. Here a past transaction or event leads to a lawsuit whose result depends on the court's decision. More generally, any future payment for a contingent liability depends on whether an uncertain future event occurs.

Accounting for Contingent Liabilities

Accounting for contingent liabilities depends on the likelihood of a future event occurring along with our ability to estimate the amount owed in the future if it occurs. Three categories are identified. (1) First, if the future event is *likely* (probable) and the amount owed can be *reasonably estimated,* we record this amount as a liability.[8] Examples are the estimated liabilities described earlier in the chapter

[8] *CICA Handbook*, section 3290, "Contingencies," par. .06

such as warranties and income taxes. (2) Second, if the future event is *unlikely* (remote), then we do not record or disclose any information regarding the contingent liability. (3) The third category covers contingent liabilities where the chance of the occurrence of the future event cannot be determined. If the future event could occur, then we disclose information about the contingent liability in the notes to the financial statements. Similarly, if the future event is likely but the amount cannot be reasonably estimated, then information about the contingent liability is disclosed in the notes to the financial statements.

Disclosing information about contingencies is motivated by the *full-disclosure principle*. This principle requires the reporting of information relevant to decision makers. The next section gives examples of contingent liabilities that require note disclosure.

Examples of Contingent Liability Disclosures

This section discusses examples of contingent liabilities that require note disclosure.

Potential Legal Claims

Many companies are sued or at risk for being sued for many reasons. The accounting question is: Should the defendant recognize a liability on its balance sheet or disclose a contingent liability in its notes while a lawsuit is outstanding and not yet settled? The answer is that a potential claim is recorded in the accounts only if payment for damages is likely and the amount can be reasonably estimated. If the potential claim cannot be reasonably estimated or it is less than likely but reasonably possible, then it is disclosed. **Canadian Tire,** for example, includes the following note in its recent annual report:

> The Corporation and certain of its subsidiaries are party to a number of legal proceedings. The Corporation believes that each such proceeding constitutes routine litigation incident to the business conducted by the Corporation and that the ultimate disposition of these matters will not have material adverse effect on its consolidated earnings, cash flow or financial position.

Debt Guarantees

Sometimes a company guarantees the payment of a debt owed by a supplier, customer, or another company. The guarantee means that if the debtor is not able to pay the debt when due, the guarantor will pay the debt on their behalf. The guarantor usually discloses the guarantee in its financial statement notes as a contingent liability. But if it is likely that the original debtor will default, the guarantor needs to record and report the guarantee in its financial statements as a liability. **Vengold Inc.** has an interesting guarantee with its officers as disclosed in their 1997 annual report:

> The Corporation has entered into employment agreements with four senior officers pursuant to which the Corporation has guaranteed housing loans in the amount of Cdn. $1,450,000.

Other Contingencies

Other examples of contingencies include environmental damages, possible tax assessments, insurance losses, and government investigations. **Suncor Inc.,** for instance, reports:

> The company is subject to various regulatory and statutory requirements relating to the protection of the environment. These requirements, in addition to contractual agreements and management decisions, result in the accrual of estimated reclamation and environmental remediation costs.

Like Suncor, many of these contingencies require both accrual and disclosure in notes to financial statements since they are likely to occur.

Eco Cops
What is it worth to be able to ski at Lake Louise? What is the cost when beaches are closed due to pollution? What is the life of a seal worth? These questions are part of measuring environmental liabilities of polluters. One method of measuring these liabilities is called contingent valuation where people are surveyed and asked to answer questions like these. Their answers are used by regulators to levy hefty fines, assess punitive damages, measure costs of clean up, and to assign penalties for damage to "environmental intangibles."

Did You Know?

Uncertainties

All organizations face uncertainties from future events such as natural disasters and the development of new competing products. If these events occur, they can damage a company's assets or drive it out of business. But these uncertainties are not contingent liabilities because they are future events not arising out of past transactions. Financial statements are not useful if they unduly speculate about the effects of possible future events such as these.

Flash back

9. A future payment is reported as a liability on the balance sheet if payment is contingent on a future event that:
   a. Is not likely but is reasonably possible and the payment cannot be reasonably estimated.
   b. Is likely and the payment can be reasonably estimated.
   c. Is not likely but the payment is known.
10. Under what circumstances is a future payment reported in financial statements as a contingent liability?

Answers—p. 642

Mid-Chapter Demonstration Problem

Lippitt Company is preparing adjusting entries at December 31. An analysis reveals the following:

1. The company is being sued by a dissatisfied customer. Legal advisors believe that it is likely that the company will have to pay damages in the amount of $7,500 which seems to be a reasonable estimate.
2. The Lippitt Company has guaranteed the $5,000 debt of a supplier. It is not likely that the supplier will default on the debt.
3. The company recognizes that $50,000 of $100,000 received in advance for products have now been earned.
4. The company provides a warranty for all of its products. However, its latest product has never been produced and sold so that it is impossible to determine the return rate for defective units.

Required

Indicate whether an adjusting entry is required for each of the above situations and why (not) at December 31.

Solution to Mid-Chapter Demonstration Problem

1. Because it is likely that the company will have to pay and the amount can be estimated an entry to record the liability and expense will be necessary.
2. No entry is necessary because the default is not likely. However, the contingent liability must be disclosed in the note to the financial statements.
3. An entry will be necessary to record the revenue and reduce the liabilty.
4. The company should record a liability for the warranty. It may be possible to determine the return rate by examining that for other, similar products. If an estimate is truly impossible, there must still be disclosure of the possible liability in the notes to the financial statements.

Long-Term Liabilities

LO 6 Describe accounting for long-term liabilities.

Long-term liabilities are obligations of a company not requiring payment within one year or a longer operating cycle. Long-term liabilities are often identical to current liabilities with the only exception being the greater time interval until an obligation comes due.

Long-term liabilities arise from many different transactions and events. Probably their most common source is when money is borrowed from a bank or when a note is issued to buy an asset. They also commonly arise when a company enters into a multiyear lease agreement that is similar to buying the asset. We explain each of these long-term liabilities in the context of discussing known, estimated, and contingent long-term liabilities. Another common source of long-term liabilities is the borrowing of money by issuing bonds to a number of creditors. Bonds are often outstanding for 30 years or more. Accounting for bonds is described in Chapter 17.

Because of the extended lives of long-term liabilities, accounting for them is often more complicated than accounting for short-term liabilities. In particular, the accountant may need to apply present value techniques to measure a long-term liability when it is created and to assign interest expense to each of the years in the liability's life.

Present Value Concepts

Information based on the concept of present value enters into many financing and investing decisions. It also enters into accounting for liabilities resulting from those decisions. Therefore, an understanding of present value is important for all business students.

LO7 Explain and calculate the present value of an amount to be paid at a future date.

Because this chapter focuses on liabilities, we explain present value concepts by referring to future cash outflows, payables, and interest expense. However, the same concepts also apply to future cash inflows, receivables, and interest income. The most fundamental **present value** concept is based on the idea that an amount of cash to be paid (or received) in the future has less value now than the same amount of cash to be paid (or received) today.

For example, $1 to be paid one year from now has a present value that is less than $1. To see why this is true, assume that $0.9259 is borrowed for one year at 8% interest. The amount of interest that will be incurred is $0.9259 × 8% = $0.0741. When the $0.0741 interest is added to the $0.9259, the sum equals the $1 payment that is necessary to repay the debt with interest, as shown here:

Amount borrowed	$0.9259
Interest for one year at 8%	$0.0741
Total debt after one year	$1.0000

In this example, the $0.9259 borrowed amount is the present value of the $1 future payment. To state the concept more generally, a borrowed amount is the present value of a future payment if the borrowed amount generates interest at a given rate and the future payment will repay the debt with interest.[9]

To carry this example of present value further, assume that the $1 payment is to be made after two years and the 8% interest is to be compounded annually. Compounding means that interest during the second period is based on the sum of the amount borrowed plus the interest accrued during the first period. In other words, the second period's interest is 8% multiplied by the sum of the original amount borrowed plus the interest earned during the first period.

In this example, where $1 is to be paid back after two years, the amount that can be borrowed (the present value) is $0.8573. The following calculation shows why $0.8573 is the present value:

Amount borrowed during first year	$0.8573
Interest during first year ($0.8573 × 8%)	0.0686
Amount borrowed during second year	$0.9259
Interest during second year ($0.9259 × 8%)	0.0741
Total debt after two years	$1.0000

Notice that the first year's interest is added to the principal amount borrowed so that the second year's interest is based on $0.9259.

Unless otherwise noted, the interest rates used in this text are annual rates and interest is compounded annually.

Present Value Tables

The present value of $1 to be paid after a number of periods in the future can be calculated by using this formula: $1/(1 + i)^n$. The symbol i in the equation is the interest rate per period and n is the number of periods until the future payment must be made. For example, the present value of $1 to be paid after two periods at 8% is $\$1/(1.08)^2$, which equals $0.8573.

[9] Exactly the same analysis applies to an investment. If $0.9259 is invested at 8%, it will generate $0.0741 interest revenue in one year, thereby amounting to a $1 receipt of principal and interest.

Although you can use this formula to find present values, other techniques are available. For example, many electronic calculators are preprogrammed to find present values. You can also use a **present value table** that shows present values computed with the formula at various interest rates for different time periods. In fact, many students find it helpful to learn how to make the calculations with the tables and then move on to use a calculator when they become comfortable with present value concepts.

Exhibit 13.5 shows present values of a future payment of $1 for up to 10 periods at five different interest rates. The present values in the table have been rounded to four decimal places.[10] (This table is taken from a larger and more complete table in Appendix II at the end of the book.)

To use this table, notice that the first value in the 8% column in Exhibit 13.5 is 0.9259. We used this value in the previous section as the present value of $1 at 8%. Go down one row in the same 8% column to find the present value of $1 discounted at 8% for two years. You should find the value of 0.8573 that we used in the second example. This value means that $0.8573 is the present value of the obligation to pay $1 after two periods, discounted at 8% per period.

Exhibit 13.5

Present Value of $1

	Rate				
Periods	**2%**	**4%**	**6%**	**8%**	**10%**
1	0.9804	0.9615	0.9434	0.9259	0.9091
2	0.9612	0.9246	0.8900	0.8573	0.8264
3	0.9423	0.8890	0.8396	0.7938	0.7513
4	0.9238	0.8548	0.7921	0.7350	0.6830
5	0.9057	0.8219	0.7473	0.6806	0.6209
6	0.8880	0.7903	0.7050	0.6302	0.5645
7	0.8706	0.7599	0.6651	0.5835	0.5132
8	0.8535	0.7307	0.6274	0.5403	0.4665
9	0.8368	0.7026	0.5919	0.5002	0.4241
10	0.8203	0.6756	0.5584	0.4632	0.3855

Using a Present Value Table

To demonstrate how an accountant can measure a liability by using a present value table like Exhibit 13.5, assume that a company plans to borrow cash and then repay it as follows:

To be paid back after one year	$ 2,000
To be paid back after two years	3,000
To be paid back after three years	5,000
Total to be paid back	$10,000

If the company will have to pay 10% interest on this loan, how much will it be able to borrow? The answer is that it can borrow the present value of the three future payments, discounted at 10%. This is calculated in Exhibit 13.6 with values from Exhibit 13.5. The illustration shows that the company can borrow $8,054 at 10% in exchange for its promise to make the three payments at the scheduled dates.

[10] Four decimal places are sufficient for the applications in this book. Other situations may require more precision.

Years from Now	Expected Payments	Present Value of $1 at 10%	Present Value of Expected Payments
1	$2,000	0.9091	$1,818
2	3,000	0.8264	2,479
3	5,000	0.7513	3,757
Total present value of the payments			$8,054

Exhibit 13.6

Finding the Present Value of a Series of Unequal Payments

Present Values of Annuities

The $8,054 present value of the loan in Exhibit 13.6 is the sum of the present values of the three different payments. If the expected cash flows for a liability are not equal, their combined present value must be found by calculating each of their individual present values. In other cases, a loan may create an **annuity;** this is a series of equal payments occurring at equal time intervals. The present value of an annuity can be found with fewer calculations.

For example, suppose that a company can repay a 6% loan by making a $5,000 payment at the end of each year for the next four years. The amount to be borrowed under this loan equals the present value of the four payments discounted at 6%. The present value is calculated in Exhibit 13.7 by multiplying each payment by the appropriate value from Exhibit 13.5. The exhibit shows that the company can borrow $17,326 under these terms.

Because the series of $5,000 payments is an annuity, the accountant can determine the present value with either of two shortcuts. As shown in the third column of Exhibit 13.7, the total of the present values of $1 at 6% for periods one through four equals 3.4651. One shortcut multiplies this total of 3.4651 by the $5,000 annual payment to get the combined present value of $17,326. This shortcut requires only one multiplication instead of four.

Years from Now	Expected Payments	Present Value of $1 at 6%	Present Value of Expected Payments
1	$5,000	0.9434	$ 4,717
2	5,000	0.8900	4,450
3	5,000	0.8396	4,198
4	5,000	0.7921	3,961
Total		3.4651	$17,326

Exhibit 13.7

Finding the Present Value of a Series of Equal Payments (an Annuity) by Discounting Each Payment

The second shortcut uses an annuity table such as Exhibit 13.8.[11] (Exhibit 13.8 is taken from a more complete table in Appendix II at the end of the book.) Instead of having to take the sum of the individual present values from Exhibit 13.5, you can go directly to the annuity table to find the present (table) value that relates to a specific number of payments and a specific interest rate. Then, you multiply this table value by the amount of the payment to find the present value of all the payments in the annuity.

To continue the example, the second shortcut proceeds as follows: Enter Exhibit 13.8 on the row for four payments and go across until you reach the column for 6%; you will find the value 3.4651. This amount equals the present value of an annuity with four payments of $1, discounted at 6%. Then, multiply 3.4651 times $5,000 to get the $17,326 present value of the annuity.

[11] The present values in Exhibit 13.8 can be found by adding the individual payments in Exhibit 13.7.

Exhibit 13.8

Present Value of an Annuity of $1

	Rate				
Payments	2%	4%	6%	8%	10%
1	0.9804	0.9615	0.9434	0.9259	0.9091
2	1.9416	1.8861	1.8334	1.7833	1.7355
3	2.8839	2.7751	2.6730	2.5771	2.4869
4	3.8077	3.6299	3.4651	3.3121	3.1699
5	4.7135	4.4518	4.2124	3.9927	3.7908
6	5.6014	5.2421	4.9173	4.6229	4.3553
7	6.4720	6.0021	5.5824	5.2064	4.8684
8	7.3255	6.7327	6.2098	5.7466	5.3349
9	8.1622	7.4353	6.8017	6.2469	5.7590
10	8.9826	8.1109	7.3601	6.7101	6.1446

Compounding Periods Shorter Than a Year

In the previous examples, the interest rates were applied to periods of one year. However, in many situations, interest is compounded over shorter periods. For example, the interest rate on bonds is usually described as an annual rate but the interest is actually paid every six months. As a result, the present value of the interest payments to be received from these bonds must be based on interest periods that are six months long.

To illustrate a calculation based on six-month interest periods, suppose that a borrower wants to know the present value of a series of ten $4,000 semiannual payments to be made over five years. These payments are to be discounted with an annual interest rate of 8%. Although the interest rate is described as an annual rate of 8%, it is actually a rate of 4% per six-month interest period. To find the present value of the series of $4,000 payments, enter Exhibit 13.8 on row 10 and go across to the 4% column. The table value is 8.1109, and the present value of the annuity is $32,444 (8.1109 × $4,000).

Study Appendix II at the end of the book to learn more about present value concepts. The appendix includes more complete present value tables and provides future value tables. It also includes exercises that will help you understand discounting.

Flash back

11. A company enters into an agreement to make four annual payments of $1,000 each, starting one year from now. The annual interest rate is 8%. The present value of these four payments is (a) $2,923, (b) $2,940, (c) $3,312, (d) $4,000, or (e) $6,733.

12. Suppose that a company has an option to pay either $10,000 after one year or $5,000 after six months and another $5,000 after one year. Which choice always has the smaller present value?

Answers—p. 642

Applying Present Value Concepts to Long-Term Notes

LO 8 Describe how present value concepts are used in accounting for long-term notes.

Earlier in the chapter, we stated that accountants use present value concepts to measure liabilities and to assign or allocate interest expense to each reporting period in a liability's life. In doing this, the liability is initially measured as the present value of the future payments. Over the life of the note, the amount of interest allocated to each period equals the product of multiplying the original interest rate by the balance of the liability at the beginning of the period. The balance at any point in time equals the original balance plus any allocated interest less any payments.[12]

Interest-Bearing Notes That Require a Single Payment

Suppose that a company buys equipment on January 2 with a fair market value of $45,000 by issuing an 8%, three-year note, with all of the interest paid at maturity. If the 8% interest is at the prevailing market rate, the face value of the note should be $45,000. The buyer records the purchase with this entry:

1999			
Jan. 2	Store Equipment	45,000.00	
	Notes Payable		45,000.00
	Issued a $45,000, three-year, 8% note payable for store equipment.		

Over the life of the note, the issuer reports annual interest expense equal to the original interest rate times each year's beginning balance for the liability. Exhibit 13.9 shows the interest allocation. Note that the interest is allocated by multiplying each year's beginning balance by the original 8% interest rate. Then, the interest is added to the beginning balance to find the ending balance, which then becomes the next year's beginning balance. Because the balance grows through compounding, the amount of interest allocated to each year increases over the life of the note. The final ending balance of $56,687 equals the original $45,000 borrowed plus the total interest of $11,687.

Exhibit 13.9

Allocation of Interest on a Note with All Interest Paid at Maturity

Beginning balance	$45,000	$48,600	$52,488
Interest rate	× 8%	× 8%	× 8%
Inertest expense	$ 3,600	$ 3,888	$ 4,199
Ending balance	$48,600	$52,488	$56,687

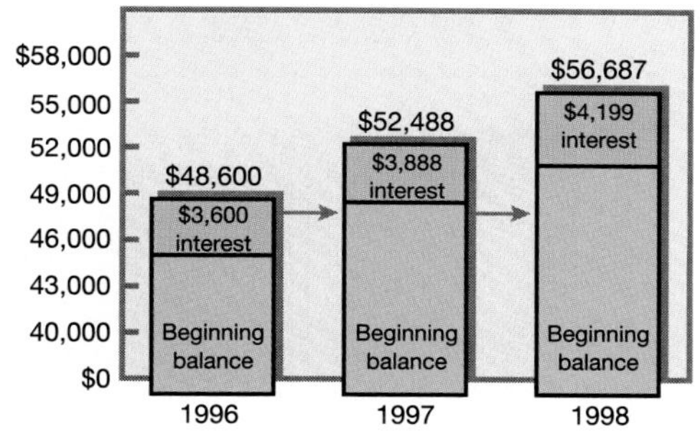

Non-Interest-Bearing Notes

Earlier in the chapter, we described so-called non-interest-bearing notes, which include the interest in their initial face values. When a non-interest-bearing note is used to purchase an asset, the note's face value is greater than the asset's fair value. As a result, the asset and the note should be recorded at the asset's fair value or at the note's fair value, whichever is more clearly determinable. The note's fair value can be estimated by finding the present value of its payments discounted at the market interest rate when it was issued.

[12] The liability's balance at any date is the present value of all the remaining future payments, discounted at the original interest rate.

For example, suppose that Harborg Company buys machinery on January 2, 1999, by issuing a non-interest-bearing, five-year, \$10,000 note payable. The company's managers conclude that their estimate of the asset's fair value is less reliable than is the current 10% interest rate available to the company.

When the note is issued, its fair value equals the present value of the \$10,000 payment due after five years discounted at 10%. Exhibit 13.5 shows us that the present value of 1 discounted at 10% for five years is 0.6209. Thus, the present (fair) value of the note is calculated as \$10,000 × 0.6209 = \$6,209. This is also the implied fair value of the asset. The following entry records the purchase:

1999			
Jan. 2	Machinery	6,209.00	
	Discount on Notes Payable	3,791.00	
	Long-Term Notes Payable		10,000.00
	Exchanged a five-year non-interest-bearing note for a machine.		

By recording the maturity value in one account and the discount in a contra account, the entry follows the typical approach of recording a non-interest-bearing note. In the entry, the \$3,791 debit to Discount on Notes Payable equals the total amount of interest that must be allocated to the five years in the note's life.

In Exhibit 13.10, we calculate each year's interest and show the effect of the allocation on the discount and the net liability. The net liability balance grows over the five years until it reaches the maturity amount of \$10,000. Note also that the discount balance decreases to \$0 after five years. Because the discount is gradually reduced to zero, this process is often referred to as amortizing the discount.

Exhibit 13.10

Allocating Interest Expense over the Life of a Non-Interest-Bearing Loan

	1996	1997	1998	1999	2000
Beginning balance	\$6,209	\$6,830	\$7,513	\$8,264	\$ 9,090
Interest rate	× 10%	× 10%	× 10%	× 10%	× 10%
Inertest expense	\$ 621	\$ 683	\$ 751	\$ 826	\$ 910
Ending balance	\$6,830	\$7,513	\$8,264	\$9,090	\$10,000

*Adjusted for rounding

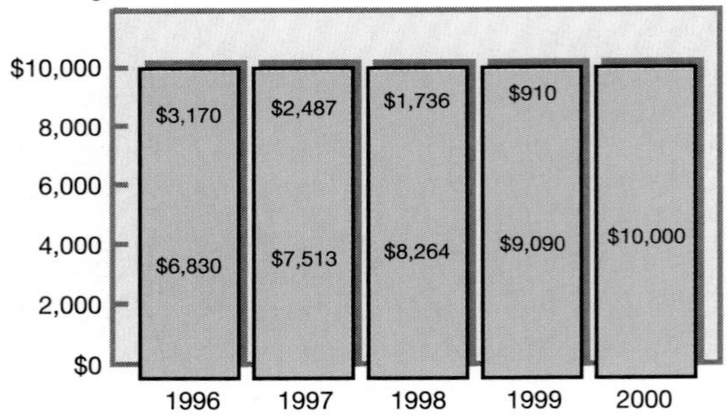

Notice that the process of calculating each year's interest is the same as it was in the previous discussion of interest-bearing notes that require a single payment. The net liability balance at the beginning of each year is multiplied by the 10% interest rate to determine the interest for the year.

The first year's interest and reduction of the discount are recorded when the accountant makes this year-end adjusting entry:

1999			
Dec. 31	Interest Expense	621.00	
	Discount on Notes Payable		621.00
	To record interest expense accrued on a non-interest-bearing note.		

Similar entries are recorded at the end of each year until the balance of the discount account equals $0, and the net liability balance equals $10,000.

When the note matures on January 2, 2005, the issuer records the payment with this entry:

2005			
Jan. 2	Long-Term Notes Payable	10,000.00	
	Cash		10,000.00
	Paid non-interest-bearing note.		

Known (Determinable) *Long-Term* Liabilities

Many known or determinable liabilities are long-term. These include certain unearned revenues and notes payable. To illustrate, if ***Maclean's*** sells a special five-year magazine subscription, then it records amounts received for this subscription in an Unearned Subscription Revenues account. We know amounts in this account are liabilities, but are they current or long-term liabilities? The answer is both. The portion of *Maclean's* Unearned Subscription Revenues account that will be fulfilled in the next year is reported as a current liability. But the remaining portion is reported as a long-term liability.

The same analysis applies to notes payable. The borrower, for instance, reports a two-year note payable as a long-term liability in the first year it is outstanding. But in the second year, the borrower reclassifies this note as a current liability since it is due within one year or the longer operating cycle. Certain other known liabilities are rarely, if ever, reported in long-term liabilities. These include accounts payable, sales taxes, and wages and salaries.

The remainder of this section discusses two additional known liabilities: leases and the current portion of long-term debt.

Lease Liabilities

Leasing is one alternative to purchasing an asset and, in certain situations, is reported like a known liability. A company can lease an asset by agreeing to make a series of rental payments to the property owner, called the *lessor*. Because a lease gives the asset's user (called the lessee) exclusive control over the asset's usefulness, the lessee can use it to earn revenues. A lease creates a liability if it has essentially the same characteristics as a purchase of an asset on credit.

According to GAAP, the lessee must report a leased asset and a lease liability if the lease qualifies as a capital lease. A **capital lease** is a lease agreement transferring the risks and benefits associated with ownership to the lessee. This type of lease spans a number of years and creates a long-term liability that is paid off in a series of equal payments. **Loblaw Companies Limited,** for instance, reports "capital leases—building and equipment" with a book value of $56.4 million at December 31, 1996. The net present value of these long-term capital lease liabilities is $38 million.

When a capital lease is entered into, the lessee records a leased asset and amortizes it over its useful life. The lessee also records a lease liability and allocates interest expense to the years of the lease. This interest allocation process is the same as that for notes payable.

Leases that are not capital leases are called **operating leases.** The lessee does not record an operating lease as an asset nor as a liability. Instead, the lessee's income statement reports rent expense. It also does not report either interest or amortization expense related to an operating lease. Loblaw's rent expense on its operating leases totalled more than $125 million for the year ended December 31, 1996. Advanced courses provide details about the characteristics of both capital and operating leases, and accounting for them by both the lessor and lessee.

Flash back

13. Which one of the following requires a lessee to record a liability? (a) operating lease, (b) lessor, (c) contingent liability, (d) capital lease.

Answer—p. 642

Current Portion of Long-Term Debt

The **current portion of long-term debt** refers to a part of long-term debt that is due within one year. While long-term debt is *reported under long-term liabilities*, the portion due within the year is reported under current liabilities. To illustrate, let's assume a $7,500 debt is paid in installments of $1,500 per year for five years. The $1,500 due within the year is reported as a current liability. No journal entry is necessary. Instead, we properly classify the amounts for debt as either current or long-term when the balance sheet is prepared.

Estimated *Long-Term* Liabilities

Estimated liabilities are both current and long-term. These include employee benefits and future income taxes. Pension liabilities to employees are long-term to those workers who will not retire within one year or the longer operating cycle. But for employees who are retired or will retire within the year, a portion of pension liabilities is current in nature. The same analysis applies to employee health benefits, deferred income taxes payable, and warranties. For example, many warranties are for 30 or 60 days in length. Estimated costs under these warranties are properly reported in current liabilities. Yet many automobile warranties are for three years or 80,000 kilometres. A portion of these warranties is reported as long-term.

Contingent *Long-Term* Liabilities

Contingent liabilities are both current and long-term in nature. This extends to nearly every contingent liability including litigation, debt guarantees, environmental costs, government investigation, and tax assessments.

Times Interest Earned

USING THE INFORMATION

LO 9 Compute times interest earned ratio and use it to analyze liabilities.

A company incurs interest expense on many of its current and long-term liabilities. Examples extend from its short-term notes and current portion of long-term liabilities to its long-term notes, bonds, and capital leases. Many of these liabilities are likely to remain obligations in one form or another for a substantial period of time even if a company experiences a decline in operations. Because of this, interest expense is often viewed as a "fixed cost." This means the amount of interest is unlikely to fluctuate much from changes in sales.

While fixed costs can be advantageous when a company is growing, they create risk. This risk stems from the possibility a company might be unable to pay them if sales decline. Let's consider **X-Caliber's** results for 1999 and two possible outcomes for the year 2000 shown in Exhibit 13.11 ($ millions). X-Caliber is a manufacturer of water sports equipment and remains a family-owned operation.

Exhibit 13.11

X-Caliber's Actual and Possible Results for 1999–2000

	Year 1999	Year 2000 If Sales Increase	Year 2000 If Sales Decrease
Sales	$600	$900	$300
Expenses (75% of sales)	450	675	225
Income before interest	$150	$225	$ 75
Interest expense (fixed)	60	60	60
Net income	$ 90	$165	$ 15

Exhibit 13.11 shows expenses other than interest are projected to remain at 75% of sales. Expenses changing with sales volume are called *variable expenses.* But interest is expected to remain at $60,000 per year due to its fixed nature.

The second column of Exhibit 13.11 shows X-Caliber's income nearly doubles (100%) if sales increase by 50%. But also see that X-Caliber's profits fall sharply if sales decline by 50%. These numbers show a company's risk is affected by the amount of fixed interest charges it incurs each period.

The risk created by these fixed expenses is captured numerically with the **times interest earned** ratio. We use the formula in Exhibit 13.12 to compute this ratio.

Exhibit 13.12

Times Interest Earned Formula

$$\textbf{Times interest earned} = \frac{\textbf{Income before interest and taxes}}{\textbf{Interest expense}}$$

For 1999, X-Caliber's income before interest is $150,000. This means its ratio is computed as $150,000/$60,000, or 2.5 times. This ratio suggests X-Caliber faces relatively low risk. Its sales must decline sharply before it would be unable to cover its interest expenses. This result is comforting to the company's owners and creditors.

We must use care when computing the times interest earned ratio for a corporation. Since interest is deducted in determining taxable income for a corporation, this ratio is adjusted for a *corporation* and expressed as:

$$\text{Times interest earned (corporation)} = \frac{\text{Net income} + \text{Interest expense} + \text{Income tax expense}}{\text{Interest expense}}$$

Best Buy's times interest earned ratio for 1995–1997 is shown in Exhibit 13.13. Best Buy's ratio has fallen sharply from 4.37 in 1995 to 1.06 in 1997. This is a combination of several factors including reduced operating income and increased interest charges. Experience shows when this ratio falls below 1.5 for companies and remains at that level or lower for several periods, the default rate on liabilities increases sharply. This implies

Exhibit 13.13

Best Buy's Times Interest Earned Ratio

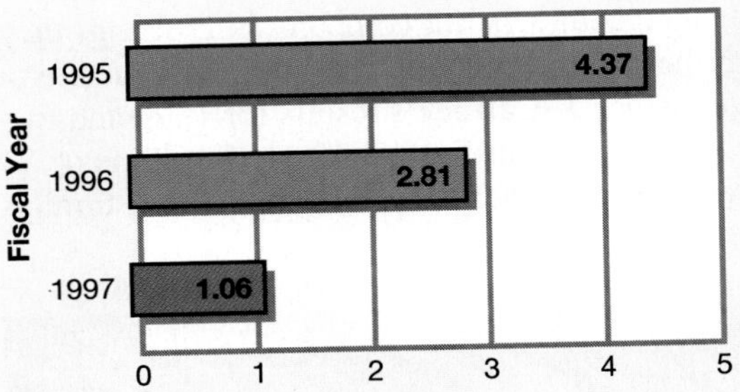

increased risk for those decision makers involved with these types of companies and their liabilities.

We must also interpret the times interest earned ratio in light of information about the variability of a company's net income before interest. If this amount is stable from year to year or is growing, the company can afford to take on added risk by borrowing. But if a company's income before interest varies greatly from year to year, fixed interest charges can increase the risk that an owner will not earn a positive return and be unable to pay interest charges.

You Make the Call

Entrepreneur

You are an entrepreneur looking to invest in and operate a local franchise of a national chain. You narrow your alternatives to two. Each has an expected annual net income *after* interest of $100,000. Net income for the first franchise included an expected fixed interest charge of $200,000. But expected fixed interest charge for the second franchise is $40,000. Which franchise is more risky to you if sales forecasts are not met? Does your decision change if the first franchise likely has more variability in its income before interest?

Answer—p. 641

Flash back

14. Times interest earned ratio:

a. Equals interest expense divided by net income.

b. Is larger as the amount of fixed interest charges gets larger.

c. Is best interpreted in light of information about the variability of a company's net income before interest.

Answers—p. 642

Summary

LO 1 Describe current and long-term liabilities and their characteristics. Liabilities are probable future payments of assets or services an entity is presently obligated to make as a result of past events. Current liabilities are due within one year or one operating cycle, whichever is longer. All other liabilities are long-term liabilities. One distinguishing characteristic among liabilities is uncertainly about the identity of the creditor, due date, and amount to be paid.

LO 2 Identify and describe known current liabilities. Known (or determinable) current liabilities are set by agreements or laws and are measurable with little uncertainly. The key is to identify known current liabilities. They include accounts payable, sales taxes payable, unearned revenues, notes payable, payroll liabilities, and the current portion of long-term debt.

LO3 **Prepare entries to account for short-term notes payable.** Short-term notes payable are current liabilities and most bear interest. When a short-term note is interest-bearing, its face value equals the amount borrowed. This type of note also identifies a rate of interest to be paid at maturity. When a short-term note in non-interest-bearing, its face value equals the amount to be paid at maturity. This is because its face value includes interest.

LO4 **Account for estimated liabilities including warranties and income taxes.** Liabilities for warranties and income taxes are recorded with estimated amounts. Both warranties and income taxes are recognized as expenses when incurred. Deferred income tax liabilities are recognized if temporary differences between GAAP and tax rules result in recording more income tax expense than the amount to be currently paid.

LO5 **Explain how to account for contingent liabilities.** If an uncertain future payment depends on a probable future event and the amount is reasonably estimated, the payment is reported as a liability. But the future payment is reported as a contingent liability if (a) the future event is reasonably possible but not probable, or (b) the event is probable but the amount of the payment cannot be reasonably estimated.

LO6 **Describe accounting for long-term liabilities.** Long-term liabilities are obligations not requiring payment within one year or the longer operating cycle. Long-term liabilities are similar to current liabilities with the exception being the length of time until payment and the likely use of present value concepts. Lease liabilities are one type of long-term liability often used as an alternative to asset purchases. Capital leases are recorded as assets and liabilities. Other leases, called operating leases, are recorded as rent expense when the asset is used.

LO7 **Explain and calculate the present value of an amount to be paid at a future date.** The primary present value concept is that today's value of an amount of cash to be paid or received in the future is less than today's value of the same amount of cash to be paid or received today. Another present value concept is that interest is compounded, which means that the interest is added to the balance and used to determine interest for succeeding periods. An annuity is a series of equal payments occurring at equal time intervals.

LO8 **Describe how present value concepts are used in accounting for long-term notes.** Accountants may use present value concepts to measure liabilities and to determine the fair value of assets purchased in return for issuing debt. They also use present value concepts to allocate interest expense among the periods in a note's life by multiplying the note's beginning-of-period balance by the original interest rate. Non-interest-bearing notes are normally recorded with a discount account that is contra to the liability account. The balance in the account is amortized in the process of recognizing interest expense over the note's life.

LO9 **Compute times interest earned ratio and use it to analyze liabilities.** Times interest earned is computed by dividing a company's net income before interest by the amount of fixed interest charges incurred. If this company is a corporation, the numerator is net income before interest and taxes. This ratio reflects the company's ability to pay interest and earn a profit for its owners against declines in sales.

Guidance Answers to **You Make the Call**

Rock Band

Both banks have agreed to give the band $15,000, and both loans require repayment in six months. Provided terms in these contracts are similar, the only potential difference is in the amount of interest the band must pay. The second bank's contract makes this clear—since $15,000 is borrowed and the band must pay $16,000, the interest charged is $1,000. We must compute interest on the first bank's contract—it is $1,050, computed as $15,000 × 14% × 6/12. The band prefers the contract requiring less interest, which is the one reading: "Band promises to pay $16,000 within six months."

Entrepreneur

The risk is reflected by the ratio showing the number of times fixed interest charges are covered by net income *before* interest, known as the times interest earned ratio. This ratio for the first franchise is 1.5 [($100,000 + $200,000)/$200,000]. Whereas the ratio for the second franchise is 3.5 [($100,000 + $40,000)/$40,000]. This analysis shows the first franchise is more susceptible to the risk of incurring a loss if its sales decline and, therefore, is more risky. The second question asks about variability of income before interest. If income before interest varies greatly from year to year, this increases the risk an owner will not earn income. Since the first franchise has the greater variability, it makes it look an even worse investment.

Guidance Answers to Flash backs

1. Liabilities are probable future payments of assets or services that an entity is presently obligated to make as a result of past transactions or events.
2. No, an expected future payment is not a liability unless an existing obligation was created by a past event or transaction.
3. In most cases, a liability due in 15 months is classified as long term. But it is classified as a current liability if the company's operating cycle is 15 months or longer.
4. A creditor might want to have a note payable instead of an account payable in order to (a) start charging interest and/or (b) have positive evidence of the debt and its terms.
5. The amount borrowed was $1,000 ($1,050 − $50). The rate of interest was 5% ($50/$1,000) for six months, which is an annual rate of 10%.
6. *a*
7. *a*
8. A corporation accrues an income tax liability for its interim financial statements because income tax expense is incurred when income is earned, not just at the end of the year.
9. *b*
10. A future payment is reported as a contingent liability if (a) the uncertain future event is likely but the amount of payment cannot be reasonably estimated, and (b) the uncertain future event is not likely but has a reasonable possibility of occurring.
11. *c*
12. The delayed payments would always have the lower present value.
13. *d*
14. *c*

Demonstration Problem

The following series of transactions and other events took place at the Kern Company during its calendar reporting year. Describe their effects on the financial statements by presenting the journal entries described in each situation.

a. Throughout September 19X1, Kern sold $140,000 of merchandise that was covered by a 180-day warranty. Prior experience shows that the costs of fulfilling the warranty will equal 5% of the sales revenue. Compute September's warranty expense and the increase in the warranty liability and show how it would be recorded with a September 30 adjusting entry. Also show the journal entry that would be made on October 8 to record an expenditure of $300 cash to provide warranty service on an item sold in September.

b. On October 12, Kern arranged with a supplier to replace an overdue $10,000 account payable by paying $2,500 cash and signing a note for the remainder. The note matured in 90 days and had a 12% interest rate. Show the entries that would be recorded on October 12, December 31, and January 10, 19X2 (when the note matures).

c. In late December the company learns that it is facing a product liability suit filed by an unhappy customer. The company's lawyer is of the opinion that although the company will likely suffer a loss from the lawsuit it is not possible to estimate the amount of the damages at the present time.

d. Kern Company has made and recorded its quarterly income tax payments. After final tax return preparation for the year the company discovers an additional $50,000 of income tax expense that should be recorded. A portion of this additional expense, $10,000 is deferrable to future years. Record the year-end income tax expense adjustment entry for the company.

e. Kern Company's net income for the year is $1,000,000. The interest expense and income tax expense for the years are $275,000 and $225,000 respectively. Calculate the number of times that fixed interest charges are earned.

f. On November 1 Kern Company borrows $5,000.00 from the bank on a 60-day, 14% note. Record the issuance of the note on November 1. Also record the repayment of the note with interest on December 30.

g. Kern Company signs a non-interest-bearing note promising to pay $2,050 within 60 days after December 16. Record the signing of the note, the interest accrual on December 31, and the repayment of the note on February 14 ($50 of interest is included in the note's face value of $2,050).

Planning the Solution

- For (a), compute the warranty expense for September and record it with an estimated liability. Record the October expenditure as a decrease in the liability.
- For (b), eliminate the liability for the account payable and create the liability for the note payable. Compute the interest expense for the 80 days that the note is outstanding in 19X1 and record it as an additional liability. Record the payment of the note, being sure to include the interest for the 10 days in 19X2.
- For (c) decide if the contingent liability for the company needs to be disclosed or accrued according to the two necessary criteria—probable loss and reasonably estimable.
- For (d) determine how much of the income tax expense is payable in the current year and how much needs to be deferred.
- For (e) calculate number of times interest charges are earned according to the formula given in the chapter. Remember that the numerator reflects income before interest and tax expense.
- For (f) record the issuance of the note. Calculate 60 days interest due and the payment of the note plus interest.
- For (g) record the note as a non-interesting-bearing note. Use the contra account Discount on Notes Payable for the interest portion of the proceeds upon issuance. Make the year-end adjustment for 15 days interest owed to Interest Expense and Discount on Notes Payable. Record the repayment of the note being sure to include the interest for the 45 days in 19X2.

Solution to Demonstration Problem

a. Warranty expense = 5% × $140,000 = $7,000

Sept.30	Warranty Expense	7,000.00	
	Estimated Warranty Liability		7,000.00
	To record warranty expense and liability at 5% of sales for the month.		

Oct. 8	Estimated Warranty Liability	300.00	
	Cash		300.00
	To record the cost of the warranty service.		

b. Interest expense for 19X1 = 12% × $7,500 × 80/365 = $197.26
Interest expense for 19X2 = 12% × $7,500 × 10/365 = $24.66

Oct. 12	Accounts Payable	10,000.00	
	Notes Payable		7,500.00
	Cash		2,500.00
	Paid $2,500 cash and gave a 90-day, 12% note to extend the due date on the account.		

Dec. 31	Interest Expense	197.26	
	Interest Payable		197.26
	To accrue interest on note payable.		

Jan. 10	Interest Expense	24.66	
	Interest Payable	197.26	
	Notes Payable	7,500.00	
	Cash		7,721.92
	Paid note with interest, including accrued interest payable.		

c. The pending lawsuit should be disclosed only in the financial statement notes. Although the loss is likely, no liability can be accrued since the loss cannot be reasonably estimated.

d.

Dec. 31	Income Taxes Expense	50,000.00	
	Income Taxes Payable		40,000.00
	Deferred Income Tax Liability		10,000.00
	To record income tax expense and the deferred tax liability		

e. $$\text{Times interest earned} = \frac{\text{Income before interest and taxes}}{\text{Interest expense}}$$

Income before interest = Net income + Interest expense + Income taxes expense

$$\text{Times interest earned} = \frac{\$1{,}000{,}000 + \$275{,}000 + \$225{,}000}{\$275{,}000} = 5.45 \text{ times}$$

f.

Nov. 1	Cash	5,000.00	
	Notes Payable		5,000.00
	Borrowed cash with a 60-day, 14% note.		

When the note and interest are paid 60 days later, Kern Company records the event with this entry:

Dec. 30	Notes Payable	5,000.00	
	Interest Expense	115.07	
	Cash		5,115.07
	Paid note with interest ($5,000 × 14% × 60/365).		

g.

Dec. 16	Cash	2,000.00	
	Discount on Notes Payable	50.00	
	Notes Payable		2,050.00
	Borrowed cash with a 60-day, non-interest-bearing note.		

Dec. 31	Interest Expense	12.50	
	Discount on Notes Payable		12.50
	To record accrued interest on note payable (15/60 days × $50).		

When the note matures on February 14, 19X2, Kern Company records this entry:

19X2			
Feb. 14	Interest Expense (45/60 days × $50)	37.50	
	Interest Payable	12.50	
	Notes Payable	2,000.00	
	Cash		2,050.00
	Paid note with interest.		

Glossary

Annuity A series of equal payments occurring at equal time intervals. (p. 633)

Capital lease A lease that gives the lessee the risks and benefits normally associated with ownership. (p. 637)

Contingent liability A potential liability that depends on a future event arising out of a past transaction; is not an existing liability. (p. 627)

Current liability Obligations due within a year or the company's operating cycle whichever is longer; paid using current assets or by creating other current liabilities. (p. 616)

Current portion of long-term debt The portion of long-term debt that is due within one year; reported under current liabilities on the balance sheet. (p. 638)

Deferred (future) income tax liability Payments of income taxes that are deferred until future years because of temporary differences between GAAP and tax rules. (p. 626)

Discount on note payable The difference between the face value of a non-interest-bearing note payable and the amount borrowed; represents interest that will be paid on the note over its life. (p. 620)

Estimated liability Obligation of an uncertain amount that can be reasonably estimated. (p. 624)

Known liability Obligations of a company with little uncertainty; set by agreements, contracts or laws; also called definitely determinable liabilities. (p. 618)

Long-term liability Obligations of a company not requiring payment within one year or a longer operating cycle. (p. 617)

Non-interest-bearing note A note that does not have a stated rate of interest; the interest is included in the face value of the note. (p. 621)

Operating lease A lease that is not a capital lease. (p. 637)

Present value The amount that can be invested (borrowed) at a given interest rate to generate a total future investment (debt) that will equal the amount of a specified future receipt (payment). (p. 631)

Present value table A table that shows the present value of an amount to be received when discounted at various interest rates for various periods of time, or the present value of a series of equal payments to be received for a varying number of periods when discounted at various interest rates. (p. 632)

Short-term note payable Current obligation in the form of a written promissory note. (p. 619)

Times interest earned The ratio of a company's income before interest divided by the amount of interest charges; used to evaluate the risk of being committed to make interest payments when income varies. (p. 639)

Warranty An agreement that obligates the seller or manufacturer to repair or replace a product when it breaks or otherwise fails to perform properly within a specified period. (p. 624)

Questions

1. What is the difference between a current and a long-term liability?
2. What is an estimated liability?
3. What are the three important questions concerning the certainty of liabilities?
4. Suppose that a company has a facility located in an area where disastrous weather conditions often occur. Should it report a probable loss from a future disaster as a liability on its balance sheet? Why?
5. Why are warranty liabilities usually recognized on the balance sheet as liabilities even when they are uncertain?
6. What factors affect the present value of a future $2,000 payment?
7. How would a lease create an asset and a liability for the lessee?
8. Find the note on commitments and contingencies following the financial statements of **Alliance** in Appendix I. What is the total minimum amount of operating lease payments in future years?
9. Refer to **Atlantis'** balance sheet in Appendix I. What accounts related to income taxes are on the balance sheet? Identify the meaning of each income tax account you identify.

Quick Study

QS 13-1
Distinguishing between current and long-term liabilities
LO 1, 2

Which of the following items would normally be classified as a current liability for a company that has a 15-month operating cycle?

a. Salaries payable.
b. A note payable due in 18 months.
c. Bonds payable that mature in two years.
d. A note payable due in 11 months.
e. The portion of a long-term note that is due to be paid in 15 months.

QS 13-2
Estimating warranty liabilities
LO 4

On September 11, Valentine's Department Store sold a lawn mower for $400 with a one-year warranty that covers parts and labour. Warranty expense was estimated at 5% of sales. On July 24, the mower was brought in for repairs covered under the warranty requiring $15 in parts and $20 of labour. Prepare the July 24 journal entry to record the warranty repairs.

QS 13-3
Interest-bearing note transactions
LO 3

On November 7, 19X1, the Eggemeyer Company borrowed $150,000 and signed a 90-day, 8% note payable with a face value of $150,000. Compute the accrued interest payable on December 31, and present the journal entry to record the paying of the note at maturity.

QS13-4
Non-interest-bearing note transactions
LO 3

The Katie Company signs a non-interest-bearing note promising to pay $4,100 within 60 days after December 16. Record the signing of the note, the interest accrual on December 31, and the repayment of the note on February 14 ($100 of interest is included in the note's face value of $4,100).

QS 13-5
Recording an income tax liability.
LO 4

Longfellow Company has made and recorded its monthly income tax payments. After final tax return preparation for the year the company discovers an additional $30,000 of income tax expense that should be recorded. A portion of this additional expense, $8,000 can be deferred to future years. Record the year-end income tax expense adjustment entry for Longfellow Company.

QS 13-6
Accounting for contingent liabilities
LO 5

The following legal claims exist for the CT Company. Classify the required accounting treatment for each legal situation as (a) a liability that should be recorded or (b) an item that need only be described in the notes of the financial statement.

1. CT company estimates that one lawsuit could result in a damages award of $1,000,000; however, it is only reasonably possible that the plaintiff will win the case.
2. CT faces a probable loss on a pending lawsuit; however, the amount of the judgment cannot be reasonably estimated.
3. CT company estimates damages of another case at $2,500,000 with a high probability of losing the case.

QS 13-7
Accounting for sales tax payable
LO 2

Palm Computing sells $5,000 of merchandise for cash on September 30. The sales tax law requires Palm Computing to collect 4% sales tax on every dollar of merchandise sold. Record the entry for the $5,000 sale and applicable sales tax. Also record the entry that shows the remittance of the 4% tax on this sale to the government on October 15.

QS 13-8
Unearned revenue
LO 2

Ticketmaster receives $4,000,000 in advance cash ticket sales for a four date tour for the Rolling Stones. Record the advance ticket sales as a lump sum as of October 31. Record the revenue earned for the first concert date played on November 5.

QS 13-9
Note transaction
LO 6

On January 1, 19X1, a company borrowed $40,000 in exchange for an interest-bearing note. The note plus compounded interest at an annual rate of 12% is due on January 1, 19X3. Determine the amount that the company will pay on the due date.

QS 13-10
Times interest earned
LO 9

Compute the times interest earned for a company that has income after interest expense and before taxes of $1,575,500 and interest expense of $137,000.

Exercises

Exercise 13-1
Classifying liabilities
LO 1

The following list of items might appear as liabilities on the balance sheet of a company that has a two-month operating cycle. Identify the proper classification of each item. In the space beside each item write a *C* if it is a current liability, an *L* if it is a long-term liability, or an *N* if it is not a liability.

_____ **a.** Income taxes payable.
_____ **b.** Notes receivable in 30 days.
_____ **c.** Mortgage payable (payments due in the next 12 months).
_____ **d.** Notes payable in 6 to 12 months.
_____ **e.** Bonds payable (mature in 5 years).
_____ **f.** Notes payable in 13 to 24 months.
_____ **g.** Wages payable.
_____ **h.** Accounts receivable.
_____ **i.** Notes payable in 120 days.
_____ **j.** Mortgage payable (payments due after the next 12 months).

Exercise 13-2
Warranty expense and liability
LO 4

Mikado Co. sold a copier with a cost of $3,800 and a two-year parts and labour warranty to a customer on August 16, 19X1, for $5,500 cash. Mikado uses the perpetual system to account for inventories. Based on prior experience, Mikado expects to eventually incur warranty costs equal to 4% of this selling price. The liability expense is recorded with an adjusting entry at the end of the year. On November 22, 19X2, the copier required on-site repairs that were completed the same day. The cost of the repairs consisted of $69 for the materials taken from the parts inventory and $130 of labour that was fully paid with cash. These were the only repairs required in 19X2 for this copier.

a. How much warranty expense should the company report in 19X1 for this copier?

b. How much is the warranty liability for this copier as of December 31, 19X1?

c. How much warranty expense should the company report in 19X2 for this copier?

d. How much is the warranty liability for this copier as of December 31, 19X2?

e. Show the journal entries that would be made to record (1) the sale; (2) the adjustment on December 31, 19X1, to record the warranty expense; and (3) the repairs that occurred in November 19X2. Mikado uses the perpetual method system to account for merchandise inventories.

Exercise 13-3
Accounting for income taxes
LO 4

Constructo Company prepares interim financial statements each month. As part of the process, estimated income taxes are accrued each month for 30% of the current month's net income. The estimated income taxes are paid on the 15th of the following month for the amount accrued. These facts are known about the last quarter of 19X1:

a.	October net income	$27,900
	November net income	18,200
	December net income	32,700

b. After the tax return was completed in early January, the accountant determined that the Income Tax Payable for the last quarter should have been $29,100.

Required

1. Determine the amount of the adjustment needed on December 31 to produce the proper ending balance in the Income Tax Payable account.

2. Present the journal entries to record the adjustment to the Income Tax Payable account and to record the January 15 payment of the December taxes.

Exercise 13-4
Interest-bearing and non-interest-bearing notes payable
LO 3

Portable Systems borrowed $94,000 on May 15, 19X1, for 60 days at 12% interest by signing a note.

a. On what date will this note mature?
b. How much interest expense is created by this note?
c. Suppose that the face value of the note equals the principal of the loan. Show the general journal entries to record issuing the note and paying it at maturity.
d. Suppose that the face value of the note is $95,880 which includes both the principal of the loan ($94,000) and the interest to be paid at maturity. Show the general journal entries to record issuing the note and paying it at maturity.

Exercise 13-5
Interest-bearing and non-interest-bearing short-term notes payable with year-end adjustments
LO 3

Accura Co. borrowed $150,000 on November 1, 19X1, for 90 days at 9% interest by signing a note.

a. On what date will this note mature?
b. How much interest expense is created by this note in 19X1? (Assume a 365-day year.)
c. How much interest expense is created by this note in 19X2? (Assume a 365-day year.)
d. Suppose that the face value of the note equals the principal of the loan. Show the general journal entries to record issuing the note, to accrue interest at the end of 19X1, and to record paying the note at maturity.
e. Suppose that the face value of the note ($153,375) includes both the principal of the loan ($150,000) and the interest to be paid at maturity. Show the general journal entries to record issuing the note, to accrue interest at the end of 19X1, and to record paying the note at maturity.

Exercise 13-6
Various liabilities
LO 4

Lawrence Company is preparing adjusting entries at December 31. An analysis reveals the following:

1. During December, Lawrence Company sold 3,000 units of a product that carries a 60-day warranty. The sales for this product totalled $120,000. The company expects 8% of the units to need repair under warranty and it estimates that the average repair cost per unit will be $15.
2. The company is being sued by a disgruntled employee. Legal advisors believe that it is probable that the company will have to pay damages the amount of which cannot be reasonably estimated.
3. The Lawrence company has guaranteed the $5,000 debt of a supplier. It is not probable that the supplier will default on the debt.
4. The company records previously unrecorded cash sales of $2,000,000 and sales taxes payable at a rate of 5%.
5. The company recognizes that $50,000 of $100,000 received in advance for products has now been earned.

Required

Prepare any required adjusting entries at December 31 and indicate which items require financial statement disclosure.

Exercise 13-7
Financial statement presentation—current liabilities
LO 2

The Rashad Company has the following selected accounts after posting adjusting entries:

Accounts Payable	$50,000
Notes Payable, six month	10,000
Accumulated Amortization, Equipment	20,000
Accrued Payroll Payable	5,000
Estimated Warranty Liability	12,000
Discount on Notes Payable, six month	1,000
Mortgage Payable	100,000

Prepare the current liability section of The Rashad Company's balance sheet, assuming $10,000 of the mortgage payable is due within the next year.

Exercise 13-8
Asset purchased with a note
LO 6

The Carson Company purchased some machinery on March 10 that had a cost of $56,000. Show the journal entry that would record this purchase under these three separate situations:

a. The company paid cash for the full purchase price.
b. The company gave an interest-bearing note for the full purchase price.
c. The company gave a non-interest-bearing one-year note for $61,600.

Exercise 13-9
Calculations for a non-interest-bearing note
LO 6

On January 2, 1996, the Brewster Co. acquired land by issuing a non-interest-bearing note for $20,000. The fair market value of the land was not reliably known, but the company knew that the market interest rate for the note was 6%. The note matures in three years on January 1, 1999.

a. What is the present value of the note at the time of the purchase?
b. What is the initial balance of the discount on the note payable?
c. Prepare a table that shows the amount of interest that will be allocated to each of the three years in the note's life and the ending balance of the net liability for each year.
d. Prepare a table that determines the ending balance of the discount on the note for each of the three years.

Exercise 13-10
Journal entries for non-interest-bearing note
LO 6

Use the data in Exercise 13-9 to prepare journal entries for these dates:

a. January 2, 1996 (land purchase).
b. December 31, 1996 (accrual entry).
c. December 31, 1997 (accrual entry).
d. December 31, 1998 (accrual entry).
e. January 1, 1999 (the payment of the note).

Exercise 13-11
Times interest earned
LO 9

Use the following information to compute times interest earned:

	Net Income or (Loss)	Interest Expense
a.	$140,000	$48,000
b.	140,000	15,000
c.	140,000	8,000
d.	265,000	12,000
e.	79,000	12,000
f.	(4,000)	12,000

Analysis component:

Which of the situations above demonstrates the strongest ability to pay fixed interest charges as they come due?

Problems

Problem 13-1
Estimated product warranty liabilities
LO 4

P0-6

On October 29, 19X1, Sharp Products began to buy and resell electric razors for $80 each. Sharp uses the perpetual method to account for inventories. The razors are covered under a warranty that requires the company to replace any nonworking razor within 90 days. When a razor is returned, the company simply throws it away and mails a new one from inventory to the customer. The company's cost for a new razor is $18. The manufacturer has advised the company to expect warranty costs to equal 7% of the total sales. These events occurred in 19X1 and 19X2:

19X1

Nov. 11 Sold 75 razors for $6,000 cash.
30 Recognized warranty expense for November with an adjusting entry.
Dec. 9 Replaced 15 razors that were returned under the warranty.
16 Sold 210 razors for $16,800 cash.

29 Replaced 30 razors that were returned under the warranty.
31 Recognized warranty expense for December with an adjusting entry.

19X2

Jan. 5 Sold 130 razors for $10,400 cash.
17 Replaced 50 razors that were returned under the warranty.
31 Recognized warranty expense for January with an adjusting entry.

Required

Check Figure Estimated liability balance, $786

1. How much warranty expense should be reported for November and December 19X1?
2. How much warranty expense should be reported for January 19X2?
3. What is the balance of the estimated warranty liability as of December 31, 19X1?
4. What is the balance of the estimated warranty liability as of January 31, 19X2?
5. Prepare journal entries to record the transactions and adjustments.

Problem 13-2
Transactions with short-term notes payable
LO 3

The Langley Company entered into the following transactions involving short-term liabilities during 19X1 and 19X2:

19X1

Apr. 20 Purchased merchandise on credit from Franken, Inc., for $38,500. The terms were 1/10, n/30. Assume Franken uses a perpetual inventory system.
May 19 Replaced the account payable to Franken with a 90-day note bearing 9% annual interest. Langley paid $8,500 cash, with the result that the balance of the note was $30,000.
July 8 Borrowed $60,000 from Bank of the North by signing an interest-bearing note for $60,000. The annual interest rate was 10%, and the note has a 120-day term.
? Paid the note to Franken, Inc., at maturity.
? Paid the note to Bank of the North at maturity.
Nov. 28 Signed a non-interest-bearing note with a face value of $21,280 from Western Bank that matures in 60 days. The face value includes a principal amount of $21,000.
Dec. 31 Recorded an adjusting entry for the accrual of interest on the note to Western Bank.

19X2

? Paid the note to Western Bank at maturity.

Required

Check Figure Total interest for Western Bank note, $280

1. Determine the maturity dates of the three notes just described.
2. Determine the interest due at maturity for the three notes.
3. Determine the interest to be recorded in the adjusting entry at the end of 19X1.
4. Determine the interest to be recorded in 19X2.
5. Present journal entries for all the preceding events and adjustments.

Problem 13-3
Present value of possible liabilities
LO 6

Sherlock Enterprises is negotiating the purchase of a new building. The seller has offered Sherlock the following three payment plans:

Plan A: $100,000 cash would be paid at once.
Plan B: $114,000 cash would be paid after two years.
Plan C: $58,000 cash would be paid at the end of each of the next two years.

The company's owner knows that the market interest rate is 8%.

Required

Check Figure Cost of building, plan B, $97,732

1. Use the market interest rate to determine present value of each of the three possible payment plans.
2. Show the journal entry that would be made to record the acquisition under each of the three plans. (Assume that the note's face value would include all interest to be paid.)

3. Identify the plan that creates the lowest cost for the company.
4. Assume that Plan B is adopted and the present value of the cash flows is used as the building's cost. Determine the amount of interest expense that will be reported in each of the two years in the note's life.

Problem 13-4
Exchanging a note for a capital asset

LO 6, 7, 8

On January 2, 19X1, Watts Company acquired an item of equipment by issuing a $55,000 non-interest-bearing five-year note payable on December 31, 19X5. A reliable cash price for the equipment was not readily available. The market annual rate of interest for similar notes was 4% on the day of the exchange.

Required

(Round all amounts in your answers to the nearest whole dollar.)

1. Determine the initial net liability created by issuing this note.
2. Present a table showing the calculation of the amount of interest expense allocated to each year the note is outstanding and the carrying amount of the net liability at the end of each of those years.
3. Present a table that shows the balance of the discount at the end of each year the note is outstanding.
4. Prepare general journal entries to record the purchase of the equipment, the accrual of interest expense at the end of 19X1 and 19X2, and the accrual of interest expense and the payment of the note on December 31, 19X5.
5. Show how the note should be presented on the balance sheet as of December 31, 19X3.

Check Figure 19X3 ending discount, $4,150

Problem 13-5
Times interest earned

LO 9

Here are condensed income statements for two unrelated companies:

Foxtrot Co.	
Sales	$500,000
Variable expenses (80%)	400,000
Net income before interest	$100,000
Interest (fixed)	30,000
Net income	$ 70,000

Tango Co.	
Sales	$500,000
Variable expenses (60%)	300,000
Net income before interest	$200,000
Interest (fixed)	130,000
Net income	$ 70,000

Required

Preparation component:

1. What is the times interest earned for Foxtrot Co.?
2. What is the times interest earned for Tango Co.?
3. What happens to each company's net income if sales increase by 30%?
4. What happens to each company's net income if sales increase by 50%?
5. What happens to each company's net income if sales increase by 80%?
6. What happens to each company's net income if sales decrease by 10%?
7. What happens to each company's net income if sales decrease by 20%?
8. What happens to each company's net income if sales decrease by 40%?

Check Figure Part 3, net income for Foxtrot Co., $100,000

Analysis component:

9. Comment on what you observe in relation to the fixed cost strategies of the two companies and the ratio values you computed in Parts 1 and 2.

Alternate Problems

Problem 13-1A

Estimated product warranty liabilities

LO 4

On November 10, 19X1, Gourmet Co. began to buy and resell electric coffee grinders for $35 each. Gourmet uses the perpetual method to account for inventories. The coffee grinders are covered under a warranty that requires the company to replace any nonworking coffee grinder within 60 days. When a grinder is returned, the company simply throws it away and mails a new one from inventory to the customer. The company's cost for a new grinder is only $14. The manufacturer has advised the company to expect warranty costs to equal 10% of the total sales. These events occurred in 19X1 and 19X2:

19X1

Nov.	16	Sold 50 coffee grinders for $1,750 cash.
	30	Recognized warranty expense for November with an adjusting entry.
Dec.	12	Replaced six grinders that were returned under the warranty.
	18	Sold 150 coffee grinders for $5,250 cash.
	28	Replaced 17 grinders that were returned under the warranty.
	31	Recognized warranty expense for December with an adjusting entry.

19X2

Jan.	7	Sold 60 coffee grinders for $2,100 cash.
	21	Replaced 38 grinders that were returned under the warranty.
	31	Recognized warranty expense for January with an adjusting entry.

Required

1. How much warranty expense should be reported for November and December 19X1?
2. How much warranty expense should be reported for January 19X2?
3. What is the balance of the estimated warranty liability as of December 31, 19X1?
4. What is the balance of the estimated warranty liability as of January 31, 19X2?
5. Prepare journal entries to record the transactions and adjustments.

Problem 13-2A

Transactions with short-term notes payable

LO 3

Palermo Company entered into the following transactions involving short-term liabilities during 19X1 and 19X2:

19X1

Apr. 22	Purchased merchandise on credit from Omni Products for $4,000. The terms were 1/10, n/30. Assume Omni uses a perpetual inventory system.
May 23	Replaced the account payable to Omni Products with a 60-day note bearing 15% annual interest. Palermo paid $400 cash, with the result that the balance of the note was $3,600.
July 15	Borrowed $9,000 from the Liberty Bank by signing an interest-bearing note for $9,000. The annual interest rate was 10%, and the note has a 120-day term.
?	Paid the note to Omni Products at maturity.
?	Paid the note to Liberty Bank at maturity.
Dec. 6	Signed a non-interest-bearing note with a face value of $16,180 from Metro Bank that matures in 45 days. The principal amount on the note is $16,000.
31	Recorded an adjusting entry for the accrual of interest on the note to the Metro Bank.

19X2

?	Paid the note to Metro Bank at maturity.

Required

1. Determine the maturity dates of the three notes just described.
2. Determine the interest due at maturity for the three notes.
3. Determine the interest to be recorded in the adjusting entry at the end of 19X1.
4. Determine the interest to be recorded in 19X2.
5. Present journal entries for all the preceding events and adjustments.

Problem 13-3A
Present value of possible liabilities
LO 6

Holmes Enterprises is negotiating the purchase of a new building. The seller has offered Holmes the following three payment plans:

Plan A: $122,000 cash would be paid at once.
Plan B: $136,000 cash would be paid after two years.
Plan C: $70,000 cash would be paid at the end of each of the next two years.

The company's owner knows that the market interest rate is 6%.

Required

1. Use the market interest rate to determine present value of each of the three possible payment plans.
2. Show the journal entry that would be made to record the acquisition under each of the three plans. (Assume that the note's face value would include all interest to be paid.)
3. Identify the plan that creates the lowest cost for the company.
4. Assume that Plan B is adopted and the present value of the cash flows is used as the building's cost. Determine the amount of interest expense that will be reported in each of the two years in the note's life.

Problem 13-4A
Exchanging a note for a plant asset
LO 6, 7, 8

On January 2, 20X1, Watts Company acquired an item of equipment by issuing a $77,000 non-interest-bearing five-year note payable on December 31, 20X5. A reliable cash price for the equipment was not readily available. The market annual rate of interest for similar notes was 6% on the day of the exchange.

Required

(Round all amounts in your answers to the nearest whole dollar.)

1. Determine the initial net liability created by issuing this note.
2. Present a table showing the calculation of the amount of interest expense allocated to each year the note is outstanding and the carrying amount of the net liability at the end of each of those years.
3. Present a table that shows the balance of the discount at the end of each year the note is outstanding.
4. Prepare general journal entries to record the purchase of the equipment, the accrual of interest expense at the end of 20X1 and 20X2, and the accrual of interest expense and the payment of the note on December 31, 20X5.
5. Show how the note should be presented on the balance sheet as of December 31, 20X3.

Problem 13-5A
Times interest earned
LO 9

Here are condensed income statements for two unrelated companies:

Solstice Co.	
Sales	$120,000
Variable expenses (50%)	60,000
Net income before interest	$ 60,000
Interest (fixed)	45,000
Net income	$ 15,000

Equinox Co.	
Sales	$120,000
Variable expenses (75%)	90,000
Net income before interest	$ 30,000
Interest (fixed)	15,000
Net income	$ 15,000

Required

Preparation component:

1. What is the times interest earned for Solstice?
2. What is the times interest earned for Equinox?
3. What happens to each company's net income if sales increase by 10%?
4. What happens to each company's net income if sales increase by 40%?

5. What happens to each company's net income if sales increase by 90%?
6. What happens to each company's net income if sales decrease by 20%?
7. What happens to each company's net income if sales decrease by 50%?
8. What happens to each company's net income if sales decrease by 80%?

Analysis component:

9. Comment on what you observe in relation to the fixed cost strategies of the two companies and the ratio values you computed in Parts 1 and 2.

Analytical and Review Problems

A & R Problem 13-1

Roger Rocket, ace righthander with the York Bluebirds, is negotiating for renewal of his contract. Prior to making an offer to Rocket, George Megabucks—owner of the team—asks you to check out three alternatives he intends to present to the pitcher. George is only willing to offer a three-year contract but is offering three different payment schemes as follows:

a. $300,000 payable at the end of each year for 10 years.
b. $750,000 payable at the end of each year for 3 years.
c. $1,800,000 payable on signing the three-year contract.

Required

Prepare journal entries for each of the alternatives as of the date of signing the contract and at the end of the first year. Also indicate balance sheet presentation as of the end of the first year. Assume:

1. The going rate of interest is 8%.
2. The company amortizes assets on a straight-line basis.

A & R Problem 13-2

On September 1, 20X1, Chang Company acquired a machine by paying $15,000 cash and signing a two-year note that carried a face amount of $90,000 due at the end of the two-year period; the note did not specify interest. Assume the going rate of interest for this company for this type of loan is 6%. The accounting period ends December 31.

Required

Give the entry to record the purchase of the machine and complete a tabulation as follows (round amounts to nearest dollar):

	Straight-Line Method	Interest Method Method
1. Cash to be paid at maturity	$________	$________
2. Total interest expense	$________	$________
3. Interest expense on income statement for 20X1	$________	$________
4. Amount of the liability reported on balance sheet at end of 20X1	$________	$________
5. Amortization expense for 20X1 (assume straight-line, partial year, no residual value, and useful life of five years)	$________	$________

Comprehensive Problem

Aardvark Exterminators

(Review of Chapters 1–13)

Aardvark Exterminators provides pest control services and sells pool extermination products manufactured by other companies. The following six-column table contains the company's unadjusted trial balance as of December 31, 19X4.

AARDVARK EXTERMINATORS
Six-Column Table
December 31, 19X4

	Unadjusted Trial Balance		Adjustments		Adjusted Trial Balance	
Cash	$ 17,000					
Accounts receivable	4,000					
Allowance for doubtful accounts		$ 828				
Merchandise inventory	13,000					
Trucks	32,000					
Accum. amortization, trucks		-0-				
Equipment	45,000					
Accum. amort., equipment		12,200				
Accounts payable		5,000				
Estimated warranty liability		1,500				
Unearned extermination services revenue		-0-				
Long-term notes payable		15,000				
Discount on notes payable	3,974					
K. Jones, capital		59,600				
K. Jones, withdrawals	10,000					
Extermination services revenue		60,000				
Interest earned		872				
Sales		75,000				
Purchases	45,000					
Amort. expense, trucks	-0-					
Amort. expense, equip.	-0-					
Wages expense	35,000					
Interest expense	-0-					
Rent expense	9,000					
Bad debt expense	-0-					
Miscellaneous expenses	1,226					
Repairs expense	8,000					
Utilities expense	6,800					
Warranty expense	-0-					
Totals	$230,000	$230,000				

The following information applies to the company and its situation at the end of the year:

a. The bank reconciliation as of December 31, 19X4, includes these facts:

Balance per bank	$15,100
Balance per books	17,000
Outstanding cheques	1,800
Deposit in transit	2,450
Interest earned	52
Service charges (miscellaneous expense)	15

Included with the bank statement was a cancelled cheque that the company had failed to record. (This information allows you to determine the amount of the cheque, which was a payment of an account payable.)

b. An examination of customers' accounts shows that accounts totalling $679 should be written off as uncollectible. In addition, it has been determined that the ending balance of the Allowance for Doubtful Accounts account should be $700.

c. A truck was purchased and placed in service on July 1, 19X4. Its cost is being amortized with the straight-line method using these facts and predictions:

Original cost	$32,000
Expected salvage value	8,000
Useful life (years)	4

d. Two items of equipment (a sprayer and an injector) were purchased and put into service early in January 19X2. Their costs are being amortized with the straight-line method using these facts and predictions:

	Sprayer	Injector
Original cost	$27,000	$18,000
Expected salvage value	3,000	2,500
Useful life (years)	8	5

e. On August 1, 19X4, the company was paid $3,840 in advance to provide monthly service on an apartment complex for one year. The company began providing the services in August. When the cash was received, the full amount was credited to the Extermination Services Revenue account.

f. The company offers a warranty for all of the products it sells. The expected cost of providing warranty service is 2.5% of sales. No warranty expense has been recorded for 19X4. All costs of servicing products under the warranties in 19X4 were properly debited to the liability account.

g. The $15,000 long-term note is a five-year, non-interest-bearing note that was given to First National Bank on December 31, 19X2. The market interest rate on the date of the loan was 8%.

h. The ending inventory of merchandise was counted and determined to have a cost of $11,700. (Note that Aardvark's unadjusted trial balance includes a Purchases account. Thus, you know that Aardvark uses a periodic inventory system.)

Required

1. Use the preceding information to determine the amounts of the following items:
   - **a.** The correct ending balance of Cash and the amount of the omitted cheque.
   - **b.** The adjustment needed to obtain the correct ending balance of the Allowance for Doubtful Accounts.
   - **c.** The annual amortization expense for the truck that was acquired during the year (computed to the nearest month).
   - **d.** The annual amortization expense for the two items of equipment that were used during the year.
   - **e.** The correct ending balances of the Extermination Services Revenue and Unearned Extermination Services Revenue accounts.
   - **f.** The correct ending balances of the accounts for Warranty Expense and Estimated Warranty Liability.
   - **g.** The correct ending balances of the accounts for Interest Expense and Discount on Notes Payable. (Round amounts to nearest whole dollar.)
   - **h.** The cost of goods sold for the year.

2. Use the results of requirement 1 to complete the six-column table by first entering the appropriate adjustments for items *a* through *g* and then completing the adjusted trial balance columns. (Hint: Item *b* requires two entries.)

3. Present general journal entries to record the adjustments entered on the six-column table. Assume that Aarkvark uses the closing entry approach to account for changes in Merchandise Inventory.
4. Present a single-step income statement, a statement of changes in owner's equity, and a classified balance sheet.

BEYOND THE NUMBERS

Reporting in Action

LO 5,7

Refer to the financial statements and related information for **Alliance** in Appendix I. Answer the following questions by analyzing the information in Appendix I:

1. Compute times interest earned for the years ended March 31, 1997 and 1996 and comment on Alliance's ability to cover its interest expense.
2. Does Alliance's note on commitments provide information allowing one to determine whether the company has entered into any operating or capital leases?
3. What evidence would you look for as an indication that Alliance has any temporary differences between the income reported on the income statement and the income reported on its tax return? Can you find any evidence of these differences for Alliance?

Comparative Analysis

LO 7

Both **Alliance** and **Atlantis** develop, produce and market movies and TV programs. Key comparative figures ($thousands) for these two organizations follow:

	Alliance		Atlantis	
Key Figures	**1997**	**1996**	**1997**	**1997**
Net Income	$18,188	$10,365	$5,565	$6,866
Income Tax Expense	9,788	1,935	4,262	3,547
Interest Expense	$ 1,296	$ 893	$ 947	$1,339

* Alliance figures are from the annual reports for the fiscal years ended March 31, 1997 and 1996. Atlantis figures are from the annual reports for the fiscal years ended December 31, 1997 and 1996.

Required

1. Compute times interest earned for the two years presented for each company.
2. Comment on which company appears stronger in its ability to commit to interest payments if income should vary.

Ethics Challenge

LO 4

Mike Thatcher is a sales manager for an automobile dealership in Alberta. Mike earns a bonus each year based on revenue generated by the number of autos sold in the year less related warranty expenses. The quality of automobiles sold each year seems to vary since the warranty experience related to autos sold is highly variable. The actual warranty expenses have varied over the past 10 years from a low of 3% of an automobile's selling price to a high of 10%. In the past Mike has tended toward estimating warranty expenses on the high end just to be conservative. It is the end of the year and once again he must work with the dealership's accountant in arriving at the warranty expense accrual for the cars sold this year.

1. Does the warranty accrual decision present any kind of ethical dilemma for Mike Thatcher?
2. Since the warranty experience is not constant what percent do you think Mike should choose for this year? Justify your response.

Communicating in Practice

LO 5

Norma Yagerhofer is the new manager of accounting and finance for a manufacturing company. Now that the end of the year is approaching, her problem is determining whether and how to describe the company's contingencies in financial statements. The general manager, Jonas Perlman, raised an objection to a specific contingency in Yagerhofer's proposal. Perlman objects to Yagerhofer's proposal to recognize an expense and a liability for warranty service on units of a new product that was just introduced in the company's fourth quarter. His scribbled comment on this point was, "There is no way that we can estimate this warranty cost. Besides, we don't owe anybody anything until the products break down and are returned for service. Let's just report an expense if and when we do the repairs."

Required

Develop a short written response for Yagerhofer to send to Perlman addressing his objection in a one-page memorandum dated December 21.

Taking It to the Net

LO 1

Visit the Canadian Bankers' Association Web site at **http://www.cbc.ca**. Find the link on the homepage to the Managing Money page. Once you have located the page find the section on "Checking Your Credit Rating." How can you correct any errors that might exist in your file?

Teamwork in Action

LO 2, 3

Your team is to assume you are in business and need to borrow $6,000 for short-term working capital. You have been shopping banks for a loan. To obtain the funds you have the following options:

1. Sign a $6,000, 90-day, 11% interest-bearing note, or
2. Sign a $6,172.50, 90-day, non-interest-bearing note.

Required

1. Discuss these options. Determine the best choice. Ensure all teammates concur with the decision and understand the rationale. Explain your decision to your instructor.
2. Each member of the team is to prepare one of the following entries:
   a. Option 1—date of borrowing
   b. Option 2—date of borrowing
   c. Option 1—maturity date
   d. Option 2—maturity date
3. In rotation, each member is to explain the entry prepared in (2) to the team. Ensure all team members concur with and understand the entries.
4. Assume the funds were borrowed on December 1 and your business has a fiscal year that coincides with a calendar year. Each member of the team is to prepare one of the following entries:
   a. Option 1—the year-end adjustment
   b. Option 2—the year-end adjustment
   c. Option 1—maturity date
   d. Option 2—maturity date
5. In rotation, each member is to explain the entry prepared in (4) to the team. Ensure all team members concur with and understand the entries.

Hitting the Road

LO 6

Obtain a recent copy of *The Globe and Mail's Report on Business* or *The Financial Post*. Find three notices of offerings of long-term debt instruments and determine the interest rates charged.

a. Are the interest rates the same?

b. What seems to determine the interest rate? For example, is it the size of the offering, the size of the company, or some other factor(s)?

Business Break

LO 4

Extended warranties of up to five years on automobiles and other long-lived consumer products have raised issues in connection with the recognition of income. Up to now, when an extended warranty was sold, all the revenue was recognized in the year of sale. Some accountants, however, have advocated that the revenue from the sale of the warranty should be recognized as the warranty period expires.

Required

1. Why should the revenue from the sale of extended warranties be deferred and recognized over the life of the warranty?
2. Contrast the rules now in effect with the proposed rules with respect to the effect on the income statements of companies selling extended warranties.
3. What accounting principle likely governed those who proposed to change the accounting rules for recognizing warranty revenue?
4. Is the rule for accounting for revenue from warranties consistent with the rules for accounting for expenses related to warranties?

14

CHAPTER

Partnerships

A Look Back

Chapter 13 focused on current and long-term liabilities. We explained how liabilities are identified, computed, recorded, and reported in financial statements.

A Look at This Chapter

This chapter explains both the partnership and corporate forms of organization. Important characteristics of both forms of organization are described along with the accounting for important transactions.

A Look Forward

Chapter 15 extends our discussion of corporate accounting to dividends and other equity transactions. We also explain how income, earnings per share, and retained earnings are reported.

Chapter Outline

- **Partnership Form of Organization**
  - Characteristics of General Partnerships
- **Basic Partnership Accounting**
  - Organizing a Partnership
  - Dividing Income or Loss
  - Partnership Financial Statements
- **Admission and Withdrawal of Partners**
  - Admission of a Partner
  - Withdrawal of a Partner
  - Death of a Partner
- **Liquidation of a Partnership**
  - No Capital Deficiency
  - Capital Deficiency

Go for It

Toronto, ON—What do we say to an 18-year-old who wants some extra spending money? Maybe, check the "help wanted" at **Zellers, Eatons, McDonald's** or **The Bay.** But do we ever say, "What do *you* want to do?" Well, Jennifer Wong did what she wanted to do. Wong decided to block print cotton T-shirts and dresses in her parent's garage to be sold at craft shows and festivals. One would not normally expect much success from such a venture.

But Wong's efforts paid off. In her first full year of business, at the ripe age of 19, her sales climbed to $110,000. In her second year, with a loan co-signed by her parents, she set up a small factory in a leased building in Scarborough. Jennifer formed a partnership with her friend, Malu Balizar, who invested $10,000 into the business. A partnership agreement was drawn up specifying how profits and losses would be divided between Jennifer and Malu and how the assets would be allocated if they decided to end the partnership. Wong has never looked back. Wong's clothing is funky, flowing and artsy. Each product is individually hand block printed with evocative designs and symbols, and signed by the artist. Jennifer's clothing isn't cheap—a T-shirt can cost $60 and a dress, $200 to $300—but the style holds up from year to year. Wong says her clothing "is customer driven and says something meaningful about our times." All clothing is made with natural dyes and uses only organic cotton.

Learning Objectives

LO 1 Identify characteristics of partnerships and similar organizations and explain the concepts of mutual agency and unlimited liability in a partnership.

LO 2 Prepare entries when forming a partnership.

LO 3 Allocate and record income and loss among partners.

LO 4 Account for the admission and withdrawal of a partner.

LO 5 Prepare entries for partnership liquidation.

CHAPTER PREVIEW

There are three common types of business organizations: corporations, partnerships and proprietorships. Partnerships are similar to proprietorships, except with more than one owner. This chapter explains partnerships. While corporations are fewest in number, they transact more business than all others combined. They are very important players in our global economy, with dollar sales at least 10 times the combined sales of unincorporated companies. Understanding the advantages and disadvantages of these forms of business organization was important for Jennifer Wong in her T-shirt venture. The opening article revealed her choice to form a partnership with her friend Malu, but this is not always best. This chapter focuses on partnerships.

Partnership Form of Organization

A **partnership** is an unincorporated association of two or more people to pursue a business for profit as co-owners. General partnerships are governed by provincial law and registration requirements. Many businesses are organized as partnerships. They are especially common in small retail and service businesses. Many professional practitioners also organize their practices as partnerships, including physicians, lawyers, and accountants. Two forms of partnerships are recognized by Canadian law: general partnerships and limited partnerships.

Characteristics of General Partnerships

LO 1 Identify characteristics of partnerships and similar organizations and explain the concepts of mutual agency and unlimited liability in a partnership.

Partnerships are an important type of organization because of certain advantages they offer with their unique characteristics. We describe these characteristics in this section.

Voluntary Association

A partnership is a voluntary association between partners. Since joining a partnership involves increased risk to your personal financial position, your participation is voluntary.[1]

Partnership Agreement

Forming a partnership requires that two or more legally competent people (who are of age and of sound mental capacity) agree to be partners. Their agreement becomes a **partnership contract.** While it should be in writing to protect partners in the event of disagreement or dissolution of the business, the contract is binding even if it is only expressed verbally.[2] Lawyers prepare partnership contracts but it is common for public accountants to review these contracts and advise partners on tax matters relating to their share of partnership income.

Limited Life

The life of a partnership is limited. Death, bankruptcy, or any event taking away the ability of a partner to enter into or fulfill a contract ends a partnership. A partnership also can be terminated at will by any one of the partners. Conditions of termination may also be specified in the partnership contract.

---

[1] Some courts have ruled that partnerships are created by the actions of partners even when there is no expressed agreement to form one.

[2] Partnership agreements normally include the partners': (a) names and contributions, (b) rights and duties, (c) sharing of income and losses, (d) withdrawal arrangement, (e) dispute procedures, (f) admission and withdrawal of new partners, and (g) rights and duties in event a partner dies.

Strategic Alliances
A more recent form of partnership is the strategic alliance. A strategic alliance is formed when a firm combines with one or more firms for a specific period of time to accomplish a common goal. A recent survey by Ernst & Young of 822 Canadian high-tech firms found that 41% were involved in such alliances. Pharmaceutical companies, such as Glaxo Canada Inc., have formed alliances with other companies to combat particular diseases. Although businesses forming alliances are frequently corporations, the alliances they have formed are a type of partnership.

Did You Know?

Taxation

A partnership is not subject to taxes on its income. It has the same tax status as a proprietorship. The income or loss of a partnership is allocated to the partners according to the partnership agreement, and is included for determining the taxable income of each partner's tax return.[3] Allocation of partnership income or loss is done each year whether or not cash is distributed to partners.

Getting Along
An important advantage of a partnership form of organization over a proprietorship form is that a partner usually brings in extra resources with which to run the business. Partnership agreements can help avoid potential disputes about issues such as: Who invested what amounts of money in the partnership? Who performs what activities, and who reports to whom? Who will receive what share of partnership profits? How will assets be distributed in the event of liquidation? Not all potential disputes, however, can be anticipated in advance. It is important when selecting a partner to give serious thought about the character and personality of those with whom we are forming long-term relationships and not be blinded by the economic resources that a potential partner may be offering. Disputes are common in partnerships and can lead to disastrous consequences for the business and for the well-being of all involved.

Did You Know?

Mutual Agency

The relationship between partners in a general partnership involves **mutual agency.** This means each partner is a fully authorized agent of the partnership. As its agent a partner can commit or bind the partnership to any contract within the scope of the partnership's business. For instance, a partner in a merchandising business can sign contracts binding the partnership to buy merchandise, lease a store building, borrow money, or hire employees. These activities are all within the scope of business of a merchandising firm. But a partner in a law firm, acting alone, cannot bind the other partners to a contract to buy snowboards for resale or rent an apartment for parties. These actions are outside the normal scope of a law firm's business.

Partners can agree to limit the power of any one or more of the partners to negotiate contracts for the partnership. This agreement is binding on the partners and on outsiders who know it exists. But it is not binding on outsiders who don't know it exists. Outsiders unaware of the agreement have the right to assume each partner has normal agency powers for the partnership. Because mutual agency exposes all partners to the risk of unwise actions by any one partner, people should evaluate each potential partner before agreeing to join a partnership.

---

[3] The Income Tax Act requires that proper records be maintained by partnerships and all other forms of business ownership that fall under its provisions.

Unlimited Liability

When a general partnership can't pay its debts, the creditors usually can apply their claims to personal assets of partners. If a partner does not have enough assets to meet his or her share of the partnership debt, the creditors can apply their claims to the assets of the other partners. Because partners can be called on to pay the debts of a partnership, each partner is said to have **unlimited liability** for the partnership's debts. Mutual agency and unlimited liability are two main reasons why most partnerships have only a few members.

Co-Ownership of Property

Partnership assets are owned jointly by all partners. Any investment by a partner becomes the joint property of all partners. Partners have a claim on partnership assets based on their capital account.

Limited Partnerships

Some individuals who want to invest in a partnership are unwilling to accept the risk of unlimited liability. Their needs may be met with a **limited partnership.** Limited partnerships are established under provincial statutes that require registration. One or more partners in a limited partnership may be designated as a **general partner** who assumes management duties and unlimited liability for the debts and obligations of the partnership. The **limited partners** have no personal liability beyond the investment they invest in the partnership. A limited partnership is managed by the general partner(s). Limited partners have no active role except as specified in the partnership agreement. A limited partnership agreement must be drawn up for a limited partnership. This legal document often specifies unique procedures for allocating incomes and losses between general and limited partners. The same basic accounting procedures are used for both limited and **general partnerships.**

Flash back

1. A partnership is terminated in the event (a) a partnership agreement is not in writing, (b) a partner dies, (c) a partner exercises mutual agency.
2. What does the term *unlimited liability* mean when applied to a general partnership?

Answers—p. 676

You Make the Call

Advisor
Your roommate has hair-dressing skills and is thinking of opening a barbershop that would cater to university students. He has a financially well off aunt with whom he would like to enter into partnership. His aunt is interested in the venture and would like a stake in the operation. However, she is heavily involved in other ventures and simply has no time to devote to another business activity. She is concerned about the extent of her liability should the business not succeed. What type of business organization might you recommend to your roommate?

Answers—p. 676

Basic Partnership Accounting

Accounting for a partnership is the same as accounting for a proprietorship except for transactions directly affecting partners' equity. Because ownership rights in a partnership are divided among partners, partnership accounting:

- Uses a capital account for each partner.

- Uses a withdrawals account for each partner.
- Allocates net income or loss to partners according to the partnership agreement.

This section describes partnership accounting for organizing a partnership, distributing income and losses, and preparing financial statements.

Organizing a Partnership

When partners invest in a partnership, their capital accounts are credited for the invested amounts. Partners can invest both assets and liabilities. Each partner's investment is recorded at an agreed upon value, normally the fair market value of the assets and liabilities at their date of contribution.

LO 2 Prepare entries when forming a partnership.

To illustrate, Olivia Tsang and David Breck organize a partnership in 1999 called **BOARDS**. Their business offers year-round facilities for skateboarding and snowboarding. Tsang's initial net investment in BOARDS is $30,000, made up of cash ($7,000), boarding facilities ($33,000), and a note payable reflecting a bank loan for the business of ($10,000). Breck's initial investment is cash of $10,000. These amounts are the values agreed upon by both partners. The entries to record these investments are:

Tsang's Investment

Jan. 11	Cash	7,000	
	Boarding facilities	33,000	
	Note payable		10,000
	O. Tsang, Capital		30,000
	To record investment of Tsang.		

Assets = Liabilities + Equity
+7,000 +10,000 +30,000
+33,000

Breck's Investment

Jan. 11	Cash	10,000	
	D. Breck, Capital		10,000
	To record investment of Breck.		

Assets = Liabilities + Equity
+10,000 +10,000

The accounting for partnership transactions after it is formed is similar to a proprietorship. Chapters 2–5 described the basic accounting procedures for a proprietorship, and they apply here as well. The minor differences include (1) Partners' withdrawals of assets are debited to their withdrawals accounts. (2) In closing the accounts at the end of a period, the partners' capital accounts are credited or debited for their shares of net income or loss. (3) The withdrawals account of each partner is closed to that partner's capital account. These procedures are similar to those used for a single proprietorship, except that separate capital and withdrawals accounts are kept for each partner.

Dividing Income or Loss

Partners are not employees of the partnership; they are its owners. If partners devote their time and services to their partnership, they are understood to do so for profit, not for salary. This means that when partners compute the net income of a partnership, salaries to partners are not expenses on the income statement. But when net income or loss of a partnership is allocated among partners, the partners can agree to base part of their allocation on salary allowances reflecting the relative values of services they provide. Partners also can agree that division of partnership earnings includes a return based on the amount invested. For instance, since Tsang contributes three times the investment of Breck, it is only fair that this fact be considered when earnings are allocated between them. Their partnership agreement can provide for interest allowances based on their capital balances. Like salary allowances, these interest allowances are not expenses on the income statement.

LO3 Allocate and record income and loss among partners.

Partners can agree to any method of dividing income or loss. But in the absence of an agreement, the law says that income or loss of a partnership is shared equally by the partners. If partners agree on how they share income but say nothing about losses, then losses are shared in the same way as income. Several methods of sharing partnership income or loss are used. Three frequently used methods divide income or loss using: (1) a stated fractional basis, (2) the ratio of capital investments, or (3) salary and interest allowances and any remainder in a fixed ratio.

Allocated on a Stated Fractional Basis

One way to divide partnership income or loss is to give each partner a fraction of the total. Partners must agree on the fractional share each receives. A fractional basis can be expressed as a ratio or percentage. A 2:1 basis is the same as 2/3 and 1/3. A 3:2 ratio can be expressed as 3/5 and 2/5 or as 60% and 40%. The partnership agreement of O. Tsang and D. Breck says Tsang receives two-thirds and Breck one-third of partnership income and loss. If their partnership's net income is $60,000, it is allocated to the partners, and the Income Summary account is closed, with the following entry:

Assets	=	Liabilities	+	Equity
				−60,000
				+40,000
				+20,000

Dec. 31	Income Summary	60,000	
	O. Tsang, Capital		40,000
	D. Breck, Capital		20,000
	To allocate income and close the Income Summary account.		

Allocated on the Ratio of Capital Investments

Partners can also allocate income or loss on the ratio of the relative capital investments of each partner. Tsang and Breck agreed to share earnings on the ratio of their capital investments. Since Tsang invested $30,000 and Breck invested $10,000, this means Tsang receives three-fourths of any income or loss ($30,000/$40,000) and Breck receives one-fourth ($10,000/$40,000).

Allocated Using Salaries, Interest Allowance, and a Fixed Ratio

Service contributions and capital contributions of partners often are not equal. Salary allowances can make up for differences in service contributions. Also, interest allowances can make up for unequal capital contributions. When both service and capital contributions are unequal, the allocation of income and loss can include both salary and interest allowances.

In Olivia Tsang and David Breck's new partnership, both agree that Tsang's services are worth an annual salary of $36,000. Since Breck is less experienced in the business, his services are valued at $24,000 annually. To compensate Tsang and Breck fairly, given these differences in service and capital contributions, they agree to share income or loss as follows:

1. Annual salary allowances of $36,000 to Tsang and $24,000 to Breck.
2. Interest allowances equal to 10% of each partner's beginning-of-year capital balance.
3. Any remaining balance of income or loss to be shared equally.

The provisions for salaries and interest in this partnership agreement are called *allowances*. Allowances are *not* reported as salaries and interest expense on the income statement. They are a means of dividing the income or loss of a partnership.

Illustration When Income Exceeds Allowance

If BOARDS has first year income of $70,000 and Tsang and Breck apply the partnership agreement above, they allocate income or loss as shown in Exhibit 14.1. Tsang gets $42,000 and Breck gets $28,000 of the $70,000 total.

Exhibit 14.1

Dividing Income When Income Exceeds Allowances

	Tsang	Breck	Total
Net income			$70,000
Salary allowances:			
Tsang	$36,000		
Breck		$24,000	
Interest allowances:			
Tsang (10% on $30,000)	3,000		
Breck (10% on $10,000)		1,000	
Total salaries and interest	39,000	25,000	64,000
Balance of net income			$ 6,000
Balance allocated equally:			
Tsang	3,000		
Breck		3,000	
Total allocated equally			6,000
Balance of net income			$ -0-
Shares of each partner	$42,000	$28,000	$70,000

Illustration When Allowances Exceed Income

The method of sharing agreed to by Tsang and Breck must be followed even if net income is less than the total of the allowances. If BOARDS first year net income is $50,000 instead of $70,000, it is allocated to the partners as shown in Exhibit 14.2. Computations for salaries and interest are identical to those in Exhibit 14.1. When we apply the total allowances against net income, the balance of income is negative. This negative ($14,000) is allocated in the same manner as a positive balance. The equal sharing agreement means a negative ($7,000) is allocated to each partner to determine the final allocation. In this case, Tsang ends up with $32,000 and Breck gets $18,000.

Exhibit 14.2

Dividing Income When Allowances Exceed Income

	Tsang	Breck	Total
Net income			$50,000
Salary allowances:			
Tsang	$36,000		
Breck		$24,000	
Interest allowances:			
Tsang (10% on $30,000)	3,000		
Breck (10% on $10,000)		1,000	
Total salaries and interest	39,000	25,000	64,000
Balance of net income over allocated			(14,000)
Balance allocated equally:			
Tsang	(7,000)		
Breck		(7,000)	
Total allocated equally			14,000
Balance of net income			$ -0-
Shares of each partner	$32,000	$18,000	$50,000

If BOARDS had experienced a loss, then Tsang and Breck share it in the same manner as the $50,000 income. The only difference is we would begin with a negative amount because of the loss. Specifically, partners are still allocated their salary and interest allowances, which further adds to the negative balance of the loss. This *total* negative balance *after* salary and interest allowances, or ($14,000) in our case, is allocated equally between the partners. These allocations are applied against the positive numbers from any allowances to determine each partner's share of the loss.

Flash back

3. Ben and Jerry form a partnership by contributing $70,000 and $35,000, respectively. They agree to an interest allowance equal to 10% of each partner's capital balance at the beginning of the year with the remaining income shared equally. Allocate first-year income of $40,000 to each partner.
4. What fraction does each partner receive if three partners share on a 1:2:3 basis?

Answers—p. 676

Partnership Financial Statements

Partnership financial statements are similar to those of a proprietorship. The **statement of changes in partners' equity** shows the capital balances at the beginning of the period, any additional investments made by the partners, the income or loss of the partnership, withdrawals by partners, and the ending capital balances. This statement, also called *statement of partners' capital,* usually shows these changes for each partner's capital account and includes the allocation of income among partners. To illustrate, Exhibit 14.3 shows the statement of changes in partners' equity for BOARDS prepared for the sharing agreement of Exhibit 14.1. Recall that BOARDS' first year income was $70,000. Also, Tsang withdrew $20,000 and Breck $12,000 at the end of the first year.

Exhibit 14.3

Statement of Changes in Partners' Equity

BOARDS
Statement of Changes in Partners' Equity
For Year Ended December 31, 1999

		Tsang		Breck	Total
Beginning capital balances . . .		$ -0-		$ -0-	$ -0-
Plus:					
Investments by owners		30,000		10,000	40,000
Net income:					
Salary allowances	$36,000		$24,000		
Interest allowances	3,000		1,000		
Balance	3,000		3,000		
Total net income		42,000		28,000	70,000
Total		$72,000		$38,000	$110,000
Less partners' withdrawals . . .		(20,000)		(12,000)	(32,000)
Ending capital balances		$52,000		$26,000	$ 78,000

The owner's equity section of the balance sheet of a partnership usually shows the separate capital account balance of each partner. In the case of BOARDS, both O. Tsang, Capital and D. Breck, Capital are listed in the owners' equity section along with their balances of $52,000 and $26,000, respectively.

Mid-Chapter Demonstration Problem

Parker and Poon began a partnership by investing $52,000 and $78,000, respectively. During the first year, the partnership earned $180,000. Prepare calculations that show how the income should be allocated to the partners under each of the following plans for sharing net incomes and losses:

a. The partners failed to agree on a method of sharing income.
b. The partners agreed to share incomes and losses in their investment ratio.
c. The partners agreed to share income by allowing an $85,000 per year salary allowance to Parker, a $65,000 per year salary allowance to Poon, 10% interest on beginning capital balances, and the remainder equally.

Planning the Solution

1. Set up a column for each partner as well as a column to keep track of allocated income.
2. Allocate income to each partner according to the terms of the partnership agreement.

Solution to Mid-Chapter Demonstration Problem

	Share to Parker	Share to Poon	Income Allocated
Plan (a) $180,000 × (1/2)	$90,000	$ 90,000	$180,000
Plan (b) ($52,000/$130,000) × $180,000	$72,000		$ 72,000
($78,000/$130,000) × $180,000		$108,000	$108,000
	$72,000	$108,000	$180,000
Plan (c) Salary allowances	$85,000	$ 65,000	$150,000
Interest allowances:			
($52,000 × .1)	5,200		5,200
($78,000 × .1)		7,800	7,800
			$163,000
Remainder equally:			
($180,000 − $163,000)/2	8,500	8,500	17,000
	$98,700	$ 81,300	$180,000

Admission and Withdrawal of Partners

A partnership is based on a contract between individuals. When a partner is added or a partner withdraws, the old partnership ends. Still, the business can continue to operate as a new partnership among the remaining partners. This section looks at how we account for the addition and withdrawal of a partner.

LO 4 Account for the admission and withdrawal of a partner

Admission of a Partner

There are two ways a new partner is admitted to a partnership. First, a new partner can purchase an interest from one or more current partners. Second, a new partner can invest cash or other assets.

Purchase of Partnership Interest

The purchase of partnership interest is *a personal transaction between one or more current partners and the new partner.* The purchaser does not become a partner until accepted by the current partners. Accounting for the purchase of partnership interest involves a reallocation of current partners' capital to reflect the transaction.

To illustrate, at the end of BOARDS first year, David Breck sells *one-half* of his partnership interest to Cris Davis for $18,000. Breck is selling a $13,000 recorded interest ($26,000 × 1/2) in the partnership (see Exhibit 14.3). The partnership records this as:

Assets = Liabilities + Equity
−13,000
+13,000

Jan. 4	D. Breck, Capital	13,000	
	C. Davis, Capital		13,000
	To record admission of Davis by purchase.		

After this entry is posted, BOARDS' owners' equity list O. Tsang, Capital, D. Breck, Capital, and C. Davis, Capital along with their balances of $52,000, $13,000 and $13,000, respectively.

Two aspects of this transaction are important. First, the $18,000 Davis paid to Breck is not recorded by the partnership. This is regardless of the amount paid by Davis to Breck. The partnership's assets, liabilities, and total equity are unaffected by this transaction. Second, Tsang and Breck must agree if Davis is to become a partner. If they agree to accept Davis, a new partnership is formed and a new contract with a new income-and-loss-sharing agreement is prepared. If Tsang or Breck refuses to accept Davis as a partner, then (under the Uniform Partnership Act) Davis gets Breck's sold share of partnership income and loss. If the partnership is liquidated, Davis gets Breck's sold share of partnership assets. But Davis gets no voice in managing the company until being admitted as a partner.

Investing Assets in a Partnership

Admitting a partner by accepting assets is a *transaction between the new partner and the partnership*. The invested assets become partnership property. To illustrate, if Tsang (with a $52,000 interest) and Breck (with a $26,000 interest) agree to accept Davis as a partner in BOARDS with her investment of $22,000, the entry to record Davis' investment is:

Assets = Liabilities + Equity
+22,000 +22,000

Jan. 4	Cash	22,000	
	C. Davis, Capital		22,000
	To record admission of Davis by investment.		

After this entry is posted, both assets (cash) and owners' equity (C. Davis, Capital) increase by $22,000. Davis now has 22% equity in the assets of the business, computed as $22,000 divided by the entire partnership equity ($52,000 + $26,000 + $22,000). But she doesn't necessarily have a right to 22% of income. Dividing income and loss is a separate matter on which partners must agree.

Bonus to Old Partners

When the current value of a partnership is greater than the recorded amounts of equity, the partners usually require a new partner to pay a bonus for the privilege of joining. To illustrate, let's say Tsang and Breck agree to accept Davis as a partner with a 25% interest in BOARDS. But they require Davis to invest $42,000. Recall, the partnership's accounting records show Tsang's recorded equity in the business is $52,000 and Breck's recorded equity is $26,000 (see Exhibit 14.3). They agree to accept Davis' $42,000 investment in return for a 25% share in both partnership's earnings and equity. Davis' equity is determined as follows:

Equities of existing partners ($52,000 + $26,000)	$ 78,000
Investment of new partner	42,000
Total partnership equity	$120,000
Equity of Davis (25% × $120,000)	$ 30,000

Although Davis invests $42,000, her equity in the recorded net assets of the partnership is only $30,000. The $12,000 difference usually is called a bonus and allocated to existing partners (Tsang and Breck) according to their net income/loss share ratio. Assume this to be 50:50. The entry to record this is:

Jan. 4	Cash	42,000	
	Davis, Capital		30,000
	Tsang, Capital ($12,000 × 1/2)		6,000
	Breck, Capital ($12,000 × 1/2)		6,000
	To record admission of Davis and bonus to old partners.		

Assets	= Liabilities	+ Equity
+42,000		+30,000
		+6,000
		+6,000

Tsang and Breck share the $12,000 bonus according to their income-and-loss-sharing agreement. This bonus is always shared in this way because it is viewed as an increase in the value of the partnership that is not yet reflected in the accounts of the previous partners.

Bonus to New Partner

Existing partners can pay a bonus to a new partner. This usually occurs when they need additional cash or the new partner has exceptional talents. The new partner gets a larger equity than the amount invested. To illustrate, let's say Tsang and Breck agree to accept Davis as a partner with a 25% interest in both the partnership's earnings and equity, but they require Davis to only invest $18,000. Davis' equity is determined as:

Equities of existing partners ($52,000 + $26,000)	$78,000
Investment of new partner	18,000
Total partnership equity	$96,000
Equity of Davis (25% × $96,000)	$24,000

The entry to record Davis' investment is:

Jan. 4	Cash	18,000	
	Tsang, Capital ($6,000 × 1/2)	3,000	
	Breck, Capital ($6,000 × 1/2)	3,000	
	Davis, Capital		24,000
	To record Davis' admission and bonus.		

Assets	= Liabilities	+ Equity
+18,000		−3,000
		−3,000
		+24,000

The old partners in accordance with their income-and-loss-sharing ratios contribute the $6,000 bonus to Davis. Davis' 25% equity doesn't necessarily entitle her to 25% of any income or loss. This is a separate matter for agreement by the partners.

Withdrawal of a Partner

There are generally two ways a partner withdraws from a partnership. First, the withdrawing partner can sell his or her interest to another person who pays cash or other assets to the withdrawing partner. For this we need only debit the withdrawing partner's capital account and credit the new partner's capital account. The second case is when cash or other assets of the partnership are distributed to the withdrawing partner in settlement of his or her equity interest. This section explains the accounting for this case.

To illustrate, let's assume in a future period that Breck withdraws from the partnership of BOARDS. The partners (Tsang, Breck, and Davis) share income and loss equally. Their partnership shows the following capital balances: Tsang, $84,000; Breck $38,000; and Davis $38,000. Accounting for the withdrawal depends on whether a bonus is paid or not. We describe three possibilities.

No Bonus

If Breck withdraws and takes cash equal to his equity, the entry is:

Assets = Liabilities + Equity
−38,000 −38,000

Oct. 31	Breck, Capital	38,000	
	Cash		38,000
	To record withdrawal of Breck and no bonus.		

Breck can take any combination of assets to which the partners agree to settle his equity. The withdrawal of Breck creates a new partnership between remaining partners. A new partnership contract and a new income-and-loss-sharing agreement are sometimes required.

Bonus to Remaining Partners

A withdrawing partner is sometimes willing to take less than the recorded value of his or her equity just to get out of the partnership or because the recorded value of some assets are overstated. Whatever the reason, when this occurs the withdrawing partner in effect gives a bonus to remaining partners equal to the equity left behind. The remaining partners share this un-withdrawn equity in their income-and-loss-sharing ratio. To illustrate, if Breck withdraws and agrees to take $34,000 cash in settlement of his equity, the entry is:

Assets = Liabilities + Equity
−34,000 −38,000
+2,000
+2,000

Oct. 31	Breck, Capital	38,000	
	Cash		34,000
	Tsang, Capital		2,000
	Davis, Capital		2,000
	To record withdrawal of Breck and bonus to remaining partners.		

Breck withdrew $4,000 less than his recorded equity. The amount not withdrawn is divided between Tsang and Davis in their income-and-loss-sharing ratio, which in this case is shared equally among partners.

Bonus to Withdrawing Partner

There are at least two reasons why a withdrawing partner may be able to receive more than his or her recorded equity. First, the recorded equity may be understated because asset values are understated. Second, the remaining partners may want to remove this partner by giving assets of greater value than this partner's recorded equity. When either case occurs, the withdrawing partner in effect receives a bonus. The remaining partners reduce their equity for this bonus using their income-and-loss-sharing ratio. To illustrate, if Breck withdraws and receives $40,000 cash in settlement of his equity, the entry is:

Assets = Liabilities + Equity
−40,000 −38,000
−1,000
−1,000

Oct. 31	Breck, Capital	38,000	
	Tsang, Capital	1,000	
	Davis, Capital	1,000	
	Cash		40,000
	To record withdrawal of and bonus to Breck.		

Death of a Partner

A partner's death dissolves a partnership. A deceased partner's estate is entitled to receive his or her equity. The partnership contract should contain provisions for settlement in this case. These usually include provisions for (a) a closing of the books to determine income or loss since the end of the previous period and (b) a method for determining and recording current values for assets and liabilities. The remaining partners and the deceased partner's estate then must agree to a settlement of the deceased partner's equity. This can involve selling the equity to remaining partners or to an outsider, or it can involve withdrawing assets.

Lawyer
You are a lawyer hired by the two remaining partners of a three-member partnership. The third partner recently died. The three partners shared income and loss in the ratio of their capital balances, which were equal. The partnership agreement says a deceased partner's estate is entitled to the "partner's percent share of partnership assets." The estate argues it is entitled to one-third of the current value of the partnership's total assets. The remaining partners say the distribution should use the asset's book values, which are only 75% of current value. They also point to partnership liabilities, which equal 40% of the assets' book value, and 30% of current value. What do you suggest?

Judgment and Ethics

Answer—p. 676

Liquidation of a Partnership

LO5 Prepare entries for partnership liquidation.

When a partnership is liquidated, its business is ended. Four steps are involved: (1) Noncash assets are sold for cash and a gain or loss on liquidation is recorded, (2) Gain or loss on liquidation is allocated to partners' using their income-and-loss ratio, (3) Liabilities are paid, and (4) Remaining cash is distributed to partners based on their capital balances. **Partnership liquidation** often follows one of two different cases described below.

No Capital Deficiency

The case of *no capital deficiency* is where all partners have a credit balance in their capital accounts before final distribution of cash. To illustrate, let's assume Tsang, Breck, and Davis operate their partnership in BOARDS for several years, sharing income and losses equally. The partners then decide to liquidate. On that date, the books are closed, and income from operations is transferred to partners' capital accounts. The partners' recorded equity balances immediately prior to liquidation are: Tsang $70,000; Breck $66,000; and Davis $62,000.

In a liquidation, some gains or losses commonly result from the sale of noncash assets. These *losses and gains are called losses and gains from liquidation*. Just like net incomes or losses, partners generally share the losses and gains from liquidation in their income-and-loss-sharing ratio. Assume BOARDS sells its noncash assets for a net gain on realization of $6,000. This is shared by the partners using their income-and-loss-sharing agreement (that is equal for these partners) yielding the partners' revised equity balances of: Tsang $72,000; Breck $68,000; and Davis $64,000.[4]

---

[4] The concepts behind these entries are not new. For example, assume BOARDS has two noncash assets recorded as: boarding facilities, $15,000 and land, $25,000. The entry to sell these assets for $46,000 is:

Jan. 15	Cash	46,000	
	Boarding facilities		15,000
	Land		25,000
	Loss or Gain from Liquidation		6,000
	Sold noncash assets for a gain.		

We then record the allocation of any loss or gain (a gain in this case) from liquidation according to the partners' income-and-loss sharing agreement as:

Jan. 15	Loss or Gain from Liquidation	6,000	
	Tsang, Capital		2,000
	Breck, Capital		2,000
	Davis, Capital		2,000
	To allocate liquidation gain to partners.		

After partnership assets are sold and the gain or loss shared, any liabilities must be paid. Because creditors have first claim, they are paid first. After creditors are paid, the remaining cash is divided among the partners according to his or her capital account balance. BOARDS only liability at liquidation is $20,000 in accounts payable. The entries to record the creditor's payment and final distribution of cash to partners is:

Assets	= Liabilities	+ Equity
−20,000	−20,000	

Assets	= Liabilities	+ Equity
−204,000		−72,000
		−68,000
		−64,000

Jan. 15	Accounts Payable	20,000	
	Cash		20,000
	To pay claims of creditors.		
15	Tsang, Capital	72,000	
	Breck, Capital	68,000	
	Davis, Capital	64,000	
	Cash		204,000
	To distribute remaining cash to partners.		

Remember the final cash payment is distributed to partners according to their capital account balances, whereas gains and losses from liquidation are allocated according to the income-and-loss-sharing ratio.

Capital Deficiency

The case of *capital deficiency* is where at least one partner has a debit balance in his or her capital account before the final distribution of cash. This can arise from liquidation losses, excessive withdrawals before liquidation, or recurring losses in prior periods. Partners with a capital deficiency must, if possible, cover the deficit by paying cash into the partnership.

To illustrate, let's assume Tsang, Breck, and Davis operate their partnership in BOARDS for several years, sharing income and losses equally. The partners then decide to liquidate. But contrary to the case above, and immediately prior to the final distribution of cash, the partners' recorded capital balances are: Tsang $19,000; Breck $8,000; and Davis ($3,000). Davis' capital deficiency means she owes the partnership $3,000. Both Tsang and Breck have a legal claim against Davis' personal assets. The final distribution of cash in this case depends on how this capital deficiency is handled.

Partner Pays Deficiency

Davis is obligated to pay $3,000 into the partnership to cover the deficiency. If Davis is willing and able to pay, the entry to record its receipt is:

Assets	= Liabilities	+ Equity
+3,000		+3,000

Jan. 15	Cash	3,000	
	Davis, Capital		3,000
	To record payment of deficiency by Davis.		

After the $3,000 payment, the partners' capital balances are: Tsang $19,000; Breck $8,000; and Davis ($0). The entry to record the final cash distributions to partners is:

Assets	= Liabilities	+ Equity
−27,000		−19,000
		−8,000

Jan. 15	Tsang, Capital	19,000	
	Breck, Capital	8,000	
	Cash		27,000
	To distribute remaining cash to partners.		

Partner Can't Pay Deficiency

When a partner is unable to pay the deficiency, it is absorbed by the remaining partners with credit balances. This is because of unlimited liability in a partnership. To illustrate, if Davis is unable to pay the $3,000 deficiency, Tsang and Breck share it based usually on their income-and-loss-sharing ratio. Since they share equally, both Tsang and Breck absorb $1,500 each of the deficiency. This is recorded as:

Jan. 15	Tsang, Capital	1,500	
	Breck, Capital	1,500	
	Davis, Capital		3,000
	To transfer Davis' deficiency to Tsang and Breck.		

Assets = Liabilities + Equity
−1,500
−1,500
+3,000

After Davis' deficiency is absorbed by Tsang and Breck, the capital accounts of the partners are: Tsang $17,500; Breck $6,500; and Davis ($0). The entry to record the final cash distributions to the partners is:

Jan. 15	Tsang, Capital	17,500	
	Breck, Capital	6,500	
	Cash		24,000
	To distribute remaining cash to partners.		

Assets = Liabilities + Equity
−24,000 −17,500
−6,500

The inability of Davis to cover her deficiency does not relieve her of liability. If she becomes able to pay at some future date, Tsang and Breck can each collect $1,500 from her.

The sharing of an insolvent partner's deficit by the remaining partners in their original income-and-loss-sharing ratio is generally regarded as equitable. In England, however, in 1904 in the case of *Garner v. Murray*, Judge Joyce ruled that the debit balance of the insolvent partner's capital account is a personal debt due to the other partners and to be borne by them in the ratio of their capital account balances immediately prior to liquidation.

While *Garner v. Murray* still appears to be good law, it is considered by most to be inequitable. The decision applies only when the partnership agreement does not cover the situation. It is therefore important to provide agreement for the sharing of a partner's debit balance by the remaining partners according to their income-and-loss-sharing ratio.

Summary

LO 1 Identify characteristics of partnerships and similar organizations and explain the concepts of mutual agency and unlimited liability in a partnership. A partnership is a voluntary association between the partners that is based on a contract. The life of a partnership is limited by agreement or by death or incapacity of a partner. Normally, each partner can act as an agent of the other partners and commit the partnership to any contract within the apparent scope of its business. All partners in a general partnership are personally liable for all the debts of the partnership. Limited partnerships include one or more general partners plus one or more limited partners whose liabilities are limited to the amount of their investments in the partnership. The risk of becoming a partner results in part from the fact that partnership characteristics include a mutual agency and unlimited liability.

LO 2 Prepare entries when forming a partnership. When partners invest in a partnership, their capital accounts are credited for the invested amounts. Partners can invest both assets and liabilities. Each partner's investment is recorded at an agreed upon value, normally the fair market value of the assets and liabilities at their date of contribution.

LO 3 Allocate and record income and loss among partners. A partnership's net incomes or losses are allocated to the partners according to the terms of the partnership agreement. The agreement may specify that each partner will receive a given fraction, or that the allocation of incomes and losses will reflect salary allowances and/or interest allowances. When salary and/or interest allowances are granted, the residual net income or loss usually is allocated equally or on a stated fractional basis.

LO 4 **Account for the admission and withdrawal of a partner.** When a new partner buys a partnership interest directly from one or more of the existing partners, the amount of cash paid from one partner to another does not affect the total recorded equity of the partnership. The recorded equity of the selling partner(s) is simply transferred to the capital account of the new partner. Alternatively, a new partner may purchase an equity by investing additional assets in the partnership. When this occurs, part of the new partner's investment may be credited as a bonus to the capital accounts of the existing partners. Also, to gain the participation of the new partner, the existing partners may give the new partner a bonus whereby portions of the existing partners' capital balances are transferred to the new partner's capital account. Occasionally, goodwill is recorded when a partner invests in a partnership.

LO 5 **Prepare entries for partnership liquidation.** When a partnership is liquidated, losses and gains from selling the partnership assets are allocated to the partners according to their income-and-loss sharing ratio. If a partner's capital account has a balance that the partner cannot pay, the other partners generally must share the deficit in their relative income-and-loss sharing ratio.

Guidance Answers to **You Make the Call**

Advisor

One possibility is to recommend to your roommate that he consider a limited partnership. His aunt may be interested in becoming a limited partner so that her liability would be limited to her investment in the enterprise. A partnership agreement could be drawn up to reflect this arrangement as well as other matters such as how to share potential profits and losses.

Guidance Answers to **Judgment and Ethics**

Lawyer

The partnership agreement fails to mention liabilities or use the term "net assets." Still, to give the estate one-third of total assets is not fair to the remaining partners. This is because if the partner had lived and the partners had decided to liquidate, the liabilities must be paid first. Also, a settlement based on the recorded equity of the deceased partner would fail to recognize excess of current value over book value. These value increases would be realized if the partnership is liquidated. A fair settlement would seem to be a payment to the estate for the balance of the deceased partner's equity based on the *current value of net assets*.

Guidance Answers to Flash backs

1. *b*

2. Unlimited liability means that the creditors of a partnership have the right to require each partner to be personally responsible for all partnership debts.

3.

	Ben	Jerry	Total
Net income			$40,000
Interest allowance	$ 7,000	$ 3,500	10,500
Remaining balance			$29,500
Balance allocated equally	14,750	14,750	29,500
Remaining balance			$ -0-
Shares of partners	$21,750	$18,250	

4. 1/6,2/6, and 3/6

Demonstration Problem

The following events affect the partner's capital accounts in several successive partnerships. On a work sheet with six money columns, one for each of five partners and a totals column, show the effects of the following events on the partners' capital accounts.

Part 1

Apr. 14/99	Ries and Bax create R&B Co. Each invests $10,000, and they agree to share profits equally.
Dec. 31/99	R&B Co. earns $15,000 in the year. Ries withdraws $4,000 from the partnership, and Bax withdraws $7,000.
Jan. 1/00	Royce is made a partner in RB&R Co. after contributing $12,000 cash. The partners agree that each will get a 10% interest allowance on their beginning capital balances. In addition, Bax and Royce are to receive $5,000 salary allowances. The remainder of the income is to be divided evenly.
Dec. 31/00	The partnership's income for the year is $40,000, and these withdrawals occur: Ries, $5,000; Bax, $12,500; and Royce, $11,000.
Jan. 1/01	For $20,000, Ries sells her interest to Murdock, who is accepted by Bax and Royce as a partner in the new BR&M Co. The profits are to be shared equally after Bax and Royce each receive $25,000 salaries.
Dec. 31/01	The partnership's income for the year is $35,000, and these withdrawals occur: Bax, $2,500, and Royce, $2,000.
Jan. 1/02	Elway is admitted as a partner after investing $60,000 cash in the new Elway & Associates partnership. Elway is given a 50% interest in capital after the other partners transfer $3,000 to his account from each of theirs. A 20% interest allowance (on the beginning-of-year capital balances) will be used in sharing profits, but there will be no salaries. Elway will get 40% of the remainder, and the other three partners will each get 20%.
Dec. 31/02	Elway & Associates earns $127,600 for the year, and these withdrawals occur: Bax, $25,000; Royce, $27,000; Murdock, $15,000; and Elway, $40,000.
Jan. 1/03	Elway buys out Bax and Royce for the balances of their capital accounts, after a revaluation[5] of the partnership assets. The revaluation gain is $50,000, which is divided in the previous 1:1:1:2 ratio. Elway pays the others from personal funds. Murdock and Elway will share profits on a 1:9 ratio.
Feb. 29/03	The partnership had $10,000 of income since the beginning of the year. Murdock retires and receives partnership cash equal to her capital balance. Elway takes possession of the partnership assets in his own name, and the business is dissolved.

Part 2

Journalize the events affecting the partnership for the year ended December 31, 2000.

Planning the Solution

- Evaluate each transaction's effects on the capital accounts of the partners.
- Each time a new partner is admitted or a partner withdraws, allocate any bonus based on the income or loss sharing agreement.
- Each time a new partner is admitted or a partner withdraws, allocate subsequent net incomes or losses in accordance with the new partnership agreement.
- Make an entry to record Royce's initial investment. Make an entry to record the allocation of interest, salaries, and remainders for December 31/00. Make an entry to show the cash withdrawals from the partnership on December 31/00. Make an entry to close the withdrawal accounts on December 31/00.

---

[5] A revaluation is a determination of the fair value of the partnership assets.

Solution to Problem

Part 1

Event	Ries	Bax	Royce	Murdock	Elway	Total
Apr. 14/99						
Initial investment	$10,000	$10,000				$ 20,000
Dec. 31/99						
Income (equal)	7,500	7,500				15,000
Withdrawals	(4,000)	(7,000)				(11,000)
Ending balance	$13,500	$10,500				$ 24,000
Jan. 1/00						
New investment			$12,000			12,000
Dec. 31/00						
10% interest	1,350	1,050	1,200			3,600
Salaries		5,000	5,000			10,000
Remainder (equal)	8,800	8,800	8,800			26,400
Withdrawals	(5,000)	(12,500)	(11,000)			(28,500)
Ending balance	$18,650	$12,850	$16,000			$ 47,500
Jan. 1/01						
Transfer interest	(18,650)			$18,650		-0-
Dec. 31/01						
Salaries		25,000	25,000			50,000
Remainder (equal)		(5,000)	(5,000)	(5,000)		(15,000)
Withdrawals		(2,500)	(2,000)			(4,500)
Ending balance	$ -0-	$30,350	$34,000	$13,650		$ 78,000
Jan. 1/02						
New investment					$ 60,000	60,000
Bonuses to Elway		(3,000)	(3,000)	(3,000)	9,000	-0-
Adjusted balance		$27,350	$31,000	$10,650	$ 69,000	$138,000
Dec. 31/02						
20% interest		5,470	6,200	2,130	13,800	27,600
Remain. (1:1:1:2)		20,000	20,000	20,000	40,000	100,000
Withdrawals		(25,000)	(27,000)	(15,000)	(40,000)	(107,000)
Ending balance		$27,820	$30,200	$17,780	$ 82,800	$158,600
Jan. 1/03						
Gain (1:1:1:2)		10,000	10,000	10,000	20,000	50,000
Adjusted balance		$37,820	$40,200	$27,780	$102,800	$208,600
Transfer interests		(37,820)	(40,200)		78,020	-0-
Adjusted balance		$ -0-	$ -0-	$27,780	$180,820	$208,600
Feb. 29/03						
Income (1:9)				1,000	9,000	10,000
Adjusted balance				$28,780	$189,820	$218,600
Settlements				(28,780)	(189,820)	(218,600)
Final balance				$ -0-	$ -0-	$ -0-

Part 2

2000			
Jan. 1	Cash	12,000	
	Royce, Capital		12,000
	To record investment of Royce.		
Dec. 31	Income Summary	40,000	
	Ries, Capital		10,150
	Bax, Capital		14,850
	Royce, Capital		15,000
	To allocate interest, salaries, and remainders.		
Dec. 31	Ries, Withdrawals	5,000	
	Bax, Withdrawals	12,500	
	Royce, Withdrawals	11,000	
	Cash		28,500
	To record the cash withdrawals by the partners.		
Dec. 31	Ries, Capital	5,000	
	Bax, Capital	12,500	
	Royce, Capital	11,000	
	Ries, Withdrawals		5,000
	Bax, Withdrawals		12,500
	Royce, Withdrawals		11,000
	To close the withdrawal accounts.		

Glossary

General partner A partner who assumes unlimited liability for the debts of the partnership; also, the general partner in a limited partnership is responsible for its management. (p. 664)

General partnership A partnership in which all partners have mutual agency and unlimited liability for partnership debts. (p. 664)

Limited partners Partners who have no personal liability for debts of the partnership beyond the amounts they have invested in the partnership. (p. 664)

Limited partnership A partnership that has two classes of partners, limited partners and general partners. (p. 664)

Mutual agency The legal relationship among the partners whereby each partner is an agent of the partnership and is able to bind the partnership to contracts within the apparent scope of the partnership's business. (p. 663)

Partnership An unincorporated association of two or more persons to pursue a business for profit as co-owners. (p. 662)

Partnership contract The agreement between partners that sets forth the terms under which the affairs of the partnership will be conducted. (p. 662)

Partnership liquidation The dissolution of a business partnership by (1) selling noncash assets for cash and allocating the gain or loss according to partners' income-and-loss ratio, (2) paying liabilities, and (3) distributing remaining cash to partners based on capital balances. (p. 673)

Statement of changes in partners' equity Shows the capital balances at the beginning of the period, any additional investments made by partners, the income or loss of the partnership, withdrawals by partners, and the capital balances. (p. 668)

Unlimited liability of partners The legal relationship among general partners that makes each of them responsible for paying all the debts of the partnership if the other partners are unable to pay their shares. (p. 664)

Questions

1. Amey and Lacey are partners. Lacey dies, and her son claims the right to take his mother's place in the partnership. Does he have this right? Why?
2. If a partnership contract does not state the period of time the partnership is to exist, when does the partnership end?
3. As applied to a partnership, what does the term mutual agency mean?
4. Can partners limit the right of a partner to commit their partnership to contracts? Would the agreement be binding (a) on the partners and (b) on outsiders?
5. What does the term unlimited liability mean when it is applied to members of a partnership?
6. How does a general partnership differ from a limited partnership?
7. George, Burton, and Dillman have been partners for three years. The partnership is being dissolved. George is leaving the firm, but Burton and Dillman plan to carry on the business. In the final settlement, George places a $75,000 salary claim against the partnership. He contends that he has a claim for a salary of $25,000 for each year because he devoted all of his time for three years to the affairs of the partnership. Is his claim valid? Why?
8. The partnership agreement of Jenny Nelmida and Fei Abella provides for a two-thirds, one-third sharing of income but says nothing about losses. The first year of partnership operations resulted in a loss and Nelmida argues that the loss should be shared equally because the partnership agreement said nothing about sharing losses. What do you think?
9. If the partners in Blume Partnership want the financial statements to show the procedures used to allocate the partnership income among the partners, on what financial statement should the allocation appear?
10. After all partnership assets are converted to cash and all liabilities have been paid, the remaining cash should equal the sum of the balances of the partners' capital accounts. Why?
11. Kay, Kat, and Kim are partners. In a liquidation, Kay's share of partnership losses exceeds her capital account balance. She is unable to meet the deficit from her personal assets, and the excess losses are shared by her partners. Does this relieve Kay of liability?
12. A partner withdraws from a partnership and receives assets of greater value than the book value of his equity. Should the remaining partners share the resulting reduction in their equities in the ratio of their relative capital balances or in their income-and-loss-sharing ratio?

Quick Study

QS 14-1
Partnership liability
LO 1

Kurt and Ellen are partners in operating a store. Without consulting Kurt, Ellen enters into a contract for the purchase of merchandise for the store. Kurt contends that he did not authorize the order and refuses to take delivery. The vendor sues the partners for the contract price of the merchandise. Will the partnership have to pay? Why? Does your answer differ if Kurt and Ellen are partners in a public accounting firm?

QS 14-2
Liability in limited partnerships
LO 1

Furst organized a limited partnership and is the only general partner. Nexx invested $20,000 in the partnership and was admitted as a limited partner with the understanding that he would receive 10% of the profits. After two unprofitable years, the partnership ceased doing business. At that point, partnership liabilities were $85,000 larger than partnership assets. How much money can the creditors of the partnership obtain from the personal assets of Nexx in satisfaction of the unpaid partnership debts?

QS 14-3
Partnership income allocation
LO 2

Ace and Bud are partners who agree that Ace will receive a $50,000 salary allowance after which remaining incomes or losses will be shared equally. If Bud's capital account is credited $1,000 as his share of the remaining net income in a given period, how much net income did the partnership earn?

QS 14-4
Partnership income allocation
LO 2

Roger Bussey and Art Beery are partners in a business they started two years ago. The partnership agreement states that Bussey should receive a salary allowance of $30,000 and that Beery should receive $40,000. Any remaining income or loss is to be shared equally. Determine each partner's share of the current year's net income of $104,000.

QS 14-5
Admission of a partner
LO 4

Logan and Smythe are partners, each with $30,000 in their partnership capital accounts. Fontaine is admitted to the partnership by an investment of $30,000. Make the entry to show Fontaine's admission to the partnership.

QS 14-6
Partner admission through purchase of interest
LO 4

Fontaine agrees to pay Logan and Smythe $10,000 each for a one-third ($33\frac{1}{3}\%$) interest in the Logan-Smythe partnership. At the time Fontaine is admitted each partner has a $30,000 capital balance. Make the journal entry to record Fontaine's purchase of the partners' interest.

Exercises

Exercise 14-1
Forms of organization
LO 1, 6

For each scenario below recommend a form of business organization. Along with each recommendation explain how business profits would be taxed if the form of organization recommended is adopted by the owners. Also list several advantages that the owners will enjoy from the form of business organization that you recommend.

1. Keith, Scott, and Brian are new college graduates in computer science. They are thinking of starting a Web-page creation company. They all have quite a few college debts and currently do not own any of the computer equipment that they will need to get the company started.
2. Dr. Marble and Dr. Sampson are new graduates from medical residency programs. They are both family practice physicians and would like to open a clinic in an underserved rural area. Although neither has any funds to bring to the new venture a banker has expressed interest in making a loan to provide start-up funds for the practice.
3. Matthew has been out of school for about five years and has become quite knowledgeable about the commercial real estate market. Matthew would like to organize a company that buys and sells real estate. Matthew feels like he has the expertise to manage the company but needs funds to invest in the commercial property.

Exercise 14-2
Journalizing partnership entries
LO 2, 3

On March 1, 1998, Reed and Vaughn formed a partnership in the province of Ontario. Reed contributed $88,000 cash and Vaughn contributed land valued at $70,000 and a building valued at $120,000. Also, the partnership assumed responsibility for Vaughn's $80,000 long-term note payable associated with the land and building. The partners agreed to share profits as follows: Reed is to receive an annual salary allowance of $30,000, both are to receive an annual interest allowance of 10% of their original capital investment, and any remaining profit or loss is to be shared equally. On October 20, 1998, Reed withdrew cash of $32,000 and Vaughn withdrew $25,000. After the adjusting entries and the closing entries to the revenue and expense accounts, the Income Summary account had a credit balance of $79,000. Present general journal entries to record the initial capital investments of the partners, their cash withdrawals, and the December 31 closing of the income summary and withdrawals accounts. Finally, determine the balances of the partners' capital accounts as of the end of 1998.

Exercise 14-3
Income allocation in a partnership
LO 3

Newton and Berry began a partnership by investing $50,000 and $75,000, respectively. During its first year, the partnership earned $165,000.

Required

Prepare calculations showing how the income should be allocated to the partners under each of the following plans for sharing net incomes and losses:

a. The partners failed to agree on a method of sharing income.
b. The partners agreed to share incomes and losses in proportion to their initial investments.
c. The partners agreed to share income by allowing a $55,000 per year salary allowance to Newton, a $45,000 per year salary allowance to Berry, 10% interest on their initial investments, and the balance equally.

Exercise 14-4
Income allocation in a partnership
LO 3

Assume that the partners of Exercise 14-3 agreed to share net incomes and losses by allowing yearly salary allowances of $55,000 to Newton and $45,000 to Berry, 10% interest allowances on their investments, and the balance equally. (a) Determine the shares of Newton and Berry in a first-year net income of $94,400. (b) Determine the partners' shares in a first-year net loss of $15,700.

Exercise 14-5
Sale of a partnership interest
LO 4

The partners in the Royal Partnership have agreed that partner Prince may sell his $90,000 equity in the partnership to Duke, for which Duke will pay Prince $75,000. Present the partnership's journal entry to record the sale on September 30.

Exercise 14-6
Admission of a new partner
LO 4

The E-O Partnership has total partners' equity of $510,000, which is made up of Elm, Capital, $400,000, and Oak, Capital, $110,000. The partners share net incomes and losses in a ratio of 80% to Elm and 20% to Oak. On November 1, Ash is admitted to the partnership and given a 15% interest in equity and incomes and losses. Prepare the journal entry to record the entry of Ash under each of the following unrelated assumptions: Ash invests cash of (a) $90,000, (b) $125,000, and (c) $60,000.

Exercise 14-7
Retirement of a partner
LO 4

Holland, Flowers, and Wood have been partners sharing net incomes and losses in a 5:3:2 ratio. On January 31, the date Wood retires from the partnership, the equities of the partners are Holland, $350,000; Flowers, $240,000; and Wood, $180,000. Present general journal entries to record Wood's retirement under each of the following unrelated assumptions:

a. Wood is paid $180,000 in partnership cash for his equity.
b. Wood is paid $200,000 in partnership cash for his equity.
c. Wood is paid $150,000 in partnership cash for his equity.

Exercise 14-8
Liquidation of a partnership
LO 5

The Red, White & Blue partnership was begun with investments by the partners as follows: Red, $175,000; White, $220,000; and Blue, $205,000. The first year of operations did not go well, and the partners finally decided to liquidate the partnership, sharing all losses equally. On August 31, after all assets were converted to cash and all creditors were paid, only $60,000 in partnership cash remained.

Required

1. Calculate the capital account balances of the partners after the liquidation of assets and payment of creditors.
2. Assume that any partner with a deficit pays cash to the partnership to cover the deficit. Then, present the general journal entries on August 31 to record the cash receipt from the deficient partner(s) and the final disbursement of cash to the partners.
3. Now make the contrary assumption that any partner with a deficit is not able to reimburse the partnership. Present journal entries (a) to transfer the deficit of any deficient partners to the other partners and (b) to record the final disbursement of cash to the partners.

Exercise 14-9
Liquidation of a partnership
LO 5

Sandburg, McArthur, and Cox are partners who share incomes and losses in a 1:4:5 ratio. After lengthy disagreements among the partners and several unprofitable periods, the partners decided to liquidate the partnership. Before the liquidation, the partnership balance sheet showed total assets, $116,000; total liabilities, $88,000; Sandburg, Capital, $1,200; McArthur, Capital, $11,700; and Cox, Capital, $15,100. The cash proceeds from selling the assets were sufficient to repay all but $24,000 to the creditors. Calculate the loss from selling the assets, allocate the loss to the partners, and determine how much of the remaining liability should be paid by each partner.

Exercise 14-10
Liquidation of a limited partnership
LO 5

Assume that the Sandburg, McArthur, and Cox partnership of Exercise 14-9 is a limited partnership. Sandburg and McArthur are general partners and Cox is a limited partner. How much of the remaining $24,000 liability should be paid by each partner?

Problems

Problem 14-1
Methods of allocating partnership income
LO 3

Tom Katz, Kaye Reeves, and Alice Troy invested $40,000, $56,000, and $64,000, respectively, in a partnership. During its first year, the firm earned $124,500.

Required

Prepare entries to close the firm's Income Summary account as of December 31 and to allocate the net income to the partners under each of the following assumptions:

a. The partners did not produce any special agreement on the method of sharing incomes.

b. The partners agreed to share net incomes and losses in the ratio of their beginning investments.

c. The partners agreed to share income by providing annual salary allowances of $33,000 to Katz, $28,000 to Reeves, and $40,000 to Troy; allowing 10% interest on the partners' beginning investments; and sharing the remainder equally.

Problem 14-2
Allocating partnership incomes and losses; sequential years
LO 3

Linda Nuñez and Ray Parker are in the process of forming a partnership to which Nuñez will devote one-half time and Parker will devote full time. They have discussed the following alternative plans for sharing net incomes and losses.

a. In the ratio of their initial investments, which they have agreed will be $21,000 for Nuñez and $31,500 for Parker.

b. In proportion to the time devoted to the business.

c. A salary allowance of $3,000 per month to Parker and the balance in accordance with their investment ratio.

d. A $3,000 per month salary allowance to Parker, 10% interest on their initial investments, and the balance equally.

The partners expect the business to generate income as follows: Year 1, $18,000 net loss; Year 2, $45,000 net income; and Year 3, $75,000 net income.

Required

1. Prepare three schedules with the following column headings:

Income/ Loss Sharing Plan	Year______ Calculations	Nuñez	Parker

2. Complete a schedule for each of the first three years by showing how the partnership net income or loss for each year would be allocated to the partners under each of the four plans being considered. Round your answers to the nearest whole dollar

Problem 14-3
Partnership income allocation, statement of changes in partners' equity, and closing entries
LO 2, 3

Brad Marshall, Jon Spiller, and Leigh Rand formed the MSR Partnership by making capital contributions of $183,750, $131,250, and $210,000, respectively. They anticipate annual net incomes of $225,000 and are considering the following alternative plans of sharing net incomes and losses: (a) equally; (b) in the ratio of their initial investments; or (c) salary allowances of $40,000 to Marshall, $30,000 to Spiller, and $45,000 to Rand; interest allowances of 10% on initial investments, with any remaining balance shared equally.

Required

1. Prepare a schedule with the following column headings:

Income/Loss Sharing Plan Totals	Calculations	Share to Marshall	Share to Spiller	Share to Rand

Use the schedule to show how a net income of $225,000 would be distributed under each of the alternative plans being considered. Round your answers to the nearest whole dollar.

2. Prepare a statement of changes in partners' equity showing the allocation of income to the partners, assuming they agree to use alternative (c) and the net income earned is $105,000. During the year, Marshall, Spiller, and Rand withdraw $17,000, $24,000, and $32,000, respectively.
3. Prepare the December 31 journal entry to close Income Summary assuming they agree to use alternative (c) and the net income is $105,000. Also, close the withdrawals accounts.

Problem 14-4
Withdrawal of a partner
LO 4

Part 1. Godfrey, Gully, and Speck are partners with capital balances as follows: Godfrey, $84,000; Gully, $69,000; and Speck, $147,000. The partners share incomes and losses in a 3:2:5 ratio. Gully decides to withdraw from the partnership, and the partners agree to not have the assets revalued upon his retirement. Prepare general journal entries to record the February 1 withdrawal of Gully from the partnership under each of the following unrelated assumptions:

a. Gully sells his interest to Goldman for $80,000 after Godfrey and Speck approve the entry of Goldman as a partner.
b. Gully gives his interest to a son-in-law, Spain. Godfrey and Speck accept Spain as a partner.
c. Gully is paid $69,000 in partnership cash for his equity.
d. Gully is paid $107,000 in partnership cash for his equity.
e. Gully is paid $15,000 in partnership cash plus computer equipment that is recorded on the partnership books at $35,000 less accumulated amortization of $11,600.

Part 2. Assume that Gully does not retire from the partnership described in Part 1. Instead, Hatch is admitted to the partnership on February 1 with a 25% equity. Prepare general journal entries to record the entry of Hatch into the partnership under each of the following unrelated assumptions:

a. Hatch invests $100,000.
b. Hatch invests $72,500.
c. Hatch invests $131,000.

Problem 14-5
Liquidation of a partnership
LO 5

Swanson, Chapel, and Page plan to liquidate their partnership. They have always shared losses and gains in a 3:2:1 ratio, and on the day of the liquidation their balance sheet appeared as follows:

SWANSON, CHAPEL, AND PAGE
Balance Sheet
May 31, 19XX

Assets		Liabilities and Owners' Equity	
Cash	$ 90,400	Accounts payable	$122,750
Inventory	268,600	David Swanson, capital	46,500
		Annie Chapel, capital	106,250
		Maria Page, capital	83,500
Total assets	$359,000	Total liabilities and owners' equity	$359,000

Required

Under the assumption the inventory is sold and the cash is distributed to the proper parties on May 31, prepare the general journal entries for the sale, the gain or loss allocation, and the distribution of the cash in each of the following unrelated cases:

a. The inventory is sold for $300,000.
b. The inventory is sold for $250,000.
c. The inventory is sold for $160,000, and any partners with resulting deficits can and do pay in the amount of their deficits.
d. The inventory is sold for $125,000, and the partners have no assets other than those invested in the business.

Problem 14-6
Withdrawal of a partner
LO 3

Until November 16, 1999, Rohan, Kovak, and Keene were partners that shared incomes and losses in the ratio of their beginning-of-year capital account balances. On November 16, Rohan suffered a heart attack and died. Kovak and Keene immediately ended the business operations and prepared the following adjusted trail balance:

ROHAN, KOVAK, AND KEENE
Adjusted Trial Balance
November 16, 1999

Cash	$ 10,625	
Accounts receivable	30,415	
Allowance for doubtful accounts		$ 1,115
Supplies inventory	46,875	
Equipment	148,860	
Accumulated amortization, equipment		14,842
Building	227,325	
Accumulated amortization, building		56,850
Land	14,800	
Accounts payable		22,688
Note payable (secured by mortgage)		37,005
Tracy Rohan, capital		141,040
Tracy Rohan, withdrawals	5,700	
Jackie Kovak, capital		141,040
Jackie Kovak, withdrawals	5,700	
Kerry Keene, capital		70,520
Kerry Keene, withdrawals	16,200	
Services revenue		75,150
Operating expense	53,750	
Totals	$560,250	$560,250

Required

1. Prepare the November 16 general journal entries to close the revenue, expense, income summary, and withdrawals accounts of the partnership.
2. Assume the estate of Rohan agreed to accept the land and building and to assume the mortgage note thereon on settlement of its claim against the partnership assets, and that Kovak and Keene planned to continue the business and rent the building from the estate. Prepare the partnership's December 1 general journal entry to transfer the land, building, and mortgage note in settlement with the estate.
3. Assume that, instead of the foregoing, the estate of Rohan demanded a cash settlement and the business had to be sold to a competitor, who gave $298,000 for the noncash assets and assumed the mortgage note but not the accounts payable. Prepare the December 1 general journal entry to transfer the noncash assets and mortgage note to the competitor, and the entries to allocate the gain or loss to the partners and to distribute the partnership cash.

Problem 14-7
Analytical essay
LO 2

Janet Koppen and Beverly Spikes want to form a partnership and are considering two methods of sharing incomes and losses. Method *a* splits all incomes and losses in a 2:3 ratio, or 40% to Koppen and 60% to Spikes. Method *b* depends on the income or loss of the partnership. If the partnership incurs a loss, the partners share it equally. If the income is in the range of $0 to $45,000, it is allocated based on an annual salary allowance of $15,000 to Koppen and $30,000 to Spikes. If the net income exceeds $45,000, the residual after the salary allowances is shared equally.

Koppen has retained you to write an evaluation of the two methods, indicating which is more favourable to her. Your discussion should include a comparison of the two methods at each of the three possible net income levels. Also discuss the importance of asking Koppen to estimate the partnership's future earnings.

Problem 14-8
Analytical essay
LO 3

Guido, DeVito, and Vanelli have been operating a successful partnership for several years. Even though business is good, DeVito and Vanelli have disagreed with Guido on several occasions regarding the business, and Guido is now withdrawing from the partnership. The partners agree that the book values of the assets are less than their market values. However, they do not want to change the recorded values at this time. As a result, the partners have agreed that Guido should withdraw cash in an amount greater than his capital account balance.

DeVito and Vanelli are not sure how to calculate the adjustments to their capital accounts (brought about by the difference between Guido's equity and the cash he is withdrawing). DeVito thinks they should split the difference in the ratio of their capital account balances. Vanelli thinks the adjustments should be calculated using their original income-and-loss-sharing ratio. Which partner do you think is correct? Explain the reasons for your answers.

Alternate Problems

Problem 14-1A
Methods of allocating partnership income
LO 2

Paul Jones, Will Rogers, and Anne Thompson invested $82,000, $49,200, and $32,800, respectively, in a partnership. During its first year, the firm earned $135,000.

Required

Prepare entries to close the firm's Income Summary account as of December 31 and to allocate the net income to the partners under each of the following assumptions. (Round your answers to the nearest whole dollar.)

a. The partners did not specify any special method of sharing incomes.
b. The partners agreed to share net incomes and losses in the ratio of their beginning investments.
c. The partners agreed to share income by providing annual salary allowances of $48,000 to Jones, $36,000 to Rogers, and $25,000 to Thompson, allowing 10% interest on the partners' beginning investments and sharing the remainder equally.

Problem 14-2A
Allocating partnership incomes and losses, sequential years
LO 3

Jacob Jackson and K. D. Fletcher are in the process of forming a partnership to which Jackson will devote one-third time and Fletcher will devote full time. They have discussed the following alternative plans for sharing net incomes and losses.

a. In the ratio of their initial investments, which they have agreed will be $52,000 for Jackson and $78,000 for Fletcher.
b. In proportion to the time devoted to the business.
c. A salary allowance of $2,000 per month to Fletcher and the balance in accordance with their initial investment ratio.
d. A $2,000 per month salary allowance to Fletcher, 10% interest on their initial investments, and the balance equally.

The partners expect the business to generate income as follows: Year 1, $18,000 net loss; Year 2, $38,000 net income; and Year 3, $94,000 net income.

Required

1. Prepare three schedules with the following column headings:

Income/ Loss Sharing Plan	Year ______		
	Calculations	Jackson	Fletcher

2. Complete a schedule for each of the first three years by showing how the partnership income or loss for each year would be allocated to the partners under each of the four plans being considered. Round your answers to the nearest whole dollar.

Problem 14-3A
Partnership income allocation, statement of changes in partners' equity, and closing entries
LO 2

Ella Phillips, Chet Fong, and Lou Campos formed the PFC Partnership by making capital contributions of $72,000, $108,000, and $60,000, respectively. They anticipate annual net incomes of $120,000 and are considering the following alternative plans of sharing net incomes and losses: (a) equally, (b) in the ratio of their initial investments, or (c) salary allowances of $20,000 to Phillips, $15,000 to Fong, and $40,000 to Campos; interest allowances of 12% on initial investments, with any remaining balance shared equally.

Required

1. Prepare a schedule with the following column headings:

Inc./Loss Sharing Plan	Calculations	Share to Phillips	Share to Fong	Share to Campos	Totals

Use the schedule to show how a net income of $120,000 would be distributed under each of the alternative plans being considered. Round your answers to the nearest whole dollar.

2. Prepare a statement of changes in partners' equity showing the allocation of income to the partners, assuming they agree to use alternative (c) and the net income actually earned is $55,000. During the year, Phillips, Fong, and Campos withdrew $9,000, $19,000, and $12,000, respectively.

3. Prepare the December 31 journal entry to close Income Summary assuming they agree to use alternative (c) and the net income is $55,000. Also, close the withdrawals accounts.

Problem 14-4A
Withdrawal of a partner
LO 4

Part 1. Soltani, Sugimoto and Suza are partners with capital balances as follows: Soltani, $303,000; Sugimoto, $74,000; and Suza, $223,000. The partners share incomes and losses in a 5:1:4 ratio. Soltani decides to withdraw from the partnership, and the partners agree to not have the assets revalued upon her retirement. Prepare general journal entries to record the April 30 withdrawal of Soltani from the partnership under each of the following unrelated assumptions:

a. Soltani sells her interest to Samba for $250,000 after Sugimoto and Suza approve the entry of Samba as a partner.

b. Soltani gives her interest to a daughter-in-law, Shulak. Sugimoto and Suza accept Shulak as a partner.

c. Soltani is paid $303,000 in partnership cash for her equity.

d. Soltani is paid $175,000 in partnership cash for her equity.

e. Soltani is paid $100,000 in partnership cash plus manufacturing equipment recorded on the partnership books at $269,000 less accumulated amortization of $168,000.

Part 2. Assume that Soltani does not retire from the partnership described in Part 1. Instead, Sung is admitted to the partnership on April 30 with a 20% equity. Prepare general journal entries to record the entry of Sung under each of the following unrelated assumptions:

a. Sung invests $150,000.

b. Sung invests $98,000.

c. Sung invests $213,000.

Problem 14-5A
Liquidation of a partnership
LO 5

Huggins, Hart, and Love, who have always shared incomes and losses in a 2:1:2 ratio, plan to liquidate their partnership. Just prior to the liquidation their balance sheet appeared as follows:

HUGGINS, HART, AND LOVE
Balance Sheet
January 18, 19XX

Assets		Liabilities and Owner's Equity	
Cash	$174,300	Accounts payable	$171,300
Equipment	308,600	C. J. Huggins, capital.	150,200
		D. C. Hart, capital	97,900
		J. D. Love, capital	63,500
Total assets	$482,900	Total liabilities and owners' equity	$482,900

Required

Under the assumption the equipment is sold and the cash is distributed to the proper parties on January 18, prepare general journal entries for the sale, the gain or loss allocation, and the distribution of cash in each of the following unrelated cases:

a. The equipment is sold for $325,000.
b. The equipment is sold for $265,000.
c. The equipment is sold for $100,000, and any partners with resulting deficits can and do pay in the amount of their deficits.
d. The equipment is sold for $75,000, and the partners have no assets other than those invested in the business.

Problem 14-6A
Withdrawal of a partner
LO 3

Until July 3, 1999, Daily, Murray, and Dryer were partners that shared incomes and losses in the ratio of their beginning-of-year capital account balances. On July 3, Murray suffered a heart attack and died. Daily and Dryer immediately terminated the partnership and prepared the following adjusted trail balance.

DAILY, MURRAY, AND DRYER
Adjusted Trial Balance
July, 3 1999

Cash	$31,418	
Accounts receivable	18,322	
Allowance for doubtful accounts		$725
Supplies inventory	54,910	
Equipment	110,660	
Accumulated amortization, equipment		15,808
Building	303,300	
Accumulated amortization, building		68,390
Land	27,400	
Accounts payable		25,975
Note payable (secured by mortgage)		64,012
Jess Daily, capital		164,800
Jess Daily, withdrawals	21,700	
Mel Murray, capital		206,000
Mel Murray, withdrawals	38,200	
Pat Dryer, capital		41,200
Pat Dryer, withdrawals	10,500	
Services revenue		195,600
Operating expense	166,100	
Totals	$782,510	$782,510

Required

1. Prepare the July 3 general journal entries to close the revenue, expense, income summary, and withdrawals accounts of the partnership.
2. Assume the estate of Murray agreed to accept the land and building and to assume the mortgage note thereon in settlement of its claim against the partnership assets, and that Daily and Dryer planned to continue the business and rent the building from the estate. Prepare the partnership's July 16 general journal entry to transfer the land, building, and mortgage note in settlement with the estate.
3. Assume that, instead of the foregoing, the estate of Murray demanded a cash settlement and the business had to be sold to a competitor, who gave $350,000 for the noncash assets and assumed the mortgage note but not the accounts payable. Prepare the July 16 general journal entry to transfer the noncash assets and mortgage note to the competitor, and the entries to allocate the gain or loss to the partners and to distribute the partnership cash.

Problem 14-7A
Analytical essay

LO 2

Janet Koppen and Beverly Spikes want to form a partnership and are considering two methods of sharing incomes and losses in a 2:3 ratio, or 40% to Koppen and 60% to Spikes. Method *b* depends on the income or loss of the partnership. If the partnership incurs a loss, the partners share it equally. If the income is in the range of $0 to $45,000, it is allocated based on an annual salary allowance of $15,000 to Koppen and $30,000 to Spikes. If the net income exceeds $45,000, the residual after the salary allowances is shared equally.

Spikes has retained you to write an evaluation of the two methods indicating which is most favourable to her. Your discussion should include a comparison of the two methods at each of the three possible net income levels. Also, discuss the importance of asking Spikes to estimate the partnership's future earnings.

Problem 14-8A
Analytical essay

LO 3

Kay Doobie, Ed Foley, and Brian McKenzie have been operating a partnership for several years. Business has not been good recently, and Doobie is withdrawing from the partnership. The partners agree that the market values of the assets are less than their recorded book values. However, they do not want to change the recorded values at this time. As a result, the partners have agreed that Doobie should withdraw cash in an amount that is less than her capital account balance.

Foley and McKenzie are not sure how to calculate the adjustments to their capital accounts (brought about by the difference between Doobie's equity and the cash she is withdrawing). Foley thinks they should split the difference in the ratio of their capital account balances. McKenzie thinks the adjustments should be calculated using their income-and-loss-sharing ratio. Which partner do you think is correct? Explain why.

Analytical and Review Problems

A & R 14-1

Jay and Mar entered into a partnership to carry on a business under the firm name of Jay-Mar Sportsland. Prior to the final signing of the agreement Jay asks you to evaluate the "income/loss distribution clause" contained in the agreement.

Your examination revealed that the agreement called for the following: equal sharing of net income and losses after an initial allocation of $40,000 to Jay and $10,000 to Mar in order to reflect the difference in time and expertise devoted to the business by each partner. The initial allocation would be made regardless of the level of net income/loss.

Required

Prepare a report to Jay on the particular clause of the agreement. Your report should show the consequence of each partner of operating results as follows: (a) net income of $80,000, (b) net income of $20,000, (c) operation at break-even, that is, no net income or loss, (d) loss of $20,000, and (e) loss of $80,000.

A & R 14-2

The summarized balance sheet of Bell, Trunk, and Field showed:

Assets		Liabilities and Owners' Equity	
Cash	$ 20,000	Accounts payable	$60,000
Other assets	280,000	Bell, capital	80,000
		Trunk, capital	120,000
		Field, capital	40,000
Total assets	$300,000	Total equities	$300,000

The partnership has operated successfully for nearly 25 years, and Field, because of his age and health, is pushing for sale of the business. In fact, he has found Arn, a buyer who is willing to pay $320,000 cash and take over the liabilities. Both Bell and Thunk are not anxious to sell what they refer to as "our little gold mine." Field is adamant about getting out and has proposed the following:

1. Either sell to Arn, or Bell and Trunk (a new partnership) should buy out Field at an amount Field would receive if the business were sold to Arn.
2. Admit Arn to the partnership upon the purchase of Field's share for an amount Field and Arn will negotiate.

The present partnership calls for a distribution of net income/loss on a 3:5:2 basis. If Arn is admitted to partnership the ratio would not change; he would be entitled to Field's 20% share of net income/loss. If Bell and Trunk buy out for an amount based on the Arn offer, Bell and Trunk would continue to share net income/loss on the same relative basis. They would (the new partnership of Bell and Trunk) have to borrow sufficient funds from the bank to retain a minimum cash balance of $10,000.

Required

1. Prepare the general journal entry for admission of Arn to the partnership upon his purchase of Field's interest for an undisclosed amount.
2. Prepare the necessary entries to record Field's withdrawal from the partnership. The amount paid to Field is equal to the amount he would have received if the partnership were sold to Arn.

A & R 14-3
The Med Mart
LO 3

Martha Emerson and Florence Knight are partners who own and operate The Med Mart, a medical supply store. Emerson's recorded equity in the business is $129,000 and Knight's recorded equity is $69,000. They share incomes and losses by allowing annual salary allowances of $55,000 to Emerson and $30,000 to Knight, with any remaining balance being shared 70% to Emerson and 30% to Knight.

Gail Emerson, Martha Emerson's daughter, has been working in the store on a salary basis. In addition to working in the store, Gail is a registered nurse and works part-time at a nearby hospital. Because Gail is well known and liked by many of the doctors, nurses, and other employees at the hospital, she attracts a great deal of business to the store. The partners believe that at least one-third of the three years' sales can be traced directly to Gail's association with the store, and it is reasonable to assume she was instrumental in attracting even more.

Gail is paid $2,000 per month, but feels this is not sufficient to induce her to remain with the store as an employee. However, she likes the work and plans to continue in the medical field. What she really wants is to become a partner in the business.

Her mother is anxious for her to remain in the business and proposes the following.

a. That Gail Emerson be admitted to the partnership with a 20% equity in the net assets.
b. That she, Martha Emerson, transfer from her capital account to Gail's capital account one-half of the 20% interest; that Martha contribute cash to the firm for the other half of Gail's interest; and that Gail sign a note to Martha for the amount of cash paid by Martha.
c. That incomes and losses be shared by continuing the $55,000 and $30,000 salary allowance to the original partners and that Gail be given a $24,000 salary allowance, after which any remaining income or loss will be shared 50% to Martha Emerson, 30% to Florence Knight, and 20% to Gail Emerson.

Required

1. Prepare a schedule showing the partners' capital balances both before and immediately after Gail's admission to the partnership.
2. Assume the net incomes for the past three years were $87,600, $91,200, and $95,400, respectively. Prepare one schedule showing how net income was allocated during the past three years, and a second schedule showing how net income would have been allocated if Martha's proposal had been in effect all three years.
3. Describe how the admission of Gail would effect Florence's equity and share in future profits, and how the partnership might benefit from Gail's admission.

BEYOND THE NUMBERS

Ethics Challenge
LO 2

Paul, Frank and Basil formed a partnership 10 years ago and Paul is about to retire. Paul is not financially minded but he knows that he is entitled to one-third of partnership assets upon his retirement. Total assets have a book value of $900,000 and Paul feels that he is entitled to his share. Frank and Basil are aware that the market value of the firm's net assets approximates $1,500,000. Frank and Basil plan to form a new partnership.

Required

What are the financial and ethical implications of distributing $300,000 to Paul upon his retirement?

Communicating in Practice

LO 1, 3, 4

Your friend, Oliver Lung, recently completed his second year in his own business. Oliver's business is growing rapidly and he needs an infusion of funds to help finance the expansion. Oliver tells you about his friend Mary who has access to funds and is a creative individual with whom Oliver gets along very well. Oliver is considering offering Mary a piece of the business and forming a business partnership. Oliver says, "Mary and I go way back and are close friends so I don't think we need any formal written partnership agreement."

Required

Write a memo to your friend Oliver to explain the purpose of a partnership. Comment on why a written agreement is essential and what matters should be included in the agreement.

Taking It to the Net

LO 3

Visit the Edgar Web site (**http://www.sec.gov**). Search the Web site using the search word "Celtics." View the 1997 10K report filed by the Boston Celtic's partnership with the SEC. Answer the following questions:

1. What were the primary sources of revenue for the Celtics for the fiscal year ended June 30, 1997?
2. What was the net income for the limited partnership for the fiscal year ended June 30, 1997.
3. Trace the net income earned to the Statement of Partners' Capital.
4. Trace the ending capital shown on the Statement of Partners' Capital to the Balance Sheet as of June 30, 1997.

Teamwork in Action

LO 4

This activity is designed to reinforce team member's understanding of the partnership form of business.

A. A partnership is a form of multiple ownership. For legal and tax purposes no entity is recognized. Each group should consider how the entity concept relates to partnerships.

B. Creditors of a partnership may sue the partnership *jointly* or *severally*. Each group should discuss what is meant by these terms and be prepared to explain their understanding to the class.

C. Can a partner avoid paying income taxes by not withdrawing income the partnership? Each group should discuss this issue and be prepared to present their conclusion to the class.

Hitting the Road

LO 1, 5

Identify three partnership enterprises operating in your province or territory. Contact these businesses and ask how many partners comprise the partnership. Did any partners withdraw from the partnerships during the past year and did any new partners enter the partnership?

Business Break

LO 1

The effort involved in identifying the right partner is effort well spent. It can mean avoiding delays, misunderstanding, and the break-up of your relationship because of inability to get along. In the end, there is no substitute for the intensive screening of partners. Unless you are successful in finding a partner who is compatible and trustworthy, and someone with whom you can get along, you are likely better off looking for an alternative form of business ownership.

Required

The Canadian Management Network Internet site known as Strategis contain an interesting article about business partnership. The article is called *Business Turning Points: Finding A Partner*. The strategis Web site can be found at **http://strategis.ic.gc.ca**. The publication date of this article is September 22, 1997. Search for this article and answer the following questions:

a. According to this article what qualities should you look for in a good partner?

b. What qualities should you keep in mind that are indicative of poor partners?

15

CHAPTER

Corporations

A Look Back

Chapter 14 focused on partnerships. We explained the basic characteristics of partnerships and showed how to account for the division of partnership income, the admission and withdrawal of partners, and partnership liquidation.

A Look at This Chapter

This chapter explains the corporate form of organization. Important characteristics of the corporate form of organization are described along with the accounting for important transactions.

A Look Forward

Chapter 16 extends our discussion of corporate accounting to dividends and other equity transactions. We also explain how income, earnings per share, and retained earnings are reported.

Chapter Outline

- **Corporate Form of Organization**
  - Characteristics of Corporations
  - Organizing a Corporation
  - Management of a Corporation
  - Rights of Shareholders
  - Shares of a Corporation
  - Basics of Capital Stock
  - Shareholders' Equity
- **Common Shares**
  - Issuing Shares
  - Issuing Shares through Subscriptions
- **Preferred shares**
  - Issuing Preferred Shares
  - Dividend Preference
  - Convertible Preferred Shares
  - Callable Preferred Shares
  - Motivation for Preferred Shares
- **Using the Information—Book Value per Share**

Go for It

Toronto, ON—Jennifer Wong's business venture into block print cotton T-shirts is a model success story. Each product is individually hand block printed with evocative designs and symbols, and signed by the artist. After a successful first year Jennifer obtained funding from her parents and formed a partnership with her friend Malu Baltazar. Sales took off and additional funds were needed to meet the growing market demand. To complicate matters Malu had to leave the partnership for personal reasons. Malu's departure stripped the business of badly needed funds.

To finance growth of her company, Wong decided to incorporate and sold common shares to the public. The idea she says is to "sell it to people who had been supporting us so far as customers." The shares were priced at $5 per share. The issuance of shares has raised more than $5 million for working capital and expansion of her business. Wong already has plans for setting up a franchise in Vancouver. If all goes well, the biggest challenge will be "staying in tune with our customers as we grow," says Wong.

Learning Objectives

LO 1 Identify characteristics of corporations and their organization.

LO 2 Describe the components of shareholders' equity.

LO 3 Record the issuance of corporate shares.

LO 4 Explain the characteristics of common and preferred shares.

LO 5 Distribute dividends between common shares and preferred shares.

LO 6 Compute book value and explain its use in analysis.

CHAPTER PREVIEW

There are three common types of business organizations: corporations, partnerships and proprietorships. This chapter explains corporations. While corporations are fewest in number, they transact more business than all others combined. They are very important players in our global economy, with dollar sales at least ten times the combined sales of unincorporated companies. Understanding the advantages and disadvantages of these forms of business organization was important for Jennifer Wong in her T-shirt venture. The opening article revealed her choice to incorporate, but this is not always best. This chapter gives us information to make such a decision.

Corporate Form of Organization

A corporation is an entity that is created by law and is separate from its owners. It has most of the rights and privileges granted to individuals. Owners of corporations are called *shareholders* or *stockholders*. Corporations can be separated into privately held and publicly held corporations. A *privately held* corporation, also called closely held, does not offer its shares for public sale and usually has few shareholders. Most corporations formed in Canada are private corporations. Provincial securities acts generally limit the number of shareholders of private corporations to 50. A *publicly held* corporation offers its shares for public sale and can have thousands of shareholders. Public sale usually refers to trading in an organized stock market such as the Montreal, Toronto, Winnipeg, Alberta or Vancouver stock exchanges.

Characteristics of Corporations

LO1 Identify characteristics of corporations and their organization.

Corporations are important because of advantages created by the unique characteristics of the corporate structure of ownership. We describe these characteristics in this section.

Separate Legal Entity

A corporation is a separate legal entity. As a separate entity, a corporation conducts its affairs with the same rights, duties and responsibilities as a person. A corporation takes actions through its agents, who are its officers and managers.

Limited Liability of Shareholders

Because a corporation is a separate legal entity, it is responsible for its own acts and its own debt. Its shareholders are not liable for either. From the viewpoint of a shareholder, this lack of liability is one of the most important advantages of the corporate form of business. Shareholders invest in the business by contributing cash or other assets in return for ownership rights in the corporation. If the business fails the amount contributed by shareholders is the maximum loss to the shareholders. If there are insufficient assets to pay business creditor claims, creditors have no claim on the shareholders' personal assets. Because shareholder liability is limited to the amount of their investments, corporations are often referred to as limited companies.

Ownership Rights Are Transferable

Ownership of a corporation is by shares of its share capital that are usually easily bought or sold. The transfer of shares from one shareholder to another usually has no effect on the corporation or its operations.[1] Many corporations have

[1] But a transfer of ownership can create significant effects if it brings about a change in who controls the company's activities.

thousands or even millions of their shares bought and sold daily in major stock exchanges throughout the world. For example, it is not uncommon for **NIKE** to trade over 2,000,000 shares in one day.

Continuous Life

A corporation's life can continue indefinitely because it is not tied to the physical lives of its owners. The laws of the legal jurisdiction of its incorporation can sometimes initially limit a corporation's life. But a corporation's charter can be renewed and its life extended when the stated time expires. This means a corporation can have a perpetual life as long as it continues to be successful.

Shareholders Are Not Corporate Agents

A corporation acts through its agents, who are the officers or managers of the corporation. Shareholders who are not officers or managers of the corporation do not have the power to bind the corporation to contracts. This is also referred to as *lack of mutual agency*. Instead, shareholders participate in the affairs of the corporation only by voting in the shareholders' meetings.

Ease of Capital Accumulation

Buying shares in a corporation often is attractive to investors because: (1) shareholders are not liable for the corporation's actions and debts, (2) shares usually are transferred easily, (3) life of the corporation is unlimited, and (4) shareholders are not agents of the corporation. These advantages make it possible for some corporations to accumulate large amounts of capital from the combined investments of many shareholders. A corporation's capacity for raising capital is limited only by its ability to convince investors it can use their funds profitably. **Alcan Aluminum Limited**, for example, a Canadian-based company involved in ventures such bauxite mining, alumina refining, and power generation had by 1996 accumulated roughly $1,235 million from 21,500 shareholders who own 226,620,000 shares.[2]

Governmental Regulation

Corporations must meet requirements of provincial or federal incorporation laws. These laws subject a corporation to governmental regulation and control. Single proprietorships and partnerships escape some of these regulations, and often avoid having to file some governmental reports required of corporations. Private corporations or closely held corporations that restrict the transfer of shares to existing shareholders and refrain from distributing shares to the public, however, are exempt from most of the security and corporate legislation reporting requirements. According to the Canada Business Corporations Act, any company with gross revenues of $10 million or assets exceeding $5 million must make its financial statements public. This applies to both public and private corporations and their financial statements must be prepared according to Canadian generally accepted accounting principles. All public corporations that are registered with one of the provincial securities bodies, depending on which province, must file annual audited financial statements within 140–170 days of their fiscal year-end.

Many Canadian companies are also listed on U.S. stock exchanges. Those companies are required to file their annual reports with U.S. regulators. These corporations prepare forms 10-K and 10-Q which are very detailed documents of company descriptions. Some companies such as **Seagrams** actually issue their annual reports in U.S. dollars.

---

[2] *Annual Report*, Alcan Aluminum Limited, 1996.

Corporate Taxation

Corporations are subject to the same property and payroll taxes as proprietorships and partnerships. But corporations are subject to *additional* taxes not levied on either of these two forms. The combined top marginal rate for corporations is between 35% to 46% of a corporation's pretax income. For some corporations these rates are reduced by several percentage points due to various incentive provisions such as manufacturing and processing credits. According to the Micro-Economic Policy Analysis Branch of Strategis Canada, total corporate income taxes as a percent of Gross Domestic Product is about average among the G-7 countries. In comparison with our NAFTA partners, however, Canada ranks the best. When employer-paid social security contributions are factored into the corporate analysis Canada ties with the United Kingdom for the best ranking among G-7 countries.

The income of a corporation is taxed twice, first as income of the corporation and again as personal income to shareholders when cash is distributed to them as dividends. This is called *double taxation*. It differs from proprietorships and partnerships, which are not subject to income taxes as business units. Their income is taxed only as the personal income of their owners. For proprietorships and partnerships the income is taxable to the owners whether or not assets are actually withdrawn from the business.

The tax situation of a corporation is usually a disadvantage. But in some cases it can be an advantage to shareholders because corporation and individual tax rates are progressive. A progressive tax means higher levels of income are taxed at higher rates and lower levels of income are taxed at lower rates. This suggests taxes can be saved or at least delayed if a large amount of income is divided among two or more tax-paying entities. A person who has a large personal income and pays taxes at a high rate can benefit if some of the income is earned by a corporation the person owns, as long as the corporation avoids paying dividends or pays at a lower rate than the individual's rate. By not paying dividends, the corporation's income is taxed only once at the lower corporate rate, at least temporarily until dividends are paid.

Did You Know?

Choosing a Business Form

Choosing the proper form of entity for a business is crucial. Many factors should be considered including taxes, liability, tax and fiscal year-end, ownership structure, estate planning, business risks, and earnings and property distributions. The chart below gives a summary of several important characteristics of business organizations:

	Proprietorship	Partnership	Corporation
Business entity	yes	yes	yes
Legal entity	no	no	yes
Limited liability	no	no	yes
Business taxed	no	no	yes
One owner allowed	yes	no	yes

Organizing a Corporation

This section describes incorporation and treatment of the costs of organization.

Incorporation

A corporation may be created under either provincial law or federal laws. Those incorporated federally must comply with the Canada Business Corporations Act

(CBCA). Most of the provincial laws are modelled after the federal statute. Requirements vary across provinces and from the CBCA but essentially a legal document known as a charter, articles of incorporation, letters patent or memorandum of association is completed and signed by the prospective shareholders. They are called *incorporates* or *promoters*. The application should include the proposed name and address of the corporation, the name and address of the first directors, the classes and number of authorized shares and the name of the person incorporating the company. The application is then filed with the proper legal jurisdiction. Companies incorporating under the CBCA must file their applications with the Corporations Directorate of Industry Canada. When completed and all fees are paid, the charter is issued and the corporation is formed. Investors then purchase the corporation's shares, meet as shareholders, and elect a board of directors. Directors are responsible for guiding a corporation's affairs. To conduct business in a province in which the business is not incorporated, a corporation must obtain a licence from the province involved. A federally incorporated corporation may conduct business in every province but it must satisfy certain provincial registration requirements.

Netting Gold
Marc Andreessen co-founded **Netscape** at the age of 22, only four months after earning his degree in computer science. One year later at the age of 23, Andreessen and friends issued Netscape shares to the public. Netscape's shares, offered at $28 each, soared to nearly $75 before ending its first trading day at a less stratospheric $58. This made Andreessen a multimillionaire at 23. [Source: *Business Week*, October 23, 1995, and *Netscape 10K Report*.]

Did You Know?

Organization Costs

Organization costs are the costs of organizing a corporation. They include legal fees, promoters' fees, and amounts paid to get a charter. The corporation records (debits) these costs to an asset account called Organization Costs. This intangible asset benefits the corporation throughout its life and its cost is amortized over a period no longer than 40 years. Canadian standards for intangible assets are consistent with U.S. standards but vary from international Standards. For example, IAS 22 requires amortization of intangible assets over a period of five years or less unless a longer term up to a maximum of 20 years can be justified.

Although not related to the benefit period, income tax rules currently permit a corporation to record 75% of organization costs as a tax deduction at an annual rate of 7% on a diminishing balance basis. This means many corporations use the same method for financial reporting to ease recordkeeping. Because organization costs usually are small in amount, the *materiality principle* supports this arbitrary short amortization period.

Startup Money
An important concern to many potential entrepreneurs is how to raise money to get the business started. Here are a few suggestions: (1) Seek help from family and friends, (2) Search out reputable venture capitalists, investors or small business development corporations, (3) Consider paying employees, investors and even suppliers with shares, and (4) Make good use of supplier credit and leasing sources.

Did You Know?

Management of a Corporation

Corporations have different organizational structures. Yet ultimate control of a corporation rests with its shareholders. They control a corporation through election of the *board of directors*, or simply directors. Individual shareholders' rights to affect management are limited to a vote in shareholders' meetings, where each of them has one vote for each common share owned. This relation is shown in Exhibit 15.1. A corporation's board of directors is responsible for and has final authority for managing the corporation's activities. It can act only as a collective body. An individual director has no power to transact corporate business. Although the board has final authority, it usually limits its actions to establishing broad policy.

Exhibit 15.1

Corporation Authority Structure

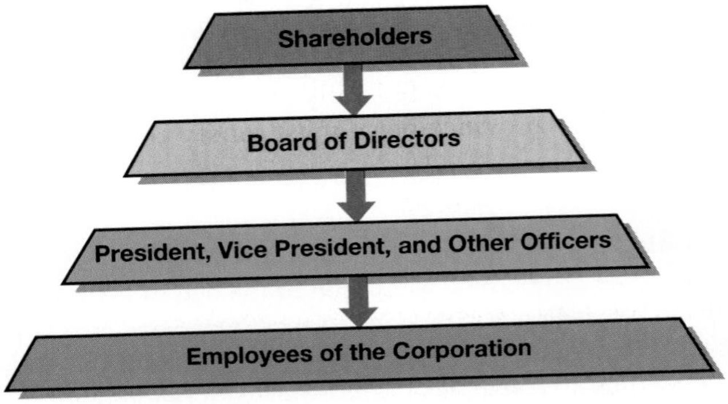

A corporation usually holds a shareholders' meeting once each year to elect directors and transact other business as required by its bylaws. The CBCA requires public corporations to have at least three directors, two of whom must not be employees or officers of the corporation. Directors are not required to be shareholders but most jurisdictions require that directors be at least 18 years of age, not bankrupt and must be residents of Canada. A group of shareholders owning or controlling votes of more than a 50% share of a corporation's shares can elect the board and control the corporation. But in many corporations few shareholders attend the annual meeting or even care about getting involved in the voting process. This means a much smaller percent is often able to dominate the election of board members.

Shareholders who don't attend shareholders' meetings must be given an opportunity to delegate their voting rights to an agent. A shareholder does this by signing a document called a proxy. A **proxy** gives a designated agent the right to vote the shares. Prior to a shareholders' meeting, a corporation's board of directors usually mails to each shareholder an announcement of the meeting and a proxy listing the existing board chairperson as the voting agent of the shareholder. The announcement asks the shareholder to sign and return the proxy.

Day-to-day direction of corporate business is delegated to executive officers appointed by the board. The chief executive officer (CEO) of a corporation is often its president. Several vice presidents who report to the president, are commonly assigned specific areas of management responsibility such as finance, production and marketing. The corporation secretary keeps minutes for meetings of shareholders and directors, and ensures that all legal responsibilities are met. In a small corporation the secretary is also responsible for keeping a record of current shareholders and amounts of their investment.

Another common corporate structure is where the chairperson of the board of directors is the CEO. In this case, the president is usually designated the chief operating officer (COO). The rest of the structure is similar.

Rights of Shareholders

When investors buy a corporation's shares they acquire all *specific* rights granted by the corporation's charter to those shareholders; they also acquire *general* rights granted shareholders by the laws of the legal jurisdiction in which the company is incorporated. When a corporation has only one class of shares, those shares are identified as **common shares.** The rights of the common shareholders are equal in all respects under the CBCA and most provincial statutes. Common shares represent *residual equity*, meaning that creditors and other shareholders (if any) rank ahead of common shareholders if a corporation is liquidated. Common shareholders usually have the general right to:

1. Vote at shareholders' meetings.
2. Share equally with other common shareholders in any dividends. This means each common share receives the same dividend per share.
3. Share equally in any assets remaining after creditors are paid when the corporation is liquidated. This means each common share receives the same amount of remaining liquidated assets.
4. Sell or otherwise dispose of their shares.
5. Purchase additional shares of common shares issued by the corporation in the future, if specifically provided for in the articles of incorporation or charter. This right is called the **preemptive right.** It protects shareholders proportionate interest in the corporation. For example, a shareholder who owns 25% of a corporation's common shares has the first opportunity to buy 25% of any new common shares issued. This enables the shareholder to maintain a 25% interest if desired.

According to the Canada Business Corporations Act the right to vote, to receive dividends that have been declared, and the right to receive property of the corporation after its dissolution are three inherent rights.The CBCA permits a company to distribute these three rights among more than one class of shares. These rights can be distributed in any combination, so long as all three rights are being assigned. In summary, viewing all of the share classes together, each of these three basic rights is assigned to at least one class but not necessarily to all. Shareholders also have the right to receive timely reports on the corporation's financial position and results of operations.

Shares of a Corporation

This section explains share certificates, their transfer, and use of registrar and transfer agents.

Share Certificates and Transfer

When investors buy a corporation's shares, they sometimes receive a *share certificate* as proof they purchased shares.[3] In many corporations, only one certificate is issued for each block of shares purchased. A certificate can be for any number of shares. Exhibit 15.2 shows an actual share certificate of 50 shares of **Westfield Publishing Company, Ltd.** A certificate shows the company name, shareholder name, number of shares, and other important items.

Exhibit 15.2

Share Certificate

C9800

INCORPORATED UNDER THE CANADA BUSINESS CORPORATIONS ACT

-50-

WESTFIELD PUBLISHING COMPANY, LTD.

THIS CERTIFIES ROBERT WETZEL is the owner of

FIFTY

FULLY PAID AND NON-ASSESSABLE COMMON SHARES OF NO PAR VALUE OF THE WESTFIELD PUBLISHING COMPANY, LTD. transferable on the books of the Corporation in person or by duly authorized lawyer upon surrender of this Certificate properly endorsed. This Certificate is not valid unless countersigned by the Transfer Agent and registered by the Registrar.

WITNESS the facsimile seal of the Corporation and the facsimile signatures of its duly authorized officers.

Dated: March 10, 1996

SEAL

SECRETARY

PRESIDENT

Registered: By Southern Trust Company Registrar Authorized Signature

Countersigned: By Transfer Agent Authorized Signature

[3] Issuance of certificates is becoming less common. Instead, many shareholders maintain accounts with the corporation or their stockbrokers and never receive certificates.

When selling shares, a shareholder completes and signs a transfer endorsement on the back of the certificate and sends it to the corporation's secretary or transfer agent. The secretary or agent cancels and files the old certificate, and issues a new certificate to the new shareholder. If the old certificate represents more shares than were sold, the corporation issues two new certificates. One certificate goes to the new shareholder for the shares purchased and the other to the selling shareholder for the remaining unsold shares. Many shareholders have their shares held in the name of their brokerage firm. When this is done, the corporation's secretary or registrar keeps a record of who owns the shares and the shareholders do not receive share certificates.

Registrar and Transfer Agents

If a corporation's shares are traded on a major stock exchange, the corporation must have a *registrar* and a *transfer agent*. A registrar keeps shareholder records and prepares official lists of shareholders for shareholders' meetings and dividend payments. A transfer agent assists purchases and sales of shares by receiving and issuing certificates as necessary. Registrars and transfer agents usually are large banks or trust companies having computer facilities and staff to do this work.

Did You Know?

Online Trading

Financial institutions such as **Scotia MacLeod**, the **Royal Bank**, the **Bank of Montreal** and the **National Bank of Canada** are taking advantage of computer technology to offer their clients discount brokerage services. Providers of brokerage services over the Internet can pass along savings in labour and order-entry to clients. Not only can clients save on brokerage fees but also they can access the Net 24 hours a day from their home computers and receive service in both English and French. Users can obtain real time share quotes and current order status as well as closing prices on hundreds of company shares that allow them to manage their own investments.

Basics of Capital Stock

LO 2 Describe the components of shareholders' equity.

Capital stock, also referred to as **share capital,** is a general term referring to all classes of a corporation's shares. The issuance of capital stock results in an increase in assets and a corresponding increase in shareholders' equity. The issuance of shares to obtain capital is often referred to as equity financing. This section introduces us to capital stock terminology and some of the basics in accounting for capital stock.

Authorized Shares

Authorized shares are the total amount of shares that a corporation's charter authorizes it to sell. Corporations formed under the Canada Business Corporations Act are permitted to issue an unlimited number of shares. Corporations disclose the number of shares authorized in the equity section of the balance sheet or its notes. **Alliance Communications Corporation** balance sheet in Appendix I reports in note 8 that the authorized capital stock of the company consists of an unlimited number of common shares comprised of Class A Voting Shares and Class B Non-Voting Shares.

Shareholders' Equity	1997	1996
Capital stock (note 8)	$88,836,000	$52,295,000

No formal journal entry is required for authorization of shares.

Selling Shares

Corporations can issue shares in at least two ways. They can either sell directly or indirectly to shareholders. *To sell directly*, a corporation advertises its shares issuance directly to potential buyers. This type of issuance is most common with privately held corporations. To *sell indirectly,* a corporation pays a brokerage house (investment banker) to issue its shares. Some brokerage houses *underwrite* an indirect issuance of shares, meaning they buy the shares from the corporation and take all gains or losses from its resale to shareholders.

Did You Know?

IPO Growth in Information Technology
Information technology is becoming increasingly important to the Canadian economy. Since 1993, 132 Canadian Information and Technology firms went public in Canada raising $3.08 billion. The largest IPO in that sector in the first six months of 1997 was the privatization of **Manitoba Telecom Services Inc.**, which raised $910 million. [Source: Strategis Canada Web Site, October 10, 1997.]

Market Value of Shares

Market value per share is the price at which a share is bought or sold. Market value is influenced by a variety of factors including expected future earnings, dividends, growth, and other company and economic events. Market values of frequently traded shares are reported daily in newspapers such as *The Globe and Mail* or are available immediately off the Web. Market values of shares not actively traded are more difficult to determine. Several techniques are used to estimate the value of these and other shares. Most all of these techniques use accounting information as an important input to this valuation process. We must remember the current market value of issued shares of a corporation (for example, buying and selling shares between investors) does not impact that corporation's shareholders' equity accounts.

Classes of Shares

A corporation's articles of incorporation authorize it to issue shares. Companies incorporated under the Canada Business Corporation Act are authorized to issue an unlimited number of shares. If all authorized shares have the same rights and characteristics, the shares are called common shares. There is no limit on the number of classes of shares set out in the articles of incorporation. Shares may be alphabetized by class such as Class A and Class B or may be assigned names such as common shares and preferred shares. We discuss preferred shares later in this chapter. **Alliance Communications Corporation**, for instance, has two types of common shares outstanding. Class A voting shares and Class B Non-Voting shares.

Did You Know?

Stock Quotes
The **Imperial Oil** stock quote below is interpreted as (left to right): **Hi,** highest price in the past 52 weeks; **Lo,** lowest price in the past 52 weeks; **Stock,** company name; **Sym,** exchange symbol; **Div,** dividends paid per share in the past year; **Yld %,** dividend divided by closing price; **PE,** ratio of share price divided by earnings; **Vol 100s,** number of shares traded in 100s; **Hi,** highest price for the day; **Lo,** lowest price for the day; **Close,** closing price for the day; **Net Chg,** change in closing price from the prior day.

52 Weeks										
Hi	Lo	Stock Sym	Div	Yld %	PE	Vol 100s	Hi	Lo	Close	Net Chg
30.77	20.80	IMO	.74	2.8	17.3	31930	27.25	26.80	26.85	−.50

Shareholders' Equity

The equity of a corporation is known as **shareholders' equity** also called *stockholders' equity* or *corporate capital*. Shareholders' equity consists of (1) contributed (or paid-in) capital and (2) retained earnings. **Contributed capital** is the total amount of cash and other assets received by the corporation from its shareholders in exchange for all classes of shares issued. **Retained earnings** is the cumulative net income retained in a corporation. Retained earnings is increased by net income and decreased by dividends and net loss.

Exhibit 15.3 compares the equity accounts of a balance sheet for the three major forms of organizations: proprietorship, partnership and corporation. Exhibits 2.4, 2.7 and 2.8 in Chapter 2 show actual equity sections for each of these three forms when applied to **FastForward**. Further details regarding the equity section of a corporation are described in this and the next chapter.

Exhibit 15.3

Equity Accounts by Organizational Form

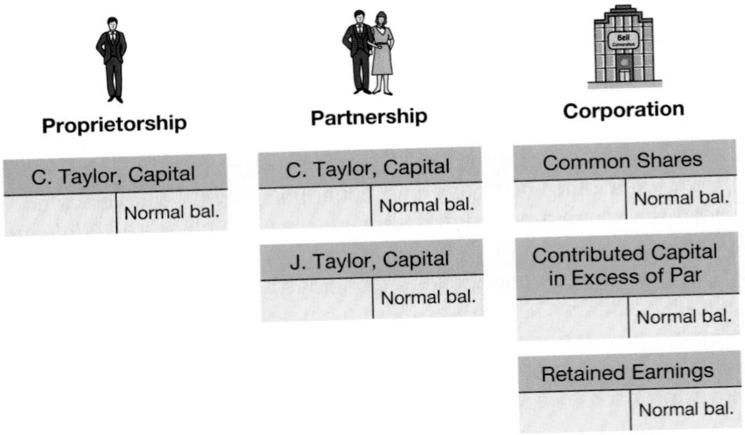

Flashback

1. Which of the following is not a characteristic of the corporate form of business? (a) ease of capital accumulation, (b) shareholders are liable for corporate debts, (c) ownership rights are easily transferred.
2. Why is income of a corporation said to be taxed twice?
3. What is a proxy?

Answers—p. 712

Common Shares

Accounting for the issuance of common shares involves (1) identifying the contributed capital and (2) keeping contributed capital separate from retained earnings. Issuance of shares affects only contributed capital accounts, no retained earnings accounts are affected.

Issuing Shares

LO 3 Record the issuance of corporate shares.

Issuing Shares for Cash

The Canada Business Corporatons Act (CBCA), 1975, as well as the more recently passed provincial counterparts, require that all shares be of **no-par** or nominal value. These acts also require the total consideration received by the corporation for each share issued to be added to the stated capital account maintained for shares of that class. Some jurisdictions permit the issuance of par value shares. **Par value** is an arbitrary value a corporation places on each share of its share capital. Because of the rarity of par value shares in Canada this text will restrict itself to the accounting treatment of no-par shares only.

Shares are most commonly issued in exchange for cash. For example, the entry to record Dillon Snowboards' immediate issuance of 30,000 shares for $300,000 on June 5, 1999 is:

June 5	Cash	300,000	
	Common Shares		300,000
	Sold and issued 30,000 common shares at $10 per share.		

Assets = Liabilities + Equity
+300,000 +300,000

Exhibit 15.4 shows the shareholders' equity of Dillon Snowboards at the end of 1999 after earnings of $65,000 and no dividend payments.

Exhibit 15.4
Shareholders' Equity

Shareholders' Equity		
Contributed capital:		
Common Shares, no-par, unlimited shares authorized;		
30,000 shares issued and outstanding	$300,000	
Retained earnings	65,000	
Total shareholders' equity		$365,000

The retained earnings balance can also be negative, reflecting accumulated losses.

Issuing Shares for Noncash Assets

A corporation can receive assets other than cash in exchange for its shares.[4] The corporation records the assets acquired at the assets' fair market values as of the date of the transaction.

To illustrate, the entry to record receipt of land valued at $105,000 in return for immediate issuance of 4,000 common shares is:

June 10	Land	105,000	
	Common Shares		105,000
	Exchanged 4,000 common shares for land.		

Assets = Liabilities + Equity
+105,000 +105,000

If reliable fair values for the assets received cannot be determined, the fair market value of the shares given up is used to estimate the assets' values.

Issuing Shares for Organization Costs

A corporation sometimes gives shares to promoters in exchange for their services in organizing the corporation. In this case the corporation receives the intangible asset of Organization Costs in exchange for its shares. The entry to record receipt of services valued at $12,000 in organizing the corporation in return for immediate issuance of 600 common shares is:

June 5	Organization Costs	12,000	
	Common Shares		12,000
	Gave promoters 600 common shares in exchange for services in organizing the corporation.		

Assets = Liabilities + Equity
+12,000 +12,000

[4] It can also assume liabilities on assets received such as a mortgage on property.

Mid-Chapter Demonstration Problem

Roberto Ltd. issued 8,000 of its common shares on January 2, 1999. Present the journal entries that the company's accountant would use to record this event under each of the following independent situations:

a. The shares were sold for $1.50 per share.

b. The shares were issued for lawyer services valued at $6,000.

c. The shares were issued to a creditor who was owed $10,000.

Solution to Mid-Chapter Demonstration Problem

a.

Jan. 2	Cash	12,000	
	Common shares		12,000
	Issued common shares for Cash.		

b.

Jan. 2	Organization Cost	6,000	
	Common shares,		6,000
	Issued common shares for incorporation fees.		

c.

Jan 2	Accounts payable	10,000	
	Common shares		10,000
	Issued common shares in payment of debt.		

Issuing Shares through Subscriptions

Shares are usually sold for cash and immediately issued. But corporations sometimes issue shares through a subscription basis. A **shares subscription** involves selling shares where the investor agrees to buy a certain number of the shares at specified future dates and prices. The typical case is when a new corporation is formed and the organizers recognize both an immediate and future need for capital. The organizers can sell shares to investors who agree to contribute some cash now and to make additional contributions in the future.

Flash back

4. A company issues 7,000 common shares and a $40,000 note payable in exchange for equipment valued at $105,000. The entry to record this transaction includes a credit to (a) Retained earnings for $65,000, (b) Common shares for $65,000, (c) Common shares for $105,000.

Answers—p. 712

Preferred Shares

As mentioned earlier there is no limit on the number of classes of shares that a corporation can issue. **Preferred shares** have special rights that give it priority (or senior status) over common shares in one or more areas. Special rights typically include a preference for receiving dividends and for the distribution of assets if the corporation is liquidated. Preferred shares carry all the rights of common shares unless they are nullified in the corporate charter. Most preferred shares, for instance, do not have the right to vote. **Alliance**, for instance, has preferred shares outstanding without general voting rights.[5] See Exhibit 15.5.

LO 4 Explain the characteristics of common and preferred shares.

Issuing Preferred Shares

A separate contributed capital account is used to record preferred shares. To illustrate, if Dillon Snowboards also had issued 50 preferred shares for $6,000 cash on July 1, 1999, the entry is:

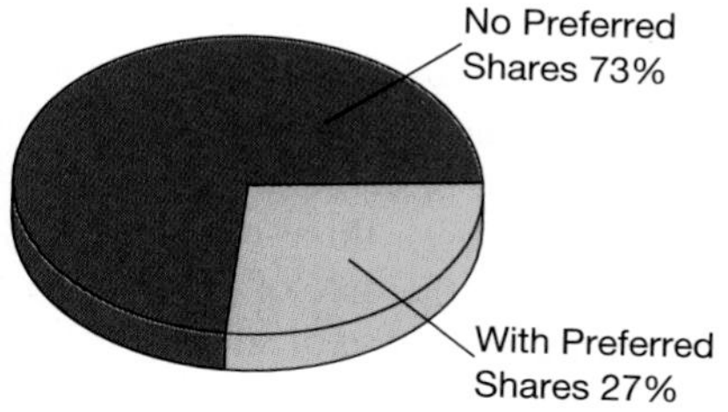

Exhibit 15.5

Corporations and Preferred Shares

July 1	Cash	6,000	
	Preferred shares		6,000
	Issued preferred shares for cash at $120 per share.		

Assets = Liabilities + Equity
+6,000 +6,000

The preferred shares account or accounts if there are more than one class of preferred shares, are included as part of contributed capital. The equity section of the year-end balance sheet for Dillon's Snowboards, including preferred shares, would appear as shown in Exhibit 15.6.

Exhibit 15.6

Shareholders' Equity with Common and Preferred shares

Shareholders' Equity		
Contributed capital:		
Preferred shares—no-par value; unlimited shares authorized; 50 shares issued and outstanding	**$ 6,000**	
Common Shares—no-par value; unlimited shares authorized; 30,000 shares issued and outstanding	300,000	
Total contributed capital		$306,000
Retained earnings		65,000
Total shareholders' equity		$371,000

Issuing no-par preferred shares is treated similar to no-par common shares. Also, issuing preferred shares for noncash assets is treated like similar entries for common shares.

Dividend Preference

Preferred shares usually carry a preference for dividends. This means preferred shareholders are allocated their dividends before any dividends are allocated to common shareholders. Simply put, a dividend cannot be paid to common shareholders unless preferred shareholders are paid first. The dividends allocated to preferred shareholders are usually expressed as a dollar amount per share or as a percent applied to the total stated value. Dividends could be expressed as $5.00 per share or as 5% of preferred shares with a total stated value of $100,000.

[5] A corporation can also issue more than one class of shares. If two classes of common shares are issued, the primary difference between them usually involves voting rights. Refer to question 9 at the end of this chapter regarding Alliance.

The reporting of preferred shares can appear complicated in practice. As an example, the December 31, 1996, annual report of **Noranda Inc.** showed among its various classes of shares that it had issued 12,000,000 cumulative, redeemable preferred shares Series F at a price of $25.00 per share that pay a fixed dividend at a rate of 5.8% per annum. A more complicated disclosure of preferred shares is found in the 1996 annual report of **Novicourt.** Novicourt was authorized to issue an unlimited number of preferred shares. The amount issued as of December 31,1996, totalled $4,984,000. These shares require Novicourt to pay dividends equal to the greater of (a) 8.50% annual rate and (b) the rate obtained by multiplying 8.5% by the ratio of the average price of gold at the second fixing on the London Metal Exchange each day during a three-month period ending on the fifteenth day of the second month prior to the date of payment of the dividend to the base price of gold established for the purpose of such dividend at U.S. $3.75 per ounce. Preferred dividends must be paid before common shareholders can receive a dividend. A preference for dividends does *not* ensure dividends. If the directors do not declare a dividend, neither the preferred nor the common shareholders receive one.

Cumulative or Noncumulative Dividend

LO 5 Distribute dividends between common shares and preferred shares.

Most preferred shares carry a cumulative dividend right. **Cumulative preferred shareholders** have a right to be paid both current and all prior periods' unpaid dividends before any dividend is paid to common shareholders. When preferred shares are cumulative and the directors either do not declare a dividend to preferred shareholders or declare a dividend that does not satisfy the cumulative dividend, then the unpaid dividend amount is called **dividend in arrears.** Accumulation of dividends in arrears on cumulative preferred shares does not guarantee they will be paid. Some preferred shares are noncumulative. **Noncumulative preferred shares** have no right to prior periods' unpaid dividends if they were not declared.

To illustrate and show the difference between cumulative and noncumulative preferred shares, let's assume a corporation's outstanding shares includes (a) 1,000 shares of 9% preferred shares amounting to $100,000 and (b) 4,000 shares common shares amounting to $200,000. During 1999, the first year of the corporation's operations, the directors declare cash dividends of $5,000. In year 2000, it declares $42,000. Allocations of total dividends are shown in Exhibit 15.7.

Exhibit 15.7
Allocation of Dividends

	Preferred	Common
If noncumulative preferred:		
Year 1999	$ 5,000	$ -0-
Year 2000		
Step 1: Current preferred dividend ($100,000 × 9%)	$ 9,000	
Step 2. Remainder to common		$33,000
If cumulative preferred:		
Year 1999	$ 5,000	$ -0-
Year 2000		
Step 1: Dividends in arrears ($9,000 − $5,000)	$ 4,000	
Step 2: Current preferred dividend	9,000	
Step 3: Remainder to common		$29,000
Totals	$13,000	$29,000

Allocation of year 2000 dividends depends on whether the preferred shares are noncumulative or cumulative. With noncumulative preferred, the preferred shareholders never receive the $4,000 skipped in 1999. But if the preferred shares are cumulative, the $4,000 in arrears is paid in 2000 before the common shareholders receive a dividend.

Participating or Nonparticipating Dividend

Nonparticipating preferred shares have dividends limited to a maximum amount each year. This maximum is often stated as a percent of the share's issuance price or as a specific dollar amount per share. Once preferred shareholders receive this amount, the common shareholders receive any and all additional dividends.

Participating preferred shares have a feature where preferred shareholders share with common shareholders in any dividends paid in excess of the percent stated on the preferred shares. This participating feature does not apply until common shareholders receive dividends equal to the preferred share's dividend percent. While many corporations are authorized to issue participating preferred shares, they are rarely issued and most managers never expect to issue them. However they do exist. **Power Corporation of Canada**, for example, recently reported participating preferred shares of $1,875,974,000. These shares were entitled to a non-cumulative dividend of $0.0375 per share per annum before dividends on the subordinate voting shares, having the right to participate, share and share alike, with the holders of the subordinate voting shares in any dividends in any year after payment of a dividend of $0.0375 per share to the subordinate shares.

What then is the purpose of participating preferred shares? They are usually authorized as a defence against a possible *takeover* of the corporation by an "unfriendly" investor (or a group of investors) who intends to buy enough voting common shares to gain control. Taking a term from spy novels, the financial world refers to this kind of plan as a *poison pill* that a company swallows if it is threatened with capture by enemy investors.

A poison pill usually works as follows: A corporation's common shareholders on a given date are granted the right to purchase a large amount of participating preferred shares at a very low price. This right to purchase preferred shares is *not* transferable. This means if these shareholders sell their common shares, the buyers do *not* gain the right to purchase preferred shares. The right to purchase preferred shares can only be exercised if the directors identify an investor of a large block of common shares as an unfriendly investor.

If an unfriendly investor buys a large block of common shares (whose right to purchase participating preferred shares did *not* transfer to this buyer), the board can issue preferred shares at a low price to the remaining common shareholders who retained the right to purchase. Future dividends must now be divided between the newly issued participating preferred shares and the common shares. This usually transfers a large value of the common shares to preferred shares. This means the common shares owned by the unfriendly investor lose much of their value, and this reduces the potential benefit of a hostile takeover.

Financial Statement Disclosure of Dividends

Dividends are not incurred as time passes. A liability for a dividend does not exist until the directors declare a dividend. This means that if a preferred dividend date passes and the corporation's board fails to declare the dividend on its cumulative preferred shares, the dividend in arrears is not a liability. But when preparing financial statements, the *full-disclosure principle* requires the corporation to report the amount of preferred dividends in arrears as of the balance sheet date. This information is usually in a note.

Convertible Preferred Shares

Preferred shares are more attractive to investors if they carry a right to be exchanged for a fixed number of common shares. **Convertible preferred shares** give holders the option of exchanging their preferred shares into common shares at a specified rate. **Laidlaw,** for example, showed in its August 31, 1997, annual report 5% cumulative, convertible first preference preferred shares of $8.7 million. This feature offers holders of convertible preferred shares a higher potential return. When a company prospers and its common shares increase in value, convertible preferred shareholders can share in this success by converting their preferred shares into more valuable common shares. Also, these holders benefit from increases in the value of common shares without converting their preferred shares because the preferred share's market value is impacted by changes in the value of common shares.

Callable Preferred Shares

Callable preferred shares gives the issuing corporation the right to purchase (retire) their shares from its holders at specified future prices and dates. Many issues of preferred shares are callable. The amount paid to call and retire a preferred share is its **call price,** or *redemption value*. This amount is set at the time the shares are issued. The call price normally includes the issue price of the shares plus a premium giving holders additional return on their investment. When the issuing corporation calls and retires preferred shares, it must pay the call price and any dividends in arrears.

Motivation for Preferred Shares

There are several reasons for a corporation to issue preferred shares. One reason is to raise capital without sacrificing control of the corporation. For example, let's suppose the organizers of a company have $100,000 cash to invest and wish to organize a corporation needing $200,000 of capital to get off to a good start. If they sold $200,000 worth of common shares, they would have only 50% control and would need to negotiate extensively with other shareholders in making policy. But if they issue $100,000 worth of common shares to themselves and sell outsiders $100,000 of 8%, cumulative preferred shares with no voting rights, they retain control of the corporation.

A second reason for issuing preferred shares is to boost the return earned by common shareholders. To illustrate, let's suppose a corporation's organizers expect their new company to earn an annual after-tax income of $24,000 on an investment of $200,000. If they sell and issue $200,000 worth of common shares, this income produces a 12% return on the $200,000 of common shareholders' equity. But if they issue $100,000 of 8% preferred shares to outsiders and $100,000 of common shares to themselves, their own return increases to 16% per year as shown in Exhibit 15.8.

Exhibit 15.8

Return to Common Shareholders

Net after-tax income	$24,000
Less preferred dividends at 8% ($100,000 × 8%)	(8,000)
Balance to common shareholders	$16,000
Return to common shareholders ($16,000/$100,000) ..	16%

Common shareholders earn 16% instead of 12% because assets contributed by preferred shareholders are invested to earn $12,000 while the preferred dividend payments amount to only $8,000.

Use of preferred shares to increase return to common shareholders is an example of **financial leverage.** Whenever the dividend rate on preferred shares is less than the rate the corporation earns on its assets, the effect of issuing preferred shares is to increase (or *lever*) the rate earned by common shareholders. Financial leverage also occurs when debt is issued and the interest rate paid on it is less than the rate earned from using the assets the creditors loaned to the corporation.

There are other reasons for issuing preferred shares. For example, a corporation's preferred shares may appeal to some investors who believe its common shares are too risky or that the dividend rate on common shares is too low. Also, if a corporation's management wants to issue common shares but believes the current market price for common shares is too low, the corporation may issue preferred shares that are convertible into common shares. If and when the price of common shares increases, the preferred shareholders can convert their shares into common shares.

Concert Organizer
You organize music concerts for profit. You've recently decided to move away from concerts targeted at under 5,000 people to those targeted at between 10,000 to 50,000 people. This demands funding. You decide to incorporate because of the increased risk of lawsuits and your desire to issue shares to meet funding demands. It is important to you that you keep control of the company for decisions on who to schedule and when. What type of shares issuance do you offer?

You Make the Call

Answer—p. 712

Flashback

5. In what ways do preferred shares often have priority over common shares?
6. Increasing the return to common shareholders by issuing preferred shares is an example of (a) financial leverage, (b) cumulative earnings, or (c) dividends in arrears.
7. A corporation has (a) $450,000 of preferred shares consisting of 9,000 shares of 10% cumulative and nonparticipating preferred shares and (b) $270,000 of common shares consisting of 27,000 shares issued and outstanding. No dividends have been declared for the past two years. During the current year, the corporation declares a $288,000 dividend. The amount paid to common shareholders is (a) $243,000, (b) $153,000, or (c) $135,000.

Answers—p. 712

Preferred Shares as Debt
According to section 3800 of the *CICA Handbook* the issuer of a financial instrument should classify it as a liability or as equity in accordance with the substance of the financial instrument. Prior to release of section 3800 debt and equity were required under GAAP to be classified according to their legal form. Now if an instrument requires the issuer to deliver cash or another financial asset under conditions that are potentially unfavourable the instrument should be classifed as a liability. Preferred shares may provide for mandatory redemption or contain a provision providing an accelerating dividend such that the dividend yield is scheduled to be so high that the issuer will be economically compelled to redeem the preferred shares. These preferred shares must be classified as liabilities for fiscal years on or after January 1,1996. Dividends relating to these preferred shares are to be shown in the income statement as a reduction similar to interest expense on long-term debt. Cumulative preferred dividends would be accrued whether or not the dividends were declared. This is a major change from previous GAAP which required that all preferred dividends be shown in the statement of retained earnings and only recorded when declared. This topic is treated in depth in more advanced accounting courses.

Did You Know?

Book Value per Share

USING THE INFORMATION

LO 6 Compute book value and explain its use in analysis.

This section explains how we compute book value and use it for analysis. We first focus on book value per share for corporations with only common shares outstanding, and then look at book value per share when both common and preferred shares are outstanding.

Book Value per Share When Only Common Shares are Outstanding

Book value per common share is the recorded amount of shareholders' equity applicable to common shares divided by the number of common shares outstanding. This ratio is defined in Exhibit 15.9.

Exhibit 15.9

Book Value per Common Share Formula

$$\text{Book Value per Common Share} = \frac{\text{Shareholders' Equity Applicable to Common Shares}}{\text{Number of Common Shares Outstanding}}$$

For instance, we can compute the book value per common share for Dillon Snowboards at the end of 1999 using data in Exhibit 15.7. Dillon has 30,000 outstanding common shares and the shareholders' equity applicable to common shares is $365,000. Common shares are entitled to total shareholders' equity when there are no preferred shares outstanding. Dillon's book value per common share is $12.17, computed as $365,000 divided by 30,000 shares.

Book Value per Share When Both Common and Preferred shares are Outstanding

To compute book value when *both common and preferred shares are outstanding*, we must first allocate total shareholders' equity between these two kinds of shares. The **book value per preferred share** is computed first, and its computation is shown in Exhibit 15.10.

Exhibit 15.10

Book Value per Preferred Share Formula

$$\text{Book Value per Preferred Share} = \frac{\text{Shareholders' Equity Applicable to Preferred Shares}}{\text{Number of Preferred Shares Outstanding}}$$

The shareholders' equity applicable to preferred shares equals the preferred share's call price (or average paid-in amount if the preferred is not callable) plus any cumulative dividends in arrears. The remaining shareholders' equity is the portion applicable to common shares.

To illustrate, let us look at the shareholders' equity section of **Music Live!** as shown in Exhibit 15.11. The preferred shares of Music Live! are callable at $108 per share, and two years of cumulative preferred dividends are in arrears.

Exhibit 15.11

Shareholders' Equity with Preferred and Common Shares

Shareholders' Equity	
Preferred shares, no-par value, $7 cumulative, 2,000 shares authorized, 1,000 shares issued and outstanding	$105,000
Common shares, no-par value, 12,000 shares authorized, 10,000 shares issued and outstanding	$260,000
Total contributed capital	$365,000
Retained Earnings	82,000
Total shareholders' equity	$447,000

The book values of Music Live! preferred and common shares are computed in Exhibit 15.12. Note the need to first allocate equity to preferred shares before we compute the book value of common shares.

Total shareholders' equity		$447,000
Less equity applicable to preferred shares:		
Call price (1,000 × $108)	$108,000	
Cumulative dividends in arrears ($100,000 × $7 × 2)	14,000	(122,000)
Equity applicable to common shares		$325,000
Book value per preferred share ($122,000/1,000)		**$ 122.00**
Book value per common share ($325,000/10,000)		**$ 32.50**

Exhibit 15.12

Computing Book Value Per Share

Book value per share is often used in analysis of a company. It reflects the amount each share is worth if a company is liquidated at amounts reported on the balance sheet. Book value is also the starting point in many share valuation methods. Other uses include merger negotiations, price setting for public utilities, and loan contracts. The main limitation in using book values is likely differences between book values and market values for both assets and liabilities. Professionals often adjust their analyses and the accounting numbers to reflect these differences.

Annual reports to shareholders sometimes disclose the book value per share. **Royal Bank's** common shares at the end of the first quarter of 1998 carried a book value of $28.66, while its market (share) value on the date of the release of the interim report was $76.35, over 266% of book value. Book value and liquidation value per share can also be different. This is because if a company is liquidated, the selling prices are often different from amounts reported on the balance sheet.

Investor

You are considering investing in **Ride**, a leading manufacturer of snowboards. Ride's current book value per common share is about $4, yet its common shares are priced at about $7 per share on the stock exchange. From this information, can you say whether Ride's net assets are priced higher or lower than their recorded values?

You Make the Call

Answer—p. 712

Flash back

8. A corporation's outstanding shares includes (a) $90,000 of cumulative preferred shares consisting of 1,000 shares and (b) 12,000 common shares. Preferred shares have a call price of $90 and dividends of $18,000 are in arrears. Total shareholders' equity is $630,000. What is the book value per common share?
9. The price at which a share is bought or sold is the (a) call price, (b) redemption value, or (c) market value.

Answers—p. 713

Summary

LO 1 Identify characteristics of corporations and their organization. Corporations are separate legal entities and their shareholders are not liable for corporate debts. Shares issued by corporations are easily transferred between shareholders, and the life of a corporation does not end with the incapacity or death of a shareholder. A corporation acts through its agents, who are its officers and managers, not its shareholders. Corporations are regulated by the government and are subject to income taxes.

LO 2 Describe the components of shareholders' equity. Authorized shares are the total amount of shares that a corporation's charter authorizes it to sell. Issued shares is the portion of authorized shares sold to shareholders. Shareholders' equity is made up of (a) contributed capital and (b) retained earnings. Contributed capital consists of funds raised by shares issuances—both common and preferred. Retained earnings consists of current and prior periods' earnings not distributed to shareholders.

LO 3 Record the issuance of corporate shares. When shares are issued, the proceeds are credited to the share capital account. This amount is contributed capital.

LO 4 Explain the characteristics of common and preferred shares. Preferred shares have a priority (or senior status) relative to common shares in one or more areas. The usual areas include preference as to (a) dividends and (b) assets in case of liquidation. But they usually do not have voting rights. Preferred shares can also be convertible or callable. Convertibility permits the holder to convert preferred shares to common shares. Callability permits the issuer to buy preferred shares under specified conditions.

LO 5 Distribute dividends between common shares and preferred shares. Preferred shareholders usually hold the right to receive dividend distributions before common shareholders. This right is known as dividend preference. When preferred shares are cumulative and in arrears, the amount in arrears must be distributed to preferred shareholders before any dividends are distributed to common shareholders.

LO 6 Compute book value and explain its use in analysis. Book value per common share is shareholders' equity applicable to common shares divided by the number of outstanding common shares. Book value per preferred share is shareholders' equity applicable to preferred shares divided by the number of outstanding preferred shares.

Guidance Answers to **You Make the Call**

Concert Organizer

Because you wish to maintain control of the company, you want to issue shares in a way that does not interfere with your ability to run the company in the way you desire. You have two basic options: (1) different classes of common shares, or (2) common and preferred shares. Your objective in this case is to issue shares to yourself that have all or a majority of the voting power. The other class of shares you issue would carry limited or no voting rights. In this way you maintain complete control and are able to raise your necessary funds.

Investor

Book value reflects recorded values. Ride's book value is about $4 per common share. The share price reflects the market's expectation of current values. Ride's market value is about $7 per common share. Comparing these figures suggests the current values of Ride's net assets is much higher than their recorded values ($7 vs. $4 per share, respectively).

Guidance Answers to Flashbacks

1. *b*
2. A corporation must pay taxes on its income and its shareholders must pay personal income taxes on dividends received from the corporation.
3. A proxy is a legal document used to transfer a shareholder's right to vote to another person.
4. *b*
5. Typically, preferred shares have a preference in receiving dividends and in the distribution of assets in the case of a company's liquidation.

6. *a*

7. *b*

Total dividend	$288,000
To preferred shareholders	135,000*
Remainder to common shareholders	$153,000

*$450,000 × .10 × 3 = $135,000

8.

Total shareholders' equity		$630,000
Less equity applicable to preferred shares:		
Call price (1,000 × $90)	$90,000	
Dividends in arrears	18,000	108,000
Equity applicable to common shares		$522,000
Book value of common shares ($522,000/12,000)		$43.50

9. *c*

Demonstration Problem

Barton Corporation was created on January 1, 1998. Barton is authorized by its articles of incorporation to issue 100,000 shares of $10 cumulative preferred shares and an unlimited number of no-par common shares. The following transactions relating to shareholders' equity occurred during the first two years of the company's operations.

1. Prepare the journal entries to record these transactions.
2. Prepare the balance sheet presentation of the organization costs, liabilities, and shareholders' equity as at December 31, 1998, and December 31, 1999. Include appropriate notes to the financial statements.

1998

Jan. 2 Issued 200,000 common shares at $12 per share.

2 Issued 100,000 common shares in exchange for a building valued at $820,000 and merchandise inventory valued at $380,000.

2 Acceped subscriptions for 150,000 common shares at $12 per share. The subscribers made no down payments, and the full purchase price was due on April 1, 1998.

3 Paid a cash reimbursement to the company's founders for $100,000 of organization costs; these costs are to be amortized over 10 years.

3 Issued 12,000 preferred shares for cash at $110 per share.

Apr. 1 Collected the full subscription price for the January 1 common shares and issued the shares.

Dec. 31 The income summary account for 1998 had a $125,000 credit balance before being closed to Retained Earnings; no dividends were declared on either common or preferred shares.

1999

June 4 Issued 100,000 common shares for cash at $15 per share.

Dec. 10 Declared dividends payable on January 10, 2,000 as follows:

To preferred shareholders for 1998	$120,000
To preferred shareholders for 1999	120,000
To common shareholders for 1999	300,000

Dec. 31 The income summary account for 1999 had a $1 million credit balance before being closed to Retained Earnings.

Planning the Solution

- Record journal entries for the events in 1998 and 1999.
- Close the accounts related to retained earnings at the end of each year.
- Determine the balance sheet amount for 1998 and 1999 for unamortized organization costs.
- Determine the balances for the 1998 and 1999 capital equity accounts for the balance sheet including information about the number of shares issued and a note regarding dividends in arrears.
- Prepare the specified portions of the 1998 and 1999 balance sheets.

Solution to Demonstration Problem

1.

1998			
Jan. 2	Cash	2,400,000	
	Common Shares		2,400,000
	Issued 200,000 common shares.		
2	Building	820,000	
	Merchandise Inventory	380,000	
	Common Shares		1,200,000
	Issued 100,000 common shares.		
3	Subscriptions receivable	1,800,000	
	Common shares subscribed		1,800,000
	Recognize subscription contract for 150,000 common shares at $12 per share.		
3	Organization Costs	100,000	
	Cash		100,000
	Reimbursed the founders for organization costs.		
3	Cash	1,320,000	
	Preferred shares		1,320,000
	Issued 12,000 preferred shares.		
Apr. 1	Cash	1,800,000	
	Subscriptions receivable		1,800,000
	Collected balance due on subscribed common shares.		
1	Common shares subscribed	1,800,000	
	Commons shares		1,800,000
	Issued 150,000 subscribed common shares.		
Dec. 31	Income Summary	125,000	
	Retained Earnings		125,000
	Close income summary and update Retained Earnings.		

1999			
June 4	Cash	1,500,000	
	Common Shares		1,500,000
	Issued 100,000 common shares.		
Dec. 10	Cash dividends declared	540,000	
	Dividends Payable, Common Shares		300,000
	Dividends Payable, Preferred Shares		240,000
	Declared current dividends and dividends in arrears to common and preferred shareholders, payable on January 10, 2000.		
Dec. 31	Income Summary	1,000,000	
	Retained Earnings		1,000,000
	To close the income summary account and update retained earnings.		
Dec. 31	Retained Earnings	540,000	
	Cash Dividends Declared		540,000
	To close to Retained Earnings the Cash Dividends Declared.		

2. Balance sheet presentations:

	As of December 31 1998	1999
Assets		
Organization Costs	$ 90,000	$ 80,000
Liabilities		
Dividends payable, common shares		$ 300,000
Dividends payable, preferred shares		240,000
Total liabilities		$ 540,000
Shareholders' Equity		
Contributed capital:		
Preferred shares, no-par value, $10 cumulative, 100,000 shares authorized, 12,000 shares issued and outstanding	$1,320,000	$1,320,000
Common shares, no-par value, unlimited shares authorized, 450,000 shares issued and outstanding in 1998, and 550,000 shares in 1999	$5,400,000	$6,900,000
Total contributed capital	$6,720,000	$8,220,000
Retained Earnings (see Note 1)	125,000	585,000
Total Shareholders' Equity	$6,845,000	$8,805,000

Note 1: As of December 31, 1998, there were $120,000 of Dividends in arrears on the preferred shares.

Glossary

Authorized shares The total amount of shares that a corporation's charter authorizes it to sell. Federally incoporated companies are authorized to issue an unlimited number. (p. 700)

Book value per common share The recorded amount of shareholder's equity applicable to common shares divided by the number of common shares outstanding. (p. 710)

Book value per preferred share The shareholder's equity applicable to preferred shares (equals the preferred share's call price—or issue price if the preferred is not callable—plus any cumulative dividends in arrears) divided by the number of preferred shares outstanding. (p. 710)

Call price The amount that must be paid to call and retire a preferred share. (p. 708)

Callable preferred shares Preferred shares that the issuing corporation, at its option, may retire by paying a specified amount (the call price) to the preferred shareholders plus any dividends in arrears. (p. 708)

Capital stock The general term referring to a corporation's stock used in obtaining its capital (owner financing); also called *share capital.* (p. 700)

Common shares Shares of a corporation that has only one class of shares. (p. 699)

Contributed capital The total amount of cash and other assets received by the corporation from its shareholders in exchange for all classes of shares issued. (p. 702)

Convertible preferred shares Preferred shares that give holders the option of exchanging their preferred shares into common shares at a specified rate. (p. 707)

Cumulative preferred shares Preferred shares on which undeclared dividends accumulate until they are paid; common shareholders cannot receive a dividend until all cumulative dividends have been paid. (p. 706)

Dividend in arrears An unpaid dividend on cumulative preferred shares; it must be paid before any regular dividends on the preferred shares and before any dividends on the common shares. (p. 706)

Financial leverage The achievement of an increased return on common shares by paying dividends on preferred shares or interest on debt at a rate that is less than the rate of return earned with the assets invested in the corporation by the preferred shareholders or creditors. (p. 708)

Market value per share The price at which stock is bought or sold. (p. 701)

Noncumulative preferred shares Preferred shares on which the right to receive dividends is lost for any year that the dividends are not declared. (p. 706)

No-par value shares A class of shares that has not been assigned a par value by the corporate charter. (p. 702)

Nonparticipating preferred shares Preferred shares on which dividends are limited to a maximum amount each year. (p. 707)

Organization costs The costs of bringing a corporation into existence, including legal fees, promoters' fees, and amounts paid to the incorporating legal jurisdiction. (p. 697)

Participating preferred shares Preferred shares with a feature that allows preferred shareholders to share with common shareholders in any dividends paid in excess of the percent stated on the preferred shares. (p. 707)

Par value An arbitrary value a corporation places on each share of its capital stock. (p. 703)

Preemptive right The right of common shareholders to protect their proportionate ownership in a corporation by having the first opportunity to buy additional common shares issued by the corporation. (p. 699)

Preferred shares Stock that gives its owners a priority status over common shareholders in one or more ways, such as the payment of dividends or the distribution of assets on liquidation. (p. 704)

Proxy A legal document that gives an agent of a shareholder the power to exercise the voting rights of that shareholder's shares. (p. 698)

Retained earnings The cumulative net income retained by a corporation. (p. 702)

Share capital Another name for capital stock. (p. 700)

Shareholders' equity The equity of a corporation; also called *stockholders' equity* or *corporate capital.* (p. 702)

Share subscription A contractual commitment by an investor to purchase unissued shares at specific future dates and prices. (p. 704)

Questions

1. Who is responsible for directing the affairs of a corporation?
2. What are organization costs? List several examples of these costs.
3. How are organization costs classified on the balance sheet?
4. List the general rights of common shareholders.
5. What is the preemptive right of common shareholders?
6. What is the meaning of the call price of a share?
7. Why would an investor find convertible preferred shares attractive?
8. Examine the balance sheet for **Atlantis** in Appendix I at the end of the book and determine the classes of shares that the company has issued.
9. Refer to the balance sheet for **Alliance** in Appendix I at the end of the book. How many classes of shares is Alliance authorized to issue?
10. What steps did Jennifer Wong have to follow in order to incorporate her business?

Quick Study

QS 15-1
Characteristics of corporations
LO 1

Of the following statements, which are true for the corporation form of business?

a. Capital often is more easily accumulated than with other forms of organization.
b. It has a limited life.
c. Owners have unlimited liability for corporate debts.
d. Distributed income is taxed twice in normal circumstances.
e. It is a separate legal entity.
f. Ownership rights cannot be easily transferred.
g. Owners are not agents of the corporation.

QS 15-2
Issuance of common shares
LO 3

On February 1, Excel Corporation issued 37,500 common shares for $252,000 cash. Present the entry to record this transaction.

QS 15-3
Interpreting journal entries for share issuances
LO 3

Each of these entries was recently recorded by a different corporation. Provide an explanation for the event or transaction described by each entry.

a.	Apr. 1	Cash	60,000	
		Common Shares		60,000
b.	Apr. 3	Organization Costs	90,000	
		Common Shares		90,000
c.	Apr. 4	Subscriptions receivable	20,000	
		Cash	60,000	
		Common shares subscribed		80,000
d.	Apr. 5	Merchandise Inventory	90,000	
		Machinery	130,000	
		Notes Payable		144,000
		Common Shares		76,000

QS 15-4
Dividend allocation between classes of shareholders
LO 5

Holden Company's shareholders' equity includes 75,000 shares of 8% cumulative preferred shares that had been issued for $375,000 and 200,000 common shares. Holden did not declare any dividends during the prior year and now declares and pays a $108,000 cash dividend. Determine the amount distributed to each class of shareholders.

QS 15-5
Book value per common share
LO 6

The shareholders' equity section of Courtland Company's balance sheet follows:

Shareholders' Equity	
Preferred shares, $5 cumulative, 10,000 shares authorized, issued and outstanding	$100,000
Common shares, 100,000 shares authorized, 75,000 shares issued and outstanding	375,000
Retained earnings	445,000
Total shareholders' equity	$920,000

The call price of the preferred shares is $30. Determine the book value per common share under the assumption that there are no dividends in arrears.

Exercises

Exercise 15-1
Recording share issuances
LO 3

Present the general journal entries that an accountant would prepare to record the following issuances of shares in three different situations:

a. Two thousand shares of common shares are issued to the corporation's promoters in exchange for their efforts in creating it. Their efforts are estimated to be worth $30,000.
b. Four thousand common shares are issued for $70,000 cash.
c. One thousand preferred shares are issued for $120,000 cash.

Exercise 15-2
Accounting for share issuances
LO 3

Hanson, Inc. issued 6,000 of its common shares on February 2. Present the journal entries that the company's accountant would use to record this event under each of the following independent situations:

a. The shares were issued for lawyers services valued at $4,000 in establishing the corporation.
b. The shares have a $2 value.
c. The shares were issued to a creditor who was owed $12,000.

Exercise 15-3
Dividends on common and noncumulative preferred shares
LO 5

The outstanding shares of Lipscomb includes 40,000 shares of 7.5% noncumulative preferred shares that had been issued for $400,000, as well as 100,000 common shares that had been issued at $1 per share. During its first four years of operation, the corporation declared and paid the following total amounts of dividends:

1999	$ 10,000
2000	24,000
2001	100,000
2002	196,000

Determine the amount of dividends paid in each year to each class of shareholders. Also determine the total dividends paid to each class in the four years combined.

Exercise 15-4
Dividends on common and cumulative preferred shares
LO 5

Use the data in Exercise 15-3 to determine the amount of dividends paid in each year to each class of shareholders, assuming that the preferred shares are cumulative. Also determine the total dividends paid to each class in the four years combined.

Exercise 15-5
Using preferred shares to create leverage
LO 2, 4

An individual entrepreneur is planning to start a new business and needs $312,500 of start-up capital. This person has $250,000 in personal assets that can be invested and thus needs to raise another $62,500 in cash. The founder will buy 5,000 common shares for $250,000 and has two alternative plans for raising the additional cash. One plan is to sell 1,250 common shares to one or more other investors for $62,500 cash. The second is to sell 625 shares of cumulative preferred shares to one or more investors for $62,500 cash (these shares have an annual 8% dividend rate).

1. If the business is expected to earn $45,000 of after-tax net income in the first year, what rate of return on beginning equity will the founder earn under each alternative? Which of the two plans will provide the higher return to the founder?
2. If the business is expected to earn $10,500 of after-tax net income in the first year, what rate of return on beginning equity will the founder earn under each alternative? Which of the two plans will provide the higher return to the founder?

Exercise 15-6
Identifying characteristics of preferred shares
LO 2, 4

Match each of the numbered descriptions with the characteristic of preferred shares that it best describes. Indicate your answer by writing the letter for the correct characteristic in the blank space next to each description.

A. Callable
B. Convertible
C. Cumulative
D. Noncumulative
E. Nonparticipating
F. Participating

_____ **1.** The holders of the shares can exchange it for common shares.
_____ **2.** The issuing corporation can retire the shares by paying a prearranged price.
_____ **3.** The holders of the shares are entitled to receive dividends in excess of the stated rate under some conditions.
_____ **4.** The holders of the shares are not entitled to receive dividends in excess of the stated rate.
_____ **5.** The holders of the shares lose any dividends that are not declared.
_____ **6.** The holders of the shares are entitled to receive current and all past dividends before common shareholders receive any dividends.

Exercise 15-7
Characteristics of corporations and partnerships
LO 1

Next to the following list of eight general characteristics of business organizations, write a brief description of how each characteristic applies to corporations and general partnerships.

		Corporations	General Partnerships
1.	Life		
2.	Owners' liability		
3.	Legal status		
4.	Tax status of income		
5.	Owners' authority		
6.	Ease of formation		
7.	Transferability of ownership		
8.	Ability to raise large amounts of capital		

Exercise 15-8
Book value per share
LO 6

The balance sheet for Kuhn Corp. includes the following information:

Shareholders' Equity	
Preferred shares, 6% cumulative, $30 call price, 5,000 shares issued and outstanding	$125,000
Common shares, 40,000 shares issued and outstanding	400,000
Retained earnings	267,500
Total shareholders' equity	$792,500

Determine the book value per share of the preferred and common shares under these two situations:

a. No preferred dividends are in arrears.

b. Three years of preferred dividends are in arrears.

Problems

Problem 15-1
Shareholders' equity transactions
LO 2, 3

Precision Products, Inc., was incorporated at the beginning of the year and engaged in a number of transactions. The following journal entries affected its shareholders' equity during its first year of operations:

		Debit	Credit
a.	Cash	150,000	
	Common Shares (5,000 shares)		150,000
b.	Organization Costs	75,000	
	Common Shares (2,500 shares)		75,000
c.	Cash	21,500	
	Accounts Receivable	7,500	
	Office Equipment	10,750	
	Building	30,000	
	Accounts Payable		11,000
	Notes Payable		18,750
	Common Shares (1,000 shares)		40,000

d.

Cash	60,000	
Accounts payable	20,000	
Common Shares (2,000 shares)		80,000

Required

1. Provide explanations for the journal entries.
2. Prepare answers for the following questions:
   a. What is the total contributed capital?
   b. What is the book value per common share at the end of the year if contributed capital plus retained earnings equals $347,500?

Problem 15-2
Share subscriptions
LO 2, 3, 4

Micron Corporation is authorized to issue 60,000 shares of $4 cumulative and nonparticipating preferred and an unlimited number of no-par-value common shares. Micron Corporation then completed these transactions:

July 6 Accepted subscriptions to 80,000 common shares at $18 per share. Down payments equal to 25% of the subscription price accompanied each subscription. The balance is due on August 10.

July 20 Gave the corporation's promoters 2,000 common shares for their services in getting the corporation organized. The board valued the services at $35,000.

Aug. 4 Accepted subscription to 6,000 shares of preferred at $65 per share. The subscriptions were accompanied by 50% down payment. The balance is due on September 5.

10 Collected the balance due on the July 6 common subscriptions and issued the shares.

30 Accepted subscriptions to 1,000 shares of preferred at $62 per share. The subscriptions were accompanied by 50% down payments. The balance is due on October 30.

Sept. 5 Collected the balance due on the August 4 preferred subscriptions and issued the shares.

Required

1. Prepare general journal entries to record the transactions.
2. Prepare the shareholders' equity section of the corporation's balance sheet as of the close of business on September 30. Assume that retained earnings are $60,000.

Problem 15-3
Shareholders' equity transactions
LO 2, 3, 4, 5

Solar Energy Company is authorized to issue an unlimited number of common shares and 100,000 shares of $10, noncumulative and nonparticipating, convertible preferred. The company completed the following transactions:

1997

Feb. 5 Issued 70,000 common shares at $10 for cash.

28 Gave the corporation's promoters 3,750 common shares for their services in organizing the corporation. The directors valued the services at $40,000.

Mar. 3 Issued 44,000 common shares in exchange for the following assets with the indicated reliable market values: land, $80,000; buildings, $210,000; and machinery, $155,000.

Dec. 31 Closed the Income Summary account. A $27,000 loss was incurred.

1998

Jan. 28 Issued 4,000 preferred shares at $100 for cash.

Dec. 15 Solar Energy Company's preferred shareholders submitted 2,500 of their convertible shares for conversion into common shares on this date. The convertible shareholders accepted nine common shares for each preferred share.

31 Closed the Income Summary account. A $98,000 net income was earned.

1999

Jan. 1 The board of directors declared a $10 cash dividend to preferred shares and $0.20 per share cash dividend to outstanding common shares, payable on February 5 to the January 24 shareholders of record.

Feb. 5 Paid the previously declared dividends.

Oct. 20 Accepted subscriptions to 4,000 common shares at $14.90 per share. Down payment of 40% accompanied the subscription contracts. The balance is due on January 20, 1995.

Dec. 31 Closed the Cash Dividends Declared and Income Summary accounts. A $159,000 net income was earned.

Required

1. Prepare general journal entries to record the transactions.
2. Prepare the shareholders' equity section of the balance sheet as of the close of business on December 31, 1999.

Problem 15-4
Computing book values and dividend allocations
LO 5, 6

Segura Corporation's common shares are currently selling on a stock exchange at $170 per share, and a recent balance sheet shows the following information:

Shareholders' Equity	
Preferred shares, 5%, cumulative, 1,000 shares authorized, issued, and outstanding	$100,000
Common shares, 4,000 shares authorized, issued, and outstanding	160,000
Retained earnings	300,000
Total shareholders' equity	$560,000

Required

Preparation component:

1. What is the market value of the corporation's common shares?
2. How much capital was contributed by the residual owners of the company? Common Shares.
3. If no dividends are in arrears, what are the book values per share of the preferred shares and the common shares?
4. If two years' preferred dividends are in arrears, what are the book values per share of the preferred shares and the common shares?
5. If two years' preferred dividends are in arrears and the preferred shares are callable at $110 per share, what are the book values per share of the preferred shares and the common shares?
6. If two years' preferred dividends are in arrears and the board of directors declares dividends of $20,000 what total amount will be paid to preferred and common shareholders? What is the amount of dividends per share for the common shares?

Analysis component:

7. What are some factors that may contribute to the difference between the book value of common shares and its market value?

Problem 15-5
Calculating book values; allocating dividends between preferred and common shares
LO 5, 6

Part 1. The balance sheet of Desktop Services Corporation includes the following information:

Shareholders' Equity	
Preferred shares, cumulative, 8%, 2,500 shares authorized, issued and outstanding	$250,000
Common shares, unlimited number authorized, 40,000 shares issued and outstanding	400,000
Retained earnings	192,500
Total shareholders' equity	$842,500

Required

Assume that the preferred has a call price of $105 plus any dividends in arrears. Calculate the book value per share of the preferred and common under each of the following assumptions:

a. There are no dividends in arrears on the preferred.
b. One year's dividends are in arrears on the preferred.
c. Three years' dividends are in arrears on the preferred.

Part 2. Since its organization. TVP Corporation had 14,000 outstanding shares of $11 preferred and 235,000 shares of no-par-value common. No dividends have been paid this year, and none were paid during either of the past two years. However, the company has recently prospered, and the board of directors wants to know how much cash would be required to provide a $1.50 per share dividend on the common. Preferred was issued at $100 per share and the common at $10 per share.

Required

Prepare a schedule that shows the amounts of cash required for dividends to each class of shareholders to provide the desired $1.50 per share dividend to the common shareholders under each of the following assumptions:

a. The preferred is noncumulative and nonparticipating.
b. The preferred is cumulative and nonparticipating.
c. The preferred is cumulative and fully participating based on stated value.
d. The preferred is cumulative and participating to 14% based on stated value.

Problem 15-6
Allocating dividends in sequential years between preferred and common shares
LO 5

Alphalon Cookware Company has 4,000 outstanding shares of $8 preferred and 56,000 shares of no-par-value common. During a seven-year period, the company paid out the following amounts in dividends:

1993	$ -0-
1994	46,000
1995	-0-
1996	60,000
1997	74,000
1998	68,400
1999	144,000

No dividends were in arrears for the years prior to 1993.

Required

1. Prepare three schedules with column headings as follows:

Year	Calculations	Preferred Dividend per Share	Common Dividend per Share

2. Complete schedules under each of the following assumptions. (Round your answers to the nearest cent.) Preferred was issued at $100 per share and common at $10 per share.
   a. The preferred is noncumulative and nonparticipating.
   b. The preferred is cumulative and nonparticipating.
   c. The preferred is cumulative and fully participating based on percentage of stated value.

Problem 15-7
Analytical essay
LO 1

Daphne Thomas and Elizabeth White want to go into business as special event promoters. Both can contribute fairly large amounts of capital, but they will need to acquire additional equity capital from other investors in about a year. Thomas has the expertise to run the business, and White will handle the administrative details. They plan to hire about three employees initially and will distribute all profits annually. White wants to operate as a general partnership, but Thomas thinks they should form a corporation. Thomas asks you to write a brief supporting her view in favour of the corporate form. What would you include in your essay to convince White that a corporation would be preferable to a partnership in their situation?

Problem 15-8
Analytical essay
LO 5, 6

Refer to the shareholders' equity section of the balance sheet in Problem 15-5. Assume, however, that an unlimited number of common shares are authorized instead of 40,000. Also, assume that the preferred is convertible into common at a rate of eight common shares for each share of preferred. If 1,000 shares of the preferred are converted into common, describe how this affects the shareholders' equity section of the balance sheet (immediately after the conversion). If you are a common shareholder in this company, and the company plans to pay total cash dividends of $300,000, does it make any difference to you whether or not the conversion takes place before the dividend declaration? Why?

Alternate Problems

Problem 15-1A
Shareholders' equity transactions
LO 2, 3, 6

Livingston Company, Inc., was incorporated at the beginning of the year and engaged in a number of transactions. Presented below are all the journal entries that affected its shareholders' equity during its first year of operations:

a.	Cash	60,000	
	Common Shares (1,500 shares)		60,000
b.	Organization Costs	20,000	
	Common Shares (500 shares)		20,000
c.	Cash	6,650	
	Accounts Receivable	4,000	
	Office Equipment	6,000	
	Building	12,500	
	Accounts Payable		2,000
	Notes Payable		7,150
	Common shares (300 shares)		20,000
d.	Cash	30,000	
	Accounts payable	10,000	
	Common shares (700 shares)		40,000

Required

1. Provide explanations for the journal entries.
2. Prepare answers for the following questions:
   a. What is the total contributed capital?
   b. What is the book value per share of the common shares at the end of the year if contributed capital plus retained earnings equals $141,500?

Problem 15-2A
Share subscriptions

LO 2, 3, 4

Conran Corporation is authorized to issue 50,000 shares of $9 cumulative and nonparticipating preferred and an unlimited number of no-par-value common shares. Conran Corporation then completed these transactions:

Apr. 4 Accepted subscriptions to 65,000 common shares at $17 per share. Downpayments equal to 25% of the subscription price accompanied each subscription. The balance is due on June 3.

11 Gave the corporation's promoters 1,300 common shares for their services in organizing the corporation. The board valued the services at $26,000.

May 1 Accepted subscriptions to 5,000 preferred shares at $120 per share. The subscriptions were accompanied by 40% down payments. The balance is due on July 31.

June 3 Collected the balance due on the April 4 common subscriptions and issued the shares.

July 1 Accepted subscriptions to 2,000 preferred shares at $122 per share. The subscriptions were accompanied by 40% down payments. The balance is due on August 15.

31 Collected the balance due on the May 1 preferred subscriptions and issued the shares.

Required

1. Prepare general journal entries to record the transactions.
2. Prepare the shareholders' equity section of the corporation's balance sheet as of the close of business on July 31. Assume that retained earnings are $23,000.

Problem 15-3A
Shareholders' equity transactions

LO 2, 3, 4, 5

Coach Motor Company is authorized by its articles of incorporation to issue an unlimited number of common shares and 50,000 shares of $10, noncumulative and nonparticipating, convertible preferred. The company completed the following transactions:

1997

Feb. 2 Issued for cash 110,000 common shares at $1 per share.

28 Gave the corporation's promoters 65,000 common shares for their services in organizing the corporation. The director's valued the services at $80,000.

Mar. 10 Issued 150,000 common shares in exchange for the following assets with the indicated reliable market values: land, $70,000; buildings, $130,000; and machinery, $89,000.

Dec. 31 Closed the Income Summary account. A $61,000 loss was incurred.

1998

Jan. 1 Issued for cash 6,000 preferred shares at $100 per share.

Dec. 1 Coach Motor Company's shareholders submitted 750 shares of their convertible preferred for conversion into common shares on this date. The convertible preferred shareholders accepted 70 common shares for each share of preferred.

31 Closed the Income Summary account. A $196,000 net income was earned.

1999

Jan. 1 The board of directors declared a $10 cash dividend to preferred shares and $0.20 per share cash dividend to outstanding common shares, payable on January 25 to the January 15 shareholders of record.

25 Paid the previously declared dividends.

Nov. 15 Accepted subscriptions to 30,000 common shares at $3.20 per share. Down payments of 25% accompanied the subscription contracts. The balance is due on February 15, 1995.

Dec. 31 Closed the Cash Dividends and Income Summary accounts. A $262,000 net income was earned.

Required

1. Prepare general journal entries to record the transactions.
2. Prepare the shareholders' equity section of the balance sheet as of the close of business on December 31, 1999.

Problem 15-4A
Computing book values and dividend allocations
LO 5, 6

Longhorn Products, Inc.'s common shares are currently selling on a stock exchange at $45 per share, and a recent balance sheet shows the following information:

Shareholders' Equity	
Preferred shares, Cumulative, 8%, 1,500 shares authorized, issued and outstanding	$ 187,500
Common shares, 18,000 shares authorized, issued, and outstanding	450,000
Retained earnings	562,500
Total shareholders' equity	$1,200,000

Required

Preparation component:

1. What is the market value of the corporation's common shares?
2. If no dividends are in arrears, what are the book values per share of the preferred shares and the common shares?
3. If two years' preferred dividends are in arrears, what are the book values per share of the preferred shares and the common shares?
4. If two years' preferred dividends are in arrears and the preferred shares are callable at $140 per share, what are the book values per share of the preferred shares and the common shares?
5. If two years' preferred dividends are in arrears and the board of directors declares dividends of $50,000 what total amount will be paid to preferred and common shareholders? What is the amount of dividends per share for the common shares?

Analysis component:

1. Discuss why the book value of common shares may not be a good estimate of its market value.

Problem 15-5A
Calculating book values: allocating dividends between preferred and common shares
LO 4, 5

Part 1. The balance sheet of Global Filter Company includes the following information:

Shareholders' Equity	
Share capital:	
Preferred, $11, cumulative and nonparticipating, 2,000 shares authorized and issued	$200,000
Common, no-par value, 60,000 shares authorized and issued	600,000
Retained earnings	120,000
Total shareholder's equity	$920,000

Required

Assume that the preferred shares have a call price of $106 plus any dividends in arrears. Calculate the book value per share of the preferred and common under each of the following assumptions:

a. No dividends are in arrears on the preferred shares.
b. One year's dividends are in arrears on the preferred shares.
c. Three years' dividends are in arrears on the preferred shares.

Part 2. Since its organization, Newhouse Corporation has had 3,200 outstanding shares of $11 preferred and 64,000 shares of no-par-value common. No dividends have been paid this year, and none were paid during either of the past two years. However, the company has recently prospered and the board of directors wants to know how much cash would be required to provide a $1.50 per share dividend on the common. The preferred was issued at $100 per share and the common at $10 per share.

Required

Prepare a schedule that shows the amounts of cash required for dividends to each class of shareholders to provide the desired $1.50 per share dividend under each of the following assumptions:

a. The preferred is noncumulative and nonparticipating.
b. The preferred is cumulative and nonparticipating.
c. The preferred is cumulative and fully participating based on stated value.
d. The preferred is cumulative and participating to 13% of stated value.

Problem 15-6A
Allocating dividends in sequential years between preferred and common shares.
LO 4

Oxford Bros. Company has 2,000 outstanding shares of $12 preferred and 30,000 shares of no-par-value common. During a seven-year period, the company paid out the following amounts in dividends:

1993	$ -0-
1994	54,000
1995	-0-
1996	30,000
1997	39,000
1998	48,000
1999	90,000

No dividends were in arrears for the years prior to 1993.

Required

1. Prepare three schedules with column headings as follows:

Year	Calculations	Preferred Dividend per Share	Common Dividend per Share

2. Complete a schedule under each of the following assumptions. (Round your calculations of dividends per share to the nearest cent.) The preferred was issued at $100 per share and common at $10 per share.

a. The preferred is noncumulative and nonparticipating.
b. The preferred is cumulative and nonparticipating.
c. The preferred is cumulative and fully participating based on a percentage of stated value.

Problem 15-7A
Analytical essay
LO 1

Daphne Thomas and Elizabeth White want to go into business as special-event promoters. Both can contribute fairly large amounts of capital, but they will need to acquire additional cash in about a year. Thomas has the expertise to run the business, and White will handle the administrative details. They plan to hire about three employees initially and will distribute all profits annually. White wants to operate as a partnership, but Thomas thinks they should form a corporation. White asks you to write a brief essay supporting her view in favour of the partnership form. What would you include in your essay to convince Thomas that a partnership might be preferable to a corporation in their situation?

Problem 15-8A
Analytical essay
LO 5, 6

Refer to the shareholders' equity section of the balance sheet in Problem 15-5A. Assume, however, that the common has 100,000 shares authorized instead of 60,000. Also, assume that the preferred shares are convertible into common at a rate of eight common shares for each of preferred. If 1,000 shares of the preferred are converted into common shares, describe how this affects the shareholders' equity section of the balance sheet (immediately after the conversion). If you are a common shareholder in this company, and cash dividends of $487,000 are to be paid out, does it make any difference to you whether or not the conversion takes place? Why?

Analytical and Review Problem

A & R Problem 15-1

Until March 2 of the current year, Knox, Lacy, and Mann were partners sharing losses and gains in a 4:4:2 ratio. On that date they received their certificate of incorporation of KLM Company, Limited. All the assets and liabilities of the partnership were taken over by the new corporation.

The trial balance of the partnership just before the transfer and the opening trail balance of the corporation appear below:

KNOX, LACY AND MANN
Post-Closing Trial Balance
March 2, 19XX

Cash	$ 4,500	
Accounts receivable	20,500	
Allowance for doubtful accounts		$ 500
Merchandise inventory	33,000	
Store equipment	13,500	
Accumulated amortization, store equipment		3,500
Land	8,500	
Building	65,000	
Accumulated amortization, building		9,500
Accounts payable		15,500
Mortgage payable		12,000
John Knox, capital		45,000
Robert Lacy, capital		40,000
George Mann, capital		19,000
	$145,000	$145,000

KLM COMPANY, LIMITED
Trial Balance
March 2. 19XX

Cash	$ 4,500	
Accounts receivable	20,500	
Allowance for doubtful accounts		$ 1,500
Merchandise inventory	25,000	
Store equipment	8,000	
Land	22,000	
Building	52,000	
Accounts payable		15,500
Mortgage payable		12,000
Share capital, common, no par value, 10,300 shares		103,000
	$132,000	$132,000

Required

Determine the number of shares of the new corporation owned by each of the three shareholders.

BEYOND THE NUMBERS

Reporting in Action

LO 2, 6

Refer to the financial statements and related information for **Atlantis** in Appendix I. Answer the following questions by analyzing the information in the report:

1. How many classes of shares is Atlantis authorized to issue?
2. Has Atlantis issued any preferred shares?
3. How many voting shares are outstanding as of December. 31, 1997, and what was their composition?
4. What is the book value of the common shares at December 31, 1997? Show calculations.
5. Obtain access to Atlantis' annual report for fiscal years ending after December 31, 1997. You may gain access to annual report information at following website: **http://www.sedar.com/dynamic_pages/issuerprofiles_e/i00002259.htm**. Have there been any issuances of preferred shares yet? Has the number of Atlantis common shares outstanding increased since December 31, 1997?

Comparative Analysis

LO 6

Both **NIKE** and **Reebok** design, produce, market, and sell sports footwear and apparel. Key comparative figures ($ thousands) for these two organizations follow:

	NIKE		Reebok	
Key Figures	**1997**	**1996**	**1996**	**1995**
Total shareholders' equity	$3,155,838	$2,431,400	$381,234	$895,289
Equity applicable to preferred	$ 300,000	$ 300,000		
Common Shares Issued	Class A&B 289,270	Class A&B 287,258	92,557	111,015
Treasury Shares Repurchased			36,716	36,211

* NIKE figures are from the annual reports for the fiscal years ended May 31, 1997 and 1996. Reebok figures are from the annual reports for the fiscal years ended December 31, 1996 and 1995.

Required

1. Compute the book value per common share for both Reebok and NIKE using the two years' data shown above.

Analysis component:

2. Identify causes of any changes in book value per share between the two years for each company.

Ethics Challenge

Jack and Bill are partners in a computer software company. They developed a word processing program that is remarkably similar to a **Corel** product. Jack telephones Bill at home one evening and says, "We should convert our partnership into a corporation before we launch this new word processing software. Let's withdraw most of our assets from the business before forming a corporate entity. If we are sued by Corel our liability will be to our business assets." Bill feels a little uneasy and replies, "Lets meet at 9 a.m. sharp to discuss this matter."

Required

Discuss the ethical issues in this case.

Communicating in Practice

LO 6

Investors use book value as a yardstick for investment in varying ways. Warren E. Buffett, one of the world's wealthiest individuals and a highly recognized investment expert, relies heavily on book value for investment decisions. But Buffet uses a slightly different computation for book value. Obtain a copy of the article "Buffet Takes Stock," by L. J. Davis, *The*

New York Times, April 1, 1990. Read the article and write a brief report that includes the following:

1. Traditional definition of the term "book value" and formulas for computation as found in this chapter.
2. Buffet's redefinition of the term "book value" and its formula for computation. Who is the source of this alternative definition and what is the person's relationship to Buffett?
3. Compute book value per share of common shares for a corporation of your choosing using (a) the traditional computation and (b) Buffet's computation. You will need an annual report which can be obtained in many ways including the following site: **http://www.sedar.com/dynamic_pages/new_docs/new**.
4. The market value of your chosen company's common shares on the date of the balance sheet in the annual report. (Research in financial press or online sites.)
5. An explanation of whether or not Buffett would have considered shares in the company you selected as a "sleeping beauty." (Hint: Answer is in article and with a comparison of two numbers.)

Teamwork in Action

LO 4

This activity in designed to reinforce team members' understanding of dividend allocation concepts.

1. Using the facts below, *each* team member is to determine the dividend allocation on a per share and per class basis for *one* of the assumptions that follow. Determine if this assumption results in arrears for future years. After determinations are complete, rotate around the team allowing each member to present their solution to the team. Do not proceed to the next team member until all team members express agreement with and understanding of the presentation. Be prepared to present to the class if you are called on to do so.

Facts:

Outstanding shares: 50,000 shares of 8% preferred shares (nonparticipating): $5,000,000
100,000 common shares: $5,000,000

Assumptions:

a. Preferred shares are noncumulative and a $200,000 dividend is declared.
b. Preferred shares are cumulative, no dividend arrears, and a $600,000 dividend is declared.
c. Preferred shares are cumulative, dividend arrears of $5 per share, and a dividend of $500,000 is declared.
d. Preferred shares are cumulative, two full years of dividend arrears, and a dividend of $1,800,000 is declared.

2. After completing a team discussion of each member's solution for the above assumptions, the team is to collaborate and determine how much of a dividend would need to be declared to ensure that a common shareholder receives $3 per share if the preferred shares are cumulative and have two full years of dividend arrears.

Hitting the Road

LO 1, 5

Review the different possible forms of business organization from the chapter. Identify a business in your area that is organized as (a) a sole proprietorship, (b) a general partnership, (c) a limited liability partnership, and (d) a corporation. You may need to confirm your identifications by placing a phone call to the various businesses.

Business Break

Visit the *Canadian Business Magazine* Web site at **http://www.canbus.com**. Explore the Web site by clicking on the following links.

1. View the Table of Contents of the latest issue of *Canadian Business Magazine.* Scan it and read an article from the issue that interests you.
2. Visit Archives and read an article that interests you.

16 CHAPTER

Corporate Reporting: Dividends, Shares, and Income

A Look Back

Chapter 15 focused on the corporate forms of organization. We described important characteristics of corporations along with accounting for many of their important transactions.

A Look at This Chapter

This chapter extends our discussion of corporate accounting to dividends, treasury shares, income reporting, and retained earnings. We also explain earnings per share, dividend yield, and the price-earnings ratio.

A Look Forward

Chapter 17 focuses on accounting for notes and bonds. This includes the characteristics of these liabilities and their implications to users of financial statements.

Chapter Outline

- **Dividends**
  - Cash Dividends
  - Stock Dividends
  - Stock Splits
- **Reacquisition of Shares**
  - Purchasing Treasury Shares
  - Reissuing Treasury Shares
- **Reporting Income Information**
  - Continuing Operations
  - Discontinued Segments
  - Extraordinary Items
  - Changes in Accounting Principles
  - Earnings per Share
  - Stock Options
- **Retained Earnings**
  - Restricted Retained Earnings
  - Appropriated Retained Earnings
  - Prior Period Adjustments
  - Changes in Accounting Estimates
  - Statement of Changes in Shareholders' Equity
- **Using the Information — Dividend Yield and Price-Earnings Ratio**
  - Dividend Yield
  - Price-Earnings

Let's Have a Ceilidh

Cape Breton, NS—Cape Breton is the heart of Scottish music. On this fun-loving island is a pub called the Bonnie Piper in the city of Sydney. It is the brainchild of Charlie "Buck" MacPherson, a farm boy from nearby Inverness.

"I always wanted to see Scotland, and so my buddy and I took a $295 charter flight and our mountain bikes to Scotland after we finished our first year in college," says MacPherson. During their tour, they dropped into a pub called "The Bonnie Piper," recalls MacPherson. "While we drank our ale, I kept thinking a pub like this would be a hit back home."

Within two years, MacPherson was running an Scottish-style pub in the hub of Cape Breton. But after three years, with a debt of $78,000, his dream was fading. "The first two years were great, and I was turning a hefty profit," boasted MacPherson. So what happened? "The next year the city took four months putting in a new sewer system on our street. At times, I was the only person in the pub. And then to top it off, we had an electrical fire closing us down for another two months."

To stay afloat, MacPherson needed cash. But who would lend him money after such a disastrous year? "I thought I was finished," says MacPherson. But, never the quitter, MacPherson took the pub's records to the local bank officer. "He really understood the situation and explained things like continuing operations, unusual losses, and extraordinary items."

The bank officer decided poor performance was tied to the sewer work and the electrical fire. The pub's normal operations were highly profitable. "In the end, I got my loan and I'm back turning a nice profit." So the next time you're in Cape Breton, enjoy a touch of Scotland at the Bonnie Piper.

Learning Objectives

LO 1 Record transactions involving cash dividends.

LO 2 Describe stock dividends and stock splits.

LO 3 Account for stock dividends and stock splits.

LO 4 Record purchases and sales of treasury shares and the retirement of shares.

LO 5 Explain the form and content of a corporate income statement.

LO 6 Compute earnings per share and describe its use.

LO 7 Explain the items reported in retained earnings.

LO 8 Compute dividend yield and explain its use in analysis.

LO 9 Compute price-earnings ratio and describe its use in analysis.

CHAPTER PREVIEW

Corporations often enter into financing transactions involving changes in shareholders' equity. The first two major sections of this chapter focus on several of these transactions including cash and stock dividends, stock splits, and a company's transactions in its own shares. The third section of this chapter describes the reporting of income information, with emphasis on the form and content of the income statement including earnings per share. The final section looks at accounting for retained earnings including prior period adjustments, retained earnings restrictions, and reporting guidelines. Understanding these topics helps us read, interpret, and use financial statements for decision making. It also assists people like Charlie MacPherson, as described in the opening article, to properly report income.

Dividends

A corporation's retained earnings is that part of shareholders' equity created by a company's income and loss activities. Retained earnings equals the total cumulative amount of reported net income less net losses and dividends declared since the beginning of operations or the shareholders' residual interest in the corporation not created by their investments. Information about retained earnings is useful in predicting the future cash flows connected with dividends and other events. This section describes how dividends affect retained eanrings and discusses dividend transactions that involve both cash and shares.

Cash Dividends

Generally a corporation is permitted to pay cash dividends if retained earnings exist. To pay a cash dividend a corporation must also have cash *in addition to* retained earnings. The decision to pay cash dividends rests with the board of directors. The directors, for instance, may decide to keep the cash to invest in corporation growth. Or they may feel the cash is needed for unforeseen emergencies, unexpected opportunities, or for paying off debt.

LO1 Record transactions involving cash dividends.

Many corporations, on the other hand, pay cash dividends to their shareholders in regular amounts at regular dates. These cash flows provide a return to investors and almost always affect the stock's market value.

Entries for Cash Dividends

We sometimes assume for simplicity that dividends are declared and paid at the same time. But in practice the payment of dividends involves three important dates: declaration, record, and payment.

Date of declaration is the date on which the directors vote to pay a dividend. Shareholders receive a dividend only if the directors vote to declare one. Declaring a dividend creates a legal liability of the corporation to its shareholders. **Date of record** is the future date specified by directors for shareholders to receive dividends. The date of record usually follows the date of declaration by at least two weeks. Shareholders listed in the corporation's records on the date of record receive dividends. **Date of payment** is the date when shareholders receive payment. This date follows the date of record by enough time to allow the corporation to arrange cheques or other means to pay dividends. If a balance sheet is prepared between the date of declaration and the date of payment, a liability for the dividend is reported as a current liability.

We must record the legal liability created by declaring a dividend. To illustrate, the entry to record a January 9 declaration of a $1 per share dividend by the directors of Z-Tech with 5,000 outstanding common shares is:

Date of Declaration

Jan. 9	Cash Dividends Declared	5,000	
	Common Dividend Payable		5,000
	Declared a $1 per share cash dividend on common shares.		

Assets	=	Liabilities	+	Equity
		+5,000		−5,000

Cash Dividends Declared is a temporary (contra equity) account that accumulates information about the total dividends declared during the reporting period. It is *not* an expense account. Common Dividend Payable reflects the corporation's current liability to its shareholders.

The date of record is January 22 and is the date on which identification is made of shareholders who will receive dividends. No journal entry is needed at the date of record:

Date of Record

Jan. 22	No entry required		

The date of payment requires an entry to record distribution of the cash dividend. The entry to record both the settlement of the liability and reduction of the cash balance on the date of payment is:

Date of Payment

Feb. 1	Common Dividend Payable	5,000	
	Cash		5,000
	Paid $1 per share cash dividend to common shareholders.		

Assets	=	Liabilities	+	Equity
−5,000		−5,000		

At the end of the reporting period, the balance of the Cash Dividends Declared account is closed to Retained Earnings. For instance, if Z-Tech declared four quarterly dividends of $5,000, the account would have a $20,000 balance at the end of the year. The required year-end closing entry is:

Dec. 31	Retained Earnings	20,000	
	Cash Dividends Declared		20,000
	To close Cash Dividends Declared account.		

Assets	=	Liabilities	+	Equity
				−20,000
				+20,000

If one of the declared dividends remains unpaid on December 31, this closing entry is still recorded because the act of declaration reduces retained earnings. The Common Dividend Payable liability account continues to carry a balance until dividends are paid. Its balance is reported on the December 31 balance sheet.

Dividend Decline

There has been a major decline in cash dividends as a percent of share prices. Cash dividends are increasingly viewed as an inefficient way to reward shareholders. Dividend tax rates can be very high, and these taxes are inescapable. Companies are instead buying back shares, paying down debt, or expanding the business.

[Source: *"Are Stocks Overpriced—Or the Yardsticks Flawed?" Business Week,* July 15, 1996.]

Deficits and Cash Dividends

A corporation with a debit (abnormal) balance for retained earnings is said to have a deficit. A **deficit** arises when a company incurs cumulative losses or pays dividends greater than total profits earned in other years. A deficit is deducted on a corporation's balance sheet as shown in Exhibit 16.1.

Exhibit 16.1

Shareholders' Equity with a Deficit

Common shares, no-par, 5,000 shares authorized and outstanding	$50,000
Retained earnings deficit	(6,000)
Total shareholders' equity	$44,000

In most jurisdictions, a corporation with a deficit is not allowed to pay a cash dividend to its shareholders. This legal restriction is designed to protect creditors of the corporation by preventing distribution of assets to shareholders at a time when the company is in financial difficulty. For example, the Canada Business Corporations Act of 1975 provides the following in section 40:

> A corporation shall not declare or pay a dividend if there are responsible grounds for believing that
> (a) the corporation is, or would after payment, be unable to pay its liabilities as they become due; or
> (b) the realizable value of the corporation's assets would thereby be less than the aggregate of its liabilities and stated capital of all classes.

The size of a company's deficit may differ depending on what GAAP the company is following. For example, the following information was extracted from the annual report of **Microcell Telecommunications Inc.**, a personal communications services operator based in Montreal:

	Dec. 31, 1996	Dec. 31, 1995
Accumulated deficit under Canadian GAAP	$ (7,767)	$ (36,623)
Accumulated deficit under U.S. GAAP	$(124,026)	$(367,479)

Liquidating Cash Dividends

The Cash Dividends Declared account is normally closed to the Retained Earnings account. But sometimes cash dividends are paid as a return of the capital contributed by shareholders. This means the Cash Dividends Declared account is closed with a debit entry to one of the contributed capital accounts instead of Retained Earnings. This kind of dividend is called a **liquidating cash dividend**, or simply *liquidating dividend*, because it returns a part of the original investment to the shareholders.

A liquidating dividend usually occurs when a company is completing a major downsizing, perhaps in preparation for a merger or closing. The equity from the outstanding shares cannot usually be used for a liquidating dividend unless all creditors are paid. This latter situation is typically limited to when a corporation is actually going out of business.

Flash back

1. The Cash Dividends Declared account is normally (a) reported on the balance sheet as a liability, (b) closed to Income Summary, (c) closed to Retained Earnings.
2. What three dates are involved in the process of paying a cash dividend?
3. When does a dividend become a legal obligation of the company?

Answers—p. 758

Stock Dividends

A corporation's directors can declare a stock dividend. A **stock dividend** occurs when a company distributes additional shares of its own stock to its shareholders without receiving any payment in return. Stock dividends and cash dividends are different. A stock dividend does not reduce a corporation's assets and shareholders' equity, while a cash dividend does both. A stock dividend simply transfers a portion of equity from retained earnings to contributed capital.

Reasons for Stock Dividends

LO 2 Describe stock dividends and stock splits.

If stock dividends do not affect assets or total shareholders' equity, then why declare and distribute them? There are several reasons. First, directors use stock dividends to keep the market price of the stock affordable. For example, if a profitable corporation grows but doesn't pay cash dividends, the price of its common shares continues to increase. The price of such a share may become so high that it discourages some investors from buying the stock. When a corporation declares a stock dividend, it increases the number of outstanding shares and lowers the per share price of its stock. Another reason for declaring a stock dividend is to provide evidence of management's confidence that the company is doing well. Finally, stock dividends conserve cash for business expansion that will hopefully lead to positive returns on shareholder investment.

Entries for Stock Dividends

A stock dividend does not affect a corporation's assets or total shareholders' equity, but it does affect the components of shareholders' equity. It does this by transferring part of retained earnings to contributed capital accounts. This is sometimes described as *capitalizing* retained earnings because it increases a company's contributed capital.

Accounting for a stock dividend depends on whether it is a small or large stock dividend. A **small stock dividend** is a distribution of less than or equal to 25% of the previously outstanding shares. It is unlikely to have a large effect on the share's market price and is, therefore, sometimes viewed as similar to a cash dividend. A small stock dividend is recorded by capitalizing retained earnings for an amount equal to the market value of the shares to be distributed.

A **large stock dividend** is a distribution of more than 25% of the previously outstanding shares. A large stock dividend is likely to have a noticeable effect on the stock's market price, and is unlikely viewed as a substitute for a cash dividend. A large stock dividend can be accounted for by a memo entry only. The main purpose of distributing it is to reduce the market price per share. Investors will own more shares but the shares are worth proportionally less.

To illustrate accounting for stock dividends, we use the shareholders' equity section of **X-Quest** shown in Exhibit 16.2 just *before* its declaration of a stock dividend.

Exhibit 16.2

Shareholders' Equity before the Stock Dividend

X-QUEST Shareholders' Equity December 31, 2000	
Common shares—no-par value, 15,000 shares authorized, 10,000 shares issued and outstanding	$108,000
Retained earnings	35,000
Total shareholders' equity	$143,000

Recording a Stock Dividend

LO 3 Account for stock dividends and stock splits.

Let's assume the directors of X-Quest declare a 10% stock dividend on December 31, 2000. This stock dividend of 1,000 shares, computed as 10% of its 10,000 outstanding shares, is to be distributed on January 20 to the shareholders of record on January 15. Since the market price of X-Quest's stock on December 31 is $15 per share, the dividend declaration is recorded as:

Assets = Liabilities + Equity
−15,000
+15,000

Date of Declaration

Dec. 31	Stock Dividends Declared	15,000	
	Common Shares Dividend Distributable		15,000
	To record declaration of a stock dividend of 1,000 common shares.		

The debit is recorded in the temporary (contra equity) account called Stock Dividends Declared. This account serves the same purpose as the Cash Dividends Declared account. A complete chart of accounts includes separate accounts for cash and stock dividends because the financial statements must report stock and cash dividends as separate events. If stock dividends are not frequently declared, a company might not keep a separate account for Stock Dividends Declared. Instead, it can record the debit directly to Retained Earnings. This approach is acceptable as long as the information is reported correctly in financial statements.

In the stock dividend declaration entry, the $15,000 credit is an increase to a contributed capital account called Common Shares Dividend Distributable. This account balance exists only until the shares are actually issued.

A stock dividend is never a liability on a balance sheet because it will never reduce assets. Instead, any declared but undistributed stock dividend appears on the balance sheet as a part of contributed capital in shareholders' equity. In particular, a balance sheet changes in three ways when declaring a stock dividend. First, the amount of equity attributed to common shares increases from $108,000 to $123,000 because 1,000 additional shares are declared for issuance. Second, retained earnings decreases by $15,000 (from $35,000 to $20,000) reflecting the transfer of amounts to contributed capital.

As part of the year-end closing process, X-Quest closes the Stock Dividends Declared account to Retained Earnings with the entry:

Assets = Liabilities + Equity
−15,000
+15,000

Dec. 31	Retained Earnings	15,000	
	Stock Dividends Declared		15,000
	To close the Stock Dividends Declared account.		

The shareholders' equity of X-Quest is shown in Exhibit 16.3 after the 10% stock dividend is declared on December 31.

Exhibit 16.3

Shareholders' Equity after Declaring a Stock Dividend

X-QUEST Shareholders' Equity December 31, 2000	
Common shares—no-par value, 15,000 shares authorized,	
10,000 shares issued and outstanding	$108,000
Common shares dividend distributable, 1,000 shares	15,000
Total contributed capital	$123,000
Retained earnings	20,000
Total shareholders' equity	$143,000

No entry is made on the date of record for a stock dividend. On January 20, the date of distribution, X-Quest distributes the new shares to shareholders and records this with the entry:

Assets = Liabilities + Equity
−15,000
+15,000

Date of Payment

Jan. 20	Common Shares Dividend Distributable . . .	15,000	
	Common Shares		15,000
	To record distribution of a 1,000-share common shares dividend.		

The combined effect of these two stock dividend entries is to transfer (or capitalize) $15,000 of retained earnings to contributed capital. The amount of capitalized retained earnings equals the market value of the 1,000 issued shares ($15 × 1,000 shares). This stock dividend has no effect on X-Quest's assets or total shareholders' equity. Nor does it affect the ownership percent of the company by individual shareholders.

To show this, assume we own 200 shares of X-Quest prior to the 10% stock dividend. When X-Quest sends each shareholder one new share for each 10 shares held, we receive 20 new shares (10% × 200 shares). Exhibit 16.4 shows the effects of this 10% stock dividend for both X-Quest and our shares. There is no change in the book value of either X-Quest or our shares. Before the stock dividend, we owned 2% of X-Quest's shares, computed as 200 divided by 10,000 outstanding shares. After the dividend we hold 220 shares, but our holding still equals 2%, computed as 220 divided by 11,000 shares now outstanding. Total book value of our holding does not change and still equals $2,860. Before the stock dividend we owned 200 shares with a book value of $14.30 per share. After this dividend we hold 220 shares with a book value of $13.00 per share. The only change in our 2% investment is that it is now divided among 220 shares instead of 200 shares. Total shareholder's equity does not change. The only effect on shareholders' equity is a transfer of $15,000 from retained earnings to contributed capital.

Exhibit 16.4

Effects of X-Quest's 10% Stock Dividend

Before 10% stock dividend	
Shareholders' equity:	
Common shares (10,000 shares)	$108,000
Retained earnings	35,000
Total shareholders' equity	**$143,000**
Book value per share = $143,000/10,000 shares = $14.30	
Book value of 200 shares = $14.30 × 200 = **$2,860**	
After 10% stock dividend is distributed	
Shareholders' equity:	
Common shares (11,000 shares)	$123,000
Retained earnings	20,000
Total shareholders' equity	**$143,000**
Book value per share = $143,000/11,000 shares = $13	
Book value of 220 shares = $13 × 220 = **$2,860**	

Amount of Retained Earnings Capitalized

The Canada Business Corporations Act requires that if a corporation declares a stock dividend, it must capitalize an amount of retained earnings that equals the market value of the shares to be distributed. On the other hand the Ontario Corporations Act allows the board of directors to determine the amount of retained earnings to be capitalized. Since there is no consistency in corporate laws regarding the amount of retained earnings to be capitalized, corporations must observe the requirements of their jurdiction of incorporation.

Engineer

You are an engineer with some savings invested in shares. One of your share investments announces a 50% stock dividend. Has the value of your share investment increased?

You Make the Call

Answer—p. 757

Stock Splits

We explained that a stock dividend can reduce a stock's market price and make it more marketable to investors. A stock dividend does this by dividing a company's outstanding shares into smaller pieces. The total value of the company is unchanged, but the price of each new share is smaller. We can accomplish the same thing with a **stock split.** A stock split is the distribution of additional shares to shareholders according to their percent ownership. When a stock split occurs, the corporation calls in its outstanding shares and issues more than one new share in exchange for each old share.[1] Splits can be done in any ratio including two-for-one, three-for-one, or higher. It does this by reducing the issued value per share. For example, in May 1998 **Shaw Industries Ltd.** announced a three-for-one stock split of its Class A Subordinate Voting Shares and its Class B Multiple Voting Shares to shareholders of record as of the close of business on June 1, 1998. Final approval of such announcements is subject to shareholder approval.

To illustrate, CompTec has 100,000 no-par value common shares outstanding with a current market value of $88 per share. A two-for-one stock split replaces 100,000 shares with 200,000 common shares. Also, market value is reduced from $88 per share to about $44 per share.

A stock split does not affect shareholders' equity reported on CompTec's balance sheet. It also does not affect individual shareholder's percent ownership of CompTec. The Contributed Capital and Retained Earnings accounts are unchanged by a split, and *no journal entry is made*. The only effect on the accounts is a change in the account description for common shares. CompTec's two-for-one split on its shares means that after the split it changes the description about these shares to reflect the additional outstanding.

The difference between stock splits and large stock dividends is often blurred in practice. Many companies report stock splits in their financial statements without calling in the original shares. The "split" results in additional shares issued to shareholders by capitalizing retained earnings or transferring other contributed capital to Common Shares. This approach avoids administrative costs of splitting the stock. **Harley-Davidson** recently declared a 2-for-1 stock split in the form of a 100% stock dividend by transferring additional paid-in capital to common shares.

A **reverse stock split** is the opposite of a stock split. It increases both the market value per share and the issued value per share. It does this by specifying the ratio to be less than one-to-one such as one-for-two. This means shareholders end up with fewer shares after a reverse stock split.

Flash back

4. Which of the following statements is correct?
   a. A large stock dividend is recorded by capitalizing retained earnings equal to the market value of the distributable shares.
   b. Stock dividends and stock splits have the same effect on the total assets and retained earnings of the issuing corporation.
   c. A stock dividend does not transfer corporate assets to the shareholders but does require retained earnings be capitalized.
5. What distinguishes a large stock dividend from a small stock dividend?
6. What amount of retained earnings is capitalized for a small stock dividend?

Answers—p. 758

[1] To reduce administrative cost, most splits are done by issuing new certificates to shareholders for the additional shares they are entitled to receive. The shareholders keep the old certificates.

Reacquisition of Shares

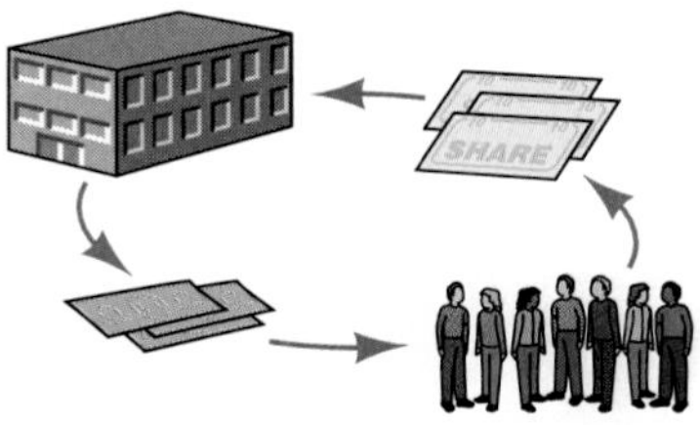

Under the Canada Business Corporations Act, as well as under the more recently passed provincial acts, such as the one in Ontario, a Corporation may purchase and retire shares of its own outstanding share capital if it can satisfy a solvency test applicable to cash dividends cited earlier in the chapter. Retiring shares reduces the number of issued shares. Purchases and retirements of shares are permissible under the CBCA only if they do not jeopardize the interests of creditors and shareholders. For instance, **Royal Bank** recently reported that "to enhance shareholder value Royal Bank repurchased 4.1 million common shares in the first half of 1997." Corporations acquire their own shares for several reasons. They can repurchase shares to avoid a hostile takeover by an investor. They can buy shares to maintain a strong or stable market. This is often done when a corporation's shares quickly and markedly decline in price. By buying shares, management shows its confidence in the price of its shares.

When shares are purchased for retirement, the stated capital account is debited at the product of the number of shares acquired multiplied by the weighted average per share invested by its shareholders. If the shares are purchased for less than the weighted average per share invested by the shareholderes, the difference is credited to a shareholders' equity account such as Contributed Capital from Retirement of Shares. On the other hand if the shares are purchased at more than the weighted average per share invested by the shareholders, the difference is debited to contributed capital from previous credit balances of share retirement transactions. Any difference remaining is debited to Retained Earnings.

For example, assume a corporation originally issued its no-par common shares at an average price of $12 per share. If the corporation later purchased and retired 1,000 of these shares at the same price for which they were issued, the entry to record the retirement is:

May 1	Common Shares	12,000	
	Cash		12,000
	Purchased and retired 1,000 common shares at $12 per share.		

Assets = Liabilities + Equity
−12,000 −12,000

If the corporation paid $11 per share, the entry would be:

May 1	Common Shares	12,000	
	Cash		11,000
	Contributed Capital, from retirement of common shares		**1,000**
	Purchased and retired 1,000 common shares at $11 per share.		

Assets = Liabilities + Equity
−11,000 −12,000
+1,000

If the corporation had paid $15 per share, the entry for the purchase and retirement is:

May 1	Cash	12,000	
	Retained Earnings	**3,000**	
	Cash		15,000
	Purchased and retired 1,000 common shares at $15 per share.		

Assets = Liabilities + Equity
+12,000 −3,000
−15,000

In addition to the reasons mentioned earlier as to why a corporation may purchase its own shares in the market there is another reason that applies to certain provincially incorporated corporations. In some provincial jurisdictions a corporation may buy these shares without having to retire them. The corporation can reissue these shares to employees as compensation. These reacquired shares are called **treasury shares.** Treasury shares are similar to unissued shares in several ways.

Neither treasury shares nor unissued shares is an asset. Neither receives cash dividends nor stock dividends. Neither allows the exercise of voting rights.

Treasury shares purchases require management to exercise ethical sensitivity. This is because corporate funds are being paid to specific shareholders instead of all shareholders. As a result, managers must be sure the purchase is in the best interest of all shareholders. These concerns cause most companies to fully disclose treasury shares transactions.

Judgment and Ethics

Director

You are a manager at Intex and a new member of its board of directors. The board is currently planning the agenda for its annual shareholders' meeting. The first item is whether to disclose a government contract Intex just signed. This contract will increase income and cash flows for current and future years. One officer said "the meeting should describe last year's activities, not future plans." After agreeing not to disclose the contract, the board moved to the next topic. It was a motion for shareholders to approve a compensation plan awarding managers options to acquire shares over the next two years. This plan gives managers a two-year option to buy shares at a fixed price equal to the stock price 30 days after the shareholders' meeting. If the share price increases in the next two years, managers can earn considerable money. Can you describe a potential problem here? What action do you take?

Answer—p. 758

Purchasing Treasury Shares

LO 4 Record purchases and sales of treasury shares and the retirement of stock.

Purchasing treasury shares reduces the corporation's assets and shareholders' equity by equal amounts.[2] We illustrate these effects on the balance sheet of **Cyber Corporation.** Exhibit 16.5 shows Cyber's account balances before any treasury shares purchase.

Exhibit 16.5

Balance Sheet before Purchasing Treasury Shares

CYBER CORP.
Balance Sheet
May 1, 1999

Assets		**Shareholders' Equity**	
Cash	$ 30,000	Contributed capital:	
Other assets	95,000	Common shares, no-par, authorized and issued 10,000 shares	$100,000
		Retained earnings	25,000
Total assets	$125,000	Total shareholders' equity	$125,000

On May 1, 1999, Cyber purchased 1,000 of its own shares for $11,500. The entry to record this purchase is:

May 1	Treasury Shares, Common	11,500	
	Cash		11,500
	Purchased 1,000 treasury shares at $11.50 per share.		

Assets	=	Liabilities	+	Equity
−11,500				−11,500

This entry reduces its shareholders' equity by debiting the Treasury shares account, which is a *contra* to equity. Exhibit 16.6 shows the effects of this transaction on Cyber's balance sheet.

[2] We describe the *cost method* of accounting for treasury shares. It is the method most widely used. The *par value* method is another method explained in advanced courses.

Exhibit 16.6

Balance Sheet after Purchasing Treasury Shares

CYBER CORP.
Balance Sheet
May 1, 1999

Assets		Shareholders' Equity	
Cash	$ 18,500	Contributed capital:	
Other assets	95,000	Common shares, no-par, authorized and issued 10,000 shares, of which 1,000 are in treasury	$100,000
		Retained earnings, of which $11,500 is restricted by treasury shares purchase.	25,000
		Total	$125,000
		Less cost of treasury shares.	(11,500)
Total assets	$113,500	Total shareholders' equity	$113,500

The treasury shares purchase reduces Cyber's cash, total assets, and total equity by $11,500. The equity reduction is reflected on the balance sheet by deducting the cost of treasury shares in the equity section. This purchase does not reduce the balance of either the Common Shares account or the Retained Earnings account. But two disclosures in this section describe the effects of the transaction. First, the shares description tells us 1,000 issued shares are in treasury, leaving only 9,000 shares outstanding. Second, the retained earnings description tells us it is partly restricted. We explain retained earnings' restrictions late in this chapter.

Did You Know?

Buybacks Explode
As a consequence of corporations buying back their own shares, share prices often rise because there are now fewer on the market. Higher prices mean higher capital gains to investors. Many investors perfer capital gains to dividends because only 3/4 of the capital gains is taxable.

Reissuing Treasury Shares

Treasury shares can be reissued by selling them at cost, above cost, or below cost. This section explains the accounting for reissuing treasury shares.

Selling Treasury Shares at Cost

If the treasury shares are reissued at cost, the entry is the opposite of the entry made to record the purchase. For instance, if on May 20 Cyber reissues 100 of the treasury shares purchased on May 1 at the same $11.50 per share cost, the entry to record this sale is:

May 21	Cash	1,150	
	Treasury Shares, Common		1,150
	Received $11.50 per share for 100 treasury shares costing $11.50 per share.		

Assets = Liabilities + Equity
+1,150 +1,150

Selling Treasury Shares above Cost

If treasury shares are sold for more than cost, the amount received in excess of cost is credited to an account called Contributed Capital, Treasury shares Transactions. For instance, if Cyber receives $12 cash per share for 400 treasury shares costing $11.50 per share, the entry to record this sale is:

June 3	Cash	4,800	
	Treasury Shares, Common		4,600
	Contributed Capital, Treasury Shares Transactions		200
	Received $12 per share for 400 treasury shares costing $11.50 per share.		

Assets = Liabilities + Equity
+4,800 +4,600
+200

The Contributed Capital, Treasury Shares Transactions account is reported as a separate item in the contributed capital section of shareholders' equity. No gain is ever reported from the sale of treasury shares.

Selling Treasury Shares below Cost

When treasury shares are sold below cost, the entry to record the sale depends on whether there is a credit balance in the Contributed Capital, Treasury Shares Transactions account. If there is no balance, the excess of cost over the sales price is debited to Retained Earnings. But if the contributed capital account has a credit balance, the excess of the cost over the sales price is debited for an amount up to the balance in this account. When the credit balance in the contributed capital account is eliminated, any remaining difference between the cost and the selling price is debited to Retained Earnings.

To illustrate, if Cyber sells its remaining 500 treasury shares at $10 per share, the company's equity is reduced by $750 (500 shares × $1.50 per share excess of cost over selling price). This reissuance is recorded with the entry:

Assets	=	Liabilities	+	Equity
+5,000				−200
				−550
				+5,750

July 10	Cash	5,000	
	Contributed Capital, Treasury Shares Transactions	200	
	Retained Earnings	550	
	Treasury Shares, Common		5,750
	Received $10 per share for 500 treasury shares costing $11.50 per share.		

This entry eliminates the $200 credit balance in the contributed capital account created on June 3 and then reduces the Retained Earnings balance by the remaining $550 excess of cost over selling price. This means the purchase and reissuance of treasury shares caused Cyber to incur a net $550 decrease in retained earnings and total shareholders' equity. A company never reports a loss from the sale of treasury shares.

Did You Know?

Online Stock Trading

The volume of online stock trading has skyrocketed. Charles Schwab, for instance, reported nearly $100 billion in online customer assets in January 1998. It also reported more than a million active online trading accounts, and over a million daily online customer visits to its Web site. The trend in Canada is catching on as well. For example, the Bank of Montreal's InvestorLine discount brokerage service trades over 700 mutual funds daily through its Web site that is available at http://www.bmo.com/investorline.

Flash back

7. Purchase of treasury shares (a) has no effect on total assets, (b) reduces total assets and total shareholders' equity by equal amounts, or (c) is recorded with a debit to Retained Earnings.
8. Southern Inc. purchases shares of Northern Corp. Should these shares be classified as treasury shares by either company?
9. How do treasury shares affect the number of authorized, issued, and outstanding shares of stock?

Answers—p. 758

Mid-Chapter Demonstration Problem

The Precision Company began 1999 with the following balances in its shareholders' equity accounts:

Common shares, no-par, 500,000 shares authorized, 200,000 shares issued and outstanding	$3,000,000
Retained earnings	5,000,000
Total	$8,000,000

All of the outstanding shares were issued for $15 when the company was created. Prepare journal entries to account for the following transactions during 1999:

Jan. 10	The board declared a $0.10 cash dividend per share to shareholders of record Jan. 28.
Feb. 15	Paid the cash dividend declared on January 10.
Mar. 31	Declared a 20% stock dividend. The market value of the stock was $18 per share.
Apr. 15	Distributed the stock dividend declared on March 31.
June 30	Purchased 30,000 treasury shares at $20 per share.
Aug. 31	Sold 20,000 treasury shares at $26 per share.
Nov. 30	Sold the remaining 10,000 treasury shares at $7 per share.

Solution to Mid-Chapter Demonstration Problem

Jan. 10	Cash Dividends Declared	20,000	
	Common Dividend Payable		20,000
	Declared a $0.10 per share cash dividend on common shares.		
Feb. 15	Common Dividend Payable	20,000	
	Cash		20,000
	Paid $0.10 per share cash dividend to common shareholders.		
Mar. 31	Stock Dividends Declared	720,000	
	Common Shares Dividend Distributable		720,000
	Declared a small stock dividend of 20% or 40,000 shares; market value is $18 per share.		
Apr. 15	Common shares Dividend Distributable	720,000	
	Common Shares		720,000
	Distributed 40,000 common shares.		
June 30	Treasury Shares, Common	600,000	
	Cash		600,000
	Purchased 30,000 common shares at $20 per share.		
Aug. 31	Cash	520,000	
	Treasury Shares, Common		400,000
	Contributed Capital, Treasury Shares Transactions		120,000
	Sold 20,000 treasury shares at $26 per share.		
Nov. 30	Cash	70,000	
	Contributed Capital, Treasury Shares Transactions	120,000	
	Retained Earnings	10,000	
	Treasury shares, Common		200,000
	Sold 10,000 treasury shares at $7 per share.		

Reporting Income Information

LO 5 Explain the form and content of a corporate income statement.

When a company's revenue and expense transactions are from routine, continuing operations, a single-step income statement is adequate for describing its performance. This format shows revenues followed by a list of operating expenses and then net income. But a company's activities often include many income-related events that are not part of a company's continuing, normal operations. Company's need to provide useful information in a format that helps users understand both current and past events and to predict future performance.

To meet this objective, companies often separate the income statement into different sections. The most important of these sections include: continuing operations, discontinued segments, extraordinary items, changes in accounting principles, and earnings per share. Exhibit 16.7 shows the entire 1999 income statement of CompCAN.

Continuing Operations

The first section of an income statement shows the revenues, expenses, and income generated by the company's continuing operations. This portion looks like the single-step income statement we first described in Chapter 6. Users especially rely on information in this section for predicting the results of future operations. This section is often viewed by users as the most important. Prior chapters have explained the nature of the items and measures included in income from continuing operations.

Discontinued Segments

Many companies have several different lines of business and deal with different groups of customers. IBM Canada, for instance, not only produces and sells computer hardware and software but also delivers systems design and repair services. Information about the segments of a company are of interest to users. A **segment of a business** is a part of a company's operations that serves a particular line of business or class of customers. A segment has assets, liabilities, and financial results of operations that can be distinguished from other parts of the company. Companies with operations in different segments are required to provide supplemental information about each of their major segments. As examples, Shaw Communications reports on the following five segments: cable television, radio, programming, telecommunications, and paging, and Canadian Tire reports its operations in three industry segments: Canadian Tire Retail, Financial Services, and Petroleum.

Reporting on Discontinued Segments

When a company incurs a gain or loss from selling or closing down a segment, this gain or loss is reported in a separate section of the income statement.[3] Section 2 of the income statement in Exhibit 16.7 includes this information. The purpose of reporting gains or losses from discontinued operations separately is to more clearly separate the results of discontinued segments from those of continuing operations. Income from operating the discontinued segment prior to its disposal also is reported in section 2. When the income statement includes results of prior years side by side, we must go back and restate prior years' results to separate out the revenues and expenses of the discontinued segment.

Separating Operating Results from Gain or Loss on Disposal

Section 2 of Exhibit 16.7 reports both (1) income from operating the discontinued segment during the year and (2) the loss from disposing of the segment's net assets. The income tax effects of each are also reported. This means the tax effects from the discontinued segment are separate from the reporting of continuing operations in section 1. If this was not so, the information would be less useful.

---

[3] *CICA Handbook*, section 1700.

Exhibit 16.7

Income Statement for a Corporation

COMPCAN
Income Statement
For Year Ended December 31, 1999

①	Net sales		$8,440,000
	Gain on sale of equipment		38,000
	Total revenues		$8,478,000
	Expenses:		
	Cost of goods sold	$5,950,000	
	Amortization expense	35,000	
	Other selling, general, and administrative expenses	515,000	
	Interest expense	20,000	
	Income taxes expense	595,500	
	Total expenses		(7,115,500)
	Unusual loss on relocating a plant		(45,000)
	Infrequent gain on sale of surplus land		72,000
	Income from continuing operations		$1,389,500
②	**Discontinued segment:**		
	Income from operating Division A (net of $180,000 income taxes)	$ 420,000	
	Loss on disposal of Division A (net of $66,000 tax benefit)	(154,000)	266,000
	Income before extraordinary items and cumulative effect of change in accounting principle		$1,655,500
③	**Extraordinary items:**		
	Gain on sale of land taken by government (net of $61,200 income taxes)	$ 142,800	
	Loss from earthquake damage (net of $270,000 income tax benefit)	(630,000)	(487,200)
	Net income		$1,168,300
④	**Earnings per common share** (200,000 outstanding shares):		
	Income from continuing operations		$ 6.95
	Discontinued operations		1.33
	Income before extraordinary items		$ 8.28
	Extraordinary items		(2.44)
	Net income (basic earnings per share)		$ 5.84

Extraordinary Items

Section 3 of the income statement in Exhibit 16.7 reports **extraordinary gains and losses.** The *CICA Handbook* identifies extraordinary gains and losses as items that have all of the following characteristics: (a) they are not expected to occur frequently over several years, (b) they do not typify the normal business activities of the entity, and (c) they do not depend primarily on decisions or determinations by management or owners.[4] Reporting extraordinary items in a separate category helps users predict future performance, absent the effects of extraordinary items.

Few items qualify as extraordinary items because they must meet both criteria of **unusual** and **infrequent.** For instance, the following items are *not* considered extraordinary:

[4] *CICA Handbook*, section 3480.

- Write-downs of inventories.
- Write-offs of receivables.
- Gains or losses from exchanging foreign currencies.
- Gains and losses from disposing segments.
- Effects of labour strikes.
- Accrual adjustments on long-term contracts.
- Sale of equipment

The list of items usually considered extraordinary include:

- Expropriation (take away) of property by a foreign government.
- Condemning of property by a domestic government body.
- Prohibition against using an asset by a newly enacted law.
- Losses or gains from an unusual and infrequent calamity ("act of God").

Gains or losses that result from the inherent risks of normal business activities are not extraordinary and are reported in the continuing operations *but* below the normal revenues, expenses, gains, and losses. For instance **Magna International Inc.**, a full systems supplier to the global automotive market, reported gains of $189.6 million on the sale of some of its ownership interests. This item is separated from Magna's "income from operations," but is still part of its $603.4 million 1997 net income from continuing operations. Magna has no extraordinary items.

Section 1 of Exhibit 16.7 includes a "Gain on sale of equipment" that is neither unusual nor infrequent with total revenues. Also note both an unusual loss and an infrequent gain are reported at the *end* of section 1 below the normal revenues, gains, expenses, and losses. Proper classification of items demands examining the facts. Accounting principles require a few special items to be reported as extraordinary gains or losses to highlight their occurrence even when they don't meet the criteria.

You Make the Call

Farmer

You are a farmer with an orchard in Kentville, Nova Scotia. This winter a bad frost wiped out about half your trees. You are currently preparing an income statement for a bank loan. Can you claim the loss of apple trees as extraordinary and separate from continuing operations?

Answer—p. 758

Changes in Accounting Principles

The *consistency principle* requires a company to continue applying the same *accounting principles* once they are chosen. The phrase accounting principles in this context refers to accounting methods such as FIFO, LIFO, and straight-line amortization. But a company can change from one acceptable accounting principle to another as long as the change improves the usefulness of information in its financial statements. A company will also have a change in accounting principles when they adopt new standards issued by the CICA or IASC.

Changes in accounting principles usually affect a company's reported income in more than one way. Let's look at CompCAN's change in accounting principle reported in its income statement of Exhibit 16.7. CompCAN purchased its only amortizable asset early in **1996** for $320,000. This asset has a $40,000 salvage value and is being amortized using the double-declining balance method for the past three years. During **1999**, CompCAN decides its income statement would be more useful if amortization is computed using the straight-line method instead of by double-declining balance.

Exhibit 16.8 compares the results of applying these two amortization methods to the initial three years of this asset's useful life. The accelerated method yielded $185,000 of amortization from **1996** through **1998**. But if the straight-line method had been used from 1996–1998, only $105,000 of amortization would have been reported. To adjust accounts to the balances they would be using the straight-line method, CompCAN needs to decrease accumulated amortization of this asset by $80,000 gross. Also, since CompCAN is subject to a 30% income tax rate, we offset this gross debit with a credit of $24,000 (30% × $80,000) for deferred income taxes to be paid in the future. The $56,000 net is the resulting credit to equity. Because this credit increases equity, CompCAN adds it to 1999's income, the year the change is made.

Exhibit 16.8

Computing Cumulative Effect of a Change in Accounting Principle

	Double-Declining Amortization	Straight-Line Amortization	Pre-Tax Difference	After-Tax Cumulative Effect
Prior to change:				
1996	$ 80,000	$ 35,000		
1997	60,000	35,000		
1998	45,000	35,000		
Subtotal	$185,000	$105,000	$80,000	$56,000*
Year of change:				
1999	33,750	35,000**		
After change:				
2000–2003		35,000		

* Reported as an adjustment to the 1999 beginning balance of retained earnings as the cumulative adjustment for differences in the three years prior to the change in 1999, net of $24,000 additional taxes to be paid (30% × $80,000).

** Reported on the 1999 income statement as amortization expense.

Reporting on Changes in Accounting Principles

CompCAN's income statement in Exhibit 16.7 shows how we report a change in an accounting principle. First, section 1 of the income statement reports $35,000 of amortization using the straight-line method for 1999. This amount is taken from the straight-line method column in Exhibit 16.8. This means income for 1999 is computed using the new accounting principle. Straight-line amortization also will be used in 2000–2003. The second effect of the change in accounting principle is the $56,000 catch-up adjustment reported as an adjustment to the beginning balance of retained earnings. This item is the cumulative effect of the change in accounting principle.

Two additional points are important. First, a note should describe the change and why it is an improvement over the old principle. Second, the note should describe what 1999's income would have been under the old method if the change had not occurred. For CompCAN, the note states 1999 amortization of $33,750 would be reported using double-declining balance instead of $35,000 under straight-line. This amount is in Exhibit 16.8 under the declining balance column for 1999.

Flashback

10. Which of the following is an extraordinary item? (a) a settlement paid to a customer injured while using a company's product, (b) a loss from damages to a plant caused by a meteorite, or (c) a loss from selling old equipment.

11. Identify the four major sections of the income statement that are potentially reported.

12. A company using FIFO for the past 15 years decides to switch to LIFO. The effect of this event on past years' net income is (a) reported as a prior period adjustment to retained earnings, (b) ignored, as it is a change in an accounting estimate, or (c) reported on the current year's income statement.

Answers—p. 758

Earnings per Share

LO 6 Compute earnings per share and describe its use.

The final section of the income statement in Exhibit 16.7 reports earnings per share results. This information is included on the face of the income statement in accordance with accounting standards. The presentation in Exhibit 16.7 for CompCAN is more complete than the minimum reporting requirements and shows the possible categories companies can and often do report.

Earnings per share is one of the most widely cited items of accounting information. **Earnings per share**, also called *net income per share*, is the amount of income earned by each share of a company's outstanding common shares. Investors find this ratio useful because it reports a company's earnings number in terms of a single common share. This aids investors in their valuation of common shares. This is especially helpful when compared with the stock market price per share discussed later in this chapter. Because of the importance and widespread use of earnings per share numbers, there are guidelines for computing it. The **basic earnings per share** formula is shown in Exhibit 16.9.

Exhibit 16.9

Basic Earnings per Share Formula

$$\text{Basic earnings per share} = \frac{\text{Net income} - \text{Preferred dividends}}{\text{Weighted-average common shares outstanding}}$$

This formula shows us the basic earnings per share computation depends on (1) preferred dividends and (2) weighted-average common shares outstanding. Our explanation begins by considering the simple case where there are no changes in shares outstanding during the period. We then look at what happens when the number of common shares outstanding changes.

No Changes in Common Shares Outstanding

Basic earnings per share is simple if (1) a company has only common shares and nonconvertible preferred shares outstanding and (2) the number of outstanding common shares does not change during the period. In this case, we take the amount of net income available to common shareholders and divide it by the number of common shares. The amount of income available to common shareholders depends on whether the preferred shares are cumulative or not. If preferred shares are *non*cumulative, the income available is the year's net income less any preferred dividends declared in that same year. If preferred shares are cumulative, the income available is the year's net income less the preferred dividends whether declared or not.

To illustrate, assume Quantum Co. earns $40,000 net income in 1999 and declares dividends of $7,500 on its noncumulative preferred shares. Quantum also had 5,000 common shares outstanding throughout 1999. This information allows us to compute Quantum's basic earnings per share as:

$$\text{Basic earnings per share} = \frac{\$40{,}000 - \$7{,}500}{5{,}000 \text{ shares}} = \$6.50$$

Changes in Common Shares Outstanding

This computation is more complex if the number of outstanding shares changes during the year. The number of shares outstanding may change for several reasons such as sales of additional shares, purchases of treasury shares, and stock dividends or splits. We consider each of these in this section.

Share Sales or Purchases in the Period

When a company sells additional shares or purchases treasury shares during the year, the denominator of the basic earnings per share formula is adjusted to equal the weighted-average number of outstanding shares. The idea behind this computation is to measure the average amount of earnings earned to the average number of shares outstanding during the year.

To illustrate, let's assume Quantum again earned $40,000 in year 2000, and it again declared preferred dividends of $7,500. But let's also assume Quantum sells 4,000 additional common shares on July 1, 2000, and purchases 3,000 shares for retirement on November 1, 2000. This means there were 5,000 shares outstanding for the first six months, and 9,000 shares outstanding for July through October (four months), but only 6,000 shares outstanding for the final two months. Exhibit 16.10 shows us how we compute Quantum's weighted-average number of shares outstanding for year 2000.

Exhibit 16.10

Computing Weighted-Average Number of Shares

Time Period	Outstanding Shares	Fraction of Year	Weighted Average
January – June	5,000	6/12	2,500
July – October	9,000	4/12	3,000
November – December	6,000	2/12	1,000
Weighted average outstanding shares			6,500

We can then compute Quantum's basic earnings per share computation using the weighted-average number of common shares outstanding as:

$$\text{Basic earnings per share} = \frac{\$40{,}000 - \$7{,}500}{6{,}500 \text{ shares}} = \$5.00$$

Quantum reports the $5 basic earnings per share number on the face of its December 31, 2000, income statement.

Stock Splits or Dividends in the Period

The number of outstanding shares is also affected by a stock split or stock dividend. These events do not produce additional assets and do not affect the amount of earnings. This means the numerator of basic earnings per share is unaffected. But earnings for the year are now spread out over a larger number of shares. This affects our computation of the weighted-average number of shares outstanding. We handle a stock split or stock dividend by restating the number of shares outstanding during the year to reflect the stock split or dividend *as if it occurred at the beginning of the year.*

To illustrate, let's assume Quantum executed a two-for-one stock split on December 1, 2000. This split causes the percent ownership of each share to be cut in half while doubling the number of shares outstanding prior to December 1. The only change in computing weighted-average shares outstanding is the inclusion of an additional multiplication reflecting the split. This effect of the split is seen with the inclusion of an additional column in Exhibit 16.11. The December outstanding shares already reflect the split and do not require any adjustment.

Exhibit 16.11

Weighted-Average Number of Post-Split Shares

Time Period	Outstanding Shares	Effect of Split	Fraction of Year	Weighted Average
January – June	5,000	2	6/12	5,000
July – October	9,000	2	4/12	6,000
November	6,000	2	1/12	1,000
December	12,000	1	1/12	1,000
Weighted-average outstanding shares				13,000

Our final step is to compute Quantum's basic earnings per share for year 2000 under the assumption of the two-for-one stock split:

$$\text{Basic earnings per share} = \frac{\$40{,}000 - \$7{,}500}{13{,}000 \text{ shares}} = \$2.50$$

We use the same sort of computations when stock dividends occur. For instance, if the two-for-one stock split had been a 10% stock dividend, the numbers of old outstanding shares are multiplied by 1.1 instead of 2.0. This is because 110% (or 1.1) of the original number of shares are now outstanding, computed as 100% +10%.

Did You Know?

Great Expectations
A company's earnings per share is a major factor in determining its share price. Even changes in earnings per share estimates can greatly affect a company's share price. For instance, an analyst recently lowered Citicorp's earnings per share forecast by 5%. Citicorp's shares fell 7 points, to 123, on this news. [Source: "Asian Flu," *Business Week*, January 19, 1998.]

Complex Capital Structure

A company can be classified as having either a simple or complex capital structure. A **simple capital structure** refers to a company with only common shares and nonconvertible preferred shares outstanding. A simple capital structure excludes dilutive securities. *Dilutive securities* include options, rights to purchase common shares, and bonds or preferred shares convertible into common shares. These securities have the potential to increase the number of common shares outstanding. A company with a simple capital structure need only report basic earnings per share as described above.

A **complex capital structure** refers to companies with dilutive securities. A company with a complex capital structure must often report two earnings per share figures: basic earnings per share and diluted earnings per share. **Diluted earnings per share** is computed by adding all dilutive securities to the denominator of the basic earnings per share computation shown in Exhibit 16.9. Diluted earnings per share reflects the decrease in basic earnings per share if all dilutive securities were converted into common shares. Fully diluted earnings per share is an assumed figure that reports what earnings per share would have been if the assumed conversions had taken place. The net result may be to reduce earnings per share or to increase earnings per share. If earnings per share after the assumed conversions exceed basic earnings per share they are said to be *anti-dilutive* and need not be reported. **Gulfstream Resources,** for example, in its 1997 annual report noted that the fully diluted earnings per share calculation for the year was anti-dilutive.

To illustrate, we show the prior two years' earnings per share figures in Exhibit 16.12 taken from the income statement of **Polyair,** the maker of high-tech outdoor gear.

For Polyair Pack Inc., basic earnings per share is nearly identical to diluted earnings per share for the second quarters of 1997–1998. This means Polyair has almost no highly dilutive securities. But this is not always the case. **Provigo,** for instance, a leader in the retail and wholesale distribution of food and general merchandise located in Montreal, announced first quarter basic earnings per share of $0.20 per share in early 1998, while its diluted earnings per share was $0.18. This is a dilution of 10%. The effects of dilutive securities on EPS is a complex topic that is given much greater coverage in intermediate accounting courses.

Corporations must report earnings per share figures on the face of their income statements. They also usually report the amount of earnings per share for net income and each of the

Exhibit 16.12
Basic and Diluted Earnings per Share Disclosure

POLYAIR INTER PACK INC.

	Quarter Ending April 30 1998	1997
Earnings per share		
Basic	$ 0.12	$ 0.08
Diluted	$ 0.12	$ 0.07
Weighted-average number of shares outstanding:		
Basic	6,820,000	6,820,000
Fully diluted	7,645,000	7,790,200

three subcategories of income (continuing operations, discontinued segments, and extraordinary items). Exhibit 16.7 shows CompCan's earnings per share in section 4. Since CompCan has a simple capital structure, it reports only basic earnings per share.

Flashback

13. During 1999, FDI reports net income of $250,000 and pays preferred dividends of $70,000. On January 1, 1999, the company had 25,000 outstanding common shares and purchased 5,000 treasury shares on July 1. The 1999 basic earnings per share is (a) $8, (b) $9, or (c) $10.

14. How are stock splits and stock dividends treated in computing the weighted-average number of outstanding common shares?

15. What two earnings per share figures are reported for a company with a complex capital structure?

Answers—p. 758

Stock Options

The vast majority of corporations whose shares are publicly traded offer stock options. A **stock option** is a right to purchase common shares at a fixed price over a specified period of time. As the share's price rises above the fixed price, the value of the option increases. Use of stock options is growing in popularity as a way to pay both managers and employees for performance. **Magna,** for instance, may grant options to purchase Class A Subordinate Voting Shares to full-time employees and **Canadian Tire** has granted stock options to certain employees for the purchase of Class A Non-Voting shares. **Starbucks** and **Home Depot** are leaders in offering stock options to both full and part-time employees. Stock options are said to motivate managers and employees to (1) focus on company performance, (2) take a long-run perspective, and (3) remain with the company. A stock option is like having an investment with no risk (or "a carrot with no stick").

To illustrate, let's say Quantum grants each of its employees the option to purchase 100 of its common shares at its current market price of $50 per share any time within the next 10 years. This means if Quantum's share price exceeds $50 per share, employees can exercise the option at a profit. For instance, if the share price rises to $70 per share, an employee can exercise the option at a gain of $20 per share ($70 share price less $50 option price). With 100 shares, a single employee has a total gain of $2,000, computed as $20 $\times$ 100 shares.

When options are granted, the difference between their estimated value and their exercise price is considered compensation expense. This expense is either recorded as compensation expense or is reported in notes to the financial statements. Most companies report this stock option compensation expense in their notes. **Alcan** in its 1996 annual report, for example, reported that 549,000 share options were excerized but not included in compensation expense. According to the notes, if Alcan had elected to recognize compensation for these shares in accordance with the methodlogy prescribed by the U.S. Financial Accounting Standards Board (FASB) net income would have been lower by $8,000,000 or $0.04 per share.

Retained Earnings

LO 7 Explain the items reported in retained earnings.

Retained earnings are made up of a company's profits and losses retained in the business. Specifically, it is the total cumulative amount of reported net income less any net losses and dividends declared since the company started operating. Retained earnings are part of the shareholders' claim on the company's net assets. Retained earnings do not imply there is a certain amount of cash available to pay shareholders, nor any other asset. This is highlighted in Exhibit 16.13 where we

Did You Know?

Future Fortunes

Some managers have fortunes to reap from stock options that have yet to be exercised. Four of the larger treasure chests are:

Michael Eisner (Walt Disney)	$360 million
Wayne Calloway (Pepsico)	120 million
Stephen Case (America Online)	115 million
Eckhard Pfeiffer (Compaq)	100 million

Protests of excessive stock options to managers are growing, often led by unions and religious organizations. [Source: "Executive Pay," *Business Week,* April 21, 1997.]

list the retained earnings, cash, and total assets from recent financial statements of **Imasco, Magna,** and **Corel.**

Exhibit 16.13

Retained Earnings, Cash, and Asset Balances

Company	Retained Earnings	Cash	Total Assets
Imasco	$ 2,502	$ 15	$ 59,749
Magna	1,302.3	878.8	5,328.7
Corel	(86.9)	6.9	398.5

This section describes important events and transactions affecting retained earnings. It also explains how we report retained earnings.

Restricted Retained Earnings

Most retained earnings are usually available for dividends. But there are sometimes restrictions placed on retained earnings. These include both legal and contractual restrictions. For instance, jurisdictions that permit treasury shares restrict the amount of treasury shares purchased to the amount of retained earnings. This is called a *statutory restriction*. Purchasing treasury shares transfers cash to shareholders and reduces assets and equity. But a treasury shares purchase does not directly reduce the balance of the Retained Earnings account. Instead, the corporation discloses this type of restriction on its retained earnings. The balance sheet in Exhibit 16.6 identifies the amount of **restricted retained earnings** created by treasury shares purchases.

Certain contracts such as loan agreements can also restrict retained earnings. These are called *contractual restrictions* and can include restrictions on paying dividends below a certain amount or percent of retained earnings. Restrictions are often described in a note to financial statements.

Appropriated Retained Earnings

In contrast to statutory or contractual retained earnings restrictions, a corporation's directors can voluntarily limit dividends because of a special need for cash such as the purchase of new facilities. When directors do this, management usually explains in a letter to shareholders or other means why dividends are being limited. They can also disclose this to users by setting up an amount of **appropriated retained earnings.** This appropriation is voluntary. It serves only to notify users of the directors' decision to not pay out cash dividends.

Prior Period Adjustments

Prior period adjustments refer to corrections of material errors in past years' financial statements. These errors may have resulted "from a mistake in computation affecting financial statements, from a misinterpretation or misrepresentation of information, from an oversight of information available at the time the financial statements were prepared that ought to have been taken into account, or from misappropriation of assets."[5] Examples include mistakenly omitting amortization, applying an unacceptable amortization method, and overlooking important facts in predicting an asset's useful life. Prior period adjustments are reported in the statement of retained earnings (or the statement of changes in shareholders' equity), net of any income tax effects. Prior period adjustments result in changing the beginning balance of retained earnings for events occurring prior to the earliest year reported on in the current set of financial statements. They do not affect the current income statement.

To illustrate, let's assume **CompCAN** makes an error in a 1997 journal entry for the purchase of land by incorrectly debiting an expense account. When this is discovered in 1999, the statement of retained earnings includes a prior period adjustment to correct this error as shown in Exhibit 16.14.

Exhibit 16.14

Prior Period Adjustment in Statement of Retained Earnings

COMPCAN
Statement of Retained Earnings
For Year Ended December 31, 1999

Retained earnings, December 31, 1998, as previously stated	$4,745,000
Prior period adjustment:	
Cost of land incorrectly expensed (net of $63,000 income taxes)	**147,000**
Retained earnings, December 31, 1998, as adjusted	$4,892,000
Plus net income	1,162,500
Less cash dividends declared	(240,000)
Retained earnings, December 31, 1999	$5,814,500

IAS 7 permits an alternative treatment of accounting errors. International accounting standards permit the amount of the correction to be included in the current period's results and comparative information presented as previously reported. Canadian GAAP does not allow this alternative treatment.

Changes in Accounting Estimates

Many items reported in financial statements are based on estimates. Future events are certain to reveal that some of these estimates were inaccurate even when based on the best data available at the time. Because these inaccuracies are not the result of mistakes, they are *not* considered accounting errors. This means any corrections due to these estimates are not reported as prior period adjustments. Instead, they are identified as **changes in accounting estimates,** and are accounted for in the current and future periods.

To illustrate, we know amortization is based on estimated useful lives and salvage values. As time passes and new information becomes available, we may need to change these estimates and the amounts reported as amortization expense. These types of changes in accounting estimates are not accounted for with a cumulative catch-up adjustment like a prior period adjustment. Instead, changes in accounting estimates are applied in determining revenues and expenses for the current and future periods. In Chapter 12, we explained one common change in an accounting estimate when we discussed revising amortization rates.

Statement of Changes in Shareholders' Equity

Many companies do not report a separate statement of retained earnings. Instead, they provide a statement of changes in shareholders' equity. A **statement of changes in shareholders' equity** lists the beginning and ending balances of each equity account and describes the changes that occurred during the year. The usual

[5] *CICA Handbook*, section 1506, par. 26.

format is to provide a column for each component of equity and use the rows to describe events occurring in the year. Exhibit 16.15 shows a condensed 1996 statement for **Z Company.**

Exhibit 16.15

Statement of Changes in Shareholders' Equity

Z COMPANY
Statement of Changes in Shareholders' Equity
December 28, 1997

	Common Shares and Capital			
(In millions)	Number of Shares	Amount	Retained earnings	Total
Balance at December 30, 1996	**821**	**$2,583**	**$9,557**	**$12,140**
Share sales	17	513	—	513
Share repurchase and retirement	(17)	(269)	(925)	(1,194)
Cash dividends declared	—	—	(156)	(156)
Other, net	—	70	342	412
Net income	—	—	5,157	5,157
Balance at December 28, 1997	**821**	**$2,897**	**$13,975**	**$16,872**

USING THE INFORMATION — Dividend Yield and the Price-Earnings Ratio

This section looks at two important ratios in investment analysis of common shares: dividend yield and the price-earnings ratio.

Dividend Yield

LO 8 Compute dividend yield and explain its use in analysis.

Investors buy a company's shares in anticipation of receiving a return from either or both cash dividends and stock price increases. Shares that pay large dividends on a regular basis are often called *income shares*. They are attractive to investors who want dependable cash flows from their investments. In contrast, some shares pay little or no dividends but are still attractive to investors because of their expected share price increases. The shares of companies that do not distribute cash but use their cash to finance expansion are often called *growth shares*.

One way to evaluate whether shares should be viewed as income shares or growth shares is to compute and analyze their dividend yield. **Dividend yield** tells us the annual amount of cash dividends distributed to common shareholders relative to the share's market value (price). More generally, it tells us the amount of cash distributed from a company relative to its total market value. The dividend yield formula in Exhibit 16.16 shows it is a rate of return based on annual cash dividends and the share's market value.

Exhibit 16.16

Dividend Yield Formula

$$\text{Dividend yield} = \frac{\text{Annual cash dividends per share}}{\text{Market value per share}}$$

Dividend yield can be computed for both current and prior periods using data on actual dividends and share prices. It can also be computed for future periods using expected values. Exhibit 16.17 shows recent dividend and share price

Exhibit 16.17

Dividend and Share Price Information

	1997		
	Common Dividend Per Share	Share Price	Dividend Yield
Viceroy Homes	$ 0.15	$ 2.15	7.0%
Nova Scotia Power	0.81	17.40	4.7%
Noranda	1.00	24.60	4.1%
CIBC	1.00	39.65	2.5%

data for **Viceroy Home, Nova Scotia Power, Noranda,** and **CIBC.** Dividend yields are also reported.

For the current low inflationery times these dividend yeilds would be considered high. Shares with high dividend yields can be classified as income shares. These shares' dividend yeilds are less than we might expect from investments in bonds but still high enough to conclude that dividends are a very important factor in assessing share values. While dividend yield is important to individuals in planning their personal cash flows (dividends now or share sales later), it is only one of many factors that we look at in analyzing companies for investment.

Flash back

16. When a corporation purchases treasury shares: (a) Retained Earnings is restricted by the amount paid, (b) it is recorded with a credit to Appropriated Retained Earnings, or (c) it is always retired.

17. Which of the following produces an expected dividend yield of 10% on common shares?

a. Dividends of $100,000 are expected to be paid next year and expected net income is $1,000,000.

b. Dividends of $50,000 were paid during the prior year and net income was $500,000.

c. Dividends of $2 per share are expected to be paid next year and the current market value of the shares is $20 per share.

Answers—p. 758

Price-Earnings

LO 9 Compute price-earnings ratio and describe its use in analysis.

We explained in prior chapters how a share's market value is affected by the stream of dividends expected to be paid out to shareholders. A share's market value is also affected by expected growth in earnings, dividends, and other items. A comparison of a company's earnings per share and its market price per share reveals information about the stock market's expectations for a company's future growth in earnings, dividends, and opportunities.

It is possible to make this comparison as a rate of return by dividing earnings per share by the market price per share. However, the comparison is traditionally done the other way and computed as a **price-earnings (or PE) ratio,** pronounced "*price earnings*" or "*price-to-earnings*" or "*PE.*" Some analysts interpret this ratio as what price the market is willing to pay for a company's current earnings. For example, **CIBC,** in January 1997 was selling at 9.7 times earnings but in January 1998 the PE ratio was 11.6. It is interesting to note that during this period the bank's dividend yield decreased from 3.4 to 2.9. Price-earnings ratios differ across companies with the same earnings because of either higher or lower expectations of future earnings for individual companies.

The price-earnings ratio is defined as the market value (price) of a company's share divided by its earnings per share as shown in Exhibit 16.18.

$$\text{Price-earnings} = \frac{\text{Market value per share}}{\text{Earnings per share}}$$

Exhibit 16.18

Price-Earnings Formula

The ratio is often computed using earnings per share reported in the most recent period. But many users compute this ratio using the expected earnings per share for the next period. To illustrate, let's assume a company's current market price is $100 per share and its next year's earnings are expected to be $8 per share. Its price-earnings ratio is 12.5, computed as $100 divided by $8.

Some analysts apply the price-earnings ratio to search for over- or underpriced shares. As a general rule, such analysts view shares with high PE ratios (say greater than 20 to 25) as more likely to be overpriced, while shares with low PE ratios (say less than 5 to 8) are more likely to be underpriced. These investors prefer to sell or avoid buying shares with high PE ratios, while they prefer to buy or hold shares with low PE ratios. The average PE ratio for the 1950–1995 period is about 14. But the PE ratio averages more than 16 when inflation is below 3.5%.

Yet investment decision making is rarely so simple as to rely on a single ratio. For instance, a company with a high PE ratio may prove to be a good investment if its earnings continue to increase beyond current expectations. Similarly, a company with a low PE ratio may prove to be a poor investment if its earnings decline below expectations. As with dividend yield, the price-earnings ratio is important in users' decisions, but it is only one piece of information. This information along with analysis of other accounting and market data must be interpreted as part of a complete analysis and not viewed in isolation.

Flash back

18. Compute the price-earnings ratio when earnings per share is $4.25 and the share price per share is $34.

19. Two companies in the same industry face similar levels of risk, have nearly the same level of earnings, and are expected to continue their historical record of paying $1.50 annual dividends per share. Yet one company has a PE ratio of 6 while the other has a PE ratio of 10. Which company has the more optimistic market expectation for future growth in earnings?

Answers—p. 758

You Make the Call

Teacher

You are a teacher and receive regular payments to a pension fund as part of your compensation. You can't withdraw these funds until age 65, but you can and do choose where to invest them. You plan to invest in one of two companies that you've concluded have identical future prospects. One has a PE of 19 and the other a PE of 25. Which do you invest in? Does it matter if your personal estimate of PE for these two companies is 29?

Answer—p. 757

Summary

LO1 Record transactions involving cash dividends. There are three important events involving cash dividends. The date of declaration is when the board of directors binds the company to pay the dividend. A dividend declaration reduces retained earnings and creates a current liability to the shareholders. The date of record is when recipients of the dividend are identified. No entry is necessary on the date of record. The date of payment is when cash is paid to shareholders of record and the current liability is removed from the books.

LO2 Describe stock dividends and stock splits. Both a stock dividend and a stock split divide a company's outstanding shares into smaller pieces. The total value of the company is unchanged, but the price of each new share is smaller. The additional shares of stock distributed to shareholders is done according to individual shareholders' percent ownership. Stock dividends and stock splits do not transfer any of the corporation's assets to shareholders. Stock dividends and stock splits do not affect assets, total shareholders' equity, or the equity attributed to each shareholder.

LO 3 Account for stock dividends and stock splits. Small stock dividends (25%) are recorded by capitalizing retained earnings equal to the market value of the distributed shares. Large stock dividends (25%) are frequently given note disclosure. Stock splits are also not recorded with journal entries but require note disclosure.

LO 4 Record purchases and sales of treasury shares and the retirement of shares. When a corporation purchases its own previously issued outstanding shares, the cost of these shares is debited to Treasury Shares. The balance of Treasury Shares is subtracted from total shareholders' equity in the balance sheet. If treasury shares are later reissued, the amount of any proceeds in excess of cost is credited to Contributed Capital, Treasury Shares Transactions. If the proceeds are less than cost, the difference is debited to Contributed Capital, Treasury Shares Transactions to the extent a credit balance exists in that account. Any remaining amount is debited to Retained Earnings. When shares are purchased for retirement, we remove all the contributed capital amounts related to the retired shares.

LO 5 Explain the form and content of a corporate income statement. Corporate income statements are similar to those for proprietorships and partnerships except for the inclusion of income taxes. The income statement consists of four potential sections: (1) continuing operations, (2) discontinued segments, (3) extraordinary items, and (4) earnings per share. Many companies need only report income from continuing operations and earnings per share because the other three items are uncommon. The cumulative effect of a change in accounting principles is reported in the statement of retained earnings as an adjustment to the beginning retained earnings balance.

LO 6 Compute earnings per share and describe its use. A company with a simple capital structure is one with no outstanding securities convertible into common shares. These companies compute basic earnings per share by dividing net income less any preferred dividends by the weighted-average number of outstanding common shares. A company with a complex capital structure has outstanding securities convertible into common shares. This company must often report both basis earnings per share and diluted earnings per share.

LO 7 Explain the items reported in retained earnings. Legal jurisdictions limit dividends and reacquisition of shares purchases to the amount of retained earnings. Companies also enter into contracts that may limit the amount of dividends, even though the companies have both the cash and the retained earnings to pay them. Corporations may voluntarily appropriate retained earnings to inform shareholders why dividends are not larger. Prior period adjustments are corrections of material errors in past years' financial statements. They result in adjustments to retained earnings.

LO 8 Compute dividend yield and explain its use in analysis. Dividend yield is the ratio of a share's annual cash dividends per share divided by its market value (price) per share. It gives the rate of return to shareholders from the company's cash dividends. Dividend yield can be compared with those of other companies and kinds of investments to determine whether the shares are income or growth shares.

LO 9 Compute price-earnings ratio and describe its use in analysis. The price-earnings ratio of a common share is computed by dividing the share's market value (price) per share by its earnings per share. Some analysts view a high ratio as suggesting the shares are overvalued while a low ratio suggests the shares are undervalued. But a stock's market value is based on expectations that may prove to be better or worse than later performance. While the price-earnings ratio is important to many users of financial statements, it is must be applied as part of a complete analysis and not viewed in isolation.

Guidance Answers to **You Make the Call**

Engineer

The 50% stock dividend provides no direct income to you. But a stock dividend often reveals management's optimistic expectations about the future. It also can improve a share's marketability by making it affordable to more investors. Accordingly, a stock dividend is usually good news.

Farmer

The frost loss is probably not extraordinary. Nova Scotia experiences enough frost damage that it would be difficult to argue this event is both unusual and infrequent. Nevertheless, you would want to highlight the frost loss, and hope the bank would view this uncommon event separately from your continuing operations.

Teacher

If you've decided to invest in one of two investments, and your analysis suggests they have identical future prospects, then you should pick the better deal. Since one requires a payment of $19 for each $1 of earnings, while the other requires $25, then you would purchase the shares with the PE of 19 since it is a better deal. You would also make sure these companies earnings computations are roughly the same—for example, no extraordinary items, unusual events, and so forth. Also, it does matter what your estimate of PE is for these companies. If you are willing to pay $29 for each $1 of earnings for these companies, then both are solid investments because you obviously expect both to exceed current market expectations.

Guidance Answers to **Judgment and Ethics**

Director

This case deals with insider trading in a company's shares. The ethical conflict is between your responsibility to Intex's shareholders (and the public) and your own interest in increasing your personal wealth with the options. If information about the new contract is kept private until after the option plan is approved and the options are priced, then you are likely to make a lot of money. (Note, insider trading laws may make nondisclosure in this case a crime.) You should try to explain the ethical and legal concerns to the board. You might also consider whether staying on the board and working for this company is appropriate since it appears there was some intent to deceive outsiders even if not eventually implemented.

Guidance Answers to Flashbacks

1. *c*
2. The three dates are the date of declaration, the date of record, and the date of payment.
3. A dividend is a legal liability at the date of declaration. It is also recorded on the date of declaration.
4. *c*
5. A small stock dividend is 25% or less of the previous outstanding shares. A large stock dividend is greater than 25%.
6. Retained earnings equal to the market value of the distributable shares should be capitalized.
7. *b*
8. No. The shares are an investment for Southern Co. and issued outstanding shares for Northern Corp.
9. Treasury shares do not affect the number of both authorized and issued shares. Treasury shares reduces the amount of outstanding shares.
10. *b*
11. The four major sections are income from continuing operations, discontinued segments, extraordinary items, and earnings per share.
12. *a*
13. *a* Weighted-average shares: (25,000 × 6/12) + (20,000 × 6/12) = 22,500
    Earnings per share: ($250,000 − $70,000)/22,500 = $8
14. The number of shares previously outstanding are retroactively restated to reflect the stock split or stock dividend as if it occurred at the beginning of the year.
15. The two types are basic earnings per share and diluted earnings per share.
16. *a*
17. *c*
18. $34/$4.25 = $8
19. The company with the higher PE ratio of 10.

Demonstration Problem

Refer back to the Mid-Chapter Demonstration Problem on page 743 and calculate the weighted average number of shares outstanding. Use the following information to prepare an income statement for 1999, including earnings per share results for each category of income.

Cumulative effect of a change in amortization method (net of tax benefit)	$ (136,500)
Expenses related to continuing operations	(2,072,500)
Extraordinary gain on expropriated land (net of tax)	182,000
Gain on disposal of discontinued segment's assets (net of tax)	29,000
Gain on sale of investment in shares	400,000
Loss from operating discontinued segment (net of tax benefit)	(120,000)
Income taxes on income from continuing operations	(225,000)
Prior period adjustment for error (net of tax benefit)	(75,000)
Sales	4,140,000
Infrequent loss	(650,000)

Planning the Solution

- Calculate the total cash dividend to be recorded by multiplying the cash dividend declared by the number of shareholders as of the date of record.
- Decide whether the stock dividend is a small or large dividend. Then, analyze each event to determine the accounts affected and the appropriate amounts to be recorded.
- Based on the shares of outstanding stock at the beginning of the year and the transactions during the year, compute the weighted-average number of outstanding shares for the year.
- Assign each of the listed items to an appropriate income statement category.
- Prepare an income statement similar to Exhibit 16.7, including appropriate earnings per share results.

Solution to Demonstration Problem

Computing the weighted-average of outstanding shares:

Time Period	Original Shares	Effect of Dividend	Post-Dividend Shares
January – April 15	200,000	1.2	240,000

Time Period	Post-Dividend Shares	Fraction of Year	Weighted Average
January – June	240,000	6/12	120,000
July – August	210,000	2/12	35,000
September – November	230,000	3/12	57,500
December	240,000	1/12	20,000
Weighted-average outstanding shares			232,500

THE PRECISION COMPANY Income Statement For Year Ended December 31, 1999		
Sales		$4,140,000
Expenses		(2,072,500)
Income taxes		(225,000)
Gain on sale of investment in shares		400,000
Infrequent loss		(650,000)
Income from continuing operations		$1,592,500
Discontinued operations:		
Loss from operating discontinued segment (net of tax benefit)	$(120,000)	
Gain on disposal of discontinued segment's assets (net of tax)	29,000	
Loss from discontinued segment		(91,000)
Income before extraordinary items and cumulative effect of a change in accounting principle		$1,501,500
Extraordinary items:		
Extraordinary gain on expropriated land (net of tax)		182,000
Net income		$1,683,500
Earnings per share (232,500 average shares outstanding):		
Income from continuing operations		$ 6.85
Loss from discontinued segment		(0.39)
Income before extraordinary gain		$ 6.46
Extraordinary gain		0.78
Net income		$ 7.24

Glossary

Appropriated retained earnings Retained earnings that are voluntarily restricted as a way of informing shareholders that dividends will be limited or not paid. (p. 752)

Basic earnings per share Calculated with the formula: (Net income − Preferred dividends)/Weighted-Average Common Shares Outstanding. (p. 748)

Changes in accounting estimates Corrections to previous estimates or predictions about future events and outcomes, such as salvage values and the useful lives of operating assets; the changes are accounted for in the current and future periods. (p. 753)

Complex capital structure A capital structure that includes outstanding rights or options to purchase common shares or securities that are convertible into common shares. (p. 750)

Date of declaration The date the directors vote to pay for a dividend. (p. 732)

Date of payment The date when shareholders receive the dividend payment. (p. 732)

Date of record The future date specified by the directors for identifying those shareholders listed in the corporation's records to receive dividends. (p. 732)

Deficit Arises when a corporation has a debit (abnormal) balance for retained earnings. (p. 733)

Diluted earnings per share An earnings per share calculation that requires that the effect of dilutive securities be added to the denominator of the basic earnings per share calculation. (p. 750)

Dividend yield A ratio that informs shareholders of the annual amount of cash dividends distributed to common shareholders relative to the share's market value (price). (p. 754)

Earnings per share The amount of income earned by each share of a company's outstanding common shares; also called net income per share. (p. 748)

Extraordinary gain or loss A gain or loss that is reported separate from continuing operations because it is not expected to occur frequently over several years, does not typify the normal business activities of the entity and does not depend primarily on decisions or determinations by management or owners. (p. 745)

Infrequent gain or loss A gain or loss that is not expected to occur again, given the operating environment of the business. (p. 745)

Large stock dividend A stock dividend that is more than 25% of the corporation's previously outstanding shares. (p. 735)

Liquidating cash dividend A distribution of corporate assets as a dividend that returns part of the original investment to the shareholders; these distributions are charged to contributed capital accounts. (p. 734)

Price-earnings ratio The ratio between a company's current market value per share and its earnings per share; used to gain understanding of the market's expectations for the stock. (p. 755)

Prior period adjustment A correction of a material error in a previous year that is reported in the statement of retained earnings (or statement of changes in shareholders' equity) net of any income tax effects. (p. 753)

Restricted retained earnings Retained earnings that are not available for dividends because of legal or contractual limitations. (p. 752)

Reverse stock split An act by a corporation to call in its stock and replace each share with less than one new share; reverse splits are opposite of stock splits as they increase both the market value per share and the issued value per share. (p. 738)

Segment of a business A component of a company's operations that serves a particular line of business or class of customers and that has assets, activities, and financial results of operations that can be distinguished from other parts of the business. (p. 744)

Simple capital structure A capital structure that consists of only common shares and nonconvertible preferred shares; it cannot include any options or rights to purchase common shares or any convertible preferred shares or bonds (dilutive securities). (p. 750)

Small stock dividend A stock dividend that is 25% or less of the corporation's previously outstanding shares. (p. 735)

Statement of changes in shareholders' equity A financial statement that lists the beginning and ending balances of each equity account and describes all the changes that occurred during the year. (p. 754)

Stock dividend A corporation's distribution of its own shares to its shareholders without receiving any payment in return. (p. 734)

Stock option A right to purchase common shares at a fixed price over a specified period of time. (p. 751)

Stock split An act by a corporation to call in its shares and replace each share with more than one new share; a stock split will decrease the market value per share and also the book per share. (p. 738)

Treasury shares Shares that were reacquired and are still held by the issuing corporation. (p. 739)

Unusual gain or loss A gain or loss that is abnormal or otherwise unrelated to the ordinary activities and environment of the business. (p. 745)

Questions

1. Identify and explain the importance of the three dates relevant to corporate dividends.
2. Why is the term *liquidating* dividend used to describe cash dividends that are debited against contributed capital accounts?
3. What effects does declaring a stock dividend have on the corporation's assets, liabilities, and total shareholders' equity? What effects does the distribution of the shares have?
4. What is the difference between a stock dividend and a stock split?
5. Courts in some countries have determined that a stock dividend is not taxable income to shareholders. What concept justifies this decision?
6. How does the purchase of treasury shares affect the purchaser's assets and total shareholders' equity?
7. Why do legal jurisdictions place limits on purchases of treasury shares?
8. Where on the income statement would a company report an abnormal gain that is not expected to occur more often than once every two years?
9. After taking five years' straight-line amortization expense for an asset that was expected to have an eight-year useful life, a company decided that the asset would last another six years. Is this decision a change in accounting principle? How would the financial statements describe this change?
10. How are earnings per share results computed for a corporation with a simple capital structure?
11. Refer to the financial statements for **Atlantis** in Appendix I at the end of the book. What is the balance of retained earnings as of December 31, 1997? What amount was paid out in dividends during 1997?
12. Refer to the financial statements for **Alliance** in Appendix I. How many voting shares were outstanding at the end of 1997?
13. Refer to the chapter's opening scenario. If you were helping MacPherson prepare documents to apply for a loan would you recommend a format such as Exhibit 16.7 in the chapter? Explain.

Quick Study

QS 16-1
Accounting for cash dividends
LO 1

Prepare journal entries to record the following transactions for Desmond Corporation:

Apr. 15	Declared a $48,000 cash dividend payable to common shareholders.
June 30	Paid the dividend declared on April 15.
Dec. 31	Closed the Cash Dividends Declared account.

QS 16-2
Accounting for a small stock dividend
LO 3

The shareholders' equity section of Jamestown Co.'s balance sheet as of April 1 follows:

Common shares, no-par value, 375,000 shares authorized, 150,000 shares issued and outstanding	$1,102,500
Retained earnings	633,000
Total shareholders' equity	$1,735,500

On April 1, Jamestown declares and distributes a 10% stock dividend. The market value of the shares on this date is $25. Prepare the shareholders' equity section for Jamestown immediately following the stock dividend.

QS 16-3
Purchase and sale of treasury shares
LO 4

On May 3, Nicholson Corp. purchased 3,000 of its own shares for $27,000. On November 4, Nicholson reissued 750 treasury shares for $7,080. Prepare the November 4 journal entry Nicholson should make to record the sale of the treasury shares.

QS 16-4
Accounting for estimate changes and error adjustments
LO 5, 7

Answer the questions about each of the following items related to a company's activities for the year:

a. After using an expected useful life of seven years and no salvage value to amortize its office equipment over the preceding three years, the company decided early this year that the equipment will last only two more years. How should the effects of this decision be reported in the current financial statements?
b. In reviewing the notes payable files, it was discovered that last year the company reported the entire amount of a payment on an installment note payable as interest expense. The mistake had a material effect on the amount of income in the prior year. How should the correction be reported in the current year financial statements?

QS 16-5
Basic earnings per share
LO 6

The Nelson company earned a net income of $450,000. The number of common shares outstanding all year long was 200,000 and preferred shareholders received dividends totalling $10,000. Compute Nelson Company's basic earnings per share.

QS 16-6
Weighted-average shares outstanding
LO 6

On January 1, Harmon Company had 100,000 common shares outstanding. On February 1, Harmon company issued 20,000 additional common shares. On June 1, another 40,000 common shares were issued. Compute Harmon Company's weighted-average shares outstanding.

QS 16-7
Weighted-average common shares outstanding
LO 6, 3

On January 1, Harrell Company had 150,000 common shares issued and outstanding. On April 1, it purchased 12,000 treasury shares and on June 2, declared a 20% stock dividend. Compute Harrell's weighted-average outstanding shares for the year.

QS 16-8
Dividend yield
LO 8

Cornerstone Company expects to pay out a $2.10 per share cash dividend next year on its common shares. The current market price per share is $28.50. Compute the expected dividend yield on the Cornerstone shares. Would you classify the Cornerstone shares as growth shares or income shares?

QS 16-9
Price-earnings ratio
LO 9

Compute a company's price-earnings ratio if its common shares have a market value of $30.75 per share and if its earnings per share are $4.10. Would an analyst viewing this stock consider that it might be over- or underpriced?

Exercises

Exercise 16-1
Stock dividends and per share values
LO 3

The shareholders' equity of Brinkman Motors, Inc., on February 5 consisted of the following:

Common shares, no-par value, 150,000 shares authorized, 60,000 shares issued and outstanding	$2,025,000
Retained earnings	675,000
Total shareholders' equity	$2,700,000

On February 5, the stock's market value was $40. On that date, the directors declared a 20% stock dividend distributable on February 28 to the February 15 shareholders of record. The stock's market value was $37 on March 2.

Required

1. Prepare entries to record the dividend declaration and distribution.
2. One shareholder owned 750 shares on February 5. Compute the per share and total book values of the investor's shares immediately before and after the dividend on February 5.
3. Compute the total market values of the investor's shares as of February 5 and March 2.

Exercise 16-2
Stock dividends and splits
LO 3

On June 30, 1999, Woodward Corporation's common shares were selling for $31 per share and the following information appeared in the shareholders' equity section of its balance sheet as of that date:

Common shares, no-par value, 60,000 shares authorized, 25,000 shares issued and outstanding	$350,000
Retained earnings	330,000
Total shareholders' equity	$680,000

Required

1. Assume that the company declares and immediately distributes a 100% stock dividend. The event is recorded by capitalizing the required minimum amount of retained earnings. Answer these questions about the shareholders' equity as it exists after issuing the new shares:
   a. What is the retained earnings balance?
   b. What is the total amount of shareholders' equity?
   c. How many shares are outstanding?
2. Assume that the company implements a two-for-one stock split instead of the stock dividend. Answer these questions about the shareholders' equity as it exists after issuing the new shares:
   a. What is the retained earnings balance?
   b. What is the total amount of shareholders' equity?
   c. How many shares are outstanding?
3. Briefly explain the difference, if any, that an investor would experience if new shares are distributed under a large dividend or a stock split.

Exercise 16-3
Reporting a purchase and retirement of common shares.
LO 4

On October 10, the shareholders' equity section of the balance sheet for Valley Systems, Inc., included this information:

Common shares, no-par value, unlimited number of shares authorized, 36,000 shares issued, and outstanding	$468,000
Retained earnings	432,000
Total shareholders' equity	$900,000

On the next day, the corporation purchased and retired 4,500 common shares at $30 per share. Explain how the equity section of Valley Systems will change after the purchase.

Exercise 16-4
Reporting a treasury shares purchase
LO 4

On October 10, the shareholders' equity section of the balance sheet for Affiliated Systems, Inc., included this information:

Common shares, no-par value, unlimited number of shares authorized, 36,000 shares issued, and outstanding	$468,000
Retained earnings	432,000
Total shareholders' equity	$900,000

On the next day, the corporation purchased and retired 4,500 common shares at $30 per share. Explain how the equity section of Affliated Systems will change after the purchase.

Exercise 16-5
Journal entries for treasury shares transactions
LO 4

Use the information in Exercise 16-4 to develop the accountant's journal entries to record these events for Affiliated Systems, Inc.:

1. The purchase of the treasury shares on October 11.
2. The sale of 1,200 treasury shares on November 1 for cash at $36 per share.
3. The sale of all the remaining treasury shares on November 25 for cash at $25 per share.

Exercise 16-6
Income statement categories
LO 5

During 1999, Burks Merchandise, Inc. sold its interest in a chain of wholesale outlets. This sale took the company out of the wholesaling business completely. The company still operates its retail outlets. Following is a lettered list of sections of an income statement:

A. Income from continuing operations
B. Income from operating a discontinued segment
C. Gain or loss from disposing of a discontinued segment
D. Extraordinary gain or loss

Indicate where each of the nine income-related items for the company would appear on the 1999 income statement by writing the letter of the appropriate section in the blank beside each item.

	Debit	Credit
A 1. Amortization expense	$ 262,500	
C 2. Gain on sale of wholesale segment (net of tax)		$ 675,000
B 3. Loss from operating wholesale segment (net of tax)	555,000	
A 4. Salaries expense	540,000	
A 5. Sales		2,700,000
D 6. Gain on condemnation of company property (net of tax)		330,000
B 7. Cost of goods sold	1,380,000	
A 8. Income taxes expense	207,000	

Exercise 16-7
Income statement presentation
LO 5

Use the data for Burks Merchandise, Inc., in Exercise 16-6 to present the income statement for 1999.

Exercise 16-8
Accounting for a change in accounting principle
LO 7

Canadian Home Company put an asset in service on January 1, 1999. Its cost was $225,000, its predicted service life was six years, and its expected salvage value was $22,500. The company decided to use double-declining-balance amortization and recorded these amounts of amortization expense in the first two years of the asset's life:

1999	$75,000
2000	50,000

The scheduled amortization expense for 2001 was $33,333. After consulting with the company's auditors, management decided to change to straight-line amortization in 2001, without changing either the predicted service life or salvage value. Under this system, the annual amortization expense for all years in the asset's life would be $33,750. The company faces a 35% income tax rate.

1. Prepare a table like Exhibit 16.8 that deals with this situation.
2. How much amortization expense will be reported on the company's income statement for this asset in 2001 and in each of the remaining years of the asset's life?
3. What amount will be reported on the company's 2001 income statement as the after-tax cumulative effect of the change?

Exercise 16-9
Weighted-average shares outstanding and earnings per share
LO 6

A company reported $1,350,000 of net income for 1999. It also declared $195,000 of dividends on preferred shares for the same year. At the beginning of 1999, the company had 270,000 outstanding common shares. These two events changed the number of outstanding shares during the year:

Apr. 30 Sold 180,000 common shares for cash.
Oct. 31 Purchased 108,000 common shares for the treasury.

a. What is the amount of net income available to the common shareholders?
b. What is the weighted-average number of common shares for the year?
c. What is the basic earnings per share for the year?

Exercise 16-10
Weighted-average shares outstanding and earnings per share
LO 6

A company reported $480,000 of net income for 1999. It also declared $65,000 of dividends on preferred shares for the same year. At the beginning of 1999, the company had 50,000 outstanding common shares. These three events changed the number of outstanding shares during the year:

June	1	Sold 30,000 common shares for cash.
Aug.	31	Purchased and retired 13,000 common shares.
Oct.	1	Completed a three-for-one stock split.

a. What is the amount of net income available to the common shareholders?
b. What is the weighted-average number of common shares for the year?
c. What is the basic earnings per share for the year?

Exercise 16-11
Computing dividend yield
LO 8

Compute the dividend yield for each of these situations:

	Annual Dividend per Share	Share's Market Price per Share
a.	$15.00	$216.00
b.	12.00	128.00
c.	6.00	61.00
d.	1.20	86.00
e.	11.00	130.00
f.	2.00	50.00

Which shares above would probably not be classified as income shares?

Exercise 16-12
Computing the price-earnings ratio
LO 9

Use the following information to compute the price-earnings ratio for each case:

	Earnings per Share	Market Value per Share
a.	$10.00	$166.00
b.	9.00	86.00
c.	6.50	90.00
d.	1.50	36.00
e.	36.00	240.00

Which of the above stocks might an analyst investigate as being undervalued by the market?

Problems

Problem 16-1
Cash dividends and retirement of shares transactions
LO 1, 4

The balance sheet for the Trevor Corporation reported the following components of shareholders' equity on December 31, 1999:

Common shares, no-par value, unlimited shares authorized, 20,000 shares issued and outstanding	$230,000
Retained earnings	135,000
Total shareholders' equity	$365,000

In 2000 Trevor Company had the following transactions affecting shareholders and the shareholder equity accounts:

Jan.	1	Purchased and retired 2,000 common shares at $20 per share.
Jan.	5	The directors declared a $2.00 per share cash dividend payable on Feb. 28 to the Feb. 5 shareholders of record.
Feb.	28	Paid the dividend declared on January 5.
July	6	Sold 750 common shares at $24 per share.
Aug.	22	Sold 1,250 common shares at $17 per share.
Sept.	5	The directors declared a $2.00 per share cash dividend payable on Oct. 28 to the Oct. 5 shareholders of record.

Oct. 28 Paid the dividend declared on September 5.
Dec. 31 Closed the $194,000 credit balance in the Income Summary account to Retained Earnings.
31 Closed the Cash Dividends Declared account.

Check Figure
Retained earnings, Dec. 31, 2000, $236,000

1. Prepare journal entries to record the transactions and closings for 2000.
2. Prepare a statement of retained earnings for the year-ended December 31, 2000.
3. Prepare the shareholders' equity section of the company's balance sheet as of December 31, 2000.

Problem 16-2
Cash dividends and retirement of shares transactions
LO 1, 4

The balance sheet for the Oppong Corporation, a provincially incorporated corporation, reported the following components of shareholders' equity on December 31, 1999:

Common shares, no-par value, unlimited shares authorized, 20,000 shares issued and outstanding	$230,000
Retained earnings	135,000
Total shareholders' equity	$365,000

In 2000 Oppong Company had the following transactions affecting shareholders and the shareholder equity accounts:

Jan. 1 Purchased 2,000 treasury shares at $20 per share.
Jan. 5 The directors declared a $2.00 per share cash dividend payable on Feb. 28 to the Feb. 5 shareholders of record.
Feb. 28 Paid the dividend declared on January 5.
July 6 Sold 750 of the treasury shares at $24 per share.
Aug. 22 Sold 1,250 of the treasury shares at $17 per share.
Sept. 5 The directors declared a $2.00 per share cash dividend payable on Oct. 28 to the Oct.. 5 shareholders of record.
Oct. 28 Paid the dividend declared on September 5.
Dec. 31 Closed the $194,000 credit balance in the Income Summary account to Retained Earnings.
31 Closed the Cash Dividends Declared account.

Check Figure
Retained earnings, Dec. 31, 2000, $252,250

1. Prepare journal entries to record the transactions and closings for 2000.
2. Prepare a statement of retained earnings for the year ended December 31, 2000.
3. Prepare the shareholders' equity section of the company's balance sheet as of December 31, 2000.

Problem 16-3
Describing equity changes with journal entries and account balances
LO 1, 3

At September 30, the end of the third quarter for Granger Co., Inc., these balances existed in its shareholders' equity accounts:

Common shares, unlimited authorized, 60,000 issued	$900,000
Retained earnings	640,000

Over the next three months, the following journal entries were recorded in the company's equity accounts:

Oct. 2	Cash Dividends Declared	120,000	
	Common Dividend Payable		120,000
25	Common Dividend Payable	120,000	
	Cash		120,000
31	Stock Dividends Declared (6,000 shares) . . .	150,000	
	Common Shares Dividend Distributable		150,000
Nov. 5	Common Shares Dividend Distributable . . .	150,000	
	Common Shares		150,000

Dec. 1	Memo—change the title of the common shares account to reflect the new number of shares outstanding of 198,000.		
31	Income Summary	420,000	
	Retained Earnings		420,000
31	Retained Earnings	270,000	
	Cash Dividends Declared		120,000
	Stock Dividends Declared		150,000

Required

1. Provide explanations for each of the journal entries.
2. Complete the following table showing the balances of the company's equity accounts (including the dividends declared accounts) at each of the indicated dates:

	Oct. 2	Oct. 25	Oct. 31	Nov. 5	Dec. 1	Dec. 31
Common shares	$____	$____	$____	$____	$____	$____
Stock dividend distributable ..	____	____	____	____	____	____
Retained earnings	____	____	____	____	____	____
Less:						
Cash dividends declared	____	____	____	____	____	____
Stock dividends declared	____	____	____	____	____	____
Combined balances of equity accounts	$____	$____	$____	$____	$____	$____

Check Figure
Total equity, Dec. 31, $1,840,000

Problem 16-4
Changes in retained earnings
LO 7

The equity sections from the 1999 and 2000 balance sheets of TRP Corporation appeared as follows:

Shareholders' Equity (As of December 31, 1999)	
Common shares, no-par value, 50,000 shares authorized, 20,000 shares issued and outstanding	$140,000
Retained earnings	160,000
Total shareholders' equity	$300,000

Shareholders' Equity (As of December 31, 2000)	
Common shares, no-par value, 50,000 shares authorized, 23,700 shares issued	$169,400
Retained earnings ($15,000 restricted)	200,000
Total shareholders' equity	$369,400

The following events occurred during 2000:

Jan. 5 A $0.50 per share cash dividend was declared, and the date of record was five days later.
Mar. 20 1,500 common shares were purchased and retired.
Apr. 5 A $0.50 per share cash dividend was declared, and the date of record was five days later.
July 5 A $0.50 per share cash dividend was declared, and the date of record was five days later.
31 A 20% stock dividend was declared when the market value was $12 per share.
Aug. 14 The dividend shares were issued.
Oct. 5 A $0.50 per share cash dividend was declared, and the date of record was five days later.

Required

1. How many shares were outstanding on each of the cash dividend dates?
2. How large were each of the four cash dividends?
3. How large was the capitalization of retained earnings for the stock dividend?
4. What was the price per share paid for the shares to be retired?
5. How much income did the company achieve during 2000?

Check Figure
Net income, $124,000

Problem 16-5
Presenting items in an income statement
LO 5

The following table shows the balances from various accounts in the adjusted trial balance for Depew Corp. as of December 31, 1999:

	Debit	Credit
a. Interest earned		$ 12,000
b. Amortization expense, equipment	$ 36,000	
c. Loss on sale of office equipment	24,750	
d. Accounts payable		42,000
e. Other operating expenses	97,500	
f. Accumulated amortization, equipment		73,500
g. Gain from settling a lawsuit		42,000
h. Cumulative effect of change in accounting principle (pre-tax)	63,000	
i. Accumulated amortization, buildings		163,500
j. Loss from operating a discontinued segment (pre-tax)	19,500	
k. Gain on court ordered early settlement of debt (pre-tax)		28,500
l. Sales		970,500
m. Amortization expense, buildings	54,000	
n. Correction of overstatement of prior year's sales (pre-tax)	15,000	
o. Gain on sale of discontinued segment's assets (pre-tax)		33,000
p. Loss from settling a lawsuit	24,000	
q. Income taxes expense	?	
r. Cost of goods sold	487,500	

Required

Answer each of these questions by providing detailed schedules:

1. Assuming that the company's income tax rate is 30%, what are the tax effects and after-tax measures of the items labelled as pre-tax?
2. What is the amount of the company's income from continuing operations before income taxes? What is the amount of the company's income taxes expense? What is the amount of the company's income from continuing operations?
3. What is the amount of after-tax income associated with the discontinued segment?
4. What is the amount of income before extraordinary items and the cumulative effect of the change in principle?
5. What is the amount of net income for the year?

Check Figure
Net income, $239,925

Problem 16-6
Changes in accounting principles
LO 5

On January 1, 1999, Pohl, Inc., purchased some equipment. Its cost was $600,000 and it was expected to have a salvage value of $30,000 at the end of its five-year useful life. Amortization was allocated to 1999, 2000, and 2001 with the declining-balance method at twice the straight-line rate. Early in 2002, the company concluded that changing to the straight-line method would produce more useful financial statements because it would be consistent with the practices of other firms in the industry.

Required

Preparation component:

1. Do generally accepted accounting principles allow Pohl, Inc., to change amortization methods in 2002?
2. Prepare a schedule that shows the amount of amortization expense allocated to 1999 through 2001 under the declining-balance method.
3. Prepare a schedule that shows the amount of amortization expense that would have been allocated to 1999 through 2001 under the straight-line method.
4. Combine the information from your answers to requirements 2 and 3 in a table like Exhibit 16.8 that computes the before- and after-tax cumulative effects of the change. The company's income tax rate is 30%. (For simplicity, round your answers to the nearest dollar.)
5. How should the cumulative effect be reported by the company? Does the cumulative effect increase or decrease net income?
6. How much amortization expense will be reported on the income statement for 2002?

Check Figure
After-tax cumulative effect, $89,880

Analysis component:

7. Assume that Pohl, Inc., makes the mistake of treating the change in amortization methods as a change in an accounting estimate. Using your answers from requirements 2, 3, and 4, describe the effect this error would have on the 2002 financial statements.

Problem 16-7
Earnings per share calculations and presentation
LO 6

The income statements for Tennison, Inc., presented the following information when they were first published in 2000, 2001, and 2002:

	2000	2001	2002
Sales	$370,000	$425,000	$412,500
Expenses	232,500	260,000	245,500
Income from continuing operations	$137,500	$165,000	$167,000
Loss on discontinued segment	(52,500)		
Income before extraordinary items	$ 85,000	$165,000	$167,000
Extraordinary gain (loss)		33,000	(70,000)
Net income	$ 85,000	$198,000	$ 97,000

The company also experienced some changes in the number of outstanding shares through the following events:

Outstanding shares on December 31, 1999	40,000
2000	
Purchase and retirement of shares on April 1	−4,000
Issuance of new shares on June 30	+12,000
10% stock dividend on October 1	+4,800
Outstanding shares on December 31, 2000	52,800
2001	
Issuance of new shares on July 1	+16,000
Purchase and retirement of shares on November 1	−4,800
Outstanding shares on December 31, 2001	64,000
2002	
Issuance of new shares on August 1	+20,000
Purchase and retirement of shares on September 1	−4,000
Three-for-one split on October 1	+160,000
Outstanding shares on December 31, 2002	240,000

Required

Preparation component:

1. Compute the weighted average of the outstanding common shares as of the end of 2000.
2. Compute the 2000 earnings per share amounts to report on the 2000 income statement for income from continuing operations, loss on discontinued segment, and net income.
3. Compute the weighted average of the outstanding common shares as of the end of 2001.
4. Compute the 2001 earnings per share amounts to report on the 2001 income statement for income from continuing operations, the extraordinary gain, and net income.
5. Compute the weighted average of the outstanding common shares as of the end of 2002.
6. Compute the 2002 earnings per share amounts to report on the 2002 income statement for income from continuing operations, the extraordinary loss, and net income.

Check Figure
2001 earnings per share for net income, $3.30

Analysis component:

7. Write a brief explanation of how you would use the earnings per share statistics from requirement 6 to estimate earnings per share for 2003.

Alternate Problems

Problem 16-1A
Retirement of shares and cash dividends

LO 1, 4

The balance sheet for Caldwell Corp. reported the following components of shareholders' equity on December 31, 1999:

Common shares, no-par value, unlimited shares authorized, 100,000 shares issued and outstanding	$ 800,000
Retained earnings	1,080,000
Total shareholders' equity	$1,880,000

The company completed these transactions during 2000:

Jan. 10 Purchased and retired 20,000 common shares at $12 cash per share.
Mar. 2 The directors declared a $1.50 per share cash dividend payable on March 31 to the March 15 shareholders of record.
31 Paid the dividend declared on March 2.
Nov. 11 Issued 12,000 common shares at $13 per share.
25 Issued 8,000 common shares at $9.50 per share.
Dec. 1 The directors declared a $2.50 per share cash dividend payable on January 2, 2001, to the December 10 shareholders of record.
31 Closed the $536,000 credit balance in the Income Summary account to Retained Earnings.
31 Closed the Cash Dividends Declared account.

Required

1. Prepare general journal entries to record the transactions and closings for 2000.
2. Prepare a statement of retained earnings for 2000.
3. Prepare the shareholders' equity section of the company's balance sheet as of December 31, 2000.

Problem 16-2A
Treasury shares transactions and cash dividends

LO 1, 4

The balance sheet for Francois Corp. reported the following components of shareholders' equity on December 31, 1999:

Common shares, no-par value, unlimited shares authorized, 100,000 shares issued and outstanding	$ 800,000
Retained earnings	1,080,000
Total shareholders' equity	$1,880,000

The company completed these transactions during 2000:

Jan.	10	Purchased 20,000 treasury shares at $12 cash per share.
Mar.	2	The directors declared a $1.50 per share cash dividend payable on March 31 to the March 15 shareholders of record.
	31	Paid the dividend declared on March 2.
Nov.	11	Sold 12,000 of the treasury shares at $13 per share.
	25	Sold 8,000 of the treasury shares at $9.50 per share.
Dec.	1	The directors declared a $2.50 per share cash dividend payable on January 2, 2001, to the December 10 shareholders of record.
	31	Closed the $536,000 credit balance in the Income Summary account to Retained Earnings.
	31	Closed the Cash Dividends Declared account.

Required

1. Prepare general journal entries to record the transactions and closings for 2000.

2. Prepare a statement of retained earnings for 2000.

3. Prepare the shareholders' equity section of the company's balance sheet as of December 31, 2000.

Problem 16-3A
Describing equity changes with journal entries and account balances

LO 1, 3

At December 31, the end of the third quarter for Hixton Co., Inc., these balances existed in its shareholders' equity accounts:

Common shares, no-par value, 48,000 shares issued	$672,000
Retained earnings	800,000

Over the next three months, the following journal entries were recorded in the company's equity accounts:

Jan. 17	Cash Dividends Declared	48,000	
	Common Dividend Payable		48,000
Feb. 5	Common Dividend Payable	48,000	
	Cash		48,000
28	Stock Dividends Declared (6,000 shares) ...	126,000	
	Common Shares Dividend Distributable		126,000
Mar. 14	Common Shares Dividend Distributable ...	126,000	
	Common shares		126,000
25	Memo—change the title of the common shares account to reflect the new number of Common Shares outstanding of 108,000.		
31	Income Summary	360,000	
	Retained Earnings		360,000
31	Retained Earnings	174,000	
	Cash Dividends Declared		48,000
	Stock Dividends Declared		126,000

Required

1. Provide explanations for each of the journal entries.

2. Complete the following table showing the balances of the company's equity accounts (including the dividend accounts) at each of the indicated dates:

	Jan. 17	Feb. 5	Feb. 28	Mar. 14	Mar. 25	Mar. 31
Common shares	$____	$____	$____	$____	$____	$____
Stock dividend distributable	____	____	____	____	____	____
Contr. capital in excess of par	____	____	____	____	____	____
Retained earnings	____	____	____	____	____	____
Less:						
Cash dividends declared	____	____	____	____	____	____
Stock dividends declared	____	____	____	____	____	____
Combined balances of equity accounts	$____	$____	$____	$____	$____	$____

Problem 16-4A
Changes in retained earnings

LO 7

The equity sections from the 1999 and 2000 balance sheets of Thornhill Corporation appeared as follows:

Shareholders' Equity (As of December 31, 1999)	
Common shares, no-par value, 15,000 shares authorized, 8,500 shares issued and outstanding	$200,000
Retained earnings	135,000
Total shareholders' equity	$335,000

Shareholders' Equity (As of December 31, 2000)	
Common shares, no-par value, 15,000 shares authorized	222,000
Retained earnings ($20,000 restricted for retirement)	147,600
Total shareholders' equity	$369,600

The following events occurred during 2000:

Feb. 15 A $0.40 per share cash dividend was declared, and the date of record was five days later.
Mar. 2 500 common shares were purchased for retirement.
May 15 A $0.40 per share cash dividend was declared, and the date of record was five days later.
Aug. 15 A $0.40 per share cash dividend was declared, and the date of record was five days later.
Oct. 4 A 12.5% stock dividend was declared when the market value was $42 per share.
20 The dividend shares were issued.
Nov. 15 A $0.40 per share cash dividend was declared, and the date of record was five days later.

Required

1. How many shares were outstanding on each of the cash dividend dates?
2. How large were each of the four cash dividends?
3. How large was the capitalization of retained earnings for the stock dividend?
4. What was the price per share paid for the retired shares?
5. How much income did the company achieve during 2000?

Problem 16-5A
Presenting items in an income statement

LO 5

The following table shows the balances from various accounts in the adjusted trial balance for Barbour Corp. as of December 31, 1999:

	Debit	Credit
a. Accumulated amortization, buildings		$ 200,000
b. Interest earned		10,000
c. Cumulative effect of change in accounting principle (pre-tax)		46,000
d. Sales		1,320,000
e. Income taxes expense	$?	
f. Loss on condemnation of property (pre-tax)	32,000	
g. Accumulated amortization, equipment		110,000
h. Other operating expenses	164,000	
i. Amortization expense, equipment	50,000	
j. Loss from settling a lawsuit	18,000	
k. Gain from settling a lawsuit		34,000
l. Loss on sale of office equipment	12,000	
m. Loss from operating a discontinued segment (pre-tax)	60,000	
n. Amortization expense, buildings	78,000	
o. Correction of overstatement of prior year's expense (pre-tax)		24,000
p. Cost of goods sold	520,000	
q. Loss on sale of discontinued segment's assets (pre-tax)	90,000	
r. Accounts payable		66,000

Required

Answer each of these questions by providing detailed schedules:

1. Assuming that the company's income tax rate is 25%, what are the tax effects and after-tax measures of the items labelled as "pre-tax"?
2. What is the amount of the company's income from continuing operations before income taxes? What is the amount of the company's income taxes expense? What is the amount of the company's income from continuing operations?
3. What is the amount of after-tax income associated with the discontinued segment?
4. What is the amount of income before extraordinary items and the cumulative effect of the change in principle?
5. What is the amount of net income for the year?

Problem 16-6A
Changes in accounting principles
LO 5

On January 1, 1999, Fricke Co., Inc., purchased some equipment. Its cost was $200,000 and it was expected to have no salvage value at the end of its five-year useful life. Amortization was allocated to 1999 through 2001 with the declining-balance method at twice the straight-line rate. Early in 2002, the company concluded that changing to the straight-line method would produce more useful financial statements because it would be consistent with the practices of other firms in the industry.

Required

Preparation component:

1. Do generally accepted accounting principles allow Fricke Co., Inc., to change amortization methods in 2002?
2. Prepare a schedule that shows the amount of amortization expense that was allocated to 1999 through 2001 under the declining-balance method.
3. Prepare a schedule that shows the amount of amortization expense that would have been allocated to 1999 through 2001 under the straight-line method.
4. Combine the information from your answers to parts 2 and 3 in a table like Exhibit 16.8 that computes the before- and after-tax cumulative effect of the change. The company's income tax rate is 25%.
5. How should the cumulative effect be reported by the company? Does the cumulative effect increase or decrease net income?
6. How much amortization expense will be reported on the income statement for 2002?

Analysis component:

7. Assume that, in error, Fricke Co., Inc., treats the change in amortization methods as a change in an accounting estimate. Using your answers from Parts 2, 3 and 4, describe the effect this error would have on the 2002 financial statements.

Problem 16-7A
Earnings per share calculations and presentation
LO 6

The original income statements for Titus, Inc., presented the following information when they were first published in 2000, 2001, and 2002:

	2000	2001	2002
Sales	$250,000	$300,000	$400,000
Expenses	160,000	215,000	270,000
Income from continuing operations	$90,000	$85,000	$130,000
Loss on discontinued segment	(26,145)		
Income before extraordinary items	$63,855	$85,000	$130,000
Extraordinary gain (loss)		14,100	(37,125)
Net income	$63,855	$99,100	$92,875

The company also experienced some changes in the number of outstanding shares over the three years through the following events:

Outstanding shares on December 31, 1999	10,000
2000	
Treasury shares purchase on July 1	−1,000
Issuance of new shares on September 30	+3,500
20% stock dividend on December 1	+2,500
Outstanding shares on December 31, 2000	15,000
2001	
Issuance of new shares on March 31	+4,000
Treasury shares purchase on October 1	−1,500
Outstanding shares on December 31, 2001	17,500
2002	
Issuance of new shares on July 1	+3,000
Treasury shares purchase on October 1	−1,750
2-for-1 split on November 1	+18,750
Outstanding shares on December 31, 2002	37,500

Required

Preparation component:

1. Compute the weighted average of the outstanding common shares as of the end of 2000.

2. Use the results of part 1 to present the original earnings per share amounts for 2000 for income from continuing operations, loss on discontinued segment, and net income.

3. Compute the weighted average of the outstanding common shares as of the end of 2001.

4. Use the results of part 3 to present the original earnings per share amounts for 2001 for income from continuing operations, the extraordinary gain, and net income.

5. Compute the weighted average of the outstanding common shares as of the end of 2002.

6. Use the results of part 5 to present the earnings per share amounts for 2002 for income from continuing operations, the extraordinary loss, and net income.

Analysis component:

7. Write a brief explanation of how you would use the earnings per share statistics from part 6 to estimate earnings per share for 2003.

Analytical and Review Problems

A & R Problem 16-1

Part 1. The more recent business corporations acts restrict the directors by the "solvency" test in the matter of declaration and payment of dividends in money or property. A similar restriction is not, however, imposed in the case of a stock dividends.

Required

Discuss why a restriction is deemed necessary in the former but not in the latter situation.

Part 2. In the case of stock dividends, the Canada Business Corporations Act prescribes that the amount of retained earnings to be capitalized is the product of the number of shares issued as a stock dividends multiplied by the market value of each share. The revised Ontario Business Corporations Act does not stipulate the amount to be capitalized, simply stating that the amount to be added to the stated capital account is the amount declared by the directors.

Required

Can a case be made for either of the positions? Support your answer.

A & R Problem 16-2

Over the last three years, Commonwealth Enterprises Ltd. has experienced the following income results (all numbers are rounded to the nearest thousand dollars):

	1996	1997	1998
Revenues	$11,000	$11,900	$14,600
Expenses	(7,000)	(7,900)	(7,700)
Gains	3,200	2,400	-0-
Losses	(1,200)	(1,900)	(3,900)
Net income	$ 6,000	$4,500	$ 3,000

Part 1. Use the information to develop a general prediction of the company's net income for 1999.

Part 2. A closer analysis of the information shows that the company discontinued a segment of its operations in 1998. The company's accountant has determined that the discounted segment produced the following amounts of income:

	1996	1997	1998
Revenues	$7,000	$2,600	$1,600
Expenses	(5,000)	(5,000)	(4,000)
Gains		400	
Losses	(1,200)	(1,500)	(900)
Loss on disposal of segment assets			(1,200)

Use the information to calculate the company's income without the discontinued segment and then develop a general prediction of the company's net income for 1999.

Part 3. A more in-depth analysis of the company's activity reveals that the company experienced these extraordinary items during the three years when it retired some of its debts before their scheduled maturity dates.

	1996	1997	1998
Extraordinary gain	$2,200	$2,000	
Extraordinary loss			$(1,700)

Use the information to calculate the company's income from continuing operations and develop a general prediction of the company's net income for 1999.

BEYOND THE NUMBERS

Reporting in Action

LO 5, 6, 8, 9

Refer to the financial statements and related information for **Atlantis** in Appendix I. Answer the following questions by analyzing the information in the report:

1. What is the per share amount of cash dividends paid on common shares during fiscal year 1997?
2. How many common shares are outstanding at the end of fiscal year 1997? How does this number compare with the weighted average number of common shares outstanding at the end of fiscal year 1997?
3. Compare Atlantis's December 31, 1997, net income per common share to the net income per common share as of December 31, 1996.
4. Does Atlantis hold any treasury shares as of December 31, 1997?
5. Does Atlantis show any changes in accounting principles or extraordinary items for fiscal years ended December 31, 1997, and December 31, 1996?
6. Did Atlantis have any gains or losses on the disposal of a business segment during 1997?
7. Obtain access to Atlantis's annual report for fiscal years ending after December 31, 1997. This access may be through a shrink-wrapped annual report included with your text or you may gain access to annual report information at Atlantis's Web site: **http://sedar.com/dynamic_assoc_docs_e/doooo2259.htm.** Has Atlantis paid out any cash dividends paid since the fiscal year-end December 31, 1997?

Comparative Analysis

LO 6, 8, 9

Both **Atlantis** and **Alliance** are in the communications business. Key comparative figures ($ thousands except for per share data) for these two organizations follow:

Key Figures	Atlantis 1997	Alliance 1997
Net income	$795,822	$18,188
Dividends paid per share of common shares	$0.00	$0.00
Common shares outstanding	10,067,074	11,919,000
Market price per share (assumed)	$11.00	$28.00

* Atlantis figures are from the annual report for the fiscal year ended December 31,1997. Alliance figures are from the annual report for the fiscal year ended March 31, 1997.

Required

1. Compute the earnings per share for each company.
2. Compute the dividend yield for each company. Does the dividend yield of the companies characterize them as income or growth stocks?
3. Compute, compare, and interpret the price-earnings ratios for Atlantis and Alliance.

Ethics Challenge

LO 5

Recall the facts outlined in the chapter regarding **CompCAN's** change in accounting principle from the double-declining balance method of amortization to the straight-line method. Recall that CompCAN decides that its income statement would be more useful if amortization is computed using the straight-line method instead of the double-declining balance method. This change in accounting principle adds $56,000 to net income in the current year. As the auditor of the company you are reviewing the decision to make the change in accounting principle. You review the equipment in question and realize that it is a piece of high-tech equipment and the risk of obsolescence in the near future is relatively high. You are also aware that all members of top management receive year-end bonuses based on net income.

Required

As an auditor in this situation, would you support the change in principle or ask management to continue using the straight-line method? Justify your response.

Communicating in Practice

LO 9

The classroom should be divided into teams. Teams are to select an industry, and each team member is to select a different company in that industry. Each team member is to acquire the annual report of the company selected. Annual reports can be obtained in many ways including accessing this book's Web page or **http://www.sedar.com/**. Use the annual report to determine the earnings per share of common shares. Use the financial press to determine the market price of this stock. Use this data to determine the price-earnings ratio. Communicate with teammates via a meeting, e-mail or telephone to discuss the meaning of this ratio, how different companies compare to each other, and the industry norm. The team must prepare a single memo reporting the ratios for each company and identify the conclusions or consensus of opinion reached during the team's discussion. The memo is to be duplicated and distributed to the instructor and all classmates.

Taking It to the Net

LO 6, 8, 9

Visit the Canadian Stock Market Reporter Inc. Web site at **http://www.canstock.com/**. This site puts key financial data about companies at your fingertips. Using the stock symbols for **Atlantis** (AAC.A or AAC.B) and **Alliance** (ATV) search for the following information: (Hint: You may want to print out the various links you visit for easy reference later.)

1. Under the sidebar category "Quote" select the Yahoo detailed quote link. Record the market price per share, earnings per share, price-earnings ratio, and dividend per share for both companies.
2. Compute the dividend yield for each company using the data you collected in requirement 1.
3. Visit the sidebar category "Earnings." View at least three of the earnings consensus links. How much difference do you find among the experts regarding the companies' future earnings prospects?
4. Under the sidebar category "Fundamentals" select the dividends and splits link. Has either company's stock split recently?

Teamwork In Action

LO 4

Let's work as a team to reinforce understanding of accounting for treasury shares.

1. After a team discussion, write a brief team statement (a) generalizing what happens to a corporation's financial position when the entity engages in a stock "buyback" and (b) identifying reasons why a corporation would engage in this activity.
2. Assume an entity reacquired 100 shares of its $100 par value common shares at a cost of $134 per share. Discuss this entry to record the acquisition. After each member understands this entry, assign each team member the preparation of *one* of the following entries (assume each entry applies to all shares):
   a. Reissue at cost
   b. Reissue at $150 per share
   c. Reissue at $120 per share—assume the related contributed capital account has a $1,500 balance.
   d. Reissue at $120 per share—assume the related contributed capital account has a $1,000 balance.
   e. Reissue at $120 per share—assume the related contributed capital account does not have a balance.
3. In sequence, each member is to present his or her entry to the team and explain the similarities and differences between that entry and the previous entry. Encourage team members to ask questions and be sure concepts are understood before proceeding.

Hitting the Road

LO 6, 8, 9

Watch a Canadian financial news television program. While watching, take notes on company happenings that are catching the attention of analysts following stocks. You might hear reference to over- and undervaluation of firms. You might also hear reporters talking about PE ratios, dividend yields, and earnings per share. Be prepared to give a brief description in class of your experience listening to the television financial news.

Business Break

LO 6

In recent year firms have become very innovative in developing and offering to the public new types of financial securities. Obtain a copy of the May 29, 1998, edition of *Canadian Business Magazine*. Read the article on pages 25–25 entitled, "A Stock Dividend" under the risk and reward section of the magazine. Answer the following questions.

1. What is the meaning of split shares according to this article?
2. How does this conception of split shares differ from stock splits as discussed in your text?
3. Why aren't split shares all they are cracked up to be?

17

Bonds and Long-Term Notes Payable

CHAPTER

A Look Back

Chapter 16 focused on corporate reporting including accounting for dividends, treasury shares, income reporting, earnings per share, and retained earnings.

A Look at This Chapter

This chapter describes the accounting for bonds and notes. We explain their characteristics, payment patterns, interest computations, retirement, and reporting requirements.

A Look Forward

Chapter 18 focuses on long-term investments in securities. We explain how to identify, account for, and report long-term investments in both debt and equity securities. We also introduce foreign exchange rates and describe accounting for foreign currency transactions.

Chapter Outline

- **Basics of Bonds**
  - Bond Financing
  - Types of Bonds
  - Bond Trading
  - Bond Issuing Procedures
- **Bond Issuances**
  - Issuing Bonds at Par
  - Determining Bond Discount or Premium
  - Issuing Bonds at a Discount
  - Amortizing a Bond Discount
  - Issuing Bonds at a Premium
  - Amortizing a Bond Premium
  - Issuing Bonds between Interest Dates
  - Accruing Bond Interest Expense
  - Bond Pricing
- **Bond Retirements**
  - Bond Retirement at Maturity
  - Bond Retirement before Maturity
  - Bond Retirement by Conversion of Shares
- **Long-Term Notes Payable**
  - Interest-Bearing Notes
  - Non-interest-Bearing Notes
  - Installment Notes
  - Mortgage Notes
- **Using the Information — Pledged Assets to Secured Liabilities**
  - Collateral Agreements for Bonds and Notes
  - Ratio of Pledged Assets to Secured Liabilities
- **Appendix—Present Values of Bonds and Notes**

Get Real!

Montreal, PQ—Yvette Bourque has overcome odds before. Three years ago she had a plan to open a natural foods store near Montreal. But she needed money. She took plans for her store to the local bank. "The banker criticized my business plan and told me to get real," says Bourque. "That really got to me."

Bourque turned to her family and friends for start-up money. Motivated by the banker's remark, Bourque is now the proud owner of **Get Real!** "I sell *real* food like farm-raised seafood and natural and organic produce. It's successful beyond my wildest expectations. It's like a dream." Get Real! now offers a line of more than 2,000 products.

But Bourque faced another obstacle. "I wanted to open two more stores, one in Quebec City and one in Ottawa." Again, Bourque met with several bankers to get a loan. "Every bank wanted me to come to four meetings and prepare five sets of forecasts. Only then would they make a loan proposal, and none of them were acceptable to me. They viewed my plans as risky and I had little collateral."

Then Bourque got an idea. "I remembered when Ben & Jerry's was a tiny ice-cream parlor and advertised its shares on its ice-cream cartons. But I didn't want the headache of shareholders." Bourque decided to issue bonds on her own and got a lawyer to draw up papers. "I put up posters in the store and printed notices on my grocery bags offering bonds for sale. I also added the notice to my regular newspaper ads." For just the $25 par value, people could buy one of my 8% bonds.

"I was flooded with requests. Some people viewed the bonds as an investment, others as a novelty. In the backroom, I typed in names and addresses and printed up bond certificates. When people sent me a cheque, I sent the bonds." Bourque ended up raising over $200,000. "I'm really fired up! I've already rented a location in Ottawa, and I'm close to a deal in Quebec City." Thanks to one banker, Get Real! is a *real* success.

Learning Objectives

LO 1 Compare bond financing versus share financing

LO 2 Explain the types of bonds and their issuing procedures.

LO 3 Prepare entries to record bond issuance and bond interest expense.

LO 4 Compute and record amortization of bond discount.

LO 5 Compute and record amortization of bond premium.

LO 6 Record the retirement of bonds.

LO 7 Explain the types and payment patterns of notes.

LO 8 Prepare entries to account for notes.

LO 9 Explain collateral agreements and their effects on loan risk.

LO 10 Compute the ratio of pledged assets to secured liabilities and explain its use.

CHAPTER PREVIEW

Bonds are issued by companies and governments for financing their activities. In return for money, bonds promise to repay the lender with interest. This chapter explains the basics of bonds and the accounting for their issuance and retirement. The chapter also describes long-term notes including interest-bearing, non-interest-bearing, and installment notes. We explain how present value concepts impact both the accounting and reporting of bonds and notes. An appendix to this chapter discusses important present value concepts in accounting for liabilities. Understanding how bonds and notes are used to the advantage of a company, as shown in the opening article, is an important goal of this chapter.

Basics of Bonds

Corporations often finance operations and borrow money by issuing bonds.[1] A **bond** is a written promise to pay an amount identified as the par value of the bond along with interest at a stated annual rate. The **par value** of the bond, also called the *face amount* or *face value*, is paid at a specified future date known as the *maturity date of the bond.* Most bonds require the borrower to make semiannual interest payments. The amount of interest paid each year is determined by multiplying the par value of the bond by the stated rate of interest determined when the bonds are issued. This section explains the motivation and basics of bonds.

Bond Financing

LO1 Compare bond financing versus share financing.

Companies can finance their business activities in several ways including issuing notes, leasing assets, and selling shares. But projects demanding large amounts of money usually require funding from either bond or shares issuances. Bond financing offers both advantages and disadvantages.

Advantages of Bonds

There are three main advantages of bond financing.

1. *Bonds do not affect shareholder control.* Shares reflect an ownership right in the corporation, whereas a bond does not. A person who owns 1,000 of a corporation's 10,000 outstanding shares controls one-tenth of all shareholders' votes. But a person who owns a $1,000, 11%, 20-year bond has no ownership right. This person, or bondholder, has a receivable from the bond issuer. The right of the bondholder is to receive (1) 11% interest, or $110, each year the bond is outstanding and (2) $1,000 when the bond matures in 20 years.
2. *Interest on bonds is tax deductible.* But dividends to shareholders are not. For instance, a company with $10,000 available to pay interest on bonds, would only have $6,000 available to pay dividends (assuming a 40% tax rate).

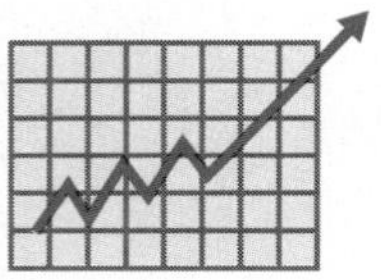

3. *Bonds can increase return on equity.* When a company earns a higher return with the borrowed funds than it is paying in interest, it increases its return on equity. This process is called *financial leverage* or *trading on the equity.*

To illustrate, let's look at **Magnum Skates.** Magnum has $1 million in equity, and is planning a $500,000 expansion to meet increasing sales. Magnum predicts the $500,000 expansion will yield $125,000 in additional income before paying any interest. Magnum currently earns $100,000 per year and has no interest expense.

---

[1] Bonds are also issued by nonprofit corporations, as well as the federal government and other governmental units, such as cities and provinces. Although the examples in this chapter deal with business situations, all issuers use the same practices to account for their bonds.

Magnum is considering three plans. Plan A is to not expand. Plan B is to expand, and raise $500,000 from issuing shares. Plan C is to sell $500,000 worth of bonds paying 10% annual interest, or $50,000. Exhibit 17.1 shows us how these three plans affect Magnum's net income, equity, and return on equity.

Exhibit 17.1

Financing with Bonds or Shares

	Plan A Don't Expand	Plan B Increase Equity	Plan C Issue Bonds
Income before interest	$ 100,000	$ 225,000	$ 225,000
Interest	—	—	(50,000)
Net income	**$ 100,000**	**$ 225,000**	**$ 175,000**
Equity	$1,000,000	$1,500,000	$1,000,000
Return on equity	**10.0%**	**15.0%**	**17.5%**

Analysis of these plans shows the owners will earn a higher return on equity if expansion occurs. The preferred plan of expansion is by issuing bonds. Even though projected net income under Plan C ($175,000) is smaller than under Plan B ($225,000), the return on equity is larger because of less equity investment. This is an important result and yields a general rule: *return on equity increases when the expected rate of return from the new assets is greater than the rate of interest on the bonds.* Also, issuing bonds allows the current owners to remain in control.

Disadvantages of Bonds

There are two main disadvantages of bond financing.

1. *Bonds require payment of both periodic interest and par value at maturity.* Bond payments can be especially burdensome when a company's income is low and when it is struggling to survive. Shares, on the other hand, do not require payment of dividends. Cash dividends on shares are paid at the discretion of the issuer.
2. *Bonds can decrease return on equity.* When a company earns a lower return with the borrowed funds than it is paying in interest, it decreases its return on equity. This is the downside risk of financial leverage. It is more likely to arise when a company has periods of low income.

A company must weigh the risks of these disadvantages against the advantages on bond financing when deciding on whether to issue bonds to finance operations.

Types of Bonds

LO 2 Explain the types of bonds and their issuing procedures.

There exist many different kinds of bonds with various characteristics. We describe the more common kinds of bonds in this section.

Secured and Unsecured Bonds

Secured bonds have specific assets of the issuing company pledged (or *mortgaged*) as collateral. This arrangement gives bondholders added protection against default by the issuer. If the issuing company fails to pay interest or par value, the secured bondholders can demand the collateral be sold and the proceeds used to pay the bond obligation.

Unsecured bonds, also called *debentures*, are backed by the issuer's general credit standing. Unsecured bonds are almost always more risky than secured bonds. Because of this added risk, a company generally must be financially strong to successfully issue debentures at a favourable rate of interest. It is common to see debentures on the balance sheets of companies such as **Air Canada, Bell Canada Enterprises, Bombardier, Canadian Tire,** and **Magna International.**

Companies can issue debentures whose claims on a company's assets are second to those of other unsecured liabilities. These debentures are called *subordinated debentures*, meaning these creditors' claims are subordinated to the claims of some others. **Magna** has issued subordinated debentures. In a liquidation, Magna's subordinated debentures would not be repaid until the claims of the more senior, unsecured liabilities are first settled.

Term and Serial Bonds

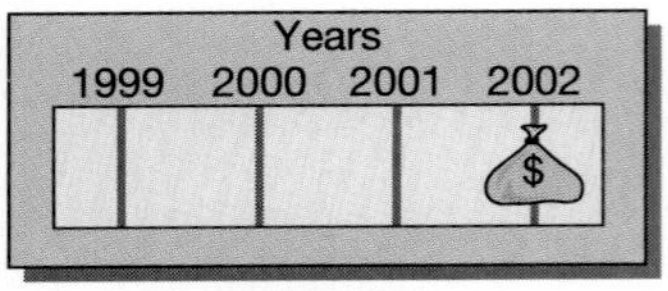

Term Bond

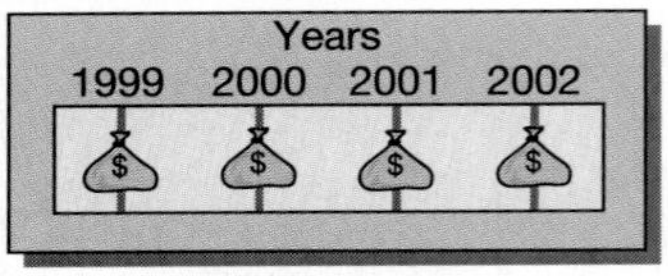

Serial Bond

Term bonds are scheduled for payment (maturity) at a single specified date. **Serial bonds** mature at several different dates (in series). This means serial bonds are repaid over a number of periods. For instance, $1 million of serial bonds might mature at the rate of $100,000 each year from 6 to 15 years after the bonds are issued. This involves 10 groups (or series) of bonds of $100,000 each where one series matures after six years, another after seven years, and another each successive year until the final series is repaid.

Many term bonds are also **sinking fund bonds.** To reduce the holder's risk, these bonds require the issuer to create a *sinking fund*, which is a group of assets used to retire the bonds at maturity. The issuer must start to set aside the assets to pay off these bonds before they mature.

Registered Bonds and Bearer Bonds

Registered Bond

Bearer Bond

Bonds issued in the names and addresses of their owners are **registered bonds.** The issuing company makes bond payments by sending cheques to these registered owners. When one investor sells a bond to another investor, the issuer must be notified of the change. Registered bonds offer the issuer the practical advantage of not having to actually issue bond certificates to investors. This arrangement protects investors against loss or theft of bonds.

Bonds payable to whoever holds them (the *bearer*) are called **bearer bonds,** or *unregistered bonds.* Since there may be no record of sales or exchanges, the holder of a bearer bond is presumed to be its rightful owner. As a result, lost or stolen bearer bonds are difficult to replace.

Many bearer bonds are also **coupon bonds.** This term reflects interest coupons that are attached to these bonds. Each coupon matures on a specific interest payment date. The owner detaches each coupon when it matures and presents it to a bank or broker for collection. At maturity, the owner follows the same process and presents the bond certificate for collection. Because there is no readily available record of who actually receives the interest, the income tax law discourages companies from issuing new coupon bonds.

Convertible and Callable Bonds

Convertible bonds can be exchanged by bondholders for a fixed number of shares of the issuing company's common shares. **Magna Corporation** for example had among its 1997 liabilities 7.25% convertible debentures with a par value of $150 million that had been issued for a net proceeds of $145.3 million net of issue costs. These debentures could be converted at any time at the option of holders into Class A Subordinate Voting Shares at a conversion price of $60.25 per share and mature on July 5, 2005. Convertible bonds offer bondholders the potential to participate in future increases in the share's market value. But if the shares do not appreciate, bondholders continue to receive periodic interest and will receive the par value when the bond matures. In most cases, the bondholders decide whether and when to convert the bonds to shares. **Callable bonds** have an option exerciseable by the issuer to retire them at a stated dollar amount prior to maturity. Callable bonds are often referred to as **redeemable bonds.**

Bond Trading

Bonds are securities and can be readily bought and sold. A large number of corporate bonds trade on major stock exchanges. A bond issue consists of a large number of bonds, usually in denominations of $1,000 or $5,000, and are sold to many different lenders. A *baby bond* is a bond with less than a $1,000 par value such as $100. Companies such as **Air Canada** and **St. Laurent Paperboard Inc.** have issued bonds in $100 denominations but such issues are rare. After bonds are issued, they often are bought and sold by investors, meaning any particular bond is probably owned by a number of people before it matures.

Because bonds are exchanged in the market, they have a market value (price). For convenience, bond market values are expressed as a percent of their par (face) value. For example, a company's bonds might be trading at $103\frac{1}{2}$, which means they can be bought or sold for 103.5% of their par value. Bonds can also trade below par value. For instance, if a company's bonds are trading at 95, they can be bought or sold at 95% of their par value.

Did You Know?

Bond Quotes

The bond quote below is interpreted as (left to right): **Bonds,** company name; **Rate,** contract interest rate ($9\frac{1}{2}$%) for this bond; **Maturity**, year (2000) in which bond's principal is paid; **Cur Yld**, yield rate (9.2%) of bond at current price; **Vol**, dollars worth ($145,000) of bonds traded in 1000s; **Close**, closing price ($1,035) for the day as % of par value; **Net Chg,** change ($1.25) in closing price as a fraction of par from the prior day.

Bonds	Rate	Maturity	Cur.Yld	Vol	Close	Net Chg
Co. Name	$9\frac{1}{2}$%	2000	9.2%	$145,000	103.5	$1.25

Bond Issuing Procedures

Bond issuances are governed by provincial and federal laws. Issuing company bonds usually requires approval by both the board of directors and shareholders. Authorization of bond issuances include the number of bonds authorized, their par value, and the contract interest rate.

The legal document identifying the rights and obligations of both the bondholders and the issuer is called the **bond indenture.** The bond indenture acts as the legal contract between the issuer and the bondholders. A bondholder may also receive a bond certificate as evidence of the company's debt. A **bond certificate,** such as shown in Exhibit 17.2, includes specifics such as the issuer's name, the bond's par value, the contract interest rate, and the maturity date. Many companies reduce costs by not issuing certificates to registered bondholders.

Exhibit 17.2

Bond Certificate

The issuing company normally sells the bonds to an investment firm called an *underwriter*. The underwriter then resells them to the public. An issuing company can also sell bonds directly to investors. When an underwriter sells bonds to a large number of investors, the bondholders' interests are represented and protected by a *trustee*. The trustee monitors the issuer to ensure it complies with the obligations in the bond indenture. Most trustees are large banks or trust companies.

Terms of a bond indenture are drawn up and accepted by the trustee before bonds are issued. When bonds are offered to the public, called *floating an issue*, they must be registered with a securities commission. Registration requires the issuer to file extensive financial information in special reports.

Bond Issuances

This section explains accounting for bond issuances at par, below par (discount), and above par (premium). We also describe the amortization of a discount or premium, and how to record bonds issued between interest payment dates.

Issuing Bonds at Par

LO 3 Prepare entries to record bond issuance and bond interest expense.

To illustrate an issuance of bonds at par value, let's suppose Barnes Company receives authorization to issue $800,000 of 9%, 20-year bonds. The bonds are dated January 1, 2000, and are due on December 31, 2019. They pay interest semiannually on each June 30 and December 31. After the bond indenture is accepted by the trustee on behalf of the bondholders, all or a portion of the bonds can be sold to an underwriter. If all bonds are sold at their par value, Barnes Company makes this entry to record the sale:

Assets = Liabilities + Equity
+800,000 +800,000

2000			
Jan. 1	Cash	800,000	
	Bonds Payable		800,000
	Sold bonds at par.		

This entry reflects increases in the company's cash and long-term liabilities.

Six months later, the first semiannual interest payment is made, and Barnes records its payment with this entry:

Assets = Liabilities + Equity
−36,000 −36,000

2000			
June 30	Bond Interest Expense	36,000	
	Cash		36,000
	Paid semiannual interest on bonds.		
	(9% × $800,000 × 1/2)		

This entry is made every six months as Barnes pays its semiannual interest obligations until the bonds mature.

When the bonds mature 20 years later, Barnes Company records its payment of the maturity value with this entry:

Assets = Liabilities + Equity
−800,000 −800,000

2019			
Dec. 31	Bonds Payable	800,000	
	Cash		800,000
	Paid bonds at maturity.		

Did You Know?

Ratings Game

Many bond buyers look to rating services such as the Dominion Bond Rating Service for assessing the risk of bonds.. These services focus on the financial strength of the issuer rather than the market attractiveness of the bond. Financial statements are a crucial part of the information these services rely on in setting ratings. Dominion's ratings, from best quality to default, are: AAA (near perfection), AA (well above average), A (up to high average, upper-medium grade), BBB (up to low average, medium grade), BB (mildly speculative), B (middle speculative),CCC (highly speculative), CC (in default), C (second tier of debt of a company in default).

Determining Bond Discount or Premium

The interest rate paid by the issuer of bonds is specified in the indenture and on the bond certificates. Because it is stated in the indenture, this rate is called the **contract rate** of the bonds. The contract rate is also called the *coupon rate*, the *stated rate*, or the *nominal rate*. The amount of interest paid each year is determined by multiplying the par value of the bonds by the contract rate.

The contract rate is usually stated on an annual basis, even if the interest is paid semiannually. For example, let's suppose a company issues a $1,000, 8% bond paying interest semiannually. The annual interest of $80 (8% × $1,000) is paid in two semiannual payments of $40 each.

The contract rate sets the amount of interest the issuer pays in *cash*. But the contract rate is not necessarily the rate of *bond interest expense* actually incurred by the issuer. Bond interest expense depends on the market value of the issuer's bonds, which is determined by market expectations on the risk of lending to this issuer. This expected risk, along with the supply of and demand for bonds, is reflected in the market rate of interest for the bond. The **market rate** is the rate that borrowers are willing to pay and that lenders are willing to earn for a particular bond and its risk level. A market rate changes in response to changes in both a bond's risk level and the supply of and demand for bonds.

Because factors that determine market rate vary across companies, different companies face different market rates for their bonds. The market rate for a specific set of bonds depends on the level of risk investors assign to them. As the level of risk increases, the rate increases. The increased market rate compensates purchasers for the increased risk of bonds. Market rates also are affected by the length of the bonds' life. Long-term bonds generally have higher rates because they are more risky. This is because of the many things that can happen to a company over a long period of time.

Many bond issuers try to set a contract rate of interest equal to the market rate they expect as of the bonds' issuance date. When the contract rate and market rate are equal, the bonds sell at their par value. But when the contract does not equal the market rate, the bonds do not sell at their par value. Instead, they are sold at a *premium* above their par value or at a *discount* below their par value. Exhibit 17.3 shows the relation between the contract rate, market rate, and a bond's issue price.

Exhibit 17.3

Relation between Bond Issue Price, Contract Rate, and Market Rate

Contract rate is:		Bond sells:
Above market rate	⇒	At a premium
Equal to market rate	⇒	At par value
Below market rate	⇒	At a discount

Some companies issue *zero-coupon bonds* that do not pay any periodic interest. This means the contract rate for zero-coupon bonds is zero. Because this 0% contract rate is always below the market rate, these bonds are always issued at a discount, meaning their prices are always less than their par values.

Flash back

1. Unsecured bonds backed only by the issuer's general credit standing are called (a) serial bonds, (b) debentures, (c) registered bonds, (d) convertible bonds, or (e) bearer bonds.
2. How do you compute the amount of interest a bond issuer pays each year?
3. When the contract rate is above the market rate, do bonds sell at a premium or a discount? Do purchasers pay more or less than the par value of the bonds?

Answers—p. 809

Issuing Bonds at a Discount

LO 4 Compute and record amortization of bond discount.

We described how a **discount on bonds payable** occurs when a company issues bonds with a contract rate less than the market rate. This means the issue price is less than the bonds' par value.

To illustrate, **Fila** announces an offer to issue bonds with a $100,000 par value, an 8% annual contract rate, and a five-year life. The market rate for Fila's bonds is 10% meaning the bonds will sell at a discount since the contract rate is less than the market rate.[2] The issue price for these bonds is 97.277 (97.277% of par value).

These bonds obligate the issuer to pay out two different future cash flows:

1. $100,000 at the end of the bonds' five-year life.
2. $4,000 (4% × $100,000) at the end of each six-month interest period of the bonds' five-year life.

The pattern of cash flows for Fila's bonds is shown in Exhibit 17.4.

Exhibit 17.4

Cash Flows of Fila's Bonds

								$100,000
	$4,000	$4,000	$4,000	$4,000	. . .	$4,000	$4,000	$4,000
0	6 mo.	12 mo.	18 mo.	24 mo.		48 mo.	54 mo.	60 mo.

If Fila accepts $92,277 cash for its bonds on the issue date of December 31, 2000, it records the sale with this entry:

Assets	=	Liabilities	+	Equity
+92,277		+100,000		
		− 7,723		

2000			
Dec. 31	Cash	92,277	
	Discount on Bonds Payable	7,723	
	Bonds Payable		100,000
	Sold bonds at a discount on the original issue date.		

These bonds are reported in the long-term liability section of the issuer's balance sheet as shown in Exhibit 17.5.

Exhibit 17.5

Balance Sheet Presentation of Bond Discount

Long-term liabilities:		
Bonds payable, 8%, due December 31, 2005	$100,000	
Less discount on bonds payable	7,723	$92,277

The discount is deducted from the par value of the bonds to produce the **carrying (or book) value** of the bonds payable. The Discount on Bonds Payable is a contra liability account.

You Make the Call

Bond Rater

You are a bond rater. It is your job to assign a rating to a bond issue that reflects its riskiness to bondholders. Identify factors you look at in assigning risk to bonds. For the factors you identify, indicate their likely levels for a bond issue sold at a discount.

Answer—p. 809

[2] The difference between the contract rate and the market rate of interest on a new bond issue is usually a fraction of a percent. But we use a difference of 2% here to emphasize the effects.

Amortizing a Bond Discount

The issuer (Fila) received $92,277 for its bonds and will pay bondholders $100,000 after five years have passed (plus interest payments). Because the $7,723 discount is eventually paid to bondholders at maturity, it is part of the cost of using the $92,277 for five years. The upper portion of Exhibit 17.6 shows that total interest cost of $47,723 is the difference between the total amount repaid to bondholders ($140,000) and the amount borrowed from bondholders ($92,277).

Exhibit 17.6

Total Bond Interest Expense for Bonds Issued at a Discount

Amount repaid:	
Ten interest payments of $4,000	$ 40,000
Par value at maturity	100,000
Total repaid to bondholders	$140,000
Less amount borrowed from bondholders	(92,277)
Total bond interest expense	**$ 47,723**
Alternative Computation	
Ten payments of $4,000	$ 40,000
Plus discount	7,723
Total bond interest expense	**$ 47,723**

Alternatively, we can compute total bond interest expense as the sum of the interest payments and the bond discount. This alternative computation is shown in the lower portion of Exhibit 17.6.

Accounting for Fila's bonds must include two procedures. First, total bond interest expense of $47,723 must be allocated across the 10 six-month periods in the bonds' life. Second, the carrying value of the bonds must be updated at each balance sheet date. Two alternative methods accomplish these objectives. They are the straight-line and the effective interest methods of allocating interest. Both methods reduce the discount on the bonds over the life of the bonds, and is often called *amortizing the bond discount.*

Junk Bond
Junk bonds are company bonds with low credit ratings. Issuers of junk bonds are more likely than average to default on repayment. On the other hand, the high risk of junk bonds can yield high returns to its bondholders if the issuer survives and repays its debt. Junk bond issuances are running at over $100 billion a year. Also, the percent of junk bond issuances in default has fallen from 33% in 1984-90 to only 9% in 1991-97. [Source: *Business Week*, March 2, 1998.]

Did You Know?

Straight-Line Method

The **straight-line method** of allocating interest is the simpler of the two methods. It allocates an equal portion of the total bond interest expense to each of the six-month interest periods.

To apply the straight-line method to Fila's bonds, we divide the five years' total expense of $47,723 by 10 (the number of semiannual periods in the bonds' life). This gives us a total bond interest expense of $4,772 per period.[3] Alternatively, we can find this number by dividing the $7,723 original discount

[3] For simplicity, all computations are rounded to the nearest whole dollar. Do the same when solving the exercises and problems at the end of the chapter.

by 10. The resulting $772 is the amount of discount to be amortized in each interest period. When the $772 of amortized discount is added to the $4,000 cash payment, the total bond interest expense for each six-month period is $4,772.

The issuer records bond interest expense and updates the balance of the bond liability for each semiannual cash payment with this entry:

Assets = Liabilities + Equity
−4,000 +772 −4,772

2001			
June 30	Bond interest expense	4,772	
	Discount on Bonds Payable		772
	Cash		4,000
	To record six months' interest and discount amortization.		

This is the entry made at the end of each of the 10 semiannual interest periods. The $772 credit to the Discount on Bonds Payable account *increases* the bonds' carrying value. This increase occurs because we *decrease* the balance of the Discount on Bonds Payable (contra) account which is subtracted from the Bonds Payable account. Exhibit 17.7 shows this pattern of decreases in the Discount on Bonds Payable account, along with increases in the bonds' carrying value.

We can summarize the following points in applying straight-line amortization to the discount on Fila's bonds over its life of 10 semiannual periods:

Exhibit 17.7

Bond Discount and Carrying Value under Straight-Line

Date	Discount Balance	Carrying Value
Dec. 31/2000	$7,723	$ 92,277
Jun. 30/2001	6,951	93,049
Dec. 31/2001	6,179	93,821
Jun. 30/2002	5,407	94,593
Dec. 31/2002	4,635	95,365
Jun. 30/2003	3,863	96,137
Dec. 31/2003	3,091	96,909
Jun. 30/2004	2,319	97,681
Dec. 31/2004	1,547	98,453
Jun. 30/2005	775*	99,225
Dec 31/2005	**-0-**	**100,000**

* Adjusted for rounding.

1. The $92,277 cash received from selling bonds equals the $100,000 par value of the bonds less the initial $7,723 discount from selling the bonds for less than par.
2. Semiannual bond interest expense of $4,772 equals total bond interest expense of $47,723 divided by 10 semiannual periods (alternatively computed as the cash paid of $4,000 plus the periodic discount amortization of $772).
3. Semiannual credit to the Discount on Bonds Payable account equals the total discount of $7,723 divided by 10 semiannual periods.
4. Semiannual $4,000 interest payment equals the bonds' $100,000 par value multiplied by the 4% semiannual contract rate.
5. Carrying (or book) value of bonds continues to grow each period by the $772 discount amortization until it equals the par value of the bonds when they mature.

Fila incurs a $4,772 bond interest expense each period but pays only $4,000. The $772 unpaid portion of expense is added to the balance of the liability by decreasing the discount contra account balance.

Effective Interest Method

The straight-line method yields changes in the bonds' carrying value (see Exhibit 17.7) while the amount for bond interest expense does not change (always equal to $4,772 for Fila bonds). This gives the impression of a changing interest rate when users divide a constant bond interest expense over a changing carrying value. As a result, the straight-line method should only be used when its results do not differ materially from those obtained by using the effective interest method.

The **effective interest method,** or simply *interest method*, allocates bond interest expense over the life of the bonds in a way that yields a constant rate of interest. This constant rate of interest is the market rate at the issue date. The effect of selling bonds at a premium or discount is the issuer incurs the prevailing market rate of interest at issuance and not the contract rate. Bond interest expense for a period is found by multiplying the balance of the liability at the beginning of that period by the bonds' original market rate. An *amortization table* can be constructed to help us keep track of interest allocation and the balances of bond-related accounts.

Exhibit 17.8 shows an amortization table for the Fila bonds. The key difference between the effective interest and straight-line methods lies in computation of bond interest expense. Instead of assigning an equal amount of interest to each interest period, the effective interest method assigns an increasing amount of interest over the Fila bonds' life because the balance of the liability increases over these five years. But both methods allocate the *same* $47,723 of total expense across the five years, but with different patterns.

Exhibit 17.8

Effective Interest Amortization of Bond Discount

Semiannual Interest Period	(A) Cash Interest Paid $100,000 × 4%	(B) Interest Expense E × 5%	(C) Discount Amortization (B-C)	(D) Unamortized Discount (D-C)	(E) Carrying Value 100,000-D
Dec. 31/2000				$7,723	$ 92,277
Jun. 30/2001	$ 4,000	$ 4,614	$ 614	$7,109	92,891
Dec. 31/2001	4,000	4,645	645	6,464	93,536
Jun. 30/2002	4,000	4,677	677	5,787	94,213
Dec. 31/2002	4,000	4,711	711	5,076	94,924
Jun. 30/2003	4,000	4,746	746	4,330	95,670
Dec. 31/2003	4,000	4,784	784	3,546	96,454
Jun. 30/2004	4,000	4,823	823	2,723	97,277
Dec. 31/2004	4,000	4,864	864	1,859	98,141
Jun. 30/2005	4,000	4,907	907	952	99,048
Dec. 31/2005	4,000	4,952	952	-0-	100,000
	$40,000	$47,723	$7,723		

Column A is the bonds' par value ($100,000) multiplied by the semiannual contract rate (4%).
Column B is the bonds' prior period carrying value multiplied by the semiannual market rate (5%).
Column C is the difference between interest paid and bond interest expense, or [(B)-(A)].
Column D is the prior period's unamortized discount less the current period's discount amortization.
Column E is the bonds' par value less unamortized discount, or [$100,000-(D)].

The amortization table shows how the balance of the discount (column D) is amortized by the effective interest method until it reaches zero. The bonds' carrying value changes each period until it equals par value at maturity. Total bond interest expense is $47,723, comprised of $40,000 of semiannual cash payments and $7,723 of the original discount below par value.

Except for differences in amounts, journal entries recording the expense and updating the liability balance are the same under the effective interest method and the straight-line method. For instance, the entry to record the interest payment at the end of the first interest period is:

2001			
June 30	Bond Interest Expense	4,614	
	Discount on Bonds Payable		614
	Cash		4,000
	To record six months' interest and discount amortization.		

Assets = Liabilities + Equity
−4000 +614 −4,614

We use the numbers in Exhibit 17.8 to make similar entries throughout the five-year life of the bonds.

Flash back

Five-year, 6% bonds with a $100,000 par value are issued at a price of $91,893. Interest is paid semiannually, and the market rate is 8% on the issue date. Use this information to answer the following questions:

4. Are these bonds issued at a discount or premium? Explain why.

5. What is the issuer's journal entry to record the sale?

6. What is the amount of bond interest expense recorded at the first semiannual cash payment using the (a) straight-line method and (b) effective interest method?

Answers—p. 809

Issuing Bonds at a Premium

LO 5 Compute and record amortization of bond premium.

When bonds carry a contract rate greater than the market rate, the bonds sell at a price greater than par value. The difference between par and market value is the **premium on bonds.** Buyers bid up the price of bonds above the bonds' par value until it reaches a level yielding the market rate.

To illustrate, assume that **Hydro Quebec** issues bonds with a $100,000 par value, a 12% annual contract rate, and a five-year life. The market rate for Hydro Quebec bonds is 10% on the issue date meaning the bonds will sell at a premium because the contract rate is greater than the market rate. This means buyers of these bonds will bid up the market price until the yield equals the market rate. The issue price for these bonds is 107.72 (107.72% of par value).

The Hydro Quebec's bonds obligate Hydro Quebec to pay out two different future cash flows:

1. $100,000 at the end of the bonds' five-year life.
2. $6,000 (6% × $100,000) at the end of each six-month interest period of the bonds' five-year life.

The pattern of cash flows for Hydro Quebec bonds is shown in Exhibit 17.9.

Exhibit 17.9

Cash Flows of Hydro Quebec Bonds

								$100,000
	$6,000	$6,000	$6,000	$6,000	. . .	$6,000	$6,000	$6,000
0	6 mo.	12 mo.	18 mo.	24 mo.		48 mo.	54 mo.	60 mo.

If Hydro Quebec accepts $107,720 cash for its bonds on the issue date of December 31, 2000, it records this sale with the entry:

2000			
Dec. 31	Cash	107,720	
	Premium on Bonds Payable		7,720
	Bonds Payable		100,000
	Sold bonds at a premium on the original issue date.		

Assets = Liabilities + Equity
+107,720 +100,000
+7,720

These bonds are reported in the long-term liability section of the issuer's balance sheet as shown in Exhibit 17.10.

Exhibit 17.10

Balance Sheet Presentation of Bond Premium

Long-term liabilities:		
Bonds payable, 12%, due December 31, 2005	$100,000	
Plus premium on bonds payable	7,720	$107,720

The premium is added to the par value of the bonds to produce the carrying value of the bonds payable. The Premium on Bonds Payable is an adjunct (also called accretion) liability account.

Amortizing a Bond Premium

The issuer (Hydro Quebec) receives $107,720 for its bonds and will pay bondholders $100,000 after five years have passed (plus interest payments). Because the $7,720 premium is not repaid to bondholders at maturity, it reduces the expense of using the $107,720 for five years. The upper portion of Exhibit 17.11 shows that total bond interest expense of $52,280 is the difference between the total amount repaid to bondholders ($160,000) and the amount borrowed from bondholders ($107,720).

Exhibit 17.11

Total Bond Interest Expense for Bonds Issued at a Premium

Amount repaid:	
Ten interest payments of $6,000	$ 60,000
Par value at Maturity	100,000
Total repaid to bondholders	$160,000
Less amount borrowed from bondholders	(107,720)
Total bond interest expense	$ 52,280
Alternative Computation	
Ten payments of $6,000	$ 60,000
Less premium	(7,720)
Total bond interest expense	$ 52,280

Alternatively, we can compute total bond interest expense as the sum of the interest payments less the bond premium. The premium is subtracted because it will not be paid to the bondholders when the bonds mature. This alternative computation is shown in the lower portion of Exhibit 17.11. Total bond interest expense is allocated over the 10 semiannual periods with either the straight-line or the effective interest method.

Straight-Line Method

We explained how the straight-line method allocates an equal portion of total bond interest expense to each of the bonds' interest periods. To apply the straight-line method to Hydro Quebec bonds, we divide the five years' total bond interest expense of $52,280 by 10 (the number of semiannual periods in the bonds' life). This gives us a total bond interest expense of $5,228 per period.

The issuer records bond interest expense and updates the balance of the bond liability for each semiannual cash payment with this entry:

2001			
June 30	Bond interest expense	5,228	
	Premium on Bonds Payable	772	
	Cash		6,000
	To record six months' interest and premium amortization.		

Assets	=	Liabilities	+	Equity
−6,000		−772		−5,228

This is the entry made at the end of each of the 10 semiannual interest periods. The $772 debit to the Premium on Bonds Payable account *decreases* the bonds' carrying value.

Effective Interest Method

Exhibit 17.12 shows an amortization table using the effective interest method for the Hydro Quebec' bonds.

Exhibit 17.12

Effective Interest Amortization of Bond Premium

Semiannual Interest Period	(A) Cash Interest Paid $100,000 × 6%	(B) Interest Expense E × 5%	(C) Premium Amortization (A − B)	(D) Unamortizated Premium (D − C)	(E) Carrying Value 100,000 + D
Dec. 31/2000				$7,720	$107,720
Jun. 30/2001	$ 6,000	$ 5,386	$ 614	7,106	107,106
Dec. 31/2001	6,000	5,355	645	6,461	106,461
Jun. 30/2002	6,000	5,323	677	5,784	105,784
Dec. 31/2002	6,000	5,289	711	5,073	105,073
Jun. 30/2003	6,000	5,254	746	4,327	104,327
Dec. 31/2003	6,000	5,216	784	3,543	103,543
Jun. 30/2004	6,000	5,177	823	2,720	102,720
Dec. 31/2004	6,000	5,136	864	1,856	101,856
Jun. 30/2005	6,000	5,093	907	949	100,949
Dec. 31/2005	6,000	5,051*	949	-0-	100,000
	$60,000	$52,280	$7,720		

Column A is the bonds' par value ($100,000) multiplied by the semiannual contract rate (6%).
Column B is the bonds' prior period carrying value multiplied by the semiannual market rate (5%).
Column C is the difference between interest paid and bond interest expense, or [(A)-(B)].
Column D is the prior period's unamortized premium less the current period's premium amortization.
Column E is the bonds' par value plus unamortized premium, or [$100,000+(D)].

Column B shows the amount of expense computed as the 5% market rate multiplied by the beginning carrying value. The amount of cash paid out in column A is larger than bond interest expense because the cash payment is based on the higher 6% contract rate. The excess cash payment over the expense reduces the principal. These amounts are shown in column C. Column E shows the new carrying value after the amortized premium in column C is deducted from the prior period's carrying value. Column D shows how the premium is reduced by the amortization process over the life of the bonds.

The effect of premium amortization on the bond interest expense and the bond liability is seen in the journal entry on June 30, 2001, when the issuer makes the first semiannual interest payment:

Assets	=	Liabilities	+	Equity
−6,000		−614		−5,386

2001			
June 30	Bond interest expense	5,386	
	Premium on Bonds Payable	614	
	Cash		6,000
	To record six months' interest and premium amortization.		

Similar entries are recorded at each payment date until the bonds mature at the end of 2005. The effective interest method yields decreasing amounts of bond interest expense and increasing amounts of premium amortization over the bonds' life.

Did You Know?

Amortization Magic

Amortization tables are made easy by spreadsheet software such as Excel and Lotus. We need only enter the bonds' par value, selling price, contract rate, market rate, and life to get a complete amortization table. All accounting entries and adjustments can be taken directly from this output.

Mid-Chapter Demonstration Problem

Randall Computer Company issued 10-year, 10% bonds with a par value of $100,000 to Chance Company for $95,083 on March 1, 1999. The bonds are dated January 1, 1999.

Required

Prepare journal entries for Randall Computer Company for 1999 of January 1, July 1, and December 31. Assume that any discount or premium is amortized only at year-end.

Solution to Mid-Chapter Demonstration Problem

1999			
Jan. 1	Cash	95,083	
	Discount on Bonds Payable	4,917	
	Bonds Payable		100,000
	Sold bonds at a discount.		
July 1	Interest Expense	5,000	
	Cash		5,000
	To record payment of six months' interest.		
Dec. 31	Interest Expense	5,000	
	Interest Payable		5,000
	To record payment of six months' interest.		
Dec. 31	Interest Expense	1,410	
	Discount on Bonds Payable		1,410
	To record amortization of the discount ($100,000 × .10 × 12/12 minus $95,083 × .12 × 12/12).		

Issuing Bonds between Interest Dates

Many bonds are sold on an interest payment date. But a company can sell its bonds at a date other than an interest payment date. When this occurs, the purchasers normally pay the issuer the purchase price plus any interest accrued since the prior interest payment date. This accrued interest is then repaid to purchasers on the next interest date.

To illustrate, let's suppose **Canadian Tire** sells $100,000 of its 9% bonds at par on March 1, 1999, which is two months after the original issue date. The interest on Canadian Tire's bonds is payable semiannually on each June 30 and December 31. Because two months have passed, the issuer collects two months' interest from the buyer at the time of the sale. This amount is $1,500 ($100,000 × 9% × 2/12). This case is reflected in Exhibit 17.13.

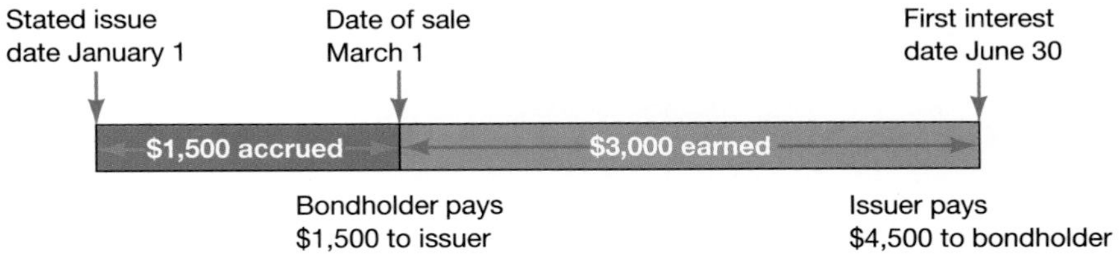

Exhibit 17.13

Accruing Interest between Interest Dates

Canadian Tire's entry to record the sale of its bonds is:

Mar. 1	Cash	101,500	
	Interest Payable		1,500
	Bonds Payable		100,000
	Sold $100,000 of bonds with two months' accrued interest.		

Assets = Liabilities + Equity
+101,500 +100,000
+1,500

The liabilities for interest payable and the bonds are recorded in separate accounts.

When the June 30 semiannual interest date arrives, Canadian Tire pays a full six months' interest of $4,500 ($100,000 × 9% × 1/2) to the bondholder. This payment includes the four months' interest of $3,000 earned by the bondholder from March 1 to June 30 *plus* the repayment of two months' accrued interest collected by Canadian Tire when the bonds were sold. Canadian Tire's entry to record this first interest payment is:

June 30	Interest Payable	1,500	
	Bond interest expense	3,000	
	Cash		4,500
	Paid semiannual interest on the bonds.		

Assets = Liabilities + Equity
−4,500 − 1,500 −3,000

The practice of collecting and then repaying accrued interest with the first interest payment is done to simplify the bond issuer's administrative efforts. To understand this, suppose a company sells bonds on 15 or 20 different dates between the original issue date and the first interest payment date. If the issuer did not collect accrued interest from buyers, it would need to pay different amounts of cash to each of them according to the time passed since they purchased the bonds. This means the issuer would need to keep detailed records of purchasers and the dates they bought their bonds. Issuers avoid this extra recordkeeping by having each buyer pay accrued interest at the time of purchase. Issuers then pay a full six months' interest to all purchasers, regardless of when they bought the bonds.

Accruing Bond Interest Expense

If a bond's interest period does not coincide with the issuing company's accounting period, an adjusting entry is necessary to recognize bond interest expense accruing since the most recent interest payment.

To illustrate, let's assume the Hydro Quebec bonds described in Exhibit 17.12 are issued on September 1, 2000, instead of December 31, 2000. As a result, four months' interest (and premium amortization) accrue before the end of the 2000 calendar year. Because the reporting period of Hydro Quebec ends on that date, an adjusting entry is needed to capture this information about the bonds.

Interest for the four months ended December 31, 2000, equals $3,591, which is 4/6 of the first six months' interest of $5,386. The premium amortization is $409, which is 4/6 of the first six months' amortization of $614. The sum of the bond interest expense and the amortization is $4,000 ($3,591 + $409), which equals 4/6 of the $6,000 cash payment due on March 1, 2001. We record these effects with this adjusting entry:

2000			
Dec. 31	Bond interest expense	3,591	
	Premium on Bonds Payable	409	
	Interest Payable		4,000
	To record four months' accrued interest and premium amortization.		

Assets = Liabilities + Equity
−409 −3,591
+4,000

Similar entries are made on each December 31 throughout the five-year life of the bonds.

When the $6,000 cash payment occurs on the next interest date, the journal entry recognizes the bond interest expense and amortization for January and February of 2001. It must also eliminate the interest payable liability created by the December 31 adjusting entry. In this case we make the following entry to record payment on March 1, 2001:

2001			
Mar. 1	Interest Payable	4,000	
	Bond Interest Expense ($5,386 × 2/6)	1,795	
	Premium on Bonds Payable ($614 × 2/6) ..	205	
	Cash		6,000
	To record two months' interest and amortization and eliminate the accrued interest liability.		

Assets	=	Liabilities	+	Equity
−6,000		−4,000		−1,795
		−205		

The interest payments made each September are recorded as normal because the entire six-month interest period is included within a single fiscal year.

Bond Pricing

Prices for bonds that are traded on an organized exchange are published in newspapers and available through online services. This information includes the bond price (called *quote*), its contract rate, and its market (called *yield*) rate. But only a fraction of bonds outstanding are actually traded on an organized exchange. Many others are rarely traded. To compute the price of a bond, we need to apply present value concepts. This can be done using special bond pricing tables or through computing the present value of a bond's cash flows. This section explains how we use *present value concepts* to price the Fila discount bond and the Hydro Quebec premium bond.

Present Value of a Discount Bond

The issue price of bonds is found by computing the present value of the bond's cash payments, discounted at the market rate of interest. When computing the present value of the Fila bond, we work with *semiannual* compounding periods because this is the time between interest payments. This means the annual market rate of 10% is changed to a semiannual rate of 5%. Also, the five-year life of the bonds is changed to 10 semiannual periods.

Our computation is twofold: (1) find the present value of the $100,000 maturity payment and (2) find the present value of the series of 10 payments of $4,000 each; see Exhibit 17.1. These present values can be found by using present value tables.[4] Appendix II lists some present value tables and explains how to use them. Table II.1 in Appendix II is used to compute the single $100,000 maturity payment, and Table II.3 in Appendix II is used to compute the $4,000 series of interest payments.

We first go to Table II.1 on row 10 and go across to the 5% column. The table value is 0.6139. Second, we go to Table II.3 on row 10 and go across to the 5% column, where the table value is 7.7217. The bond price is computed by multiplying the cash flow amounts by their corresponding table values and adding them together. Exhibit 17.14 shows this result.

Exhibit 17.14

Computing Fila's Bond Price

Cash Flow	Table	Table Value	Amount	Present Value
$100,000 par value	II.1	0.6139	$100,000	$61,390
$4,000 interest payments	II.3	7.7217	4,000	30,887
Price of Bond				$92,277

[4] Many inexpensive calculators provide present value functions for easy computation of bonds prices.

This means if 5% is semiannual market rate for Fila bonds, the maximum price that buyers will pay is $92,277. This amount is also the minimum price the issuer will accept.

Present Value of a Premium Bond

We estimate the issue price of Hydro Quebec' bonds by using the market rate to compute the present value of its future cash flows. When computing the present value of this bond, we work with *semiannual* compounding periods because this is the time between interest payments. This means the annual market rate of 10% is changed to a semiannual rate of 5%. Also, the five-year life of the bonds is changed to 10 semiannual periods.

Our computation is twofold: (1) find the present value of the $100,000 maturity payment and (2) find the present value of the series of 10 payments of $6,000 each; see Exhibit 17.9. These present values can be found by using present value tables. First, go to Table II.1 on row 10 and go across to the 5% column. The table value is 0.6139. Second, go to Table II.3 on row 10 and go across to the 5% column, where the table value is 7.7217. The bond price is computed by multiplying the cash flow amounts by their corresponding table values and adding them together. Exhibit 17.15 shows these computations.

Exhibit 17.15

Computing Hydro Quebec's Bond Price

Cash Flow	Table	Table Value	Amount	Present Value
$100,000 par value	II.1	0.6139	$100,000	$ 61,390
$6,000 interest payments	II.3	7.7217	6,000	46,330
Price of Bond				$107,720

This means if 5% is the semiannual market rate for Hydro Quebec bonds, the maximum price that buyers will pay is $107,720. This amount is also the minimum price the issuer will accept.

Flash back

Use this information to solve 7, 8, and 9: On December 31, 1999, a company issued 16%, 10-year bonds with a par value of $100,000. Interest is paid on June 30 and December 31. The bonds are sold to yield a 14% annual market rate at an issue price of $110,592.

7. Are these bonds issued at a discount or premium? Explain why.
8. Using the effective interest method of allocating bond interest expense, the issuer records the second interest payment (on December 31, 2000) with a debit to Premium on Bonds Payable in the amount of (a) $7,470, (b) $7,741, (c) $259, (d) $530, (e) $277.
9. How are the bonds reported in the long-term liability section of the issuer's balance sheet as of December 31, 2000?
10. On May 1, a company sells 9% bonds with a $500,000 par value that pays semiannual interest on each of January 1 and July 1. The bonds are sold at par value plus interest accrued since January 1. The bond issuer's entry to record the first semiannual interest payment on July 1 includes (a) a debit to Interest Payable for $15,000, (b) a debit to Bond interest expense for $22,500, (c) a credit to Interest Payable for $7,500.

Answers—p. 809

Bond Retirements

This section describes the retirement of bonds: (1) at maturity, (2) before maturity, and (3) by converting them to shares.

LO 6 Record the retirement of bonds.

Bond Retirement at Maturity

The carrying value of bonds at maturity will always equal their par value. Both Exhibits 17.9 (a discount) and 17.13 (a premium) show the carrying value of these bonds at the end of their five-year life ($100,000) equals the bonds' par value.

The entry to record retirement of the Hydro Quebec bonds in Exhibit 17.12 at maturity, assuming interest is already paid and recorded, is:

2005			
Dec. 31	Bonds Payable	100,000	
	Cash		100,000
	To record retirement of bonds at maturity.		

Assets	=	Liabilities	+	Equity
−100,000		−100,000		

Bond Retirement before Maturity

Companies sometimes wish to retire some or all of their bonds prior to maturity. For instance, if interest rates decline significantly, a company may wish to replace old high-interest paying bonds with new low-interest bonds. Two common ways of retiring bonds before maturity are to (1) exercise a call option or (2) purchase them on the open market.

In the first instance, a company can reserve the right to retire bonds early by issuing *callable bonds.* This means the bond indenture gives the issuing company an option to *call* the bonds before they mature by paying the par value plus a *call premium* to the bondholders. The second case is where the issuer retires bonds by repurchasing them on the open market at their current price. Whether bonds are called or repurchased, the issuer is unlikely to pay a price that exactly equals the bonds' carrying value. When there is a difference between the bonds' carrying value and the amount paid in a bond retirement transaction, the issuer records a gain or loss equal to the difference.

To illustrate the accounting for retiring callable bonds, let's assume a company has issued callable bonds with a par value of $100,000. The call option requires the issuer to pay a call premium of $3,000 to bondholders in addition to the par value. Immediately after the June 30, 2000, interest payment, the bonds have a carrying value of $104,500. On July 1, 2000, the issuer calls these bonds and pays $103,000 to bondholders. The issuer recognizes a $1,500 gain from the difference between the bonds' carrying value of $104,500 and the retirement price of $103,000. The entry to record this bond retirement is:

Callable Bond

July 1	Bonds Payable	100,000	
	Premium on Bonds Payable	4,500	
	Gain on Retirement of Bonds		1,500
	Cash		103,000
	To record retirement of bonds before maturity.		

Assets	=	Liabilities	+	Equity
−103,000		−100,000		+1,500
		−4,500		

A company generally must call all of its bonds when it exercises a call option. But a company can retire as many or as few bonds as it desires through open market transactions. If it retires less than the entire set of bonds, it recognizes a gain or loss for the difference between the carrying value of those bonds retired and the amount paid to acquire them.

Flashback

11. Six years ago, a company issued $500,000 of 6%, eight-year bonds at a price of 95. The current carrying value is $493,750. The company retired 50% of the bonds by buying them on the open market at a price of $102\frac{1}{2}$. What is the amount of gain or loss on retirement of these bonds?

Answers—p. 809

Bond Retirement by Conversion of Shares

We described convertible bonds earlier in the chapter, and explained how bondholders have the right to convert their bonds to common shares. When conversion occurs, the carrying value of bonds is transferred to contributed capital accounts and no gain or loss is recorded.

To illustrate, on January 1 the $100,000 par value bonds of **Converse**, with a carrying value of $100,000, are converted to 15,000 no-par value common shares. The entry to record this conversion is:

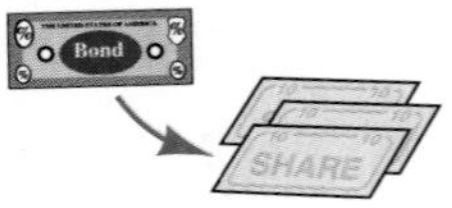

Convertible Bond

Assets	=	Liabilities	+	Equity
		−100,000		+100,000

Jan. 1	Bonds Payable	100,000	
	Common Shares, no-par value		100,000
	To record retirement of bonds by conversion into common shares.		

The market prices of the bonds and shares are not part of this entry.

Did You Know?

Cruising with Convertibles
A convertible bond has both debt and equity features. The debt feature is the economic obligation to deliver cash or other assets. The equity feature is the call option granting the investor the right to convert to common shares of the issuer. When the share price is greater than the conversion price it is probable that the debt will not have to be repaid. For purposes of measuring a firm's ratio of debt to equity the convertible bond should be treated as equity. But when the share price is less than the conversion price and it is likely that conversion will not occur, the bond should be included as debt. The *CICA Handbook* provides guidelines on the presentation of financial instruments that contain both debt and equity features. These guidelines emphasize economic substance over form and will be dealt with in later accounting courses.

Long-Term Notes Payable

LO 7 Explain the types and payment patterns of notes.

Like bonds, notes payable are issued to finance operations and borrow money. But, unlike a bond, signing a note payable is typically a transaction with a single lender such as a bank. A note is initially measured and recorded at its selling price. Selling price is the note's face value minus any discount or plus any premium. Over the life of a note, the amount of interest expense allocated to each period is computed by multiplying the interest rate at issuance of the note by the beginning-of-period balance of the note. The balance of a note at any point in time equals its face value minus any unallocated discount or plus any unallocated premium.[5]

[5] A note's balance at any date is also computed as the present value of all remaining future payments, discounted at the original interest rate.

Interest-Bearing Notes

Let's assume **Taco Bell** buys service equipment on January 2 with a fair market value of $45,000 by issuing an 8%, three-year note with a face value of $45,000. The company records the purchase with this entry:

Jan. 2	Service Equipment	45,000	
	Notes Payable		45,000
	Issued a $45,000, three-year, 8% note payable for equipment.		

Assets	=	Liabilities	+	Equity
+45,000		+45,000		

The company (note issuer) reports annual interest expense equal to the original interest rate times each year's beginning balance of the note over the life of the note. Exhibit 17.16 shows this interest expense computation and allocation.

	1999	2000	2001
Beginning balance	$45,000	$48,600	$52,488
Interest rate	× 8%	× 8%	× 8%
Interest expense	$ 3,600	$ 3,888	$ 4,199
Ending balance	$48,600	$52,488	$56,687

Exhibit 17.16

Interest-Bearing Note—Interest Paid at Maturity

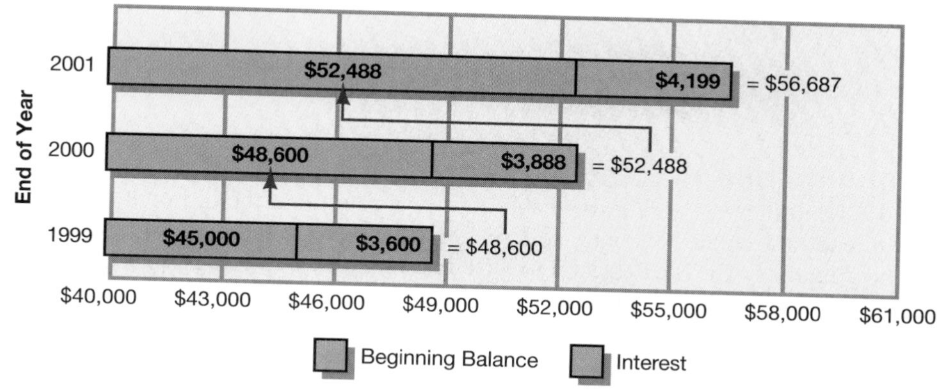

Interest is computed by multiplying each year's beginning balance by the original 8% interest rate. Interest is then added to the beginning balance to find the ending balance. A period's ending balance becomes next period's beginning balance. Because the balance grows by compounding, the amount of interest allocated to each year increases over the life of the note. The final ending balance of $56,687 equals the original $45,000 borrowed plus total interest of $11,687. A note that delays interest payments is more common for lower risk companies that wish to delay cash payments until some later period. It is often backed with assets as collateral.

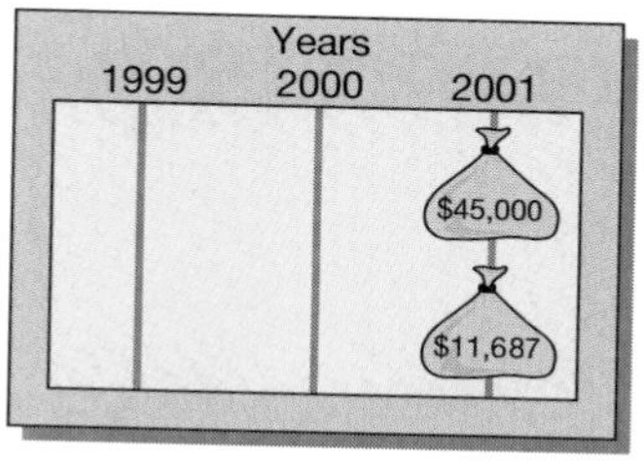

Retailer
You are a retailer in stereo components. You are planning a holiday sale on a quality stereo system requiring no payments for two years. At the end of two years, buyers must pay the full amount. Your normal selling price is $4,100, but you are willing to sell it today for $3,000 cash. What is your sale price if payment will not occur for two years and the market rate is 10%?

You Make the Call

Answer—p. 809

Non-interest-Bearing Notes

A *non-interest-bearing note* includes interest in its face (maturity) value. When a non-interest-bearing note is used to purchase an asset, the note's face value (because it includes interest) is greater than the asset's fair value. This type of note is desired by issuers who wish to avoid periodic interest payments. The asset and the note are recorded at a carrying value of either the asset's fair value or the note's fair value, whichever is more clearly determinable. A note's fair value, like that of a bond, is computed based on the market interest rate when it is issued. An asset's fair value is determined by current market transactions.

To illustrate, let's assume **Neptune Theatre** buys staging machinery on January 2, 1999, by issuing a non-interest-bearing, 5-year, $10,000 note payable. Exhibit 17.17 shows this note's cash flows.

Exhibit 17.17

Cash Flows of Non-interest-Bearing Note

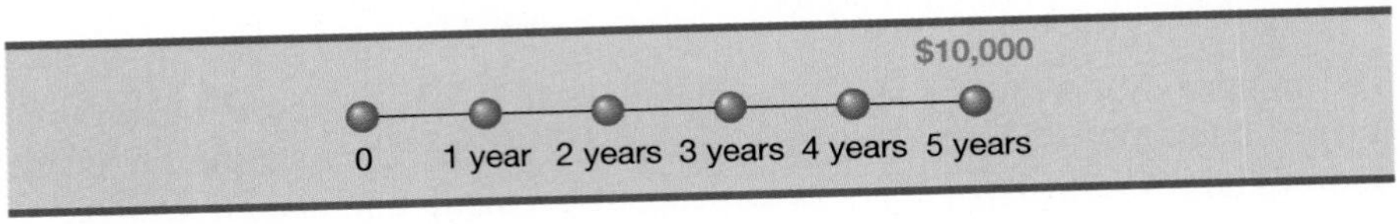

Neptune decides its estimate of the machinery's fair value is less reliable than the current 10% market interest rate available to Neptune. This note's fair value when issued is $6,209.[6] This also gives us the implied fair value of the machinery. The entry to record this purchase is:

Assets	=	Liabilities	+	Equity
+6,209		−3,791		
		+10,000		

1999			
Jan. 2	Machinery	6,209	
	Discount on Notes Payable	3,791	
	Long-Term Notes Payable		10,000
	Exchanged a five-year non-interest-bearing note for machinery.		

By recording face (maturity) value in one account and the discount in a liability contra account, this entry follows the usual way of recording a non-interest-bearing note. The $3,791 debit to Discount on Notes Payable is the *total interest expense* to be allocated to the five years of the note's life.

Exhibit 17.18 shows each year's interest, the allocation of the discount, and the note balance. The note balance grows over the five years until it reaches its face value of $10,000. The discount balance decreases to $0 after five years, and reflects *amortizing the discount*. The process of computing each year's interest is the same as in the previous discussion of the interest-bearing note. The note balance at the beginning of each year is multiplied by the 10% interest rate to determine interest for that year.

The first year's interest expense and discount amortization are recorded when we make year-end adjusting entries as follows:

Assets	=	Liabilities	+	Equity
		+621		−621

1999			
Dec. 31	Interest Expense	621	
	Discount on Notes Payable		621
	To record interest expense accrued on non-interest-bearing note.		

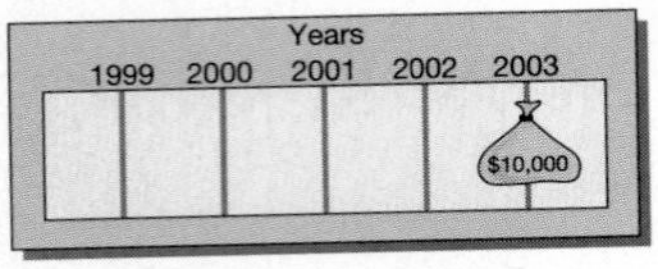

Similar entries are recorded at the end of each year until the balance of the discount account equals $0 and the net liability balance equals $10,000.

6 The note's fair value is computed as the present value of the $10,000 payment due after five years discounted at the market rate of 10%. Table II.1 in Appendix II shows the present value of 1 discounted at 10% for five years is 0.6209. The present (fair) value of the note is $6,209, computed as $10,000 × 0.6209.

	1999	2000	2001	2002	2003
Beginning balance	$6,209	$6,830	$7,513	$8,264	$9,090
Interest rate	× 10%	× 10%	× 10%	× 10%	× 10%
Interest expense	$ 621	$ 683	$ 751	$ 826	$ 910*
Ending balance	$6,830	$7,513	$8,264	$9,090	$10,000

*Adjusted for rounding.

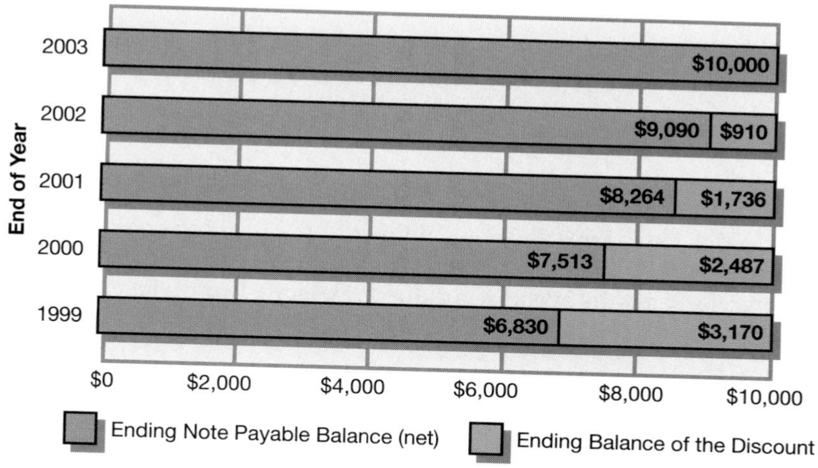

Exhibit 17.18

Non-interest-Bearing Note

When the note matures on January 2, 2004, the issuer records its payment with the entry:

2004			
Jan. 2	Long-Term Notes Payable	10,000	
	Cash		10,000
	Paid non-interest-bearing note.		

Assets = Liabilities + Equity
−10,000 −10,000

Flash back

12. On January 1, 1999, a company signs a $6,000 three-year note payable bearing 6% annual interest. The original principal and all interest is paid on December 31, 2001. Interest is compounded annually. How much interest is allocated to year 2000? (a) $0, (b) $360, (c) $381.60, or (d) $404.50.

13. A company promises to pay a lender $4,000 at the end of four years. The annual interest rate is 8% and interest is included in the $4,000 payments, meaning the note's fair value is $2,940. Record this note's issuance.

Answers—p. 809

Installment Notes

LO 8 Prepare entries to account for notes.

An **installment note** is an obligation requiring a series of periodic payments to the lender. Installments notes are common for franchises and other businesses where costs are large and the owner desires to spread these costs over several periods. When an installment note is used to borrow money or pay for assets, the borrower records the note with an entry similar to the one used for a single-payment note. This means the increase in cash or assets is recorded with a debit and the increase in the liability is recorded with a credit to Notes Payable.

To illustrate, let's assume **SuperBowl,** a bowling establishment, borrows $60,000 from a bank to purchase AMF and Brunswick bowling equipment. SuperBowl signs an 8% installment note with the bank requiring six annual payments. SuperBowl records the note's issuance as:

1999			
Dec. 31	Cash	60,000	
	Notes Payable		60,000
	Borrowed $60,000 by signing an 8% installment note.		

Assets = Liabilities = Equity
+60,000 +60,000

SuperBowl might also issue a note directly to the seller of the bowling equipment. In this case, SuperBowl would record the bowling equipment received instead of cash. One of these sellers, **Brunswick Corp.,** often provides commitments to banks in event of a buyer's default. Brunswick's annual report states:

> The company has entered into agreements ... that provide for the repurchase of its products from a financial institution in the event of repossession upon a dealer's default ... [And] provide limited recourse on marine and bowling capital equipment sales.

Payments on an installment note normally include the interest expense accruing to the date of the payment plus a portion of the amount borrowed (the *principal*). Generally, we can identify two types of payment patterns: (1) accrued interest plus equal principal payments, and (2) equal payments. The remainder of this section describes these two patterns and how we account for them.

Accrued Interest plus Equal Principal Payments

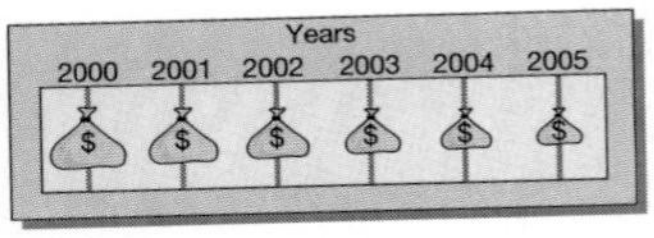

One payment pattern is accrued interest plus equal amounts of principal. This pattern creates cash flows that decrease in size over the life of the note. This decrease occurs because each payment reduces the note's principal balance, yielding less accrued interest expense for the next period.

To illustrate, let's assume the $60,000, 8% note signed by SuperBowl requires it to make six payments at the end of each year equal to *accrued interest plus $10,000 of principal*. Exhibit 17.19 describes these payments, interest, and changes in the balance of this note. Column A lists the note's beginning balance. Columns B, C, and D list each cash payment and how it is divided between interest and principal. Column B shows interest expense accruing in each year at 8% of the beginning balance. Column C shows each payment reduces principal with a $10,000 debit to the Notes Payable account. Column D is the total of B and C. Column E shows the ending balance of the note, which equals the beginning balance in column A minus the principal payment in column C.

We also include *debit* or *credit* in column headings to help understand their accounting effects. For instance, the credit to Cash equals the sum of debits to interest expense and principal. This table shows total interest expense is $16,800 and total principal is $60,000. This means total cash payments are $76,800. The graph in the lower portion of Exhibit 17.19 captures these effects and highlights the (1) decreasing total payment pattern, (2) decreasing accrued interest, and (3) constant principal payments of $10,000.

Period Ending	(A) Beginning Balance Prior (e)	(B) Debit Interest Expense 8% × (A)	+	(C) Debit Notes Payable $60,000/6	=	(D) Credit Cash (B) + (C)	(E) Ending Balance (A) − (C)
		Payments					
Dec. 31/2000	$60,000	$ 4,800		$10,000		$14,800	$50,000
Dec. 31/2001	50,000	4,000		10,000		14,000	40,000
Dec. 31/2002	40,000	3,200		10,000		13,200	30,000
Dec. 31/2003	30,000	2,400		10,000		12,400	20,000
Dec. 31/2004	20,000	1,600		10,000		11,600	10,000
Dec. 31/2005	10,000	800		10,000		10,800	-0-
		$16,800		$60,000		$76,800	

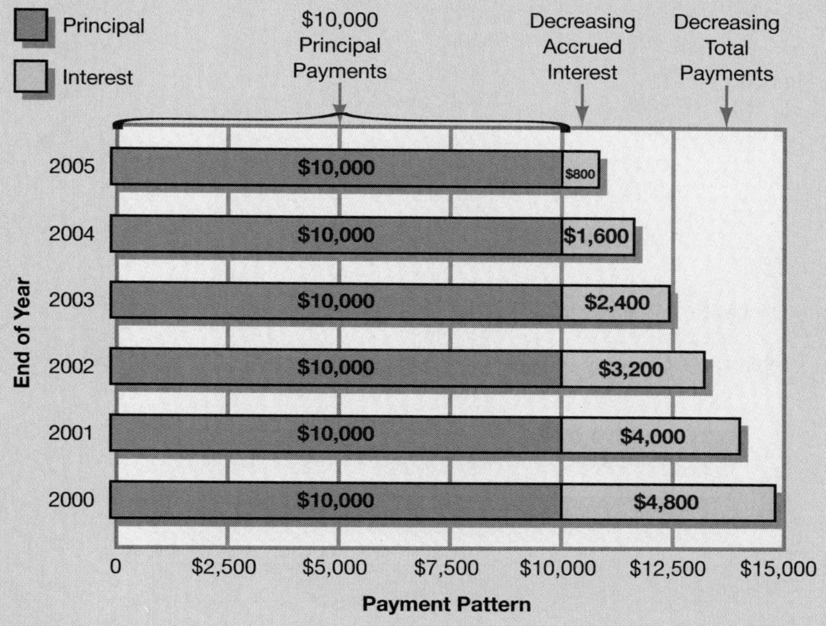

Exhibit 17.19

Installment Note—Accrued Interest plus Equal Principal Payments

SuperBowl (borrower) records the effects of the first two payments with these entries:

2000			
Dec. 31	Interest Expense	4,800	
	Notes Payable	10,000	
	Cash		14,800
	To record first installment payment.		

Assets = Liabilities + Equity
−14,800 −10,000 −4,800

2001			
Dec. 31	Interest Expense	4,000	
	Notes Payable	10,000	
	Cash		14,000
	To record second installment payment.		

Assets = Liabilities + Equity
−14,000 − 10,000 − 4,000

After all six payments are recorded, the balance of the Notes Payable account is zero.

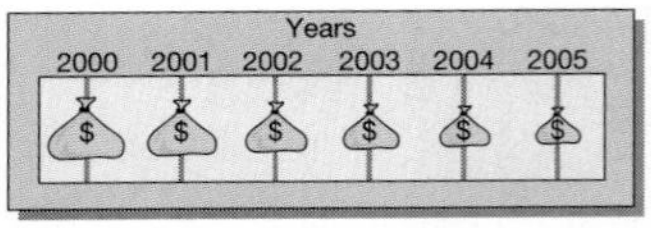

Equal Total Payments

Many installment notes require the borrower to make a series of equal payments. These payments consist of changing amounts of interest and principal.

To illustrate, let's assume the above $60,000 note requires SuperBowl (borrower) to make a series of six equal total payments of $12,979 at the end of each year.[7] Exhibit 17.20 shows the *equal total payments pattern* and its effects on the note balance. Each payment of $12,979 includes both interest and principal. See how the total amount of each payment is allocated between interest and principal.

Exhibit 17.20

Installment Note—Equal Total Payments

		Payments			
	(A)	(B)	(C)	(D)	(E)
		Debit	*Debit*	*Credit*	
Period Ending	**Beginning Balance Prior (e)**	**Interest Expense 8% × (A)** +	**Notes Payable (B) − (D)** =	**Cash Computed**	**Ending Balance (A) − (C)**
Dec. 31/2000	**$60,000**	**$ 4,800**	**$ 8,179**	**$12,979**	**$51,821**
Dec. 31/2001	51,821	4,146	8,833	12,979	42,988
Dec. 31/2002	42,988	3,439	9,540	12,979	33,448
Dec. 31/2003	33,448	2,676	10,303	12,979	23,145
Dec. 31/2004	23,145	1,852	11,127	12,979	12,018
Dec. 31/2005	12,018	961	12,018	12,979	-0-
		$17,874	**$60,000**	**$77,874**	

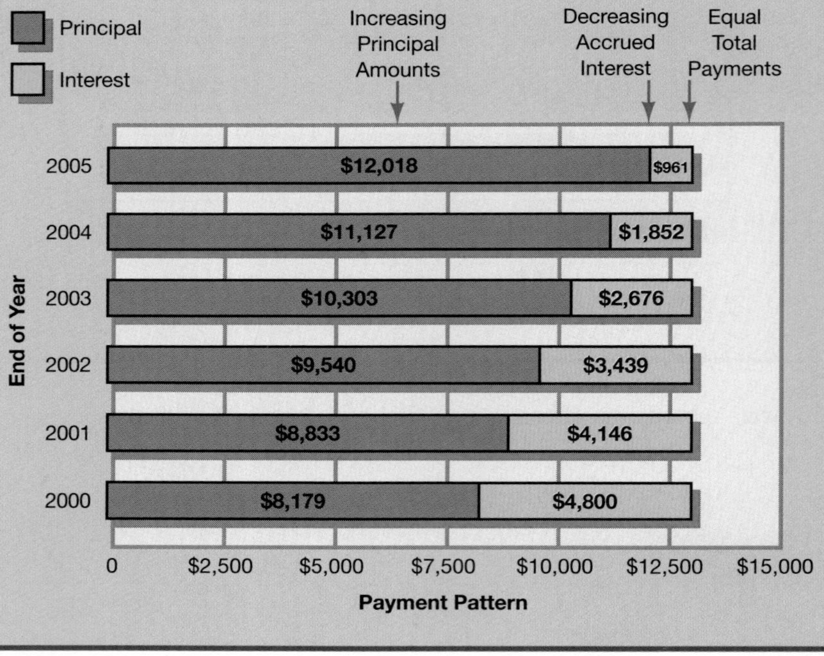

Exhibit 17.20 is very similar to Exhibit 17.19. Column A shows the note's beginning balance for each year. Column B shows accrued interest for each year at 8% of the beginning balance. Column C shows the change in the principal of the note, which equals the difference between the total payment in column D and the interest expense in column B. Column E shows the ending balance after each payment.

[7] The $60,000 equals the present value of an annuity of six annual payments of $12,979, discounted at 8% (we show this computation later in the section).

While all six payments are equal, the accrued interest decreases each year because the principal balance of the note is declining. As the amount of interest decreases each year, the amount applied to the principal increases. This pattern is graphed in the lower portion of Exhibit 17.20.

The amounts in Exhibit 17.20 are used to show how we record the first two payments toward this note with these journal entries:

2000			
Dec. 31	Interest Expense	4,800	
	Notes Payable	8,179	
	Cash		12,979
	To record first installment payment.		

Assets = Liabilities + Equity
−12,979 −8,179 −4,800

2001			
Dec. 31	Interest Expense	4,146	
	Notes Payable	8,833	
	Cash		12,979
	To record second installment payment.		

Assets = Liabilities + Equity
−12,979 −8,833 −4,146

The borrower records similar entries for each of the remaining payments. After six years, the Notes Payable account balance is zero.

It is interesting to compare the two payment patterns in Exhibits 17.19 and 17.20. The series of equal total payments leads to a greater amount of interest expense over the life of the note. This is because the first three payments in Exhibit 17.20 are smaller and do not reduce the principal as quickly as the first three payments in Exhibit 17.19.[8]

Mortgage Notes

A **mortgage** is a legal agreement that helps protect a lender if a borrower fails to make the required payments on bonds or notes. A mortgage gives the lender the right to be paid out of the cash proceeds from the sale of a borrower's specific assets identified in the mortgage. A separate legal document, called a *mortgage contract*, describes the terms of a mortgage.

Mortgage notes include a mortgage contract pledging title to specific assets as security for the note. While less common, there also exist *mortgage bonds* backed by assets of the issuer. A mortgage contract is given to the lender who accepts a note or to the trustee for the bonds. This contract usually requires the issuer (borrower) to pay all property taxes on the mortgaged assets, to maintain them properly, and to carry adequate insurance against fire and other types of losses. These requirements are designed to keep the property from losing value and avoid diminishing the lender's security. Mortgage notes are especially popular in the purchase of homes and in the acquisition of plant assets by companies. Accounting for mortgage notes and bonds is essentially the same as

[8] Table II.3 in Appendix II is used to compute the series of six payments equal to the present value of the initial note balance of $60,000 at 8% interest. We go to Table II.3 on row 6 and go across to the 8% column, where the table value is 4.6229. The present value is equal to the payment amounts multiplied by the table value as shown below:

Cash Flow	Table	Table Value	Amount	Present Value
$? interest payments	II.3	4.6229	?	60,000

We solve for the payment by dividing $60,000 by 4.6229. When a note requires a series of equal payments, we can compute the payment amount with a present value table or calculator.

accounting for unsecured notes and bonds. The primary difference is the mortgage agreement needs to be disclosed to users of financial statements

Some mortgage notes carry a variable interest rate, also called floating rate. The contract rate on these types of notes and bonds can be periodically adjusted according to changes in interest rates and terms of the contract.

Most mortgage contracts grant the lender the right to *foreclose* on the property if the borrower fails to pay in accordance with the terms of the debt agreement. If foreclosure occurs, a court either orders the property to be sold or simply grants legal title of the mortgaged property to the lender. If the property is sold, the proceeds are first applied to court costs and then to the claims of the mortgage holder. If there are any additional proceeds, the borrower is entitled to receive them depending on any claims from the borrower's unsecured creditors.

Flashback

14. Which of the following is true for an installment note requiring a series of equal payments?

a. Payments consist of an increasing amount of interest and a decreasing amount of principal.

b. Payments consist of changing amounts of principal, but the interest portion remains constant.

c. Payments consist of a decreasing amount of interest and an increasing amount of principal.

15. How is the interest portion of an installment note payment computed?

16. When a borrower records a periodic interest payment on an installment note, how are the balance sheet and income statement affected?

Answers—p. 809

Pledged Assets to Secured Liabilities

USING THE INFORMATION

This section explains how lenders can reduce their risk of loss and how borrowers can achieve more favourable terms by entering into collateral agreements. We also describe an important measure of this risk.

Collateral Agreements for Bonds and Notes

LO 9 Explain collateral agreements and their effects on loan risk.

We already explained how some bonds are secured by collateral agreements. Other bonds, called *debentures*, are unsecured. We also explained how mortgage notes can be secured by collateral. Collateral agreements reduce the risk of loss for both bonds and notes. Unsecured bonds and notes are more risky because the issuer's obligation to pay interest and principal has the same priority as all other unsecured liabilities in the event of bankruptcy. If a company's financial troubles leave it unable to pay its debts in full, the unsecured creditors (including the holders of debentures) lose a proportion or all of their balances.

A company's ability to borrow money with or without collateral agreements depends on its credit rating. In some cases, debt financing is unavailable unless the borrower can provide security to creditors with a collateral agreement. Even if unsecured loans are available, the creditors are likely to charge a higher rate of interest to compensate for the added risk. To borrow funds at a more favourable rate, many bonds and notes are secured by collateral agreements in the form of mortgages.

Information about a company's security agreements with its lenders is important to users. Notes to financial statements sometimes describe the amounts of assets pledged as security against liabilities. We next describe a ratio used to assess a borrower's situation with respect to its security agreements.

Ratio of Pledged Assets to Secured Liabilities

LO 10 Compute the ratio of pledged assets to secured liabilities and explain its use.

Lenders reduce their risk with agreements that can force borrowers to sell specific assets to settle overdue debts. Buyers (investors) of a company's secured debt obligations need to determine whether the pledged assets of the debtor provide adequate security. One method of evaluating this is to compute the ratio of **pledged assets to secured liabilities.** This is computed by dividing the book value of the company's assets pledged as collateral by the book value of the liabilities secured by these collateral agreements as shown in Exhibit 17.21.

Exhibit 17.21

Pledged Assets to Secured Liabilities

$$\text{Pledged assets to secured liabilities} = \frac{\text{Book value of pledged asset}}{\text{Book value of secured liabilities}}$$

To illustrate how we use this ratio, let's assume a company owns assets with a book value of \$230,000 pledged against loans with a balance of \$100,000. The pledged assets to secured liabilities ratio is 2.3 (often expressed as "2.3 to 1") and is computed as \$230,000/\$100,000. While there are no exact guidelines for interpreting the values for this ratio, the 2.3 value is sufficiently high to provide secured creditors with some comfort that their loans are covered by the borrower's assets.

The pledging of assets for the benefit of secured creditors also affects unsecured creditors. As an increasing portion of the assets are pledged, the unsecured creditors are less likely to receive a full repayment. In evaluating their position, unsecured creditors also gain information from the ratio of pledged assets to secured liabilities. A high ratio suggests that unsecured creditors are at greater risk for two reasons. Namely, secured creditors often demand a high ratio when they perceive (1) the values of the assets in liquidation are low, and (2) the likelihood of the company to meet its obligations from operating cash flows is weak.

When we use this ratio we must be aware that reported book values of the company's assets are unlikely to exactly reflect their market values. This ratio is improved if we can determine the assets' current market values and then use them in the ratio instead of book values. Major lenders to a company can sometimes get this information directly by asking the borrower to provide recent appraisals or other evidence of the assets' market values. Many lenders do not have this option. Using the ratio also requires knowledge about secured liabilities and pledged assets—both how they're measured and reported. This requires analysis of information in both the financial statements and their notes.

Bond Investor

You are a bond investor. You're planning to purchase debenture bonds from one of two companies that operate in the same industry and are similar in size and performance. The first company has \$350,000 of unsecured liabilities and \$575,000 of secured liabilities. The book value of this company's pledged assets is \$1,265,000. The second company has \$1,200,000 of unsecured liabilities and \$800,000 of secured liabilities, and its book value of pledged assets is \$2,000,000. Using the ratio of pledged assets to secured liabilities, determine which company's debenture bonds are less risky.

You Make the Call

Answer—p. 809

Summary

LO 1 Compare bond financing versus shares financing. Bond financing is used to fund business activities. Advantages of bond financing versus common shares include (a) no effect on shareholders' control, (b) tax savings, and (c) increased earnings due to financial leverage. Disadvantages include (a) required interest and principal payments, and (b) decreased earnings when operations turn less profitable.

LO 2 Explain the types of bonds and their issuing procedures. An issuer's bonds usually are sold to many investors. Certain bonds are secured by the issuer's assets while other bonds, called *debentures*, are unsecured. Serial bonds mature at different points in time while term bonds mature at one time. Registered bonds have each bondholder's name and address recorded by the issuing company, while bearer bonds are payable to whoever holds the bonds. Convertible bonds are exchangeable by bondholders for shares of the issuing company's shares. Callable bonds can be retired by the issuer at a set price. Bonds are often issued by an underwriter, and a bond certificate is evidence of the issuer's obligation.

LO 3 Prepare entries to record bond issuance and bond interest expense. When bonds are issued at par, Cash is debited and Bonds Payable are credited for the bonds' par value. At the bonds' interest payment dates, Bond Interest Expense is debited and Cash credited for an amount equal to the bonds' par value multiplied by the bonds' contract rate. The cash paid to bondholders on semiannual interest payment dates is computed as one-half of the result of multiplying the par value of the bonds by their contract rate.

LO 4 Compute and record amortization of bond discount. The issue price of a bond is computed using the market rate in solving for the present values of the bonds' interest payments and their par value. Bonds are issued at a discount when the contract rate is less than the market rate. This is the same as saying the issue (selling) price is less than par. When this occurs, the issuer records a credit to Bonds Payable (at par) and debits both to Discount on Bonds Payable and to Cash. The amount of bond interest expense assigned to each period is computed using either the straight-line or effective interest method. Straight-line can only be used if the results are not materially different from the effective interest method. Bond interest expense using the effective interest method equals the bonds' beginning-of-period carrying value multiplied by the original market rate at time of issuance.

LO 5 Compute and record amortization of bond premium. Bonds are issued at a premium when the contract rate is higher than the market rate. This means the issue (selling) price is greater than par. When this occurs, the issuer records a debit to Cash and credits both to Premium on Bonds Payable and to Bonds Payable (at par). The amount of bond interest expense assigned to each period is computed using either the straight-line or effective interest method. The balance of the Premium on Bonds Payable is allocated to reduce bond interest expense over the life of the bonds.

LO 6 Record the retirement of bonds. Bonds are retired at maturity with a debit to Bonds Payable and a credit to Cash for the par value of the bonds. Bonds can be retired early by the issuer by exercising a call option or by purchases on the open market. Alternatively, bondholders can retire bonds early by exercising a conversion feature on convertible bonds. The issuer recognizes a gain or loss for the difference between the amount paid out and the bonds' carrying value, unless the bonds are converted into shares in which case no gain or loss is recognized.

LO 7 Explain the types and payment patterns of notes. Notes are either interest-bearing or non-interest-bearing. Notes can require repayment of principal and interest (a) at the end of a period of time, or (b) gradually over a period of time in either equal or unequal amounts. Notes repaid over a period of time are called installment notes and usually follow one of two payment patterns: (a) decreasing payments of interest plus equal amounts of principal or (b) equal total payments.

LO 8 Prepare entries to account for notes. Interest is allocated to each period in a note's life by multiplying its carrying value by its market rate at issuance. If a note is repaid with equal payments, the amount of payment is computed by dividing the borrowed amount by the present value of an annuity number (taken from a present value table) using the market rate and the number of payments.

LO 9 Explain collateral agreements and their effects on loan risk. Some bonds and notes are secured by collateral agreements. Collateral agreements reduce the risk of loss for both bonds and notes. Unsecured bonds and notes are more risky because the issuer's obligation to pay interest and principal has the same priority as all other unsecured liabilities in the event of bankruptcy. To borrow funds at a more favourable rate, many bonds and notes are secured by collateral agreements called *mortgages*.

LO 10 Compute the ratio of pledged assets to secured liabilities and explain its use. Both secured and unsecured creditors are concerned about the relation between the amounts of assets owned by the debtor and the amounts of secured liabilities. Secured creditors are safer when the ratio of pledged assets to secured liabilities is larger. But the risks of unsecured creditors are often increased when this ratio is high because their claims to assets are secondary to secured creditors.

Guidance Answers to **You Make the Call**

Bond Rater

One factor in rating a bond is its payment pattern. Higher-risk bonds have longer repayment periods and smaller interest payments over the life of the bond. Another factor is the competitive position of the company. Higher-risk bonds are more likely issued by companies in financial difficulties or facing higher than normal uncertainties. Still another factor is the financial health of the company. Companies with higher than normal debt and with large fluctuations in earnings are considered of higher risk.

Retailer

This is a present value question where the market rate (10%) and present value ($3,000) are known, but the payment made two years later is not known. The amount we'd expect to receive at the end of two years is $3,630, computed as $3,000 × 1.10 × 1.10. (This is similar to the computation in Exhibit 17.16.) Therefore, your sale price is $3,630 with no payments for two years. This $3,630 received two years from today is equivalent to $3,000 cash today.

Bond Investor

The first company's ratio of pledged assets to secured liabilities is 2.2 ($1,265,000/$575,000), and for the second company it is 2.5 ($2,000,000/$800,000). This suggests that secured creditors of the second company are at less risk than secured creditors of the first company. But *debenture bonds are unsecured.* Therefore, since the first company has fewer secured liabilities, it is of lower risk for unsecured debenture bonds. In addition, the first company has fewer liabilities and, since the companies are of equal size, the liabilities of the first company make up a smaller portion of total assets. Consequently, as a buyer of unsecured debenture bonds, you prefer the first company.

Guidance Answers to Flashbacks

1. *b*

2. Multiply the par value of the bonds by the contract rate of interest.

3. The bonds sell at a premium, and the purchasers pay more than the par value of the bonds.

4. The bonds are issued at a discount, meaning issue price is less than par value. A discount occurs because the bonds' contract rate is less than their market rate.

5.

Cash	91,893	
Discount on Bonds Payable	8,107	
Bonds Payable		100,000

6. *a.* $3,811 (total interest equal to $38,107, or 10 payments of $3,000 plus the $8,107 discount, divided by 10 periods.)

b. $3,676 (beginning balance of $91,893 times 4% market interest rate.)

7. The bonds are issued at a premium, meaning issue price is greater than par value. A premium occurs because the bonds' contract rate is greater than their market rate.

8. *e.* (On June 30/2000: $110,592 × 7% = $7,741 bond interest expense; $8,000 − $7,741 = $259 premium amortization; $110,592 − $259 = $110,333 ending balance. On Dec. 31/2000: $110,333 × 7% = $7,723 bond interest expense; $8,000 − $7,723 = $277 premium amortization.)

9.

Bonds payable, 16%, due December 31, 2009	$100,000	
Plus premium on bonds payable .	10,056*	$110,056

*Beginning premium balance of $10,592 less $259 and $277 amortized on June 30/2000 and Dec. 31/2000.

10. *a*

11. $9,375 loss (difference between repurchase price of $256,250 [50% of ($500,000 × 102.5%)] and carrying value of $246,875 [50% of $493,750].)

12. *c* [$6,000 + ($6,000 × .06)] × .06 = $381.60

13.

Cash	2,940	
Discount on Notes Payable	1,060	
Long-Term Notes Payable . . .		4,000
Exchanged a four-year non-interest-bearing note for cash.		

14. *c*

15. The interest portion of an installment payment equals the beginning balance for the period multiplied by the original interest rate.

16. On the balance sheet, the balances of the liability and cash are decreased. On the income statement, interest expense is increased.

Demonstration Problem

The Staley Tile Company patented and successfully test-marketed a new product. However, to expand its ability to produce and market the product, the company needed to raise $800,000 of additional financing. On January 1, 1999, the company borrowed the money under these arrangements:

a. Staley signed a $400,000, 10% installment note that will be repaid with five equal annual installments. The payments will be made on December 31 of 1999 through 2003.

b. Staley issued five-year bonds with a par value of $400,000. The bonds have a 12% annual contract rate and pay interest on June 30 and December 31. The annual market interest rate for the bonds was 10% on January 1, 1999.

Required

1. For the installment note, (a) compute the size of each payment, (b) prepare an amortization table, and (c) present the entry for the first payment.

2. For the bonds, (a) estimate the issue price of the bonds, (b) present the January 1, 1999, entry to record issuing the bonds, (c) prepare an amortization table using the interest method, (d) present the June 30, 1999, entry to record the first payment of interest, and (e) present an entry to record retiring the bonds at the call price of $416,000 on January 1, 2001.

Planning the Solution

- For the installment note, divide the borrowed amount by the annuity table factor (from Exhibit 17A.6) for 10% and five payments. Prepare a table similar to Exhibit 17.20 and use the numbers in the first line for the entry.
- For the bonds, estimate the issue price by using the market rate to find the present values of the bonds' cash flows (use tables found in Appendix II). Then, use this result to record issuing the bonds. Next, develop an amortization table like Exhibit 17.8, and use it to get the numbers that you need for the journal entry. Finally, use the table to find the carrying value as of the date of the retirement of the bonds that you need for the journal entry.

Solution to Demonstration Problem

Part 1

Payment = Note balance/Table value = $400,000/3.7908 = $105,519

Table value is for five payments and an interest rate of 10%.

		Payments			
	(a)	(b) *Debit*	(c) *Debit*	(d) *Credit*	(e)
Period Ending	Beginning Balance	Interest Expense +	Notes Payable =	Cash	Ending Balance
1999	$400,000	$ 40,000	$ 65,519	$105,519	$334,481
2000	334,481	33,448	72,071	105,519	262,410
2001	262,410	26,241	79,278	105,519	183,132
2002	183,132	18,313	87,206	105,519	95,926
2003	95,926	9,593	95,926	105,519	-0-
Total		$127,595	$400,000	$527,595	

1999			
Dec. 31	Interest Expense	40,000	
	Notes Payable	65,519	
	Cash		105,519
	To record first installment payment.		

Part 2

Estimated issue price of the bonds:

Cash Flow	Table	Table Value	Amount	Present Value
Par value	App. II (PV of $1)	0.6139	$400,000	$245,560
Interest (annuity) . . .	App. II (PV of annuity)	7.7217	24,000	185,321
Total				$430,881

Table value is for 10 payments and an interest rate of 5%.

1999			
Jan. 1	Cash	430,881	
	Premium on Bonds Payable		30,881
	Bonds Payable		400,000
	Sold bonds at a premium.		

Semiannual Interest Period	(A) Cash Interest Paid 6% × $400,000	(B) Interest Expense 5% × (E)	(C) Premium Amortization (A) − (B)	(D) Unamortized Premium	(E) Carrying Value
Jan. 1/99				$30,881	$430,881
Jun. 30/99	$ 24,000	$ 21,544	$ 2,456	28,425	428,425
Dec. 31/99	24,000	21,421	2,579	25,846	425,846
Jun. 30/2000	24,000	21,292	2,708	23,138	423,138
Dec. 31/2000	24,000	21,157	2,843	20,295	420,295
Jun. 30/2001	24,000	21,015	2,985	17,310	417,310
Dec. 31/2001	24,000	20,866	3,134	14,176	414,176
Jun. 30/2002	24,000	20,709	3,291	10,885	410,885
Dec. 31/2002	24,000	20,544	3,456	7,429	407,429
Jun. 30/2003	24,000	20,371	3,629	3,800	403,800
Dec. 31/2003	24,000	20,200*	3,800	-0-	400,000
Totals	$240,000	$209,119	$30,881		

*Adjusted for rounding.

1999			
June 30	Bond interest expense	21,544	
	Premium on Bonds Payable	2,456	
	Cash		24,000
	Paid semiannual interest on the bonds.		

2001			
Jan. 1	Bonds Payable	400,000	
	Premium on Bonds Payable	20,295	
	Cash		416,000
	Gain on Retirement of Bonds		4,295
	To record the retirement of bonds (carrying value determined as of December 31, 2000).		

17A APPENDIX

Present Values of Bonds and Notes

Learning Objectives

LO 11 Explain and compute the present value of an amount to be paid at a future date.

LO 12 Explain and compute the present value of a series of equal amounts to be paid at future dates.

Accounting for long-term liabilities such as bonds and notes presents us with new challenges because of the extended time period until these obligations are settled. This appendix explains how we can apply present value techniques both to measure a long-term liability when it is created and to assign interest expense to the periods until it is settled. Appendix II provides additional discussion of present value concepts.

Present Value Concepts

The concept of present value affects accounting for liabilities. A focus on liabilities leads to a focus on the present value of future cash outflows, payables, and interest expense. But present value concepts also apply to future cash inflows, receivables, and interest income. The basic present value concept is the idea that cash paid (or received) in the future has less value now than the same amount of cash paid (or received) today.

LO 11 Explain and compute the present value of an amount to be paid at a future date.

To illustrate, if we must pay $1 one year from now, its present value is less than $1. To see this, let's assume we borrow $0.9259 today for one year at 8% interest. Our interest expense for this loan is computed as $0.9259 x 8% or $0.0741. When the $0.0741 interest is added to the $0.9259 borrowed, we get the $1 payment necessary to repay our loan with interest. This is formally computed in Exhibit 17A.1.

Exhibit 17A.1

Components of a One-Year Loan

Amount borrowed	**$0.9259**
Interest for one year at 8%	0.0741
Amount owed after one year	$1.0000

The $0.9259 borrowed is the present value of the $1 future payment. More generally, an amount borrowed equals the present value of the future payment. This relation implies that a borrowed amount can yield interest at a given rate such that its future amount will repay the loan with interest.[9]

To extend this example, let's assume we must repay the $1 after two years instead of one, and the 8% interest is compounded annually. *Compounded* means

[9] This same interpretation applies to an investment. If $0.9259 is invested at 8%, it yields $0.0741 interest revenue in one year. This amounts to $1, made up of principal and interest.

interest during the second period is based on the total of the amount borrowed plus the interest accrued from the first period. The second period's interest is then computed as 8% multiplied by the sum of the amount borrowed plus interest earned in the first period.

What then is the present value of the $1 we must repay in two years? Exhibit 17A.2 shows how we compute this amount to be $0.8573. Note the first year's interest is added to the principal so that the second year's interest is based on $0.9259.[10]

Exhibit 17A.2

Components of a Two-Year Loan

Amount borrowed in first year	**$0.8573**
Interest for first year ($0.8573 × 8%)	0.0686
Amount borrowed in second year	$0.9259
Interest for second year ($0.9259 × 8%) ..	0.0741
Amount owed after 2 years	$1.0000

Present Value Tables

The present value of $1 that we must repay several periods into the future can be computed by using the formula: $1/(1 + i)^n$. The symbol i in the formula equation is the interest rate per period and n is the number of periods until the future payment must be made. Applying this formula to our two-year loan we get: $\$1/(1.08)^2$ or $0.8573. This is the same value shown in Exhibit 17A.2.

We can use this formula to find any present value. But simpler methods are available. Perhaps the easiest is for us to use electronic calculators that are preprogrammed with present value formulas. But we can also use a present value table. A *present value table* lists present values computed with the formula for various interest rates and time periods. Many people find it helpful in learning present value concepts to first work with the table and then move to using a calculator.

Exhibit 17A.3

Present Value of $1

	Rate			
Periods	**4%**	**6%**	**8%**	**10%**
1	0.9615	0.9434	**0.9259**	0.9091
2	0.9246	0.8900	**0.8573**	0.8264
3	0.8890	0.8396	0.7938	0.7513
4	0.8548	0.7921	0.7350	0.6830
5	0.8219	0.7473	0.6806	0.6209
6	0.7903	0.7050	0.6302	0.5645
7	0.7599	0.6651	0.5835	0.5132
8	0.7307	0.6274	0.5403	0.4665
9	0.7026	0.5919	0.5002	0.4241
10	0.6756	0.5584	0.4632	0.3855

Exhibit 17A.3 shows a present value table for a future payment of $1 for up to 10 periods at five different interest rates. Present values in this table are rounded to four decimal places.[11] This table is drawn from the larger and more complete Table II.1 in Appendix II at the end of the book.

Note the first value in the 8% column is 0.9259. This is the value we computed above for the present value of a $1 loan for 1-year at 8% (see Exhibit 17A.1). Go down one row in the same 8% column and we find the present value of $1 discounted at 8% for two years, or 0.8573. Again, this value means $0.8573 is the present value of our obligation to repay $1 after two periods at 8% interest (see Exhibit 17A.2).

[10] Benjamin Franklin is said to have described compounding as: "The money, money makes, makes more money."

[11] Four decimal places are sufficient for applications in this book. Some situations require more precision.

Applying a Present Value Table

To illustrate how we measure a liability using a present value table, let's assume a company plans to borrow cash and repay it as follows:

Exhibit 17A.4

Present Value of a Series of Unequal Payments

Payment after 1 year	$ 2,000
Payment after 2 years	3,000
Payment after 3 years	5,000
Total Payments	$10,000

How much does this company receive today if the interest rate is 10% on this loan? To answer this we need to compute the present value of the three future payments, discounted at 10%. This computation is shown in Exhibit 17A.4 using values from Exhibit 17A.3. It shows the company can borrow $8,054 at 10% in exchange for its promise to make three payments at the scheduled dates.

LO 12 Explain and compute the present value of a series of equal amounts to be paid at future dates.

Years from Now	Expected Payments	Present Value of $1 at 10%	Present Value of Expected Payments
1	$2,000	0.9091	$1,818
2	3,000	0.8264	2,479
3	5,000	0.7513	3,757
Present value of all payments			$8,054

Present Value of an Annuity

The $8,054 present value of the loan in Exhibit 17A.4 equals the sum of the present values of the three payments. When payments are not equal, their combined present value is best computed by adding their individual present values as shown in Exhibit 17A.4. But sometimes payments follow an annuity. An **annuity** is a series of equal payments at equal time intervals. The present value of an annuity is readily computed.

To illustrate, let's take a company that must repay a 6% loan with a $5,000 payment at the end of each year for the next four years. The amount borrowed under this loan equals the present value of the four payments discounted at 6%. Exhibit 17A.5 shows how to compute its present value of $17,326 by multiplying each payment by its matching present value factor from Exhibit 17A.3.

Exhibit 17A.5

Present Value of a Series of Equal Payments (Annuity) by Discounting Each Payment

Years from Now	Expected Payments	Present Value of $1 at 6%	Present Value of Expected payments
1	$5,000	0.9434	$ 4,717
2	5,000	0.8900	4,450
3	5,000	0.8396	4,198
4	5,000	0.7921	3,961
Present value of all payments		3.4651	$17,326

But since the series of $5,000 payments is an annuity, we can compute present value with either of two shortcuts. First, the third column of Exhibit 17A.5 shows the sum of the present values of $1 at 6% for period 1 through 4 equals 3.4651. The shortcut is to multiply this total of 3.4651 by the $5,000 annual payment to get the combined present value of $17,326. It requires one multiplication instead of four.

The second shortcut uses an *annuity table* such as the one shown in Exhibit 17A.6.[12] Exhibit 17A.6 is drawn from the more complete Table II.3 in Appendix II. Instead of having to take the sum of individual present values from Exhibit 17A.3, we go directly to the annuity table to get the present value factor for a specific number of payments and interest rate. We then multiply this factor by the amount of the payment to find the present value of the entire annuity.

Exhibit 17A.6

Present Value of an Annuity of $1

		Rate		
Periods	**4%**	**6%**	**8%**	**10%**
1	0.9615	0.9434	0.9259	0.9091
2	1.8861	1.8334	1.7833	1.7355
3	2.7751	2.6730	2.5771	2.4869
4	3.6299	**3.4651**	3.3121	3.1699
5	4.4518	4.2124	3.9927	3.7908
6	5.2421	4.9173	4.6229	4.3553
7	6.0021	5.5824	5.2064	4.8684
8	6.7327	6.2098	5.7466	5.3349
9	7.4353	6.8017	6.2469	5.7590
10	**8.1109**	7.3601	6.7101	6.1446

Specifically, we look at Exhibit 17A.6 to find the row for four periods and go across until we reach the column for 6%, where we find the factor 3.4651. This factor equals the present value of an annuity with four payments of $1, discounted at 6%. We then multiply 3.4651 times $5,000 to get the $17,326 present value of our annuity.

Compounding Periods Shorter Than a Year

Our present value examples all involved periods of a year. But in many situations, interest is compounded over shorter periods. For example, interest rate on bonds is usually stated as an annual rate but interest is often paid every six months. This means the present value of interest payments from these bonds must be computed using interest periods of six months.

To illustrate, let's assume a borrower wants to know the present value of a series of ten $4,000 *semiannual payments* made over five years at an *annual interest rate* of 8%. While the interest rate is stated as an annual rate of 8%, it is actually a rate of 4% per six-month interest period. To compute the present value of this series of $4,000 payments, enter Exhibit 17A.6 on row 10 and go across to the 4% column to find the factor 8.1109. The present value of this annuity is $32,444 (8.1109 × $4,000).

Note: We recommend reading Appendix II to learn more about present value concepts. This appendix includes more complete present value tables and also provides a discussion of future value concepts and tables. It includes exercises to help in understanding present value concepts.

[12] The formula for finding this table's values is: $\dfrac{1 - \dfrac{1}{(1+i)^n}}{i}$ The present values in Exhibit 17A.6 are also found by adding the values of the individual payments from Exhibit 17A.3. (Since only four decimal places are shown, there are some ±0.0001 rounding differences between them).

Flashback

17. A company enters into an agreement to make four annual payments of $1,000 each, starting one year from now. The annual interest rate is 8%. The present value of these four payments is (a) $2,923, (b) $2,940, (c) $3,312, (d) $4,000, (e) $6,733.
18. Suppose a company has an option to pay either $10,000 after one year or $5,000 after six months and another $5,000 after one year. Which choice has the smaller present value?

Answers—p. 816

Summary of Appendix 17A

11. **Explain and compute the present value of an amount to be paid at a future date.** The basic concept of present value is that an amount of cash to be paid or received in the future is worth less than the same amount of cash to be paid or received today. Another important present value concept is that interest is compounded. This means interest is added to the balance and used to determine interest for succeeding periods. The present value of an amount is computed using the present value table for a single amount (or calculator).

12. **Explain and compute the present value of a series of equal amounts to be paid at future dates.** An annuity is a series of equal payments occurring at equal time intervals. The present value of an annuity can be computed as the sum of individual present values for each payment. Alternatively, and the preferred approach, is to compute the present value of the entire series using the present value table for an annuity (or calculator).

Guidance Answer to Flashbacks

17. *c.* 3.3121 × $1,000 = $3,312
18. The option of paying $10,000 after a year always has a lower present value. In effect, it postpones paying the first $5,000 by six months. As a result, the present value of the delayed payment is always less.

Glossary

Annuity A series of annual payments at equal time intervals. (p. 814)

Bearer bonds Bonds that are made payable to whoever holds them (called the bearer); also called *unregistered bonds.* (p. 782)

Bond A written promise to pay an amount identified as the par value of the bond along with interest at a stated annual amount; usually issued in denominations of $1,000. (p. 780)

Bond certificate A document containing bond specifics such as the issuer's name, the bonds' par value, the contract interest rate, and the maturity date. (p. 783)

Bond indenture The contract between the bond issuer and the bondholders; it identifies the rights and obligations of the parties. (p. 783)

Callable bonds Bonds that give the issuer an option of retiring them at a stated dollar amount prior to maturity; also called *redeemable bonds.* (p. 782)

Carrying amount The net amount at which bonds are reflected on the balance sheet; equals the par value of the bonds less any unamortized discount or plus any unamortized premium; also called the *book value* of the bonds. (p. 786)

Contract rate The interest rate specified in the bond indenture; it is multiplied by the par value of the bonds to determine the amount of interest to be paid each year; also called the *coupon rate*, the *stated rate*, or the *nominal rate.* (p. 785)

Convertible bonds Bonds that can be exchanged by the bondholders for a fixed number of shares of the issuing company's common shares. (p. 782)

Coupon bonds Bonds that have interest coupons attached to their certificates; the bondholders detach the coupons when they mature and present them to a bank or broker for collection. (p. 782)

Discount on bonds payable The difference between the par value of a bond and its lower issue price that arises when the contract rate is lower than the market rate. (p. 786)

Effective interest method Allocates interest expense over the life of the bonds in a way that yields a constant rate of interest; interest expense for a period is found by multiplying the balance of the liability at the beginning of the period by the bonds' original market rate; also called *interest method.* (p. 788)

Installment note An obligation requiring a series of periodic payments to the lender. (p. 801)

Market rate The interest rate that borrowers are willing to pay and that lenders are willing to earn for a particular bond at its risk level. (p. 785)

Mortgage A legal agreement that protects a lender by giving the lender the right to be paid out of the cash proceeds from the sale of the borrower's specific assets identified in the mortgage. (p. 805)

Par value of a bond The amount that the bond issuer agrees to pay at maturity and the amount on which interest payments are based; also called the *face amount* or *face value.* (p. 780)

Pledged assets to secured liabilities The ratio of the book value of a company's pledged assets to the book value of its secured liabilities. (p. 808)

Premium on bonds The difference between the par value of a bond and its higher issue price that arises when the contract rate is higher than the market rate. (p. 790)

Redeemable Bonds See *callable bonds.* (p. 782)

Registered bonds Bonds owned by investors whose names and addresses are recorded by the issuing company; the interest payments are made with cheques to the registered owners. (p. 782)

Secured bonds Bonds that have specific assets of the issuing company pledged as collateral. (p. 781)

Serial bonds Bonds that mature at different dates with the result that the entire debt is repaid gradually over a number of years. (p. 782)

Sinking fund bonds Bonds that require the issuing company to make deposits to a separate pool of assets; the bondholders are repaid at maturity from the assets in this pool. (p. 782)

Straight-line method (interest allocation) A method that allocates an equal amount of interest to each accounting period in the life of bonds. (p. 787)

Term bonds Bonds that are scheduled for payment (mature) at a single specified date. (p. 782)

Unsecured bonds Bonds that are backed by the issuer's general credit standing; unsecured bonds are almost always more risky than unsecured bonds; also called *debentures.* (p. 781)

Questions

1. What is the difference between notes payable and bonds payable?
2. What is the primary difference between a share and a bond?
3. What is the main advantage of issuing bonds instead of obtaining funds from the company's owners?
4. What is a bond indenture? What provisions are usually included in an indenture?
5. What are the duties of a trustee for bondholders?
6. Why does a company that issues bonds between interest dates collect accrued interest from the bonds' purchasers?
7. What are the *contract* and *market interest rates* for bonds?
8. What factors affect the market interest rates for bonds?
9. If you know the par value of bonds, the contract rate and the market interest rate, how can you estimate the market value of the bonds?
10. Does the straight-line or interest method produce an allocation of interest that creates a constant rate of interest over a bond's life? Explain your answer.
11. What is the cash price of a $2,000 bond that is sold at $98\frac{1}{4}$? What is the cash price of a $6,000 bond that is sold at $101\frac{1}{2}$?
12. Describe two alternative payment patterns for installment notes.
13. Explain why unsecured creditors should be alarmed when the pledged assets to secured liabilities ratio for a borrower has grown substantially.
14. Refer to the annual report for **Alliance** presented in Appendix I. Is there any indication that the company has issued bonds?
15. Refer to the annual report for **Atlantis** presented in Appendix I. For the fiscal year ended December 31, 1997, did Atlantis have any outstanding mortgages payable. If so how were they secured?
16. What obligation does Yvette Bourque have to the investors who purchased $200,000 of bonds to finance her natural foods store?

Quick Study

QS 17-1
Bond terms and identifications

LO 2

Match the following terms and phrases by entering the letter of the phrase that best describes each term in the blank next to the term.

_____ 1. debentures
_____ 2. bearer bonds
_____ 3. registered bonds
_____ 4. bond indenture
_____ 5. sinking fund bonds
_____ 6. serial bonds
_____ 7. secured bonds
_____ 8. convertible bonds

a. Issuer records the bondholders' names and addresses.
b. Unsecured; backed only by the issuer's general credit standing.
c. Varying maturity dates.
d. Identifies the rights and responsibilities of the issuer and bondholders.
e. Can be exchanged for shares of the issuer's common shares.
f. Unregistered; interest is paid to whoever possesses them.
g. Issuer maintains a separate pool of assets from which bondholders are paid at maturity.
h. Specific assets of the issuer are mortgaged as collateral.

QS 17-2
Quoted bond selling price and bond interest expense for bonds issued at a discount
LO 4

Lyndon Industries issued 8%, 10-year bonds with a par value of $350,000 and semiannual interest payments. On the issue date, the annual market rate of interest for the bonds was 10%, and the selling price was 87.5. The straight-line method is used to allocate the interest.

a. What are the proceeds of the bond?
b. What is the total amount of bond interest expense that will be recognized over the life of the bonds?
c. What is the amount of bond interest expense recorded on the first interest payment date?

QS 17-3
Quoted bond selling price and bond interest expense for bonds issued at a premium
LO 1,5

Top Notch, Inc., issued 10%, 15-year bonds with a par value of $120,000 and semiannual interest payments. On the issue date, the annual market rate of interest for the bonds was 8%, and they sold it at $117\frac{1}{4}$. The interest method is used to allocate the interest.

a. What are the proceeds of the Top Notch, Inc. bonds?
b. What is the total amount of bond interest expense that will be recognized over the life of the bonds?
c. What is the amount of bond interest expense recorded on the first interest payment date?

QS 17-4
Journalizing the issuance of bonds at a premium and discount
LO 3

Journalize the bonds issued in QS 17-2 and QS 17-3. Assume that both bonds are issued on January 1, 1999.

QS 17-5
Calculating bond proceeds using present values
LO 4,5

Using the facts in QS 17-2 and QS 17-3 confirm that the bond proceeds given in each problem are correct. Use the comprehensive present value tables in Appendix II.

QS 17-6
Issuing bonds between interest dates
LO 3

Lafrentz Company issues bonds as of January 1, 1999. The total bond issue was $2,000,000 of 8% bonds. The company sold $1,800,000 of the bonds on the original issue date. The final $200,000 were sold at par on March 1, 1999. The bonds pay interest semiannually as of June 30 and December 31. Record the entry for the March 1 sale of bonds.

QS 17-7
Retiring bonds before maturity
LO 6

On July 1, 1999, the Geiger Company exercises a $4,000 call option on its outstanding bonds that have a carrying value of $208,000 and par value of $200,000. The company exercises the call option immediately after the semiannual interest is paid on June 30, 1999. Record the journal entry to show retiring the bonds.

QS 17-8
Bond retirement by share conversion
LO 6

On January 1, 1999, the $1,000,000 par value bonds of Stephens Company with a carrying value of $1,000,000 are converted to 500,000 shares of $0.50 par value common shares. Journalize the conversion of the bonds.

QS 17-9
Installment note with equal payments
LO 3

New West Corp. borrowed $170,000 from a bank and signed an installment note that calls for five annual payments of equal size, with the first payment due one year after the note was signed. Use Table 17.20 to compute the size of the annual payment for each of the following annual interest rates: (a) 4%, (b) 8%, (c) 12%.

QS 17-10
Collateral Agreements
LO 9

Footnote 2 of the **Collins Industries'** annual report reads as follows:

> The credit facility [line] is collateralized by receivables, inventories, equipment and certain real property. Under the terms of the Agreement, the Company is required to maintain certain financial ratios and other financial conditions. The Agreement also prohibits the Company from incurring certain additional indebtedness, limits certain investments, advances or loans and restricts substantial asset sales, capital expenditures and cash dividends. At October 31, 1997 and 1996 the Company was in compliance with all loan covenants.

What restrictions are placed on Collins Industry by the bank which has granted the company credit?

QS 17-11
Computing the amount due on an interest-bearing note
LO 7

On January 1, 1999, The Deitrich Company borrowed $75,000 in exchange for an interest-bearing note. The note plus compounded interest at an annual rate of 8% is due on December 31, 2001. Determine the amount that Deitrich will pay on the due date. (Round to the nearest dollar.)

QS 17-12
Ratio of pledged assets to secured liabilities
LO 10

Use the following information to compute the ratio of pledged assets to secured liabilities for both companies:

	Delta Co.	Sigma Co.
Pledged assets	$387,000	$172,000
Total assets	550,000	490,000
Secured liabilities	163,000	158,000
Unsecured liabilities	266,000	390,000

Which company appears to have the riskier secured debt?

Exercises

When solving the following exercises, round all dollar amounts to the nearest whole dollar. Also assume that none of the companies use reversing entries.

Exercise 17-1
Journal entries for bond issuance and interest payments
LO 3

On January 1, 1999, Maverick Enterprises issued $1,700,000 of 20-year bonds, dated January 1, 1999. The bonds have a $1,700,000 par value, mature in 20 years, and pay 9% interest semiannually on June 30 and December 31. The bonds were sold to investors at their par value.

a. How much interest will Maverick pay to the holders of these bonds every six months?

b. Show the journal entries that Maverick would make to record (1) the issuance of the bonds on January 1, 1999, (2) the first interest payment on June 30, 1999, and (3) the second interest payment on December 31, 1999.

c. Assume the Maverick Enterprises bonds were sold at (1) 98 and (2) 102. Journalize the issuance of the bonds at 98 and 102.

Exercise 17-2
Journal entries for bond issuance with accrued interest
LO 3

On May 1, 1999, Maverick Enterprises issued bonds dated January 1, 1999. The bonds have a $1,700,000 par value, mature in 20 years, and pay 9% interest semiannually on June 30 and December 31. The bonds were sold to investors at their par value plus the four months' interest that had accrued since the original issue date.

a. How much accrued interest was paid to Maverick by the purchasers of these bonds on May 1, 1999?

b. Show the journal entries that Maverick would make to record (1) the issuance of the bonds on May 1, 1999, (2) the first interest payment on June 30, 1999, and (3) the second interest payment on December 31, 1999.

Exercise 17-3
Computing the present value of a bond and recording the issuance
LO 4

The Kloss Company issued bonds with a par value of $600,000 on their initial issue date. The bonds mature in 10 years and pay 6% annual interest in two semiannual payments. On the issue date, the annual market rate of interest for the bonds turned out to be 8%.

a. What is the size of the semiannual interest payment for these bonds?

b. How many semiannual interest payments will be made on these bonds over their life?

c. Use the information about the interest rates to decide whether the bonds were issued at par, a discount, or a premium.

d. Estimate the market value of the bonds as of the date they were issued.

e. Present the journal entry that would be made to record the bonds' issuance.

Exercise 17-4
Straight-line allocation of interest for bonds sold at a discount
LO 4

Bailey's, Inc., issued bonds with a par value of $90,000 on January 1, 2000. The annual contract rate on the bonds is 8%, and the interest is paid semiannually on June 30 and December 31. The bonds mature after three years. The annual market interest rate at the date of issuance was 10%, and the bonds were sold for $85,431.

a. What is the amount of the original discount on these bonds?

b. How much total bond interest expense will be recognized over the life of these bonds?

c. Present an amortization table like Exhibit 17.7 for these bonds; use the straight-line method of allocating the interest and amortizing the discount.

Exercise 17-5
Interest method allocation of interest for bonds sold at a discount
LO 4

Profitt Corporation issued bonds with a par value of $250,000 on January 1, 2000. The annual contract rate on the bonds is 9%, and the interest is paid semiannually. The bonds mature after three years. The annual market interest rate at the date of issuance was 12%, and the bonds were sold for $231,570.

a. What is the amount of the original discount on these bonds?

b. How much total bond interest expense will be recognized over the life of these bonds?

c. Present an amortization table like Exhibit 17.8 for these bonds; use the interest method of allocating the interest and amortizing the discount.

Exercise 17-6
Computing the present value of a bond and recording the issuance
LO 5

Innovention, Inc., issued bonds with a par value of $75,000 on their initial issue date. The bonds mature in five years and pay 10% annual interest in two semiannual payments. On the issue date, the annual market rate of interest for the bonds turned out to be 8%.

a. What is the size of the semiannual interest payment for these bonds?

b. How many semiannual interest payments will be made on these bonds over their life?

c. Use the information about the interest rates to decide whether the bonds were issued at par, a discount, or a premium.

d. Estimate the market value of the bonds as of the date they were issued.

e. Present the journal entry that would be made to record the bonds' issuance.

Exercise 17-7
Interest method allocation of interest for bonds sold at a premium
LO 5

Great Plains Power Company issued bonds with a par value of $800,000 on January 1, 2000. The annual contract rate on the bonds was 13%, and the interest is paid semiannually. The bonds mature after three years. The annual market interest rate at the date of issuance was 12%, and the bonds were sold for $819,700.

a. What is the amount of the original premium on these bonds?

b. How much total bond interest expense will be recognized over the life of these bonds?

c. Present an amortization table like Exhibit 17.12 for these bonds; use the interest method of allocating the interest and amortizing the premium.

Exercise 17-8
Retiring bonds payable
LO 6

On January 1, 1999, AeroFab, Inc., issued $350,000 of 10%, 15-year bonds at a price of $97\frac{3}{4}$. Six years later, on January 1, 2005, the corporation retired 20% of these bonds by buying them on the open market at $104\frac{1}{2}$. All interest had been properly accounted for and paid through December 31, 2004, the day before the purchase. The straight-line method was used to allocate the interest and amortize the original discount.

a. How much money did the company receive when it first issued the entire group of bonds?

b. How large was the original discount on the entire group of bonds?

c. How much amortization did the company record on the entire group of bonds between January 1, 1999, and December 31, 2004?

d. What was the carrying value of the entire group of bonds as of the close of business on December 31, 2004? What was the carrying value of the retired bonds on this date?

e. How much money did the company pay on January 1, 2005, to purchase the bonds that it retired?

f. What is the amount of the gain or loss from retiring the bonds?

g. Provide the general journal entry that the company would make to record the retirement of the bonds.

Exercise 17-9
Straight-line amortization table and accrued interest
LO 4

Piccolo Corp. issued bonds with a par value of $50,000 and a four-year life on June 1, 1999. The contract interest rate is 7%. The bonds pay interest on November 30 and May 31. They were issued at a price of $47,974.

a. Prepare an amortization table (as shown in Exhibit 17.7) for these bonds that covers their entire life. Use the straight-line method of allocating interest.

b. Show the journal entries that the issuer would make to record the first two interest payments and to accrue interest as of December 31, 1999.

Exercise 17-10
Accounting for a non-interest-bearing note
LO 8

Kern Company acquired a machine on December 1 by giving a $60,000 non-interest-bearing note due in one year. The market rate of interest for this type of debt was 10%. Show the entries that would be made when the note (a) is created on December 1, 1999, (b) as of December 31, 1999, and (c) at maturity on December 1, 2000.

Exercise 17-11
Installment note with payments of accrued interest and equal amounts of principal
LO 7, 8

On December 31, 1999, JMS, Inc. borrowed $25,000 by signing a four-year, 7% installment note. The note requires annual payments of accrued interest and equal amounts of principal on December 31 of each year from 2000 through 2003.

a. How much principal will be included in each of the four payments?

b. Prepare an amortization table for this installment note like the one presented in Exhibit 17.19.

Exercise 17-12
Journal entries for an installment note with payments of accrued interest and equal amounts of principal
LO 7, 8

Use the data in Exercise 17-11 to prepare journal entries that JMS, Inc. would make to record the loan on December 31, 1999, and the four payments starting on December 31, 2000, through the final payment on December 31, 2003.

Exercise 17-13
Installment note with equal payments
LO 7, 8

On December 31, 1999, Volks Corp. borrowed $25,000 by signing a four-year, 7% installment note. The note requires four equal payments of accrued interest and principal on December 31 of each year from 2000 through 2003.

a. Compute the size of each of the four equal payments.

b. Prepare an amortization table for this installment note like the one presented in Exhibit 17.20.

Exercise 17-14
Journal entries for an installment note with equal payments
LO 7, 8

Use the data in Exercise 17-13 to prepare journal entries that Volks Corp. would make to record the loan on December 31, 1999, and the four payments starting on December 31, 2000, through the final payment on December 31, 2003.

Exercise 17-15
Computing the ratio of pledged assets to secured liabilities
LO 9, 10

An unsecured major creditor of Telstar Corporation has been monitoring the company's financing activities. Two years before, the ratio of its pledged assets to secured liabilities had been 1.7. One year ago, the ratio had climbed to 2.3, and the most recent financial report shows that the ratio value is now 3.1. Briefly describe what this trend may indicate about the company's activities, specifically from the point of view of this creditor.

Problems

When solving the following problems, round all dollar amounts to the nearest whole dollar. Also assume that none of the companies use reversing entries.

Problem 17-1
Computing bond prices and recording issuance with journal entries
LO 3, 4, 5

Check Figure Part 1, premium, $2,718

Abbey Research, Inc., issued bonds on January 1, 1999, that pay interest semiannually on June 30 and December 31. The par value of the bonds is $20,000, the annual contract rate is 10%, and the bonds mature in 10 years.

Required

For each of these three situations, (a) determine the issue price of the bonds and (b) show the journal entry that would record the issuance.

1. The market interest rate at the date of issuance was 8%.
2. The market interest rate at the date of issuance was 10%.
3. The market interest rate at the date of issuance was 12%.

Problem 17-2
Straight-line method of allocating interest amortizing a bond discount and a bond premium.
LO 3, 4, 5

The Scofield Corporation issued $2,000,000 of bonds that pay 6% annual interest with two semiannual payments. The date of issuance was January 1, 1999, and the interest is paid on June 30 and December 31. The bonds mature after 15 years and were issued at the price of $1,728,224.

Required

1. Prepare a general journal entry to record the issuance of the bonds.
2. Calculate the cash payment, discount amortization amount, and bond interest expense to be recognized every six months.

3. Determine the total bond interest expense that will be recognized over the life of these bonds.

   Check Figure Total bond interest expense, $2,071,776

4. Prepare the first two years of an amortization table like Exhibit 17.7 based on the straight-line method of allocating the interest.
5. Present the journal entries that Scofield would make to record the first two interest payments.
6. Assume that the proceeds of the bond are $2,447,990. Repeat requirements 1–5.

Problem 17-3
Interest method of allocating bond interest and amortizing a bond discount
LO 4

Evans Materials Corp. issued $650,000 of bonds that pay 5% annual interest with two semiannual payments. The date of issuance was January 1, 1999, and the interest is paid on June 30 and December 31. The bonds mature after four years and were issued at the price of $584,361. The market interest rate was 8%.

Required

Preparation component:

1. Prepare a general journal entry to record the issuance of the bonds.
2. Determine the total bond interest expense that will be recognized over the life of these bonds.

   Check Figure Total bond interest expense, $195,639

3. Prepare the first two years of an amortization table like Exhibit 17.8 based on the interest method.
4. Present the journal entries that Evans would make to record the first two interest payments.

Analysis component:

5. Now assume that the market interest rate on January 1, 1999, was 4% instead of 8%. Without presenting any specific numbers, describe how this change would affect the amounts presented on the Evans's financial statements.

Problem 17-4
Interest method of amortizing bond interest, amortizing bond premium, and retiring bonds
LO 5, 6

Phantom Industries issued $90,000 of bonds that pay 11% annual interest with two semiannual payments. The date of issuance was January 1, 1999, and the interest is paid on June 30 and December 31. The bonds mature after three years and were issued at the price of $92,283. The market interest rate was 10%.

Required

1. Prepare a general journal entry to record the issuance of the bonds.
2. Determine the total bond interest expense that will be recognized over the life of these bonds.
3. Prepare the first four lines of an amortization table like Exhibit 17.12 based on the interest method.

   Check Figure Interest for period ending Jun 30/2000, $4,580

4. Present the journal entries that Phantom would make to record the first two interest payments.
5. Present the journal entry that would be made to record the retirement of these bonds on December 31, 2000, at a price of 98.

Problem 17-5
Bond premium amortization and finding the present value of remaining cash flows
LO 5

Ford Products, Inc., issued bonds with a par value of $500,000 and a five-year life on January 1, 1999. The bonds pay interest on June 30 and December 31. The contract interest rate is 6.5%. The bonds were issued at a price of $510,666. The market interest rate was 6% on the original issue date.

Required

1. Calculate the total bond interest expense over the life of the bonds.
2. Prepare an amortization table like Exhibit 17.12 for these bonds that covers their entire life. Use the interest method.
3. Show the journal entries that Ford Products would make to record the first two interest payments.

   Check Figure Balance as of Jun 30/2001 $505,728

4. Use the original market interest rate to compute the present value of the remaining cash flows for these bonds as of December 31, 2001. Compare your answer with the amount shown on the amortization table as the balance for that date and explain your findings.

Problem 17-6
Installment notes

LO 7,8

On October 31, 1999, Borghese Ltd. borrowed $400,000 from a bank by signing a five-year installment note bearing interest at 8%. The terms of the note require equal payments each year on October 31.

Required

1. Compute the size of each installment payment.
2. Complete an installment note amortization schedule for this note similar to Exhibit 17.20.
3. Present the journal entries that Borghese would make to record accrued interest as of December 31, 1999 (the end of the annual reporting period), and the first payment on the note.
4. Now assume that the note does not require equal payments but does require four payments that include accrued interest and an equal amount of principal in each payment. Complete an installment note amortization schedule for this note similar to Exhibit 17.19. Present the journal entries that Borghese would make to record accrued interest as of December 31, 1999 (the end of the annual reporting period), and the first payment on the note.

Check Figure Part 2, interest for period ending Oct. 31/2003, $14,292

Problem 17-7
Computing and analyzing ratio of pledged assets to secured liabilities

LO 9,10

On January 1, 2000, Dailey Company issued at par 11%, four-year bonds with a $135,000 par value. The bonds are secured by a mortgage that specifies assets totalling $225,000 as collateral. On the same date, Weekley Company issued at par 11%, four-year bonds with a par value of $60,000. Weekley is securing its bonds with a mortgage that includes $150,000 of pledged assets. Following is December 31, 1999, balance sheet information for both companies:

	Dailey Co.	Weekley Co.
Total assets	$900,000*	$450,000**
Liabilities:		
Secured	$210,000	$ 75,000
Unsecured	150,000	165,000
Shareholders' equity	540,000	210,000
Total liabilities and shareholders' equity	$900,000	$450,000

* 43% pledged
**55% pledged

Required

Preparation component:

1. Compute the ratio of pledged assets to secured liabilities for each company after January 1, 2000.

Check Figure Dailey, 1.8 to 1; Weekley, 2.9 to 1

Analysis component:

2. Which company's bonds appear to offer the best security? What other information might be helpful in evaluating the risk of the bonds?

When solving the following alternate problems, round all dollar amounts to the nearest whole dollar. Also assume that none of the companies use reversing entries.

Alternate Problems

Problem 17-1A
Computing bond prices and recording issuance with journal entries
LO 3, 4, 5

Strata Systems, Inc., issued a group of bonds on January 1, 1999, that pay interest semiannually on June 30 and December 31. The par value of the bonds is $45,000, the annual contract rate is 12%, and the bonds mature in five years.

Required

For each of these three situations, (a) determine the issue price of the bonds and (b) show the journal entry that would record the issuance.

1. The market interest rate at the date of issuance was 10%.
2. The market interest rate at the date of issuance was 12%.
3. The market interest rate at the date of issuance was 14%.

Problem 17-2A
Straight-line method of allocating interest and amortizing a bond discount and a bond premium
LO 3, 4, 5

The Poole Corporation issued $1,700,000 of bonds that pay 10% annual interest with two semiannual payments. The date of issuance was January 1, 1999, and the interest is paid on June 30 and December 31. The bonds mature after ten years and were issued at the price of $1,505,001.

Required

1. Prepare a general journal entry to record the issuance of the bonds.
2. Calculate the cash payment, discount amortization amount, and bond interest expense to be recognized every six months.
3. Determine the total bond interest expense that will be recognized over the life of these bonds.
4. Prepare the first two years of an amortization table like Exhibit 17.7 based on the straight-line method of allocating the interest.
5. Present the journal entries that Poole would make to record the first two interest payments.
6. Assume that the proceeds on the bond are $2,096,466. Repeat requirements 1–5.

Problem 17-3A
Interest method of allocating interest and amortizing a bond discount
LO 4

Joseph Manufacturing Corp. issued $120,000 of bonds that pay 6% annual interest with two semiannual payments. The date of issuance was January 1, 1999, and the interest is paid on June 30 and December 31. The bonds mature after 15 years and were issued at the price of $99,247. The market interest rate was 8%.

Required

1. Prepare a general journal entry to record the issuance of the bonds.
2. Determine the total bond interest expense that will be recognized over the life of these bonds.
3. Prepare the first four lines of an amortization table like Exhibit 17.8 based on the interest method.
4. Present the journal entries that Joseph Manufacturing would make to record the first two interest payments.

Problem 17-4A
Interest method of allocating interest, amortizing bond premium and retiring bonds
LO 5, 6

Adams Brothers, Inc., issued $900,000 of bonds that pay 13% annual interest with two semiannual payments. The date of issuance was January 1, 1999, and the interest is paid on June 30 and December 31. The bonds mature after four years and were issued at the price of $987,217. The market interest rate was 10%.

Required

Preparation component:

1. Prepare a general journal entry to record the issuance of the bonds.
2. Determine the total bond interest expense that will be recognized over the life of these bonds.
3. Prepare the first two years of an amortization table like Exhibit 17.12 based on the interest method.

4. Present the journal entries that Adams Brothers would make to record the first two interest payments.
5. Present the journal entry that would be made to record the retirement of these bonds on December 31, 2000, at the price of 106.

Analysis component:

6. Instead of the facts described in the problem, assume that the market interest rate on January 1, 1999, was 14% instead of 10%. Without presenting any specific numbers, describe how this change would affect the amounts presented on the company's financial statements.

Problem 17-5A
Bond premium amortization and finding the present value of remaining cash flows
LO 5

LaRue Company issued bonds with a par value of $160,000 and a five-year life on January 1, 1999. The bonds pay interest on June 30 and December 31. The contract interest rate is 9%. The bonds were issued at a price of $166,494. The market interest rate was 8% on the original issue date.

Required

1. Calculate the total bond interest expense over the life of the bonds.
2. Prepare an amortization table like Exhibit 17.12 for these bonds that covers their entire life. Use the interest method.
3. Show the journal entries that LaRue would make to record the first two interest payments.
4. Use the original market interest rate to compute the present value of the remaining cash flows for these bonds as of December 31, 2001. Compare your answer with the amount shown on the amortization table as the balance for that date, and explain your findings.

Problem 17-6A
Installment notes
LO 7, 8

On September 30, 1999, Rome Enterprises borrowed $300,000 from a bank by signing a three-year installment note bearing interest at 10%. The terms of the note require equal payments each year on September 30.

Required

1. Compute the size of each installment payment.
2. Complete an installment note amortization schedule for this note similar to Exhibit 17.20.
3. Present the journal entries that Rome would make to record accrued interest as of December 31, 1999 (the end of the annual reporting period), and the first payment on the note.
4. Now assume that the note does not require equal payments but does require three payments that include accrued interest and an equal amount of principal in each payment. Complete an installment note amortization schedule for this note similar to Exhibit 17.19. Present the journal entries that Rome would make to record accrued interest as of December 31, 1999 (the end of the annual reporting period) and the first payment on the note.

Problem 17-7A
Computing and analyzing ratio of pledged assets to secured liabilities
LO 9, 10

On January 1, 2002, Spruce Company issued $45,000 of 12%, ten-year bonds secured by a mortgage that specifies assets totalling $120,000 as collateral. On the same date, Willow Company issued 12%, ten-year bonds on January 1, with a par value of $150,000. Willow's bonds are secured by a mortgage that includes $225,000 of pledged assets. Following is December 31, 2001, balance sheet information for both companies:

	Spruce Co.	Willow Co.
Total assets	$180,000*	$750,000**
Liabilities:		
Secured	$ 39,000	$ 57,000
Unsecured	42,000	505,500
Owners' equity	99,000	187,500
Total liabilities and owners' equity	$180,000	$750,000

*59% pledged
**10% pledged

Required

Preparation component:

1. Compute the ratio of pledged assets to secured liabilities for each company after January 1, 2002.

Analysis component:

2. Which company's bonds appear to offer the best security? What other information would be helpful in evaluating the risk of the bonds?

Analytical and Review Problem

A & R Problem 17-1

The accounts of Clues Corporation showed the following balances as of December 31, 1999:

Bonds Payable	$1,500,000
Bond Discount	$ 30,900

The 9%, 10-year bonds dated August 1, 1998, were issued on December 1, 1998, and the cash proceeds were $1,510,200. Interest is payable semiannually. Assume that bond discount is amortized on a straight-line basis over the bond's useful life.

Required

Reconstruct the entries pertaining to the bond issue that were made on the company's books during 1998 and 1999. Assume that the company's fiscal year coincides with the calendar year.

BEYOND THE NUMBERS

Reporting in Action

LO 1, 2

Refer to the financial statements and related information for **Alliance** in Appendix I. Answer the following questions by analyzing the information in the report:

1. Has Alliance issued any bonds or long-term notes payable?
2. What is the due date of the company's long-term loans payable?
3. Are any assets pledged as security for the long-term loans payable?
4. At whose option are the debentures convertible?
5. Obtain access to Alliance's annual report for fiscal years ending after March 31, 1997. Has Alliance issued additional long-term debt since the fiscal year ended May 31, 1997?

Comparative Analysis

LO 10

Both **NIKE** and **Reebok** design, produce, market and sell sports footwear and apparel. Key comparative figures ($ millions) for these two organizations follow:

Key Figures	NIKE 1997	Reebok 1996
Accounts receivable, net	$1,754	$591
Inventory	1,339	545
Property and equipment, net	922	186
Long-term debt (includes current portion)	298	907

* NIKE figures are from the annual report for the fiscal year ended May 31,1997.
Reebok figures are from the annual report for the fiscal year ended December 31, 1996.

Required

1. Assume that both NIKE and Reebok have pledged substantially all of their accounts receivables, inventories, and property and equipment to collateralize their long-term debt. Compute the ratio of pledged assets to secured liabilities for both companies.
2. Using the ratio you computed in part 1 of this question, determine which company's long-term debt is less risky.

Ethics Challenge

LO 1

A few years ago the politicians needed a new headquarters building for their municipal government. The price tag for the building approached $24 million. The politicians felt that it was unlikely that the voters would approve a bond issue to raise money for the headquarters since approving the bond issue would cause taxes to increase. The politicians opted for a different approach. They had a bank issue $24 million worth of securities to pay for the construction of the building. The municipality then agreed to make a yearly lease payment (comprised of repayment of principal and interest) to repay the obligation. Unlike conventional municipal bonds the lease payments are not binding obligations on the municipal government and, therefore, no voter approval is required.

Required

1. Do you think the actions of the politicians and the investment bankers were ethical in this situation?
2. How does the security issued to pay for the building compare in riskiness to a regular municipal bond issued by a municipal government?

Communicating in Practice

LO 5

Your business associate mentioned he is considering investing in the corporate bond market. He recently sent you an e-mail to say he is considering investing in bonds currently selling at a premium. He says that since the bonds are selling at a premium, they are highly valued and his investment will yield more than the going rate of return for the risk involved. Reply via e-mail (or memo) to confirm or correct your associate's analysis.

Taking It to the Net

LO 1

Visit the Canadian Bond Rating Service at **http://www.cbrs.com.**

Required

1. Click on Rating. Then click on rating methodology. What seven major areas does CBRS consider when rating a particular issuer?
2. Go back to the table of contents and click on CBRS rating scales. Describe the ratings for long-term debt.
3. Go back to the table of contents and click on ratings process. What factors make CBRS change a company rating?

Teamwork in Action

LO 4, 5

Let's work as a team to reinforce understanding of how to prepare an effective interest method amortization table for bond premiums and discounts.

1. Each member of the team is to independently prepare a blank table with the appropriate headings for amortization of bond premiums. When each member is done, compare tables and ensure all are in agreement.

Steps 2 and 3 require use of the following facts: January 1, 1999—Issued $100,000, 9%, five-year bonds at 104.1. Market rate at issue was 8%. Rates specified are annual rates and interest is to be paid semiannually on June 30 and December 31.

2. In rotation, *each* member of the team will fully explain how to complete *one* line of the table. Each member must completely verbalize any formula used and the specific numbers for their table line. (Round all amounts to the nearest dollar) All members are to fill in their tables during this process. You need not finish the table; stop when each member has an opportunity to explain a line.
3. In rotation, team members are to identify a column from which we can readily project the final number, explain what that number is, and how this number is known.
4. Come to a team consensus as to what the total bond interest expense on this bond issue would be if the bond is not retired before maturity.
5. As a team, you are to prepare a list of similarities and differences between the amortization table just prepared and the necessary table if the bond had been issued at a discount. You may again use a rotation system to identify these items.

Hitting the Road

LO 1

Visit your local library. Ask a librarian to help you locate the recent financial records of your city or municipal government. Examine the records of the municipality you choose.

Required

1. Determine the amount of long-term debt in the form of bonds that the municipality currently has outstanding.
2. Read the supporting information to the financial statements and record:
   a. Interest rate the debt was issued at.
   b. When the debt will be retired.
   c. Whether the debt has received a rating from the Canadian Bond Rating Service, Moody's, Standard and Poor's, or another rating agency.

Business Break

LO 1, 2

Read the article "The Bond Boom in the Former Soviet Bloc," in the September 15, 1997, issue of *Business Week*.

Required

1. Historically have companies in central and eastern Europe relied on debt financing?
2. How does the yield on a Eurobond issued by a Russian bank compare to comparable North American securities?
3. Do experts feel the yields on bonds issued in central Europe compensate investors for the risks?
4. Refer to the chart in the article and list the top five eastern and central European companies in terms of Eurobond amounts issued in 1997.

18 CHAPTER

Long-Term Investments and International Accounting

A Look Back

Chapter 17 focused on a special group of long-term liabilities: notes payable and bonds. We described both of these liabilities and explained how they are both accounted for and reported.

A Look at This Chapter

This chapter emphasizes another special category, that of long-term investments in securities. We explain how to identify, account for, and report long-term investments in both debt and equity securities. We also introduce foreign exchange rates and describe accounting for transactions listed in a foreign currency.

A Look Forward

Chapter 19 focuses on reporting and analyzing a company's cash flows. Special emphasis is directed at the statement of cash flows.

Chapter Outline

- **Classifying Investments**
  - Temporary versus Long-Term
  - Classes of Long-Term Investments
- **Long-Term Investments in Securities**
  - Investment in Debt Securities Held to Maturity
  - Investment in Equity Securities with Significant Influence
  - Investment in Equity Securities with Controlling Influence
- **Investments in International Operations**
  - Exchange Rates between Currencies
  - Sales or Purchases Listed in a Foreign Currency
  - Consolidated Statements with International Subsidiaries
- **Using the Information—Componented Return on Total Assets**
- **Appendix 18A—Parent and Subsidiary Corporations**

Investing: The Next Generation

Bay Street, Toronto, ON—It was the worst day in Sara Brempong's young career as a financial analyst. She had just failed to land a major client and her boss removed her from a special analyst training program. Brempong's response? She quit. "Nothing fit," says Brempong. "Here I was, 23-years-old, in a stuffy old-boys' firm, advising clients twice my age on securities investments. I knew what I was doing, but no one believed in me."

That was five years ago. Today, Brempong is running her own investment firm, **Brempong & Brempong**. The other Brempong? "Well," laughs Brempong, "I asked my grandfather to sign on as joint partner because, like all the big firms, I thought I needed multiple names for the title of an investment firm." Adds Brempong, "Actually, he is the person who started me on my career. When he gave gifts to us grandchildren, he always tucked in some shares of the manufacturer."

Grandpa must now be proud, for Brempong's upstart firm pulled in over $485,000 in commissions and consulting revenues this past year. And the current year is running 28% ahead of last year. What's the secret? "Two things," says Brempong. "First, I work hard at knowing my investments and client needs. Second, I pursue a niche market for clients." What Brempong does is work tirelessly at attracting young investors, the twenty- and thirty-something crowd. "There is a large untapped market that I've only begun to break into," says Brempong. "Larger investment houses don't pursue these clients—I do." She also relies heavily on analysis of annual reports.

"My fundamental analysis is twofold," says Brempong. "I analyze the financial statements of potential investments to assess their strengths and weaknesses. Then I use their products and services, and ask others about them." Brempong also usually insists on visiting a company before she invests, or recommends investment, in it. "If I'm looking at a camera company, I use its cameras. I ask other people for their opinions too." Still, she cautions, "there is always a risk, but I try to minimize it through smart investing." Seems like grandpa was a good teacher.

Learning Objectives

LO 1 Distinguish long-term investments from temporary investments.

LO 2 Identify classes of securities in long-term investments.

LO 3 Account for debt securities held to maturity.

LO 4 Account for equity securities using the cost method.

LO 5 Account for equity securities having significant influence.

LO 6 Describe how equity securities having controlling influence are reported.

LO 7 Explain foreign exchange rates between currencies.

LO 8 Record transactions listed in a foreign currency.

LO 9 Compute and analyze the components of return on total assets.

CHAPTER PREVIEW

This chapter completes our study of assets by focusing on long-term investments. Many companies have long-term investments, and many of these are in the form of debt and equity securities issued by other companies. This chapter describes long-term investments in these securities and how they are accounted for. An increasing number of companies also invest in international operations. The financial statement effects of these investments are often very important. We explain how transactions listed in foreign currencies are accounted for and reported. Our understanding of the topics in this chapter are important in our ability to read and interpret financial statements. This knowledge is the type used by Sara Brempong as described in the opening article for investment decisions in shares and bonds.

Classifying Investments

This section explains how we classify investments. We first describe the distinction between short- and long-term investments. We then describe the different classification of long-term investments.

Temporary versus Long-Term

LO 1 Distinguish long-term investments from temporary investments.

We explained in Chapter 10 how to account for temporary investments in debt and equity securities. Temporary investments are usually held as an investment of cash for use in current operations. Temporary investments are current assets and must meet two requirements. First, they are expected to be converted into cash within one year or the current operating cycle of the business, whichever is longer. Second, they are readily convertible to cash, sometimes called *marketable*.[1]

Long-term investments are investments not meeting the two requirements for temporary investments. This means long-term investments include investments in bonds and shares that are not marketable or, if marketable, are not intended to be converted into cash in the short-term. Long-term investments also include funds earmarked for a special purpose. Examples are bond sinking funds, and investments in land or other assets not used in the company's operations. Long-term investments are reported in the noncurrent section of the balance sheet often in its own separate section titled *Long-term investments*.

Classes of Long-Term Investments

LO 2 Identify classes of securities in long-term investments.

Accounting for investments depends on several factors. One is whether securities are classified as (1) *trading* securities, (2) debt securities *held-to-maturity*, or (3) debt and equity securities *available-for-sale*. Investments in trading securities always are temporary investments and are reported as current assets. The other two classes of investments are either long-term or temporary depending on what the company intends to do with them. Another factor for equity securities is a company (investor's) percent ownership in the other company's (investee's) shares.

Exhibit 18.1 classifies long-term securities investments on these two factors. The four classifications shown are: (1) debt securities *held-to-maturity*, (2) debt and equity securities *available-for-sale*, (3) equity securities giving an investor a significant influence over an investee, and (4) equity securities giving an investor control over an investee. We next describe each of these four important classes of securities and how to account for them.

[1] It is helpful to review the section on temporary investments in Chapter 10 before studying this chapter.

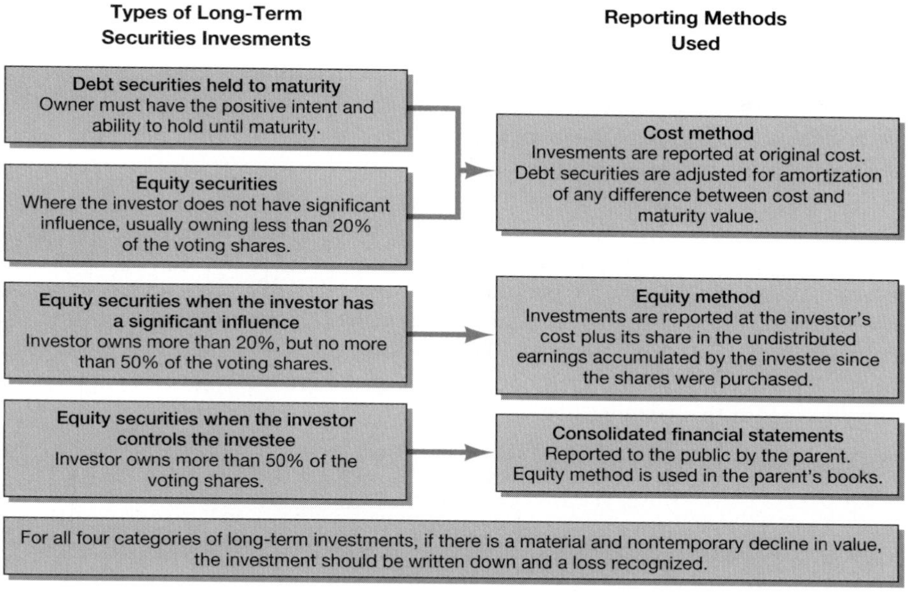

Exhibit 18.1

Accounting for Long-Term Investments in Securities

Flashback

1. Give at least two examples of assets classified as long-term investments.
2. What are the requirements for a security to be classified as a long-term investment?

Answers—p. 848

Long-Term Investments in Securities

Similar to the accounting for temporary investments, a long-term investment is recorded at cost when purchased. Cost is defined as all necessary expenditures to acquire the investment, including any commissions or brokerage fees paid. Recall that temporary investments are current assets; they are expected to be converted into cash within one year or the current operating cycle of the business, whichever is longer. In general, temporary investments such as T-bills and term deposits are those that are "capable of reasonably prompt liquidation."[2] Temporary investments either mature in one year or the current operating cycle or are easily sold and therefore qualify as *marketable*. Securites that do not qualify as current assets are called long-term investments. Long-term investments include investments in bonds and shares that are not marketable or that, although marketable, are not *intended* to serve as a ready source of cash. Long-term investments also include funds earmarked for a special purpose, such as bond sinking funds, and land or other assets owned but not used in the regular operations of the business. In general, these assets are reported on the balance sheet in a separate *Long-term investments* section. But after the purchase, the accounting treatment for long-term investments depends on the class of investments.

Investments in Debt Securities Held to Maturity

LO 3 Account for debt securities held to maturity.

Long-term investments in *debt* securities are those that a company intends and is able to hold until maturity. Debt securities are recorded at cost when purchased. Also, long-term investments in debt securities require us to record interest revenue as it accrues.

[2] *CICA Handbook*, par. 3010.02.

The cost of an investment in a long-term debt security can be either higher or lower than the maturity value of the debt security. When the investment is long-term, the difference between cost and maturity value is amortized over the remaining life of the security. Chapters 13 and 17 explain how we amortize this difference. For this chapter, *we assume for ease of computations that the cost of a debt security equals its maturity value.*

Illustration of a Debt Security Held-to-Maturity

Music City paid $29,500 plus a brokerage fee of $500 to buy Power Corp. 7% bonds payable with a $30,000 par value on August 31,1998. The bonds pay interest semiannually on August 31 and February 28. The amount of each interest payment is $1,050, computed as $30,000 face value × 7% interest × 6/12 year. Music City intends to hold the bonds until they mature on August 31, 2000. The entry to record this purchase is:

Assets = Liabilities + Equity
+30,000
−30,000

1998			
Aug. 31	Investment in Power Corp. Bonds	30,000	
	Cash		30,000
	Purchased bonds to be held to maturity.		

On December 31, 1998, at the end of its accounting period, Music City accrues interest receivable in the following entry:

Assets = Liabilities + Equity
+700 +700

Dec. 31	Interest Receivable	700	
	Interest Earned		700
	$1,050 × 4/6 = $700.		

The $700 reflects 4/6 of the semiannual cash receipt of interest. This is the portion earned by Music City. Music City's financial statements at December 31, 1998, are show in Exhibit 18.2.

Exhibit 18.2

Financial Statement Effects of Debt Securities

On the income statement for 1998:	
Interest earned	$ 700
On the December 31, 1998, balance sheet:	
Assets:	
Current Assets:	
Interest receivable	$ 700
Long-term investments:	
Investment in Power Corp. bonds	$30,000

On February 28, 1999, and each interest payment date thereafter, Music City records receipt of the semiannual interest as:

Assets = Liabilities + Equity
+1,050 +350
−700

1999			
Feb. 28	Cash	1,050	
	Interest Receivable		700
	Interest Earned		350
	Received six months' interest on Power Corp. bonds.		

When the bonds mature, the entry to record proceeds from the matured bonds is:

Assets = Liabilities + Equity
+30,000
−30,000

2000			
Aug. 31	Cash	30,000	
	Investment in Power Corp. Bonds ...		30,000
	Received cash from matured bonds.		

This illustration reflects the *cost method* for recording and reporting long-term investments in long-term debt securities. This method is required in practice.

Money Manager
You are a money manager for a company. You currently manage a fund with a large amount of investments in other companies' fixed-rate bonds and notes. You expect interest rates to both sharply fall within a few weeks and remain at this lower rate. What is the strategy for your investments in fixed-rate bonds and notes?

You Make the Call

Answer—p. 847

Trading Secrets
Mutual fund companies keep secret their trading records for many reasons including regulatory requirements and potential lawsuits. But a mystery arose when top-secret trading records of the $55 billion **Fidelity Magellan** fund appeared in the *Washington Post*. This resulted in several lawsuits filed against Fidelity. Fidelity's fund managers have since been barred from talking about individual shares with the press, and the company has stopped its internal circulation of daily fund trading for security reasons. [Source: *Business Week*, May 27, 1996.]

Did You Know?

Investments in Equity Securities

LO 4 Account for equity securities using the cost method.

The accounting for long-term investments in portfolio securities is similar to accounting for temporary investments. First, these investments are recorded at cost. Second, dividends received are credited to Dividends Earned and reported in the income statement. Third, when the shares are sold, proceeds from the sale are compared with the cost of the investment and any gain or loss on the sale is reported in the income statement.

A portfolio investment could consist of the same securities as a temporary investment. The difference is that management intends not to dispose of the securities of a portfolio in the short term. Portfolio investments are held to generate investment income. For example, a company that holds shares of **B.C. Tel** with the intention of selling them within six months would classify this investment as temporary. If the intent were to hold on to these shares for the long-term the investment in B.C. Tel would be classified as long term. An important requirement for a security to be classified as a long-term portfolio investment in equity securities is that it must not enable its investor to have significant influence over the investee. This usually is interpreted as an investor who owns less than 20% of the investee company's voting shares.[3]

Illustration of the Cost Method of Accounting for an Equity Security

Music City purchased 1,000 shares of **Intex's** common shares at its par value of $86,000 on October 10, 1998. The entry to record this purchase is:

Oct. 10	Investment in Intex Common Shares	86,000	
	Cash		86,000
	Purchased 1,000 shares.		

Assets	=	Liabilities	+	Equity
+86,000				
−86,000				

[3] The 20% limit is not an absolute rule. Other factors may overrule. See *CICA Handbook*, section 3050, "Long-term Investments," par. .04.

On November 2, Music City receives a $1,720 quarterly dividend on the Intex shares. The entry to record the dividend receipt is:

Assets = Liabilities + Equity
+1,720 +1,720

Nov. 2	Cash	1,720	
	Dividends Earned		1,720
	Received dividend of $1.72 per share.		

On December 20, Music City sells 500 of the Intex shares for $45,000. The entry to record this sale is:

Assets = Liabilities + Equity
+45,000 +2,000
−43,000

Dec. 20	Cash	45,000	
	Investment in Intex Common Shares		43,000
	Gain on Sale of Long-Term Investment		2,000
	$86,000/2 = $43,000		

Reporting Long-Term Investments

Long-term investments are stated at cost with market value disclosed even if market value is below cost as long as the decline in value is temporary. However, when there has been a loss in value that is other than temporary, the investment is written down to recognize the loss.[4] The writedown (loss) would be included in determining net income. When a long-term investment has been written down to recognize the loss, the new carrying value is deemed to be the new cost basis for subsequent accounting purposes. A subsequent increase in value would be recognized only when realized, i.e., when the shares are sold. For purposes of calculating the gain or loss on sale of the investment, the cost of the investment sold should be calculated on the basis of the average carrying value (total cost of the shares ÷ number of shares held).[5]

Investment in Equity Securities with Significant Influence

LO 5 Account for equity securities having significant influence.

A long-term investment in **equity securities with significant influence** is defined as an investor who is able to exert significant influence over the investee. This is usually the result of an investor buying a large block of a company's voting shares. An investor who owns 20% or more (but not more than 50%) of a company's voting shares is usually presumed to have a significant influence over the investee. Yet there are cases where the 20% test of significant influence is overruled by other, more persuasive, evidence. This evidence can either lower the 20% requirement or increase it. According to section 3050.04 of the *CICA Handbook:*

> An investor may be able to exercise significant influence over strategic operating, investing and financing policies of an investee even though the investor does not control or jointly control the investee. The ability to exercise significant influence may be indicated by, for example, representation on the board of directors, participation in policy-making processes, material intercompany transactions, interchange of managerial personnel or provision of technical information. If the investor holds less than 20% of the voting interest in the investee, it is presumed that the investor does not have the ability to exercise significant influence, unless such influence is clearly demonstrated. On the other hand, the holding of 20% or more of the voting interest in the investee does not in itself confirm the ability to exercise significant influence. A substantial or majority ownership by another investor would not necessarily preclude an investor from exercising significant influence.

[4] Ibid., par. 3050.20.

[5] Ibid., par. 3050.27.

The **equity method** of accounting and reporting is used for long-term investments in equity securities with significant influence. We now illustrate this method.

Illustration of an Equity Security with Significant Influence.

This section illustrates the equity method of accounting for long-term investments in equity securities with significant influence. The investor records the purchase of these securities at cost when acquired. To illustrate, Micron Company purchased 3,000 shares (30%) of JVT common shares for a total cost of $70,650 on January 1, 1998. The entry to record this purchase on Micron's books is:

Jan. 1	Investment in JVT Common Shares	70,650	
	Cash		70,650
	Purchased 3,000 shares.		

Assets = Liabilities + Equity
+70,650
−70,650

Under the equity method, earnings of the investee (JVT) increase both the investee's net assets and the investor's (Micron) equity claims against the investee's assets. This means when the investee closes its books and reports its earnings, the investor records its share of those earnings in its investment account. JVT reported net income of $20,000 for 1998. Micron's entry to record its 30% share of these earnings is:

Dec. 31	Investment in JVT Common Shares	6,000	
	Earnings from Investment in JVT		6,000
	To record 30% equity in investee's earnings of $20,000.		

Assets = Liabilities + Equity
+6,000 +6,000

The debit reflects the increase in Micron's equity in JVT. The credit means 30% of JVT's net income appears on Micron's income statement as earnings from the investment. As with all revenues, Micron closes these earnings to Income Summary.

If the investee incurs a net loss instead of a net income, the investor records its share of the loss and reduces (credits) its investment account. The investor closes a loss to Income Summary. For example assume that JVT had reported a loss of $15,000. The following entries would be made by Micron:

Dec. 31	Loss from Investment in JVT Common Shares	4,500	
	Investment in JVT		4,500
	To record 30% decrease in equity from investee's loss of $15,000.		

Assets = Liabilities + Equity
−4,500 −4,500

Dec. 31	Income Summary	4,500	
	Loss from Investment in JVT Common Shares		4,500
	To close the loss from investments to income summary.		

Assets = Liabilities + Equity
−4,500
+4,500

The receipt of cash dividends is not recorded as revenue when using the equity method. This is because the investor has already recorded its share of the earnings reported by the investee. Instead, dividends received from an investee convert the form of the investor's asset from a shares investment to cash. This means dividends reduce the balance of the investment account, but increase cash. To illustrate, JVT declared and paid $10,000 in cash dividends on its common shares. Micron's entry to record its 30% share of these dividends received on January 9, 1999 is:

Jan. 9	Cash	3,000	
	Investment in JVT Common Shares . .		3,000
	To record receipt of 30% of $10,000 dividend paid by JVT.		

Assets = Liabilities + Equity
+3,000
−3,000

The book value of an investment in equity securities when using the equity method is equal to the cost of the investment plus the investor's equity in the *undistributed* earnings of the investee. Once we record the above transactions for Micron, its investment account appears as in Exhibit 18.3.

Exhibit 18.3

Investment in JVT Common Shares Ledger Account

Date		Explanation	Debit	Credit	Balance
1998					
Jan.	1	Investment	70,650		70,650
Dec.	31	Share of earnings	6,000		76,650
1999					
Jan.	9	Share of dividend		3,000	73,650

Micron's account balance on January 9, 1999, for the Investment in JVT is $73,650. This is the investment's cost *plus* Micron's equity in JVT's earnings since its purchase *less* Micron's equity in JVT's cash dividends since its purchase.

When an investment in equity securities is sold, the gain or loss is computed by comparing proceeds from the sale with the book value of the investment on the date of sale. If Micron sells its JVT shares for $80,000 on January 10, 1999, the entry to record the sale is:

Assets = Liabilities + Equity
+80,000 +6,350
−73,650

Jan. 10	Cash	80,000	
	Investment in JVT Common Shares . .		73,650
	Gain on Sale of Investments		6,350
	Sold 3,000 shares for $80,000		

In most cases shares are purchased at amounts greater than their net book value. If the acquisition cost is greater than the book value at the date of acquisition the investor must adjust the earnings recorded by amortizing the excess of cost over book value. This added complexity is discussed in detail in intermediate accounting texts.

Did You Know?

Tinseltown Securities

Did you ever wish you could share in the profits of Hollywood films like *Independence Day*, *The Lost World*, *Titanic*, or *Speed*? Well, you can now. Both **Fox** and **Universal Studios** are selling equity shares in their upcoming movies to outside investors. **Citicorp**, who is handling these shares, forecasts a minimum annualized rate of return of 15%. But the possibility of big hits is what is drawing many investors. [Source: *Business Week*, August 11, 1997.]

Investment in Equity Securities with Controlling Influence

LO 6 Describe how equity securities having controlling influence are reported.

A long-term investment in **equity securities with controlling influence** is defined as an investor who is able to exert a controlling influence over the investee. An investor who owns more than 50% of a company's voting shares is presumed to have a controlling influence over the investee. This investor can dominate all other shareholders in electing the corporation's board of directors. This investor usually has control over the investee corporation's management. The controlling corporation (investor) is known as the **parent company** and the company whose shares are held by the parent (investee) is referred to as a **subsidiary.**

Many large companies are parents with subsidiaries. For example, **George Weston Limited** is the parent of several subsidiaries, including **Loblaw, Neilson/Cadbury, Zehrmart, E.B. Eddy Paper,** and **National Grocers.**

When a corporation owns all the outstanding shares of a subsidiary, it can take over the subsidiary's asssets, cancel the subsidiary's shares, and merge the subsidiary into the parent company. However, there often are financial, legal, and tax advantages if a large business is operated as a parent corporation that controls one or more subsidiary corporations. In fact, many large companies are parent corporations that own one or more subsidiaries. A summary of accounting for equity investments by percent of ownership is provided in Exhibit 18.4.

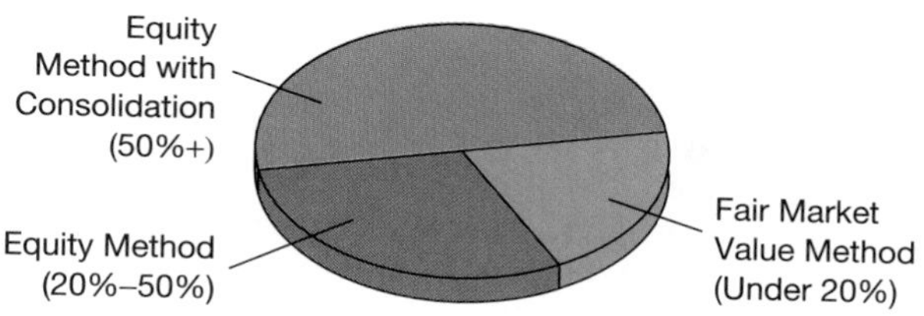

Exhibit 18.4

Accounting for Equity Investments by Percent of Ownership

When a business operates as a parent company with subsidiaries, separate accounting records are maintained by each corporation. From a legal viewpoint, the parent and each subsidiary are still separate entitites with all the rights, duties, and responsibilities of individual corporations. However, investors in the parent company indirectly are investors in the subsidiaries. To evaluate their investments, parent company investors must consider the financial status and operations of the subsidiaries as well as the parent. This information is provided in consolidated financial statements.

Consolidated financial statements show the financial position, results of operations, and cash flows of all companies under the parent's control, including all subsidiaries. These statements are prepared as if the company is organized as one entity. The parent uses the equity method in its accounts, but the investment account is *not* reported on the parent's financial statements. Instead, the individual assets and liabilities of the parent and its subsidiaries are combined on one balance sheet. Their revenues and expenses also are combined on one income statement and their cash flows are combined on one statement of changes in financial position. The detailed procedures for preparing consolidated financial statements are included in advanced courses. Some of the basics procedures however are provided in the appendix at the end of this chapter.

Flashback

3. What are the three classes of long-term equity investments? Describe the criteria for each class and the method used to account for each.

Answers—p. 848

Mid-Chapter Demonstration Problem

The following transactions relate to Brown Company's long-term investment activities during 19X1 and 19X2. Brown did not own any long-term investments prior to 19X1. Show the appropriate journal entries and the portions of each year's balance sheet and income statement that describe these transactions.

19X1

Sept.	9	Purchased 1,000 shares of **Packard, Inc.,** common shares for $80,000 cash. These shares represent 30% of Packard's outstanding shares.
Oct.	2	Purchased 2,000 shares of **MT&T** common shares for $60,000 cash. These shares represent less than a 1% ownership in MT&T.
	17	Purchased as a long-term investment 1,000 shares of **Four Seasons** common shares for $40,000 cash. These shares are less than 1% of Four Seasons's outstanding shares.
Nov.	1	Received $5,000 cash dividend from Packard.
	30	Received $3,000 cash dividend from MT&T.
Dec.	15	Received $1,400 cash dividend from Four Seasons.
	31	Packard's 19X1 net income was $70,000.
	31	Market values for the investments in equity securities are Packard, $84,000; MT&T, $48,000; and Four Seasons Hotels, $45,000.

19X2

Jan. 1 Packard, Inc., was taken over by other investors, and Brown sold its shares for $108,000 cash.

May 30 Received $3,100 cash dividend from MT&T.

June 15 Received $1,600 cash dividend from Four Seasons.

Aug. 17 Sold the MT&T shares for $52,000 cash.

19 Purchased 2,000 shares of **Loblaw** common shares for $50,000 as a long-term investment. The shares represent less than a 5% ownership in Loblaw.

Dec. 15 Received $1,800 cash dividend from Four Seasons.

31 Market values of the investments in marketable equity securities are Four Seasons, $39,000 and Loblaw, $48,000.

Planning the Solution

- Account for the investment in Packard under the equity method.
- Account for the investments in MT&T, Four Seasons, and Loblaw as long-term investments in securities.
- Prepare the information for the two balance sheets by including the appropriate assets and shareholders' equity accounts.

Solution to Mid-Chapter Demonstration Problem

Journal Entries during 19X1

Date	Account and Explanation	Debit	Credit
Sept. 9	Investment in Packard Common Shares . . .	80,000	
	Cash		80,000
	Acquired 1,000 shares representing a 30% equity in Packard, Inc.		
Oct. 2	Investment in MT&T Common Shares	60,000	
	Cash		60,000
	Acquired 2,000 shares as a long-term investment in securities available for sale.		
17	Investment in Four Seasons Common Shares	40,000	
	Cash		40,000
	Acquired 1,000 shares as a long-term investment in securities available for sale.		
Nov. 1	Cash	5,000	
	Investment in Packard Common Shares		5,000
	Received dividend from Packard, Inc.		
30	Cash	3,000	
	Dividends Earned		3,000
	Received dividend from MT&T		
Dec. 15	Cash	1,400	
	Dividends Earned		1,400
	Received dividend from Four Seasons.		
31	Investment in Packard Common Shares . . .	21,000	
	Earnings from Investment in Packard .		21,000
	To record our 30% share of Packard's annual earnings of $70,000		

Assets = Liabilities + Equity
+80,000
−80,000

Assets = Liabilities + Equity
+60,000
−60,000

Assets = Liabilities + Equity
+40,000
−40,000

Assets = Liabilities + Equity
+5,000
−5,000

Assets = Liabilities + Equity
+3,000 +3,000

Assets = Liabilities + Equity
+1,400 +1,400

Assets = Liabilities + Equity
+21,000 +21,000

	Cost	Fair (Market) Value
MT&T	$ 60,000	$ 48,000
Four Seasons	40,000	45,000
Total	$100,000	$ 93,000

Given the usual fluctuations in market prices, it is reasonable to assume that the reduction is temporary. Therefore, no adjustment is necessary.

December 31, 19X1, Balance Sheet Items

Assets		
Long-term investments:		
Equity securities, at cost (market value, $93,000)	$100,000	
Investment in Packard, Inc. (market value, $84,000)	96,000	
Total		$196,000

Income Statement Items for the Year Ended December 31, 19X1

Dividends earned	$ 4,400
Earnings from equity method investment	21,000

Journal Entries during 19X2

Date	Account	Debit	Credit	Assets = Liabilities + Equity
Jan. 1	Cash	108,000		Assets = Liabilities + Equity
	Investment in Packard Common Shares		96,000	+108,000 +12,000
	Gain on Sale of Investments		12,000	−96,000
	Sold 1,000 shares for cash.			
May 30	Cash	3,100		Assets = Liabilities + Equity
	Dividends Earned		3,100	+3,100 +3,100
	Received dividend from MT&T.			
June 15	Cash	1,600		Assets = Liabilities + Equity
	Dividends Earned		1,600	+1,600 +1,600
	Received dividend from Four Seasons.			
Aug. 17	Cash	52,000		Assets = Liabilities + Equity
	Loss on Sale of Investments	8,000		+52,000 −8,000
	Investment in MT&T Common Shares		60,000	+60,000
	Sold 2,000 shares for cash.			
19	Investment in Loblaw Common Shares	50,000		Assets = Liabilities + Equity
	Cash		50,000	+50,000
	Acquired 2,000 shares as a long-term investment in securities available for sale.			−50,000
Dec. 15	Cash	1,800		Assets = Liabilities + Equity
	Dividends Earned		1,800	+1,800 +1,800
	Received dividend from Four Seasons.			

	Cost	Fair (Market) Value
Four Seasons	$ 40,000	$ 39,000
Loblaw	50,000	48,000
Total	$ 90,000	$ 87,000

December 31, 19X2, Balance Sheet Items

Assets	
Long-term investments:	
Equity securities, at cost (market value, $87,000)	$90,000

Income Statement Items for the Year Ended December 31, 19X2

Dividends earned	$ 6,500
Gain on sale of investments	12,000
Loss on sale of investments	(8,000)

Investments in International Operations

Many companies from small entrepreneurs to large corporations conduct business internationally. The operations of some large corporations take place in so many different countries that they are called **multinationals.** Many of us, for example, think of **Alcan** and **Bombardier** as primarily Canadian companies. Yet both companies earn over three-quarters of their sales from outside Canada. Other corporations such as **Magna, McCain Foods, CAE Electronics,** and **Molson's** are major players in the world of international business.

Two major accounting challenges arise when companies have international operations. Both relate to transactions that occur using more than one currency. The two challenges can be described as (1) accounting for sales or purchases listed in a foreign currency and (2) preparing consolidated financial statements with international subsidiaries. For ease in discussion of these challenges, we use companies with a base of operations in Canada and with a need to prepare financial statements in Canadian dollars. This means the *reporting currency* of these companies is the Canadian dollar.

Exchange Rates between Currencies

LO 7 Explain foreign exchange rates between currencies.

Markets for the purchase and sale of foreign currencies exist all over the world. In these markets, Canadian dollars can be exchanged for U.S. dollars, British pounds, French francs, Japanese yen, or any other legal currencies. The price of one currency stated in terms of another currency is called a **foreign exchange rate.**

Exhibit 18.5 lists foreign exchange rates for selected currencies at April 13, 1998. We see the exchange rate for British pounds and Canadian dollars is $2.3839 on January 1, 1998. This rate means one British pound can be purchased for $2.3839. On the same day, the exchange rate between German marks and Canadian dollars is $0.7822. This rate means one German mark can be purchased for $0.7822. Foreign exchange rates fluctuate due to changing economic and political conditions. These include the supply and demand for currencies and expectations about future events.

Exhibit 18.5

Foreign Exchange Rates for Selected Currencies*

Country (unit)	Price in $Can.	Country (unit)	Price in $Can.
Britain (pound)	$ 2.3839	U.S. (dollar)	$ 1.4212
Germany (mark)	0.7822	France (franc)	0.2334
Mexico (peso)	0.1680	Japan (yen)	0.0195
Taiwan (dollar)	0.0433	Europe (ECU)	1.5524

*Rates for April 13, 1998, http://www.traveloco.com/index2.html?loco=/tools/currency

Did You Know?

Rush to Russia

In New York, London, Frankfurt, and Tokyo, investors are swarming to buy Russian equities even in the face of rampant crime, corruption, and slow economic growth. Why? Many argue Russia remains a bargain-priced, if risky, bet on future growth. They focus on Russia not only as a way to buy into natural-resource companies for a song, but also as a play on growth. Some analysts argue resource-rich Russia is one of the cheapest emerging markets.
[Source: *Business Week*, March 24, 1997.]

Sales or Purchases Listed in a Foreign Currency

LO 8 Record transactions listed in a foreign currency.

When a Canadian company makes a credit sale to an international customer, accounting for the sale and the account receivable requires special treatment when the terms of the sale require payment in a foreign currency.

Did You Know?

Greenback Effects

What do changes in foreign exchange rates mean? Exchange rate movements, particularly between the Canadian dollar and the U.S. dollar can have a major impact on the bottom line. For **Alcan** each US$0.01 permanent change in the value of the Canadian dollar has an after-tax impact of about $11 million on the company's long-term profitability. Alcan benefits from a weakening of the Canadian dollar but is disadvantaged by a strengthening of the Canadian dollar.
[Source: Alcan 1997 annual report.]

Consider the case of the Canadian-based manufacturer, **Quebec Company,** who makes credit sales to **London Outfitters,** a British retail company. A sale occurred on December 12, 1998, for a price of £10,000, payment due on February 10, 1999. Quebec Company keeps its accounting records in Canadian dollars. To record the sale, Canadian Company must translate the sales price from pounds to dollars. This is done using the exchange rate on the date of the sale. Assuming the exchange rate on December 12, 1998 is $2.36, Quebec records this sale as:

Dec. 12	Accounts Receivable — London Outfitters .	23,600	
	Sales (£10,000 × $2.36)		23,600
	To record a sale at £10,000, when the exchange rate equals $2.36.		

Assets = Liabilities + Equity
+23,600 +23,600

Quebec Company prepares its annual financial statements on December 31, 1998. On that date, the current exchange rate increases to $2.38. This means the current dollar value of Quebec Company's receivable is $23,800 (10,000 × $2.38). This amount is $200 greater than the amount recorded on December 12. Accepted accounting principles require a receivable to be reported in the balance sheet at its current dollar value. Quebec Company must make the following entry to record the increase in the dollar value of this receivable:

Dec. 31	Accounts Receivable—London Outfitters . .	200	
	Foreign Exchange Gain or Loss		200
	To record the increased value of the British pound on the receivable.		

Assets = Liabilities + Equity
+200 +200

Quebec Company receives London Outfitters' payment of £10,000 on February 10, 1999. Quebec Company immediately exchanges the pounds for Canadian dollars. On this date, the exchange rate for pounds is \$2.35. This means Quebec Company receives only \$23,500 (10,000 × \$2.35). It records the cash receipt and the loss associated with the decline in the exchange rate as follows:

Assets	= Liabilities	+ Equity
+23,500		−300
−23,800		

Feb. 10	Cash	23,500	
	Foreign Exchange Gain or Loss	300	
	Accounts Receivable — London Outfitters		23,800
	Received foreign currency payment of an account and converted it into dollars.		

Gains and losses from foreign exchange transactions are accumulated in the Foreign Exchange Gain or Loss account. After year-end adjustments, the balance in the Foreign Exchange Gain or Loss account is reported on the income statement and closed to the Income Summary account.

Accounting for credit purchases from an international supplier is similar to the case of a credit sale to an international customer. In particular, if the Canadian company is required to make payment in a foreign currency, the account payable must be translated into dollars before the Canadian company can record it. If the exchange rate is different when preparing financial statements and when paying for the purchase, the Canadian company must recognize an exchange gain or loss at those dates.

You Make the Call

Home Builder

You are a Canadian home builder who regularly purchases lumber from mills in both the U.S. and Canada. Lumber prices have been similar across both countries. But today the price of the Canadian dollar in terms of the U.S. dollar jumped from U.S.\$0.70 to U.S.\$0.80. Are you now more or less likely to buy lumber from Canadian or U.S. mills?

Answer—p. 847

Consolidated Statements with International Subsidiaries

A second challenge in accounting for international operations involves preparing consolidated financial statements when the parent company has one or more international subsidiaries. Consider the Canadian-based company, **Classic Winery,** which owns a controlling interest in a French subsidiary. The reporting currency of the Canadian parent is the dollar. The French subsidiary maintains its financial records in francs. Before preparing consolidated statements, the parent must translate financial statements of the French company into Canadian dollars. After this translation is complete, we prepare consolidated statements the same as with domestic subsidiaries.[6]

Procedures for translating an international subsidiary's account balances depend on the nature of the subsidiary's operations. The process requires the parent company to select appropriate foreign exchange rates and to apply those rates to the account balances of the foreign subsidiary. This concept is introduced; however, it is beyond the scope of first year accounting.

[6] The problem is more challenging when the accounts of the French subsidiary are maintained in accordance with the French version of GAAP. The French statements then must be converted to Canadian GAAP before consolidation.

Flashback

4. If a Canadian company makes a credit sale of merchandise to a French customer and the sales terms require payment in francs:
   a. The Canadian company incurs an exchange loss if the foreign exchange rate between francs and dollars increases from $0.234 at the date of sale to $0.239 at the date the account is settled.
   b. The French company may eventually need to record an exchange gain or loss.
   c. The Canadian company may be required to record an exchange gain or loss on the date of the sale.

Answer—p. 848

Components of Return on Total Assets

USING THE INFORMATION

LO 9 Compute and analyze the components of return on total assets.

Chapter 1 described a company's *return on total assets* (or simply *return on assets*) and explained its importance in assessing financial performance. The **return on total assets** can be separated into two components to help us in this analysis. The two components are: net profit margin and total asset turnover. Net profit margin was explained in Chapter 4 and total asset turnover in Chapter 13. Exhibit 18.6 shows how these two components determine return on total assets.

Exhibit 18.6

Components of Return on Total Assets

Return on Total Assets	=	Profit Margin	×	Total Asset Turnover
$\frac{\text{Net Income}}{\text{Average Total Assets}}$	=	$\frac{\text{Net Income}}{\text{Net Sales}}$	×	$\frac{\text{Net Sales}}{\text{Average Total Assets}}$

Net profit margin (net income / net sales) is the first component and reflects the percent of net income in each dollar of net sales. Total asset turnover (net sales / average total assets) is the second component and reflects a company's ability to produce net sales from total assets. All companies desire a high return on total assets. By looking at these two components, we can often discover strengths and weaknesses not revealed by return on total assets. This improves our ability to assess future performance and company strategy.

To illustrate, we look at return on total assets and its components for **Reebok** and **NIKE**. Reebok's return on total assets and its components are shown in Exhibit 18.7.

Exhibit 18.7

Reebok's Components of Return on Total Assets

Year	Return on Total Assets	=	Profit Margin	×	Total Asset Turnover
1996	8.08%	=	3.99%	×	2.02
1995	9.98%	=	4.73%	×	2.11
1994	16.74%	=	7.76%	×	2.16

At least three results emerge. First, Reebok's return on total assets declines from 1994 through 1996. Second, total asset turnover also declines over this period, but not significantly. And third, Reebok's net profit margin sharply falls between 1994 and 1996. These components show the dual role of net profit margin and total asset turnover for Reebok. More important, it shows the cause of Reebok's decline is not total asset turnover, but net profit margin. Reebok's costs and expenses have increased as a percent of sales, and cost management is necessary.

Generally, if a company is to maintain its return on total assets, then a decline in either profit margin or total asset turnover must be met with an increase in the other. If not, then return on assets will decline. Companies look at these components in planning future strategies. A component analysis can also reveal where a company is weak and where changes are needed.

We also look at these two components in comparing competitors. If asset turnover is lower than the industry norm, for instance, a company should focus on getting asset turnover at least up to the norm. The same applies to profit margin. Exhibit 18.8 shows NIKE's components for its fiscal year ending May 31, 1997.

Exhibit 18.8
NIKE's Components of Return on Total Assets

Fiscal Year	Return on Total Assets	=	Profit Margin	x	Total Asset Turnover
1997	17.09%	=	8.66%	x	1.97

NIKE's most recent return on total assets is much higher than Reebok's. But the components show Reebok is as good and slightly better than NIKE on total asset turnover. This highlights Reebok's sharp decline in net profit margin in recent years. One potential cause is Reebok's increased Cost of Goods Sold and Selling, General and Administrative Expenses as a percent of net sales. Reebok should focus on reducing these expenditures as a percent of sales.[7]

You Make the Call

Retailer
You are an entrepreneur and owner of a retail sporting goods store. The store's recent year's performance reveals (industry norms in parenthesis): return on total assets = 11% (11.2%); profit margin = 4.4% (3.5%); and total asset turnover = 2.5 (3.2). What does your analysis of these figures suggest?

Answer—p. 847

Summary

LO 1 Distinguish long-term investments from temporary investments. Temporary investments in securities are current assets that meet two criteria. First, they are expected to be converted into cash within one year or the current operating cycle of the business, whichever is longer. Second, they are readily converted to cash, sometimes called marketable. All other investments in securities are long-term investments. Long-term investments also include assets not used in operations and those held for a special purpose such as land for expansion.

LO 2 Identify classes of securities in long-term investments. Long-term investments in securities are classified into one of four groups: (a) debt securities held-to-maturity, (b) debt and equity securities available-for-sale, (c) equity securities where an investor has a significant influence over the investee, and (d) equity securities where an investor has a controlling influence over the investee.

LO 3 Account for debt securities held to maturity. Debt securities held-to-maturity are reported at cost when purchased. Interest revenue is recorded as it accrues. The cost of held-to-maturity securities is adjusted for amortization of any difference between cost and maturity value.

LO 4 Account for equity securities using the cost method. Debt and equity securities available-for-sale are recorded at cost when purchased. Available-for-sale securities are reported at their fair market values with unrealized holding gains or losses shown in the shareholders' equity section of

[7] Another base of comparison is to compute average figures for manufacturers of athletic footwear and apparel. Industry averages are available through publications such as Dun & Bradstreet's *Industry Norms and Key Ratios*.

the balance sheet. Gains and losses realized on the sale of these investments are reported in the income statement.

LO 5 **Account for equity securities having significant influence.** The equity method is used when an investor has a significant influence over an investee. This usually exists when an investor owns 20% or more of the investee's voting shares, but not exceeding 50% ownership. The equity method means an investor records its share of the investee's earnings with a debit to the investment account and a credit to a revenue account. Dividends received satisfy the investor's equity claims and reduce the investment account balance.

LO 6 **Describe how equity securities having controlling influence are reported.** If an investor owns more than 50% of another company's voting shares and controls the investee, the investor's financial reports are prepared on a consolidated basis. These reports are prepared as if the company is organized as one entity. The individual assets and liabilities of the parent and its subsidiaries are combined on one balance sheet. Similarly, their revenues and expenses are combined on one income statement and their cash flows are combined on one statement of changes in financial position.

LO 7 **Explain foreign exchange rates between currencies.** A foreign exchange rate is the price of one currency stated in terms of another. A company with transactions in a foreign currency when the exchange rate changes between the time of the transactions and its settlement will experience an exchange gain or loss.

LO 8 **Record transactions listed in a foreign currency.** When a company makes a credit sale to a foreign customer and sales terms call for payment in a foreign currency, the company must translate the foreign currency into dollars to record the receivable. If the exchange rate changes before payment is received, foreign exchange gains or losses are recognized in the year they occur. The same treatment is used when a company makes a credit purchase from a foreign supplier and is required to make payment in a foreign currency. Also, a company with a foreign subsidiary that maintains its accounts in a foreign currency must translate these account balances into dollars before they are consolidated with the parent's accounts.

LO 9 **Compute and analyze the components of return on total assets.** Return on total assets is made up of two components we can use to assess a company's ability in using its assets: net profit margin and total asset turnover. A decline in one component must be met with an increase in another if profits are to be maintained. The components are also helpful in assessing company performance compared to competitors. For instance, if one component is worse than the industry norm, then a company should focus on getting its performance on this component at least up to the industry norm.

Guidance Answers to **You Make the Call**

Money Manager

If you have investments in fixed-rate bonds and notes when interest rates fall, then the value of your investments increase. This is because the bonds and notes you hold continue to pay the same (high) rate while the market is demanding a new lower interest rate. Your strategy is to continue holding your investments in bonds and notes, and potentially to increase these holdings through additional purchases.

Home Builder

You are now more likely to buy Canadian lumber. This is because it takes more U.S. money to buy a Canadian dollar (and lumber). For instance, the purchase of lumber from a U.S. mill with a $1,000 (Canadian dollars) price cost the builder $700 (U.S. dollars, computed as C.$1,000 × U.S.$0.70) before the rate change and $800 (U.S. dollars, computed as C.$1,000 × U.S.$0.80) after the rate change.

Retailer

Your analysis of return on assets shows your store to be competitive. In particular, your store's return on assets is 11%, which is similar to the industry norm of 11.2%. However, disaggregation of return on assets reveals additional information. Your store's profit margin of 4.4% is much higher than the norm of 3.5%. But your total asset turnover of 2.5 is much lower than the norm of 3.2. These results suggest you are less efficient in using assets as compared with competitors. You need to focus on increasing sales or reducing your assets. You might wish to consider reducing prices to increase sales. You need to make sure such a strategy doesn't reduce your return on total assets. For instance, you could reduce your profit margin to 4% to increase sales. If total asset turnover increases to more than 2.75 when profit margin is lowered to 4%, then your return on total assets is improved.

Guidance Answers to Flash backs

1. Long-term investments include funds earmarked for a special purpose, bonds and shares that do not meet the test of a current asset, and other assets that are not used in the regular operations of the business.
2. A shares investment is classified as a long-term investment if it is not marketable or, if marketable, it is not held as an available source of cash to meet the needs of current operations.
3. Long-term equity investments are placed in one of the following three categories and accounted for using the method indicated:
   a. Available-for-sale (noninfluential, less than 20% of outstanding shares) — cost method.
   b. Significant influence (20% to 50% of outstanding shares) — equity method.
   c. Controlling influence (holding more than 50% of outstanding shares) — consolidation to report.
4. *a*

Demonstration Problem

Boudreau Co. is a Canadian corporation that has customers in several foreign countries. Following are some of Boudreau's 19X1 and 19X2 transactions:

19X1

Apr. 8 Sold merchandise to Lejeune Co. of France for 125,000 francs to be received in 60 days. The exchange rate for francs was $0.02822.

July 21 Sold merchandise for $8,880 cash to Vongurp Corp. of Germany. The exchange rate for marks was $0.5920 on this date.

Oct. 14 Received the Lejeune Company's payment for its purchase of Apr. 8 and exchanged the francs for dollars. The current foreign exchange rate for francs into dollars was $0.02840.

Nov. 18 Sold merchandise on credit to British Imports, Ltd., a company located in London, England. The price of 3,000 pounds was to be paid 90 days from the date of sale. On Nov. 18, the exchange rate for pounds into dollars was $1.7730.

Dec. 20 Sold merchandise for 350,000 yen to Yamoto Company of Japan;, payment in full to be received in 60 days. On this day, the foreign exchange rate for yen was $0.007710.

31 Prepared adjusting entries to recognize exchange gains or losses on the annual financial statements. Rates for exchanging foreign currencies on this day included the following:

Francs (Belgium)	$0.1335
Yen (Japan)	0.007897
Pounds (Britain)	1.7125
Marks (Germany)	0.5944

19X2

Jan. 12 Received full payment from British Imports, Ltd. for the sale of November 18 and immediately exchanged the pounds for dollars. The exchange rate for pounds was $1.7628.

19 Received Yamoto's full payment for the sale of December 20 and immediately exchanged the yen for dollars. The exchange rate for marks was $0.007779.

Required

1. Prepare general journal entries to account for these transactions on Boudreau's books.
2. Compute the foreign exchange gain or loss to be reported on Boudreau's 19X1 income statement.
3. What actions might Boudreau consider to reduce its risk of foreign exchange gains or losses?

Planning the Solution

- Account for each transaction.
- Calculate any foreign exchange gain or loss at year-end by multiplying the number of foreign currency units by the difference between the foreign exchange rate on the transaction date and the year-end foreign exchange rate.
- Calculate any foreign exchange rate on the date cash is received by multiplying the number of foreign currency units by the difference between the foreign exchange rate on the cash collection date and the foreign exchange rate at the previous year-end.

Solution to Demonstration Problem

Part 1.

19X1			
Apr. 8	Accounts receivable/Lejeune	3,527.50	
	Sales (125,000 × $0.02822)		3,527.50

July 21	Cash	8,880.00	
	Sales		8,880.00

Oct. 14	Cash (125,000 × $0.028400)	3,550.00	
	Foreign exchange gain or loss		22.50
	Accounts receivable — Lejeune		3,527.50

Nov. 18	Accounts Receivable		
	British Imports (1.773 × 3,000)	5,319.00	
	Sales		5,319.00

Dec. 20	Accounts Receivable — Yomoto	2,698.50	
	Sales (350,000 × $0.007710)		2,698.50
31	Foreign Exchange Gain or Loss	181.50	
	Accounts Receivable — British Imp. . .		181.50
	Original measure =		
	(3,000 × $1.773) = $5,319.00		
	Year-end measure =		
	(3,000 × $1.7125) = 5,137.50		
	Loss for the period = $181.50		
31	Accounts Receivable — Yomoto	65.45	
	Foreign Exchange Gain or Loss		65.45
	Original measure =		
	(350,000 × $0.007710) = $2,698.50		
	Year-end measure =		
	(350,000 × $0.007897) = 2,763.95		
	Gain for the period = $65.45		

19X2			
Jan. 12	Cash (3,000 × $1.7628)	5,288.40	
	Accounts Receivable — British Imp. ($5,319.00 − $155.00)		5,164.00
	Foreign Exchange Gain or Loss		124.40
19	Cash (350,000 × $0.007779)	2722.65	
	Foreign Exchange Gain or Loss	41.30	
	Accounts Receivable—Yomoto ($2,698.50 + $65.45)		2,763.95

Part 2. Foreign exchange loss to be reported on the 19X1 income statement:

October 14	$ 22.50
December 31	(181.50)
December 31	65.45
Total	$ (93.55)

Part 3. To reduce the risk of foreign exchange gain or loss, Boudreau could attempt to negotiate foreign customer sales that are denominated in Canadian dollars. To accomplish this, Boudreau may be willing to offer favourable terms, such as price discounts or longer credit terms. Another possibility that may be of limited potential is for Boudreau to make credit purchases denominated in foreign currencies, planning the purchases so that the payables in foreign currencies match the foreign currency receivables in time and amount.

Parent and Subsidiary Corporations

18A

APPENDIX

Learning Objectives

LO 10 Prepare consolidated balance sheets and explain how to report any excess of investment cost over book value or minority interests.

Corporations commonly own shares in and may even control other corporations. For example, if Par Company owns more than 50% of the voting shares of Sub Company, Par company can elect Sub Company's board of directors and thus control its activities and resources. In this case, the controlling corporation, Par Company, is known as the *parent company*, and Sub Company is called the *subsidiary*.

When a corporation owns all the outstanding shares of a subsidiary, it can take over the subsidiary's assets, cancel its shares, and merge the subsidiary into the parent company. However, instead of operating the business as a single corporation, there often are financial, legal, and tax advantages if a large business is operated as a parent corporation that controls one or more subsidiary corporations. Actually, most large companies are parent corporations that own one or more subsidiaries.

When a business is operated as a parent company with subsidiaries, separate accounting records are kept for each corporation. Also, from a legal viewpoint, the parent and each subsidiary are separate entities with all the rights, duties, and responsibilities of a separate corporation. However, investors in the parent company depend on the parent to present consolidated financial statements. Consolidated statements show the financial position and results of all operations under the parent's control, including those of any subsidiaries. These statements are prepared as if the business were organized as a single company. In other words, the assets and liabilities of all affiliated companies are combined on a single balance sheet. Also, their revenues and expenses are combined on a single income statement and their cash flows are combined on a single income statement and their cash flows are combined on a single statement of cash flows. The relationships between the consolidated entity and the separate parent and subsidiary corporations is shown in the top portion of Exhibit 18A.1.

Consolidated Balance Sheets

The bottom portion of Exhibit 18A.1 shows the process of preparing a consolidated balance sheet from the separate balance sheets of the parent and the subsidiary. When parent and subsidiary balance sheets are consolidated, duplications in items are eliminated so that the combined figures do not show more assets and equities than actually exist. For example, a parent's investment in a subsidiary is evidenced by shares that are carried as an asset in the parent company's records. However, these shares actually represent an equity in the subsidiary's assets. Therefore, if the parent's investment in a subsidiary and the subsidiary's assets were both shown on the consolidated balance sheet, the same resource would be counted twice. To prevent this, the parent's investment and the subsidiary's capital accounts are offset and eliminated in preparing a consolidated balance sheet.

Exhibit 18A.1

A Consolidated Entity's Relationship to the Parent and Subsidiary Corporations

Parent and subsidiary corporations

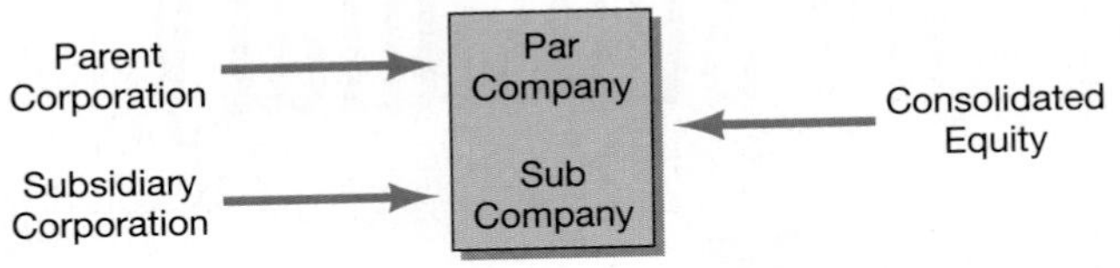

Consolidating the balance sheet of the parent and subsidiary corporations

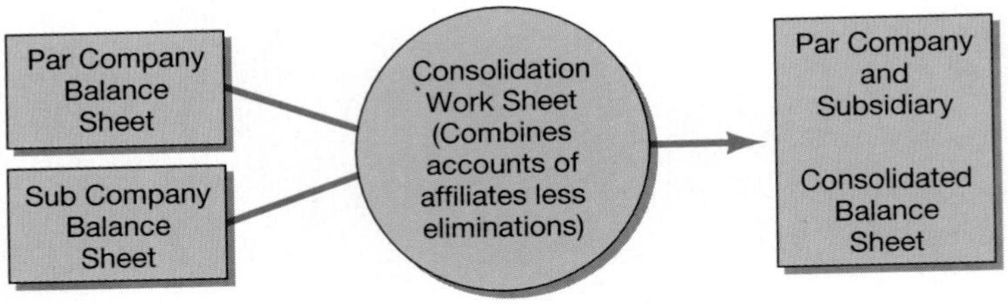

Likewise, a single enterprise cannot owe a debt to itself. This would be like a student who "borrows" $20 for a date from funds saved for next semester's expenses and who then prepares a balance sheet that shows the $20 as both a receivable from himself and a payable to himself. To prevent such double counting, intercompany debts and receivables are also eliminated in preparing a consolidated balance sheet.

Balance Sheets Consolidated at Time of Acquisition

When a parent's and a subsidiary's assets are combined in the preparation of a consolidated balance sheet, a work sheet normally is used to organize the data. For example, Exhibit 18A.2 shows a work sheet to consolidate the accounts of Par Company and its subsidiary called Sub Company. In the work sheet, the account balances are on December 31, 1998, which was the day Par Company acquired Sub Company. On that day, Par Company paid cash to purchase all of Sub Company's outstanding common shares. The shares had a book value of $115,000, or $11.50 per share, on the books of Sub Company. In this first illustration, we assume that Par Company paid $115,000, or book value, for the outstanding shares.

In Exhibit 18A.2, notice that the eliminations columns include two sets of debts and credits. One set is identified by the letter (a), and the other set is identified by the letter (b).

Elimination (a)

On the day it acquired Sub Company, Par Company loaned Sub Company $10,000 to use in the subsidiary's operations. In exchange for the cash, Sub Company signed a promissory note to Par Company. This intercompany debt was in reality a transfer of funds within the consolidated entity. Therefore, since it did not increase the total assets and total liabilities of the affiliated companies, elimination (a) prevents these balances from appearing on the consolidated balance sheet. To understand this elimination, recall that the subsidiary's promissory note appears as a $10,000 debit in Par Company's Notes Receivable account. Then, observe that the first credit in the Eliminations column exactly offsets or eliminates this item. Next, recall that the subsidiary's note appears as a credit in its Notes Payable account. In the Eliminations columns, the $10,000 debit completes the elimination of this intercompany debt.

Par Company and Sub Company Work Sheet for a Consolidated Balance Sheet December 31, 1998					
			Eliminations		
	Par Company	Sub Company	Debit	Credit	Consolidated Amount
Assets					
Cash	5,000	15,000			20,000
Notes receivable	10,000			(a) 10,000	
Investment in Sub Company	115,000			(b) 115,000	
Other assets	190,000	117,000			307,000
	320,000	132,000			327,000
Liabilities and Equities					
Accounts payable	15,000	7,000			22,000
Notes payable		10,000	(a) 10,000		
Common shares	250,000	100,000	(b) 100,000		250,000
Retained earnings	55,000	15,000	(b) 15,000		55,000
	320,000	132,000	125,000	125,000	327,000

Exhibit 18A.2

Consolidated Work Sheet for 100% Owned Subsidiary—Shares Purchased at Book Value

Elimination (b)

When a parent company buys a subsidiary's shares, the investment is recorded in the accounts of the parent as an asset. This investment represents an equity in the subsidiary's net assets. However, you must not show both the subsidiary's (net) assets and the parent company's investment in the subsidiary on a consolidated balance sheet. To do so would be to double count those resources. On the work sheet, the credit portion of elimination (b) prevents double counting of Sub company's net assets.

Also, shareholders' equity accounts represent the equity of outside parties that own the company's shares. But from a consolidated point of view, there are no outside parties that own the subsidiary's shares. Therefore, the shareholders' equity account balances of Sub Company should not appear on a consolidated balance sheet. On the work sheet, the debits of elimination (b) prevent Sub Company's shareholders' equity balances from appearing on the consolidated balance sheet.

After the intercompany items are eliminated on a work sheet as in Exhibit 18A.2, the assets of the parent and the subsidiary and the remaining equities in these assets are combined and carried into the work sheet's last column. The combined amounts are then used to prepare a consolidated balance sheet that shows all the assets and equities of the parent and its subsidiary.

Parent Company Does Not Buy All of Subsidiary's Shares and Pays More Than Book Values

In the above example, Par Company purchased all of its subsidiary's shares and paid book value for it. However, a parent company often purchases less than 100% of a subsidiary's shares and commonly pays a price that is either more or less than book value. To illustrate, assume Par Company purchased only 80% of Sub Company's outstanding shares. Also assume that Par company paid $13 per share, a price that was $1.50 more than the shares's book value.

These new assumptions result in a more complicated work sheet entry to eliminate the parent's investment and the subsidiary's shareholders' equity accounts. The entry is complicated by (1) the minority interest in the subsidiary and (2) the excess over book value paid by the parent company for the subsidiary's shares.

Minority Interest

When a parent buys a controlling interest in a subsidiary, the parent company is the subsidiary's majority shareholder. However, when the parent owns less than 100% of the subsidiary's shares, the subsidiary has other shareholders who own a **minority interest** in its assets and share in its earnings.

When you prepare a consolidated work sheet for a parent and a subsidiary that has a minority interest, the equity of the minority interest must be recognized. This is done in the process of eliminating the shareholders' equity balances of the subsidiary, as shown in Exhibit 18A.3. In this case, the minority shareholders have a 20% interest in the subsidiary. Therefore, on the work sheet, 20% of the subsidiary' shareholders' equity amounts [($100,000 + $15,000) × 20% = $23,000] is reclassified as the minority interest.

Exhibit 18A.3

Consolidated Work Sheet—80% of Subsidiary Shares Purchased at More Than Book Value

Par Company and Sub Company
Work Sheet for a Consolidated Balance Sheet
December 31, 1998

	Par Company	Sub Company	Eliminations Debit	Eliminations Credit	Consolidated Amount
Assets					
Cash	16,000	15,000			31,000
Notes receivable	10,000			(a) 10,000	
Investment in Sub Company	104,000			(b) 104,000	
Other assets	190,000	117,000			307,000
Excess of cost over book Value			(b) 12,000		12,000
	320,000	132,000			350,000
Liabilities and Equities					
Accounts payable	15,000	7,000			22,000
Notes payable		10,000	(a) 10,000		
Common shares	250,000	100,000	(b) 100,000		250,000
Retained earnings	55,000	15,000	(b) 15,000		55,000
Minority interest				(b) 23,000	23,000
	320,000	132,000	137,000	137,000	350,000

Excess of Investment Cost over Book Value

In Exhibit 18A.3, we assume that Par Company paid $13 per share for its 8,000 shares of Sub Company. Therefore, the cost of these shares exceeded their book value by $12,000, calculated as follows:

Cost of shares (8,000 shares at $13 per share)	$104,000
Book value (8,000 shares at $11.50 per share)	92,000
Excess of cost over book value	$ 12,000

Now observe how in the process of eliminating the parent's investment in the subsidiary, this excess of cost over book value is set out on the work sheet. Then, it is carried into the Consolidated Amounts columns as an asset.

After the work sheet of Exhibit 18A.3 was completed, the consolidated amounts in the last column were used to prepare the consolidated balance sheet of Exhibit 18A.4. Note the treatment of the minority interest in the balance sheet. The minority shareholders have a $23,000 equity in the consolidated assets of the affiliated companies. Some accountants argue that this item should be disclosed in the shareholders' equity section. Others believe it should be shown in the long-term liabilities section. However, the minority interest usually is shown as a separate item between the liabilities and shareholders' equity sections, as shown in Exhibit 18A.4.

Par Company and Subsidiary
Consolidated Balance Sheet
December 31,1998

Assets		
Cash		$ 31,000
Other assets		307,000
Goodwill from consolidation		12,000
Total assets		$ 350,000
Liabilities and Shareholders' Equity		
Liabilities:		
Accounts payable		$ 22,000
Minority interest		23,000
Shareholders' equity:		
Common shares	$250,000	
Retained earnings	55,000	
Total shareholders' equity		305,000
Total liabilities and shareholders' equity		$ 350,000

Exhibit 18A.4

Consolidated Balance Sheet of Par Company and Subsidiary

Next, observe that the $12,000 excess over book value that Par Company paid for Sub Company's shares appears on the consolidated balance sheet as an asset called "Goodwill from consolidation." There are several reasons why a parent might pay more than book value for its equity in a subsidiary. (1) One reason may be that certain of the subsidiary's assets are carried on the subsidiary's books at less than fair value. (2) Another reason may be that certain of the subsidiary's liabilities are carried at book values that are greater than fair values. (3) Also, the subsidiary's earnings prospects may be good enough to justify paying more than the net fair (market) value of its assets and liabilities. In this illustration, we assume that the book values of Sub Company's assets and liabilities are equal to their fair values. However, Sub Company's expected earnings justified paying $104,000 for an 80% equity in the subsidiary's net assets (assets less liabilities).

When a company pays more than book value because the subsidiary's assets are undervalued, the cost in excess of book value must be allocated to those assets and liabilities so that they are restated at fair values. After the subsidiary's assets and liabilities have been restated to reflect fair values, any remaining cost in excess of book value is reported on the consolidated balance sheet as "Goodwill from consolidation."

Occasionally, a parent company pays less than book value for its interest in a subsidiary. The probable reason for a price below book value is that some of the subsidiary's assets are carried on its books at amounts in excess of fair value. Therefore, the CICA ruled that the excess of book value over cost should be allocated to reduce the balance sheet valuations of the overvalued assets.

Earnings and Dividends of a Subsidiary

As you already learned, a parent uses the equity method in its books to account for its investment in a subsidiary. As a result, the parent's recorded net income and Retained Earnings account include the parent's equity in the net income earned by the subsidiary since the date of acquisition. Also, the balance of the parent's Investment in Subsidiary account increases (or decreases) each year by an amount equal to the parent's equity in the subsidiary's earnings (or loss) less the parent's share of any dividends paid by the subsidiary.

For example, assume that Sub Company earned $12,500 during 1999, its first year as a subsidiary, and at year-end paid out $7,500 in dividends. Par Company records its 80% equity in these earnings and dividends as follows:

Assets = Liabilities + Equity
+10,000 +10,000

Assets = Liabilities + Equity
+6,000
−6,000

Dec. 31	Investment in Sub Company	10,000	
	Earnings from Investment in Subsidiary		10,000
	To record 80% of the net income reported by Sub Company.		
31	Cash	6,000	
	Investment in Sub Company		6,000
	To record the receipt of 80% of the $7,500 Dividends paid by Sub Company.		

Consolidated Balance Sheets at a Date after Acquisition

Exhibit 18A.5 shows the December 31, 1999, work sheet to consolidate the balance sheets of Par Company and Sub Company. To simplify the illustration, it is assumed that Par Company had no transactions during the year other than to record its equity in Sub Company's earnings and dividends. Also, the other assets and liabilities of Sub Company did not change, and the subsidiary had not paid its note to Par Company.

Compare Exhibit 18A.5 with 18A.3 to see the changes in Par Company's balance sheet (the first column). Par Company's cash increased from $16,000 to $22,000 because of the dividends received from Sub Company. The Investment in Sub Company account increased from $104,000 to $108,000 as a result of the equity method entries during the year. Finally, Par Company's Retained Earnings increased by $10,000 which was the Parent's equity in the subsidiary's earnings.

Exhibit 18A.5

Work Sheet for a Consolidated Balance Sheet, One Year after Acquisition

Par Company and Sub Company
Work Sheet for a Consolidated Balance Sheet
December 31, 1999

	Par Company	Sub Company	Eliminations Debit	Eliminations Credit	Consolidated Amount
Assets					
Cash	22,000	20,000			42,000
Notes receivable	10,000			(a) 10,000	
Investment in Sub Company . . .	108,000			(b) 108,000	
Other assets	190,000	117,000			307,000
Excess of cost over book value . .			(b) 12,000		12,000
	330,000	137,000			361,000
Liabilities and Equities					
Accounts payable	15,000	7,000			22,000
Notes payable		10,000	(a) 10,000		
Common shares	250,000	100,000	(b) 100,000		250,000
Retained earnings	65,000	20,000	(b) 20,000		65,000
Minority interest				(b) 24,000	24,000
	330,000	137,000	142,000	142,000	361,000

In the second column of Exhibit 18A.5 note only two changes: (a) Sub Company's cash balance increased by $5,000, which is the difference between its $12,500 net income and $7,500 payment of dividends; and (2) retained earnings also increased from $15,000 to $20,000, which is explained by the $12,500 net income less $7,500 dividends. Note that the $20,000 balance is eliminated on the work sheet.

Two additional items need explanation. First, the minority interest set out on the December 31, 1999, work sheet (Exhibit 18A.3) is greater than on the December 31, 1998, work sheet. The minority shareholders have a 20% equity in Sub Company. So, the $24,000 shown on the December 31, 1999, work sheet is 20% of Sub Company's Common Shares and Retained Earnings balances on December 31, 1999. This $24,000 is $1,000 greater than the beginning-of-year minority interest because the subsidiary's retained earnings increased $5,000 during the year; the minority shareholder's share of this increase is 20%, or $1,000.

Second, the $12,000 excess cost over book value shown in Exhibit 18A.5 is unchanged from a year earlier. However, generally accounting principles require that this cost be amortized. The procedures of amortizing this cost are explained in a more advanced course.

Other Consolidated Statements

In addition to the balance sheet, the consolidated financial statements include a consolidated income statement, consolidated retained earnings statement, and consolidated statement of cash flows. However, you can have a general understanding of these statements without further discussion of the procedures to prepare them. At this point, you need only recognize that all duplications in items are eliminated. Also, when one affiliate records profit on sales to the other affiliate, the profit is eliminated in the consolidated statements. Finally, the amounts of net income and retained earnings that are reported in consolidated statements are equal to the amounts recorded by the parent under the equity method.

Summary of Appendix 18A

LO 10 **Prepare consolidated balance sheets and explain how to report any excess of investment cost over book value or minority interests.** Consolidated balance sheets are prepared by combining the accounts of the separate corporations as if they were a single entity. When the purchase price of a sub's identifiable assets exceed book values the book values should be revalued. Any remaining excess of the purchase price over the revalued net assets should be shown on the consolidated financial statements as goodwill. In combining these accounts the effects of intercompany transactions must be eliminated to avoid double counting. Since 100% of subsidiary net assets are reported on the consolidated balance sheet any claim not represented by the parent company is to be reported as minority interest.

Glossary

Consolidated financial statements Financial statements that show the results of all operations under the parent's control, including those of any subsidiaries; assets and liabilities of all affiliated companies are combined on a single balance sheet, revenues and expenses are combined on a single income statement, and cash flows are combined on a single statement of cash flows as though the business were in fact a single company. (p. 839)

Equity method An accounting method used for long-term investments when the investor has significant or controlling influence over the investee; the investment account is initially debited for cost and then is increased to reflect the investor's share of the investee's earnings and decreased to reflect the investor's receipt of dividends paid by the investee. (p. 837)

Equity securities with controlling influence The definition for a long-term investment when the investor is able to exert controlling influence over the investee; investors owning 50% or more of a company's voting shares are presumed to exert controlling influence over the investee. (p. 838)

Equity securities with significant influence The definition for a long-term investment when the investor is able to exert significant influence over the investee; usually investors owning 20% or more of a company's voting shares are presumed to exert significant influence over the investee. (p. 836)

Foreign exchange rate The price of one currency stated in terms of another currency. (p. 842)

Long-term investments Investments in shares and bonds that are not marketable or, if marketable, are not intended to be converted into cash in the short-term; also funds earmarked for a special purpose, such as bond sinking funds, and land or other assets not used in the company's operations. (p. 832)

Minority interest The portion of a subsidiary company's shareholders' equity that is not owned by the parent corporation. (p. 854)

Multinational business A company that operates in a large number of different countries. (p. 842)

Parent company A corporation that owns a controlling interest in another corporation (more than 50% of the voting shares is required). (p. 838)

Return on total assets A measure of a company's operating efficiency, computed by expressing net income as a percentage of average total assets. (p. 845)

Subsidiary A corporation that is controlled by another corporation (the parent) because the parent owns more than 50% of the subsidiary's voting shares. (p. 838)

A superscript letter A identifies assignment material based on Appendix 18A.

Questions

1. Under what conditions should investments be classified as current assets? As long-term assets?
2. Identify the classes for long-term investments.
3. On a balance sheet, what valuation must be reported for debt securities held to maturity? How is interest recognized on these securities?
4. In accounting for common shares investments, when should the equity method be used?
5. Under what circumstances would a company prepare consolidated financial statements?
6. Under what circumstances are long-term investments in debt securities reported at their original cost adjusted for amortization of any difference between cost and maturity value?
7. What are two basic problems of accounting for international operations?
8. If a Canadian company makes a credit sale to a foreign customer and the customer is required to make payment in Canadian dollars, can the Canadian company have an exchange gain or loss as a result of the sale?
9. A Canadian. company makes a credit sale to a foreign customer, and the customer is required to make payment in a foreign currency. The foreign exchange rate was $1.40 on the date of the sale and is $1.30 on the date the customer pays the receivable. Will the Canadian company record an exchange gain or an exchange loss?
10. Refer to the financial statements of **Alliance Company** in Appendix I. What percent of Alliance's other assets consists of long-term investments?
11. Refer to the 1997 financial statements of **Atlantis** in Appendix I. How much revenue is derived from non-Canadian sources?
12. In the chapter's opening scenario how does Brempong employ fundamental analysis of companies she invests in or makes recommendations on?

Quick Study

QS 18-1
Short and long-term investments
LO 1, 2, 6

Fill in the blanks.

1. Trading securities are classified as ____________________ assets.
2. Equity securities giving an investor significant influence are accounted for using the ______________ ________________.
3. Debt securities held to maturity are presented on the balance sheet at ______________ ______________ ______________.
4. Accrual of interest on bonds held as investments will require a credit to ___________ ___________.
5. The controlling investor is called the _____________ ____________ and the investee company is called the _______________.

QS 18-2
Distinguishing short and long-term investments
LO 1

Which of the following are true of long-term investments?

a. They are held as an investment of cash available for current operations.
b. They may include debt securities held-to-maturity.
c. They may include bonds and shares that are not intended to serve as a ready source of cash.
d. They may include funds earmarked for a special purpose, such as bond sinking funds.
e. They may include investments in trading securities.
f. They are easily sold and therefore qualify as being marketable.

QS 18-3
Debt securities
LO 3

On February 1, 19X1, Tom LeJeune purchased 6% bonds issued by Aberdeen Utilities Corp. at a cost of $30,000, which equals their par value. The bonds pay interest semiannually on July 31 and January 31. Prepare the entries to record the July 31 receipt of interest and the December 31 accrual.

QS 18-4
Equity securities
LO 4

On May 20, 19X1, Castle Co. paid $750,000 to acquire 25,000 (10%) of B&G Corp.'s outstanding common shares as a long-term investment. On August 5, 19X3, Castle sold half of the shares for $475,000. What method should be used to account for this shares investment? Prepare entries to record the acquisition and sale of the shares.

QS 18-5
Equity method
LO 5

Assume the same facts as in QS 18-4, except assume that the shares acquired represented 40% of B&G Corp.'s outstanding shares. Also assume that B&G Corp. paid a $125,000 dividend on November 1, 19X1, and reported a net income of $550,000 for 19X1. Prepare the entry to record the receipt of the dividend and the year-end adjustment of the investment account.

QS 18-6
Foreign currency transactions
LO 8

On March 1, 19X1, a Canadian company made a sale with credit terms requiring payment in 30 days to a German company, Bittner Corp. The amount of the sale was 20,000 marks. Assuming the exchange rate between German marks and Canadian dollars was $0.6811 on March 1 and $0.6985 on March 31, prepare the entries to record the sale and the cash receipt on March 31.

QS 18-7
Foreign currency transactions
LO 8

A Canadian company sells a British company a product with the transaction listed in British pounds. On the date of the sale the transaction of $16,000 was billed as 10,000 pounds, reflecting an exchange rate of 2.20 (that is, $2.20 per pound). Show the entry to record the sale and also the receipt of the payment when the exchange rate has fallen to 2.10.

QS 18-8
Return on total assets
LO 9

How is the return on total assets computed? What does this ratio evaluate?

QS 18-9
Disaggregated return on total assets
LO 9

State the formula to disaggregate the return on total assets. Explain how disaggregation of the return on total assets is useful to users of financial statements.

Exercises

Exercise 18-1
Transactions involving temporary and long-term investments
LO 1, 3, 4

Prepare general journal entries to record the following transactions involving the temporary and long-term investments of Morton Financial Corp., all of which occurred during 19X1. Use an account titled "Temporary Investments" for any transactions that you determine are short-term.

a. On February 15, paid $150,000 to purchase $150,000 of Canada General's 90-day short-term notes payable, which are dated February 15 and pay 10% interest.
b. On March 22, bought 700 shares of Royal Industries common shares at 25 1/2 plus a $250 brokerage fee.
c. On May 16, received a cheque from Canadian General in payment of the principal and 90 days' interest on the notes purchased in transaction *a*.
d. On July 30, paid $50,000 to purchase $50,000 of OMB Electronics' 8% notes payable, dated July 30, 19X1, and due January 30, 19X2.
e. On September 1, received a $0.50 per share cash dividend on the Royal Industries common shares purchased in transaction *b*.
f. On October 8, sold 350 shares of Royal Industries common shares for $32 per share, less a $175 brokerage fee.
g. On October 30, received a cheque from OMB Electronics for three months' interest on the notes purchased in transaction *d*.

Exercise 18-2
Classifying share investments
LO 2

During 19X1, GeoMass Company's investments in securities included five items. These securities, with their December 31, 19X1, market values, are as follows:

a. Weller Company bonds payable: $418,500 cost; $455,000 market value. GeoMass positively intends and is able to hold these bonds until they mature in 19X6.
b. BayShore common shares: 29,500 shares; $332,450 cost; $361,375 market value. GeoMass owns 32% of Bayshore's voting shares and has a significant influence over Bayshore.
c. Carrollton common shares: 12,000 shares; $169,750 cost; $183,000 market value. The goal of this investment, which amounts to 3% of Carrollton's outstanding shares, is to earn dividends over the next few years.
d. Zetech common shares: 18,000 shares; $95,300 cost; $93,625 market value. The goal of this investment is an expected increase in market value of the shares over the next three to five years. Zetech has 30,000 common shares outstanding.
e. Flavius common shares: 16,300 shares; $102,860 cost; $109,210 market value. These shares are marketable and are held as an investment of cash available for operations.

State whether each of these investments should be classified as a current asset or as a long-term investment. Also, for each of the long-term items, indicate in which of the four types of long-term investments the item should be classified. Assume that GeoMass had no long-term investments prior to 19X1. Show how the long-term investments would be reported in the year-end financial statements.

Exercise 18-3
Investments in securities
LO 3

Vallejo Services began operations in 19X1 and regularly makes long-term investments in securities. The total cost and fair value of these investments at the end of several years were:

	Cost	Market Value
On December 31, 19X1	$374,000	$362,560
On December 31, 19X2	426,900	453,200
On December 31, 19X3	580,700	686,450
On December 31, 19X4	875,500	778,800

Prepare journal entries to record the lower of cost or market of Vallejo's investments at the end of each year.

Exercise 18-4
Shares investment transactions; equity method
LO 5

Prepare general journal entries to record the following events on the books of Kedgewick Co.:

19X1

Jan. 2 Purchased 30,000 shares of Lintex Co. common shares for $204,000 plus a broker's fee of $3,480. Lintex has 90,000 shares of common shares outstanding and has acknowledged the fact that its policies will be significantly influenced by Kedgewick.

Sept. 1 Lintex declared and paid a cash dividend of $3.10 per share.

Dec. 31 Lintex announced that net income for the year amounted to $624,900.

19X2

June 1 Lintex declared and paid a cash dividend of $3.60 per share.

Dec. 31 Lintex announced that net income for the year amounted to $699,750.

31 Kedgewick sold 10,000 shares of Lintex for $162,500.

Exercise 18-5
Receivables listed in a foreign currency
LO 8

On May 8, 19X1, Laurier Company (a Canadian company) made a credit sale to Devereaux (a French company). The terms of the sale required Devereaux to pay 800,000 francs on February 10, 19X2. Laurier prepares quarterly financial statements on March 31, June 30, September 30, and December 31. The foreign exchange rates for francs during the time the receivable was outstanding were:

May 8, 19X1	$ 0.1984
June 30, 19X1	0.2013
September 30, 19X1	0.2029
December 31, 19X1	0.1996
February 10, 19X2	0.2047

Compute the foreign exchange gain or loss that Jefferson should report on each of its quarterly income statements during the last three quarters of 19X1 and the first quarter of 19X2. Also compute the amount that should be reported on Jefferson's balance sheets at the end of the last three quarters of 19X1.

Exercise 18-6
Foreign currency transactions
LO 8

Red Rover of Calgary sells its products to customers in Canada and in Great Britain. On December 16, 19X1, Red Rover sold merchandise on credit to Bronson Ltd. of London, England, at a price of 17,000 pounds. The exchange rate on that day for 1 pound was $2.1838. On December 31, 19X1, when Red Rover prepared its financial statements, the exchange rate was 1 pound for $2.0890. Bronson paid its bill in full on January 15, 19X2, at which time the exchange rate was 1 pound for $2.1656. Red Rover immediately exchanged the 17,000 pounds for Canadian dollars. Prepare journal entries on December 16, December 31, and January 15, to account for the sale and account receivable on Red Rover's books.

Exercise 18-7
Return on total assets
LO 9

The following information is available from the financial statements of Rawhide Industries:

	19X1	19X2	19X3
Total assets, December 31	$190,000	$320,000	$750,000
Net income	28,200	36,400	58,300

Compute Rawhide's return on total assets for 19X2 and 19X3. (Round answers to one decimal place.) Comment on the company's efficiency in using its assets in 19X2 and 19X3.

Problems

Problem 18-1
Entries for long-term investments
LO 4

Franklin Security, Inc., has relatively large idle cash balances and invests them in common shares that it holds as a long-term investment. Following is a series of events and other facts relevant to the long-term investment activity of the company:

19X1

Jan. 20 Purchased 900 shares of **Magna** Corporation at 18 3/4 plus a $590 commission.
Feb. 9 Purchased 2,200 shares of **Sony** Corp. at 46 7/8 plus a $2,578 commission.
June 12 Purchased 500 shares of **Corel**, Inc., at 55 1/2 plus an $832 commission.
Dec. 31 These per share market values were known for the shares in the portfolio: Magna Corporation, 20 3/8; Corel, 57 1/4; Sony, 39. The losses are not considered permanent.

19X2

Apr. 15 Sold 900 shares of Magna Corporation at 21 3/4 less a $685 commission.
July 5 Sold 500 shares of Corel at 49 1/8 less a $491 commission.
22 Purchased 1,600 shares of Microcel Corp. at 36 1/4 plus a $1,740 commission.
Aug. 19 Purchased 1,800 shares of Paragon Communications at 28 plus a $1,260 commission.
Dec. 31 These per share market values were known for the shares in the portfolio: **Paragon**, 31 3/4; **Microcel**, 30; **Sony**, 36 1/2.

19X3

Feb. 27 Purchased 3,400 shares of **Microsoft Corp.** at 23-5/8 plus a $1,606 commission.
June 21 Sold 2,200 shares of Sony at 40 less a $2,640 commission.
30 Purchased 1,200 shares of **Canadian Tire Corp.** at 47 1/2 plus a $1,995 commission.
Aug 3 Sold 1,600 shares of Microcel at 31 1/4 less a $1,750 commission.
Nov. 1 Sold 1,800 shares of Paragon at 42 3/4 less a $2,309 commission.
Dec. 31 These per share market values were known for the shares in the portfolio: Canadian Tire, 56 1/2; Microsoft, 28.

Required

1. Prepare journal entries to record each of the above transactions.

2. For each year, prepare a schedule that shows the realized gains and losses included in earnings and the total unrealized gain or loss at the end of each year. Are the unrealized gains and losses recorded?

Check Figure
Nov. 1/ 19X3
Gain on sale of investment, $22,981

Problem 18-2
Accounting for share investments
LO 5

Hammerman Steel Works was organized on January 4, 19X1. The following investment transactions and events subsequently occurred:

19X1

Jan. 5 Hammerman purchased 30,000 shares (20%) of Falcon International's outstanding common shares for $780,000.
Oct. 23 Falcon declared and paid a cash dividend of $1.60 per share.
Dec. 31 Falcon announced that its net income for 19X1 was $582,000. Market value of the shares was $27.75 per share.

19X2

Oct. 15 Falcon declared and paid a cash dividend of $1.30 per share.
Dec. 31 Falcon announced that its net income for 19X2 was $738,000. Market value of the shares was $30.45 per share.

19X3
Jan. 2 Hammerman sold all of its investment in Falcon for $947,000 cash.

Part 1. Assume that Hammerman has a significant influence over Falcon because it owns 20% of the shares.

Required

1. Give the entries to record the preceding events in Hammerman's books.
2. Compute the carrying value per share of Hammerman's investment as reflected in the investment account on January 1, 19X3.
3. Compute the change in Hammerman's equity from January 5, 19X1, through January 2, 19X3, resulting from its investment in Falcon.

Check Figure
Carrying value per share, $31.90

Part 2. Assume that even though Hammerman owns 20% of Falcon's outstanding shares, a thorough investigation of the surrounding circumstances indicates that it does not have a significant influence over the investee.

Required

1. Give the entries to record the preceding events in Hammerman's books.
2. Compute the cost per share of Hammerman's investment as reflected in the investment account on January 1, 19X3.
3. Compute the change in Hammerman's equity from January 5, 19X1, through January 2, 19X3, resulting from its investment in Falcon.

Problem 18-3
Accounting for long-term investments
LO 4

Decker Manufacturing Co.'s long-term investment portfolio at December 31, 19X1, consisted of the following:

Securities Available-for-Sale	Cost	Fair Market Value
80,000 shares of Company A common shares	$1,070,600	$980,000
14,000 shares of Company B common shares	318,750	308,000
35,000 shares of Company C common shares	1,325,500	1,281,875

Decker had the following long-term investment transactions during 19X2:

Jan. 29 Sold 7,000 shares of Company B common shares for $158,375 less a brokerage fee of $3,100.
Apr. 17 Purchased 20,000 shares of Company W common shares for $395,000 plus a brokerage fee of $6,800. The shares represent a 30% ownership in Company W.
July 6 Purchased 9,000 shares of Company X common shares for $253,125 plus a brokerage fee of $3,500. The shares represent a 10% ownership in Company X.
Aug. 22 Purchased 100,000 shares of Company Y common shares for $750,000 plus a brokerage fee of $8,200. The shares represent a 45% ownership in Company Y.
Nov. 13 Purchased 17,000 shares of Company Z common shares for $533,800 plus a brokerage fee of $6,900. The shares represent a 5% ownership in Company Z.
Dec. 9 Sold 80,000 shares of Company A common shares for $1,030,000 less a brokerage fee of $8,200.
Dec. 31 Company W anounced a net loss of $15,000 and Company Y announced a net loss of $15,000.

The fair (market) values of Decker's investments at December 31, 19X2, are: B, $162,750; C, $1,220,625; W, $382,500; X, $236,250; Y, $562,500; Z, $557,600.

Required

1. Determine what amount should be reported on Decker's December 31, 19X2, balance sheet for its investments in equity securities.
2. What amount of gain or loss on those transactions relating to these securities should be reported on Decker's December 31, 19X2, income statement?

Check Figure
(2) Realized holding loss, ($52,900)

Problem 18-4
Foreign currency transactions
LO 8

Savannah Co. is a Canadian corporation that has customers in several foreign countries. Following are some of Savannah's 19X1 and 19X2 transactions:

19X1

Apr. 8 Sold merchandise to Salinas & Sons of Mexico for $7,938 cash. The exchange rate for pesos was $0.1323.

July 21 Sold merchandise on credit to Sumitomo Corp. located in Japan. The price of 1.5 million yen was to be paid 120 days from the date of sale. The exchange rate for yen was $0.009646 on this date.

Oct. 14 Sold merchandise for 19,000 pounds to Smithers Ltd. of Great Britain, payment in full to be received in 90 days. The exchange rate for pounds was $1.5181.

Nov. 18 Received Sumitomo's payment for its purchase of July 21, and exchanged the yen for dollars. The current foreign exchange rate for yen was $0.009575.

Dec. 20 Sold merchandise for 17,000 marks to Schmidt Haus of Germany, payment in full to be received in 30 days. On this day, the foreign exchange rate for marks was $0.6852.

31 Prepared adjusting entries to recognize exchange gains or losses on the annual financial statements. Rates for exchanging foreign currencies on this day included the following:

Pesos (Mexico)	$0.1335
Yen (Japan)	0.009551
Pounds (Britain)	1.5235
Marks (Germany)	0.6807

19X2

Jan. 12 Received full payment from Smithers for the sale of October 14 and immediately exchanged the pounds for dollars. The exchange rate for pounds was $1.5314.

19 Received Schmidt Haus's full payment for the sale of December 20 and immediately exchanged the marks for dollars. The exchange rate for marks was $0.6771.

Required

Preparation component:

1. Prepare general journal entries to account for these transactions on Savannah's books.
2. Compute the foreign exchange gain or loss to be reported on Savannah's 19X1 income statement.

Analysis component:

3. What actions might Savannah consider to reduce its risk of foreign exchange gains or losses?

Problem 18-5A
Consolidated statements, at acquisition and one year later
LO 4

On January 1, 1998, Northwood Company purchased 80% of Souther Company's outstanding shares at $48 per share. On that date, Northwood Company had retained earnings of $517,500. Souther Company had retained earnings of $135,000 and had 15,000 shares outstanding.

Part 1.

Required

1. Give the elimination entry to be used on a work sheet for a consolidated balance sheet dated January 1, 1998.
2. Determine the amount of consolidated retained earnings that should be shown on a consolidated balance sheet dated January 1, 1998.

Part 2. During the year December 31, 1998, Northwood Company paid cash dividends of $67,500 and earned net income of $127,500 excluding earnings from its investment in Souther Company. Souther Company earned net income of $63,000 and paid dividends of $30,000. Except for Northwood Company's Retained Earnings account and the Investment in Souther Company account, the balance sheet accounts for the two companies on December 31, 1998, are as follows:

Assets	Northwood Company	Souther Company
Cash	$157,800	$124,200
Notes receivable	54,000	
Merchandise	367,200	178,200
Building, net	348,000	216,000
Land	210,000	189,000
Investment in Souther Company	?	
Total assets	$?	$707,400
Liabilities and Shareholders' Equity		
Accounts payable	$439,500	$260,400
Note payable		54,000
Common shares	672,000	225,000
Retained earnings	?	168,000
Total liabilities and shareholders' equity	$?	$707,400

Northwood Company loaned $54,000 to Souther Company during 1998 for which Souther Company signed a note. On December 31, 1998, the note had not been repaid.

Required

1. Calculate the December 31, 1998, balances in Northwood Company's Investment in Souther Company account and Retained Earnings account.
2. Complete a work sheet to consolidate the balance sheets of the two companies.

Problem 18-6A
Consolidated work sheet and balance sheet

LO 4

The following items appeared in the first columns of a work sheet prepared to consolidate the balance sheets of Upper Company and Lower Company on the day Upper Company gained control of Lower Company by purchasing 6,375 of its common shares at $65 per share. Lower Company has a total of 7,500 shares outstanding.

Assets	Upper Company	Lower Company
Cash	$ 28,125	$ 41,250
Note receivable, Lower Company	37,500	
Accounts receivable, net	105,000	90,000
Inventories	157,500	131,250
Investment in Lower Company	414,375	
Equipment, net	300,000	262,500
Buildings, net	318,750	
Land	75,000	
Total assets	$1,436,250	$525,000
Liabilities and Shareholders' Equity		
Accounts payable	$ 78,750	$ 37,500
Note payable, Upper Company		37,500
Common shares	937,500	375,000
Retained earnings	420,000	75,000
Total liabilities and shareholders' equity	$1,436,250	$525,000

At the time Upper Company acquired control of Lower Company, it took Lower Company's note in exchange for $37,500 in cash, and it sold and delivered $7,500 of equipment at cost to Lower Company on open account (account receivable). Both transactions are reflected in the foregoing accounts.

Required

1. Prepare a work sheet to consolidate the balance sheets of the two companies and prepare a consolidated balance sheet.
2. Under the assumption that Lower Company earned $37,500 during the first year after it was acquired by Upper Company, paid out $22,500 in dividends, and retained the balance of its earnings in its operations, give the entry to eliminate Upper Company's investment in the subsidiary and Lower Company's shareholders' equity accounts at the year's end

Alternate Problems

Problem 18-1A
Entries for long-term investments

LO 4

Dayton Enterprises has idle cash balances and invests them in common shares of Canadian and foreign companies as a long-term investment. Following is a series of events and other facts relevant to the long-term investment activity of the company:

19X1

Mar. 10 Purchased 2,400 shares of **Four Seasons Hotels**, at $33 1/4 plus $1,995 commission.
Apr 7 Purchased 5,000 shares of **Royal Bank** at $17 1/2 plus $2,625 commission.
Sept. 1 Purchased 1,200 shares of **Polaroid Corp.** at $49 plus $1,176 commission
Dec. 31 These per share market values were known for the shares in the portfolio: Four Seasons, $35 1/2; Royal Bank, $17; Polaroid, $51 3/4.

19X2

Apr. 26 Sold 5,000 shares of Royal Bank at $16 3/8 less $2,237 commission.
June 2 Purchased 3,600 shares of **Duracell Int'l, Inc.,** at $18 7/8 plus $2,312 commission.
14 Purchased 900 shares of **Sears Canada Inc.** at 24 1/2 plus $541 commission.
Nov. 27 Sold 1,200 shares of Polaroid at $52 less $1,672 commission.
Dec. 31 These per share market values were known for the shares in the portfolio: Four Seasons, $36 1/4; **Duracell**, $18 1/8; Sears, $26.

19X3

Jan. 28 Purchased 2,000 shares of **Loblaw Co.** at $41 plus $3,280 commission.
Aug. 22 Sold 2,400 shares of Four Seasons at $29 3/4 less $2,339 commission.
Sept. 3 Purchased 1,500 shares of **Motorola, Inc.,** at $29 plus $870 commission.
Oct. 9 Sold 900 shares of Sears at $27 1/2 less $619 commission.
31 Sold 3,600 shares of Duracell at $16 5/8 less $1,496 commission
Dec. 31 These per share market values were known for the shares in the portfolio: Loblaw, $46 7/8; Motorola, $22 1/2.

Required

1. Prepare journal entries to record the events and any year-end adjustments needed to record the fair values of the long-term investments.
2. For each year, prepare a schedule that shows the realized gains and losses included in earnings and the total unrealized gain or loss at the end of each year. Are the unrealized gains and losses recorded?

Problem 18-2A
Accounting for share investments

LO 5

Main Street Company was organized on January 3, 19X1. The following investment transactions and events subsequently occurred:

19X1

Jan. 5 Main Street purchased 15,000 shares (25%) of Cornerstone Industries's outstanding common shares for $187,500.
Aug. 1 Cornerstone declared and paid a cash dividend of $0.95 per share.
Dec. 31 Cornerstone announced that its net income for 19X1 was $92,000. Market value of the shares was $12.90 per share.

19X2

Aug. 1 Cornerstone declared and paid a cash dividend of $1.25 per share.
Dec. 31 Cornerstone announced that its net income for 19X2 was $76,000. Market value of the shares was $13.55 per share.

19X3

Jan. 8 Main Street sold all of its investment in Cornerstone for $204,750 cash.

Part 1. Assume that Main Street has a significant influence over Cornerstone because it owns 25% of the shares.

Required

1. Give the entries to record the preceding events in Main Street's books.
2. Compute the carrying value per share of Main Street's investment as reflected in the investment account on January 7, 19X3
3. Compute the change in Main Street's equity from January 5, 19X1, through January 8, 19X3, resulting from its investment in Cornerstone.

Part 2. Assume that even though Main Street owns 25% of Cornerstone's outstanding shares, a thorough investigation of the surrounding circumstances indicates that it does not have a significant influence over the investee.

Required

1. Give the entries to record the preceding events in Main Street's books.
2. Compute the cost per share of Main Street's investment as reflected in the investment account on January 7, 19X3.
3. Compute the change in Main Street's equity from January 5, 19X1, through January 8, 19X3, resulting from its investment in Cornerstone.

Problem 18-3A
Accounting for long-term investments

LO 4

Certifax Co.'s long-term investment portfolio at December 31, 19X1, consisted of the following:

Securities Available-for-Sale	Cost	Fair (Market) Value
45,000 shares of Company R common shares	$1,118,250	$1,198,125
17,000 shares of Company S common shares	616,760	586,500
22,000 shares of Company T common shares	294,470	303,600

Certifax had the following long-term investment transactions during 19X2:

Jan. 13 Sold 4,250 shares of Company S common shares for $144,500 less a brokerage fee of $2,390.
Mar. 24 Purchased 31,000 shares of Company U common shares for $565,750 plus a brokerage fee of $9,900. The shares represent a 62% ownership in Company U.
Apr. 5 Purchased 85,000 shares of Company V common shares for $267,750 plus a brokerage fee of $4,500. The shares represent a 10% ownership in Company V.
Sept. 2 Sold 22,000 shares of Company T common shares for $313,500 less a brokerage fee of $5,400.
27 Purchased 5,000 shares of Company W common shares for $101,000 plus a brokerage fee of $2,100. The shares represent a 25% ownership in Company W.
Oct. 30 Purchased 10,000 shares of Company X common shares for $97,500 plus a brokerage fee of $2,340. The shares represent a 13% ownership in Company X.

The fair (market) values of Certifax's investments at December 31, 19X2, are: R, $1,136,250; S, $420,750; U, $545,600; V, $269,875; W, $109,375; X, 91,250.

Required

1. Determine what amount should be reported on Certifax's December 31, 19X2, balance sheet for its investments in equity securities.
2. Prepare a December 31, 19X2, adjusting entry, if necessary, to record the fair value adjustment of the long-term investments in securities available for sale.
3. What amount of gain or loss on those transactions relating to securities should be reported on Certifax's December 31, 19X2, income statement?

Problem 18-4A
Foreign currency transactions
LO 8

C. D. Howe Co. is a Canadian corporation that has customers in several foreign countries. Following are some of C. D. Howe's 19X1 and 19X2 transactions:

19X1

May 26 Sold merchandise for 6.5 million yen to Fuji Company of Japan, payment in full to be received in 60 days. On this day, the foreign exchange rate for yen was $0.009412.

June 1 Sold merchandise to Fordham Ltd. of Great Britain for $72,613 cash. The foreign exchange rate for pounds was $1.5277.

July 25 Received Fuji's payment for its purchase of May 26, and exchanged the yen for dollars. The current exchange rate for yen was $0.009368.

Oct. 15 Sold merchandise on credit to Martinez Brothers of Mexico. The price of 373,000 pesos was to be paid 90 days from the date of sale. On this date, the foreign exchange rate for pesos was $0.1341.

Dec. 6 Sold merchandise for 242,000 francs to LeFevre Company of France, payment in full to be received in 30 days. The exchange rate for francs was $0.1974.

31 Prepared adjusting entries to recognize exchange gains or losses on the annual financial statements. Rates of exchanging foreign currencies on this day included the following:

Yen (Japan)	$0.009447
Pounds (Britain)	1.5318
Pesos (Mexico)	0.1562
Francs (France)	0.1998

19X2

Jan. 5 Received LeFevre's full payment for the sale of December 6, and immediately exchanged the francs for dollars. The exchange rate for francs was $0.2063.

13 Received full payment from Martinez Brothers for the sale of October 15, and immediately exchanged the pesos for dollars. The exchange rate for pesos was $0.1419.

Required

Preparation component:

1. Prepare general journal entries to account for these transactions on C. D. Howe's books.
2. Compute the foreign exchange gain or loss to be reported on C. D. Howe's 19X1 income statement.

Analysis component:

3. What actions might C. D. Howe consider to reduce its risk of foreign exchange gains or losses?

Problem 18-5A[A]
Consolidated statements, at acquisition and one year later
LO 4

On January 1, 1998, Larger Company purchased 90% of Smaller Company's outstanding shares at $24 per share. On that date, Larger Company had retained earnings of $350,500. Smaller Company had retained earnings of $225,000 and had outstanding 20,000 common shares issued at $10 per share.

Part 1.

Required

1. Give the elimination entry to be used on a work sheet for a consolidated balance sheet dated January 1, 1998.
2. Determine the amount of consolidated retained earnings that should be shown on a consolidated balance sheet dated January 1, 1998.

Part 2. During the year ended December 31, 1998, Larger Company paid cash dividends of $45,000 and earned net income of $90,000 excluding earnings from its investment in Smaller Company. Smaller Company earned net income of $45,000 and paid dividends of

$25,000. Except for Larger Company's Retained Earnings account and the Investment in Smaller Company account, the balance sheet accounts for the two companies on December 31, 1998, are as follows:

Assets	Larger Company	Smaller Company
Cash	$140,200	$106,800
Notes receivable	45,000	
Merchandise	220,800	175,300
Building, net	284,250	240,000
Land	186,000	183,500
Investment in Smaller Company	?	
Total assets	$?	$705,600
Liabilities and Shareholders' Equity		
Accounts payable	$215,250	$215,600
Note payable		45,000
Common shares	675,000	200,000
Retained earnings	?	245,000
Total liabilities and shareholders' equity	$?	$705,600

Larger Company loaned $45,000 to Smaller Company during 1998, for which Smaller Company signed a note. On December 31, 1998, the note had not been repaid.

Required

1. Calculate the December 31, 1998, balances in Larger Company's Investment in Smaller Company account and Retained Earnings account.
2. Complete a work sheet to consolidate the balance sheets of the two companies.

Problem 18-6A[A]
Consolidated work sheet and balance sheet
LO 4

The following items appeared in the first two columns of a work sheet prepared to consolidate the balance sheets of Parent Company and Subsidiary Company on the day Parent Company gained control of Subsidiary Company by purchasing 29,750 shares of its common stock at $13 per share. Subsidiary Company has a total of 35,000 common shares outstanding.

Assets	Parent Company	Subsidiary Company
Cash	$ 37,250	$ 72,500
Note receivable, Subsidiary Company	54,000	
Accounts receivable, net	110,000	80,000
Inventories	215,000	162,500
Investment in Subsidiary Company	386,750	
Equipment, net	461,250	257,500
Buildings, net	337,500	
Land	150,000	
Total assets	$1,751,750	$572,500
Liabilities and Shareholders' Equity		
Accounts payable	$ 257,500	$ 98,500
Note payable, Parent Company		54,000
Common shares	875,000	350,000
Retained earnings	619,250	70,000
Total liabilities and shareholders' equity	$1,751,750	$572,500

At the time Parent Company acquired control of Subsidiary Company, it took Subsidiary Company's note in exchange for $54,000 in cash, and it sold and delivered $3,000 of equipment at cost to Subsidiary Company on open account (account receivable). Both transactions are reflected in the foregoing accounts.

Required

1. Prepare a work sheet to consolidate the balance sheets of the two companies and prepare a consolidated balance sheet.
2. Under the assumption that Subsidiary Company earned $50,000 during the first year after it was acquired by Parent Company, paid out $32,500 in dividends, and retained the balance of its earnings in its operations, give the entry to eliminate Parent Company's investment in the subsidiary and Subsidiary Company's shareholders' equity accounts at the year's end.

Analytical and Review Problems

A & R Problem 18-1

On January 1, 1997, Tony Company purchases 40% of Danny Company's outstanding voting shares. On December 31, 1998, Tony Company's account Investment in Danny Company showed a balance of $400,000. Danny Company reported the following information for the years of 1997 and 1998:

	Net Income	Dividends Paid
1997	$150,000	$50,000
1998	200,000	50,000

Required

Calculate the purchase price paid by Tony Company for the Danny Company shares.

A & R Problem 18-2

The following is an excerpt from the notes to the financial statements if **ABC Sciences Ltd.:**

> ABC Sciences holds a 35.4% interest in Halifax-based Eastern Laboratories which develops, manufactures, and distributes chemicals solely in the Canadian market. ABC Sciences accounts for its investment in Eastern Chemicals by the equity method. During 1998, Eastern had a strong year, with revenues increasing 79.6% while net income more than doubled to $7.6 million. ABC Science's share of this net income was . . .

Required

1. Is ABC Sciences using the cost or equity method to account for its investment in Eastern Chemicals? Support your answer.
2. Prepare the journal entry to record ABC Sciences's share of Eastern's net income.
3. If Eastern paid out 50% of its 1998 net income as cash dividends, what entry would ABC Sciences make to record the receipt of cash?

BEYOND THE NUMBERS

Reporting in Action

LO 7, 10

Refer to the financial statements and related information for **Alliance** in Appendix I. Answer the following questions by analyzing the information in Alliance's report:

1. Are Alliance's financial statements consolidated? How can you tell?
2. Does Alliance have more than one subsidiary? How can you tell?
3. Does Alliance have any foreign operations? How can you tell?
4. Is there a foreign exchange gain or loss on the income statement (consolidated statement of operations)? Describe what you find or do not find.
5. Compute Alliance's return on total assets for the year ended March 31, 1997.
6. Obtain access to Alliance's annual report for fiscal years ending after March 31, 1997. This access may be through a shrink-wrapped annual report included with your text or you may gain access to annual report information at Alliance's Web site: **http://info.Alliance.com/ar/contents.htm**. Recompute Alliance's return on total assets for the years subsequent to March 31, 1997 for which you have information.

Comparative Analysis

LO 9

Both **NIKE** and **Reebok** design, produce, market and sell sports footwear and apparel. Key comparative figures ($ millions) for these two organizations follow:

	NIKE		Reebok	
Key Figures	**1997**	**1996**	**1996**	**1995**
Net income	$ 796	$ 553	$ 139	$ 165
Net Sales	$9,187	$6,471	$3,479	$3,481
Total Assets	$5,361	$3,952	$1,786	$1,652

* NIKE figures are from the annual reports for the fiscal years ended May 31,1997, and 1996.
Reebok figures are from the annual reports for the fiscal years ended December 31, 1996, and 1995.

Required

1. Compute the return on total assets for NIKE as of May 31, 1997, and Reebok as of December 31, 1996.
2. Disaggregate the return on total assets computed in part 1 of this question for both companies according to the formula given in the chapter.
3. Which company has the higher return on total assets? The higher profit margin? The higher total asset turnover? Compare your answers to the chapter's discussion of return on total asset which compared NIKE and Reebok.

Ethics Challenge

LO 1, 2

Jack Phelps is the controller for Jayhawk Company. Jayhawk has numerous long-term investments in debt securities. About 18 months ago the company had significant amounts of idle cash that were invested in 10-year bonds. Management's intent was to dispose of the bonds within two years from the date of purchase. Jack is preparing the year-end financial statements. In accounting for investments, he knows he must designate each investment as temporary or long-term. Since the bonds were purchased, interest rates have risen sharply meaning the market values of the bonds have declined significantly. Jack earns a bonus each year which is computed as a percent of the net income of the company.

Required

1. Will Jack's bonus be dependent in any way on the classification of the debt securities?
2. What criteria must Jack consider to properly classify the securities as temporary or long-term?
3. Are there any likely checks in the company to review the classification that Jack chooses for the securities?

Communicating in Practice

LO 4, 5, 6

You are the accountant for Jackson Company. The owner of the company, Abel Terrio, has finished reviewing the financial statements you prepared for 19X3 and questions the $6,000 loss reported on the company's sale of its investment in the common shares of Blackhawk Co. Jackson acquired 50,000 shares of Blackhawk's outstanding common shares on December 31, 19X1, at a cost of $500,000. This shares purchase represented a 40% interest in Blackhawk. The 19X2 income statement showed the investments made by Jackson proved very profitable, and the earnings from all investments were $126,000. On January 3, 19X3, Jackson Company sold the Blackhawk shares for $575,000. Blackhawk did not pay any dividends during 19X2 and reported a net income of $202,500 for the year. Terrio believes that because the purchase price of the Blackhawk shares was $500,000, and it was sold for $575,000, the 19X3 income statement should report a $75,000 gain on the sale.

Required

Draft a memo to Terrio explaining why the $6,000 loss on the sale of the Blackhawk shares is correctly reported.

Taking It to the Net

LO 7

Visit the Web site **www.royalbank.com/travel/fxconvert.html**. The Web site affords the opportunity to convert over 40 different currencies into any one of the other currencies. Use the website's currency converter and convert the Canadian. dollar into five other currencies.

Teamwork in Action

LO 1, 2, 6, 3, 4, 5

Each member of the team has the responsibility to become an expert on a specific classification of long-term investments. This expertise will be used to facilitate their teammates understanding of the concepts and procedures relevant to the classification they have chosen. Follow the procedure outlined below:

1. Each team member is to quickly select her or his area for expertise development by choosing one of the classifications of long-term investments listed below.
   a. Held-to-maturity debt securities
   b. Long-term investments in debt securities and equity securities without significant influence.
   c. Equity securities with significant influence
   d. Equity securities with controlling influence
2. Learning teams are to disburse and expert teams are to be formed. Expert teams are made up of students who all select the same area of expertise. The instructor will identify the location where each expert team will meet.
3. Using data below, expert teams will collaborate to develop a presentation following requirements listed below. Each student must write up the presentation in a format they can show to their learning teams in the next step in the activity.

Requirements for expert presentation:

   a. Write a transaction for the acquisition of this investment. The transaction narrative is to include all necessary data to reflect the chosen classification.
   b. Prepare the journal entry to record the acquisition.

      (Note: The expert team on "Equity securities with controlling influence" will substitute requirements e–f below with a discussion of the reporting phase when this type of investment is owned.)
   c. Identify information necessary to complete the end-of-period accounting for this investment.
   d. Design information that will allow your expert team to illustrate possible end-of-period accounting.
   e. Assuming this is the only investment your business owns, prepare any necessary year-end entries.
   f. Present relevant Balance Sheet section(s).

4. Re-form learning teams. In rotation, each expert is to present to the team the presentation he or she developed in 3. Experts are to encourage and respond to questions.

Hitting the Road

LO 7

Assume that you are planning a spring break trip to Europe. Identify three different locations where you can find exchange rates for the dollar relative to European currencies.

Business Break

LO 7

Read the article "Uniquely Canadian Number Crunching" in *The Financial Post* weekend edition July 25–27, 1998.

1. What is the central concern of this article?
2. What are the reported earnings of **Bombardier Inc.** and **Doman Industries Ltd.** for 1997 under Canadian GAAP? What would be their bottom line figures if U.S. GAAP had been used?
3. How do the accounting rules for currency losses in Canada differ from those of other countries?
4. Is the CICA proposing any changes?

19 Reporting and Analyzing Cash Flows

CHAPTER

A Look Back

Chapter 18 focused on long-term investments in securities. We explained how to identify, account for, and report for them. We also described accounting for transactions listed in a foreign currency.

A Look at This Chapter

Chapter 19 focuses on reporting and analyzing cash inflows and cash outflows. We emphasize how to prepare and interpret the statement of cash flows.

A Look Forward

Chapter 20 focuses on tools to help us analyze financial statements. We describe comparative analysis and the application of ratios for financial analysis.

Chapter Outline

- **Basics of Cash Flow Reporting**
  - Purpose of the Statement of Cash Flows
  - Importance of Cash Flows
  - Measuring Cash Flows
  - Classifying Cash Flows
  - Classification Issues
  - Noncash Investing and Financing Activities
  - Format of the Statement of Cash Flows
  - Preparing the Statement of Cash Flows
- **Cash Flows from Operating Activities**
  - Methods of Reporting Operating Cash Flows
  - Direct Method of Reporting Operating Cash Flows
  - Indirect Method of Reporting Operating Cash Flows
- **Cash Flows from Investing Activities**
  - Capital Asset Transactions
- **Cash Flows from Financing Activities**
  - Bonds Payable Transactions
  - Common Shares Transactions
  - Retained Earnings Transactions
  - Proving Cash Balances
- **Using the Information—Cash Flow Analysis**
  - Analyzing Cash Sources and Uses
  - Cash Flow on Total Assets
- **Appendix 19A—Using a Spreadsheet to Prepare the Statements of Cash Flows**

Ginseng Rich, Cash Poor

Moncton, NB—Dennis Chen is a grower of ginseng, a herb whose root is valued for its health benefits. But this summer, high winds and hail swept through Chen's 20 hectare plot of ginseng. Chen needed lumber and screening to repair the covering that protected his ginseng capital from nature's elements. But he neither had cash, nor the sympathy of bankers.

"Every banker wanted to see my financial statements, especially my cash flows. But I tried to explain that I'd only been in business four years, and had never received any cash from any customer," says Chen. "The bankers just didn't understand." What they didn't understand is that ginseng takes about five years to mature from planting until harvest. And since Chen began his business only four years ago, all of his cash flows were negative and large.

"When I finally showed them my statement of cash flows, there was a look of disbelief on their faces," says Chen. "One banker told me flat out he wouldn't touch my loan with a ten-foot pole!" Chen's income statement didn't help much either. Most accounting professionals won't accept recognition of revenue for agricultural products in their growth stage. Especially when growth extends over five years or more. So Chen's prospects were fading.

"I was lucky," says Chen. "I got an appointment with a small town credit union. The loan officer grew up on a farm, and was familiar with ginseng. While it wasn't the best terms, I got it." What Chen got was cash to do the necessary repairs and save his ginseng and four years of work. Chen accepted a higher than average interest rate and a collateral agreement giving the credit union access to his ginseng if he defaulted.

"That loan officer really saved me," says Chen. "He looked beyond the numbers and the cash flows to see what was happening. I think it'll be a win-win situation for both of us." And ginseng lovers alike.

Learning Objectives

LO 1 Explain the purpose and importance of cash flow information.

LO 2 Distinguish among operating, investing, and financing activities.

LO 3 Identify and disclose noncash investing and financing activities.

LO 4 Describe the format of the statement of cash flows.

LO 5 Prepare a statement of cash flows.

LO 6 Compute cash flows from operating activities using the direct method.

LO 7 Compute cash flows from operating activities using the indirect method.

LO 8 Determine cash flows from both investing and financing activities.

LO 9 Analyze the statement of cash flows.

LO 10 Compute and apply the cash flow on total assets ratio.

CHAPTER PREVIEW

Profitability is a primary goal of most managers. But it is not the only goal. A company cannot achieve or maintain profits without careful management of cash. Managers and other users of information pay close attention to a company's cash position and the events and transactions affecting cash. Information about these events and transactions is reported in the statement of cash flows. This chapter explains how we prepare, analyze, and interpret a statement of cash flows. It also discusses the importance of cash flow information for predicting future performance and making managerial decisions. Understanding the statement of cash flows is especially important in obtaining a small business loan and one with favourable terms. Dennis Chen's experience with the importance of this statement as described in the opening article is common.

Basics of Cash Flow Reporting

This section describes the basics of cash flow reporting including its purpose, measurement, classification, format, and preparation.

Purpose of the Statement of Cash Flows (SCF)

LO1 Explain the purpose and importance of cash flow information.

The purpose of the **statement of cash flows** is to assist users of financial statements to evaluate the liquidity and solvency of an enterprise and to assess the enterprise's ability to generate cash from internal sources, to repay its liabilities, and to reinvest and to make distributions to owners.[1] The SCF provides details of the major items comprising cash receipts and cash payments during a period. This includes separately identifying the cash flows related to operating, investing, and financing activities.

The statement of cash flows does more than simply report changes in cash. It is the detailed disclosure of individual cash flows that makes this statement useful to users. Information in this statement helps users answer questions such as:

- How does a company obtain its cash?
- Where does a company spend its cash?
- What is the change in the cash balance?

The statement of cash flows addresses these important questions by summarizing, classifying, and reporting a company's periodic cash inflows and outflows.

Importance of Cash Flows

Information about cash flows, its sources and uses, can influence decision makers in important ways. For instance, we look more favourably at a company that is financing its expenditures with cash from operations than one that does it by selling its assets. Information about cash flows helps users decide whether a company has enough cash to pay its existing debts as they mature. It is also relied upon to evaluate a company's ability to meet unexpected obligations and pursue unexpected opportunities. External information users especially want to assess a company's ability to take advantage of new business opportunities. Internal users such as managers use cash flow information to plan day-to-day operating activities and make long-term investment decisions.

[1] *CICA Handbook*, section 1540.

There are many striking examples of how careful analysis and management of cash flows have lead to improved financial stability. **Kasten Chase Applied Research,** a company specializing in wireless technologies support, obtained temporary protection from bankruptcy in 1992 and desperately needed to improve its cash flows. It turned around its cash flows from operations from a deficit of $4.3 million in 1996 to $1.3 million in 1997. It did so by engaging in aggressive cost-cutting measures. Cash flows are important to businesses in all sectors. At the time of writing this chapter it is uncertain whether **Eaton's** will be successful in solving its cash flow problems with restructuring that involves closing down unprofitable stores and engaging in strategic planning that is more customer focused.

The case of **W. T. Grant Co.** is a classic North American example of why cash flow information is important in predicting a company's future performance and financial strength. Grant reported net income of more than $40 million per year for three consecutive years. At the same time, it was experiencing an alarming decrease in cash provided by operations. For instance, net cash *outflow* was more than $90 million by the end of that three-year period.[2] Grant soon was bankrupt. Users who relied solely on Grant's earnings numbers were unpleasantly surprised. This reminds us that cash flows as well as income statement and balance sheet information is crucial in making business decisions.

Cash Valuation

Financial analysts who value private companies sometimes do so on the basis of a multiple of operating cash flow. Medium-sized private companies usually sell for five to seven times operating cash flows. Larger companies can command higher multiples. Rules of thumb, however, should not be used as a primary valuation technique but can be used as a reasonableness test of value reached through the application of other more rigorous techniques. You will learn about these valuation techniques in more advanced courses.

Measuring Cash Flows

Cash flows are defined to include both "cash and cash equivalents" in the statement of cash flows. This means the statement explains the difference between the beginning and ending balances of *cash and cash equivalents*. While we continue to use the term cash flows we must remember that cash flows include both cash and cash equivalents.

As we discussed in Chapter 9, a cash equivalent is an investment that must satisfy two criteria:

1. It must be readily convertible to a known amount of cash.
2. It must be sufficiently close to its maturity date so its market value is not significantly affected by interest rate changes.

A new section on Cash Flow Statements was issued in August 1998 to replace *CICA Handbook* section 1540 on the Statement of Changes in Financial Position (SCFP). This chapter will reflect the new recommendations which are now in line with IASC and FASB standards. A cash flow statement is now

[2] J. Largay and C. Stickney, "Cash Flow, Ratio Analysis and the W. T. Grant Company Bankruptcy," *Financial Analysts Journal*, July–August 1980, pp. 51–56.

required in every set of GAAP financial statements. The definition of *cash equivalents* is changed to short-term, highly liquid investments that are readily convertible to known amounts of cash and are subject to an insignificant risk of changes in value. In most cases cash and cash equivalents would include cash and temporary investments[3] of three months or less from the date of acquisition. Equity investments are not included as cash equivalents. Classifying short-term, highly liquid investments as cash equivalents is based on the idea that companies make these investments to earn a return on idle cash balances.

Items meeting the criteria of cash equivalents are sometimes not held as temporary investments of idle cash. For instance, an investment company that specializes in the purchase and sale of securities often buys cash equivalents as part of its investing strategy. Companies in this situation are allowed to exclude these securities from the cash equivalents account. These companies must follow a clear policy for determining the items to include and not include. These policies are disclosed in notes to their financial statements and must be followed consistently from period to period. **Canadian Tire** defines its cash as:

> ...cash and short-term investments less bank indebtedness. Short-term investments held include Canadian and United States government securities and notes of other creditworthy parties within one year.

Under the new provisions of section 1540 of the *CICA Hanbook*, Canadian Tire will no longer deduct bank indebtedness.

Classifying Cash Flows

LO 2 Distinguish among operating, investing, and financing activities.

Since we treat cash and cash equivalents as a single item on the statement of cash flows, transactions between cash and cash equivalents such as cash paid to purchase cash equivalents and cash received from selling cash equivalents are not reported in the statement. But all other cash receipts and payments are classified and reported on the statement as operating, investing, or financing activities. Individual cash receipts and payments within each of these three categories are labelled to identify their source transactions or events. Cash receipts and payments are then summarized for each category by netting them against each other. A net cash inflow (source) occurs when the receipts in a category exceed the payments. A net cash outflow (use) occurs when the payments in a category exceed receipts.

Operating Activities

Operating activities include the cash effects of transactions and events that determine net income. But remember that not all items in income such as unusual gains and losses are operating activities. We discuss these exceptions later in the chapter. Examples of operating activities are the production and purchase of merchandise, the sale of goods and services to customers, and expenditures toward administering the business. Exhibit 19.1 lists the more common cash inflows and outflows from operating activities.

[3] In recent years cash equivalents have been determined net of short-term borrowings. Short-term borrowings will no longer be deducted.

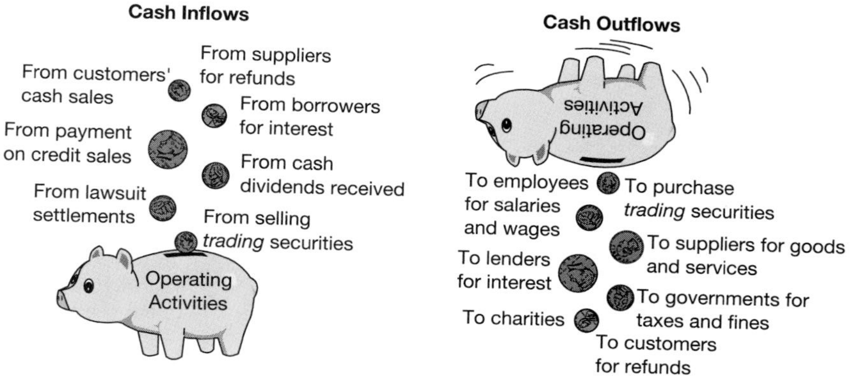

Exhibit 19.1

Cash Flows from Operating Activities

Investing Activities

Investing activities include the (a) purchase and sale of long-term assets, (b) the purchase and sale of short-term investments that are not cash equivalents, and (c) lending and collecting on loans other than those made by a financial institution. Exhibit 19.2 lists examples of cash flows from investing activities. Proceeds from collecting the principal amounts of loans deserve special attention. If the loan results from sales to customers, its cash receipts are classed as operating activities whether short-term or long-term. But if the loan results from a loan to another party, then its cash receipts from collecting the principal of the note is classed as an investing activity. Collection of interest on a loan is *not* part of investing activities but rather part of operating activities.

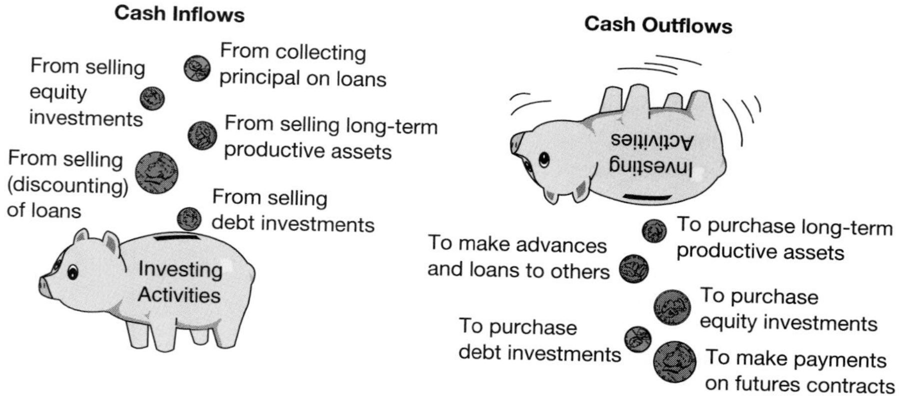

Exhibit 19.2

Cash Flows from Investing Activities*

* Investing activities exclude transactions in trading securities.

Financing Activities

Financing activities are those that result in changes in the size and composition of the equity capital and borrowings of the enterprise. They include (a) getting cash from issuing debt and repaying the amounts borrowed, and (b) getting cash from or distributing cash to owners. These activities all involve transactions with a company's owners and creditors. They also involve borrowing and repaying of principal amounts relating to both short- and long-term debt. But payments of interest expense are classified as operating activities. Also, cash payments to settle credit purchases of merchandise, whether on account or by note, are operating activities. Exhibit 19.3 lists examples of cash flows from financing activities.

Exhibit 19.3

Cash Flows from Financing Activities

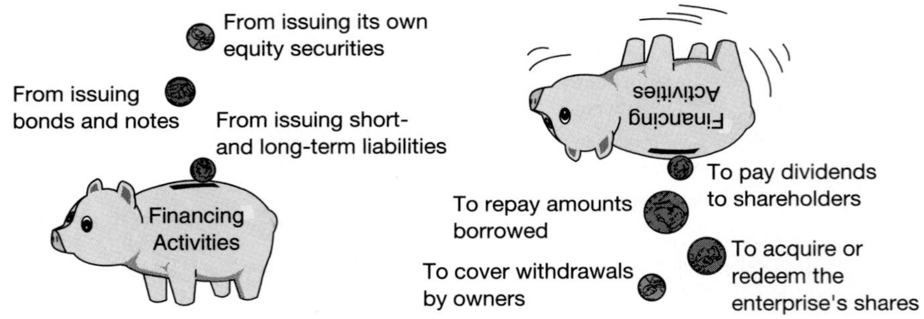

Classification Issues

Earlier in the chapter we classified dividends received as an operating cash flow. This seems logical because dividends received enter into the determination of net income. However, it is arguable that dividends received can also be classified as financing cash flows because they are a cost of obtaining funds or as investing cash flows because they reflect returns on investments made by the enterprise. Similar arguments can be made for interest received and paid. The *CICA Handbook* requires that interest and dividends received and paid that are included in the determination of net income should be classified as cash flows from operating activities. Alernative treatments, however, is permitted according to the nature of the transaction:

> Interest and dividends not included in the determination of net income should be classified according to their nature. Dividends and interest paid and charged to retained earnings should be presented separately as cash flows used in financing activities. Cash flows from dividends paid by subsidiaries to non-controlling interests should be presented separately as cash flows used in financing activities. (section 1540.35)

Noncash Investing and Financing Activities

LO 3 Identify and disclose noncash investing and financing activities.

There are often important investing and financing activities that do not affect cash receipts or payments. Yet because of their importance and the *full disclosure* principle, these important noncash investing and financing activities are disclosed in a note to the statement in a way that provides all the relevant information about these investing and financing activities. One example of such a transaction is the purchase of long-term assets by giving a long-term note payable. This transaction involves both investing and financing activities, but it does not affect any cash inflow and outflow and is not reported in any of the three sections of the statement of cash flows. Another example is where investing and financing activities involve cash receipts or payments but only for part of the entire transaction. The *CICA Handbook* includes the following examples: (a) acquisition of assets by assuming directly related liabilities or by means of a capital lease, (b) the acquisition of an enterprise in exchange for share of the acquirer and (c) the conversion of debt to equity.[4] A more exhaustive list is provided in Exhibit 19.4.

[4] *CICA Handbook*, section 1540.47.

To illustrate, let's assume Burton purchases machinery for $12,000 by paying cash of $5,000 and trading in old machinery with a market value of $7,000. The statement of cash flows reports only the $5,000 cash outflow for purchase of machinery. This means the $12,000 investing transaction is only partially described in the body of the statement of cash flows. Yet this information is potentially important to users in that it changes the make up of assets. According to section 1540.46 of the *CICA Handbook:*

> Investing and financing transactions that do not require the use of cash or cash equivalents should be excluded from a cash flow statement. Such transactions should be disclosed elsewhere in the financial statements in a way that provides all the relevant information about these investing and financing activities.

Companies use one of two ways to disclose noncash investing and financing activities not reported in the body of the statement of cash flows. They must be disclosed in either (1) a note, or (2) a separate schedule attached to (often the bottom of) the statement. In the case of Burton, it could either describe the transaction in a note or include a small schedule at the bottom of its statement that lists the $12,000 asset investment along with financing of $5,000 and a $7,000 trade-in of old machinery. Union Camp provides an example of disclosure of noncash investing and financing activities as follows:

Fair value of assets acquired	$8,345
Less: cash paid	7,115
Liabilities incurred or assumed	$1,230

The Union Camp schedule attached to the statement describes an exchange of assets involving both cash and noncash aspects. The $7,115 cash payment is reported in Union Camp's statement of cash flows as an investing activity. But the note tells us that the purchase of certain assets involves a noncash aspect—that is, a liability to pay in the future. Exhibit 19.4 lists some transactions that are disclosed as noncash investing and financing activities.

- Retirement of debt by issuing equity securities.
- Conversion of preferred shares to common shares.
- Leasing of assets in capital lease transaction.
- Purchase of long-term asset by issuing note payable.
- Exchange of noncash assets for other noncash assets.
- Purchase of noncash assets by issuing equity or debt.

Exhibit 19.4

Examples of Noncash Investing and Financing Activities

Community Activist

You are a community activist trying to raise public awareness of pollution emitted by a local manufacturer. The manufacturer complains about the high costs of pollution controls and points to its recent $4 million annual loss as evidence. But you also know its net cash flows were a positive $8 million this past year. How are these results possible?

You Make the Call

Answer—p. 911

Format of the Statement of Cash Flows

LO 4 Describe the format of the statement of cash flows.

Accounting standards require companies to include a statement of cash flows in a complete set of financial statements. This statement must report information about a company's cash receipts and cash payments during the period.

Exhibit 19.5 shows us the usual format of the statement of cash flows. This exhibit shows that a company must report cash flows from three activities: operating, investing, and financing. Cash inflows and cash outflows are reported for each category. The statement explains how transactions and events impact the beginning-of-period cash (and cash equivalents) balance to produce its end-of-period balance.

Exhibit 19.5

Format of the Statement of Cash Flows

COMPANY NAME Statement of Cash Flows Period Covered	
Cash flows from operating activities:	
[List of individual inflows and outflows]	
Net cash provided (used) by operating activities	$ ###
Cash flows from investing activities:	
[List of individual inflows and outflows]	
Net cash provided (used) by investing activities	###
Cash flows from financing activities:	
[List of individual inflows and outflows]	
Net cash provided (used) in financing activities	###
Net increase (decrease) in cash	$ ###
Cash (and equivalents) balance at beginning of period	###
Cash (and equivalents) balance at end of period	$ ###

Note disclosure of "Noncash investing and financing transactions."

Flash back

1. Does a statement of cash flows disclose payments of cash to purchase cash equivalents? Does it disclose receipts of cash from selling cash equivalents?
2. Identify the categories of cash flows reported separately on the statement of cash flows.
3. Identify the category for each of the following cash flow activities: (a) purchase equipment for cash, (b) payment of wages, (c) sale of common shares for cash, (d) receipt of cash dividends from share investment, (e) cash collection from customers, (f) issuance of bonds for cash.

Answers—p. 911

Preparing the Statement of Cash Flows

LO 5 Prepare a statement of cash flows.

Preparation of a statement of cash flows involves five steps: (1) compute the net increase or decrease in cash, (2) compute and report net cash provided (used) by operating activities (using either the direct or indirect method—both are explained in this chapter), (3) compute and report net cash provided (used) by investing activities, (4) compute and report net cash provided (used) by financing activities, and (5) compute net cash flow by combining net cash provided (used) by operating, financing and investing activities and prove it by adding it to the beginning cash balance to show it equals the ending cash balance. Noncash investing and financing activities are disclosed in a note or a separate schedule to the statement.

The first step in preparing the statement—computing the net increase or decrease in cash—is a simple but crucial computation. It equals the current period's cash balance minus the prior period's cash balance. This is the "bottom line" figure for the statement of cash flows and is a helpful check on the accuracy of our work.

The information we need to prepare a statement of cash flows comes from a variety of sources. These include comparative balance sheets at the beginning and end of the period, an income statement for the period, and a careful analysis of each noncash balance sheet account in the general ledger. Because cash inflows and cash outflows are captured in our accounting system, we can also examine transactions affecting the Cash account.

The remaining sections of this chapter explain the important steps in preparing the statement of cash flows. But first we describe the two different approaches to preparing the statement: (1) analyzing the Cash account, and (2) analyzing noncash accounts.

Step 1: Compute net increase or decrease in cash

Step 2: Compute net cash from operating activities

Step 3: Compute net cash from investing activities

Step 4: Compute net cash from financing activities

Step 5: Prove and report beginning and ending cash balances

Analyzing the Cash Account

All of a company's cash receipts and cash payments are recorded in the Cash account in the General Ledger. The Cash account is therefore a natural place to look for information about cash flows from operating, investing, and financing activities.

To illustrate, let's look at the summarized Cash account of **Genesis** in Exhibit 19.6.

Exhibit 19.6

Summarized Cash Account

Summarized Cash Account

Balance, Dec. 31/1999	12,000		
Receipts from customers	570,000	Payments for goods	319,000
Proceeds from asset sales	12,000	Payments for wages and operating expenses	218,000
Proceeds from share issuance	15,000	Interest payments	8,000
		Tax payments	5,000
		Payments for assets	10,000
		Payments to retire bonds	18,000
		Dividend payments	14,000
Balance, Dec. 31/2000	17,000		

Individual cash transactions are summarized in this Cash account according to the major types of cash receipts and cash payments. For instance, only the total cash receipts from all customers is listed. Individual cash transactions underlying these totals can number into the thousands. Accounting software programs are available to provide us with summarized cash accounts similar to the one illustrated.

Preparing a statement of cash flows from Exhibit 19.6 requires us to determine whether the cash inflow or outflow is an operating, investing, or financing activity. We then list these individual cash flows according to their activity. This yields the statement shown in Exhibit 19.7.

Exhibit 19.7

Statement of Cash Flows—Direct Method

GENESIS Statement of Cash Flows For Year Ended December 31, 2000		
Cash flows from operating activities:		
Cash received from customers	$570,000	
Cash paid for merchandise	(319,000)	
Cash paid for wages and other operating expenses	(218,000)	
Cash paid for interest	(8,000)	
Cash paid for taxes	(5,000)	
Net cash provided by operating activities		$20,000
Cash flows from investing activities:		
Cash received from sale of capital assets	$ 12,000	
Cash paid for purchase of capital assets	(10,000)	
Net cash provided by investing activities		2,000
Cash flows from financing activities:		
Cash received from issuing shares	$ 15,000	
Cash paid to retire bonds	(18,000)	
Cash paid for dividends	(14,000)	
Net cash used in financing activities		(17,000)
Net increase in cash		$ 5,000
Cash balance at beginning of 2000		12,000
Cash balance at end of 2000		$17,000

Preparing the statement of cash flows from an analysis of the summarized Cash account presents two limitations. First, most companies have many individual cash receipts and payments making it difficult to review them all. While accounting software greatly minimizes this burden, it is still a task requiring professional judgment. Second, the Cash account does not usually carry a description of each cash transaction. This makes it difficult to assign cash transactions according to activity.

Analyzing Noncash Accounts

The second approach to preparing the statement of cash flows is based on analyzing noncash accounts. This approach uses the fact that when a company records cash inflows and outflows with debits and credits to the Cash account (as reflected in the prior section), it also records credits and debits in other noncash accounts. Many of these noncash accounts are balance sheet accounts. For instance, the sale of land for cash. Others are revenue and expense accounts that are closed to Retained Earnings, also a balance sheet account. For instance, the sale of services for cash yields a credit to services revenue that is closed to Retained Earnings. In sum, *all cash transactions eventually affect noncash balance sheet accounts.* This means we can determine cash inflows and cash outflows by analyzing changes in noncash balance sheet accounts. We are not limited to analyzing the Cash account.

Exhibit 19.8 uses the accounting equation to show the important relation between the Cash account and noncash balance sheet accounts.

Exhibit 19.8 starts with the familiar accounting equation at the top. We then expanded it in line (2) so that cash is separated from noncash asset accounts. Next, we move noncash asset accounts to the right-hand side of the equality in line (3) where they become a negative. This shows cash is equal to the sum of the liability and equity accounts minus the noncash asset accounts. Line (4) points out that *changes* in one side of the accounting equation are equal to changes on the other side. It also shows we can explain changes in cash by analyzing changes

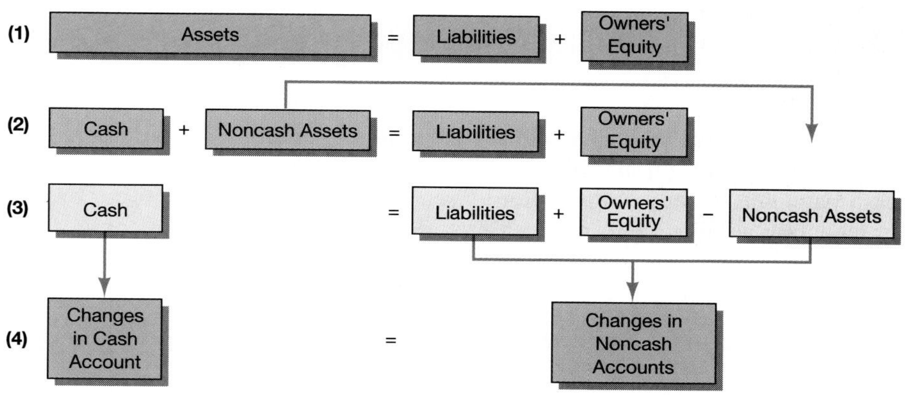

Exhibit 19.8

Relation between Cash and Noncash Accounts

in the noncash accounts consisting of liabilities, equity accounts, and noncash assets. By analyzing all noncash balance sheet accounts and related income statement accounts, we have the information for preparing a statement of cash flows.

Information to Prepare the Statement

Information to prepare the statement of cash flows usually comes from three sources: (a) comparative balance sheets, (b) current income statement, and (c) additional information. Comparative balance sheets give us changes in noncash accounts from the beginning to the end of the period. The current income statement gives us details to help compute cash flows from operating activities. Additional information often includes details on transactions and events helping us explain both cash flows and noncash investing and financing activities.

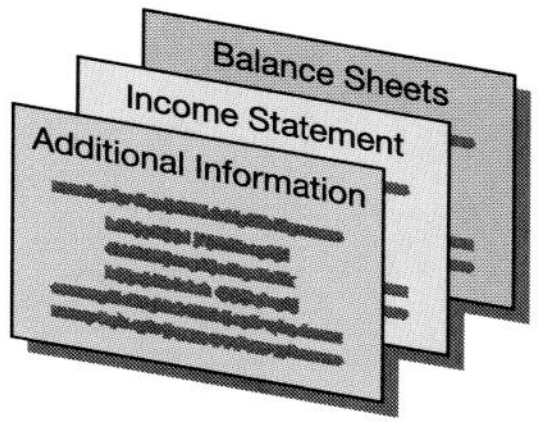

E-Cash

The electronic payment industry is advancing rapidly in Canada. Electronic cash or e-cash is based on smart card technology that makes use of a microcomputer chip embedded in a plastic card that allows a consumer to load digital cash and use the card to anonymously pay e-cash to retailers, banks, and even vending machines. However to gain mass market acceptance of this technology some kind of home-loading device probably needs to be developed.

Cash Flows from Operating Activities

This section describes the reporting of cash flows from operating activities using two different methods: direct method and indirect method. These two different methods apply only to the operating activities section.

Methods of Reporting Operating Cash Flows

The net cash flows provided (used) by operating activities can be reported in one of two ways: the *direct method* or the *indirect method*. The direct method separately lists each major item of operating cash receipts (such as cash received from customers) and each major item of operating cash payments (such as cash paid for merchandise). The cash payments are subtracted from cash receipts to determine the net cash provided (used) by operating activities. The operating activities section of Exhibit 19.7 is an example of the direct method of reporting operating cash flows.

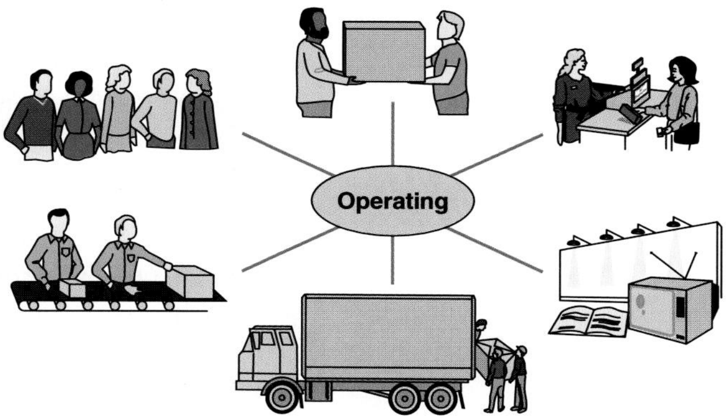

The **indirect method** reports net income and then adjusts it for items necessary to give us net cash provided (used) by operating activities. It does *not* report individual items of cash inflows and cash outflows from operating activities. Instead, the indirect method reports the necessary adjustments to reconcile net income to net cash provided (used) by operating activities. A common adjustment is an addition for amortization. Since amortization expense is not a current cash payment, we add amortization expense back to net income in our process of adjusting net income to net cash provided (used) by operating activities.

The operating activities section prepared under the indirect method appears as shown in Exhibit 19.9.

Exhibit 19.9

Operating Activities Section—Indirect Method

Cash flows from operating activities:		
Net income	$38,000	
Adjustments to reconcile net income to net cash provided by operating activities:		
Increase in accounts receivable	(20,000)	
Increase in merchandise inventory	(14,000)	
Increase in prepaid expenses	(2,000)	
Decrease in accounts payable	(5,000)	
Decrease in interest payable	(1,000)	
Increase in income taxes payable	10,000	
Amortization expense	24,000	
Loss on sale of capital assets	6,000	
Gain on retirement of bonds	(16,000)	
Net cash provided by operating activities		$20,000

It is important to see that the amount of net cash provided by operating activities is *identical* under both the direct and indirect methods. This equality always exists. The difference in these methods is with computation of this amount.

The indirect method of reporting operating cash flows does not provide as much detailed information as the direct method. The direct method is *recommended* by the CICA. But since the direct method is not required and the indirect method is arguably easier to compute, companies are likely to continue reporting operating cash flows using the indirect method. We describe both methods in this chapter.

Since the direct method is the cash flow version of an income statement, many people find the direct method easier to understand when first learning about cash flow reporting. It allows decision makers to know how much of revenues and costs are actually received or paid in cash. It also follows the same format as the income statement. Many internal users such as managers and budget officers use the direct method to predict future cash requirements and availability.

To illustrate both methods, we prepare the operating activities section of the statement of cash flows for Genesis. The December 31, 1999, and 2000, balance sheets of Genesis along with its 2000 income statement are shown in Exhibit 19.10. Our objective is to prepare a statement of cash flows explaining the $5,000 increase in cash for year 2000 as seen from its balance sheets. This is computed as Cash of $17,000 at the end of year 2000 minus Cash of $12,000 at the end of 1999.

Genesis also discloses additional information about year 2000 transactions:

a. All accounts payable balances result from merchandise purchases.

b. Capital assets costing $70,000 are purchased by paying $10,000 cash and issuing $60,000 of bonds payable.

c. Capital assets with an original cost of $30,000 and accumulated amortization of $12,000 are sold for $12,000 cash. This yields a $6,000 loss.

d. Proceeds from issuing 3,000 common shares are $15,000.

e. Paid $18,000 to retire bonds with a book value of $34,000. This yields a $16,000 gain from bond retirement.

f. Cash dividends of $14,000 are declared and paid.

Exhibit 19.10

Financial Statements

GENESIS
Balance Sheet
December 31, 2000 and 1999

	2000	1999
Assets		
Current assets:		
Cash	$ 17,000	$ 12,000
Accounts receivable	60,000	40,000
Merchandise inventory	84,000	70,000
Prepaid expenses	6,000	4,000
Total current assets	$167,000	$126,000
Long-term assets:		
Capital assets	$250,000	$210,000
Less accumulated amortization	(60,000)	(48,000)
Total assets	$357,000	$288,000
Liabilities		
Current liabilities:		
Accounts payable	$ 35,000	$ 40,000
Interest payable	3,000	4,000
Income taxes payable	22,000	12,000
Total current liabilities	$ 60,000	$ 56,000
Long-term liabilities:		
Bonds payable	90,000	64,000
Total liabilities	$150,000	$120,000
Shareholders' Equity		
Contributed capital:		
Common shares, no-par value	$95,000	$80,000
Retained earnings	112,000	88,000
Total shareholders' equity	207,000	168,000
Total liabilities and shareholders' equity	$357,000	$288,000

GENESIS
Income Statement
For Year Ended December 31, 2000

Sales		$590,000
Cost of goods sold	$300,000	
Wages and other operating expenses	216,000	
Interest expense	7,000	
Income taxes expense	15,000	
Amortization expense	24,000	(562,000)
Loss on sale of capital assets		(6,000)
Gain on retirement of debt		16,000
Net income		$ 38,000

The next section describes the direct method. The section following this one describes the indirect method. An instructor may choose to cover one or the other in preparing a statement of cash flows. Neither section depends on the other.

Direct Method of Reporting Operating Cash Flows

LO 6 Compute cash flows from operating activities using the direct method.

We compute cash flows from operating activities under the direct method by adjusting accrual-based income statement items to a cash basis. The usual approach is to adjust income statement accounts related to operating activities for changes in their related balance sheet accounts as follows:

Revenue or Expense → Adjustments for Changes in Related Balance Sheet Accounts → Cash Receipts or Cash Payments

We follow this same approach in this section.

The framework for reporting major classes of cash receipts and cash payments is shown in Exhibit 19.11. This framework is for the operating section of the cash flow statement prepared using the **direct method.**

Exhibit 19.11

Major Classes of Operating Cash Flows

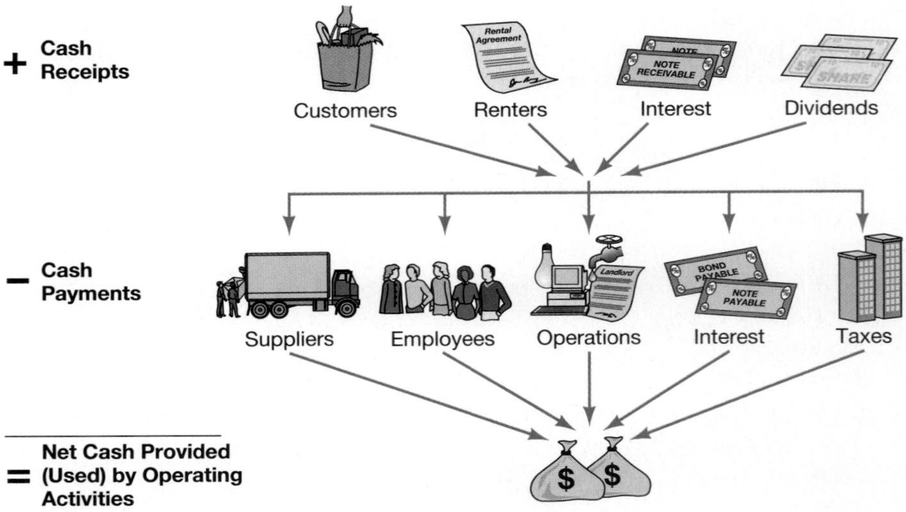

In preparing the operating section for Genesis, we first look at its cash receipts and then its cash payments.

Operating Cash Receipts

Exhibit 19.10 and the additional information from Genesis identifies only one potential cash receipt—that of sales to customers. This section takes sales from the accrual-based income statement and adjusts it as necessary to give us cash received from customers.

Cash Received from Customers

If all sales are for cash, the amount of cash received from customers is equal to sales. But when sales are on account, we must adjust the amount of sales revenue for the change in Accounts Receivable. It is often helpful to use *account analysis* for this purpose. This usually involves setting up a T-account and reconstructing its major entries, including its cash receipts and payments.

To illustrate, the T-account below reports accounts receivable balances on December 31, 1999, and 2000. The beginning balance is $40,000, and the ending balance is $60,000. The income statement shows sales is $590,000, and we enter it on the debit side of this account. With this information, we can reconstruct the Accounts Receivable account and determine the amount of cash received from customers.

Accounts Receivable			
Balance, Dec. 31/1999	40,000		
Sales	590,000	Collections =	570,000
Balance, Dec. 31/2000	60,000		

This T-account shows the balance of accounts receivable begins at $40,000 and increases to $630,000 from sales of $590,000. But then its ending balance is reported at only $60,000. This implies that cash receipts from customers are $570,000, computed as $40,000 + $590,000 − [?] = $60,000. This computation can be rearranged to express cash received as equal to sales of $590,000 minus a $20,000 increase in accounts receivable. This computation is summarized in Exhibit 19.12.

Exhibit 19.12

Formula to Compute Cash Received from Customers—Direct Method

Cash received from customers = Sales { − Increase in accounts receivable *or* + Decrease in accounts receivable }

The statement of cash flows for Genesis in Exhibit 19.7 shows the $570,000 cash received from customers as a cash inflow from operating activities.

Other Cash Receipts

While cash receipts of Genesis are limited to collections from customers, we sometimes see other types of cash receipts. The most common are cash receipts involving rent, interest, and dividends. We compute cash received from these items by subtracting an increase in their respective receivable account or adding a decrease. For instance, if rent receivable increases in the period, it implies cash received is less than rent revenue reported on the income statement. But if rent receivable decreases, it implies cash received is more than reported rent revenue. The same logic applies to interest and dividends. The formulas for these computations are summarized in Exhibit 19.16 later in this section.

Operating Cash Payments

Exhibit 19.10 and the additional information from Genesis identifies four operating expenses. We analyze each of these expenses to compute their operating cash payments for the statement of cash flows.

Cash Paid for Merchandise

We compute cash paid for merchandise by analyzing both cost of goods sold and merchandise inventory. If all merchandise purchases are for cash and the ending balance of Merchandise Inventory is unchanged from the beginning balance, then the amount of cash paid for merchandise equals cost of goods sold. But this situation is uncommon. We usually see some change in the Merchandise Inventory balance in a period. Also, merchandise purchases are often made on credit, and yield changes in the Accounts Payable balance.

When the balances of Merchandise Inventory and Accounts Payable change, we must adjust cost of goods sold for changes in both of these accounts to compute cash paid for merchandise. This adjustment has two steps. First, we use the change in the balance of Merchandise Inventory along with the amount of cost of goods sold to compute cost of purchases for the period. If inventory increases, it implies we bought more than was sold and we add the inventory change to cost of goods sold to compute cost of purchases. If inventory decreases, it implies we bought less than was sold and we subtract the inventory change from cost of goods sold to compute purchases.

The second step uses the change in the balance of Accounts Payable along with the amount of cost of purchases to compute cash paid for merchandise. If accounts payable decreases, it implies we paid for more goods than was acquired this period and we add the accounts payable change to cost of purchases to compute cash paid for merchandise. If accounts payable increases, it implies we paid less than was acquired and we subtract the accounts payable change from purchases to compute cash paid for merchandise.

We illustrate this two-step process for Genesis. First, we use account analysis of merchandise inventory to compute cost of purchases. We do this by reconstructing the Merchandise Inventory account:

Merchandise Inventory			
Balance, Dec. 31/1999	70,000		
Purchases =	**314,000**	**Cost of goods sold**	**300,000**
Balance, Dec. 31/2000	84,000		

The beginning balance is $70,000, and its ending balance is $84,000. The income statement shows cost of goods sold is $300,000, and we enter it on the credit side of this account. With this information, we can determine the amount for cost of purchases at $314,000. This computation can be rearranged to express cost of purchases as equal to cost of goods sold of $300,000 plus the $14,000 increase in inventory.

Our second step is to compute cash paid for merchandise by adjusting purchases for the change in accounts payable. This is done by reconstructing the Accounts Payable account:

Accounts Payable			
		Balance, Dec. 31/1999	40,000
Payments =	**319,000**	**Purchases**	**314,000**
		Balance, Dec. 31/2000	35,000

This account shows us that its beginning balance of $40,000 plus purchases of $314,000 minus an ending balance of $35,000 gives us cash paid of $319,000 (or $40,000 + $314,000 − [?] = $35,000). Alternatively, we can express cash paid for merchandise as equal to purchases of $314,000 plus the $5,000 decrease in accounts payable.

We summarize the two-step adjustment to cost of goods sold to compute cash paid for merchandise in Exhibit 19.13.

Exhibit 19.13

Two Steps to Compute Cash Paid for Merchandise—Direct Method

Step 1:

Purchases = Cost of goods sold
- + Increase in merchandise inventory
- *or*
- − Decrease in merchandise inventory

Step 2:

Cash paid for merchandise = Purchases
- + Decrease in accounts payable
- *or*
- − Increase in accounts payable

Exhibit 19.7 shows the $319,000 cash paid by Genesis for merchandise is reported on the statement of cash flows as a cash outflow for operating activities.

Cash Paid for Wages and Operating Expenses (Excluding Amortization)

The income statement of Genesis shows wages and other operating expenses of $216,000; see Exhibit 19.10. To compute cash paid for wages and other operating expenses, we adjust this amount for changes in their related balance sheet accounts.

We begin by looking for prepaid expenses and accrued liabilities relating to wages and other operating expenses in the beginning and ending balance sheets of Genesis in Exhibit 19.10. These balance sheets show Genesis has prepaid expenses but no accrued liabilities. This means its adjustment to this expense item is limited to the change in prepaid expenses. The amount of adjustment is computed by assuming all cash paid for wages and other operating expenses is initially debited to Prepaid Expenses. This assumption allows us to reconstruct the Prepaid Expenses account:

Prepaid Expenses			
Balance, Dec. 31/1999	4,000		
Payments =	**218,000**	Wages and other operating expenses	216,000
Balance, Dec. 31/2000	6,000		

This account shows prepaid expenses increase by $2,000 in the period. This means cash paid for wages and other operating expenses exceeded the reported expense by $2,000. Alternatively, we can express cash paid for wages and other operating expenses of Genesis as equal to its expenses of $216,000 plus the $2,000 increase in prepaid expenses.

Our analysis assumes all cash payments for wages and operating expenses are initially debited to Prepaid Expenses in reconstructing the Prepaid Expenses account. But this assumption is not necessary for our analysis to hold. If cash payments are debited directly to the expense account, the total amount of cash paid for wages and other operating expenses will still equal the $216,000 expense plus the $2,000 increase in prepaid expenses.

Exhibit 19.14 summarizes the adjustments to wages (including salaries) and other operating expenses. While the balance sheet of Genesis did not report accrued liabilities, we add these to the exhibit to explain the adjustment to cash when they do exist. If accrued liabilities decrease, it implies we paid for more goods or services than received this period, and we must add the change in accrued liabilities to the expense amount to get cash paid for these goods or services. If accrued liabilities increase, it implies we paid less than was acquired and we must subtract the change in accrued liabilities from the expense amount to get cash paid.

Cash paid for wages and other operating expenses	=	Wages and other operating expenses	+ Increase in prepaid expenses *or* − Decrease in prepaid expenses	+ Decrease in accrued liabilities *or* − Increase in accrued liabilities

Exhibit 19.14

Formula to Compute Cash Paid for Wages and Operating Expenses—Direct Method

Cash Paid for Both Interest and Income Taxes

Our analysis for computing operating cash flows for interest and taxes is similar to that for operating expenses. Both require adjustments to their amounts on the income statement for changes in their related balance sheet accounts.

We begin with the income statement of Genesis showing interest expense of $7,000 and income taxes expense of $15,000. To compute the cash paid, we adjust interest expense for the change in interest payable and we adjust income taxes expense for the change in income taxes payable. These computations involve reconstructing both liability accounts:

Interest Payable			
		Balance, Dec.31/1999	4,000
Interest paid =	8,000	Interest expense	7,000
		Balance, Dec. 31/2000	3,000

Income Taxes Payable			
		Balance, Dec. 31/1999	12,000
Income taxes paid =	5,000	Income taxes expense	15,000
		Balance, Dec. 31/2000	22,000

These accounts reveal cash paid for interest of $8,000 and cash paid for income taxes of $5,000. The formulas to compute these amounts are shown in Exhibit 19.15.

Exhibit 19.15

Formulas to Compute Cash Paid for Both Interest and Taxes—Direct Method

$$\text{Cash paid for interest} = \text{Interest expense} \begin{cases} + \text{ Decrease in interest payable} \\ \quad or \\ - \text{ Increase in interest payable} \end{cases}$$

$$\text{Cash paid for taxes} = \text{Income taxes expense} \begin{cases} + \text{ Decrease in income taxes payable} \\ \quad or \\ - \text{ Increase in income taxes payable} \end{cases}$$

Both of these cash payments are reported as operating cash outflows on the statement of cash flows for Genesis in Exhibit 19.7.

Analysis of Other Operating Expenses

Genesis has three other operating expenses reported on its income statement: amortization, loss on sale of assets, and gain on retirement of debt. We consider each of these for their potential cash effects.

Amortization Expense Amortization expense for Genesis is $24,000. It is known as a *noncash expense* because there are no cash flows associated with amortization. Amortization expense is an allocation of the amortizable cost of a purchased asset. The cash outflow associated with an asset is reported as part of investing activities when it is paid for. This means amortization expense is *never* reported on a statement of cash flows using the direct method.

Loss on Sale of Assets Sales of assets frequently result in gains and losses reported as part of net income. But the amount of recorded gain or loss does *not* reflect cash flows in these transactions. Asset sales result in cash inflow equal to the actual amount received, regardless of whether the asset was sold at a gain or a loss. This cash inflow is reported under investing activities. This means the loss or gain on a sale of assets is never reported on a statement of cash flows using the direct method.

Gain on Retirement of Debt Retirements of debt usually yield gains and losses reported as part of net income. But the amount of recorded gain or loss does *not* reflect cash flows in these transactions. Debt retirement results in cash outflow equal to the actual amount paid to settle the debt, regardless of whether the debt was retired at a gain or loss. This cash outflow is reported under financing activities. This means the loss or gain from retirement of debt is never reported on a statement of cash flows using the direct method.

Summary of Adjustments for Direct Method

Exhibit 19.16 summarizes the adjustments to the revenues and expenses making up net income to give us net cash provided (used) by operating activities under the direct method.

Exhibit 19.16

Summary of Selected Adjustments for Direct Method

Item	From Income Statement	Adjustments to Get Cash Flow Numbers	
Receipts:			
From customers	Sales Revenue	+ Decrease in Accounts Receivable − Increase in Accounts Receivable	
Of rent	Rent Revenue	+ Decrease in Rent Receivable − Increase in Rent Receivable	
Of interest	Interest Revenue	+ Decrease in Interest Receivable − Increase in Interest Receivable	
Of dividends	Dividend Revenue	+ Decrease in Dividends Receivable − Increase in Dividends Receivable	
Payments:			
To suppliers	Cost of Goods Sold	+ Increase in Inventory − Decrease in Inventory	+ Decrease in Accounts Payable − Increase in Accounts Payable
For operations	Operating Expense	+ Increase in Prepaids − Decrease in Prepaids	+ Decrease in Accrued Liabilities − Increase in Accrued Liabilities
To employees	Wages (Salaries) Expense	+ Decrease in Wages (Salaries) Payable − Increase in Wages (Salaries) Payable	
For interest	Interest Expense	+ Decrease in Interest Payable − Increase in Interest Payable	
For income tax	Income Tax Expense	+ Decrease in Income Tax Payable − Increase in Income Tax Payable	

While computation for computing net cash provided (used) by operating activities is different for the direct and indirect methods, the result is identical. Both methods yield the same $20,000 amount for net cash provided (used) by operating activities; see Exhibits 19.7 and 19.17.

Direct Method Format of Operating Activities Section

Exhibit 19.7 shows the statement of cash flows for Genesis using the direct method. Major items of cash inflows and cash outflows are listed separately in the operating activities section. The format requires that operating cash outflows are subtracted from operating cash inflows to get net cash provided (used) by operating activities.

Flash back

4. Is the direct or indirect method of reporting operating cash flows more informative? Explain. Which method is more common in practice?
5. Net sales in a period are $590,000, beginning accounts receivable are $120,000, and ending accounts receivable are $90,000. What amount is collected from customers in the period?
6. The Merchandise Inventory account balance decreases in a period from a beginning balance of $32,000 to an ending balance of $28,000. Cost of goods sold for the period is $168,000. If the Accounts Payable balance increases $2,400 in the period, what is the amount of cash paid for merchandise?
7. Reported wages and other operating expenses incurred total $112,000. At the end of the prior year, prepaid expenses totalled $1,200, and this year the balance is $4,200. The current balance sheet shows wages payable of $5,600, whereas last year's did not show any accrued liabilities. How much is paid for wages and other operating expenses this year?

Answers—p. 911

Mid-Chapter Demonstration Problem

The following financial information refers to Mitchel Company:

MITCHELL COMPANY
Balance Sheets

Assets	Dec. 31, 1998	Dec. 31, 1999
Current Assets:		
Cash	$ 20,000	$ 15,000
Account receivable (net)	25,000	23,000
Inventory	34,000	37,000
Prepaid expenses	8,000	6,000
Total current assets	$ 87,000	$ 81,000
Long-term investments	40,000	37,000
Capital assets	170,000	191,000
Accumulated amortization	(25,000)	(31,000)
Total assets	$272,000	$280,000
Liabilities and Shareholders' Equity		
Current Liabilities:		
Accounts payable	$ 30,000	$ 38,000
Accrued liabilities	65,000	68,000
Total current liabilities	95,000	106,000
Bonds payable	90,000	100,000
Common shares	37,000	40,000
Retained earnings	50,000	34,000
	$272,000	$280,000

Income Statement
For Year Ended December 31, 1999

Sales	$250,000
Cost of goods sold	165,000
Gross margin	85,000
Operating expenses	40,000
Operating income before taxes	45,000
Gain on sale of investment	8,000
Income before taxes	53,000
Less income taxes	14,800
Net income	$ 38,200

Required

a. Calculate sales adjusted to a cash basis.
b. Calculate cost of goods sold adjusted to a cash basis.
c. How much cash was paid for operating expenses?
d. How much cash was provided by operating activities?

Solution to Mid-Chapter Demonstration Problem

a.		
Sales revenue reported per income statement	$250,000	
Adjustments to cash basis:		
Decrease in accounts receivable	2,000	(source of cash)
Sales adjusted to a cash basis	$252,000	
b.		
Cost of goods sold per income statement	$165,000	
Adjustments to a cash basis:		
Increase in inventory	3,000	(use of cash)
Increase in accounts payable	(8,000)	(source of cash)
Cost of goods sold adjusted to a cash basis	$160,000	
c.		
Operating expenses per income statements	$ 40,000	
Adjusted to a cash basis:		
Decrease in prepaid expenses	(2,000)	(noncash expense)
Increase in accrued liabilities	(3,000)	(increase in expense not using cash)
Amortization	(6,000)	(noncash expense)
Cash paid for operating expenses	$ 29,000	
d.		
Sales adjusted to a cash basis	$525,000	
Less: Cost of goods sold adjusted to a cash basis	160,000	
Cash paid for operating expenses	29,000	
Cash paid for income tax	14,800	
Cash provided by operating activities	$ 48,200	

Indirect Method of Reporting Operating Cash Flows

We know net income is computed using accrual accounting. Accrual accounting recognizes revenues when earned and expenses when incurred. But revenues and expenses do not necessarily reflect the receipt and payment of cash. The indirect method of computing and reporting net cash flows from operating activities involves adjusting the net income figure to get the net cash provided (used) by operating activities. This includes subtracting noncash credits from net income and adding noncash charges back to net income.

LO7 Compute cash flows from operating activities using the indirect method.

We draw on the financial statements of Genesis in Exhibit 19.10 to illustrate application of the indirect method. The indirect method of reporting begins with net income of $38,000 for Genesis. Net income is then adjusted to give us net cash provided (used) by operating activities. Exhibit 19.17 shows the results of the indirect method of reporting operating cash flows for Genesis. The net cash provided by operating activities is $20,000. This amount is the same as that for the direct method of reporting operating cash flows; see Exhibit 19.7. *The two methods always yield the same net cash flow provided (used) by operating activities.* It is only the computations and presentation that are different.

The indirect method does not report individual operating cash inflows or cash outflows. Instead, the indirect method adjusts net income for three types of adjustments as shown in Exhibit 19.17. First, there are adjustments for changes in noncash current assets and current liabilities relating to operating activities (the first

6 items). Second, there are adjustments to income statement items involving operating activities that do not affect cash inflows or outflows in the period (amortization). Third, there are adjustments to eliminate gains and losses resulting from investing and financing activities (those not part of operating activities—the loss on sale of capital assets and gain on retirement of bonds). This section describes each of these three types of adjustments in applying the indirect method.

Exhibit 19.17

Statement of Cash Flows—Indirect Method

GENESIS
Statement of Cash Flows
For Year Ended December 31, 2000

Cash flows from operating activities:		
Net income	$38,000	
Adjustments to reconcile net income to net cash provided by operating activities:		
Increase in accounts receivable	(20,000)	
Increase in merchandise inventory	(14,000)	
Increase in prepaid expenses	(2,000)	
Decrease in accounts payable	(5,000)	
Decrease in interest payable	(1,000)	
Increase in income taxes payable	10,000	
Amortization expense	24,000	
Loss on sale of capital assets	6,000	
Gain on retirement of bonds	(16,000)	
Net cash provided by operating activities		$20,000
Cash flows from investing activities:		
Cash received from sale of capital assets	$12,000	
Cash paid for purchase of capital assets	(10,000)	
Net cash provided by investing activities		2,000
Cash flows from financing activities:		
Cash received from issuing shares	$15,000	
Cash paid to retire bonds	(18,000)	
Cash paid for dividends	(14,000)	
Net cash used in financing activities		(17,000)
Net increase in cash		$ 5,000
Cash balance at beginning of 1999		12,000
Cash balance at end of 2000		$17,000

Adjustments for Operating Items Not Providing or Using Cash

The income statement usually includes certain expenses that do not reflect cash outflows in the period. Examples are amortization of capital assets and amortization of bond discount. The indirect method for reporting operating cash flows requires that:

Expenses with no cash outflows are added back to net income

To see this logic, recall that items such as amortization of capital assets are recorded with debits to expense accounts and credits to noncash accounts. There is no cash effect in these entries. Yet because items such as amortization expense are proper deductions in computing accrual income, we need to add them back to net income when computing net cash flows from operations. Adding them back cancels their deductions.

Similarly, when net income includes revenues that do not reflect cash inflows in the period, the indirect method for reporting operating cash flows requires that:

Revenues with no cash inflows are subtracted from net income

Both types of adjustments to net income are a necessary part of the computations to get net cash provided by operating activities. We now look at the individual operating items of Genesis that fit this category and do not provide or use cash.

Amortization

Amortization expense is the only operating item for Genesis that does not affect cash flows in the period. Our discussion indicates we must add $24,000 amortization expense back to net income as part of our adjustments to get net cash provided by operating activities. Later in the chapter we explain that the cash outflow for a capital asset is reported as an investing activity on the statement of cash flows when paid.

Adjustments for Nonoperating Items

The income statement sometimes includes losses that are not part of operating activities, and are classified as either investing or financing activities. Examples are a loss from sale of a capital asset and a loss from retirement of a bond payable. Under the indirect method for reporting operating cash flows:

Nonoperating losses are added back to net income

To see the logic, consider that items such as a capital asset sale and bond retirement are normally recorded by recognizing the cash, removing all capital asset or bond accounts, and recognizing the loss or gain. The cash received or paid is not part of operating activities. Instead it is recorded under either investing or financing activities. There is *no* operating cash flow effect. But because the nonoperating loss is a deduction in computing accrual income, we need to add it back to net income when computing the net cash flow effect from operations. Adding it back cancels the deduction.

Similarly, when net income includes gains that are not part of operating activities, the indirect method for reporting operating cash flows requires:

Nonoperating gains are subtracted from net income

These net income adjustments are part of computations to get net cash provided by operating activities. We now look at the individual nonoperating items of Genesis.

Loss on Sale of Capital Assets

Genesis reports a $6,000 loss on sale of capital assets in its income statement. This loss is a proper deduction in computing net income, but it is *not part of operating activities*. Instead, a sale of capital assets is part of investing activities. This means the $6,000 nonoperating loss is added back to net income as part of our adjustments to get net cash provided by operating activities. Adding it back cancels the recorded loss. Later in the chapter we explain how the cash inflow from the capital asset sale is reported in investing activities.

Gain on Retirement of Debt

There is a $16,000 gain on retirement of debt reported in the income statement of Genesis. This gain is properly included in net income, but it is *not part of operating activities*. This means the $16,000 nonoperating gain is subtracted from net income as part of our adjustments to get net cash provided by operating activities. Subtracting it cancels the recorded gain. Later in the chapter we describe how the cash outflow to retire debt is reported in financing activities.

Adjustments for Changes in Current Assets and Current Liabilities

This section describes adjustments for changes in noncash current assets and current liabilities as part of the procedure for determining operating cash flows using the indirect method.

Adjustments for Changes in Noncash Current Assets

Changes in noncash current assets are normally the result of operating activities. Examples are sales affecting accounts receivable and use of rented assets affecting prepaid rent expense. Our adjustments to net income in computing operating cash flows must therefore include changes in noncash current assets. Under the indirect method for reporting operating cash flows:

Decreases in noncash current assets are added to net income

To see this logic, consider that a decrease in a noncash current asset such as accounts receivable suggests more available cash at the end of the period compared to the beginning of the period. This is because a decrease in accounts receivable implies greater cash receipts. We add these greater cash receipts from decreases in noncash current assets to net income when computing net cash flow from operations.

Similarly, an increase in noncash current assets such as accounts receivable implies more credit sales than cash collections. An increase in prepaid rent expense suggests more cash was paid for rent than was deducted as rent expense. We must therefore subtract this increase in prepaid rent from net income in computing the amount of cash flow from operations. The indirect method for reporting operating cash flows requires:

Increases in noncash current assets are subtracted from net income

These adjustments to net income are a necessary part of the computations to get net cash provided by operating activities. We now turn to the individual noncash current assets of Genesis as shown in Exhibit 17.10.

Accounts Receivable Accounts receivable of Genesis *increased* $20,000 in the period, from a beginning balance of $40,000 to an ending balance of $60,000. This increase implies Genesis collected less cash than its reported sales amount for this period. It also means some of these sales were in the form of accounts receivable, leaving accounts receivable with an increase. This lesser amount of cash collections compared with sales is reflected in the Accounts Receivable account as shown here:

Accounts Receivable			
Balance, Dec. 31/1999	40,000		
Sales, 2000	590,000	Collections =	570,000
Balance, Dec. 31/2000	60,000		

This $20,000 increase in accounts receivable is subtracted from net income as part of our adjustments to get net cash provided by operating activities. Subtracting it adjusts sales to the cash receipts amount.

Merchandise Inventory Merchandise inventory *increased* $14,000 in the period, from a beginning balance of $70,000 to an ending balance of $84,000. This increase implies Genesis had a greater amount of cash purchases than goods sold this period. This greater amount of cash purchases ended up in the form of inventory, resulting in an inventory increase. This greater amount of cash purchases compared to the amount subtracted from income as cost of goods sold is reflected in the Merchandise Inventory account increase:

Merchandise Inventory			
Balance, Dec. 31/1999	70,000		
Purchases =	314,000	Cost of goods sold	300,000
Balance, Dec. 31/2000	84,000		

The $14,000 increase in inventory is subtracted from net income as part of our adjustments to get net cash provided by operating activities.

Prepaid Expenses Prepaid expenses *increased* $2,000 in the period, from a beginning balance of $4,000 to an ending balance of $6,000. This increase implies Genesis' cash payments exceeded its operating expenses incurred this period. These larger cash payments ended up increasing the amount of prepaid expenses. This is reflected in the Prepaid Expenses account:

Prepaid Expenses			
Balance, Dec. 31/1999	4,000		
Payments =	218,000	Wages and other operating expenses	216,000
Balance, Dec. 31/2000	6,000		

This $2,000 increase in prepaid expenses is subtracted from net income as part of our adjustments to get net cash provided by operating activities. Subtracting it adjusts operating expenses to a cash payments amount.

Adjustments for Changes in Current Liabilities

Changes in current liabilities are normally the result of operating activities. An example is purchases affecting accounts payable. Our adjustments to net income in computing operating cash flows must therefore include changes in current liabilities. Under the indirect method for reporting operating cash flows:

Increases in current liabilities are added to net income

To see the logic, an increase in accounts payable suggests that cash payments are less than its related expense. As another example, an increase in wages payable implies that wages expense exceeded cash paid for the period. Because more was deducted as an expense than was paid in cash, we add the increase in wages payable to net income when computing net cash flow from operations.

Similarly, when current liabilities decrease in the period, the indirect method for reporting operating cash flows requires:

Decreases in current liabilities are subtracted from net income

These adjustments to net income are a necessary part of the computations to get net cash provided by operating activities. We now turn to the individual current liabilities of Genesis as shown in Exhibit 17.10.

Accounts Payable Accounts payable of Genesis *decreased* $5,000 in the period, from a beginning balance of $40,000 to an ending balance of $35,000. This decrease implies its cash payments exceeded its merchandise purchases by

$5,000 for the period. This larger amount for cash payments compared to purchases is reflected in the Accounts Payable account:

Accounts Payable			
		Balance, Dec. 31/1999	40,000
Payments =	319,000	Purchases	314,000
		Balance, Dec. 31/2000	35,000

The $5,000 decrease in accounts payable is subtracted from net income as part of our adjustments to get net cash provided by operating activities.

Interest Payable Interest payable *decreased* $1,000 in the period, from a beginning balance of $4,000 to an ending balance of $3,000. This decrease indicates cash payments for interest exceeded interest expense for the period by $1,000. This larger cash payment compared to the reported interest expense is reflected in the Interest Payable account:

Interest Payable			
		Balance, Dec. 31/1999	4,000
Interest paid =	8,000	Interest expense	7,000
		Balance, Dec. 31/2000	3,000

The $1,000 decrease in interest payable is subtracted from net income as part of our adjustments to get net cash provided by operating activities.

Income Taxes Payable Income taxes payable *increased* $10,000 in the period, from a beginning balance of $12,000 to an ending balance of $22,000. This increase implies the amount owed for income taxes exceeded the cash payments for the period by $10,000. This smaller cash payment compared to income taxes owed is reflected in the Income Taxes Payable account:

Income Taxes Payable			
		Balance, Dec. 31/1999	12,000
Income taxes paid =	5,000	Income taxes expense	15,000
		Balance, Dec. 31/2000	22,000

The $10,000 increase in income taxes payable is added to net income as part of our adjustments to get net cash provided by operating activities.

Did You Know?

Cash or Income

The difference between net income and operating cash flows can be large. As examples, Alcan reported a net income of $410 million and operating cash flows of $981 million in its 1996 annual report and CAE reported a net income of $60,276,000 and an operating cash outflow of $(44,485,000) in its 1997 annual report.

Summary of Adjustments for Indirect Method

Exhibit 19.18 summarizes the adjustments to net income to get net cash provided (used) by operating activities for the indirect method.

Exhibit 19.18

Summary of Selected Adjustments for Indirect Method

Net Income
- \+ Amortization
- \+ Loss on disposal of long-term asset
- \+ Loss on retirement of debt
- − Gain on disposal of long-term asset
- − Gain on retirement of debt
- \+ Decrease in noncash current asset
- − Increase in noncash current asset
- \+ Increase in current liability*
- − Decrease in current liability*

Net cash provided (used) by operating activities

*Excludes current portion of long-term debt and any short-term notes payable if unrelated to sales. Both are financing activities.

While the computations in determining net cash provided (used) by operating activities is different for the direct and indirect methods, the result is identical. Both methods yield the same $20,000 figure for net cash provided (used) by operating activities; see Exhibits 19.7 and 19.17.

Flash back

8. Determine the net cash provided (or used) by operating activities using the following data:

Net income	$74,900
Decrease in accounts receivable	4,600
Increase in inventory	11,700
Decrease in accounts payable	1,000
Loss on sale of equipment	3,400
Payment of dividends	21,500

9. Why are expenses such as amortization added to net income when cash flow from operating activities is computed by the indirect method?

10. A company reports net income of $15,000 that includes a $3,000 gain on the sale of capital assets. Why is this gain subtracted from net income in computing cash flow from operating activities using the indirect method?

Answers—p. 911

Cash Flows from Investing Activities

The third step in preparing the statement of cash flows is to compute and report net cash flows from investing activities. Cash flows for investing activities reveal the extent to which expenditures have been made for the purpose of generating future income cash flows. We determine investing activities by identifying changes in all noncurrent asset accounts and both current and long-term notes receivable. These accounts include capital assets, investments, and notes. Changes in these accounts are then analyzed using available information to determine their effect, if any, on cash. Results of this analysis are reported in the investing activities section of the statement. *Reporting of investing activities is identical under the direct method and indirect method.*

Investing activities include transactions such as the (a) purchase and sale of property, plant and equipment, intangibles and other long-term assets, (b) lending and collecting on notes receivable, and (c) purchase and sale of debt or equity instruments other than those instruments considered to be cash equivalents. Information to compute cash flows from investing activities is usually taken from beginning and ending balance sheets and from the income statement. Information provided earlier in the chapter about the transactions of Genesis reveals it both purchased and sold capital assets during the period. Both transactions are investing activities.

LO 8 Determine cash flows from both investing and financing activities.

Capital Asset Transactions

We use a three-step process in determining net cash provided (used) by investing activities. (1) Identify changes in investing-related accounts. (2) Explain these changes using reconstruction analysis. (3) Report cash flow effects.

For capital assets, we need to deal with both the capital asset account and its related accumulated amortization account. Comparative balance sheet information for these accounts is in Exhibit 19.10. The first step reveals a $40,000 increase in capital assets from $210,000 to $250,000, and a $12,000 increase in accumulated amortization from $48,000 to $60,000. We need to explain these changes.

The second step begins by reviewing ledger accounts and any additional information at our disposal. A capital asset account is affected by both purchases and sales of capital assets. An accumulated amortization account is increased by additional amortization and reduced by removing accumulated amortization on asset disposals. Items (b) and (c) of the additional information reported on page 886 for Genesis are relevant for these accounts. To explain changes in these accounts and to help us understand the cash flows effects, we prepare *reconstructed entries*. A reconstructed entry is our reproduction of an entry from a transaction; *it is not the actual entry made by the preparer*. Item (b) reports Genesis purchased capital assets costing $70,000 by issuing $60,000 in bonds payable to the seller and paying $10,000 in cash. The reconstructed entry for our analysis of item (b) is:

Assets = Liabilities + Equity
+70,000 +60,000
−10,000

Capital Assets	70,000	
Bonds Payable		60,000
Cash		**10,000**

This entry reveals a $10,000 cash outflow for assets purchased. It also reveals a noncash investing and financing transaction involving $60,000 bonds given up for $60,000 of capital assets.

Item (c) reports Genesis sold capital assets costing $30,000 (with $12,000 of accumulated amortization) for cash received of $12,000, resulting in a loss of $6,000. The reconstructed entry for item (c) is:

Assets = Liabilities + Equity
+12,000 −6,000
−30,000
+12,000

Cash	**12,000**	
Accumulated Amortization	12,000	
Loss on Sale of Capital Assets	6,000	
Capital Assets		30,000

This entry reveals a $12,000 cash inflow for assets sold. Also, notice the $6,000 loss is computed by comparing the asset book value to the cash received, and does not reflect any cash inflow or outflow.

We can also reconstruct the entry for amortization expense using information from the income statement:

Assets = Liabilities + Equity
−24,000 −24,000

Amortization Expense	24,000	
Accumulated Amortization		24,000

This entry shows that amortization expense results in no cash flow effects.

These reconstructed entries are reflected in the ledger accounts for both capital assets and accumulated amortization.

Capital Assets			
Balance, Dec. 31/1999	210,000		
Purchase	70,000	Sale	30,000
Balance, Dec. 31/2000	250,000		

Accumulated Amortization, Capital Assets			
		Balance, Dec. 31/1999	48,000
Sale	12,000	Amort. expense	24,000
		Balance, Dec. 31/2000	60,000

In performing an actual cash flow analysis we have the entire ledger and additional information at our disposal. For brevity reasons, we are given the additional information for reconstructing accounts and verifying that our analysis of the investing-related accounts is complete.

The third step is to make the necessary disclosures on the statement of cash flows. Disclosure of the two cash flow effects in the investing section of the statement appears as (also see Exhibit 19.7 or 19.17):

Cash flows from investing activities:	
Cash received from sale of capital assets	$ 12,000
Cash paid for purchase of capital assets	(10,000)

The $60,000 portion of the purchase described in item (b) and financed by issuance of bonds is a noncash investing and financing activity. This can be reported in a note to the statement as:

Noncash investing and financing activity:
Purchased capital assets with issuance of bonds........ $60,000

We have now reconstructed these accounts by explaining how the beginning balances of both accounts are affected by purchases, sales, and amortization in yielding their ending balances. For instance, the change in capital assets from $210,000 to $250,000 is fully explained by the $70,000 purchase and the $30,000 sale. Also, the change in accumulated amortization from $48,000 to $60,000 is fully explained by the sale of assets (with $12,000 of accumulated amortization) and $24,000 of amortization expense.

Flash back

11. Equipment costing $80,000 with accumulated amortization of $30,000 is sold at a loss of $10,000. What is the cash receipt from the sale? In what category of the statement of cash flows is it reported?

Answers—p. 911

Cash Flows from Financing Activities

The fourth step in preparing the statement of cash flows is to compute and report net cash flows from financing activities. We normally do this by identifying changes in all note payable (current and noncurrent), noncurrent liability, and equity accounts. These accounts include long-term debt, notes payable, bonds payable, owner's capital, common shares, and retained earnings. Changes in these accounts are then analyzed using available information to determine their effect, if any, on cash. Results of this analysis are reported in the financing activities section of the statement. *Reporting of financing activities is identical under the direct method and indirect method.*

Financing activities include transactions such as (a) receiving cash from issuing debt and repaying the amounts borrowed, and (b) receiving cash from or distributing cash to owners. Information provided earlier about the transactions of Genesis reveals four transactions involving financing activities. We already analyzed one of these, the $60,000 issuance of bonds payable to purchase capital assets as a noncash investing and financing activity. The remaining three transactions are retirement of bonds, issuance of common shares, and payment of cash dividends. We again use a three-step process in determining net cash provided (used) by financing activities. (1) Identify changes in financing-related accounts. (2) Explain these changes using reconstruction analysis. (3) Report cash flow effects.

Bonds Payable Transactions

Comparative balance sheet information from Exhibit 19.10 for bonds payable is our starting point. The first step reveals an increase in bonds payable from $64,000 to $90,000. We need to explain this change.

The second step is to review the bonds payable ledger account and any additional information available. Item (e) of the additional information given earlier for Genesis is relevant to bonds payable. Item (e) reports bonds with a carrying value of $34,000 are retired for $18,000 cash, resulting in a $16,000 gain. The reconstructed entry for our analysis of item (e) is:

Assets	= Liabilities	+ Equity
−18,000	−34,000	+16,000

Bonds Payable	34,000	
Gain on retirement of debt		16,000
Cash		**18,000**

This entry reveals an $18,000 cash outflow for retirement of bonds. It also shows a $16,000 gain from comparing the bonds payable carrying value with the cash received. This gain does not reflect any cash inflow or outflow.

Item (b) also involves bonds payable. It reports Genesis purchased capital assets costing $70,000 by issuing $60,000 in bonds payable to the seller and paying $10,000 in cash. We already reconstructed its entry for our analysis of investing activities. Recall it increased bonds payable by $60,000 and is reported as a noncash investing and financing transaction. These reconstructed entries are reflected in the ledger account for bonds payable:

Bonds Payable			
		Balance, Dec. 31/1999	64,000
Retired bonds	34,000	Issued bonds	60,000
		Balance, Dec. 31/2000	90,000

The third step is to make the necessary disclosures on the statement of cash flows. Disclosure of the cash flow effect from the bond retirement in the financing section of the statement appears as (also see Exhibit 19.7 or 19.17):

Cash flows from financing activities:	
Cash paid to retire bonds	(18,000)

We have now reconstructed the bonds payable account by explaining how its beginning balance is affected by a bond retirement and bond issuance in yielding its ending balance. In particular, the change in bonds payable from $64,000 to $90,000 is fully explained by the $34,000 retirement and the $60,000 issuance.

Common Shares Transactions

We use comparative balance sheet information from Exhibit 19.10 for the first step in analyzing the common shares account. This first step reveals an increase in common shares from $80,000 to $95,000. We need to explain this change.

Our second step is to review the common shares ledger account and any additional information available. Item (d) of the additional information given earlier for Genesis reports it issued 3,000 common shares for $5 per share. The reconstructed entry for our analysis of item (d) is:

Cash	**15,000**	
Common Shares		15,000

Assets = Liabilities + Equity
+15,000 +15,000

This entry reveals a $15,000 cash inflow from the issuance of shares. This reconstructed entry is reflected in the ledger account for common shares:

Common Shares		
	Balance, Dec. 31/1999	80,000
	Issued shares	15,000
	Balance, Dec. 31/2000	95,000

The third step is to make the necessary disclosure on the statement of cash flows. Disclosure of the cash flow effect from shares issuance in the financing section of the statement appears as (also see Exhibit 19.7 or 19.17):

Cash flows from financing activities:	
Cash received from issuing shares	$ 15,000

The $15,000 shares issue fully explains the change in the Common Shares account.

Retained Earnings Transactions

The first step in analyzing the Retained Earnings account is to review comparative balance sheet information from Exhibit 19.10. The first step reveals an increase in retained earnings from $88,000 to $112,000. We need to explain this change.

Our second step is to analyze the Retained Earnings account and any additional information available. Item (f) of the additional information given earlier for Genesis reports it paid cash dividends of $14,000. The reconstructed entry for our analysis of item (f) is:

Retained Earnings	14,000	
Cash		**14,000**

Assets = Liabilities + Equity
−14,000 −14,000

This entry reveals a $14,000 cash outflow to pay cash dividends. We must also remember retained earnings is affected by net income from the income statement. Net income was already dealt with under the operating section of the statement of cash flows. This reconstruction analysis is reflected in the ledger account for retained earnings:

Retained Earnings			
		Balance, Dec. 31/1999	88,000
Cash dividend	14,000	Net income	38,000
		Balance, Dec. 31/2000	112,000

The third step is to make the necessary disclosure on the statement of cash flows. Disclosure of the cash flow effect from the cash dividend appears in the financing section of the statement as (also see Exhibit 19.7 or 19.17):

Cash flows from financing activities:	
Cash paid for dividends	(14,000)

The $14,000 dividend payment along with the reported net income of $38,000 fully explain the change in Retained Earnings.

Proving Cash Balances

We have now explained all of the cash inflows and outflows of Genesis, along with one noncash investing and financing transaction. Our analysis has reconciled changes in all noncash balance sheet accounts. The fifth and final step in preparing the statement is to report the beginning and ending cash balance and prove the *net change in cash* is explained by operating, investing, and financing net cash flows. This step is shown below for Genesis:

Net cash provided by operating activities	$20,000
Net cash provided by investing activities	2,000
Net cash used in financing activities	(17,000)
Net increase in cash and cash equivalents	**$ 5,000**
Cash and cash equivalents at beginning of 2000 .	12,000
Cash and cash equivalents at end of 2000	$17,000

This schedule shows the $5,000 net increase in cash from $12,000 at the beginning of the period to $17,000 at the end is reconciled by net cash flows from operating ($20,000 inflow), investing ($2,000 inflow), and financing ($17,000 outflow) activities. This is formally reported at the bottom of the statement of cash flows as shown in either Exhibit 19.7 or 19.17.

You Make the Call

Reporter

You are a newspaper reporter covering a workers' strike. Management grants you an interview and complains about recent losses and negative cash flows. It shows you financial numbers revealing a recent $600,000 net loss which included a $930,000 extraordinary loss. It also shows you the company's total net cash outflow of $550,000 which included net cash outflows of $850,000 for investing activities and $350,000 for financing activities. What is your initial reaction to management's complaints?

Answer—p. 911

Cash Flow Analysis

USING THE INFORMATION

Numerous ratios are used to analyze income statement and balance sheet data. By comparison, ratios related to the statement of cash flows are fewer in number. One of these ratios is cash flow per share. One must be careful not to interpret it as a measure of earnings performance.

Analyzing Cash Sources and Uses

LO 9 Analyze the statement of cash flows.

Most managers stress the importance of understanding and predicting cash flows. Many business decisions are based on cash flow evaluations. For instance, creditors evaluate a company's ability to generate cash before deciding whether to loan money. Many investors make similar evaluations before buying shares. Specifically, information in the statement of cash flows helps us address questions such as:

- How much cash is generated from or used in operations?
- What expenditures are made with cash from operations?
- How are dividends paid when losses occur?
- What is the source of cash for debt payments?
- What is the source of cash for distributions to owners?
- How is the increase in investments financed?
- What is the source of cash for new capital assets?
- Why is cash lower when income increased?
- What is the use of cash from financing?

While cash flows from investing and financing activities are important in these decisions, we pay special attention to operating cash flows. A statement of cash flows helps in this regard by separating investing, financing, and operating activities.

To illustrate the importance of separately analyzing cash flows by activities, we look at data from three different companies in Exhibit 19.19. These companies operate in the same industry and have been in business for several years.

Exhibit 19.19
Cash Flows of Competitors

(in thousands)	Foster	Smith	Tower
Cash provided (used) by operating activities	$90,000	$40,000	$(24,000)
Cash provided (used) by investing activities:			
Proceeds from sale of operating assets			26,000
Purchase of operating assets	(48,000)	(25,000)	
Cash provided (used) by financing activities:			
Proceeds from issuance of debt			13,000
Repayment of debt	(27,000)		
Net increase (decrease) in cash	$15,000	$15,000	$15,000

These three companies each generated a $15,000 net increase in cash flows. But their sources and uses of cash flows are very different. Foster's operating activities provided net cash flows of $90,000. This allowed it to purchase additional operating assets for $48,000 and repay $27,000 of debt. Smith's operating activities provided $40,000 of operating cash flows. This limited its purchase of operating assets to $25,000. Tower's net cash increase is due to selling operating assets and incurring additional debt. Its operating activities resulted in a net cash outflow of $24,000.

Our analysis of these cash flow data reveals that Foster is more capable of generating cash to meet its future obligations than is Smith or Tower. Also, the strong operating cash flows of Foster bode well for future performance, while Tower's operating outlook is poor. This evaluation is, of course, tentative and may be contradicted by other information, including data in the balance sheet or income statement.

Managers analyze cash flows for making many short-term and long-term decisions. A decision on the necessity of short-term borrowing is made using many of the procedures we discussed in this chapter. Short-term planning also can lead to decisions about investing idle cash balances. Managers' setting of sales prices is also influenced by cash flow data.

Managers' long-term decisions involving new investments are based on cash flow predictions. They estimate cash inflows and outflows over the life of the investment, often extending many years into the future. Other long-term decisions based on cash flow data include deciding whether a product is manufactured by the company or purchased from an outside supplier, and whether a product or a department is eliminated or retained.

Flash back

12. Refer to the statement of cash flows for **Atlantis** in Appendix I. What was the major investing activity that took place during the year ended December 31, 1997?

Answer—p. 911

Cash Flow on Total Assets

LO 10 Compute and apply the cash flow on total assets ratio.

We described the importance of return on total assets in both Chapters 1 and 18. Return on total assets is a valuable measure of financial performance and is computed as net income divided by average total assets. The numerator of return on total assets is net income based on accrual accounting. Accrual accounting records revenue when earned and expenses when incurred.

Cash flow accounting is different from accrual accounting. Cash flow accounting recognizes cash inflows when received (not necessarily earned) and cash outflows when paid (not necessarily incurred). While cash flow information has limitations, it can help us measure a company's ability to meet its obligations, pay dividends, expand operations, and obtain financing.

Because of the importance of cash flows, users often look at a cash-based measure called cash flow on total assets. It is somewhat similar to return on total assets, but its numerator is net cash flows from operating activities (not net income). Specifically, the *cash flow on total assets* is computed as shown in Exhibit 19.20.

Exhibit 19.20

Cash Flow on Total Assets

$$\textbf{Cash flow on total assets} = \frac{\textbf{Operating cash flows}}{\textbf{Average total assets}}$$

This ratio can add to our analysis of company performance. The cash flow on total assets ratio reflects actual cash flows and is not affected by the accounting constraints of recognition and measurement for net income. It is important for companies to recognize its cash flow amounts and patterns in planning and analyzing operating activities. The cash flow on total assets ratio is one measure to help us assess cash flows.

To illustrate, we look at the cash flow on total assets for **NIKE** at May 31, 1997. It is computed as ($ in thousands):

$$\text{Cash flow on total assets} = \frac{\$323{,}120}{(\$5{,}361{,}207 + \$3{,}951{,}628)/2} = 6.94\%$$

Is a 6.94% cash flow on total assets good or bad for NIKE? To help answer this question and others like it, we can compare NIKE's ratio with its prior performance, the ratios of competitors, and with ratios of other noncompeting companies. As a first step, we show NIKE's cash flow on total assets ratio for each of the prior three-years in the second column of Exhibit 19.21. Its return on total assets is provided for comparison purposes in the third column.

Exhibit 19.21

NIKE's Cash Flow on Total Assets

Year	Cash Flow on Total Assets	Return on Total Assets
1997	6.94%	17.09%
1996	9.58	15.60
1995	9.24	14.49

We see that NIKE's cash flow on total assets has declined steadily over the period 1995–97, while its return on total assets has slightly grown. This result suggests NIKE's *earnings quality* has declined over this period. This decline in earnings quality for NIKE means less of its earnings is realized in the form of cash.

We also compare NIKE's cash flow on total assets to some other companies including **PepsiCo, McDonald's, Wal-Mart,** and **Wendy's.** A bar chart of these results is shown in Exhibit 19.22.

Exhibit 19.22

Cash Flow on Total Assets of Selected Companies

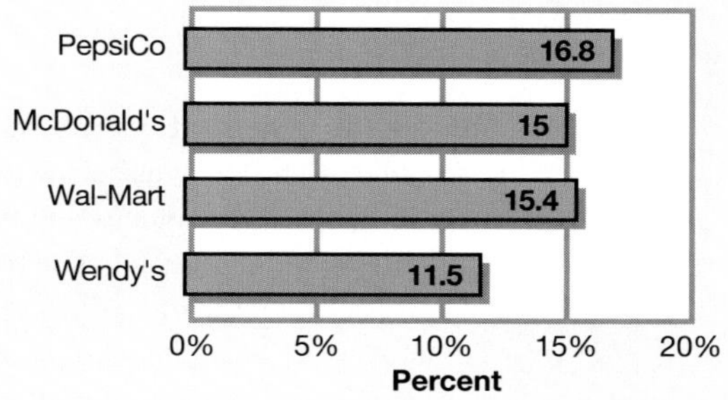

We see that NIKE's cash flow on total assets ratio is lower than the same ratio for these companies. This finding adds to our concern from the resulting decline in the cash flow on total assets ratio as evidenced in Exhibit 19.21.

Overall, the statement of cash flows is an important bridge between the income statement and balance sheet, and valuable in financial analysis. The cash flow on total assets ratio is a useful part of this analysis, and is used as an indicator of earnings quality.

Free Cash Flow

Free cash flow is a common term in financial analysis. It refers to operating cash flows available after allowing for investing and financing requirements. Free cash flow is usually defined as operating cash flows minus capital expenditures and cash dividends. Growth and financial flexibility depend on adequate free cash flow.

Did You Know?

Summary

LO1 **Explain the purpose and importance of cash flow information.** The main purpose of the statement of cash flows is to report the items comprising cash receipts and cash payments for a period. This includes identifying these cash flows as relating to either operating, investing, or financing activities. Many business decisions involve evaluating cash flows. Examples are investor and creditor decisions to invest in or loan money to a company. Users' evaluations include focusing on the activities that provide or use cash.

LO2 **Distinguish among operating, investing, and financing activities.** Operating activities include the cash effects of transactions and events that determine net income. Investing activities include the (a) purchase and sale of long-term assets, (b) the purchase and sale of short-term investments other than cash equivalents, and (c) lending and collecting on loans. Financing activities include (a) getting cash from issuing debt and repaying the amounts borrowed, and (b) obtaining cash from or distributing cash to owners and giving owners a return on investment.

LO3 **Identify and disclose noncash investing and financing activities.** For external reporting, a company must supplement its statement of cash flows with a description of its noncash investing and financing activities. These activities are disclosed in either a note to the statement or in a separate schedule usually reported at the bottom of the statement. Two examples of these activities are the retirement of debt by issuing equity securities and the exchange of a note payable for capital assets.

LO4 **Describe the format of the statement of cash flows.** The statement of cash flows reports cash receipts and disbursements into one of three categories: operating, investing, or financing activities. Cash inflows and cash outflows are reported for each category.

LO5 **Prepare a statement of cash flows.** Preparation of a statement of cash flows involves five steps: (1) compute the net increase or decrease in cash, (2) compute net cash provided (used) by operating activities [using either the direct or indirect method], (3) compute net cash provided (used) by investing activities, and (4) compute net cash provided (used) by financing activities. Noncash investing and financing activities are disclosed in either a note or in a separate schedule to the statement. (5) report the beginning and ending cash balance and prove it is explained by operating, investing and financing net cash flows.

LO6 **Compute cash flows from operating activities using the direct method.** The direct method for reporting net cash provided (used) by operating activities involves listing separately the major classes of operating cash inflows and outflows. The operating cash outflows are then subtracted from operating cash inflows to get the net inflow or outflow from operating activities. The direct method is recommended by the CICA. The direct method should also include a separate schedule reporting the reconciliation between net income and net cash provided (used) by operating activities.

LO7 **Compute cash flows from operating activities using the indirect method.** The indirect method for reporting net cash provided (used) by operating activities starts with net income and then adjusts it for three items: (1) revenues and expenses not providing (using) cash, (2) gains and losses from investing and financing activities, and (3) changes in noncash current assets and current liabilities related to operating activities.

LO8 **Determine cash flows from both investing and financing activities.** Cash flows from both investing and financing activities are determined by identifying the cash flow effects of transactions and events affecting each balance sheet account related to these activities. All cash flows from these activities are identified when we can explain changes in these accounts from the beginning to the end of the period.

LO9 **Analyze the statement of cash flows.** To understand and predict cash flows, users stress the importance of separately identifying the sources and uses of cash flows by operating, investing, and financing activities. Special emphasis is placed on operating cash flows since they derive from a company's continuing operations.

LO10 **Compute and apply the cash flow on total assets ratio.** The cash flow on total assets ratio is defined as operating cash flows divided by average total assets. Companies prefer to maintain a regular and positive level of net cash flows from operating activities, and analysis of current and past cash flow on total assets ratios is one measure of a company's success in achieving this goal. It is also viewed as a measure of earnings quality.

Guidance Answers to **You Make the Call**

Community Activist

Several reasons can explain an increase in net cash flows when a loss is reported. Possibilities include: (1) early recognition of expenses relative to revenues generated (research and development), (2) valuable long-term sales contracts not yet recognized in income, (3) issuances of debt or equity to finance expansion, (4) selling of assets, (5) delayed cash payments, and (6) prepayment on sales. Your analysis of this manufacturer needs to focus on the components of both net income and net cash flows, and their implications for future performance.

Reporter

Your initial course of action is to verify management's claims about poor performance. A $600,000 loss along with a $550,000 decrease in net cash flows seemingly supports its claim. But a closer scrutiny reveals a different picture. You compute its cash flow from operating activities at a positive $650,000, computed as [?] − $850,000 − $350,000 = ($550,000). You note also net income *before* the extraordinary loss is a positive $330,000, computed as [?] − $930,000 = ($600,000). This is powerful information to confront management. A serious and directed discussion is likely to reveal a far more positive picture of this company's financial performance.

Guidance Answers to Flashbacks

1. No. The statement of cash flows reports changes in the sum of cash plus cash equivalents. It does not report transfers between cash and cash equivalents.
2. The three categories of cash inflows and outflows are operating activities, investing activities, and financing activities.
3. a. Investing
   b. Operating
   c. Financing
   d. Operating
   e. Operating
   f. Financing
4. The direct method is most informative because it separately lists each major item of operating cash receipts and each major item of operating cash payments. The indirect method is used most often.
5. $590,000 + ($120,000 − $90,000) = $620,000
6. $168,000 − ($32,000 − $28,000) − $2,400 = $161,600
7. $112,000 + ($4,200 − $1,200) − $5,600 = $109,400
8. $74,900 + $4,600 − $11,700 − $1,000 + $3,400 = $70,200
9. In the calculation of net income, expenses such as amortization are subtracted from revenue. These expenses do not require current cash outflows. Therefore, adding these expenses back to net income eliminates noncash items from the net income number, converting it to a cash basis.
10. In the process of reconciling net income to net cash provided (or used) by operating activities, a gain on the sale of capital assets is subtracted from net income because a sale of capital assets is not an operating activity; it is an investing activity.
11. $80,000 − $30,000 − $10,000 = $40,000

    The $40,000 cash receipt is reported as an investing activity.
12. Investing activities during the year ended December 31, 1997, showed that the largest use of cash was the completion of programs costing $129,945,000.

Demonstration Problem

Umlauf's beginning and ending balance sheet, income statement, and supplementary information follow.

Required

1. Prepare a statement of cash flows using the direct method for the year ended 2000.
2. Prepare a statement of cash flows using the indirect method for the year ended 2000.

UMLAUF COMPANY
Balance Sheet
December 31, 2000 and 1999

	December 31	
	2000	1999
Assets		
Cash	$ 43,050	$ 23,925
Accounts receivable	34,125	39,825
Merchandise inventory	156,000	146,475
Prepaid expenses	3,600	1,650
Equipment	135,825	146,700
Accumulated amortization, equipment	(61,950)	(47,550)
Totals	$310,650	$311,025
Liabilities and Shareholders' Equity		
Accounts payable	28,800	33,750
Income taxes payable	5,100	4,425
Dividends payable	-0-	4,500
Bonds payable	-0-	37,500
Common shares no-par value	168,750	168,750
Retained earnings	108,000	62,100
Totals	$310,650	$311,025

An examination of the company's statements and accounts showed:

a. All sales were made on credit.
b. All merchandise purchases were on credit.
c. Accounts Payable balances resulted from merchandise purchases.
d. Prepaid expenses relate to other operating expenses.
e. Equipment costing $21,375 with accumulated amortization of $11,100 was sold for cash.
f. Equipment was purchased for cash.
g. The change in the balance of Accumulated Amortization resulted from amortization expense and from the sale of equipment.
h. The change in the balance of Retained Earnings resulted from dividend declarations and net income.

UMLAUF COMPANY
Income Statement
For Year Ended December 31, 2000

Sales (see note 1)		$446,100
Cost of goods sold (see note 2)	$222,300	
Other operating expenses (see note 3)	120,300	
Amortization expense	25,500	
Income taxes expense (see note 4)	13,725	(381,825)
Loss on sale of equipment (see note 5)		(3,300)
Loss on retirement of bonds (see note 6)		(825)
Net income (See note 7)		$60,150

Planning the Solution

- Prepare a blank statement of cash flows with sections for operating, investing, and financing activities using the direct method format.
- Compute cash received from customers, cash paid for merchandise, cash paid for other operating expenses and taxes as illustrated in the chapter.
- Compute the cash paid for equipment and the cash received from the sale of equipment according to the supplementary information provided, the amount for amortization expense, and the change in the balances of equipment and accumulated amortization. Use a T-account to help chart the effects of the sale and purchase of the equipment on the balances of the equipment account and the accumulated amortization account.
- Calculate the effect of net income on the change in the retained earnings balance. Ascribe the difference between the change in retained earnings and the amount of net income to dividends declared. Adjust the dividends declared amount for the change in the dividends payable balance.
- Enter the cash effects of the entry in the appropriate section of the statement,
- Total each section of the statement, determine the total change in cash, and add the beginning balance to get the ending balance.
- Now prepare a blank statement of cash flows with sections for operating, investing, and financing activities using the indirect method format.

Solution to Demonstration Problem

Notes:

(1)	Sales	$446,100
	Add decrease in accounts receivable	5,700
	Cash received from customers	$451,800
(2)	Cost of goods sold	$222,300
	Plus increase in merchandise inventory	9,525
	Purchases	231,825
	Plus decrease in accounts payable	4,950
	Cash paid for merchandise	$236,775
(3)	Other operating expenses	$120,300
	Plus increase in prepaid expenses	1,950
	Cash paid for other operating expenses	$122,250
(4)	Income taxes expense	$13,725
	Less increase in income taxes payable	(675)
	Payments of income taxes	$ 13,050
(5)	Cost of equipment sold	$21,375
	Accumulated amortization of equipment sold	(11,100)
	Book value of equipment sold	10,275
	Loss on sale of equipment	(3,300)
	Cash receipt from sale of equipment	$ 6,975
	Cost of equipment sold	$ 21,375
	Less decrease in the equipment account balance	(10,875)
	Cash paid for new equipment	$ 10,500

Equipment			
Balance, Dec. 31/1999	146,700		
Purchase	10,500	Sale	21,375
Balance, Dec. 31/2000	135,825		

Accumulated Amortization, Equipment			
		Balance, Dec. 31/1999	47,550
Sale	11,100	Amort. expense	25,500
		Balance, Dec. 31/2000	61,950

(6)	Loss on retirement of bonds	$ 825
	Carrying value of bonds retired	37,500
	Cash payment to retire bonds	$38,325
(7)	Net income	$ 60,150
	Less increase in retained earnings	45,900
	Dividends declared	14,250
	Plus decrease in dividends payable	4,500
	Cash paid for dividends	$ 18,750

UMLAUF COMPANY
Statement of Cash Flows (Direct Method)
For Year Ended December 31, 2000

Cash flows from operating activities:		
Cash received from customers	$451,800	
Cash paid for merchandise	(236,775)	
Cash paid for other operating expenses	(122,250)	
Cash paid for income taxes	(13,050)	
Net cash provided by operating activities		$79,725
Cash flows from investing activities:		
Cash received from sale of office equipment	$ 6,975	
Cash paid for store equipment	(10,500)	
Net cash used in investing activities		(3,525)
Cash flows from financing activities:		
Cash paid to retire bonds payable	$ (38,325)	
Cash paid for dividends	(18,750)	
Net cash used in financing activities		(57,075)
Net increase in cash		$19,125
Cash balance at beginning of year		23,925
Cash balance at end of year		$43,050

UMLAUF COMPANY
Statement of Cash Flows (Indirect Method)
For Year Ended December 31, 2000

Cash flows from operating activities:		
Cash flows from operating activities:		
Net income	$ 60,150	
Adjustments to reconcile net income to net cash provided by operating activities:		
Decrease in accounts receivable	5,700	
Increase in merchandise inventory	(9,525)	
Increase in prepaid expenses	(1,950)	
Decrease in accounts payable	(4,950)	
Increase in income taxes payable	675	
Amortization expense	25,500	
Loss on sale of capital assets	3,300	
Loss on retirement of bonds	825	
Net cash provided by operating activities		$79,725
Cash flows from investing activities:		
Cash received from sale of office equipment	$ 6,975	
Cash paid for store equipment	(10,500)	
Net cash used in investing activities		(3,525)
Cash flows from financing activities:		
Cash paid to retire bonds payable	$(38,325)	
Cash paid for dividends	(18,750)	
Net cash used in financing activities		(57,075)
Net increase in cash		$19,125
Cash balance at beginning of year		23,925
Cash balance at end of year		$43,050

19A Using a Spreadsheet to Prepare the Statement of Cash Flows

APPENDIX

Learning Objective

LO 11 Illustrate use of a spreadsheet in preparing a statement of cash flows.

We compute net cash flows provided (or used) by operating activities under the indirect method by using balance sheets at the beginning and end of the period, the current period's income statement, and information about selected transactions. Exhibit 19.10 shows the income statement and balance sheet information for **Genesis.** Based on this information, Exhibit 19.17 presented the indirect method of reconciling net income to net cash provided by operating activities. This appendix explains how we can use a spreadsheet (work sheet) analysis to prepare the statement of cash flows using the indirect method.

Preparing the Indirect Method Spreadsheet

Analyzing noncash accounts can be challenging when a company has a large number of accounts and many operating, investing, and financing transactions. A *spreadsheet*, also called *working paper*, can help us organize the information needed to prepare a statement of cash flows. A spreadsheet also makes it easier to check the accuracy of our work.

To illustrate how we use this spreadsheet, we return to the comparative balance sheets and income statement shown in Exhibit 19.10. Information needed for the spreadsheet in preparing the statement of cash flows is listed below along with identifying letters:

a. Net income is $38,000.
b. Accounts receivable increases by $20,000.
c. Merchandise inventory increases by $14,000.
d. Prepaid expenses increases by $2,000.
e. Accounts payable decreases by $5,000.
f. Interest payable decreases by $1,000.
g. Income taxes payable increases by $10,000.
h. Amortization expense is $24,000.
i. Capital assets costing $30,000 with accumulated amortization of $12,000 are sold for $12,000 cash. Loss on sale of assets is $6,000.
j. Bonds with a book value of $34,000 are retired with a cash payment of $18,000. Gain on retirement of bonds is $16,000.
k. Capital assets costing $70,000 are purchased with a cash payment of $10,000 and an issuance of bonds payable for $60,000.
l. Issued 3,000 common shares for $15,000.
m. Paid cash dividends of $14,000.

Exhibit 19A.1 shows the indirect method spreadsheet for Genesis. Both beginning and ending balance sheets are recorded on the spreadsheet. We enter information in the Analysis of Changes columns for the cash flows from operating, investing, and financing activities. We also include information about noncash investing and financing activities near the bottom. The spreadsheet does not reconstruct the income statement. Instead, net income is entered as the first item used in computing the amount of cash flows from operating activities.

Exhibit 19A.1

Spreadsheet for Preparing Statement of Cash Flows—Indirect Method

GENESIS
Spreadsheet for Statement of Cash Flows—Indirect Method
For Year Ended December 31, 2000

	December 31, 1999	Analysis of Changes Debit	Analysis of Changes Credit	December 31, 2000
Balance sheet—debits:				
Cash	12,000			17,000
Accounts receivable	40,000	(b) 20,000		60,000
Merchandise inventory	70,000	(c) 14,000		84,000
Prepaid expenses	4,000	(d) 2,000		6,000
Capital assets	210,000	(k1)70,000	(i) 30,000	250,000
	336,000			417,000
Balance sheet — credits:				
Accumulated amortization	48,000	(i) 12,000	(h) 24,000	60,000
Accounts payable	40,000	(e) 5,000		35,000
Interest payable	4,000	(f) 1,000		3,000
Income taxes payable	12,000		(g) 10,000	22,000
Bonds payable	64,000	(j) 34,000	(k2)60,000	90,000
Common shares no-par value	80,000		(l) 15,000	95,000
Retained earnings	88,000	(m) 14,000	(a) 38,000	112,000
	336,000			417,000
Statement of cash flows:				
Operating activities:				
Net income		(a) 38,000		
Increase in accounts receivable			(b) 20,000	
Increase in merchandise inventory			(c) 14,000	
Increase in prepaid expenses			(d) 2,000	
Decrease in accounts payable			(e) 5,000	
Decrease in interest payable			(f) 1,000	
Increase in income taxes payable		(g) 10,000		
Amortization expense		(h) 24,000		
Loss on sale of capital assets		(i) 6,000		
Gain on retirement of bonds			(j) 16,000	
Investing activities:				
Receipts from sale of capital assets		(i) 12,000		
Payment for purchase of capital assets			(k1)10,000	
Financing activities:				
Payments to retire bonds			(j) 18,000	
Receipts from issuing shares		(l) 15,000		
Payments of dividends			(m) 14,000	
Noncash investing and financing activities disclosed in note:				
Purchase of capital assets financed by bonds		(k2)60,000	(k1) 60,000	
		337,000	337,000	

Entering the Analysis of Changes on the Spreadsheet

The following sequence of procedures are used to complete the spreadsheet after the balance sheet accounts are entered:

1. Enter net income as an operating cash inflow (debit) and as a credit to Retained Earnings.
2. In the statement of cash flows section, adjustments to net income are entered as debits if they increase cash inflows and as credits if they decrease cash inflows. Applying this rule, adjust net income for the change in each noncash current asset and current liability related to operating activities. For each adjustment to net income, the offsetting debit or credit helps reconcile the beginning and ending balances of a current asset or current liability.
3. Enter adjustments to net income for income statement items not providing or using cash in the period. For each adjustment, the offsetting debit or credit helps reconcile a noncash balance sheet account.
4. Adjust net income to eliminate any gains or losses from investing and financing activities. Because the cash from a gain must be excluded from operating activities, the gain is entered as a credit in the operating activities section. Losses are entered as debits. For each of these adjustments, the related debits and/or credits help reconcile balance sheet accounts and involve entries to show the cash flow from investing or financing activities.
5. After reviewing any unreconciled balance sheet accounts and related information, enter the reconciling entries for all remaining investing and financing activities. Examples are purchases of capital assets, issuances of long-term debt, sales of capital stock, and dividend payments. Some of these may require entries in the noncash investing and financing activities section of the spreadsheet.
6. Check accuracy by totalling the Analysis of Changes columns and by determining that the change in each balance sheet account has been explained.

We illustrate these steps in Exhibit 19A.1 for Genesis:

Step	Entries
1	(a)
2	(b) through (g)
3	(h)
4	(i) through (j)
5	(k) through (m)

Because adjustments *i*, *j*, and *k* are more challenging, we show them in the debit and credit format. *These entries are for purposes of our understanding—they are not the entries actually made in the journals.* The format we use is similar to the one used for general journal entries, except that changes in the Cash account are identified as sources or uses of cash.

i.	Loss from sale of capital assets	6,000	
	Accumulated amortization	12,000	
	Receipt from sale of capital assets (source of cash)	12,000	
	Capital assets		30,000
	To describe sale of capital assets.		
j.	Bonds payable	34,000	
	Payments to retire bonds (use of cash)		18,000
	Gain on retirement of bonds		16,000
	To describe retirement of bonds.		

k1.	Capital assets	70,000	
	Payment to purchase capital assets (use of cash)		10,000
	Purchase of capital assets financed by bonds		60,000
	To describe purchase of capital assets, cash payment, and use of noncash financing.		
k2.	Purchase of capital assets financed by bonds	60,000	
	Bonds payable		60,000
	To show issuance of bonds payable to finance purchase of capital assets.		

Flashback

13. In using a spreadsheet for preparing the operating section of a statement of cash flows reported using the indirect method, which of the following is true?

a. Decrease in accounts receivable is analyzed with a debit in the statement of cash flows section and a credit in the balance sheet section.

b. Cash dividend paid is analyzed with a debit to retained earnings and a credit in the investing activities section.

c. Analysis of a cash payment to retire bonds payable at a loss requires one debit and two credits.

d. Amortization expense does not require analysis on the spreadsheet because there is no cash inflow or outflow.

Answers—p. 919

Summary of Appendix 19A

LO 11 **Illustrate use of a spreadsheet in preparing a statement of cash flows.** A spreadsheet is a useful tool in preparing a statement of cash flows. Six key steps (described in the Appendix) are applied when using the spreadsheet. The result is a properly classified statement of cash flows.

Guidance Anwser to Flashbacks

13. *c*

Glossary

Direct method A calculation of the net cash provided or used by operating activities that lists the major classes of operating cash receipts, such as receipts from customers, and subtracts the major classes of operating cash disbursements, such as cash paid for merchandise. This method is recommended by the CICA. (p. 888)

Financing activities Transactions with a company's owners and creditors which include getting cash from issuing debt and repaying the amounts borrowed, and getting cash from or distributing cash to owners and giving owners a return on investments. (p. 879)

Indirect method A calculation that reports net income and then adjusts the net income amount by adding and subtracting items that are necessary to yield net cash provided or used by operating activities. (p. 886)

Investing activities The acquisition and disposal of long-term assets and other investments that are not classified as cash equivalents. (p. 879)

Operating activities The principal revenue-producing activities that are not investing or financing activities. Operating activities involve the production or purchase of merchandise and the sale of goods and services to customers, including expenditures related to administering the business. (p. 878)

Statement of cash flows A financial statement that reports the cash inflows and outflows for an accounting period, and that classifies those cash flows as operating activities, investing activities, and financing activities. (p. 876)

A superscript letter A identifies questions based on Appendix 19A.

Questions

1. What are some examples of items reported on a statement of cash flows as investing activities?
2. What are some examples of items reported on a statement of cash flows as financing activities?
3. When a statement of cash flows is prepared by the direct method, what are some examples of items reported as cash flows from operating activities?
4. If a corporation pays cash dividends, where on the corporation's statement of cash flows should the payment be reported?
5. A company purchases land for $100,000, paying $20,000 cash and borrowing the remainder on a long-term note payable. How should this transaction be reported on a statement of cash flows?
6. What is the direct method of reporting cash flows from operating activities?
7. What is the indirect method of reporting cash flows from operating activities?
8. Is amortization a source of cash?
9. On June 3, a company borrowed $50,000 by giving its bank a 60-day, interest-bearing note. On the statement of cash flows, where should this item be reported?
10. If a company reports a net income for the year, is it possible for the company to show a net cash outflow from operating activities? Explain your answer.
11. Refer to **Alliance's** consolidated statement of changes in financial position shown in Appendix I. (a) Which method was used to compute net cash provided by operating activities? (b) Although the consolidated balance sheet shows that there was an increase in receivables from fiscal year 1996 to fiscal year 1997, why were receivables subtracted rather than added in the calculation of net cash provided by operating activities during the March 31, 1997, fiscal year-end as indicated in note 14?
12. Refer to **Atlantis's** consolidated statement of changes in financial position shown in Appendix I. How much cash was generated from interim financing in 1997, compared with 1996?
13. Refer to Alliance's consolidated statement of changes in financial position shown in Appendix I. What activities comprised the two largest investing activities resulting in cash outflows for the year ended March 31, 1997?
14. What do the loan terms given to Chen in the opening scenario suggest regarding the loan officer's risk assessment of the loan to the ginseng farm?

Quick Study

QS 19-1
Explaining statement of cash flows
LO 1

Describe the content of a statement of cash flows.

QS 19-2
Classifying transactions by activity
LO 2

Classify the following cash flows as operating, investing, or financing activities:

1. Issued common shares for cash.
2. Received interest on investment.
3. Paid interest on outstanding bonds.
4. Sold delivery equipment at a loss.
5. Paid property taxes on the company offices.

6. Collected proceeds from sale of long-term investments.
7. Received payments from customers.
8. Paid wages.
9. Purchased merchandise for cash.
10. Paid dividends.

QS 19-3
Identifying noncash transactions
LO 2

List three examples of transactions that are noncash financing and investing transactions.

QS 19-4
Computing cash from customers
LO 6

Use the following information in QS 19-4 through QS 19-9.

BRIGHTWELL CO., INC.
Comparative Balance Sheet
December 31, 2000 and 1999

Assets	2000	1999
Cash	$ 95,800	$ 25,000
Accounts receivable (net)	42,000	52,000
Inventory	86,800	96,800
Prepaid expenses	6,400	5,200
Furniture	110,000	120,000
Accumulated amortization, furniture	(18,000)	(10,000)
Total assets	$323,000	$289,000
Liabilities and Shareholders' Equity		
Accounts payable	$ 16,000	$ 22,000
Wages payable	10,000	6,000
Income taxes payable	2,400	3,600
Notes payable (long-term)	30,000	70,000
Common shares no-par value	230,000	180,000
Retained earnings	34,600	7,400
Total liabilities and shareholders' equity	$323,000	$289,000

BRIGHTWELL CO., INC.
Income Statement
For Year Ended June 30, 2000

Sales		$468,000
Cost of goods sold		312,000
Gross profit		$156,000
Operating expenses:		
Amortization expense	$ 38,600	
Other expenses	57,000	
Total operating expenses		95,600
Net income from operations		$ 60,400
Income taxes		24,600
Net income		$ 35,800

How much cash was received from customers during 2000?

QS 19-5
Computing cash paid for merchandise
LO 6

Refer to the facts in QS 19-4. How much cash was paid for merchandise during 2000?

QS 19-6
Computing cash paid for expenses
LO 6

Refer to the facts in QS 19-4. How much cash was paid for operating expenses during 2000?

QS 19-7
Computing cash from an asset sale
LO 3, 8

Refer to the facts in QS 19-4 and assume furniture that cost $54,000 is sold at its book value and all furniture acquisitions are for cash. What is the cash inflow related to the sale of furniture?

QS 19-8
Computing cash paid for dividends
LO 8

Refer to the facts in QS 19-4 and assume all shares are issued for cash. How much cash is paid for dividends?

QS 19-9
Computing cash from operations (indirect)
LO 7

Refer to the facts in QS 19-4. Using the indirect method, compute cash provided or used from operating activities.

QS 19-10
Analyzing sources and uses of cash
LO 9, 10

(in thousands)	Foxtail	Spiral	Tetris
Cash provided (used) by operating activities	$80,000	$70,000	$ (34,000)
Cash provided (used) by investing activities:			
Proceeds from sale of operating assets			36,000
Purchase of operating assets	(38,000)	(35,000)	
Cash provided (used) by financing activities:			
Proceeds from issuance of debt			33,000
Repayment of debt	(7,000)		
Net increase (decrease) in cash	$35,000	$35,000	$ 35,000
Average assets	$800,000	$650,000	$400,000

Required

1. Which of the three competitors is in the strongest position as indicted by their comparative cash flow statements?
2. Compare the strength of Foxtail's cash flow on total assets ratio to Spiral's.

QS 19-11A
Explaining noncash accounts on a spreadsheet
LO 5

When a spreadsheet for a statement of cash flows is prepared, all changes in noncash balance sheet accounts are explained using the spreadsheet. Explain how we can use noncash balance sheet accounts to account for cach.

Exercises

Exercise 19-1
Classifying transactions on statement of cash flows (direct)

LO 2, 3

The following events occurred during the year. Assuming that the company uses the direct method of reporting cash provided by operating activities, indicate the proper accounting treatment for each event by placing an *x* in the appropriate column.

	Statement of Cash Flows			Footnote Describing Noncash Investing and Financing Activities	Not Reported on Statement or in Footnote
	Operating Activities	Investing Activities	Financing Activities		
a. Borrowed cash from the bank by signing a nine-month note payable.					
b. Paid cash to purchase a patent.					
c. A six-month note receivable was accepted in exchange for a building that had been used in operations.					
d. Long-term bonds payable were retired by issuing common shares.					
e. Recorded amortization expense on all capital assets.					
f. A cash dividend that was declared in a previous period was paid in the current period.					
g. Surplus merchandise inventory was sold for cash.					

Exercise 19-2
Organizing the statement of cash flows and supporting footnote

LO 2, 3, 4

Use the following information about the 2000 cash flows of Ulrich Company to prepare a statement of cash flows using the direct method and a footnote describing noncash investing and financing activities.

Cash and cash equivalents balance, December 31, 1999	$25,000
Cash and cash equivalents balance, December 31, 2000	70,000
Cash received as interest	2,500
Cash paid for salaries	72,500
Bonds payable retired by issuing common shares (there was no gain or loss on the retirement)	187,500
Cash paid to retire long-term notes payable	125,000
Cash received from sale of equipment	61,250
Cash borrowed on six-month note payable	25,000
Land purchased and financed by long-term note payable	106,250
Cash paid for store equipment	23,750
Cash dividends paid	15,000
Cash paid for other expenses	40,000
Cash received from customers	485,000
Cash paid for merchandise	252,500

Exercise 19-3
Computing cash flows
LO 6

For each of the following cases, use the information provided about the 1999 operations of Milwood Company to compute the required cash flow information:

Case A: Compute cash paid for salaries:	
Salaries expense	$ 51,000
Salaries payable, January 1	3,150
Salaries payable, December 31	3,750
Case B: Compute cash received from customers:	
Sales revenue	$510,000
Accounts receivable, January 1	25,200
Accounts receivable, December 31	34,800
Case C: Compute cash paid for insurance:	
Insurance expense	$ 68,400
Prepaid insurance, January 1	11,400
Prepaid insurance, December 31	17,100

Exercise 19-4
Computing cash flows
LO 6

In each of the following cases, use the information provided about the 1999 operations of Roche Company to compute the required cash flow information:

Case A: Compute cash received from interest:	
Interest revenue	$ 34,000
Interest receivable, January 1	3,000
Interest receivable, December 31	3,600
Case B: Compute cash paid for rent:	
Rent expense	$ 40,800
Rent payable, January 1	8,800
Rent payable, December 31	7,200
Case C: Compute cash paid for merchandise:	
Cost of goods sold	$528,000
Merchandise inventory, January 1	159,600
Accounts payable, January 1	67,800
Merchandise inventory, December 31	131,400
Accounts payable, December 31	84,000

Exercise 19-5
Cash flows from operating activities (direct)
LO 6

Use the following income statement and information about changes in noncash current assets and current liabilities to present the cash flows from operating activities using the direct method:

RYLANDER COMPANY
Income Statement
For Year Ended December 31, 1999

Sales		$ 1,818,000
Cost of goods sold		891,000
Gross profit from sales		$ 927,000
Operating expenses:		
Salaries expense	$248,535	
Amortization expense	43,200	
Rent expense	48,600	
Amortization expense, patents	5,400	
Utilities expense	19,125	364,860
Total		$ 562,140
Gain on sale of equipment		7,200
Net income		$ 569,340

Changes in current asset and current liability accounts during the year, all of which related to operating activities, were as follows:

Accounts receivable	$40,500 increase
Merchandise inventory	27,000 increase
Accounts payable	13,500 decrease
Salaries payable	4,500 decrease

Exercise 19-6
Cash flows from operating activities (indirect)
LO 7

Refer to the information about Rylander Company presented in Exercise 19-5. Use the indirect method and compute the cash provided (or used) by operating activities.

Exercise 19-7
Cash flows from operating activities (indirect)
LO 7

Eden Company's 1999 income statement showed the following: net income, $364,000; amortization expense, building, $45,000; amortization expense, equipment, $8,200; and gain on sale of capital assets, $7,000. An examination of the company's current assets and current liabilities showed that the following changes occurred because of operating activities: accounts receivable decreased $18,100; merchandise inventory decreased $52,000; prepaid expenses increased $3,700; accounts payable decreased $9,200; other payables increased $1,400. Use the indirect method to compute the cash flow from operating activities.

Exercise 19-8
Classifying transactions on statement of cash flows (indirect)
LO 2, 7

The following events occurred during the year. Assuming that the company uses the indirect method of reporting cash provided by operating activities, indicate the proper accounting treatment for each event listed below by placing an *x* in the appropriate column.

	Statement of Cash Flows			Footnote Describing Noncash Investing and Financing Activities	Not Reported on Statement or in Footnote
	Operating Activities	Investing Activities	Financing Activities		
a. Sold capital equipment at a loss.	______	______	______	______	______
b. Recorded amortization expense.	______	______	______	______	______
c. Income taxes payable increased by 15% from prior year.	______	______	______	______	______
d. Declared and paid a cash dividend.	______	______	______	______	______
e. Paid cash to purchase merchandise inventory.	______	______	______	______	______
f. Land for a new plant was purchased by issuing common shares.	______	______	______	______	______
g. Accounts receivable decreased during the year.	______	______	______	______	______

Exercise 19-9
Preparation of statement of cash flows (direct)
LO 5, 6, 9

The following summarized journal entries show the total debits and credits to the Pyramid Corporation's Cash account for the year 2000.

Part 1. Use the information to prepare a statement of cash flows for the year 2000. The cash provided (or used) by operating activities should be presented according to the direct method. In the statement, identify the entry that records each item of cash flow. Assume that the beginning balance of cash was $133,200.

a.	Cash	1,440,000	
	Common Shares No-Par Value		1,440,000
	Issued common shares for cash.		
b.	Cash	2,400,000	
	Notes Payable		2,400,000
	Borrowed cash with a note payable.		
c.	Purchases	480,000	
	Cash		480,000
	Purchased merchandise for cash.		
d.	Accounts Payable	1,200,000	
	Cash		1,200,000
	Paid for credit purchases of merchandise.		
e.	Wages Expense	600,000	
	Cash		600,000
	Paid wages to employees.		
f.	Rent Expense	420,000	
	Cash		420,000
	Paid rent for buildings.		
g.	Cash	3,000,000	
	Sales		3,000,000
	Made cash sales to customers.		
h.	Cash	1,800,000	
	Accounts Receivable		1,800,000
	Collected accounts from credit customers.		
i.	Machinery	2,136,000	
	Cash		2,136,000
	Purchased machinery for cash.		
j.	Investments	2,160,000	
	Cash		2,160,000
	Purchased investments for cash.		
k.	Interest Expense	216,000	
	Notes Payable	384,000	
	Cash		600,000
	Paid notes and accrued interest.		
l.	Cash	206,400	
	Dividends Earned		206,400
	Collected dividends from investments.		
m.	Cash	210,000	
	Loss on Sale of Investments	30,000	
	Investments		240,000
	Sold investments for cash.		
n.	Cash	720,000	
	Accumulated Amortization, Machinery	420,000	
	Machinery		960,000
	Gain on Sale of Machinery		180,000
	Sold machinery for cash.		

o.	Common Dividend Payable	510,000	
	Cash		510,000
	Paid cash dividends to shareholders.		
p.	Income Taxes Payable	480,000	
	Cash		480,000
	Paid income taxes owed for the year.		
q.	Common Shares	228,000	
	Cash		228,000
	Purchased and retired common shares for cash.		

Part 2. Consult the statement of cash flows you have prepared for Part 1 and answer the following questions:

1. Of the three activity sections (operating, investing, or financing), which section shows the largest cash flow for the year?
2. What is the purpose of the largest investing cash outflow for the year?
3. Are the proceeds larger from issuing debt or equity for the year?
4. Did the company have a net cash inflow or outflow from borrowing activity in 2000?

Exercise 19-10
Preparation of statement of cash flows (direct)
LO 5, 6, 10

Part 1. Use the Benton, Inc. financial statements and supplementary information given to prepare a statement of cash flows for the year ended June 30, 2000, using the direct method.

BENTON INC.
Comparative Balance Sheet
June 30, 2000

Assets	2000	1999
Cash	$ 85,800	$ 45,000
Accounts receivable (net)	70,000	52,000
Inventory	66,800	96,800
Prepaid expenses	5,400	5,200
Equipment	130,000	120,000
Accumulated amortization, furniture	(28,000)	(10,000)
Total assets	$330,000	$309,000
Liabilities and Shareholders' Equity		
Accounts payable	$ 26,000	$ 32,000
Wages payable	7,000	16,000
Income taxes payable	2,400	3,600
Notes payable (long-term)	40,000	70,000
Common shares, no-par value	230,000	180,000
Retained earnings	24,600	7,400
Total liabilities and shareholders' equity	$330,000	$309,000

Additional information follows:

a. The note is retired at carrying value.
b. The only changes affecting retained earning during 2000 are net income and cash dividends paid.
c. New equipment is acquired during 2000 for $58,600.
d. Sold equipment costing $48,600 for a $2,000 gain.
e. Prepaid expenses and wages expense affect other expenses on the Income Statement.
f. All sales and purchases of merchandise were on credit.

Part 2. Compute the cash flow on total assets ratio for Benton, Inc. for the fiscal year 2000.

BENTON INC.
Income Statement
For Year Ended June 30, 2000

Sales		$668,000
Cost of goods sold		412,000
Gross profit		$256,000
Operating expenses:		
Amortization expense	$58,600	
Other expenses	67,000	
Total operating expenses		125,600
Net income from operations		$130,400
Income taxes		45,640
Gain on sale of equipment		2,000
Net income		$ 86,760

Problems

Problem 19-1
Statement of cash flows (direct method)
LO 5, 6

Infinity Corporation's balance sheet and income statement are as follows:

INFINITY CORPORATION
Comparative Balance Sheet
December 31, 2000

	December 31	
Assets	**2000**	**1999**
Cash	$ 174,000	$117,000
Accounts receivable	93,000	81,000
Merchandise inventory	609,000	534,000
Equipment	333,000	297,000
Accumulated amortization, equipment	(156,000)	(102,000)
Totals	$1,053,000	$927,000
Liabilities and Shareholders' Equity		
Accounts payable	$ 69,000	$ 96,000
Income taxes payable	27,000	24,000
Common shares, no-par value	780,000	720,000
Retained earnings	177,000	87,000
Totals	$1,053,000	$927,000

INFINITY CORPORATION
Income Statement
For Year Ended December 31, 2000

Sales		$1,992,000
Cost of goods sold		1,194,000
Gross profit		$ 798,000
Operating expenses:		
Amortization expense	$ 54,000	
Other expenses	501,000	
Total operating expenses		555,000
Income from operations		$ 243,000
Income taxes		42,000
Net income		$ 201,000

Other information regarding Infinity: (1) all sales were credit sales, (2) all credits to accounts receivable in a period were receipts from customers, (3) all purchases of merchandise were on credit, (4) all debits to accounts payable in a period resulted from payments for merchandise, (5) other operating expenses were cash expenses, and (6) the decrease in income taxes payable was for payment of taxes.

Additional information regarding Infinity's activities during the year 2000:

a. Purchased equipment for $36,000 cash.
b. Issued 12,000 common shares at $5 per share.
c. Declared and paid $111,000 of cash dividends.

Required

Prepare a statement of cash flows that reports the cash inflows and outflows from operating activities according to the direct method. Show your supporting calculations.

Check Figure Net cash provided by operating activities, $144,000

Problem 19-2
Statement of cash flows (indirect method)
LO 5, 7

Refer to Infinity Corporation's balance sheets presented in Problem 19-1.

Required

Prepare a statement of cash flows that reports the cash inflows and outflows from operating activities according to the indirect method.

Check Figure Net cash provided by operating activities, $144,000

Problem 19-3A
Cash flows spreadsheet (indirect method)
LO 5, 7, 11

Refer to the facts about Infinity Corporation presented in Problem 19-1.

Required

Prepare a statement of cash flows using a spreadsheet that follows the indirect method of computing cash flows from operating activities. Identify the debits and credits in the Analysis of Changes columns with letters that correspond to the following list of transactions and events:

a. Net Income is $201,000
b. Accounts receivable increased.
c. Merchandise inventory increased
d. Accounts payable decreased.
e. Income taxes payable increased
f. Amortization expense is $54,000.
g. Purchased equipment for $36,000.
h. Issued 12,000 shares at $5 per share.
i. Declared and paid $111,000 of cash dividends.

Check Figure Analysis of Changes column totals, $579,000

Problem 19-4
Statement of cash flows (direct method)
LO 5, 6, 9

Comptex Company's balance sheet and income statement are as follows:

COMPTEX COMPANY
Comparative Balance Sheet
December 31, 2000

	December 31	
Assets	**2000**	**1999**
Cash	$ 53,875	$ 76,625
Accounts receivable	65,000	49,625
Merchandise inventory	273,750	252,500
Prepaid expenses	5,375	6,250
Equipment	159,500	110,000
Accumulated amortization, equipment	(34,625)	(44,000)
Totals	$522,875	$451,000
Liabilities and Shareholders' Equity		
Accounts payable	$ 88,125	$116,625
Short-term notes payable	10,000	6,250
Long-term notes payable	93,750	53,750
Common shares, no-par value	201,250	156,250
Retained earnings	129,750	118,125
Totals	$522,875	$451,000

COMPTEX COMPANY Income Statement For Year Ended December 31, 2000		
Sales		$496,250
Cost of goods sold		250,000
Gross profit		$246,250
Operating expenses:		
Amortization expense	$ 18,750	
Other expenses	136,500	
Total operating expenses		155,250
Loss on sale of equipment		5,125
Income from operations		$ 85,875
Income taxes		12,125
Net income		$ 73,750

Comptex Company recently completed its year 2000 operations. Other information regarding Comptex: (1) all sales were credit sales, (2) all credits to accounts receivable in the period were receipts from customers, (3) purchases of merchandise were on credit, (4) all debits to accounts payable in the period resulted from payments for merchandise, (5) the income tax expenses were cash expenses, and (6) the other expenses were paid in advance and were initially debited to Prepaid expenses.

Additional information regarding Comptex's activities during 2000:

a. Loss on sale of equipment is $5,125.
b. Sold equipment costing $46,875, with accumulated amortization of $28,125, for $13,625.
c. Purchased equipment costing $96,375 by paying cash of $25,000 and signing a long-term note payable for the balance.
d. Borrowed $3,750 by signing a short-term note payable.
e. Paid $31,375 to reduce a long-term note payable.
f. Issued 2,500 common shares for cash at $18 per share.
g. Declared and paid cash dividends of $62,125.

Required

Preparation component:

1. Prepare a statement of cash flows that reports the cash inflows and outflows from operating activities according to the direct method. Show supporting calculations. Also prepare a footnote describing noncash investing and financing activities.

Analysis component:

2. Analyze and discuss the information contained in your answer to requirement 1, giving special attention to the wisdom of the dividend payment.

Check Figure Net cash provided by operating activities, $33,375

Problem 19-5
Statement of cash flows (indirect method)
LO 5, 7

Refer to Comptex Company's balance sheets presented in Problem 19-4.

Required

Prepare a statement of cash flows that reports the cash inflows and outflows from operating activities according to the indirect method.

Check Figure Net cash provided by operating activities, $33,375

Problem 19-6A
Cash flows spreadsheet (indirect method)
LO 5, 7, 8, 11

Refer to the facts about Comptex Company presented in Problem 19-4 and Problem 19-5.

Required

Prepare a statement of cash flows spreadsheet that follows the indirect method of computing cash flows from operating activities. Identify the debits and credits in the Analysis of Changes columns with letters that correspond to the transactions presented in Problem 19-5.

Check Figure Analysis of Changes column totals, $515,375

Alternate Problems

Problem 19-1A
Statement of cash flows (direct method)
LO 5, 6

Tanaka Company's balance sheet and income statement are as follows:

TANAKA COMPANY
Comparative Balance Sheet
December 31, 2000

	December 31	
	2000	**1999**
Assets		
Cash	$ 53,925	$ 31,800
Accounts receivable	19,425	23,250
Merchandise inventory	175,350	139,875
Equipment	105,450	76,500
Accumulated amortization, equipment	(48,300)	(30,600)
Totals	$305,850	$240,825
Liabilities and Shareholders' Equity		
Accounts payable	$ 38,475	$ 35,625
Income taxes payable	4,500	6,750
Common shares, no-par value	207,000	165,000
Retained earnings	55,875	33,450
Totals	$305,850	$240,825

TANAKA COMPANY
Income Statement
For Year Ended December 31, 2000

Sales		$609,750
Cost of goods sold		279,000
Gross profit		$330,750
Operating expenses:		
Amortization expense	$ 17,700	
Other expenses	179,775	
Total operating expenses		197,475
Income from operations		$133,275
Income taxes		44,850
Net income		$ 88,425

Other information regarding Tanaka: (1) all sales were credit sales, (2) all credits to accounts receivable in the period were receipts from customers, (3) purchases of merchandise were on credit, (4) all debits to accounts payable in the period resulted from payments for merchandise, (5) the other operating expenses were cash expenses, and (6) the decrease in income taxes payable was for payment of taxes.

Additional information regarding Tanaka's activities during the year 2000:

a. Purchased equipment for $28,950 cash.
b. Issued 3,000 common shares at $14 per share.
c. Declared and paid $66,000 of cash dividends.

Required

Prepare a statement of cash flows that reports the cash inflows and outflows from operating activities according to the direct method. Show your supporting calculations.

Problem 19-2A
Statement of cash flows (indirect method)
LO 5, 7

Refer to Tanaka Company's balance sheets presented in Problem 19-1A.

Required

Prepare a statement of cash flows that reports the cash inflows and outflows from operating activities according to the indirect method.

Problem 19-3A^A
Cash flows spreadsheet (indirect method)
LO 7, 8, 11

Refer to the facts about Tanaka Company presented in Problem 19-1A.

Required

Prepare a statement of cash flows using a spreadsheet that follows the indirect method of computing cash flows from operating activities. Identify the debits and credits in the Analysis of Changes columns with letters that correspond to the following list of transactions and events:

a. Net income is $88,425
b. Accounts receivable increased.
c. Merchandise inventory increased.
d. Accounts payable decreased
e. Income taxes payable increased.
f. Amortization expense is $17,700.
g. Purchased equipment for $28,950.
h. Issued 3,000 shares at $14 per share.
i. Declared and paid $66,000 of cash dividends.

Problem 19-4A
Statement of cash flows (direct method)
LO 5, 6, 9

Kirby Corporation's balance sheet and income statement are as follows:

KIRBY CORPORATION
Comparative Balance Sheet
December 31, 2000

	December 31	
	2000	**1999**
Assets		
Cash	$136,500	$ 71,550
Accounts receivable	74,100	90,750
Merchandise inventory	454,500	490,200
Prepaid expenses	17,100	19,200
Equipment	278,250	216,000
Accumulated amortization, equipment	(108,750)	(93,000)
Totals	$851,700	$794,700
Liabilities and Shareholders' Equity		
Accounts payable	$117,450	$123,450
Short-term notes payable	17,250	11,250
Long-term notes payable	112,500	82,500
Common shares, no-par value	483,000	450,000
Retained earnings	121,500	127,500
Totals	$851,700	$794,700

KIRBY CORPORATION Income Statement For Year Ended December 31, 2000		
Sales		$1,083,000
Cost of goods sold		585,000
Gross profit		$ 498,000
Operating expenses:		
Amortization expense	$ 36,600	
Other expenses	392,850	
Total operating expenses		429,450
Loss on sale of equipment		2,100
Income from operations		$ 66,450
Income taxes		9,450
Net income		$ 57,000

Kirby Company recently completed its year 2000 operations. Other information regarding Kirby: (1) all sales were credit sales, (2) all credits to accounts receivable in the period were receipts from customers, (3) purchases of merchandise were on credit, (4) all debits to accounts payable in the period resulted from payments for merchandise, (5) the decrease in income taxes payable resulted from cash payments (6) the other expenses were paid in advance and were initially debited to prepaid expenses.

Additional information regarding Kirby's activities during 2000:

a. Loss on sale of equipment is $2,100.
b. Sold equipment costing $51,000, with accumulated amortization of $20,850, for 28,050.
c. Purchased equipment costing $113,250 by paying cash of $38,250 and signing a long-term note payable for the balance.
d. Borrowed $6,000 by signing a short-term note payable.
e. Paid $45,000 to reduce a long-term note payable.
f. Issued 3,000 common shares for cash at $11 per share.
g. Declared and paid cash dividends of $63,000.

Required

Preparation component:

1. Prepare a statement of cash flows that reports the cash inflows and outflows from operating activities according to the direct method. Show supporting calculations. Also prepare a footnote describing noncash investing and financing activities.

Analysis component:

2. Analyze and discuss the information contained in your answer to requirement 1, giving special attention to the wisdom of the dividend payment.

Problem 19-5A
Statement of cash flows (indirect method)
LO 5, 7, 8

Refer to Kirby Corporation's balance sheets presented in Problem 19-4A.

Required

Prepare a statement of cash flows that reports the cash inflows and outflows from operating activities according to the indirect method.

Problem 19-6A^A
Cash flows spreadsheet (indirect method)
LO 5, 7, 8, 11

Refer to the facts about Kirby Corporation presented in Problem 19-4A and Problem 19-5A.

Required

Prepare a statement of cash flows spreadsheet that follows the indirect method of computing cash flows from operating activities. Identify the debits and credits in the Analysis of Changes columns with letters that correspond to the transactions presented in Problem 19-5A.

Analytical and Review Problems

A & R 19-1

Morgan Corporation earned a $168,000 net income during 2000. Machinery was sold for $232,000 and a $48,000 loss on the sale was recorded. Machinery purchases totalled $660,000 including a July purchase for which a $160,000 promissory note was issued. Bonds were retired at their face value, and the issuance of new common shares produced an infusion of cash. Morgan's comparative balance sheets were as follows (in thousands):

MORGAN CORPORATION
Comparative Balance Sheet
December 31, 2000

	December 31	
	2000	1999
Assets		
Cash	$ 208	$ 168
Accounts receivable	392	444
Merchandise inventory	648	620
Machinery	2,700	2,520
Accumulated amortization, machinery	(380)	(420)
Totals	$3,568	$3,332
Liabilities and Shareholders' Equity		
Accounts payable	$ 476	$ 572
Notes payable	544	420
Dividends payable	64	40
Bonds payable	456	640
Common shares, no-par value	1,400	1,120
Retained earnings	628	540
Totals	$3,568	$3,332

1. What was Morgan's amortization expense in 2,000?
2. What was the amount of cash flow from operations?
3. What was the amount of cash flow from investing activities?
4. What was the amount of dividends declared? Paid?
5. By what amount would you expect the total sources of cash to differ from the total uses of cash?
6. What was the amount of cash flow from financing activities?

A & R 19-2

For each item, identify both the dollar amount and its classification—that is, whether it would appear as a positive or a negative adjustment to net income in the calculation of cash flow from operations or as some other source or use of cash.

1. Declared a $22,000 cash dividend; paid $19,000 during the year.
2. Sold land that cost $95,000 for $120,000 cash.
3. Sold for cash 2,000 shares for $14 a share.
4. Bought machinery for $37,000 in exchange for a note due in eight months.
5. Bought a computer that had a fair value of $140,000 by giving in exchange real estate that had cost $95,000 in an earlier period.
6. Equipment amortization, $56,000.
7. Issued for cash on December 31, 1998, 10-year, 10% $500,000 bonds at a $24,000 discount.
8. Bought its own shares for $13,500.
9. Paid a lawyer $13,500 for services performed, billed, and recorded correctly in 1997.
10. Reported net income of $86,000 for the year ended December 31, 1998.

BEYOND THE NUMBERS

Reporting in Action

LO 2, 6, 7, 9

Refer to the financial statements and related information for Alliance in Appendix I. Answer the following questions by analyzing the information in the report:

1. Alliance's annual report contains a consolidated statement of changes in financial position that reports cash flow information. Was this statement of cash flows prepared according to the direct method or the indirect method?
2. During each of the fiscal years 1997 and 1996 was cash provided by operating activities more or less than net income?
3. How much was Alliance's gain on sale of investments? How does it affect the reporting of cash flows?
4. What was the net amount spent on investing activities? How were these investments financed?
5. Obtain access to Alliance's annual report for fiscal years ending after March 31, 1997. This access may be through a securities investment firm or you may gain access to annual report information at the following Web site: http://www.sedar.com. Since March 31, 1997, what have been Alliance's largest cash outflows and inflows in the investing and financing sections of the cash flow statement?

Comparative Analysis

LO 9, 10

Both Atlantis and Alliance are actively engaged in producing and broadcasting filmed entertainment. Key comparative figures ($ millions) for these two organizations follow:

	Alliance		Atlantis	
Key Figures	**1997**	**1996**	**1997**	**1996**
Operating cash flows	$240.7	$174.5	$136.9	$136.9
Total assets	$353.7	$238.8	$333.2	$334.8

* Alliance figures are from the annual reports for the fiscal years ended March 31,1997, and 1996. Atlantis figures are from the annual reports for the fiscal years ended December 31, 1996, and 1995.

Required

1. Compute the cash flow on total assets ratio for (a) Alliance for 1997 and (b) Atlantis for 1997.
2. What does the cash flow on total assets ratio measure?
3. Which company has the higher cash flow on total assets ratio?
4. Does the cash flow on total assets ratio provide any information as to the quality of earnings of a firm?
5. What are the two largest sources of cash for Alliance in 1997? For Atlantis in 1997?

Ethics Challenge

LO 9

Wendy Geiger is working late on a Friday night in preparation for a meeting with her banker early Monday morning. Her business is just finishing its fourth quarter. In the first year the business experienced negative cash flows from operations. In the second and third years, cash flows from operations turned positive. Unfortunately, her inventory costs rose significantly in year four and her net income will probably be down about 25% after this year's adjusting entries. Wendy is hoping to secure a line of credit from her banker which will be a nice financing buffer. From prior experience with her banker she knows a focus of the meeting on Monday will be cash flows from operations. The banker will scrutinize the cash flow numbers for years one through four and will want a projected number for year five. Wendy knows that a steady upward progression of cash flows in years one through four will really help her case for securing the line of credit. Wendy decides to use her discretion as owner of the business and proposes several adjusting entries and business actions which will help turn her cash flow number in year four from negative to positive.

Required

1. Identify three possible entries or business actions Wendy might use to improve the cash flow from operations number on the statement of cash flows for year four.
2. Comment on the ethics and possible consequences of Wendy's decision to propose the adjustments/actions for year four.

Communicating in Practice

LO 1, 4

Your friend, Maddy Massola, recently completed his second year in his own business. Maddy just received annual financial statements from his accountant. Maddy says he finds the income statement and balance sheet quite informative but he does not understand the statement of cash flows. He says the first section is particularly confusing and he cannot get much beyond it. He says it contains a lot of additions and subtractions that do not make sense to him. Maddy added "I'm not concerned. It's probably just one of those extra forms accountants are required to fill out. The Income Statement tells me the business was more profitable than last year and that is what's most important. If I want to know about cash or cash changes, I can look at the Balance Sheets from this year and last."

Required

Write a memo to your friend to explain the purpose of the statement of cash flows. Comment on why he found the first section so confusing and suggest what he might do to rectify this problem.

Taking It to the Net

LO 9

Use the Sedar database at **http://www.sedar.com** to access the December 31, 1997, annual report for **Canadian Pacific Corporation**. Locate this company's consolidated statement of changes in financial position for the years ended December 31, 1997, 1996, and 1995. (Note that under the current accounting recommendations this statement would be called a statement of cash flows.) Answer the following questions.

1. Which method, direct or indirect, does Canadian Pacific use to prepare a statement of cash flow?
2. What is the largest adjustment needed to reconcile cash flow from operations to net income in each of the two years?
3. What is the largest investment requiring cash in each of the three years presented?
4. For the fiscal year ended December 31, 1997, did Canadian Pacific issue a long-term debt? Was any long-term debt repaid during 1997?

Teamwork in Action

LO 1, 4, 9, 6, 7

The aim of this activity is to provide team support for "putting it all together" with the statement of cash flows. After completing *each* of the three sections below, members should report to the team. Team members are to confirm or correct teammate's responses.

1. Each member of the team is to prepare notes to present a response to one of the following questions about the statement of cash flows:
   a. What is this statement's reporting objectives?
   b. What methods or formats can be used to prepare it? Describe each by identifying their similarities and differences.
   c. What steps are followed to prepare it?
   d. What kinds of analysis are often made from its information?
2. Each member of the team is to prepare notes to identify *and explain* the formula for computing cash flows from operating activities using the direct method for one of the following items:
   a. Cash receipts from customers
   b. Cash paid for merchandise
   c. Cash paid for wages and operating expenses
   d. Cash paid for interest and taxes

3. Each member of the team is to prepare notes to identify *and explain* the adjustment from net income to cash flows from operating activities using the indirect method for one of the following items:
   a. Noncash operating revenues and expenses
   b. Gains and Losses
   c. Increases and decreases in current assets
   d. Increases and decreases in current liabilities

Hitting the Road

LO1

Visit the Motley Fool Investment Web site at **http://www.fool.com**. Click on the sidebar link entitled "School." Select the link "Valuation: Principles and Practice." How does the Fool's school define cash flow? Per the school's instruction why do analysts focus on earnings before interest and taxes (EBIT)? Visit other links at the Web site that may interest you such as "A Journey Through the Balance Sheet" or find out what the "Fool's Ratio" is.

Business Break

Read the article, "Are profits shakier than they look?" in the August 5, 1996, issue of *Business Week*.

Required

1. How is the free cash flow number derived from cash flow from operations?
2. How does **Allied's** explanation of their cash concerns differ from the analyst Jeff Fotta's interpretation?
3. How does Fotta conduct the dual cash flow analysis?

20 CHAPTER

Analyzing Financial Statements

A Look Back

Chapter 19 focused on reporting and analyzing cash inflows and cash outflows. We explained how to prepare and interpret the statement of cash flows.

A Look at This Chapter

This chapter emphasizes the analysis and interpretation of financial statement information. We learn to apply horizontal, vertical, and ratio analyses to better understand company performance and financial condition.

A Look Forward

Chapter 21 introduces us to managerial accounting. We discuss its purposes, concepts, and roles in helping managers gather and organize information for decision making. Management principles are also explained.

Chapter Outline

- **Basics of Analysis**
  - Purpose of Analysis
  - Building Blocks of Analysis
  - Information for Analysis
  - Standards for Comparisons
  - Tools of Analysis
- **Horizontal Analysis**
  - Comparative Statements
  - Trend Analysis
- **Vertical Analysis**
  - Common-Size Statements
  - Common-Size Graphics
- **Ratio Analysis**
  - Liquidity and Efficiency
  - Solvency
  - Profitability
  - Market
  - Summary of Ratios
  - Analysis Reporting

Say It Ain't So!

Beardstown—Is nothing sacred? The Beardstown Ladies, those homespun, grandmotherly investors whose supposed success created a mini-industry, are being called frauds. The ladies may have fudged the figures.

With three books to their name in North American bookstores, the Beardstown Ladies are a fixture on the lecture circuit, riding a bull market in homespun advice. But their best advice might have been "Know your accounting." The ladies' *Common-Sense Investment Guide* claims an annual return of 23.4% over the decade covered in the book. But this return is computed by averaging the ladies two best years—1991 and 1992—and ignoring the other eight years.

Oops, that's not the way it's done. This would mean their total returns were nowhere near as great as claimed. The accounting firm Price Waterhouse, which did an audit of the ladies' books, says the actual return over the period covered in the book is 9.1%. This figure is well below the 23.4% claimed by the ladies, and less than the 15% return of the overall stock market for the same period.

Experts in accounting and analysis are not surprised. The ladies' investment strategy was simple and not fundamentally sound. They pooled their money and bought shares of big, low-risk companies, then watched as the share price rose with the general increase in the stock market. An index fund would have returned about double that of the ladies' return over the same period.

Still, their apparent success and their folksiness make them popular guests on television shows and brought some work as money management experts. Their first book sold more than 800,000 copies in Canada and the U.S. Senior partner Betty Sinnock says she is "just sick" about what's happened. A piece of homespun advice they didn't give—if it looks too good to be true, it probably is.

Source: *Globe and Mail*, May 30, 1998; *Fortune* Web site (March 30, 1998), Paul Krugman "There'll Always Be a Soros"; CNN Web site, "Moneyweek" (Aired March 1, 1998); CNN Web site, "Your Money" (Aired February 28, 1998); *Wisconsin State Journal* (February 28, 1998) "Well! I never! Beardstown Ladies didn't mean to deceive"; and CNN Web site, "Moneyline" (Aired March 17, 1998).]

Learning Objectives

LO 1 Explain the purpose of analysis.

LO 2 Identify the building blocks of analysis.

LO 3 Describe standards for comparisons in analysis.

LO 4 Identify the tools of analysis.

LO 5 Explain and apply methods of horizontal analysis.

LO 6 Describe and apply methods of vertical analysis.

LO 7 Define and apply ratio analysis.

LO 8 Summarize and report results of analysis.

CHAPTER PREVIEW

This chapter shows us how to use the information in financial statements to evaluate the financial performance and condition of a company. We describe the purpose of analysis, its basic building blocks, the information available, standards for comparisons, and tools of analysis. Three major analysis tools are emphasized—horizontal analysis, vertical analysis, and ratio analysis. We illustrate the application of each of these tools using Ralco's financial statements. This chapter also expands and organizes the ratio analyses introduced at the end of each of the prior nineteen chapters. Understanding financial statement analysis is crucial to sound business decision making. Its proper application avoids our reliance on little old ladies from Beardstown.

Basics of Analysis

Financial statement analysis is the application of analytical tools to general-purpose financial statements and related *data* for making business decisions. It involves transforming data into useful information. Financial statement analysis reduces our reliance on hunches, guesses, and intuition. It reduces our uncertainty in decision making. But it does not lessen the need for expert judgment. Instead, it provides us an effective and systematic basis for business decisions. This section describes the purpose of financial statement analysis, its information sources, the use of comparisons, and some issues in computations.

Purpose of Analysis

LO1 Explain the purpose of analysis.

The purpose of financial statement analysis is to help users make better business decisions. These users include decision makers both internal and external to the company.

Internal users of accounting information are those individuals involved in managing and operating the company. They include managers, officers, internal auditors, consultants, and many other important internal decision makers. Internal users make the strategic and operating decisions of a company. The purpose of financial statement analysis for these users is to provide information helpful in improving the company's efficiency or effectiveness in providing products or services.

External users of accounting information are *not* directly involved in running the company. They include shareholders, lenders, directors, customers, suppliers, regulators, lawyers, financial advisors, brokers and the press. Yet these users are affected by, and sometimes affect, the company's activities. External users rely on financial statement analysis to make better and more informed decisions in pursuing their own goals.

We can identify many examples of how financial statement analysis is used. Shareholders and creditors assess future company prospects for investing and lending decisions. A board of directors analyzes financial statements in monitoring management's decisions. Employees and unions use financial statements in labour negotiations. Suppliers use financial statements in establishing credit terms. Customers analyze financial statements in deciding whether to establish supply relationships. Public utilities set customer rates by analyzing financial statements. Auditors use financial statements in assessing the "fair presentation" of their clients' financial statement numbers. And analyst services such as *Dun & Bradstreet, Moody's*, and *Standard & Poor's* use financial statements in making buy-sell recommendations and setting credit ratings.

The common goal of all these users is to evaluate company performance. This includes evaluation of (1) past and current performance, (2) current financial position, and (3) future performance and risk.

Building Blocks of Analysis

LO2 Identify the building blocks of analysis.

Financial statement analysis focuses on one or more elements of a company's financial condition or performance. Our analysis emphasizes four areas of inquiry—with varying degrees of importance. These four areas are described and illustrated in this chapter and are considered the *building blocks* of financial statement analysis.

- *Liquidity and Efficiency*—ability to meet short-term obligations and to efficiently generate revenues.
- *Solvency*—ability to generate future revenues and meet long-term obligations.
- *Profitability*—ability to provide financial rewards sufficient to attract and retain financing.
- *Market*—ability to generate positive market expectations.

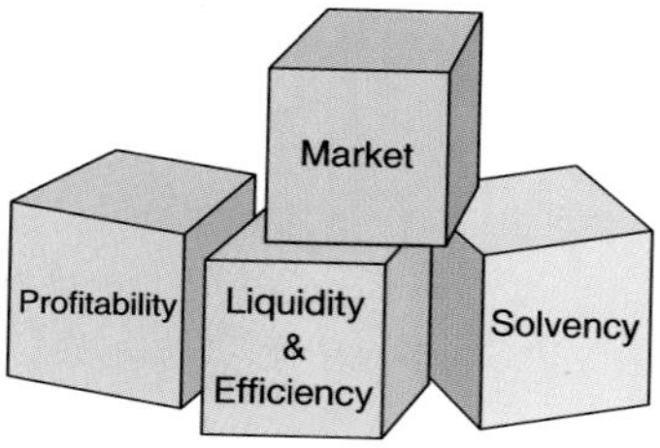

Applying the building blocks of financial statement analysis involves determining (1) the objectives of analysis, and (2) the relative emphasis among the building blocks. An investor, for instance, when evaluating the investment merit of common shares often emphasizes earnings and returns analyses. This involves assessing profitability and efficiency. But a thorough analysis requires an investor to assess other building blocks although with perhaps lesser emphasis. Attention to these other areas is necessary to assess risk exposure. This usually involves some analysis of liquidity and solvency. Further analysis can reveal important risks that outweigh earning power, and may lead to major changes in the financial statement analysis of a company.

We distinguish among these four building blocks to emphasize the different aspects of a company's financial condition or performance. Yet we must remember these areas of analysis are interrelated. For instance, a company's operating performance is affected by availability of financing and short-term liquidity conditions. Similarly, a company's credit standing is not limited to satisfactory short-term liquidity, but depends also on its profitability and efficiency in using assets. Early in our analysis, we need to tentatively determine the relative emphasis of each building block and their order of analysis. Emphasis and analysis can later change due to evidence collected.

Did You Know?

Chips and Brokers

Blue chips is used to refer to shares of big, profitable companies. The term comes from poker—where the most valuable chips are the blue ones. *Brokers* execute orders to buy or sell shares. The term comes from wine retailers—individuals who broach (break) wine casks.

Information for Analysis

We explained how decision makers such as managers, employees, directors, customers, suppliers, current and potential owners, current and potential lenders, brokers, regulatory authorities, lawyers, economists, labour unions, analysts, and consultants need to analyze financial statements. Some of these people such as managers and a few regulatory agencies are able to receive special financial reports prepared to meet their needs. But most must rely on general-purpose financial statements that companies publish periodically. **General-purpose financial statements** include the (1) income statement, (2) balance sheet, (3) statement of changes in shareholders' equity (or statement of retained earnings), (4) statement of cash flows, and (5) notes related to the statements.

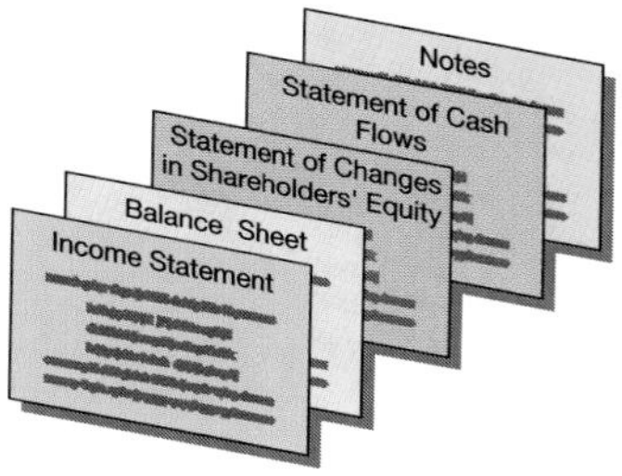

General-purpose financial statements are part of financial reporting. **Financial reporting** refers to the communication of relevant financial information to decision makers. It includes financial statements, but it also involves information from any filings with the securities commissions, news releases, shareholders' meetings, forecasts, management letters, auditor's report, and analyses published in annual reports. Financial reporting broadly refers to useful information for decision makers to make investment, credit, and other decisions. It should help users assess the amounts, timing, and uncertainty of future cash inflows and outflows.

One example of useful information outside the traditional financial statements is the Management Discussion and Analysis (MD&A) section. **Atlantis's** annual report in Appendix I provides us a typical example. The MD&A begins with a brief description of its television production and television distribution activities. It then proceeds with a discussion of operating results by summarizing its main revenues and expenses and net earnings. This is followed by a discussion of the company's financial position. The MD&A next examines liquidity and capital resources—roughly equivalent to investing and financing activities and ends with an outlook based on its positioning within the industry. While this analysis is not complete, it is an excellent starting point for us in understanding the business activities of a company.

Did You Know?

Data Web
Reviewing financial numbers used to involve mountains of paper in dark library basements. We can now do it from the convenience of our home via the Net. Many companies offer Web sites with free access and screening of numerous key financial numbers like earnings and sales. Most sites are updated daily with closing share prices. For instance, Standard & Poor's has information for more than 10,000 companies (**www.stockinfo.standardpoor.com**). [Source: *Business Week*, September 22, 1997.]

Standards for Comparisons

LO 3 Describe standards for comparisons in analysis.

When computing and interpreting analysis measures as part of our financial statement analysis, we need to decide whether these measures suggest good, bad, or average performance. To make these judgments, we need standards for comparisons. Standards for comparisons can include:

- *Intracompany.* The company under analysis provides standards for comparisons based on prior performance and relations between its financial items. **Atlantis's** current net income, for instance, can be compared with prior years' net income and its relation to revenues.
- *Competitor.* One or more direct competitors of the company under analysis can provide standards for comparisons. **Coca-Cola's** profit margin, for instance, can be compared with the profit margin of **PepsiCo.**
- *Industry.* Industry statistics can provide standards of comparisons. Published industry statistics are available from several services such as Dun & Bradstreet, Standard and Poor's, and Moody's.
- *Guidelines (Rules-of-Thumb).* General standards of comparisons can develop from past experiences. Examples are the 2 to 1 level for the current ratio or 1 to 1 level for the acid-test ratio. These guidelines, or rules-of-thumb, must be carefully applied since their context is often crucial.

All of these standards of comparisons are useful when properly applied. Yet analysis measures taken from a selected competitor or group of competitors are often the best standards of comparisons. Also, intracompany and industry measures are important parts of all analyses. Guidelines or rules-of-thumb should be applied with care, and then only if they seem reasonable in light of past experience and industry's norms.

Flashback

1. Who are the intended users of general-purpose financial statements?
2. What statements are usually included in general-purpose financial statements published by corporations?
3. Which of the following are not useful as a basis for comparison when analyzing ratios and turnovers? (a) companies operating in a different economy, (b) subjective standards from past experience, (c) rule-of-thumb standards, or (d) averages within a trade or industry.
4. What basis of comparison for ratios is usually best?

Answers—pp. 968–969

Tools of Analysis

LO 4 Identify the tools of analysis.

There are several tools of financial statement analysis. Three of the most common tools are:

- *Horizontal Analysis.* Tools comparing a company's financial condition and performance across time.
- *Vertical Analysis.* Tools comparing a company's financial condition and performance to a base amount.
- *Ratio Analysis.* Tools using key relations among financial statement items.

The remainder of this chapter describes these tools of analysis and how we apply them.

Did You Know?

Ticker Prices
Ticker prices refer to a band of moving information on a computer or television screen carrying up-to-the-minute share prices. The terms comes from ticker tape—a one-inch wide strip of paper spewing share prices and transactions from a printer that ticked as it ran. While most of today's investors have never actually seen ticker tape, the term survives.

Horizontal Analysis

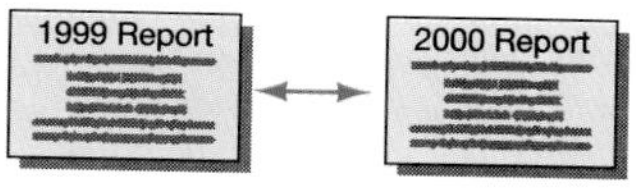

Our analysis of a single financial item is important but is of limited value. Instead, important relations exist between items and across time, and our financial analysis needs to use this information. Much of financial statement analysis involves identifying and describing relations between items and groups of items and changes in those items. Horizontal analysis is a tool to evaluate changes in financial statement data *across time.*[1]

Comparative Statements

LO 5 Explain and apply methods of horizontal analysis.

Our analysis of financial statement data is often helped by comparing amounts for two or more successive periods. **Comparative financial statements** are reports where financial amounts are placed side by side in columns on a single

[1] The term *horizontal analysis* arises from the left-to-right (or right-to-left) movement of our eyes as we review comparative financial statements across time.

statement for analysis purposes. Each financial statement can be presented in a *comparative format*. For instance, **Alliance's** *annual* report in Appendix I is a comparative statement based on three years of financial performance. This section explains how we compute dollar changes and percent changes in comparative statements and illustrates their application to the financial statements of **Ralco Corporation**.

Computation of Dollar Changes and Percent Changes

Comparing financial statements over relatively short time periods—two to three years—is often done by analyzing changes in line items. A change analysis usually includes an analysis of both changes in absolute dollar amounts as well as percent changes. Both analyses are relevant since dollar changes can sometimes yield large percent changes inconsistent with their importance. For instance, a 50% change from a base figure of $100 is less important than the same percent change from a base amount of $100,000 in the same statement. Reference to dollar amounts is necessary to retain a proper perspective and for assessing the importance of changes.

We compute the *dollar change* for a financial statement item as:

$$\text{Dollar change} = \text{Analysis period amount} - \text{Base period amount}$$

where *analysis period* is the point or period of time for the financial statements under analysis, and *base period* is the point or period of time for the financial statements used for comparison purposes. We commonly use the prior year as the base period.

We compute the *percent change* by dividing the dollar change by the base period amount, and then multiplying this quantity by 100:

$$\text{Percent change} = \frac{\text{Analysis period amount} - \text{Base period amount}}{\text{Base period amount}} \times 100$$

While we can always compute a dollar change, we must be aware of a few rules in working with percent changes. To illustrate, let's look at four separate cases in the chart below:

Case No.	Base Period	Analysis Period	Change Analysis Dollar	Change Analysis Percent
A	$(4,500)	$1,500	$6,000	—
B	2,000	(1,000)	(3,000)	—
C	—	8,000	8,000	—
D	10,000	-0-	(10,000)	(100%)

When a negative amount appears in the base period and a positive amount in the analysis period (or vice versa), we cannot compute a meaningful percent change; see cases A and B. Also, when there is no value in the base period, no percent change is computable; see case C. Finally, when an item has a value in the base period and zero in the next period, the decrease is 100 percent; see case D.

It is also common for horizontal analysis to compare amounts to average (or median[2]) values from prior periods. Comparing changes to average (or median)

---

[2] *Median* is the middle value in a group of numbers. For instance, if five prior years' incomes are (in 000s) $15, $19, $18, $20, and $22, their median value is $18. When there are two middle numbers, we can take their average. For instance, if four prior years' sales are (in 000s) $84, $91, $96, and $93, then the median is $92 (computed as the average of $91 and $93).

values computed over a number of years highlights unusual happenings, as average values smooth out erratic or unusual fluctuations. We also commonly round percents and ratios to one or two decimal places. But there is no uniform practice on this matter. Computations are as detailed as necessary. This is judged by whether or not they potentially affect users' decisions. Computations should not be excessively detailed so as to lose important relations among a mountain of decimal points.

Comparative Balance Sheet

One of the most useful comparative statements is the comparative balance sheet. It consists of amounts from two or more balance sheet dates arranged side by side. The usefulness of comparative financial statements is often improved by also showing each item's dollar change and percent change. This type of presentation highlights large dollar and percent changes for decision makers. Exhibit 20.1 shows the comparative balance sheet for Ralco.

Exhibit 20.1

Comparative Balance Sheet

RALCO CORPORATION
Comparative Balance Sheets
Nov. 30, 19x8, and Nov. 30, 19x7

(in thousands)	19X8	19X7	Amount of Increase or (Decrease) in 19X8	Percent of Increase or (Decrease) in 19X7
Assets				
Current Assets:				
Cash and short-term investments	$ 85,618	$ 57,000	$28,618	50.2
Accounts receivable				
Trade	50,586	36,327	14,259	39.3
Other	2,264	2,185	79	3.6
Inventory	13,417	7,361	6,056	82.3
Prepaid expenses	1,348	812	536	66.0
Total current assets	153,233	103,685	49,548	47.8
Capital assets	38,189	28,605	9,584	33.5
Total assets	$191,422	$132,290	$59,132	44.7
Liabilities and Shareholders' Equity				
Current liabilities:				
Accounts payable	$ 8,487	$ 5,391	$ 3,096	57.4
Accrued liabilities	10,722	6,073	4,649	76.6
Income taxes payable	4,930	7,400	(2,470)	(33.4)
Total current liabilities	24,139	18,864	5,275	28.0
Deferred income taxes	2,330	2,192	$ 138	6.3
Total liabilities	26,469	21,056	5,413	25.7
Shareholders' equity:				
Common share capital	89,380	67,792	21,588	31.8
Contributed surplus	352	352	-0-	0.0
Foreign currency adjustment	372	(372)	(100.0)	
Retained earnings	75,221	42,718	32,503	76.1
Total shareholders' equity	164,953	111,234	53,719	48.3
Total liabilities and shareholders' equity	$191,422	$132,290	$59,132	44.7

Our analysis of comparative financial statements begins by focusing on items that show large dollar or percent changes. We then try to identify the reasons for these changes and, if possible, determine whether they are favourable or unfavourable. We also follow up on items with small changes when we expected the changes to be large.

Regarding Ralco's comparative balance sheet, its first line item, "Cash and short-term investments," in Exhibit 20.1 stands out and shows a $28.6 million increase (50.2%). To a large extent, this increase may be explained by the increase in two other items: the $21.6 million increase in share capital and the $32.5 million increase in Retained Earnings.

Note that Ralco's liabilities increased by $5.4 million. In light of this, the $28.6 million increase in Cash and short-term investments might appear to be an excessive investment in highly liquid assets that usually earn a low return. However the company's very strong and liquid financial position indicates an outstanding ability to respond to new opportunities such as the acquisition of other companies.

Comparative Income Statement

A comparative income statement is prepared similar to the comparative balance sheet. Amounts for two or more periods are placed side by side, with additional columns for dollar and percent changes. Exhibit 20.2 shows Ralco's comparative income statement.

Exhibit 20.2

Comparative Income Statements

RALCO CORPORATION
Comparative Statements of Income
For Years Ended November 30, 19x8 and 19x7

(in thousands)	19X8	19X7	Amount of Increase or (Decrease) in 19X8	Percent of Increase or (Decrease) in 19X7
Sales	$164,313	$105,027	$59,286	56.4
Cost of sales	35,940	24,310	11,630	47.8
Gross profit	128,373	80,717	47,656	59.0
Expenses:				
Advertising	34,390	20,579	13,811	67.1
Selling, general and administrative	30,833	18,005	12,828	71.2
Research and development	10,888	6,256	4,632	74.0
Depreciation and amortization	6,137	4,079	2,058	50.5
Loss (gain) on foreign exchange	1,546	(480)	2,026	422.1
Total expenses:	83,794	48,439	35,355	73.0
Income from continuing operations	44,579	32,278	12,301	38.1
Interest income	2,861	2,389	472	19.8
Income from continuing operations before income taxes	47,440	34,667	12,773	36.8
Income taxes	14,937	13,814	1,123	8.1
Net income	$ 32,503	$ 20,853	$11,650	55.9

All of the income statement items (except foreign exchange) reflect the company's rapid growth. The increases ranged from 67.1 to 19.8%. Expecially note the large $13.8 million or 67.1% increase in advertising. This suggests the company's leadership and strong response to competition in the software industry. Although the dollar increase in Interest income was only $.5 million, this amounted to a 19.8% increase. This is consistent with the increase in Cash and short-term investments reported in the balance sheet.

Output-Made-Easy
Today's accounting programs and spreadsheets can produce outputs with horizontal, vertical, and ratio analyses. These analyses include graphical depiction of financial relations. The key is being able to use this information properly and effectively for business decision making.

Trend Analysis

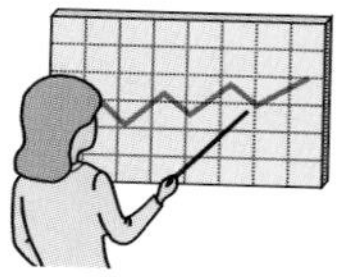

Trend analysis, also called *trend percent analysis* or *index number trend analysis*, is used to reveal patterns in data covering successive periods. It involves computing trend percents for a series of financial numbers. This method of analysis is a variation on the use of percent changes for horizontal analysis. The difference is that trend analysis does not subtract the base period amount in the numerator. To compute trend percents we need to:

1. Select a *base period* and assign each item for the base period statement a weight of 100%.
2. Express financial numbers from other periods as a percent of its base period number.

Specifically, a *trend percent*, also called an *index number*, is measured as the amount in the analysis period divided by the amount of the same item in the base period, and then multiplying this quotient by 100 to get it in percent form:

$$\text{Trend percent} = \frac{\text{Analysis period amount}}{\text{Base period amount}} \times 100$$

To illustrate trend analysis, we use selected financial data of Ralco as shown in Exhibit 20.3.

Exhibit 20.3

Revenues and Expenses

	19X8	19X7	19X6	19X5	19X4
Revenues	$164,313	$105,027	$67,515	$52,242	$29,230
Costs of Sales	35,940	24,310	19,459	7,735	6,015
Gross profit	$128,373	$ 80,717	$48,056	$44,507	$23,215

We select 19X4 as the base period and compute the trend percent for each year and each item by dividing each year's dollar amount by its 19X4 dollar amount. For instance, the revenue trend percent for 19X7 is 359.3%, computed as $105,027/$29,230. The trend percents for the data from Exhibit 20.3 are shown in Exhibit 20.4.

Exhibit 20.4

Trend Percents of Revenues and Expenses

	19X8	19X7	19X6	19X5	19X4
Revenues	562.1%	359.3%	231.0%	178.7%	100%
Costs of Sales	597.5	404.2	323.5	128.6	100
Gross Profit	553.0	347.7	207.0	191.7	100

Our analysis of trend percents is often aided by graphical depictions. Exhibit 20.5 presents the trend percents from Exhibit 20.4 in a line graph. A *line graph* can help us identify trends and detect changes in direction or magnitude. For example, note that the gross profit line was bending upward from 19X4 to 19X5 but was essentially flat from 19X5 to 19X6. The gross profit increased

Exhibit 20.5

Trend Percent Lines for Revenues and Selected Expenses

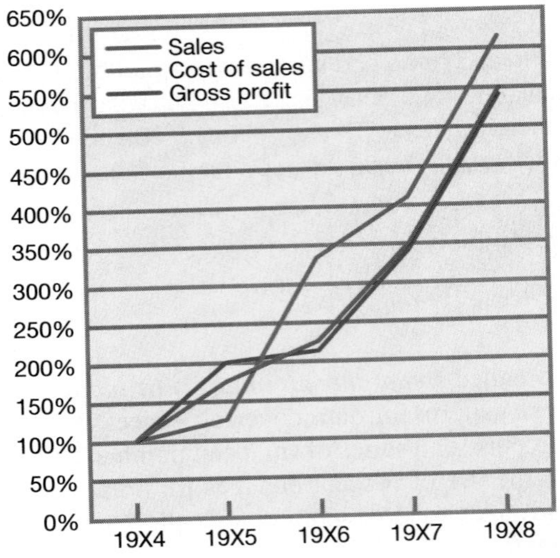

at a lower rate from 19X5 to 19X6 but then parallels the sales line from 19X6 to 19X8.

The line graph in Exhibit 20.5 also helps us understand the relationships between items. For example, the graph in Exhibit 20.5 shows that through 19X7, cost of sales increased at a rate that was somewhat more than the increase in sales. Further, the differing trends in these two items had a clear effect on the percentage changes in gross profit. That is, gross profit increased each year at a somewhat slower rate than sales.

Trend analysis of financial statement items also can include comparisons of relations between items on different financial statements. For instance, Exhibit 20.6 shows a comparison of Ralco's total assets and revenues.

Exhibit 20.6

Revenues and Total Assets Data

	19X8	19X4	Trend Percent (19X8 vs 19X4)
Revenues	$164.3	$29.2	562.7%
Total assets (fiscal year-end)	191.4	41.9	456.8

The rate of increase in total assets was not quite as large as the increase in revenues. Is this change favourable? We cannot say for sure. It might suggest that the company is no longer able to use assets as efficiently as in earlier years. On the other hand, it might mean that the company can expect slower growth in future years. Financial statement analysis often leads the analyst to ask questions, without providing one clear answer.

You Make the Call

Auditor

You are an auditor testing the "reasonableness" of a client's income. Your tests reveal a 3% increase in sales from $200,000 to $206,000, and a 4% decrease in expenses from $190,000 to $182,400. Both changes are within your reasonableness criterion of ±5% and, therefore, you do not pursue additional tests of the accounts. The partner in charge questions your lack of follow-up and notes the *joint relation* between sales and expenses. What is the partner referring to?

Answer—p. 968

Vertical Analysis

Vertical analysis is a tool to evaluate individual financial statement items or groups of items in terms of a specific base amount. This base amount is commonly defined as 100%. When analyzing financial statements, we usually define a key aggregate figure as the base. For instance, an income statement's base is usually revenue and a balance sheet's base is usually total assets. Since the sum of individual items in vertical analysis is 100%, this analysis is also called *common-size analysis*. This section explains vertical analysis and applies it to Ralco's statements.[3]

Common-Size Statements

LO 6 Describe and apply methods of vertical analysis.

The comparative statements in Exhibits 20.1 and 20.2 show how each item has changed over time, but they do not emphasize the relative importance of each item. We use **common-size statements** to reveal changes in the relative importance of each financial statement item. All individual amounts in common-size statements are redefined in terms of common-size percents. A *common-size percent* is measured by taking each individual financial statement amount under analysis and dividing it by its base amount:

$$\text{Common-size percent} = \frac{\text{Analysis amount}}{\text{Base amount}} \times 100$$

Common-Size Balance Sheet

Common-size statements express each item as a percent of a *base amount*. The base amount for a common-size balance sheet is usually total assets. It is assigned a value of 100%. This also implies the total amount of liabilities plus shareholders' equity equals 100% since this amount equals total assets. Next, we compute a common-size percent for each asset, liability, and shareholders' equity item where the base amount is total assets. When we present a company's successive balance sheets in this way, changes in the mixture of assets, liabilities, and equity are more apparent.

For example, look at the common-size comparative balance sheet for Ralco in Exhibit 20.7. Note that Cash and short-term investments amounted to 43.1% of total assets at the end of 19X7 fiscal year. By comparison, they were 44.7% of total assets at the end of 19X8.

Common-Size Income Statement

Our analysis also usually benefits from an examination of a common-size income statement. In this case the amount of revenues is usually the base amount. It is assigned a value of 100%. Each common-size income statement item appears as a percent of revenues. If we think of the 100% revenues amount as representing one sales dollar, the remaining items show how each revenue dollar is distributed among costs, expenses, and profit.

Exhibit 20.8 shows the comparative income statement for each dollar of Ralco's revenues for 19X8 and 19X7. The exhibit shows expenses, as a percent of revenues, have increased from 46.1% to 51.0%. The largest change is an

[3] The term *vertical analysis* arises from the up-down (or down-up) movement of our eyes as we review common-size financial statements.

Exhibit 20.7

Common-Size Comparative Balance Sheet

RALCO CORPORATION Common-Size Comparative Balance Sheet November, 19X8, and November, 19X7			Common-Size Percentages	
(in thousands)	19X8	19X7	19X8	19X7
Assets				
Current assets:				
Cash and short-term investments	$ 85,618	$ 57,000	44.7	43.1
Accounts receivable				
Trade	50,586	36,327	26.4	27.4
Other	2,264	2,185	1.2	1.7
Inventory	13,417	7,361	7.0	5.6
Prepaid expenses	1,348	812	0.7	0.6
Total current assets	153,233	103,685	80.0	78.4
Capital assets	38,189	28,605	20.0	21.6
Total assets	$191,422	$132,290	$100.0	100.0
Liabilities and Shareholders' Equity				
Current liabilities:				
Accounts payable	$ 8,487	$ 5,391	4.4	4.1
Accrued liabilities	10,722	6,073	5.6	4.6
Income taxes payable	4,930	7,400	2.6	5.6
Total current liabilities	24,139	18,864	12.6	14.3
Deferred income taxes	2,330	2,192	1.2	1.6
Total liabilities	26,469	21,056	13.8	15.9
Shareholders' equity				
Common share capital	89,380	67,792	46.7	51.2
Contribution surplus	352	352	0.2	0.3
Foreign currency adjustment		372		0.3
Retained earnings	75,221	42,718	39.3	32.3
Total shareholders' equity	164,953	111,234	86.2	84.1
Total liabilities and shareholders' equity	$191,422	$132,290	100.0	100.0

increase in selling and administrative expenses, from 17.1 cents on the dollar to 18.8 cents on the dollar. The only expense that decreased as a percentage of revenues is amortization which is a noncash expense.

One of the advantages of computing common-size percents for successive income statements is in helping us uncover potentially important changes in a company's expenses. For Ralco, the relative size of each expense changed very little from 19X7 to 19X8. Evidence of no changes is also valuable information for our analysis.

Common-Size Graphics

There are several tools of common-size analysis. Two of the most common are trend analysis of common-size statements and graphical analysis. The trend analysis of common-size statements is similar to the trend analysis of comparative statements discussed under vertical analysis. The only difference is the substitution of common-size percents for percent changes and, therefore, is not illustrated here. Instead, this section discusses graphical analysis of common-size statements.

Exhibit 20.8

Common-Size Comparative Income Statement

RALCO CORPORATION
Common-Size Comparative Income Statement
For Years Ended November 30, 19X8 and 19X7

			Common-Size Percentages	
(in thousands)	19X8	19X7	19X8	19X7
Sales	$164,313	$105,027	100.0	100.0
Cost of sales	35,940	24,310	21.9	23.1
Gross profit	128,373	80,717	78.1	76.9
Expenses:				
Advertising	34,390	20,579	20.9	19.6
Selling, general and administrative	30,833	18,005	18.8	17.1
Research and development	10.888	6,256	6.6	6.0
Depreciation and amortization	6,137	4,079	3.7	3.9
Loss (gain) on foreign exchange	1,546	(480)	0.9	(0.5)
Total expenses	83,794	48,439	51.0	46.1
Income from continuing operations	44,579	32,278	27.1	30.7
Interest income	2,861	2,389	1.7	2.3
Income from continuing operations before income taxes	47,440	34,667	28.9	33.0
Income taxes	14,937	13,814	9.1	13.2
Net income	$ 32,503	$ 20,853	19.8	19.8
Earnings per share	$ 0.63	$ 0.45		
Weighted-average share outstanding	51,768	46,146		

An income statement readily lends itself to common-size graphical analysis. Revenues affect nearly every item in an income statement. It is also usually helpful for our analysis to know what portion of revenues is taken up by various geographical regions. Exhibit 20.9 shows Ralco's common-size income statement in graphical form. This pie chart highlights the contribution of each component of revenues.

Exhibit 20.9

Common-Size Graphic of Ralco's Income Statement

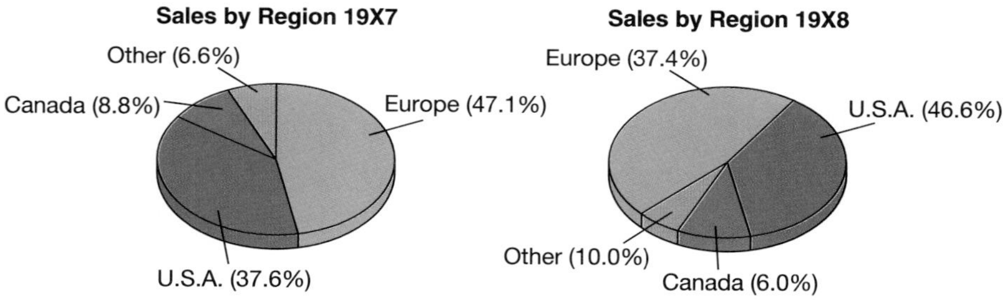

The pie chart on the left side of the illustration shows the sales generated by each of the company's geographic regions in 19X7. The pie chart on the right shows the revenues by sales by region for 19X8. In the annual report, the data for these charts did not appear in the financial statements. Instead they were included as part of the discussion and analysis by management.

Common-size financial statements are useful in comparing different companies. This is because financial statements of different companies are recast in common-size format. But common-size statements fail to reflect the relative sizes of companies under analysis. Comparison of a company's common-size statements with competitors' or industry common-size statistics alerts our attention to differences in the structure or distribution of its financials. Major differences should be explored and explained.

Flash back

5. On common-size comparative statements, which of the following is true? (a) Each item is expressed as a percent of a base amount. (b) Total assets is assigned a value of 100%. (c) Amounts from two or more successive periods are placed side by side. (d) All of the above are true.
6. What is the difference between the percents shown on a comparative income statement and those shown on a common-size comparative income statement?
7. Trend percents (a) are shown on comparative income statement and comparative balance sheet, (b) are shown on common-size comparative statements, or (c) are also called index numbers.

Answers—p. 969

Mid-Chapter Demonstration Problem

Use the financial Statements of Precision Company to satisfy the following requirements.

1. Prepare a comparative income statement showing the percent increase or decrease for 2000 over 1999.
2. Prepare a common-size comparative balance sheet for 2000 and 1999.

PRECISION COMPANY
Comparative Income Statement
For Years Ended December 31, 2000 and 1999

	2000	1999
Sales	$2,486,000	$2,075,000
Cost of goods sold	1,523,000	1,222,000
Gross profit from sales	$963,000	$853,000
Operating expenses:		
Advertising expense	$ 145,000	$ 100,000
Sales salaries expense	240,000	280,000
Office salaries expense	165,000	200,000
Insurance expense	100,000	45,000
Supplies expense	26,000	35,000
Amortization expense	85,000	75,000
Miscellaneous expenses	17,000	15,000
Total operating expenses	$ 778,000	$ 750,000
Operating income	$ 185,000	$ 103,000
Less interest expense	44,000	46,000
Income before taxes	$ 141,000	$ 57,000
Income taxes	47,000	19,000
Net income	$ 94,000	$ 38,000
Earnings per share	$ 0.99	$ 0.40

PRECISION COMPANY
Comparative Balance Sheet
December 31, 2000, and December 31, 1999

	2000	1999
Assets		
Current assets:		
Cash	$ 79,000	$ 42,000
Short-term investment	65,000	96,000
Accounts receivable (net)	120,000	100,000
Merchandise inventory	250,000	265,000
Total current assets	$ 514,000	$ 503,000
Capital Assets:		
Store equipment (net)	$ 400,000	$ 350,000
Office equipment (net)	45,000	50,000
Buildings (net)	625,000	675,000
Land	100,000	100,000
Total capital assets	$1,170,000	$1,175,000
Total assets	$1,684,000	$1,678,000
Liabilities		
Current liabilities:		
Accounts payable	$ 164,000	$ 190,000
Short-term notes payable	75,000	90,000
Taxes payable	26,000	12,000
Total current liabilities	$ 265,000	$ 292,000
Long-term liabilities:		
Notes payable (secured by mortgage on building and land)	400,000	420,000
Total liabilities	$ 665,000	$ 712,000
Shareholders' Equity		
Contributed capital:		
Common shares no-par value	$ 475,000	$ 475,000
Retained earnings	544,000	491,000
Total shareholders' equity	$1,019,000	$ 966,000
Total liabilities and shareholders' equity.	$1,684,000	$1,678,000

Planning the Solution

- Set up a four-column income statement; enter the 2000 and 1999 amounts in the first two columns and then enter the dollar change in the third column and the percent change from 1999 in the fourth column.
- Set up a four-column balance sheet; enter the 2000 and 1999 amounts in the first columns and then compute and enter the amount of each item as a percent of total assets.

Solution to Mid-Chapter Demonstration Problem

PRECISION COMPANY
Comparative Income Statement
For Years Ended December 31, 2000 and 1999

	2000	1999	Increase (Decrease) in 2000 Amount	Increase (Decrease) in 2000 Percent
Sales	$2,486,000	$2,075,000	$411,000	19.8%
Cost of goods sold	1,523,000	1,222,000	301,000	24.6
Gross profit from sales	$963,000	$ 853,000	$110,000	12.9
Operating expenses:				
Advertising expense	$ 145,000	$100,000	$45,000	45.0
Sales salaries expense	240,000	280,000	(40,000)	(14.3)
Office salaries expense	165,000	200,000	(35,000)	(17.5)
Insurance expense	100,000	45,000	55,000	122.2
Supplies expense	26,000	35,000	(9,000)	(25.7)
Amortization expense	85,000	75,000	10,000	13.3
Miscellaneous expenses	17,000	15,000	2,000	13.3
Total operating expenses	$ 778,000	$ 750,000	$ 28,000	3.7
Operating income	$ 185,000	$ 103,000	$ 82,000	79.6
Less interest expense	44,000	46,000	(2,000)	(4.3)
Income before taxes	$ 141,000	$ 57,000	$ 84,000	147.4
Income taxes	47,000	19,000	28,000	147.4
Net income	$ 94,000	$ 38,000	$ 56,000	147.4
Earnings per share	$0.99	$0.40	$ 0.59	147.5

PRECISION COMPANY
Common-Size, Comparative Balance Sheet
December 31, 2000, and December 31, 1999

	2000	1999	Common-Size Percents 2000*	Common-Size Percents 1999*
Assets				
Current assets:				
Cash	$ 79,000	$ 42,000	4.7%	2.5%
Short-term investments	65,000	96,000	3.9	5.7
Accounts receivable (net)	120,000	100,000	7.1	6.0
Merchandise inventory	250,000	265,000	14.8	15.8
Total current assets	$ 514,000	$ 503,000	30.5	30.0
Capital Assets:				
Store equipment (net)	$ 400,000	$ 350,000	23.8	20.9
Office equipment (net)	45,000	50,000	2.7	3.0
Buildings (net)	625,000	675,000	37.1	40.2
Land	100,000	100,000	5.9	6.0
Total capital assets	$1,170,000	$1,175,000	69.5	70.0
Total assets	$1,684,000	$1,678,000	100.0	100.0

Liabilities				
Current liabilities:				
Accounts payable	$ 164,000	$ 190,000	9.7	11.3
Short-term notes payable ..	75,000	90,000	4.5	5.4
Taxes payable	26,000	12,000	1.5	0.7
Total current liabilities	$ 265,000	$ 292,000	15.7	17.4
Long-term liabilities:				
Notes payable (secured by mortgage on buildings and land)	400,000	420,000	23.8	25.0
Total liabilities	$ 665,000	$ 712,000	39.4	42.4
Shareholders' Equity				
Contributed capital:				
Common shares no-par value	$ 475,000	$ 475,000	28.2	28.3
Retained earnings	544,000	491,000	32.3	29.3
Total shareholders' equity	$1,019,000	$ 966,000	60.5	57.6
Total liabilities and equity	$1,684,000	$1,678,000	100.0	100.0

*Columns may not foot due to rounding.

Solution to Mid-Chapter Demonstration Problem

Ratio Analysis

LO7 Define and apply ratio analysis.

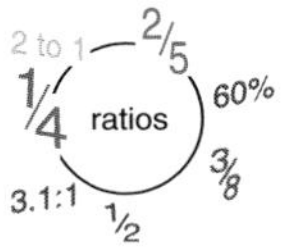

Ratios are among the most popular and widely used tools of financial analysis. They provide us with clues and symptoms of underlying conditions. Ratios, properly interpreted, identify areas requiring further investigation. A ratio can help us uncover conditions and trends difficult to detect by inspecting individual components comprising the ratio. Ratios, like other analysis tools, are usually future oriented. This means they are often adjusted for their probable future trend and magnitude. In this sense ratios can be used to prepare forecasted financial statements. Usefulness of ratios depends on our skillful interpretation of them, and is the most challenging aspect of ratio analysis.

A ratio expresses a mathematical relation between two quantities. It can be expressed as a percent, rate, or proportion. For instance, a change in an account balance from $100 to $250 can be expressed as: (1) 250%, (2) 2.5 times, or (3) 2.5 to 1 [or 2.5:1]. While computation of a ratio is a simple arithmetic operation, its interpretation is not. To be meaningful, a ratio must refer to an economically important relation. For example, there is a direct and crucial relation between an item's sales price and its cost. Accordingly, the ratio of cost of goods sold to sales is a significant one. In contrast, there is no obvious relation between freight costs and the balance of temporary investments in securities.

This section describes an important set of financial ratios and shows how to apply them. The selected ratios are organized into the four building blocks of financial statement analysis: (1) liquidity and efficiency, (2) solvency, (3) profitability, and (4) market. All of these ratios have been previously explained at relevant points in prior chapters. The purpose here is to organize and apply them under a summary framework.

Liquidity and Efficiency

Liquidity refers to the availability of resources to meet short-term cash requirements. A company's short-term liquidity is affected by the timing of cash inflows and outflows along with its prospects for future performance. Our analysis of liquidity is aimed at a company's capital requirements. **Efficiency** refers to how productive a company is in using its assets. Efficiency is usually measured relative to how much revenue is generated for a certain level of assets.

Both liquidity and efficiency are important and complementary in our analysis. If a company fails to meet its current obligations, its continued existence is doubtful. Viewed in this light, all other measures of analysis are of secondary importance. While accounting measurements assume indefinite existence (going-concern assumption) of the company, our analysis must always assess the validity of this assumption using liquidity measures. Efficiency is how well a company uses its assets. Inefficient use of assets can yield liquidity problems.

For users, a lack of liquidity often precedes lower profitability and opportunity. It can foretell a loss of owner control or loss of investment. When a company's owners possess unlimited liability (proprietorships and certain partnerships) a lack of liquidity endangers their personal assets. To creditors of a company, lack of liquidity can yield delays in collecting interest and principal payments or the loss of amounts due them. A company's customers and suppliers of goods and services are affected by short-term liquidity problems. Implications include a company's inability to execute contracts and potential damage to important customer and supplier relationships. This section describes and illustrates ratios relevant to accessing liquidity and efficiency.

Working Capital and Current Ratio

The amount of current assets less current liabilities is called **working capital** or *net working capital*. A company needs an adequate amount of working capital to meet current debts, carry sufficient inventories, and take advantage of cash discounts. A company that runs low on working capital is less likely to meet current obligations or continue operating.

When evaluating a company's working capital we must look beyond the dollar amount of current assets less current liabilities. We also need to consider the relation between the amounts of current assets and current liabilities. Recall from Chapter 5 that the *current ratio* describes a company's ability to pay its short-term obligations. The current ratio relates current assets to current liabilities as follows:

$$\text{Current ratio} = \frac{\text{Current assets}}{\text{Current liabilities}}$$

Drawing on information in Exhibit 20.1, Ralco's working capital amounts and current ratios for both 19X8 and 19X7 are shown in Exhibit 20.10

Exhibit 20.10

Working Capital and Current Ratio

(in millions)	Nov. 30, 19X8	Nov. 30, 19X7
Current assets	$153,233	$103,685
Current liabilities	24,139	18,864
Working capital	**$129,094**	**$ 84,821**
Current ratio:		
$153,233/$24,139	6.35 to 1	
$103,685/$18,864		5.50 to 1

A high current ratio suggests a strong liquidity position. A high ratio means a company should be able to meet its current obligations. But a company also can have a current ratio that is too high. An excessively high ratio means the company has invested too much in current assets compared to its current obligations. Since current assets do not normally generate much additional revenue, an excessive investment in current assets is not an efficient use of funds.

Many users apply a guideline of 2 to 1 for the current ratio in helping evaluate the debt-paying ability of a company. A company with a 2 to 1 or higher current ratio is generally thought to be a good credit risk in the short run. But this analysis is only one step in our process of assessing a company's debt-paying ability. We also need to analyze at least three additional factors:

1. Type of business.
2. Composition of current assets.
3. Turnover rate of current asset components.

Type of Business

The type of business a company operates affects our assessment of its current ratio. A service company that grants little or no credit and carries no inventories other than supplies can probably operate on a current ratio of less than 1 to 1 if its revenues generate enough cash to pay its current liabilities on time. On the other hand, a company selling high-priced clothing or furniture requires a higher ratio. This is because of difficulties in judging customer demand and other factors. For instance, if demands falls, this company's inventory may not generate as much cash as expected. A company facing these risks should maintain a current ratio of more than 2 to 1 to protect its creditors.

The importance of the type of business to our analysis implies an evaluation of a company's current ratio should include a comparison with ratios of other successful companies in the same industry. Another important part of our analysis is to observe how the current ratio changes over time. We must also recognize that the current ratio is affected by a company's accounting methods, especially choice of inventory method. For instance, a company using LIFO tends to report a smaller amount of current assets than if it uses FIFO when costs are rising. These factors should be considered before we decide whether a given current ratio is adequate.

Composition of Current Assets

The composition of a company's current assets is important to our evaluation of short-term liquidity. For instance, cash, cash equivalents, and temporary investments are more liquid than accounts and notes receivable. Also, receivables normally are more liquid than merchandise inventory. We know cash can be used to immediately pay current debts. But items such as accounts receivable and merchandise inventory must be converted into cash before payments can be made. An excessive amount of receivables and inventory weakens a company's ability to pay current liabilities. One way to take account of the composition of current assets is to evaluate the acid-test ratio. We discuss this in the next section.

Turnover Rate of Asset

Asset turnover measures the efficiency of a company's use of assets. One relevant measure of asset efficiency is the revenues generated. The general measure of asset turnover is revenues divided by total assets. But evaluation of turnover for individual assets is also useful in our analysis. We discuss total asset turnover along with both receivables and inventories turnover below.

You Make the Call

Banker

You are a banker, and a company calls on you for a one-year, $200,000 loan to finance expansion. This company's current ratio is 4:1 with current assets of $160,000. Key competitors carry a current ratio of about 1.9:1. Using this information, do you approve the loan application? Does your decision change if the application is for a 10-year loan?

Answer—p. 968

Acid-Test Ratio

Chapter 6 introduced us to the *acid-test ratio*, also called *quick ratio*. This ratio focuses on current asset composition. Quick assets are cash, short-term investments, accounts receivable, and notes receivable. These are the most liquid types of current assets. We compute the acid-test ratio as:

$$\text{Acid-test ratio} = \frac{\text{Quick assets}}{\text{Current liabilities}}$$

Using information in Exhibit 20.1, we compute Ralco's acid-test ratios as shown in Exhibit 20.11.

Exhibit 20.11
Acid-Test Ratio

(in millions)	November 30, 19X8	November 30, 19X7
Cash and short-term investments	$85,618	$57,000
Accounts receivable, trade	50,586	36,327
Total quick assets	$136,204	$93,327
Current liabilities	$ 24,139	$18,864
Acid-test ratio:		
$136,204/$24,139	5.64 to 1	
$93,327/$18,864		4.95 to 1

Ralco
Acid-Test Ratio = 5.64

A traditional rule-of-thumb for an acceptable acid-test ratio is 1 to 1. Similar to our analysis of the current ratio, we need to consider other factors. For instance, the working capital requirements of a company are affected by how frequently the company converts its current assets into cash. This implies our analysis of the company's short-term liquidity should also include analysis of receivables and inventories. We next look at these analyses.

Accounts Receivable Turnover

We can measure how frequently a company converts its receivables into cash by computing *accounts receivable turnover*. As we explained in Chapter 10, this is computed as:

$$\text{Accounts receivable turnover} = \frac{\text{Net sales}}{\text{Average accounts receivable}}$$

While this ratio is called accounts receivable turnover, all short-term receivables (including notes receivable) from customers are normally included in the denominator amount along with accounts receivable. The numerator of this ratio is more precise if credit sales are used. But net sales (or revenues) is usually used by external users because information about credit sales is typically not reported.

Ralco's 19X8 accounts receivable turnover is computed as:

$$\frac{\$164,313}{(\$50,586 + \$36,327)/2} = 3.78 \text{ times}$$

If accounts receivable are collected quickly, then accounts receivable turnover is high. A high turnover is favourable because it means the company need not commit large amounts of capital to accounts receivable. An accounts receivable turnover can be too high. This can occur when credit terms are so restrictive they negatively affect sales volume.

Ending accounts receivable is sometimes substituted for the average balance in computing accounts receivable turnover. This is acceptable if the difference between these figures is not material. Also, some users prefer using gross accounts receivable (before subtracting the allowance for doubtful accounts). But many balance sheets report only the net amount of accounts receivable.

Merchandise Inventory Turnover

Working capital requirements are affected by how long a company holds merchandise inventory before selling it. One measure of this effect is the *merchandise inventory turnover*, or simply *inventory turnover*. Merchandise turnover is defined in Chapter 7 as:

$$\text{Merchandise turnover} = \frac{\text{Cost of goods sold}}{\text{Average merchandise inventory}}$$

Using the costs of sales and inventories information in Exhibits 20.1 and 20.2, we compute Ralco's merchandise turnover for 19X8 as (cost of goods sold is called *costs of sales* on Ralco's income statement):

$$\frac{\$35{,}940}{(\$13{,}417 + \$7{,}361)/2} = 3.46 \text{ times}$$

Average inventory is estimated by averaging the beginning and the ending inventories for 19X8. If the beginning and ending inventories do not represent the amount normally on hand, an average of quarterly inventories may be used if available.

A company with a high turnover requires a smaller investment in inventory than one producing the same sales with a lower turnover. But merchandise turnover can be too high if a company keeps such a small inventory on hand that it restricts sales volume.

Days' Sales Uncollected

We already described how accounts receivable turnover can be used to evaluate how frequently a company collects its accounts. Another measure of this activity is *days' sales uncollected*. In Chapter 9 we defined it as:

$$\text{Days' sales uncollected} = \frac{\text{Accounts receivable}}{\text{Net sales}} \times 365$$

This formula takes the usual approach of placing accounts receivable in the numerator. Any short-term notes receivable from customers are also normally included in the numerator.

We illustrate this ratio's application by using Ralco's information in Exhibits 20.1 and 20.2. The days' sales uncollected on November 30, 19x8, is:

$$\frac{\$50{,}586}{\$164{,}313} \times 365 = 112.4 \text{ days}$$

Days' sales uncollected is more meaningful if we know the company's credit terms. A rough guideline is days' sales uncollected should not exceed one and one-third times the days in its: (a) credit period, if discounts are not offered; (b) discount period, if discounts are offered.

Days' Sales in Inventory

Chapter 7 explained how *days' sales in inventory* is a measure useful in evaluating the liquidity of a company's inventory. Days' sales in inventory is linked to inventory in a similar manner as days' sales uncollected is linked to receivables. Days' sales in inventory is computed as:

$$\text{Days' sales in inventory} = \frac{\text{Ending inventory}}{\text{Cost of goods sold}} \times 365$$

Applying this formula to Ralco's 19X8 financial statements, we compute days' sales in inventory as:

$$\frac{\$13{,}417}{\$35{,}940} \times 365 = 136.3 \text{ days}$$

If the products in Ralco's inventory are in demand by customers, this formula estimates that its inventory will be converted into receivables (or cash) in 136.3 days. If all of Ralco's sales are credit sales, the conversion of inventory to receivables in 136.3 days plus the conversion of receivables to cash in 112.4 days suggest that inventory will be converted to cash in about 248.7 days (136.3 + 112.4 = 248.7).

Total Asset Turnover

Total asset turnover describes the ability of a company to use its assets to generate sales. We explained in Chapter 13 that this ratio is computed as:

$$\text{Total asset turnover} = \frac{\text{Revenues}}{\text{Average total assets}}$$

In computing Ralco's total asset turnover for 19X8, we follow the usual practice of averaging total assets at the beginning and the end of the year. Taking the information from Exhibits 20.1 and 20.2, this computation is:

$$\frac{\$164{,}313}{(\$191{,}422 + \$132{,}290)/2} = 1.015 \text{ times}$$

Flashback

8. The following information is from the Dec. 31/2000 balance sheet of Paff Company: cash, \$820,000; accounts receivable, \$240,000; inventories, \$470,000; capital assets, \$910,000; accounts payable, \$350,000; and income taxes payable, \$180,000. Compute the (a) current ratio and (b) acid-test ratio.

9. On Dec. 31/1999, Paff Company (in prior question) had accounts receivable of \$290,000 and inventories of \$530,000. During 2000, net sales amounted to \$2,500,000 and cost of goods sold was \$750,000. Compute the (a) accounts receivable turnover, (b) days' sales uncollected, (c) merchandise turnover, and (d) days' sales in inventory.

Answers—p. 969

Solvency

Solvency refers to a company's long-run financial viability and its ability to cover long-term obligations. All business activities of a company—financing, investing, and operating—affect a company's solvency. One of the most important components of solvency analysis is the composition of a company's capital structure. *Capital structure* refers to a company's sources of financing.

Analyzing solvency of a company is different from analyzing short-term liquidity. Analysis of solvency is long-term and uses less precise but more encompassing measures. Analysis of capital structure is one key in evaluating solvency. Capital structure ranges from relatively permanent equity capital to more risky or temporary short-term financing. Assets represent secondary sources of security for lenders ranging from loans secured by specific assets to the assets available as general security to unsecured creditors. There are different risks associated with different assets and financing sources.

This section describes tools of solvency analysis. Our analysis is concerned with a company's ability to meet its obligations and provide security to its creditors over the long run. Indicators of this ability include *debt* and *equity* ratios, the relation between *pledged assets* and *secured liabilities*, and the company's capacity to earn sufficient income to *pay fixed interest charges.*

Debt and Equity Ratios

One element of solvency analysis is to assess the portion of a company's assets contributed by its owners and the portion contributed by creditors. This relation is reflected in the debt ratio described in Chapter 3. Recall the *debt ratio* expresses total liabilities as a percent of total assets. The **equity ratio** provides complementary information by expressing total shareholders' equity as a percent of total assets.

Ralco's debt and equity ratios are computed as:

	Nov.30, 19X8	Ratios	
Total liabilities	$ 26,469	13.8%	[Debt Ratio]
Total shareholders' equity	164,953	86.2	[Equity Ratio]
Total liabilities and shareholders' equity	$191,422	100.0%	

Ralco's financial statements reflect very little debt compared to most companies. The company has only one long-term liability and, at the end of 19X8, its liabilities provide only 13.8% of the total assets. A company is considered less risky if its capital structure (equity and long-term debt) is comprised more of equity. One source of this increased risk is the required payments under debt contracts for interest and principal amounts. Another factor is the amount of financing provided by shareholders. The greater is shareholder financing, the more losses a company can absorb through its shareholders before the remaining assets become inadequate to satisfy the claims of creditors.

From the shareholders' point of view, including debt in the capital structure of a company is desirable so long as risk is not too great. If a company earns a return on borrowed capital that is higher than the cost of borrowing, the difference represents increased income to shareholders. Because debt can have the effect of increasing the return to shareholders, the inclusion of debt is sometimes described as *financial leverage*. Companies are said to be highly leveraged if a large portion of their assets is financed by debt.

Pledged Assets to Secured Liabilities

We explained in Chapter 17 how we use the ratio of pledged assets to secured liabilities to evaluate the risk of nonpayment faced by secured creditors. This ratio also is relevant to unsecured creditors. The ratio is computed as:

$$\text{Pledged assets to secured liabilities} = \frac{\text{Book value of pledged assets}}{\text{Book value of secured liabilities}}$$

The information needed to compute this ratio is not usually reported in published financial statements. This means the ratio is used primarily by persons who have the ability to obtain information directly from the company such as bankers and certain lenders.

A generally agreed minimum value for this ratio is about 2 to 1. But the ratio needs careful interpretation because it is based on the *book value* of pledged assets. Book values are not necessarily intended to reflect amounts to be received for assets in event of liquidation. Also, the long-term earning ability of a company with pledged assets may be more important than the value of its pledged assets. Creditors prefer that a debtor be able to pay with cash generated by operating activities rather than with cash obtained by liquidating assets.

Times Interest Earned

Chapter 14 explained the *times interest earned ratio*. Its purpose is to reflect the riskiness of repayments with interest to creditors. The amount of income before the deduction of interest charges and income taxes is the amount available to pay interest charges. We compute this ratio as:

$$\text{Times interest earned} = \frac{\text{Income before interest and income taxes}}{\text{Interest expense}}$$

The larger this ratio, the less risky is the company for lenders. A guideline for this ratio says that creditors are reasonably safe if the company earns its fixed interest charges two or more times each year.

Exhibit 20.2 does not report interest expense as a separate item for Ralco. Apparently interest expense is not material; probably it is offset against interest income. Also, recall from Exhibit 20.1 that Ralco did not have any long-term debt. Furthermore, few if any of the company's current liabilities would be likely to generate interest expense. As a result, we are not able to calculate times interest earned for Ralco.

Did You Know?

Bears and Bulls
Bear market is a declining market. It comes from bear skin jobbers who often sold bear skins before the bears were caught. The term bear was then used to describe investors who sold shares they did not own in anticipation of a price decline. *Bull market* is a rising market. It comes from the once popular sport of bear and bull baiting. The term bull came to mean the opposite of bear.

Profitability

We are especially interested in the ability of a company to use its assets efficiently to produce profits (and positive cash flows). **Profitability** refers to a company's ability to generate an adequate return on invested capital. Return is judged by assessing earnings relative to the level and sources of financing. Profitability is also relevant to solvency.

This section describes profitability measures and their importance to financial statement analysis. We also explain variations in return measures and their interpretation. We analyze the components of return on invested capital for additional insights into company performance.

Profit Margin

The operating efficiency and profitability of a company can be expressed in two components. The first is the company's *profit margin*. We explained in Chapter 4 how profit margin reflects a company's ability to earn a net income from sales. It is measured by expressing net income as a percent of revenues (sales and revenues are treated as similar in ratio analysis). We can use the information in Exhibit 20.2 to compute Ralco's 19X8 profit margin as:

$$\text{Profit margin} = \frac{\text{Net income}}{\text{Revenues}} = \frac{\$32{,}503}{\$164{,}313} = 19.8\%$$

To evaluate the profit margin of a company, we must consider the industry in which it operates. For instance, a publishing company might be expected to have a profit margin between 10% and 15%, while a retail supermarket might have a normal profit margin of 1% or 2%.

The second component of operating efficiency is *total asset turnover*. We described this ratio earlier in this section. Both profit margin and total asset turnover make up the two basic components of operating efficiency. These ratios also reflect on management performance since managers are ultimately responsible for operating efficiency. The next section explains how we use both measures in analyzing return on total assets.

Return on Total Assets

The two basic components of operating efficiency, profit margin and total asset turnover, are used to compute a summary measure. This summary measure is the *return on total assets* we described in Chapters 1 and 18. It is computed as:

$$\text{Return on total assets} = \frac{\text{Net income}}{\text{Average total assets}}$$

Ralco's 19X8 return on total assets is:

$$\frac{\$32{,}503}{(\$191{,}422 + \$132{,}290)/2} = 20.1\%$$

Ralco's 20.1% return on total assets is favourable compared to most businesses; however, this is a risky industry and good times can turn into bad very quickly. The following computation shows the relation between profit margin, total asset turnover, and return on total assets:

$$\text{Profit margin} \times \text{Total asset turnover} = \text{Return on total assets}$$

or

$$\frac{\text{Net income}}{\text{Net sales}} \times \frac{\text{Net sales}}{\text{Average total assets}} = \frac{\text{Net income}}{\text{Average total assets}}$$

Notice that both profit margin and total asset turnover contribute to overall operating efficiency, as measured by return on total assets. If we apply this formula to Ralco we get:

$$19.8\% \times 1.015 = 20.1\%$$

Return on Common Shareholders' Equity

Perhaps the most important goal in operating companies is to earn net income for its owners. The *return on common shareholders' equity* measures the success of a company in reaching this goal. We explained in Chapter 2 how we compute this return measure:

$$\text{Return on common shareholders' equity} = \frac{\text{Net income} - \text{Preferred dividends}}{\text{Average common shareholders' equity}}$$

Recall from Exhibit 20.1 that Ralco did not have any preferred shares outstanding. As a result we determine Ralco's return as follows:

$$\frac{\$32{,}503 - \$0}{(\$164{,}953 + \$111{,}234)/2} = 23.5\%$$

The denominator in this computation is the book value of common shares. In the numerator, the dividends on cumulative preferred shares must be subtracted whether they are declared or are in arrears. If preferred is noncumulative, its dividends are subtracted only if declared.

Market

Market measures are useful when analyzing corporations having publicly traded shares. These market measures use share price in their computation. Share price reflects what the market (public) expectations are for the company. This includes both the return and risk characteristics of a company as currently perceived by the market.

Price-Earnings Ratio

We explained in Chapter 18 how the *price-earnings ratio* is computed as:

$$\text{Price-earnings ratio} = \frac{\text{Market price per share}}{\text{Earnings per share}}$$

We also described how the predicted earnings per share for the next period is often used in the denominator of this computation. But reported earnings per share for the most recent period is also commonly used. In both cases, the ratio is an indicator of the future growth of and risk related to a company's earnings as perceived by investors who establish the market price of the shares.

The market price of Ralco's common shares during 19X8 ranged from a low of \$14.50 to a high of \$23.25. Ralco's management reported that it did not expect 19X9 revenue growth rates to be as high as those for 19X8. Management also indicated that operating expenses as a percentage of revenues might increase. Nevertheless, the price earnings ratios are much higher than those of most companies. Using Ralco's \$0.63 earnings per share that was reported at the end of 19X8, we compute its price-earnings ratios using both the low and high share prices:

$$\text{Low: } \frac{\$14.50}{\$0.63} = 23$$

$$\text{High: } \frac{\$23.25}{\$0.63} = 36.9$$

Ralco's higher ratios reflect the expectation of investors that the company will continue to grow at a rate faster than the normal company.

Dividend Yield

We explained in Chapter 16 how to use *dividend yield* as a means to compare the dividend-paying performance of different investment alternatives. Dividend yield is computed as:

$$\text{Dividend yield} = \frac{\text{Annual dividends per share}}{\text{Market price per share}}$$

Some companies decide not to declare dividends because they prefer to reinvest the cash. Ralco, for instance, does not pay cash dividends on its common shares.

Summary of Ratios

Exhibit 20.12 presents a summary of the major financial statement analysis ratios illustrated in this chapter and throughout the book. This summary includes each ratio's title, formula, and common use.

Exhibit 20.12

Financial Statement Analysis Ratios

Ratio	Formula	Measure of:
Liquidity and Efficiency		
Current ratio	$= \frac{\text{Current assets}}{\text{Current liabilities}}$	Short-term debt-paying ability
Acid-test ratio	$= \frac{\text{Cash + Temporary investments + Current receivables}}{\text{Current liabilities}}$	Immediate short-term debt-paying ability
Accounts receivable turnover	$= \frac{\text{Net sales}}{\text{Average accounts receivable}}$	Efficiency of collection
Merchandise turnover	$= \frac{\text{Cost of goods sold}}{\text{Average merchandise inventory}}$	Efficiency of inventory
Days' sales uncollected	$= \frac{\text{Accounts receivable}}{\text{Net sales}} \times 365$	Liquidity of receivables
Days' sales in inventory	$= \frac{\text{Ending inventory}}{\text{Cost of goods sold}} \times 365$	Liquidity of inventory
Total asset turnover	$= \frac{\text{Net sales}}{\text{Average total assets}}$	Efficiency of assets in producing sales
Solvency		
Debt ratio	$= \frac{\text{Total liabilities}}{\text{Total assets}}$	Creditor financing and leverage
Equity ratio	$= \frac{\text{Total shareholders' equity}}{\text{Total assets}}$	Owner financing
Pledged assets to secured liabilities	$= \frac{\text{Book value of pledged assets}}{\text{Book value of secured liabilities}}$	Protection to secured creditors
Times interest earned	$= \frac{\text{Income before interest and taxes}}{\text{Interest expense}}$	Protection in meeting interest payments

Exhibit 20.12

(Continued)

Ratio	Formula	Measure of:
Profitability		
Profit margin	$= \dfrac{\text{Net income}}{\text{Net sales}}$	Net income in each sales dollar
Gross margin	$= \dfrac{\text{Net sales} - \text{Cost of goods sold}}{\text{Net sales}}$	Gross margin in each sales dollar
Return on total assets	$= \dfrac{\text{Net income}}{\text{Average total assets}}$	Overall profitability of assets
Return on common shareholders' equity	$= \dfrac{\text{Net income} - \text{Preferred dividends}}{\text{Average common shareholders' equity}}$	Profitability of owner's investment
Book value per common share	$= \dfrac{\text{Shareholders' equity applicable to common shares}}{\text{Number of common shares outstanding}}$	Liquidation at reported amounts.
Basic earnings per share	$= \dfrac{\text{Net income} - \text{Preferred dividends}}{\text{Weighted-average common shares outstanding}}$	Net income on each common share
Market		
Price-earnings ratio	$= \dfrac{\text{Market price per common share}}{\text{Earnings per share}}$	Market value based on earnings
Dividend yield	$= \dfrac{\text{Annual dividends per share}}{\text{Market price per share}}$	Cash return to each common share

Flash back

10. Which ratio best reflects the ability of a company to meet immediate interest payments? (a) debt ratio, (b) equity ratio, (c) times interest earned, or (d) pledged assets to secured liabilities.
11. Which ratio measures the success of a company in earning net income for its owners? (a) profit margin, (b) return on common shareholders' equity, (c) price earnings ratio, or (d) dividend yield.
12. If a company has net sales of $8,500,000, net income of $945,000, and total asset turnover of 1.8 times, what is its return on total assets?

Answers—p. 969

Analysis Reporting

LO 8 Summarize and report results of analysis.

Understanding the purpose of our financial statement analysis is crucial to its quality. This understanding leads to efficiency of effort, effectiveness in application, and relevance in focus. Most analyses face constraints on availability of information and decisions must be made using incomplete or inadequate information.

A goal of most financial statement analyses is reducing uncertainty through a rigorous and sound evaluation. A *financial statement analysis report* helps by directly addressing the building blocks of analysis. It also helps identify weaknesses in inference by requiring explanation, and it forces us to organize our reasoning and to verify the flow and logic of analysis. A report serves as our communication device with readers. The writing process reinforces our judgments and vice versa. It helps us refine conclusions from evidence on key building blocks.

A good report separates interpretations and conclusions of analysis from the information underlying them. This separation enables readers to see our process and rationale of analysis. It also enables the reader to draw personal conclusions and make modifications as appropriate. A good analysis report often consists of six sections devoted to:

- *Executive Summary.* The executive summary is brief and focuses on important analysis results and conclusions.
- *Analysis Overview.* Background material on the company, its industry, and its economic environment.
- *Evidential Matter.* Financial statements and information used in the analysis. This includes ratios, trends, comparisons, statistics, and all analytical measures assembled. Often organized under the building blocks of analysis.
- *Assumptions.* Identification of important assumptions regarding a company's industry and economic environment, and other important assumptions for estimates.
- *Important Factors.* Listing of important favourable and unfavourable factors, both quantitative and qualitative, for company performance—usually listed by areas of analysis.
- *Inferences.* Includes forecasts, estimates, interpretations, and conclusions drawing on all sections of the report.

We must remember that "importance" is defined by the user. This means our analysis report should include a brief table of contents to help readers focus on those areas most relevant to their decisions. All irrelevant matter must be eliminated. For example, decades-old details of the beginnings of a company and a detailing of the miscues of our analysis are irrelevant. Ambiguities and qualifications to avoid responsibility or hedge inferences should be eliminated. Finally, writing is important. Mistakes in grammar and errors of fact compromise the credibility of our analysis.

Short Selling

Short selling refers to selling shares before you buy them. Here's an example of how it works: You borrow 100 **Atlantis** shares, sell them in the market at $40 each and receive money from their sale. You then wait. Your hope is that Atlantis's share price falls to say $35 each and you can replace the borrowed shares for less money than you sold them for—reaping a profit of $5 each less any transaction fees.

Did You Know?

Summary

LO1 **Explain the purpose of analysis.** The purpose of financial statement analysis is to help users make better business decisions. Internal users want information helpful in improving the company's efficiency or effectiveness in providing products or services. External users want information to make better and more informed decisions in pursuing their personal goals. The common goals of all users is to evaluate a company's (1) past and current performance, (2) current financial position, and (3) future performance and risk.

LO2 **Identify the building blocks of analysis.** Financial statement analysis focuses on mainly four areas of inquiry. These four areas are the building blocks of analysis: (1) liquidity and efficiency—ability to meet short-term obligations and to efficiently generate revenues; (2) solvency—ability to generate future revenues and meet long-term obligations; (3) profitability—ability to provide financial rewards sufficient to attract and retain financing; and (4) market—ability to generate positive market expectations.

LO3 **Describe standards for comparisons in analysis.** To make conclusions from analysis we need standards for comparisons. Standards for comparisons include: (1) intracompany—prior performance and relations between financial items of company under analysis; (2) competitor—one or more direct competitors of the company under analysis provide standards for comparisons; (3) industry—industry statistics can provide standards of comparisons; and (4) guidelines (rules-of-thumb)—general standards of comparisons can develop from past experiences and personal judgments.

LO4 **Identify the tools of analysis.** The three most common tools of financial statement analysis: (1) horizontal analysis—comparing a company's financial condition and performance across time; (2) vertical analysis—comparing a company's financial condition and performance to a base amount such as revenues or total assets; and (3) ratio analysis—using key relations among financial statement items.

LO5 **Explain and apply methods of horizontal analysis.** Horizontal analysis is a tool to evaluate changes in financial statement data across time. Two important tools of horizontal analysis are comparative statements and trend analysis. Comparative statements show amounts for two or more successive periods, often with changes disclosed in both absolute and percent terms. Trend analysis is used to reveal important changes occurring from one period to the next.

LO6 **Describe and apply methods of vertical analysis.** In common-size statements, each item is expressed as a percent of a base amount. The base amount for the balance sheet is usually total assets, and the base amount for the income statement is usually net sales. Vertical analysis is a tool to evaluate each financial statement item or group of items in terms of a specific base amount. This base amount is commonly defined as 100%. Two important tools of vertical analysis are common-size statements and graphical analyses.

LO7 **Define and apply ratio analysis.** Ratio analysis provides clues and symptoms of underlying conditions. Ratios, properly interpreted, identify areas requiring further investigation. A ratio expresses a mathematical relation between two quantities such as a percent, rate, or proportion. Selected ratios are organized into the building blocks of analysis: (1) liquidity and efficiency, (2) solvency, (3) profitability, and (4) market.

LO8 **Summarize and report results of analysis.** A financial statement analysis report is often organized around the building blocks of analysis. It serves as a communication device with readers. A good report separates interpretations and conclusions of analysis from the information underlying them. This separation enables readers to see the process and rationale of analysis. It also enables the reader to draw personal conclusions and make modifications as appropriate. An analysis report often consists of six sections: (1) executive summary; (2) analysis overview; (3) evidential matter; (4) assumptions; (5) important factors; and (6) inferences.

Guidance Answers to **You Make the Call**

Auditor

The *joint relation* referred to here is where the increase in sales and the decrease in expenses yield a greater than 5% increase in income. In particular, both *individual* accounts (sales and expenses) yielded percent changes within the ±5% acceptable range. However, a joint analysis suggests a different picture. For example, consider a joint analysis using the profit margin ratio (net income/sales). The client's profit margin is 11.46% ($206,000 – $182,400 / $206,000) for the current year compared with 5.0% ($200,000 – $190,000 / $200,000) for the prior year—a 129% increase in profit margin! This is what the partner is concerned with, and it suggests expanding audit tests to verify or refute the client's figures.

Banker

Your decision on the loan application is positive for at least two reasons. First, the current ratio suggests a strong ability to meet short-term obligations. Second, current assets of $160,000 and a current ratio of 4:1 imply current liabilities of $40,000 (one-fourth of current assets) and a working capital excess of $120,000. This working capital excess is 60% of the loan amount. However, if the application is for a 10-year loan, our decision is less optimistic. While the current ratio and working capital suggest a good safety margin, there are indications of inefficiency in operations. In particular, a 4:1 current ratio is more than double its competitors' ratio. This is characteristic of inefficient asset use.

Guidance Answers to Flashbacks

1. General-purpose financial statements are intended for the large variety of users who are interested in receiving financial information about a business but who do not have the ability to require the company to prepare specialized financial reports designed to meet their specific interests.
2. General-purpose financial statements include the income statement, balance sheet, statement of changes in shareholders' equity (or statement of retained earnings), and statement of cash flows, plus notes related to the statements.
3. *a*

4. Data from one or more direct competitors of the company under analysis are usually preferred for developing standards for comparisons.
5. *d*
6. Percents on a comparative income statement show the increase or decrease in each item from one period to the next. On a common-size comparative income statement, each item is shown as a percent of net sales for a specific period.
7. *c*
8. *a* ($820,000 + $240,000 + $470,000)/($350,000 + $180,000) = 2.9 to 1
   b ($820,000 + $240,000)/($350,000 + $180,000) = 2 to 1
9. *a* $2,500,000/[($290,000 + $240,000)/2] = 9.43 times
   b ($240,000/$2,500,000) × 365 = 35 days
   c $750,000/[($530,000 + $470,000)/2] = 1.5 times
   d ($470,000/$750,000) × 365 = 228.7 days
10. *c*
11. *b*
12. Profit margin × Total asset turnover = Return on total assets ($945,000/$8,500,000) × 1.8 = 20%

Demonstration Problem

Use the financial statements of Precision Company to satisfy the following requirements: Compute and identify the appropriate building block statement analysis for the following ratios as of December 31, 2000, or for the year ended December 31, 2000:

a. Current ratio
b. Acid-test ratio
c. Accounts receivable turnover
d. Days' sales uncollected
e. Merchandise turnover
f. Debt ratio
g. Pledged assets to secured liabilities
h. Times interest earned
i. Profit margin
j. Total asset turnover
k. Return on total assets
l. Return on common shareholders' equity

PRECISION COMPANY
Comparative Income Statement
For Years Ended December 31, 2000 and 1999

	2000	1999
Sales	$2,486,000	$2,075,000
Cost of goods sold	1,523,000	1,222,000
Gross profit from sales	$ 963,000	$ 853,000
Operating expenses:		
Advertising expense	$ 145,000	$ 100,000
Sales salaries expense	240,000	280,000
Office salaries expense	165,000	200,000
Insurance expense	100,000	45,000
Supplies expense	26,000	35,000
Amortization expense	85,000	75,000
Miscellaneous expenses	17,000	15,000
Total operating expenses	$ 778,000	$ 750,000
Operating income	$ 185,000	$ 103,000
Less interest expense	44,000	46,000
Income before taxes	$ 141,000	$ 57,000
Income taxes	47,000	19,000
Net income	$ 94,000	$ 38,000
Earnings per share	$ 0.99	$ 0.40

PRECISION COMPANY Comparative Balance Sheet December 31, 2000, and December 31, 1999	2000	1999
Assets		
Current assets:		
Cash	$ 79,000	$ 42,000
Short-term investments	65,000	96,000
Accounts receivable (net)	120,000	100,000
Merchandise inventory	250,000	265,000
Total current assets	$ 514,000	$ 503,000
Capital Assets:		
Store equipment (net)	$ 400,000	$ 350,000
Office equipment (net)	45,000	50,000
Buildings (net)	625,000	675,000
Land	100,000	100,000
Total capital assets	$1,170,000	$1,175,000
Total assets	$1,684,000	$1,678,000
Liabilities		
Current liabilities:		
Accounts payable	$ 164,000	$ 190,000
Short-term notes payable	75,000	90,000
Taxes payable	26,000	12,000
Total current liabilities	$ 265,000	$ 292,000
Long-term liabilities:		
Notes payable (secured by mortgage on building and land)	400,000	420,000
Total liabilities	$ 665,000	$ 712,000
Shareholders' Equity		
Contributed capital:		
Common shares no-par value	$ 475,000	$ 475,000
Retained earnings	544,000	491,000
Total shareholders' equity	$1,019,000	$ 966,000
Total liabilities and shareholders' equity	$1,684,000	$1,678,000

Planning the Solution

- Compute the given ratios using the provided numbers; be sure to use the average of the beginning and ending amounts where appropriate.

Solution to Demonstration Problem

Ratios for 2000:

a. Current ratio: $514,000/$265,000 = 1.9 to 1 (Liquidity and Efficiency)

b. Acid-test ratio: ($79,000 + $65,000 + $120,000)/$265,000 = 1.0 to 1 (Liquidity and Efficiency)

c. Average receivables: ($120,000 + $100,000)/2 = $110,000

Accounts receivable turnover: $2,486,000/$110,000 = 22.6 times (Liquidity and Efficiency)

d. Days' sales uncollected: ($120,000/$2,486,000) × 365 = 17.6 days (Liquidity and Efficiency)

e. Average inventory: ($250,000 + $265,000)/2 = $257,500
Merchandise turnover: $1,523,000/$257,500 = 5.9 times (Liquidity and Efficiency)

f. Debt ratio: $665,000/$1,684,000 = 39.5% (Solvency)

g. Pledged assets to secured liabilities: ($625,000 + $100,000)/$400,000 = 1.8 to 1 (Solvency)

h. Times interest earned: $185,000/$44,000 = 4.2 times (Solvency)

i. Profit margin: $94,000/$2,486,000 = 3.8% (Profitability)

j. Average total assets: ($1,684,000 + $1,678,000)/2 = $1,681,000
Total asset turnover: $2,486,000/$1,681,000 = 1.48 times (Liquidity and Efficiency)

k. Return on total assets: $94,000/$1,681,000 = 5.6% or 3.8% × 1.48 = 5.6% (Profitability)

l. Average total equity: ($1,019,000 + $966,000)/2 = $992,500
Return on common shareholders' equity: $94,000/$992,500 = 9.5% (Profitability)

Glossary

Common-size statements Comparative financial statements in which each amount is expressed as a percent of a base amount. In the balance sheet, the amount of total assets is usually selected as the base amount and is expressed as 100%. In the income statement, net sales is usually selected as the base amount. (p. 949)

Comparative financial statement A financial statement with data for two or more successive accounting periods placed in columns side by side, sometimes with changes shown in dollar amounts and percents. (p. 943)

Efficiency Refers to how productive a company is in using its assets; usually measured relative to how much revenue is generated for a certain level of assets. (p. 956)

Equity ratio The portion of total assets provided by shareholders' equity, computed as shareholders' equity divided by total assets. (p. 961)

Financial reporting The process of communicating information that is relevant to investors, creditors, and others in making investment, credit, and similar decisions. (p. 942)

Financial statement analysis The application of analytical tools to general-purpose financial statements and related data for making business decisions. (p. 940)

General-purpose financial statements Statements published periodically for use by a wide variety of interested parties; include the income statement, balance sheet, statement of changes in shareholders' equity (or statement of retained earnings), statement of cash flows, and notes related to the statements. (p. 941)

Liquidity Refers to the availability of resources to meet short-term cash requirements. (p. 956)

Profitability Refers to a company's ability to generate an adequate return on invested capital. (p. 962)

Solvency Refers to a company's long-run financial viability and its ability to cover long-term obligations. (p. 961)

Vertical analysis A tool to evaluate each financial statement item or group of items in terms of a specific base amount; the base amount is commonly defined as 100% and is usually revenue on the income statement and total assets on the balance sheet. (p. 949)

Working capital Current assets minus current liabilities. (p. 956)

Questions

1. Explain the difference between financial reporting and financial statements.
2. What is the difference between comparative financial statements and common-size comparative statements?
3. Which items are usually assigned a value of 100% on a common-size comparative balance sheet and a common-size comparative income statement?
4. Why is working capital given special attention in the process of analyzing balance sheets?
5. What are three factors that would influence your decision as to whether a company's current ratio is good or bad?
6. Suggest several reasons why a 2 to 1 current ratio may not be adequate for a particular company.
7. What does a relatively high accounts receivable turnover indicate about a company's short-term liquidity?
8. What is the significance of the number of days' sales uncollected?
9. Why does merchandise turnover provide information about a company's short-term liquidity?
10. Why is the capital structure of a company, as measured by debt and equity ratios, of importance to financial statement analysts?

11. Why must the ratio of pledged assets to secured liabilities be interpreted with caution?
12. Why would a company's return on total assets be different from its return on common shareholders' equity?
13. What ratios would you compute for the purpose of evaluating management performance?
14. Using the financial statements for **Atlantis** in Appendix I, compute Atlantis's return on total assets for the fiscal year ended December 31, 1997.
15. Refer to the financial statements for **Alliance** in Appendix I. Compute Alliance's equity ratio as of March 31, 1997.
16. Reread the chapter's opening article about the Beardstown Ladies. Identify three factors that impact the return computation for a group of shares and that may have contributed to the error made by Betty Sinnock.

Quick Study

QS 20-1
Building blocks of analysis
LO 2

Which of the following items are means of accomplishing the objective of financial reporting but are not included within general-purpose financial statements? (a) income statements, (b) company news releases, (c) balance sheets, (d) certain reports filed with the Ontario Securities and Exchange Commission, (e) statements of cash flows, or (f) management discussions and analyses of financial performance.

QS 20-2
Horizontal and vertical analysis
LO 5, 6

Given the following information for Heffington Corporation, determine (a) the common-size percents for gross profit from sales and (b) the trend percents for net sales, using 1999 as the base year.

	2000	1999
Net sales	$201,600	$114,800
Cost of goods sold	109,200	60,200

QS 20-3
Tools of analysis
LO 4

a. Which two short-term liquidity ratios measure how frequently a company collects its accounts?
b. Which two terms are used to describe the difference between current assets and current liabilities?
c. Which two ratios are the basic components in measuring a company's operating efficiency? Which ratio summarizes these two components?

QS 20-4
Standards for comparisons
LO 3

What are five possible standards of comparison you can use when analyzing financial statement ratios? Which of these is generally considered to be the most useful? Which one is least likely to provide a good basis for comparison?

QS 20-5
Purpose and tools of analysis
LO 1, 4

Match the ratio to the building block of financial statement analysis to which it relates:

A. Liquidity and efficiency
B. Solvency
C. Profitability
D. Market

_____ 1. Dividend yield
_____ 2. Return on total assets
_____ 3. Gross Margin
_____ 4. Acid-test ratio
_____ 5. Equity ratio
_____ 6. Times interest earned
_____ 7. Pledged assets to secured liabilities
_____ 8. Book value per common share
_____ 9. Days' sales in inventory
_____ 10. Accounts receivable turnover

QS 20-6
Define and apply ratio analysis
LO 5, 7

For each ratio below identify whether the change in the ratio from 1999 to 2000 would generally be regarded as favourable or unfavourable.

Ratio	2000	1999
1. Profit Margin	8%	6%
2. Debt Ratio	45%	40%
3. Gross Margin	33%	45%
4. Acid-test Ratio	.99	1.10
5. Accounts Receivable Turnover	5.4	6.6
6. Basic Earnings Per Share	$1.24	$1.20
7. Merchandise Turnover	3.5	3.3
8. Dividend Yield	1%	.8%

Exercises

Exercise 20-1
Computing trend percents
LO 5

Compute trend percents for the following items, using 1998 as the base year. Then, state whether the situation shown by the trends appears to be favourable or unfavourable.

	2002	2001	2000	1999	1998
Sales	$283,880	$271,800	$253,680	$235,560	$151,000
Cost of goods sold	129,200	123,080	116,280	107,440	68,000
Accounts receivable	19,100	18,300	17,400	16,200	10,000

Exercise 20-2
Reporting percent changes
LO 5

Where possible, compute percents of increase and decrease for the following:

	2000	1999
Temporary investments	$217,800	$165,000
Accounts receivable	42,120	48,000
Notes payable	57,000	-0-

Exercise 20-3
Computing common-size percents
LO 6

Express the following income statement information in common-size percents and assess whether the situation is favourable or unfavourable.

HARBISON CORPORATION
Comparative Income Statement
For Years Ended December 31, 2000, and 1999

	2000	1999
Sales	$720,000	$535,000
Cost of goods sold	475,200	280,340
Gross profit from sales	$244,800	$254,660
Operating expenses	151,200	103,790
Net income	$ 93,600	$150,870

Exercise 20-4
Evaluating short-term liquidity
LO 7

Mixon Company's December 31 balance sheets included the following data:

	2001	2000	1999
Cash	$ 30,800	$ 35,625	$ 36,800
Accounts receivable, net	88,500	62,500	49,200
Merchandise inventory	111,500	82,500	53,000
Prepaid expenses	9,700	9,375	4,000
Capital assets,net	277,500	255,000	229,500
Total assets	$518,000	$445,000	$372,500
Accounts payable	$128,900	$ 75,250	$ 49,250
Long-term notes payable secured by mortgages on capital assets	97,500	102,500	82,500
Common shares, no-par value	162,500	162,500	162,500
Retained earnings	129,100	104,750	78,250
Total liabilities and shareholders' equity	$518,000	$445,000	$372,500

Required

Compare the short-term liquidity positions of the company at the end of 2001, 2000, and 1999 by computing: (a) the current ratio and (b) the acid-test ratio. Comment on any changes that occurred.

Exercise 20-5
Calculating common-size percentage
LO 6

Refer to Mixon Company's balance sheets in Exercise 20-4. Express the balance sheets in common-size percents. Round to the nearest tenth percent.

Exercise 20-6
Evaluating short-term liquidity
LO 7

Refer to the information in Exercise 20-4 about Mixon Company. The company's income statements for the years ended December 31, 2001, and 2000 included the following data:

	2001	2000
Sales	$672,500	$530,000
Cost of goods sold	$410,225	$344,500
Other operating expenses	208,550	133,980
Interest expense	11,100	12,300
Income taxes	8,525	7,845
Total costs and expenses	$638,400	$498,625
Net income	$ 34,100	$ 31,375
Earnings per share	$ 2.10	$ 1.93

Required

For the years ended December 31, 2001, and 2000, assume all sales were on credit and compute the following: (a) days' sales uncollected, (b) accounts receivable turnover, (c) merchandise turnover, and (d) days' sales in inventory. Comment on any changes that occurred from 2000 to 2001.

Exercise 20-7
Evaluating long-term risk and capital structure
LO 7

Refer to the information in Exercises 20-4 and 20-5 about Mixon Company. Compare the long-term risk and capital structure positions of the company at the end of 2001 and 2000 by computing the following ratios: (a) debt and equity ratios, (b) pledged assets to secured liabilities, and (c) times interest earned. Comment on any changes that occurred.

Exercise 20-8
Evaluating operating efficiency and profitability
LO 7

Refer to the financial statements of Mixon Company presented in Exercises 20-4 and 20-5. Evaluate the operating efficiency and profitability of the company by computing the following: (a) profit margin, (b) total asset turnover, and (c) return on total assets. Comment on any changes that occurred.

Exercise 20-9
Evaluating profitability
LO 7

Refer to the financial statements of Mixon Company presented in Exercises 20-4 and 20-5. This additional information about the company is known:

Common shares market price, December 31, 2001	$15.00
Common shares market price, December 31, 2000	14.00
Annual cash dividends per share in 2001	.30
Annual cash dividends per share in 2000	.15

Required

To evaluate the profitability of the company, compute the following for 2001 and 2000: (a) return on common shareholders' equity, (b) price-earnings ratio on December 31, and (c) dividend yield.

Exercise 20-10
Determining income effects from common-size and trend percents
LO 5,7

Common-size and trend percents for a company's sales, cost of goods sold, and expenses follow:

	Common-Size Percents			Trend Percents		
	2001	2000	1999	2001	2000	1999
Sales	100.0%	100.0%	100.0%	104.4%	103.2%	100.0%
Cost of goods sold	62.4	60.9	58.1	102.0	100.1	100.0
Expenses	14.3	13.8	14.1	94.0	90.0	100.0

Required

Determine whether the company's net income increased, decreased, or remained unchanged during this three-year period.

Exercise 20-11
Evaluating short-term liquidity
LO 8

Huff Company and Mesa Company are similar firms that operate within the same industry. The following information is available:

	Huff			Mesa		
	2001	2000	1999	2001	2000	1999
Current ratio	1.6	1.7	2.0	3.1	2.6	1.8
Acid-test ratio	.9	1.0	1.1	2.7	2.4	1.5
Accounts receivable turnover	29.5	24.2	28.2	15.4	14.2	15.0
Merchandise turnover . .	23.2	20.9	16.1	13.5	12.0	11.6
Working capital	$60,000	$48,000	$42,000	$121,000	$93,000	$68,000

Required

Write a brief essay comparing Huff and Mesa based on the preceding information. Your discussion should include their relative ability to meet current obligations and to use current assets efficiently.

Exercise 20-12
Analyze and report results of analysis
LO 8

Kampa Company and Arbor Company are similar firms that operate within the same industry. Arbor began operations in 2005 and Kampa in 1999. In 2007, both companies paid 7% interest to creditors. The following information is available:

	KAMPA COMPANY			ARBOR COMPANY		
	2007	2006	2005	2007	2006	2005
Total asset turnover ...	3.0	2.7	2.9	1.6	1.4	1.1
Return on total assets .	8.9	9.5	8.7	5.8	5.5	5.2
Profit margin	2.3	2.4	2.2	2.7	2.9	2.8
Sales	$400,000	$370,000	$386,000	$200,000	$160,000	$100,000

Required

Write a brief essay comparing Kampa and Arbor based on the preceding information. Your discussion should include their relative ability to use assets efficiently to produce profits. Also comment on their relative success in employing financial leverage in 2007.

Problems

Problem 20-1
Computing ratios and percents
LO 5, 6, 7

The condensed statements of Thornhill Company follow:

THORNHILL COMPANY
Comparative Income Statement ($000)
For Years Ended December 31, 2001, 2000, and 1999

	2001	2000	1999
Sales	$444,000	$340,000	$236,000
Cost of goods sold	267,288	212,500	151,040
Gross profit from sales	$176,712	$127,500	$ 84,960
Selling expenses	$ 62,694	$ 46,920	$ 31,152
Administrative expenses	40,137	29,920	19,470
Total expenses	$102,831	$ 76,840	$ 50,622
Income before taxes	$ 73,881	$ 50,660	$ 34,338
Income taxes	13,764	10,370	6,962
Net income	$ 60,117	$ 40,290	$ 27,376

THORNHILL COMPANY
Comparative Balance Sheet ($000)
December 31, 2001, 2000, and 1999

Assets	2001	2000	1999
Current assets	$ 48,480	$ 37,924	$ 50,648
Long-term investments	- 0 -	500	3,720
Capital assets	90,000	96,000	57,000
Total assets	$138,480	$134,424	$111,368
Liabilities and Shareholders' Equity			
Current liabilities	$ 20,200	$ 19,960	$ 19,480
Common shares	72,000	72,000	54,000
Other contributed capital	9,000	9,000	6,000
Retained earnings	37,280	33,464	31,888
Total liabilities and shareholders' equity ...	$138,480	$134,424	$111,368

Required

Preparation component:

1. Compute each year's current ratio.
2. Express the income statement data in common-size percents.
3. Express the balance sheet data in trend percents with 1999 as the base year.

Check Figure 2001, total assets, 124.34

Analysis component:

4. Comment on any significant relationships revealed by the ratios and percents.

Problem 20-2
Calculation and analysis of trend percents
LO 5

The condensed comparative statements of Cohorn Company follow:

COHORN COMPANY
Comparative Income Statement ($000)
For Years Ended December 31, 2005–1999

	2005	2004	2003	2002	2001	2000	1999
Sales	$1,594	$1,396	$1,270	$1,164	$1,086	$1,010	$ 828
Cost of goods sold	1,146	932	802	702	652	610	486
Gross profit from sales	$ 448	$ 464	$ 468	$ 462	$ 434	$ 400	$ 342
Operating expenses	340	266	244	180	156	154	128
Net income	$ 108	$ 198	$ 224	$ 282	$ 278	$ 246	$ 214

COHORN COMPANY
Comparative Balance Sheet ($000)
December 31, 2005–1999

Assets	2005	2004	2003	2002	2001	2000	1999
Cash	$ 68	$ 88	$ 92	$ 94	$ 98	$ 96	$ 99
Accounts receivable, net	480	504	456	350	308	292	206
Merchandise inventory	1,738	1,264	1,104	932	836	710	515
Other current assets	46	42	24	44	38	38	19
Long-term investments	-0-	-0-	-0-	136	136	136	136
Capital assets, net	2,120	2,114	1,852	1,044	1,078	960	825
Total assets	$4,452	$4,012	$3,528	$2,600	$2,494	$2,232	$1,800
Liabilities and Equity							
Current liabilities	$1,120	$ 942	$ 618	$ 514	$ 446	$ 422	$ 272
Long-term liabilities	1,194	1,040	1,012	470	480	520	390
Common shares	1,000	1,000	1,000	840	840	640	640
Other contributed capital	250	250	250	180	180	160	160
Retained earnings	888	780	648	596	548	490	338
Total liabilities and equity	$4,452	$4,012	$3,528	$2,600	$2,494	$2,232	$1,800

Required

Preparation component:

1. Compute trend percents for the items of the statements using 1999 as the base year.

Check Figure 2005 total assets, 247.3

Analysis component:

2. Analyze and comment on the situation shown in the statements.

Problem 20-3
Calculation of financial statement ratios
LO7

The 2000 financial statements of Hoffman Corporation follow:

HOFFMAN CORPORATION
Income Statement
For Year Ended December 31, 2000

Sales		$348,600
Cost of goods sold:		
Merchandise inventory, December 31, 1999	$ 32,400	
Purchases	227,900	
Goods available for sale	$260,300	
Merchandise inventory, December 31, 2000	31,150	
Cost of goods sold		229,150
Gross profit from sales		$119,450
Operating expenses		52,500
Operating income		$ 66,950
Interest expense		3,100
Income before taxes		$ 63,850
Income taxes		15,800
Net income		$ 48,050

HOFFMAN CORPORATION
Balance Sheet
December 31, 2000

Assets		Liabilities and Shareholders' Equity	
Cash	$ 9,000	Accounts payable	$ 16,500
Temporary investments	7,400	Accrued wages payable	2,200
Accounts receivable, net	28,200	Income taxes payable	2,300
Notes receivable (trade)	3,500	Long-term note payable, secured by mortgage on capital assets	62,400
Merchandise inventory	31,150		
Prepaid expenses	1,650		
Capital assets, net	152,300	Common shares, no-par value	90,000
		Retained earnings	59,800
Total assets	$233,200	Total liabilities and shareholders' equity	$233,200

Assume that all sales were on credit. On the December 31, 1999, balance sheet, the assets totalled $182,400, common shares were $90,000, and retained earnings amounted to $31,300.

Required

Compute the following: (a) current ratio, (b) acid-test ratio, (c) days' sales uncollected, (d) merchandise turnover, (e) days' sales in inventory, (f) ratio of pledged assets to secured liabilities, (g) times interest earned, (h) profit margin, (i) total asset turnover, (j) return on total assets, and (k) return on common shareholders' equity.

Problem 20-4
Comparative analysis of financial statement ratios

LO7

Two companies that compete in the same industry are being evaluated by a bank that can lend money to only one of them. Summary information from the financial statements of the two companies follows:

	Datatech Company	Sigma Company
Data from the current year-end balance sheets:		
Assets		
Cash	$ 18,500	$ 33,000
Accounts receivable	36,400	56,400
Notes receivable (trade)	8,100	6,200
Merchandise inventory	83,440	131,500
Prepaid expenses	4,000	5,950
Capital assets, net	284,000	303,400
Total assets	$434,440	$536,450
Liabilities and Shareholders' Equity		
Current liabilities	$ 60,340	$ 92,300
Long-term notes payable	79,800	100,000
Common shares, no-par value	175,000	205,000
Retained earnings	119,300	139,150
Total liabilities and shareholders' equity	$434,440	$536,450
Data from the current year's income statements:		
Sales	$660,000	$780,200
Cost of goods sold	485,100	532,500
Operating expenses	87,430	112,400
Interest expense	6,900	11,000
Income tax expense	12,800	19,300
Net income	67,770	105,000
Earnings per share	$ 1.94	$ 2.56
Beginning-of-year data:		
Accounts receivable, net	$ 28,800	$ 53,200
Notes receivable	-0-	-0-
Merchandise inventory	54,600	106,400
Total assets	388,000	372,500
Common shares, no par value	175,000	205,000
Retained earnings	94,300	90,600

Required

1. Compute the current ratio, acid-test ratio, accounts (including notes) receivable turnover, merchandise turnover, days' sales in inventory, and days' sales uncollected for the two companies. Then, identify the company that you consider to be the better short-term credit risk and explain why.
2. Compute the profit margin, total asset turnover, return on total assets, and return on common shareholders' equity for the two companies. Assuming that each company paid cash dividends of $1.50 per share and each company's shares can be purchased at $25 per share, compute their price-earnings ratios and dividend yields. Also, identify which company's shares you would recommend as the better investment and explain why.

Problem 20-5
Analysis of working capital
LO 7

Providence Corporation began the month of May with $650,000 of current assets, a current ratio of 2.5 to 1, and an acid-test ratio of 1.1 to 1. During the month, it completed the following transactions:

May 2 Bought $75,000 of merchandise on account. (The company uses a perpetual inventory system.)
8 Sold merchandise that cost $58,000 for $103,000.
10 Collected a $19,000 account receivable.
15 Paid a $21,000 account payable.
17 Wrote off a $3,000 bad debt against the Allowance for Doubtful Accounts account.
22 Declared a $1 per share cash dividend on the 40,000 shares of outstanding common shares.
26 Paid the dividend declared on May 22.
27 Borrowed $75,000 by giving the bank a 30-day, 10% note.
28 Borrowed $90,000 by signing a long-term secured note.
29 Used the proceeds from notes plus another $100,000 to buy additional machinery.

Required

Prepare a schedule showing Providence's current ratio, acid-test ratio, and working capital after each of the transactions. Round calculations to two decimal places.

Check Figure May 29 working capital, $310,000

Alternate Problems

Problem 20-1A
Computing ratios and percents
LO 5, 6, 7

The condensed statements of Temptron Corporation follow:

TEMPTRON CORPORATION
Comparative Income Statement ($000)
For Years Ended December 31, 2001, 2000, and 1999

	2001	2000	1999
Sales	$199,800	$167,000	$144,800
Cost of goods sold	109,890	87,175	67,200
Gross profit from sales	$ 89,910	$ 79,825	$ 77,600
Selling expenses	$ 23,680	$ 20,790	$ 19,000
Administrative expenses	17,760	15,610	16,700
Total expenses	$ 41,440	$ 36,400	$ 35,700
Income before taxes	$ 48,470	$ 43,425	$ 41,900
Income taxes	5,050	4,910	4,300
Net income	$ 43,420	$ 38,515	$ 37,600

TEMPTRON CORPORATION
Comparative Balance Sheet ($000)
December 31, 2001, 2000, and 1999

	2001	2000	1999
Assets			
Current assets	$ 55,860	$ 33,660	$ 37,300
Long-term investments	-0-	2,700	11,600
Capital assets	113,810	114,660	80,000
Total assets	$169,670	$151,020	$128,900
Liabilities and Shareholders' Equity			
Current liabilities	$ 23,370	$ 20,180	$ 17,500
Common shares	47,500	47,500	38,000
Other contributed capital	14,850	14,850	12,300
Retained earnings	83,950	68,490	61,100
Total liabilities and shareholders' equity	$169,670	$151,020	$128,900

Required

Preparation component:

1. Compute each year's current ratio.
2. Express the income statement data in common-size percents.
3. Express the balance sheet data in trend percents with 1999 as the base year.

Analysis component:

4. Comment on any significant relationships revealed by the ratios and percents.

Problem 20-2A
Calculation and analysis of trend percents
LO 5

The condensed comparative statements of Hensley Company follow:

HENSLEY COMPANY
Comparative Income Statement ($000)
For Years Ended December 31, 2005–1999

	2005	2004	2003	2002	2001	2000	1999
Sales	$660	$710	$730	$780	$840	$870	$960
Cost of goods sold	376	390	394	414	440	450	480
Gross profit from sales	$284	$320	$336	$366	$400	$420	$480
Operating expenses	184	204	212	226	240	244	250
Net income	$100	$116	$124	$140	$160	$176	$230

HENSLEY COMPANY
Comparative Balance Sheet ($000)
December 31, 2005–1999

	2005	2004	2003	2002	2001	2000	1999
Assets							
Cash	$34	$36	$42	$44	$50	$52	$58
Accounts receivable, net	120	126	130	134	140	144	150
Merchandise inventory	156	162	168	170	176	180	198
Other current assets	24	24	26	28	28	30	30
Long-term investments	26	20	16	100	100	100	100
Capital assets, net	410	414	420	312	320	328	354
Total assets	$770	$782	$802	$788	$814	$834	$890
Liabilities and Equity							
Current liabilities	$138	$146	$176	$180	$200	$250	$270
Long-term liabilities	82	110	132	138	184	204	250
Common shares	150	150	150	150	150	150	150
Other contributed capital	60	60	60	60	60	60	60
Retained earnings	340	316	284	260	220	170	160
Total liabilities and equity	$770	$782	$802	$788	$814	$834	$890

Required

Preparation component:

1. Compute trend percents for the items of the statements using 1999 as the base year.

Analysis component:

2. Analyze and comment on the situation shown in the statements.

Problem 20-3A
Calculation of financial statement ratios
LO 7

The 2000 financial statements of Nowland Corporation follow:

NOWLAND CORPORATION
Income Statement
For Year Ended December 31, 2000

Sales		$215,500
Cost of goods sold:		
Merchandise inventory, December 31, 1999	$ 16,400	
Purchases	132,200	
Goods available for sale	$148,600	
Merchandise inventory, December 31, 2000	12,500	
Cost of goods sold		136,100
Gross profit from sales		$ 79,400
Operating expenses		50,200
Operating income		$ 29,200
Interest expense		1,200
Income before taxes		$ 28,000
Income taxes		2,200
Net income		$ 25,800

NOWLAND CORPORATION
Balance Sheet
December 31, 2000

Assets		Liabilities and Shareholders' Equity	
Cash	$5,100	Accounts payable	$10,500
Temporary investments	5,900	Accrued wages payable	2,300
Accounts receivable, net	11,100	Income taxes payable	1,600
Notes receivable (trade)	2,000	Long-term note payable, secured by mortgage on capital assets	25,000
Merchandise inventory	12,500		
Prepaid expenses	1,000	Common shares, no-par value	41,000
Capital assets, net	72,900	Retained earnings	30,100
Total assets	$110,500	Total liabilities and and shareholders' equity	$110,500

Assume that all sales were on credit. On the December 31, 1999, balance sheet, the assets totalled $95,900, common shares were $41,500, and retained earnings were $19,800.

Required

Compute the following: (a) current ratio, (b) acid-test ratio, (c) days' sales uncollected, (d) merchandise turnover, (e) days' sales in inventory, (f) ratio of pledged assets to secured liabilities, (g) times interest earned, (h) profit margin, (i) total asset turnover, (j) return on total assets, and (k) return on common shareholders' equity.

Problem 20-4A
Comparative analysis of financial statement ratios

LO7

Two companies that operate in the same industry as competitors are being evaluated by a bank that can lend money to only one of them. Summary information from the financial statements of the two companies follows:

	Lutz Comapny	Highland Company
Data from the current year-end balance sheets		
Assets		
Cash	$ 22,000	$ 38,500
Accounts receivable	79,100	72,500
Notes receivable (trade)	13,600	11,000
Merchandise inventory	88,800	84,000
Prepaid expenses	11,700	12,100
Capital assets, net	178,900	254,300
Total assets	$394,100	$472,400
Liabilities and Shareholders' Equity		
Current liabilities	$ 92,500	$ 99,000
Long-term notes payable	95,000	95,300
Common shares, no-par value	135,000	143,000
Retained earnings	71,600	135,100
Total liabilities and shareholders' equity	$394,100	$472,400
Data from the current year's income statements		
Sales	$395,600	$669,500
Cost of goods sold	292,600	482,000
Operating expenses	51,550	97,100
Interest expense	7,900	12,400
Income tax expense	7,700	14,300
Net income	35,850	63,700
Earnings per share	$ 1.33	$ 2.23
Beginning-of-year data		
Accounts receivable, net	$ 74,200	$ 75,300
Notes receivable	-0-	-0-
Merchandise inventory	107,100	82,500
Total assets	385,400	445,000
Common shares, no-par value	135,000	143,000
Retained earnings	51,100	111,700

Required

1. Compute the current ratio, acid-test ratio, accounts (including notes) receivable turnover, merchandise turnover, days' sales in inventory, and days' sales uncollected for the two companies. Then, identify the company that you consider to be the better short-term credit risk and explain why.
2. Compute the profit margin, total asset turnover, return on total assets, and return on common shareholders' equity for the two companies. Assuming that each company paid cash dividends of $3 per share and each company's shares can be purchased at $25 per share, compute their price earnings ratios and dividend yields. Also, identify which company's shares you would recommend as the better investment and explain why.

Problem 20-5A
Analysis of working capital

LO 7

Resource Corporation began the month of June with $280,000 of current assets, a current ratio of 2.80 to 1, and an acid-test ratio of 1.2 to 1. During the month, it completed the following transactions:

June 1 Sold merchandise that cost $62,000 for $101,000.
3 Collected a $78,000 account receivable.
5 Bought $130,000 of merchandise on account. (The company uses a perpetual inventory system.)
7 Borrowed $90,000 by giving the bank a 60-day, 10% note.
10 Borrowed $180,000 by signing a long-term secured note.
12 Used $280,000 cash to buy additional machinery.
15 Declared a $1 per share cash dividend on the 60,000 shares of outstanding common shares.
19 Wrote off a $7,000 bad debt against Allowance for Doubtful Accounts.
22 Paid a $11,000 account payable.
31 Paid the dividend declared on June 15.

Required

Prepare a schedule showing the company's current ratio, acid-test ratio, and working capital after each of the transactions. Round to two decimal places.

Analytical and Review Problems

A & R 20-1

In your position as controller of Skinner Company, you are responsible for keeping the board of directors informed about the financial activities and status of the company. In preparing for the next board meeting, you have calculated the following ratios, turnovers, and percentages to enable you to answer questions:

Year	1998	1997	1996
Sales trend	137.00	125.00	100.00
Selling expenses to net sales	9.8%	13.7%	15.3%
Sales to capital assets	3.5 to 1	3.3 to 1	3 to 1
Current ratio	2.6 to 1	2.4 to 1	2.1 to 1
Acid-test ratio	0.8 to 1	1.1 to 1	1.2 to 1
Merchandise turnover	7.5 times	8.7 times	9.9 times
Accounts receivable turnover	6.7 times	7.4 times	8.2 times
Total asset turnover	2.6 times	2.6 times	3.0 times
Return on total assets	8.8 %	9.4%	10.1%
Return on shareholders' equity	9.75%	11.5%	12.25%
Profit margin	3.3%	3.5%	3.7%

Required

Using the preceding data, answer each of the following questions and explain your answers:

a. Is it becoming easier for the company to meet its current debts on time and to take advantage of cash discounts?
b. Is the company collecting its accounts receivable more rapidity?
c. Is the company's investment in accounts receivable decreasing?
d. Are dollars invested in inventory increasing?
e. Is the company's investment in capital assets increasing?
f. Is the shareholders' investment becoming more profitable?
g. Is the company using its assets efficiently?
h. Did the dollar amount of selling expenses decrease during the three-year period?

A & R 20-2

PETER LAU CORPORATION
Balance Sheet
December 31, 2000

Assets		Liabilities and Shareholders' Equity	
Cash	$	Current liabilities	$
Accounts receivable, net		8% bonds payable	
Merchandise inventory		Common shares, no-par value	$15,000
Capital assets, net		Retained earnings	
		Total liabilities and	
Total assets	$	shareholders' equity	$

Sales (all credit)	$40,000
Cost of goods sold	24,000
Expenses	13,000
Income taxes	1,000
Net income	2,000
Net income/shareholders' equity	10%
Bonds payable/shareholders'equity	1 to 4
Inventory turnover	4 times
Accounts receivable collection period (360-day year)	45 days
Current ratio	2 to 1
Total asset turnover	1.25 times

Required

Complete the above balance sheet for Peter Lau Corporation.

A & R 20-3

A company began the month of May with $200,000 of current assets, a 2 to 1 current ratio, and a 1 to 1 acid-test (quick) ratio. During the month the following transactions were completed:

a. Bought $20,000 of merchandise on account.
b. Sold $25,000 of merchandise costing $15,000.
c. Collected an $8,500 account receivable.
d. Paid a $12,000 account payable.
e. Wrote off a $1,000 bad debt against the allowance account.
f. Declared a $1 per share cash dividend on the 10,000 common shares outstanding.
g. Paid the dividend declared in (f).
h. Borrowed $12,000 by giving the bank a 60-day, 10% note.
i. Borrowed $30,000 by placing a 10-year mortage on the capital assets.
j. Used $20,000 of proceeds of the mortgage to buy additional machinery.

Required

1. State the effect of each of the above transactions on working capital and on the current ratio. Give the effect in terms of increase, decrease or no effect. (Working capital is defined as "current assets minus current liabilities.")
2. For the end of May, calculate the
   i) current ratio
   ii) Acid-test ratio
   iii) Working capital

BEYOND THE NUMBERS

Reporting in Action

LO 5, 6

Refer to the financial statements and related information for **Alliance** in Appendix I. Answer the following questions by analyzing the available information.

1. Using 1995 as the base year, compute trend percents for 1995–1997 for revenues, gross profit, other expenses, income taxes, and net income. (Round to the nearest whole percent).
2. Compute common-size percents for 1997 and 1996 for the following categories of assets: (a) cash and short-term investments, (b) investment in film and television, (c) property and equipment, and (d) other assets. (Round to the nearest tenth percent).
3. Comment on any significant changes between years for the income statement trends and balance sheet percents.
4. Obtain access to Alliances's annual report for fiscal years ending after March 31, 1997. This access may be through alternative sources including the following Web site: **http:www.sedar.com.** Update your work for 1 and 2 above for any new information you have accessed.

Comparative Analysis

LO 6

Both **NIKE** and **Reebok** design, produce, market and sell sports footwear and apparel. Key comparative figures ($ thousands) for these two organizations follow:

	NIKE	Reebok
Key Figures	**1997**	**1996**
Cash and equivalents	$445,421	$232,365
Accounts receivable	1,754,137	590,504
Inventory	1,338,640	544,522
Retained earnings	2,973,663	992,563
Cost of sales	5,502,993	2,144,422
Income taxes	499,400	84,083
Revenues (NIKE)	9,186,539	
Net sales (Reebok)		3,478,604
Total assets	5,361,207	1,786,184

* NIKE figures are from the annual report for the fiscal year ended May 31,1997.
Reebok figures are from the annual report for the fiscal year ended December 31, 1996.

Required

1. Compute common-size percents for the two companies for both years using the selected data provided.
2. Which company incurred a higher percent of their revenues or net sales as income tax expense?
3. Which company has retained a higher portion of total earnings in the company?
4. Which company has a higher gross margin on sales?
5. Which company is holding a higher percent of total assets as inventory?

Ethics Challenge

LO 8

In your position as controller of Tallman Company, you are responsible for keeping the board of directors informed about the financial activities and status of the company. At the board meeting you present the following report:

	2004	2003	2002
Sales trend	147.00	135.00	100.00
Selling expenses to net sales	10.1%	14.0%	15.6%
Sales to capital assets	3.8 to 1	3.6 to 1	3.3 to 1
Current ratio	2.9 to 1	2.7 to 1	2.4 to 1
Acid-test ratio	1.1 to 1	1.4 to 1	1.5 to 1
Merchandise turnover	7.8 times	9.0 times	10.2 times
Accounts receivable turnover	7.0 times	7.7 times	8.5 times
Total asset turnover	2.9 times	2.9 times	3.3 times
Return on total assets	9.1%	9.7%	10.4%
Return on shareholders' equity	9.75%	11.50%	12.25%
Profit margin	3.6%	3.8%	4.0%

After the meeting is over you overhear the company's CEO holding a press conference with analysts in which she mentions the following ratios.

	2004	2003	2002
Sales trend	147.00	135.00	100.00
Selling expenses to net sales	10.1%	14.0%	15.6%
Sales to capital assets	3.8 to 1	3.6 to 1	3.3 to 1
Current ratio	2.9 to 1	2.7 to 1	2.4 to 1

1. Why do think the CEO decided to report 4 ratios instead of the full 11 that you prepared?
2. Comment on the possible consequences of the CEO's decision.

Communicating in Practice

LO 7, 8

The class should be divided into teams. Each team is to select a different industry, and each team member is to select a different company in that industry. Each team member is to acquire the annual report of the company selected. Annual reports can be obtained in many ways including the following Web site: **http://www.sedar.com.** Use the annual reports to analyze the company using at least one ratio from each of the four categories presented in this chapter. Where necessary use the financial press to determine the market price of the firm's shares. Communicate with teammates via a meeting, e-mail, or telephone to discuss how different companies compare to each other, and to industry norms. The team is to prepare a single memo reporting a comparison of the companies analyzed. The memo is also to present any conclusions reached from the comparison. Duplicate the memo and distribute it to the instructor and all classmates.

Taking It to the Net

LO 1, 4

A focus of both financial press and public is the TSE 100. While many people monitor the TSE 100 the majority of the public may not know what companies comprise the average. Visit the Web site **http://www.tse.com.**

1. Name five companies included as part of the TSE 100.
2. What are the stock symbols of the five companies you have chosen?
3. Click on "Quote look-up" on the top bar and search for any two of the five companies you have chosen. Report on the information retrieved by your search.

Teamwork in Action

LO 2, 4, 5, 6, 7

The aim of this activity is to provide team support for understanding the various approaches to analyzing information in financial statements.

A. After a team discussion of the meaning of horizontal and vertical analysis, write up a description of each that all team members agree with and understand. Illustrate each description with an example.

B. *Each* member of the team is to select *one* of the categories of ratio analysis listed below. Prepare notes to explain what the ratios in that category measure. Choose one specific ratio from the category selected. In your notes, present the formula for this ratio, and explain what it specifically measures.

1. Liquidity and Efficiency
2. Solvency
3. Profitability
4. Market

C. Each member is to report their notes from (B) to teammates. Team members are to confirm or correct teammate's presentation.

Hitting the Road

LO 1

This chapter and this course have given you tools to become a successful investor upon graduation. Devise a savings/investment strategy whereby you are able to accumulate $1,000,000 by age 65. Start by making some assumptions about your starting salary once you graduate from university or college. Next compute the percent of your salary that you will be able to save each year. If you will receive any lump-sum monies upon graduation you can also factor those amounts into your calculations. Historically, investments in shares have delivered average annual returns of 10–11%. Given this history you should probably not assume that you will earn above 10% on the money you invest. It is not necessary to specify in this assignment exactly what types of assets you will buy for your investments, just make an assumption about an interest rate that you expect to earn. Use the future value tables in Appendix II to calculate how your savings will grow. Experiment a bit with your figures to see how much less you have to save if you start at age 25 versus age 35 or 40. (For this assignment do not worry about factoring inflation into your calculations.)

Read the article, "Debt-to-equity ratio proves fundamental," in the July 25–27, 1998 weekend edition of *The Financial Post.*

Business Break
LO1

Required

1. What is it that the article says is most often ignored during a rising stock market?
2. What surprises the author of this article about the performance of companies with high or low debt levels during a rising market?
3. How do companies with high dividend yields perform during a market correction (falling share prices) compared with the performance of firms with low debt ratios?
4. What problems can too much debt bring to a company? What first piece of advice does the author offer for the investor who desires to find companies that are less likely to fall apart during a downturn?

I

Financial Statement Information

APPENDIX

This appendix includes financial statement information from (a) **Alliance Communications Corporation** and (b) **Atlantis Communications Inc.** All of this information is taken from their annual reports. An **annual report** is a summary of the financial results of a company's operations for the year and its future plans. It is directed at external users of financial information, but also affects actions of internal users.

An annual report is also used by a company to showcase itself and its products. Many include attractive pictures, diagrams and illustrations related to the company. But the *financial section* is its primary objective. This section communicates much information about a company, with most data drawn from the accounting information system.

The layout of the financial section of an annual report is fairly standard and usually includes:

- Financial History and Highlights
- Message to Shareholders
- Management Discussion and Analysis
- Management Report
- Auditor's Report
- Financial Statements
- Notes to Financial Statements
- List of Directors and Managers

This appendix provides most of this information for Alliance Communications Corporation and Atlantis Communications Inc. This appendix is organized as follows:

- Alliance: I-1 to I-33
- Atlantis: I-34 to I-60

Many assignments at the end of each chapter refer to information in this appendix. We encourage readers to spend extra time with these assignments as they are especially useful in reinforcing and showing the relevance and diversity of financial reporting.

1 CORPORATE HIGHLIGHTS

3 MESSAGE TO SHAREHOLDERS

10 OPERATIONS

25 MANAGEMENT'S DISCUSSION AND ANALYSIS

32 AUDITORS' REPORT

33 CONSOLIDATED BALANCE SHEETS

34 CONSOLIDATED STATEMENTS OF EARNINGS AND RETAINED EARNINGS

35 CONSOLIDATED STATEMENTS OF CHANGES IN FINANCIAL POSITION

36 NOTES TO THE FINANCIAL STATEMENTS

CORPORATE PROFILE

Alliance Communications Corporation is a global producer, distributor and broadcaster of filmed entertainment. Headquartered in Toronto with offices in Montreal, Vancouver, Los Angeles, Paris and Shannon, Alliance shares trade in Toronto and Montreal under AAC, and on NASDAQ under the symbol ALLIF.

ALLIANCE

CORPORATE HIGHLIGHTS

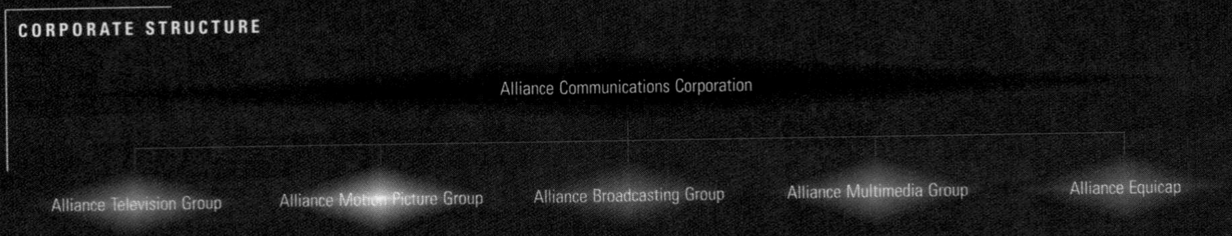

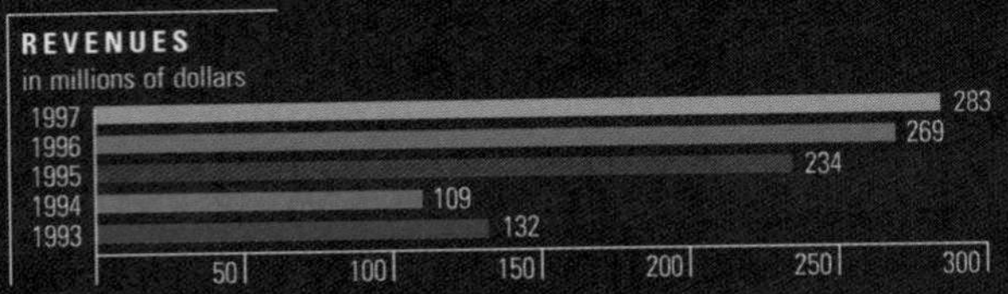

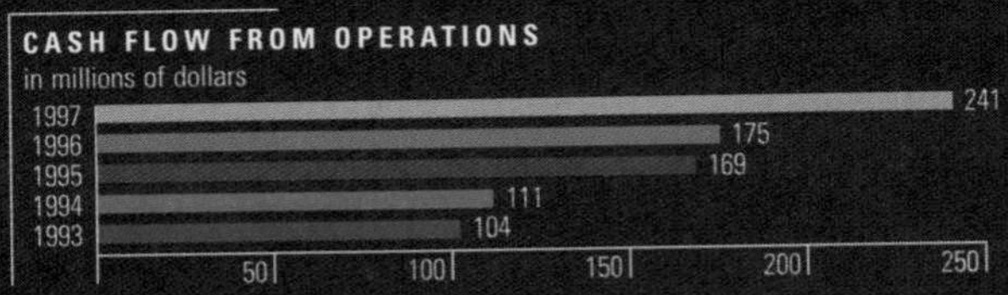

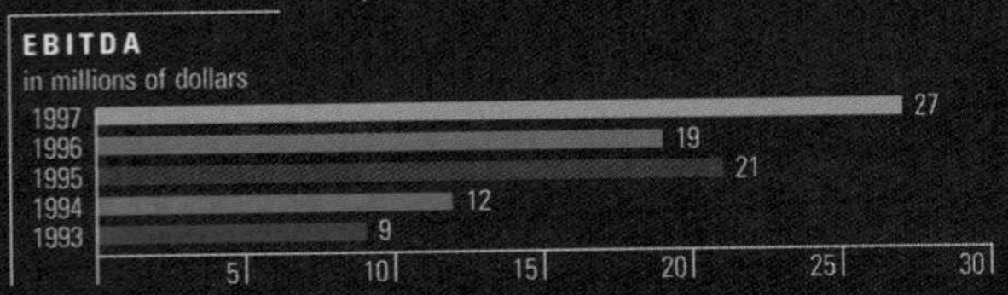

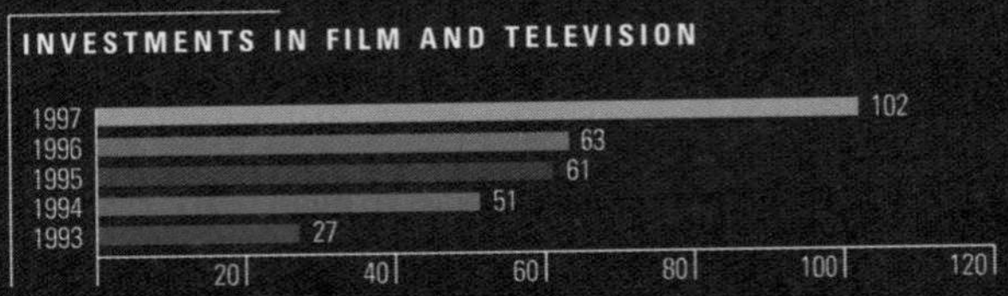

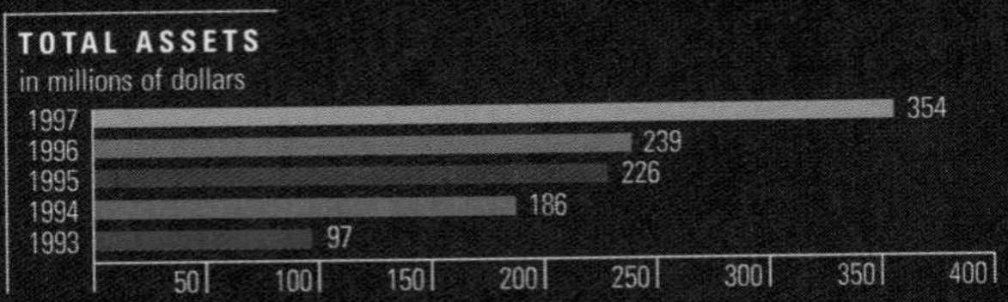

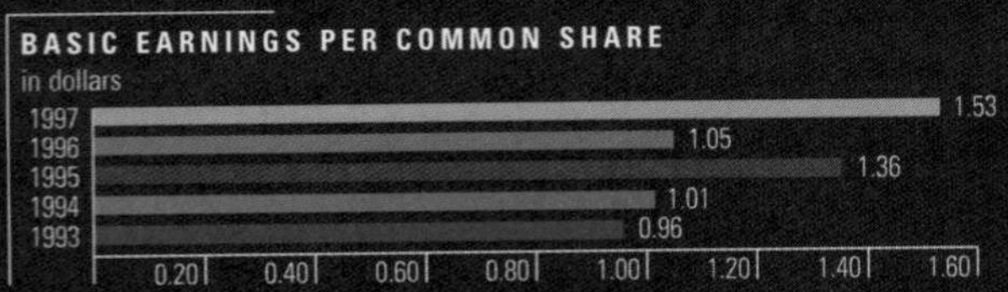

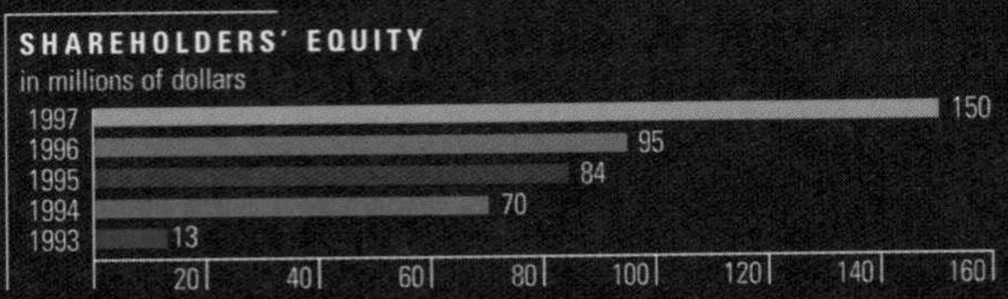

CORPORATE HIGHLIGHTS

AWARDS AND HONOURS

MOTION PICTURE AWARDS

Berlin Film Festival	C.I.C.A.E. Award	Welcome to the Dollhouse
Cannes International Film Festival	Special Jury Prize	Crash
Fantasporto, Portugal	Critics Award	Denise Calls Up
Fantasporto, Portugal	Audience Award	Denise Calls Up
Genie Awards	Best Achievement in Sound Editing	Crash
Genie Awards	Best Achievement in Film Editing	Crash
Genie Awards	Best Achievement in Art Direction	Lilies
Genie Awards	Best Achievement in Costume Design	Lilies
Genie Awards	Golden Reel Award	Crash
Genie Awards	Best Motion Picture	Lilies
Genie Awards	Best Overall Sound	Lilies
Genie Awards	Best Adapted Screenplay	Crash
Genie Awards	Best Achievement in Cinematography	Crash
Genie Awards	Best Achievement in Direction	Crash
Deauville Festival of American Cinema	Grand Prize	The Daytrippers
Sundance Film Festival	Filmmaker's Trophy Award	In the Company of Men

CANNES INTERNATIONAL FILM FESTIVAL AWARDS (MAY 1997)

Cannes International Film Festival	Grand Prix	The Sweet Hereafter
Cannes International Film Festival	International Critics Prize	The Sweet Hereafter
Cannes International Film Festival	Ecumenical Prize	The Sweet Hereafter

TELEVISION AWARDS

Banff International Television Festival	Best Continuing Series	Due South
Banff International Television Festiva	Best Animated Program	ReBoot
Golden Gates, San Francisco	Golden Gate Award	Due South
Worldfest Houston	Gold Award	Mirror Mirror
Worldfest Houston	Silver Award	Reboot
Gemini Awards	Chrysler Canada Award	Due South
Gemini Awards	Best Dramatic Series	Due South
Gemini Awards	Best Performance by an Actress	North of 60
Gemini Awards	Best Animated Program or Series	Reboot
Gemini Awards	Best Performance by a Supporting Actor	North of 60
Gemini Awards	Best Direction	Straight Up
Gemini Awards	Best Performance by an Actress	Mother Trucker: The Diana Kilmury Story
Worldfest Houston	Gold Special Jury Award	The Hunchback

PRIMETIME EMMY AWARDS NOMINATIONS (JULY 1997)

Outstanding Art Direction for a Miniseries or a Special	The Hunchback
Outstanding Costume Design for a Miniseries or a Special	The Hunchback
Outstanding Hairstyling for a Miniseries or a Special	The Hunchback
Outstanding Makeup for a Miniseries or a Special	The Hunchback
Outstanding Costume Design for a Miniseries or a Special	The Inheritance

SELECTED HIGHLIGHTS

May 20/96	Crash wins Special Jury Prize at Cannes Film Festival.
June 1/96	Diane Keaton signs first look deal with Alliance.
June 25/96	Alliance signs exclusive television deal with Director John Woo.
July 23/96	Crash becomes first Canadian motion picture to capture, in its opening week, first place at the French box office.
Aug. 22/96	Alliance completes cross border offering, realizing net proceeds of $32.9 million.
Sept. 4/96	Alliance wins coveted analog license to launch History Television.
Sept. 18/96	Alliance realizes profit in Mainframe investment and retains international distribution deal.
Sept. 19/96	Alliance forms Equicap Financial Corporation. Robert Beattie named division head.
Oct. 30/96	Principal photography begins on Atom Egoyan's The Sweet Hereafter.
Nov. 15/96	The English Patient opens in Canada culminating in $13 million at the box office.
Nov. 27/96	Crash wins 6 Genie awards including the Golden Reel Award for top grossing film. Lilies wins Genie award for Best Motion Picture.
Jan. 13/97	Alliance/Shaw Partnership files application for a national Video on Demand programming service.
Jan. 13/97	Alliance begins production with international partners on Captain Star, the Company's first conventional animation series.
Jan. 23/97	Alliance increases ownership in Showcase Television to 99%.
Jan. 23/97	Alliance acquires 20% interest in La Fete Group.
Feb. 27/97	Alliance forms joint venture with UK theatrical distributor, Electric Pictures.
Mar. 2/97	Alliance wins 7 Gemini Awards including Best Dramatic Series for Due South.
Mar. 4/97	Alliance begins principal photography on John Woo's Once a Thief, the series, for delivery on fiscal 1998.
Mar. 24/97	Films distributed in Canada by Alliance Releasing win 12 Academy Awards led by The English Patient.

MESSAGE TO SHAREHOLDERS

Fiscal 1997 was a year of success for Alliance. On the one hand, the company experienced earnings growth momentum, particularly in the core production, distribution and broadcasting businesses. On the other hand, Alliance's long term strategies began to bear fruit as the company achieved a number of its targeted objectives.

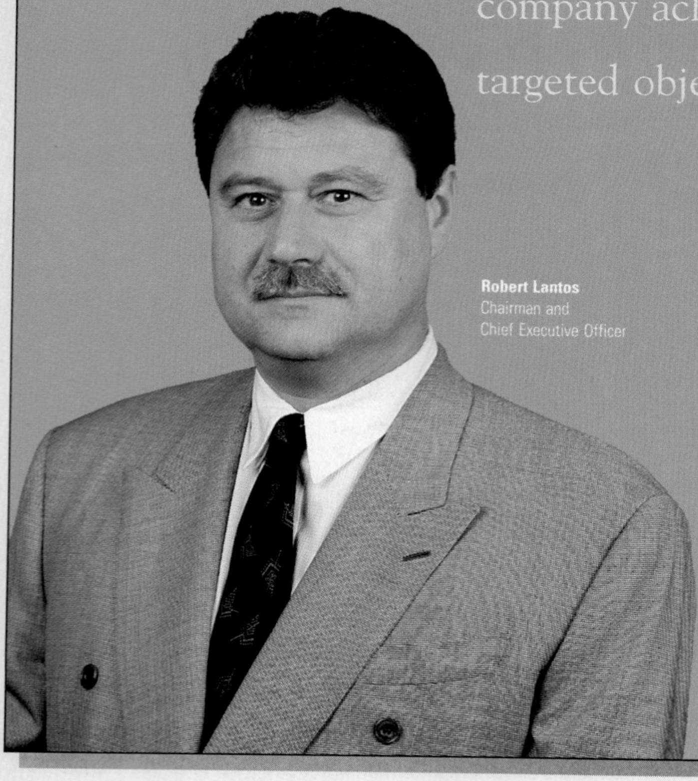

Robert Lantos
Chairman and
Chief Executive Officer

MESSAGE TO SHAREHOLDERS

We pursued our two-pronged strategy with determination and confidence:

1. TO MAXIMIZE OUR ACCESS TO THE MARKET BY BUILDING OUR DIRECT DISTRIBUTION REACH.

- We renewed long term Canadian distribution agreements with the two top US independent motion picture producers, Miramax and New Line.

- We successfully applied to the CRTC for a license to launch a new specialty network - History Television - a highly-prized and fiercely contested service which was awarded one of the last analog licenses and which will be launched on a new specialty tier by all major Canadian Cable Systems in September 1997.

- We consolidated our ownership of Showcase Television through the acquisition of most of the minority interest thereby increasing our equity from 55% to 99%.

- We ensured long term revenue growth for Showcase Television, obtaining the CRTC's approval to increase the service's permitted advertising time to 12 minutes per hour from its original 8 minute maximum.

- We expanded the reach of the now profitable Showcase Television to 3.5 million homes which will grow to 4 million in September 1997 through a new carriage agreement with Videotron and CF Cable in Montreal.

- Through a 50-50 joint venture with Shaw Communications, we applied for and received a license to launch a national Video-On-Demand service in English and French, a new distribution medium which we believe will have a significant long term impact on revenues.

- We entered the UK theatrical distribution market, teaming with distributor Electric Pictures.

- We expanded into the US first-run syndication market through distribution agreements with Polygram Filmed Entertainment.

- We acquired a 20% interest in Canada's leading childrens' film producer, Quebec's Les Productions La Fete, with an option to double our equity.

- We launched an in-house ad sales division in our Broadcasting Group, replacing the previous agency arrangements and resulting in immediate revenue growth.

- We acquired Canadian distribution rights to approximately 100 hours of drama from producer Telescene.

- We expanded our Canadian video operations into the distribution of non-theatrical product, including titles from Nelvana's animation catalogue.

Victor Loewy
President - Alliance Motion Picture Distribution
Vice Chairman - Alliance Communications Corporation

2. TO BUILD AND IMPROVE OUR CONTENT LIBRARY.

- We retain long term distribution rights by producing proprietary projects. We ensure continued production growth through increased investment in in-house development, exclusive deals with carefully targeted high profile talent, and by recruiting skilled creative executives. This philosophy has already begun to yield dividends as highlighted in television by John Woo's *Once A Thief*, Diane Keaton's *Northern Lights* and Larry Gelbart's *Fast Track*, and in motion pictures by Atom Egoyan's *The Sweet Hereafter* and by the upcoming David Cronenberg's *eXistenZ*, Istvan Szabo's *Sunshine*, and Costa-Gavras' *No Other Life*.

Throughout the year, we continued our relentless pursuit of excellence. The quality of our product determines our stature in the industry and the prices we command in the international marketplace.

In turn, our peers rewarded us with some of the industry's highest laurels:

- Once again we won the top Canadian television and film honours. At the Gemini Awards, *Due South* was named Best Dramatic Series for the third consecutive year – the tenth time an Alliance produced series won this award. Also for the third time, *Due South* won the Chrysler Canada Award for Most Popular Television Program and *ReBoot* won the Gemini for Best Animated Program.

- *Crash* won a Special Jury Prize at the 1996 Cannes Film Festival.

- In May 1997, *The Sweet Hereafter*, the fourth Alliance collaboration with director Atom Egoyan, was the most decorated film at this year's Cannes Film Festival, winning three major awards including the Grand Prix. It is now three years in a row that an Alliance film has won an award in Cannes.

- Motion pictures acquired for Canada by Alliance such as *The English Patient*, *Shine*, *Secrets & Lies* and *Sling Blade* won 12 Academy Awards this year.

- In July 1997, Alliance received five prime time Emmy nominations, four for *The Hunchback* and one for *The Inheritance*.

Ultimately, our strategy is – to put it bluntly – to make money – which is exactly what we accomplished in fiscal 1997 with a 27% growth in earnings from $10.4 million to $13.2 million, a 42% growth in EBITDA from $18.8 million to $26.7 million, and a 66% growth in pre-tax earnings from $12.3 million to $20.4 million. (These results are exclusive of the Mainframe related gain). Our distribution-driven, diversified production strategy ensures that this growth will continue in fiscal 1998 and in the years to follow.

From left to right:
Atom Egoyan, director and producer of *The Sweet Hereafter*. **John Woo**, director and executive producer of *Once a Thief*, the movie. **David Cronenberg**, writer, director and producer of *Crash*. **Dianne Keaton**, executive producer and star of *Northern Lights*

MESSAGE TO SHAREHOLDERS

A report to our shareholders must be more than just corporate cheerleading. A critical analysis of the company must also take into account its vulnerabilities and unfulfilled expectations. This year at Alliance:

1. We targeted the UK market because, after the US, it is the world's strongest source of independent movies. To support the initiative we competed for a lottery franchise in order to better access British film subsidies.

We assembled a strong and diverse group of partners. Under the name Studio Pictures, we competed for a franchise award which, had it succeeded, would have triggered some $60 million of off-balance sheet production financing over five years. Although we were not successful, we achieved our goal of expanding Alliance's production reach into the UK, forging an important tie with one of the UK's leading film production executives, George Faber, the former head of BBC Films. Mr. Faber's Company Pictures, in which Alliance is a shareholder, now has an overall production deal with Alliance. The British distributor Electric Pictures formed the platform for our move into the UK distribution market.

2. Our television production slate suffered from an imbalance between series and movies. With only two series in production, television movies dominated the slate. Movies are more costly per hour than series. This negatively impacted our gross margins. The imbalance has been addressed. Fiscal 1998 features our largest television production slate ever with 120 hours confirmed for delivery this year. The slate is now dominated by series, with six in production and several pilots underway. Because we own extensive rights in perpetuity to all our productions, even the less profitable television movies are valuable additions to our library and will continue to generate revenues well beyond their amortization cycle.

3. In 1994, we invested in a start-up television station in Hungary, Budapest TV3. Our strategy was to create a new market for our library and, parallel with our investment, we entered into a long term product supply agreement with TV3.

The Company's diverse day to day business activities are managed by a Management Executive Committee comprised of Robert Lantos, Victor Loewy and shown here from left to right:

Roman Doroniuk
Chief Financial Officer,
George Burger
Executive Vice-President,
Jeff Rayman
Chairman,
Alliance Multimedia
President ,
Alliance Equicap

While the station has been modestly successful, we are experiencing collection difficulties on our supply agreement which has now been suspended. Our investment in TV3 is not material (approximately $1.3 million) and we believe that its value is not at present impaired. With TV3 not proving to be of strategic value to our library sales, the Company may sell its interest in the station.

THE EQUICAP FACTOR

Our focus on expansion and the strengthening of our core businesses over the past three years has significantly reduced Equicap's share of the overall earnings picture of Alliance. The potential negative impact of ending Equicap's tax shelter activities on the Company's earnings has been minimized.

In fiscal 1997, Equicap's tax shelter business contributed approximately $4.5 million to our net earnings, or 34% excluding the Mainframe gain, down from 38% in fiscal 1996. Net earnings in our core businesses increased from 1996 to 1997 by 34%, excluding the Mainframe gain.

Our growing production slate, renewed distribution output deals, growth in our broadcasting business and revenues generated by our library will ensure that our overall earnings growth is not compromised by a reduced contribution from Equicap in fiscal 1998 and beyond. We are confident that we have successfully replaced Equicap's tax shelter earnings with valuable and predictable profits from our growing core activities.

While we anticipate no earnings from tax shelters in fiscal 1999, we do expect growing revenue and earning streams from Equicap's new ventures led by Equicap Financial Corporation.

HIDDEN ASSETS

A brief inventory of some extraordinary assets whose value is not fully reflected on the balance sheet:

1. We have amassed a world class library of movies, television drama and animation — the largest and most valuable library ever assembled by a Canadian company. It consists of over 1,000 hours of international rights and more than 8,000 hours of Canadian rights (including nearly 3,000 motion pictures). The growth of our international rights library is propelled by our philosophy to produce proprietary projects. Our Canadian rights library is the beneficiary of our strong theatrical distribution operation which consistently feeds our Canadian library with new titles.

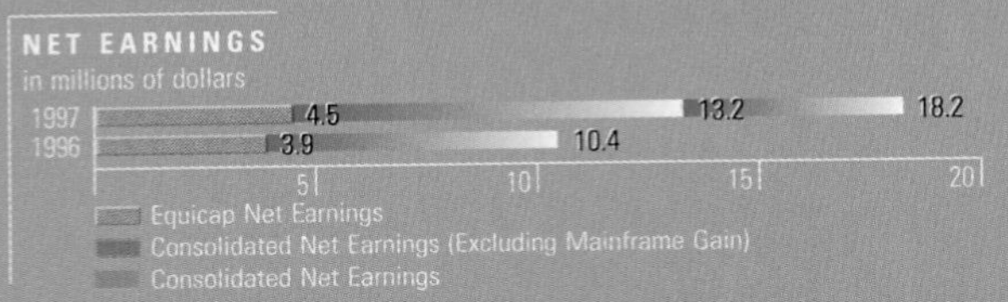

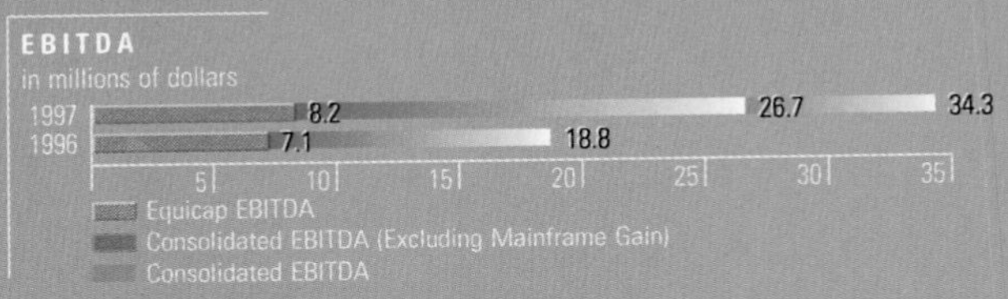

In the business of filmed entertainment, library revenues are an essential pillar of strength. They represent a steadily increasing high margin income stream from off-balance sheet assets. For a library to generate meaningful revenues it has to achieve a certain critical mass and it must contain some highly desirable lead titles. Alliance's library has both. Since fiscal 1994, library revenues have grown at a compound annual rate of 42% from $4.5 million to $13.0 million and all of the titles in our library have been principally fully amortized. We define library revenues as sales of programs after their first cycle, typically three years after completion. There are more aggressive definitions practised in the industry which, in our opinion, mix library revenues with current revenues.

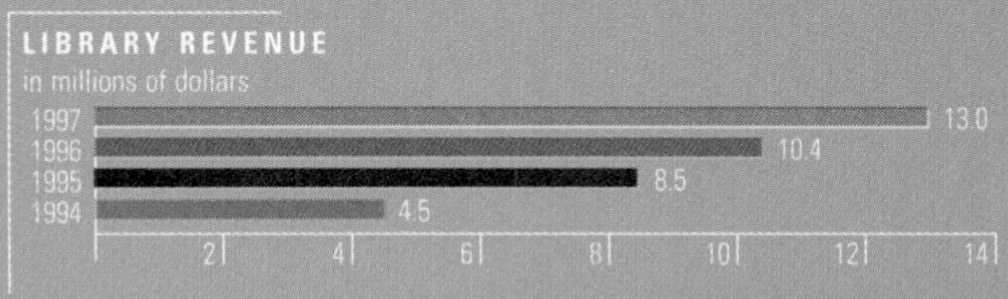

A major portion of Alliance's product is still in its first cycle of exploitation thus ensuring future growth in library revenue as these rights revert to the Company.

2. When we took Alliance public four years ago, we had no broadcast assets. Today, we have three specialty services:

I) Showcase Television, which is now generating operating revenue of $20 million with a subscriber growth rate of 20,000 households per month.

II) History Television, which even prior to its September 1997 launch, has begun to generate advertising sales.

The launching of History Television will bring economies of scale to Showcase Television as the two services share origination facilities, advertising sales force, administration and management.

One of the reasons we acquired the minority interests in Showcase Television was to be free to fully realize upon these efficiencies.

We consider Showcase Television and History Television to be "beachfront properties" as they are among the last specialty services to receive wide national cable carriage. With all analog slots now occupied, future specialty licences in English Canada will likely be issued on the basis of digital carriage only and will require a long period before achieving the level of consumer penetration necessary for profitability.

Our specialty networks have value beyond their earnings multiple. They are irreplaceable. Together with our strength in Canadian theatrical and home video distribution, our broadcast assets provide us with a uniquely diversified reach into the Canadian market.

III) Video-On-Demand (in partnership with Shaw Communications) which will bring the video store to the consumer's living room.

All three services are important new opportunities for Alliance's library.

3. In the years since our IPO, we have built a growing animation business from a start-up position. The two computer generated series which we co-produce with Mainframe and distribute world-wide, *ReBoot* and *Beast Wars*, are at the leading edge of CGI. They are widely sold internationally and are in the US market in first-run syndication. Both are ratings hits in Canada where they are among the top-rated shows on YTV.

Our first 2-D conventional animated series, *Captain Star*, is an international co-production with various European partners such as the UK's HTV.

It debuts in Canada in September on the new cartoon network, Teletoon.

An Alliance animation library is now beginning to take shape, containing 91 episodes of high-end animation to which we control international distribution rights.

Our 1994 investment in Mainframe Entertainment has strengthened our balance sheet with a ten-fold after tax cash return on our capital plus a 7% carried interest in the now publicly traded company. While we have reduced our equity position, we have maintained our principal strategic objective through a distribution agreement which provides us with international rights to Mainframe product.

Thanks to our strategic focus, we have carefully laid the groundwork for future growth. We have identified our weak spots and have replaced them with new building blocks, positioning the Company to focus on its strengths.

In closing, we record with great regret the passing of our friend and distinguished colleague, Andrew Sarlos, O.C., LL.D.(Hon), F.C.A., who served Alliance with distinction as a Director of the Company from 1992. He is greatly missed. At the same time, we record with pleasure the election to the Board in 1996 of Donald Sobey, Chairman of the Empire Group. We warmly welcome Mr. Sobey.

Robert Lantos

MANAGEMENTS DISCUSSION AND ANALYSIS

ALLANCE COMMUNICATIONS CORPORATION

RESULTS OF OPERATIONS

Fiscal 1997 marked renewed earnings growth with record net earnings, revenues and cash flow from operations.

Net earnings for the year ended March 31, 1997 increased 75.0% to $18.2 million compared to $10.4 million for the year ended March 31, 1996. Excluding the gain on sale of investment, net earnings in fiscal 1997 increased 26.9% to $13.2 million. EBITDA increased 42.0% to $26.7 million for the year ended March 31, 1997 from $18.8 million for the year ended March 31, 1996.

Revenues in fiscal 1997 increased 5.1% to $282.6 million compared to fiscal 1996 revenues of $268.9 million. Revenues increased in all businesses with the exception of Motion Pictures, where revenues declined due to the timing of the delivery of Alliance-produced motion pictures. Gross profit increased 16.2% to $68.8 million in fiscal 1997 from $59.2 million in fiscal 1996 while the gross margin increased to 24.3% in fiscal 1997 from 22.0% in fiscal 1996.

Cash flow from operations in fiscal 1997 increased 37.9% to $240.7 million from $174.5 million in fiscal 1996.

The following table presents a consolidated financial summary of the Company's businesses.

For the years ended March 31, 1997, March 31, 1996 and March 31, 1995
(In thousands of Canadian dollars)

							% Increase (Decrease)	
	1997	%	1996	%	1995	%	1997 over 1996	1996 over 1995
REVENUES BY BUSINESS:								
Alliance Television	$ 110,463	39.1	$ 104,676	38.9	$ 106,540	45.5	5.5	(1.7)
Alliance Motion Pictures	113,331	40.1	121,416	45.1	100,709	43.1	(6.7)	20.6
Alliance Equicap	24,967	8.8	23,204	8.6	23,582	10.1	7.6	(1.6)
Alliance Broadcasting	19,884	7.0	16,836	6.3	2,586	1.1	18.1	551.0
Alliance Multimedia	13,954	5.0	2,813	1.1	394	0.2	396.1	614.0
Total Revenues	$ 282,599	100.0	$ 268,945	100.0	$ 233,811	100.0	5.1	15.0
DIRECT OPERATING EXPENSES BY BUSINESS:								
Alliance Television	$ 88,699	80.3	$ 80,486	76.9	$ 83,282	78.2	10.2	(3.4)
Alliance Motion Pictures	90,762	80.1	109,331	90.0	87,743	87.1	(17.0)	24.6
Alliance Equicap	12,372	49.6	11,920	51.4	11,573	49.1	3.8	3.0
Alliance Broadcasting	11,218	56.4	7,299	43.4	827	32.0	53.7	782.6
Alliance Multimedia	10,765	77.1	753	26.8	260	66.0	1329.6	189.6
Total Direct Operating Expenses	$ 213,816	75.7	$ 209,789	78.0	$ 183,685	78.6	1.9	14.2
GROSS PROFIT BY BUSINESS:								
Alliance Television	$ 21,764	19.7	$ 24,190	23.1	$ 23,258	21.8	(10.0)	4.0
Alliance Motion Pictures	22,569	19.9	12,085	10.0	12,966	12.9	86.8	6.8
Alliance Equicap	12,595	50.4	11,284	48.6	12,009	50.9	11.6	(6.0)
Alliance Broadcasting	8,666	43.6	9,537	56.6	1,759	68.0	(9.1)	442.2
Alliance Multimedia	3,189	22.9	2,060	73.2	134	34.0	54.8	1,437.3
Total Gross Profit	$ 68,783	24.3	$ 59,156	22.0	$ 50,126	21.4	16.3	18.0

MANAGEMENTS DISCUSSION AND ANALYSIS

ALLANCE COMMUNICATIONS CORPORATION

FISCAL 1997 COMPARED TO FISCAL 1996

Revenues in fiscal 1997 were $282.6 million, an increase of $13.7 million or 5.1%, compared to $268.9 million in fiscal 1996. This increase was due to revenue growth in all businesses, with the exception of a slight decline in Alliance Motion Pictures.

Alliance Television revenues in fiscal 1997 were $110.5 million, an increase of $5.8 million or 5.5%, compared to $104.7 million in fiscal 1996. This increase was due to an $8.1 million increase in production revenues, partially offset by a $2.3 million decrease in distribution revenues. In the current year, 56 hours of television production were delivered compared to 57 hours in the prior year. These hours were comprised of 35 hours of series delivered in fiscal 1997 compared to 46 hours in fiscal 1996, 18 hours of television movies delivered in fiscal 1997 compared to 10 hours in fiscal 1996 and three hours of television pilots delivered in fiscal 1997 compared to one hour in fiscal 1996. On average, therefore, the size of the average hourly production budget increased substantially over the prior year as television movie budgets per hour are generally much higher than television series' budgets per hour. The decreased distribution revenues were due to exceptional revenues being earned in the prior year on certain titles which was not repeated in the same magnitude in the current year.

Alliance Motion Pictures revenues in fiscal 1997 were $113.3 million, a decrease of $8.1 million or 6.7%, compared to $121.4 million in fiscal 1996. This decrease was due primarily to the production division where revenues decreased by $15.2 million over the prior year from $32.2 million in fiscal 1996 to $17.0 million in the current year. In the current year, the production division delivered one motion picture, Crash, whereas in the prior year three motion pictures were delivered. In Alliance Releasing, the Company's Canadian distribution business, revenues in fiscal 1997 were $82.0 million, an increase of $2.2 million or 2.8%, compared to $79.8 million in fiscal 1996. Within Alliance Releasing, theatrical revenues increased $1.4 million compared to the prior year, video revenues decreased $2.4 million compared to the prior year and television revenues increased $3.0 million compared to the prior year, due primarily to the timing of the releases in the various media formats. Theatrical successes in the current year included: The English Patient; Shine; Michael; and Trainspotting. Le Monde revenues were $11.7 million, an increase of $7.2 million or 160.0%, compared to $4.5 million in fiscal 1996 due to the growing library of titles. Top revenue performers in the current year included: Lethal Tender; Dead Silence; Hostile Intent; and Ravager. Alliance Independent Films' revenues of $2.7 million decreased $2.2 million or 44.9%, compared to $4.9 million in the prior year due to the decline in the amount of new product acquired and delivered in the current year. Deliveries in the current year included: Denise Calls Up; Welcome to the Dollhouse; and When Night is Falling.

Alliance Equicap revenues in fiscal 1997 were $25.0 million an increase of $1.8 million or 7.8%, compared to fiscal 1996 revenues of $23.2 million due primarily to the success of production services deals in the current year. In addition, the current year's revenues include Equicap Financial Corporation, which started up operations in the fall of 1996. Equicap Financial Corporation closed six deals in the period October 1996 to March 1997 for arrangement fee revenues and interest income of $0.6 million.

Alliance Broadcasting revenues in fiscal 1997 were $19.9 million, an increase of $3.1 million or 18.5%, compared to $16.8 million in fiscal 1996 due primarily to increased advertising sales. Cable revenues were slightly higher due to an increase in the subscriber base net of the impact of a lower average subscriber rate.

MANAGEMENTS DISCUSSION AND ANALYSIS

ALLANCE COMMUNICATIONS CORPORATION

Alliance Multimedia revenues in fiscal 1997 were $14.0 million, an increase of $11.2 million or 400.0%, compared to $2.8 million in fiscal 1996. Distribution revenues of $12.0 million were recognized in fiscal 1997 as 26 episodes of Beastwars were delivered. TMP-The Music Publisher ("TMP") revenues increased to $2.0 million, an increase of $0.9 million or 81.8%, compared to $1.1 million in fiscal 1996 due to the timing of collections of foreign royalties and also from the successes of Amanda Marshall's debut album which contained five TMP songs and the TMP song "Heaven Help My Heart", recorded by both Wynonna Judd and Tina Arena.

Gross profit in fiscal 1997 was $68.8 million, an increase of $9.6 million or 16.2%, compared to $59.2 million in fiscal 1996. This increase was due primarily to Alliance Motion Pictures where the gross profit increased $10.5 million year-over-year. As a percentage of revenues, gross profit in fiscal 1997 was 24.3%, compared to 22.0% in fiscal 1996, due to increased margins in Alliance Motion Pictures and the change in the revenue mix, partially offset by decreased margins in Alliance Television. The increased margins in Alliance Motion Pictures were due primarily to an increased margin in the production division where the margin improved from - 11.8% on the motion pictures delivered in the prior year to 15.9% on Crash, which was delivered in the current year. The decreased margins in Alliance Television were due to the increased production costs per hour of delivering higher quality television movies in the current year such as: The Hunchback; The Inheritance and Toe Tags (pilot) as well as an increased proportion of television movies versus television series. Television series generally have better margins but accounted for a lower percentage of production in fiscal 1997.

Other operating expenses in fiscal 1997 were $42.0 million, an increase of $1.6 million or 4.0%, compared to $40.4 million in fiscal 1996. Other operating expenses as a percentage of revenues decreased slightly to 14.9% compared to 15.0% in fiscal 1996. Other operating expenses are comprised of corporate overhead and operating expenses other than direct operating expenses. These expenses include such items as general and administrative expenses, salaries and benefits, office rental, communications costs and professional fees. In fiscal 1997, $13.9 million of operating expenses related to corporate overhead, compared to $12.3 million in fiscal 1996. Corporate overhead included non-recurring charges of $2.1 million in fiscal 1997: $1 million relating to Equicap bonus costs; $600,000 relating to the Company's unsuccessful UK franchise bid; and $500,000 relating to head office moving costs, compared to $1.3 million in fiscal 1996: $800,000 relating to severance costs; and $500,000 relating to the Company's unsuccessful efforts to acquire the broadcast assets of John Labatt Limited. Before non-recurring charges, corporate overhead increased to $11.8 million in fiscal 1997 from $11.0 million in fiscal 1996. The increase in other operating expenses was primarily due to head count increases in new and expanding businesses such as Alliance Pictures International and Equicap Financial Corporation.

Net interest expense in fiscal 1997 was $1.3 million, an increase of $0.4 million or 44.4%, compared to $0.9 million in fiscal 1996, reflecting increased cash requirements in the current year, partially offset by the equity offering proceeds and lower interest rates.

The Company's effective tax rate for fiscal 1997 increased to 35.0% from 15.7% in fiscal 1996 due to a shift in the mix of earnings before income taxes to income tax jurisdictions with less favourable income tax rates. In addition, in the current year, the gain on sale of investment was taxed at approximately 34%.

Net earnings in fiscal 1997 were $18.2 million, an increase of $7.8 million or 75.0%, compared to $10.4 million in fiscal 1996.

MANAGEMENTS DISCUSSION AND ANALYSIS
ALLANCE COMMUNICATIONS CORPORATION

FISCAL 1996 COMPARED TO FISCAL 1995

Revenues in fiscal 1996 were $268.9 million, an increase of $35.1 million or 15.0%, compared to $233.8 million in fiscal 1995. This increase was due primarily to significant revenue growth in Alliance Motion Pictures, as well as the inclusion of revenues for a full year in Alliance Broadcasting, which started commercial operations in January 1995.

Alliance Television revenues in fiscal 1996 were $104.7 million, a decrease of $1.8 million or 1.7%, compared to $106.5 million in fiscal 1995. This decrease was due primarily to lower international revenues partially offset by higher North American revenues.

Alliance Motion Pictures revenues in fiscal 1996 were $121.4 million, an increase of $20.7 million or 20.6%, compared to $100.7 million in fiscal 1995. This increase was due primarily to increased revenues in Alliance Releasing, where revenues in fiscal 1996 were $79.8 million, an increase of $21.3 million or 36.4%, compared to $58.5 million in fiscal 1995. Within Alliance Releasing, this increase was due primarily to increased Canadian home video revenues as a result of a number of successful home video releases, including Pulp Fiction, Mortal Kombat, Don Juan DeMarco and Johnny Mnemonic, as well as the continued exploitation of Dumb and Dumber, The Swan Princess and The Mask, which were released theatrically in fiscal 1995. These increases were slightly offset by a $3.0 million decrease in Canadian theatrical revenues in fiscal 1996.

Alliance Equicap revenues in fiscal 1996 were $23.2 million which was approximately the same as fiscal 1995. In fiscal 1996, Equicap focused on structured production financings, which provided private investors with access to tax incentives provided by the Canadian government.

Alliance Broadcasting revenues in fiscal 1996 were $16.8 million, an increase of $14.2 million or 546.2%, compared to $2.6 million in fiscal 1995. This increase was due primarily to fiscal 1996 revenues reflecting the first full year of operations of Showcase, while the previous year reflected only one quarter of operations. Revenues were recognized in the first quarter of operations.

Alliance Multimedia revenues in fiscal 1996 were $2.8 million, an increase of $2.4 million or 600.0%, compared to $0.4 million in fiscal 1995. Distribution revenues of $1.7 million were recognized in fiscal 1996 as episodes of ReBoot were delivered to YTV. Fiscal 1996 also reflected the first full year of operations of TMP where revenues were $1.1 million, an increase of $0.7 million or 175.0%, compared to $0.4 million in fiscal 1995.

Gross profit in fiscal 1996 was $59.2 million, an increase of $9.1 million or 18.2%, compared to $50.1 million in fiscal 1995. This increase was due primarily to the inclusion of gross profit realized from Showcase Television's first full year of operations and distribution revenues realized upon the delivery of ReBoot. Gross profit in fiscal 1996 was 22.0%, compared to 21.4% in fiscal 1995, due to the change in the revenue mix and increased margins in Alliance Television, partially offset by decreased margins in Alliance Motion Pictures. Decreased margins in Alliance Motion Pictures were due primarily to an increase in the provision for investment in film and television programs in fiscal 1996. In addition, margins on films delivered in fiscal 1996 were not as favourable as the margins on films delivered in fiscal 1995.

Other operating expenses in fiscal 1996 were $40.4 million, an increase of $11.8 million or 41.3%, compared to $28.6 million in fiscal 1995. In fiscal 1996, $12.3 million of other operating expenses related to corporate overhead, compared to $11.7 million in fiscal 1995. Corporate overhead included non-recurring charges of $1.3 million in fiscal 1996 compared to $0.6 million in fiscal 1995. Before non-recurring charges, corporate overhead decreased to $11.0 million in fiscal 1996 from $11.1 million in fiscal 1995. The overall increase in other operating expenses was due to expansion of the Los Angeles office and international operations, increased expenses in Alliance Broadcasting associated with Showcase Television's first full year of operations, overall head count and wage increases and certain one-time expenditures, such as severance costs and costs associated with the company's unsuccessful efforts to acquire the broadcast assets of John Labatt Limited.

Net interest expense in fiscal 1996 was $0.9 million, an increase of $0.6 million or 200.0%, compared to $0.3 million in fiscal 1995, reflecting increased interest costs as the opening cash balance was drawn down early in the fiscal year to finance production costs, acquisitions of distribution product and development costs.

The Company's effective tax rate for fiscal 1996 decreased to 15.7% from 22.0% in fiscal 1995 due to a shift in the mix of earnings before income taxes to non-Canadian operations with favourable income tax rates.

Net earnings in fiscal 1996 were $10.4 million, a decrease of $2.6 million or 20.0%, compared to $13.0 million in fiscal 1995.

LIQUIDITY AND CAPITAL RESOURCES

Cash flow from operations increased significantly during fiscal 1997 to $240.7 million from $174.5 million for fiscal 1996 and $169.1 million for fiscal 1995. Earnings before interest, provision for income taxes, depreciation, amortization and minority interest ("EBITDA") increased to $26.7 million during fiscal 1997 after dropping to $18.8 million in fiscal 1996 from $21.5 million in fiscal 1995.

Alliance has traditionally financed its working capital requirements principally through cash generated by operations, revolving bank credit facilities and sales of equity. The greatest demand for working capital exists in the start-up phase of production, which traditionally occurs in August and September, although it is progressively becoming less and less seasonal in nature as the company diversifies its business.

The nature of the Company's business is such that significant initial expenditures are required to produce and acquire television programs and films, while revenues from these television programs and films are earned over an extended period of time after their completion and acquisition. As Alliance's activities grow, its financing requirements are expected to grow. The Company believes it has sufficient resources to fund its operations through fiscal 1998 from cash generated by operations, existing bank facilities and the net proceeds of the U.S. equity offering in August 1996.

Alliance typically borrows from banks to provide interim production financing. All revenues associated with these productions are pledged as security for these loans. The majority of these borrowings relate specifically to television program and film production.

On October 28, 1994, prior to the reorganization of the share capital of the Company, the Company issued an unsecured, subordinated 6.5% convertible debenture maturing April 5, 2002 to Onex Corporation for $16.5 million cash. The debenture is convertible into common shares of the Company at any time at $19 per share. Interest is payable in cash or additional convertible debentures at the Company's option. Commencing October 28, 1999, the debenture or any portion thereof will be redeemable at the option of the Company, provided certain conditions are met, at the issue price, together with accrued and unpaid interest to the date of redemption. The debenture provides the Company with the option to pay for the redemption of the debenture by issuing common shares to the debenture holder at a price equal to 90% of the weighted average trading price of the common shares for the last 20 consecutive trading days prior to redemption or the maturity date.

In fiscal 1995, the Company obtained a $75 million credit facility from a Canadian chartered bank. The bank facility provided for a $20 million demand operating line, a $50 million term production financing facility and a $5 million facility to hedge foreign exchange exposure.

In August 1996, the Company completed a cross-border offering of 3,020,000 class B non-voting shares for net proceeds of $32.9 million.

In December 1996, the Company's bank facility was increased to $122 million to provide for a $65 million demand operating line, a $50 million term production financing facility, a $5 million facility to hedge foreign exchange exposure and a $2 million lease facility. As at March 31, 1997, the Company had loans outstanding under its term production facility on productions in progress in the amount of $15.9 million. The Company applied $12.5 million of its cash against the $15.9 million loans for net operating loan and bank indebtedness of $3.4 million as at March 31, 1997. See note 5 to the Consolidated Financial Statements.

In March 1997, Equicap Financial Corporation obtained a $25 million non-recourse revolving line of credit with a Canadian Chartered bank. The line of credit forms part of the funds made available for film projects financed by Equicap Financial Corporation.

RISKS AND UNCERTAINTIES

The Company capitalizes production and distribution costs as incurred to investment in film and television programs and such costs are amortized to direct operating expenses in accordance with SFAS 53. Under SFAS 53, all costs incurred in connection with an individual film or television program, including production costs, release prints and advertising costs, are capitalized as investment in film and television programs. These costs are stated at the lower of unamortized cost and estimated net realizable value. Estimated total production costs for an individual film or television program are amortized in the proportion that revenues realized relates to management's estimate of the total revenues expected to be received from such film or television program. As a result, if revenue estimates change with respect to a film or television program, the Company may be required to write down all or a portion of the unamortized costs of such film or television program. No assurance can be given that a write down will not have a significant impact on the Company's results of operations and financial condition.

Results of operations for any period are significantly dependent on the number and timing of television programs and films delivered or made available to various media. Consequently, the Company's results of operations may fluctuate materially from period to period and the results for any one period are not necessarily indicative of results for future periods. Ultimately, profitability depends not only on revenues but on the amount paid to acquire or produce the film or television program and the amount spent on the prints and advertising campaign used to promote it.

The Company currently finances a portion of its production budgets from Canadian governmental agencies and incentive programs, such as Telefilm Canada and federal and provincial tax credits, as well as international sources in the case of the Company's co-productions. There can be no assurance that local cultural incentive programs which the Company may access in Canada and internationally, will not be reduced, amended or eliminated. Any change in these incentive programs may have an adverse impact on the Company.

MANAGEMENTS DISCUSSION AND ANALYSIS

ALLANCE COMMUNICATIONS CORPORATION

A significant portion of the Company's revenues and expenses is in U.S. dollars, and therefore subject to fluctuation in exchange rates. There is risk that a significant fluctuation in exchange rates may have an adverse impact on the Company's results of operations.

Commissions earned by Alliance Equicap have been principally related to sales of limited partnership units to private investors in connection with structured production financings. Recent changes to Canadian income tax legislation have eliminated tax incentives available to investors in connection with certain financings. Consequently, it is expected that Alliance Equicap's revenues in fiscal 1998 will be substantially less than in fiscal 1997.

OUTLOOK

The Company achieved record results in fiscal 1997 and plans to continue to build on this success. The Company will continue to pursue its long term strategy of expanding its libraries and increasing its direct distribution reach. The Company's proven ability to deliver and distribute high quality product combined with its strong financial position, makes it well positioned to achieve its aggressive growth strategy.

QUARTERLY REVIEW

The business of the Company fluctuates during the year as indicated by the table below, which summarizes quarterly results for the fiscal year ended March 31, 1997:

(In thousands of Canadian dollars except share information)

	1st Qtr.	2nd Qtr.	3rd. Qtr.	4th Qtr.	Total
Revenues	$ 63,516	$ 54,617	$ 64,956	$ 99,510	$ 282,599
Gross Profit	12,402	15,688	16,066	24,627	68,783
EBITDA	3,026	3,529	6,850	13,341	26,746
Net Earnings	955	6,260	4,081	6,892	18,188
Basic Earnings Per Share	$ 0.10	$ 0.53	$ 0.32	$ 0.53	$ 1.53

AUDITORS' REPORT

ALLIANCE COMMUNICATIONS CORPORATION

To the shareholders of Alliance Communications Corporation:

We have audited the consolidated balance sheets of Alliance Communications Corporation as at March 31, 1997 and 1996 and the consolidated statements of earnings and retained earnings and changes in financial position for each of the years in the three year period ended March 31, 1997. These financial statements are the responsibility of the company's management. Our responsibility is to express an opinion on these financial statements based on our audits.

We conducted our audits in accordance with Canadian generally accepted auditing standards. Those standards require that we plan and perform an audit to obtain reasonable assurance whether the financial statements are free of material misstatement. An audit includes examining, on a test basis, evidence supporting the amounts and disclosures in the financial statements. An audit also includes assessing the accounting principles used and significant estimates made by management, as well as evaluating the overall financial statement presentation.

In our opinion, these consolidated financial statements present fairly, in all material respects, the financial position of the company as at March 31, 1997 and 1996 and the results of its operations and the changes in its financial position for each of the years in the three year period ended March 31, 1997 in accordance with Canadian generally accepted accounting principles.

Coopers & Lybrand

Chartered Accountants

North York, Ontario, Canada
May 30, 1997
(except as to note 21 which is as of June 17, 1997)

CONSOLIDATED BALANCE SHEETS

ALLIANCE COMMUNICATIONS CORPORATION

As at March 31, 1997 and March 31, 1996
(In thousands of Canadian dollars)

	1997	1996
ASSETS		
Cash and short-term investments	$ 10,777	$ 5,090
Accounts receivable	82,184	53,081
Distribution contracts receivable	76,272	64,948
Loans receivable	9,283	-
Investment in film and television programs (note 2)	101,531	63,274
Film and television programs in progress	22,955	22,398
Program exhibition rights	11,821	9,151
Development costs and investment in scripts	13,103	7,762
Property and equipment (note 3)	10,314	6,848
Broadcasting licences, net of accumulated amortization of $30 (1996 - $nil)	7,236	-
Other assets (note 4)	8,246	6,346
	$ 353,722	$ 238,898
LIABILITIES		
Operating loan and bank indebtedness (note 5)	$3,361	$ 5,617
Accounts payable and accrued liabilities	86,268	47,440
Distribution revenues payable	23,223	26,238
Loans payable (note 6)	-	2,083
Income taxes (note 12)	10,927	10,818
Deferred revenue	62,980	32,706
Convertible debenture (note 7)	16,500	16,500
Minority interest	39	2,116
	203,298	143,518
SHAREHOLDERS' EQUITY		
Capital stock (note 8)	88,836	52,295
Retained earnings	60,893	42,705
Cumulative translation adjustments	695	380
	150,424	95,380
	$ 353,722	$ 238,898

Signed on behalf of the Board,

David J Kassie
Director

Ellis Jacob
Director

The accompanying notes form an integral part of these financial statements.

CONSOLIDATED STATEMENTS OF EARNINGS AND RETAINED EARNINGS

ALLIANCE COMMUNICATIONS CORPORATION

For the years ended March 31, 1997, March 31, 1996 and March 31, 1995
(In thousands of Canadian dollars, except per share data)

	1997	1996	1995
REVENUES	$ 282,599	$ 268,945	$ 233,811
DIRECT OPERATING EXPENSES	213,816	209,789	183,685
GROSS PROFIT	68,783	59,156	50,126
OTHER EXPENSES			
Other operating expenses	42,037	40,363	28,643
Amortization	5,160	5,038	5,164
Interest (note 10)	1,296	893	282
Minority interest	(142)	562	(596)
	48,351	46,856	33,493
EARNINGS BEFORE UNDERNOTED	20,432	12,300	16,633
GAIN ON SALE OF INVESTMENT (NOTE 11)	7,544	-	-
EARNINGS BEFORE INCOME TAXES	27,976	12,300	16,633
PROVISION FOR INCOME TAXES (NOTE 12)	9,788	1,935	3,658
NET EARNINGS FOR THE YEAR	18,188	10,365	12,975
RETAINED EARNINGS, BEGINNING OF YEAR	42,705	32,340	19,365
RETAINED EARNINGS, END OF YEAR	$ 60,893	$ 42,705	$ 32,340
BASIC EARNINGS PER COMMON SHARE (NOTE 13)	$ 1.53	$ 1.05	$ 1.36

The accompanying notes form an integral part of these financial statements

CONSOLIDATED STATEMENTS OF CHANGES IN FINANCIAL POSITION

ALLIANCE COMMUNICATIONS CORPORATION

For the years ended March 31, 1997, March 31, 1996 and March 31, 1995
(In thousands of Canadian dollars)

	1997	1996	1995
CASH AND SHORT-TERM INVESTMENTS PROVIDED BY (USED IN):			
OPERATING ACTIVITIES			
Net earnings for the year	$ 18,188	$ 10,365	$ 12,975
Items not affecting cash:			
Amortization of investment in film and television programs	190,226	185,534	169,460
Amortization of program exhibition rights	9,363	6,807	-
Amortization of development costs and investment in scripts	2,351	1,800	1,342
Amortization of property and equipment and pre-operating costs	2,401	2,934	3,518
Amortization of broadcasting licences and goodwill	408	304	304
Gain on sale of investment (note 11)	(7,544)	-	-
Minority interest	(142)	562	(596)
Deferred income taxes	3,529	1,594	3,284
Net changes in other non-cash balances related to operations (note 14)	21,950	(35,373)	(21,173)
	240,730	174,527	169,114
INVESTING ACTIVITIES			
Investment in films and television programs	(228,483)	(188,156)	(177,414)
Film and television programs in progress	(557)	7,516	(5,328)
Program exhibition rights	(12,033)	(6,333)	(10,236)
Development costs and investment in scripts	(7,692)	(5,226)	(2,278)
Net additions to property and equipment	(5,237)	(2,973)	(6,280)
Net proceeds from sale of investment (note 11)	7,684	-	-
Business acquisitions	(9,425)	135	(2,765)
Cash balances of acquired businesses	-	-	4,308
Long-term investments	(2,219)	(992)	(617)
	(257,962)	(196,029)	(200,610)
FINANCING ACTIVITIES			
Operating loan and bank indebtedness	(2,256)	5,617	-
Increase in loans receivable	(9,283)	-	-
Increase (decrease) in loans payable	(2,083)	712	1,086
Issue of convertible debenture	-	-	16,500
Issue of common shares	36,541	1,403	21,818
Exercise of warrants	-	-	(20,984)
	22,919	7,732	18,420
INCREASE (DECREASE) IN CASH AND SHORT-TERM INVESTMENTS	5,687	(13,770)	(13,076)
CASH AND SHORT-TERM INVESTMENTS, BEGINNING OF YEAR	5,090	18,860	31,936
CASH AND SHORT-TERM INVESTMENTS, END OF YEAR	$ 10,777	$ 5,090	$ 18,860

The accompanying notes form an integral part of these financial statements

NOTES TO THE FINANCIAL STATEMENTS

ALLIANCE COMMUNICATIONS CORPORATION

Alliance Communications Corporation ("the Company") is a fully integrated global supplier of entertainment products whose origins are in television and motion picture production and distribution. The Company also has interests in broadcasting, computer generated animation facilities, music publishing and financing services.

1. SIGNIFICANT ACCOUNTING POLICIES

(a) Generally Accepted Accounting Principles
These consolidated financial statements have been prepared in accordance with Canadian generally accepted accounting principles ("Canadian GAAP"). These principles conform in all material respects with the accounting principles generally accepted in the United States ("U.S. GAAP") except as described in note 20.

(b) Principle of Consolidation
The consolidated financial statements include the accounts of Alliance Communications Corporation and all of its subsidiaries.

(c) Revenue Recognition
Revenue is derived from sale of distribution rights and equity in productions and theatrical or television exhibition. Revenue is recognized as earned when the film or television program is completed and delivered, when amounts are due from the exhibitor or when a contract is executed that irrevocably transfers distribution rights to a licensee or equity to an investor, and there is reasonable assurance of collectability of proceeds.

The Company recognizes as revenue only the net benefits from sales to limited partnerships when the investor has irrevocably committed to acquire the related equity.

Fees related to loan origination, including loan restructuring or renegotiating, are recognized as revenue over the expected term of the loan.

Cable service subscriber fee revenue is accrued as earned. Advertising revenue is recognized when advertisements are aired.

Revenue for music publishing is derived from the collection of royalties on the rights owned and is recognized when received.

Amounts received and receivable and not recognized as revenue are included in deferred revenue.

(d) Short-term Investments
Short-term investments are carried at the lower of cost and market value.

(e) Loans Receivable
Loans receivable are stated net of unearned income and an allowance for credit losses. An allowance for credit losses is maintained in an amount considered adequate to absorb estimated credit-related losses. The allowance is increased by provisions for credit losses which are charged to income, and reduced by write-offs net of expected recoveries. The Company conducts ongoing credit assessments of its loan portfolio on an account-by-account basis and establishes specific allowances when doubtful accounts are identified.

(f) Investment in Film and Television Programs
Investment in film and television programs represents the unamortized costs of motion picture and television programs which have been produced by the Company or for which the Company has acquired distribution rights. Such costs include all production, print and advertising costs which are expected to be recovered from future revenues, net of estimated future liabilities related to the product.

Amortization is determined based on the ratio that current revenues earned from the film and television programs bear to expected gross future revenues. Based on management's estimates of gross future revenues as at March 31, 1997, it is expected that the investment in film and television programs will be absorbed principally over the next three years.

Investment in film and television programs is written down to the net recoverable amount if the investment is greater than the net recoverable amount. Net recoverable amount is defined as the total future revenues expected to be earned from film and television programs, net of future costs.

(g) Film and Television Programs in Progress
Film and television programs in progress represents the accumulated costs of uncompleted motion picture and television programs which are being produced by the Company.

(h) Program Exhibition Rights
Program exhibition rights represents the rights to various long-term contracts acquired from third parties to broadcast television programs and motion pictures. Program exhibition rights and corresponding liabilities are recorded at the time the Company becomes committed under a license agreement and the product is available for telecast. The carrying value of the program exhibition rights is amortized over the lesser of two years and the contracted exhibition period beginning in the month the film or television program is premiered.

(i) Development Costs and Investment in Scripts
Development costs and investment in scripts represents expenditures made on projects prior to production. Advances or contributions received from third parties to assist in development are deducted from these expenditures. Upon commencement of production, development costs and investment in scripts are charged to the production. Development costs and investment in scripts are amortized on the straight-line basis over three years commencing in the year following the year such costs are incurred when production has not commenced. Development costs and investment in scripts are written off when determined not to be recoverable.

(j) Government Financing and Assistance
The Company has access to several government programs that are designed to assist film and television production and distribution in Canada. Amounts received in respect of production assistance are recorded as revenue in accordance with the Company's revenue recognition policy for completed film and television programs. Government assistance with respect to distribution rights is recorded as a reduction of investment in film and television programs. Government assistance towards current expenses is included in net earnings for the year.

(k) Property and Equipment
Property and equipment are carried at cost less accumulated amortization. Amortization is provided, commencing in the year after acquisition, using the following rates and methods:

Computer hardware
- 30% principally by declining balance
Computer software
- 100% principally by declining balance
Furniture and fixtures
- 20% principally by declining balance
Equipment
- 30% principally by declining balance
Leasehold improvements
- straight-line over the lease term
Broadcast and transmission equipment
- straight-line over 5 years

(l) Broadcasting Licences
In acquisitions involving broadcasting undertakings, fair value is assigned to the broadcasting licences acquired. Broadcasting licences are amortized on a straight-line basis over a period of forty years. When there is an expectation that the net carrying amount of the licence will not be recovered, the licence is written down to its net recoverable amount.

(m) Other Assets
Other assets include pre-operating costs related to the period before commencement of commercial operations of Showcase Television Inc. and other businesses. The amount is being amortized on a straight-line basis over a period of five years.

Other assets also include long-term investments which are accounted for at cost when the conditions for equity accounting are not present and goodwill which is amortized on a straight-line basis over a period of five years.

(n) Distribution Revenues Payable
Distribution revenues payable represents the excess of receipts from the distribution of film and television programs over commissions earned and distribution costs incurred and are payable to the licensor of the film or television program.

(o) Foreign Currency
Assets and liabilities denominated in currencies other than Canadian dollars are translated at exchange rates in effect at the balance sheet date. Revenue and expense items are translated at average rates of exchange for the year. Translation gains or losses are included in the determination of earnings except for gains or losses arising on the translation of the accounts of the foreign subsidiaries considered to be self-sustaining, which are deferred as a separate component of shareholders' equity.

(p) Non-Cash Balances Related to Operations
Non-cash balances related to operations are comprised of the aggregate of the following assets and liabilities: accounts receivable; distribution contracts receivable; other assets excluding long-term-investments and goodwill; accounts payable and accrued liabilities; distribution revenues payable; income taxes; deferred revenue; and cumulative translation adjustments.

(q) Use of Estimates
The preparation of financial statements in conformity with generally accepted accounting principles requires management to make estimates and assumptions that affect the reported amounts of assets and liabilities and disclosure of contingent assets and liabilities at the dates of the financial statements and the reported amounts of revenues and expenses during the reporting periods. Actual results could differ from those estimates.

(r) Comparative Amounts
Certain amounts presented in the prior period have been reclassified to conform with the presentation adopted in the current year.

2. INVESTMENT IN FILM AND TELEVISION PROGRAMS
(In thousands of Canadian dollars)

	1997	1996
Completed film and television programs produced, net of amortization	$ 37,218	$ 22,837
Film and television programs acquired, net of amortization	64,313	40,437
	$ 101,531	$ 63,274

The Company expects that 92% of completed film and television programs produced, net of amortization, and 72% of acquisition costs related to film and television programs acquired, net of amortization, will be amortized during the three year period ending March 31, 2000.

The Company earns revenues from films and television programs which are fully amortized and are not valued in the accounts.

3. PROPERTY AND EQUIPMENT

(In thousands of Canadian dollars)

	1997		1996	
	Cost	Accumulated Amortization	Cost	Accumulated Amortization
Computer hardware and software	$ 5,243	$ 2,142	$ 4,040	$ 1,387
Furniture and fixtures	3,206	985	2,061	742
Equipment	1,438	975	1,316	704
Leasehold improvements	4,340	881	1,876	771
Broadcast and transmission equipment	1,570	500	1,482	323
	15,797	5,483	10,775	3,927
Net property and equipment		$ 10,314		$ 6,848

4. OTHER ASSETS

(In thousands of Canadian dollars)

	1997	1996
Pre-operating costs, net of accumulated amortization of $1,338 (1996 - $708)	$ 2,507	$ 2,231
Prepaid expenses	1,344	1,622
Long-term investments	3,688	1,609
Goodwill, net of accumulated amortization of $1,162 (1996 - $784)	707	884
	$ 8,246	$ 6,346

5. OPERATING LOAN AND BANK INDEBTEDNESS

(In thousands of Canadian dollars)

	1997	1996
Bank indebtedness - gross	$ 15,871	$ 18,760
Interest expense on bank indebtedness	$ 1,010	$ 961
Weighted average interest rate	6.09%	9.04%

Operating loan and bank indebtedness is netted on the balance sheet with cash and short-term investments to the extent a right of offset exists.

The Company's assets and the assets of its subsidiaries have been pledged as collateral for the bank indebtedness.

At March 31, 1997, the Company had unused credit facilities aggregating $131,729,000 (1996 - $61,240,000) subject to margin calculations. These facilities are primarily used for bridge financing of productions.

6. LOANS PAYABLE

(In thousands of Canadian dollars)

	1997	1996
Interest bearing loans at prime plus 1%, unsecured with no specific repayment date	$ nil	$ 2,083

7. CONVERTIBLE DEBENTURE

On October 28, 1994, the Company issued a convertible, unsecured, subordinated debenture for $16,500,000 cash, bearing interest at 6.5% per year and maturing on April 5, 2002. The debenture is convertible at the option of the holder into common shares of the Company at any time after October 28, 1995 at a conversion price of $19 per share. Interest is payable in cash or additional convertible debentures at the Company's option.

Commencing October 28, 1999, the debenture will be redeemable at the option of the Company, provided certain conditions are met, at the issue price, together with accrued and unpaid interest to the date of redemption. The Company has the option to pay for the redemption of the debenture by issuing its own common shares to the debenture holder at a price equal to 90% of the weighted average trading price of the common shares for the last 20 consecutive trading days prior to redemption or the maturity date.

8. CAPITAL STOCK

a) The authorized capital stock of the Company consists of an unlimited number of common shares. The common shares are comprised of Class A Voting Shares (the "Voting Shares") and Class B Non-Voting Shares (the "Non-Voting Shares") which have identical attributes except that the Non-Voting Shares are non-voting and each of the Voting Shares is convertible at any time at the holder's option into one fully paid and non-assessable Non-Voting Share. The Non-Voting Shares may be converted into Voting Shares only in certain circumstances.

b) During fiscal 1997, the following transactions occurred:
In August 1996, 3,020,000 Non-Voting Shares were issued pursuant to a public offering at a gross price of US$8.50 per share for proceeds of CDN$32,920,000, net of issue expenses and income tax benefits;

In September 1996, 10,000 Non-Voting Shares were issued in connection with the acquisition of film and television programs at $13.62 per share for proceeds of $136,000;

In January 1997, 95,421 Non-Voting Shares were issued in connection with a long-term investment in another company at $11.79 per share for proceeds of $1,125,000;

In January and February 1997, 162,807 Non-Voting Shares were issued in connection with the acquisition of an additional 44% ownership interest in Showcase Television Inc. at $11.84 per share for proceeds of $1,927,000 (note 9); and

During fiscal 1997, 62,100 Voting Shares were converted into Non-Voting Shares. In addition, 37,020 employee stock options for 18,509 Voting Shares and 18,511 Non-Voting Shares were exercised pursuant to the Company stock option plan for proceeds of $433,000.

c) During fiscal 1996, the following transactions occurred:
On April 26, 1995, the Company reorganized its share capital and created the Voting Shares and Non-Voting Shares, converted each existing common share into one-half of a Voting Share and one-half of a Non-Voting Share, and cancelled all of the existing authorized and issued common shares; and

During fiscal 1996, 117,478 employee stock options were exercised pursuant to the Company stock option plan for proceeds of $1,403,000.

d) During fiscal 1995, the following transactions occurred:
In May 1994, 1,530,000 shares were issued pursuant to the exercise of 1,530,000 warrants to acquire common shares and the receipt of proceeds of $20,984,000 released from escrow net of issue expenses and income tax benefits;

NOTES TO THE FINANCIAL STATEMENTS
ALLIANCE COMMUNICATIONS CORPORATION

In October 1994, 13,900 shares were issued in connection with the purchase of a 75% interest in Partisan Music Productions Inc., carrying on business as TMP - The Music Publisher, at $16.33 per share for aggregate proceeds of $227,000; and

During fiscal 1995, 51,936 employee stock options were exercised pursuant to the Company stock option plan for proceeds of $607,700.

e) As a result, the issued capital stock is as follows:
(In thousands of Canadian dollars)

	1997	1996
Common shares:		
Voting Shares, 4,905,134 (1996 - 4,948,725)	$ 26,057	$ 26,169
Non-Voting Shares, 8,313,882 (1996 - 4,945,043)	62,779	26,126
	$ 88,836	$ 52,295

f) The Company has an Amended and Restated 1993 Employee Stock Option Plan which provides for the issuance of up to 1,750,000 common shares. These options generally vest in equal annual amounts over three to five years. No options are exercisable for periods of more than ten years after date of grant. Options granted under the plan may not have an option price less than the fair market value of the Non-Voting Shares on the date the option is granted.

Options outstanding were split 50% Voting Shares and 50% Non-Voting Shares on May 15, 1995. All new options granted after May 15, 1995 are options to purchase Non-Voting Shares.

Stock option activity for 1995, 1996 and 1997 is as follows:

(In thousands of Canadian dollars)

	Number of Shares			Weighted Average
	Voting	Non-Voting	Total	Exercise Price
Outstanding at March 31, 1994	360,633	360,633	721,266	$ 11.80
Granted	276,203	276,203	552,406	14.24
Exercised	(25,968)	(25,968)	(51,936)	13.29
Cancelled	(14,850)	(14,850)	(29,700)	11.34
Outstanding at March 31, 1995	596,018	596,018	1,192,036	12.88
Granted	-	537,520	537,520	14.75
Exercised	(58,739)	(58,739)	(117,478)	11.70
Cancelled	(99,409)	(99,416)	(198,825)	12.85
Outstanding at March 31, 1996	437,870	975,383	1,413,253	13.69
Granted	5,000	121,120	126,120	14.25
Exercised	(18,509)	(18,511)	(37,020)	11.71
Cancelled	(17,934)	(17,925)	(35,859)	12.85
Outstanding at March 31, 1997	406,427	1,060,067	1,466,494	$ 13.81
Exercisable at March 31, 1997	291,628	503,604	795,232	$ 13.20
Exercisable at March 31, 1996	216,962	216,962	433,924	12.47
Exercisable at March 31, 1995	172,943	172,944	345,887	11.78

At March 31, 1997, 1,466,494 options were outstanding with exercise prices ranging from $11.70 to $16.375 and with a weighted average remaining contractual life of 4.9 years.

NOTES TO THE FINANCIAL STATEMENTS
ALLIANCE COMMUNICATIONS CORPORATION

9. BUSINESS ACQUISITIONS

During fiscal 1997, the Company acquired an additional 44% ownership interest in Showcase Television Inc. for total consideration of $9,207,000. The consideration was in the form of $7,280,000 cash and 162,807 common shares of the Company. The fair value assigned to the broadcasting licence in this acquisition was $7,266,000. After completion of this acquisition, the Company had a 99% ownership interest in Showcase Television Inc.

10. INTEREST

(In thousands of Canadian dollars)

	1997	1996	1995
Interest expense on long-term debt	$ 1,073	$ 1,195	$ 476
Interest income	(1,282)	(1,550)	(359)
Other	1,505	1,248	165
	$ 1,296	$ 893	$ 282

Interest paid for the year ended March 31, 1997 amounted to $1,925,000 (1996 - $2,040,000, 1995 - $1,332,000).

11. GAIN ON SALE OF INVESTMENT

In September 1996, Mainframe Entertainment Inc. repurchased a portion of the Company's investment in Mainframe for net proceeds of $7,684,000 resulting in a pre-tax gain on sale of $7,544,000. The Company retained a 15% ownership interest in Mainframe (note 21).

12. INCOME TAXES

The differences between the effective tax rate reflected in the provision for income taxes and the Canadian statutory income tax rate are as follows:

	1997	1996	1995
Corporate statutory income tax rate	44.6%	44.6%	44.0%
Add (deduct) the income tax rate effect of:			
Foreign operations subject to different income tax rates	(11.9)	(31.9)	(24.6)
Expenses not deductible for income tax purposes	2.8	2.3	3.4
Other	(0.5)	0.7	(0.8)
	35.0%	15.7%	22.0%

The subsidiaries' non-capital tax losses are approximately $1,180,000, which are available for offset against those subsidiaries' future taxable income. The benefits of these losses, which have not been reflected in these accounts, expire in various years to fiscal 2002.

Details of income taxes are as follows:

(In thousands of Canadian dollars)

	1997	1996
Depreciation	$ 388	$ 185
Financing fees	(1,803)	(995)
Prepaid royalties	5,217	20,067
Development costs	-	3,450
Investment in film and television programs	-	7,622
Other	1,719	1,927
Net operating loss carry-forwards	(2,822)	(21,438)
Deferred income taxes	2,699	10,818
Taxes payable	8,228	-
	$ 10,927	$ 10,818

13. EARNINGS PER SHARE

Earnings per common share is calculated on the basis of 11,919,000 (1996 - 9,840,000, 1995 - 9,543,000) weighted average common shares outstanding.

Fully diluted earnings per common share for 1997 is $1.44 (1996 - $0.99, 1995 - $1.31). This reflects the effects of employee stock options and convertible debenture outstanding as at March 31, 1997 and 1996 and 1995.

14. STATEMENT OF CHANGES IN FINANCIAL POSITION

(In thousands of Canadian dollars)

	1997	1996	1995
Cash provided by (used in):			
Accounts receivable and distribution contracts receivable	$ (40,427)	$ (26,569)	$ (22,388)
Accounts payable and accrued liabilities	38,828	(248)	5,551
Distribution revenue payable	(3,015)	(6,532)	13,223
Deferred revenue	30,274	(498)	(14,607)
Other	(3,710)	(1,526)	(2,952)
Net changes in non-cash working capital balances related to operations	$ 21,950	$ (35,373)	$ (21,173)

15. GOVERNMENT FINANCING AND ASSISTANCE

Revenues include $14,101,000 of production financing obtained from the government for the year ended March 31, 1997 (1996 - $13,824,000, 1995 - $8,881,000). This financing is repayable from distribution revenues in respect of which the financing was made. As revenues from these productions are not currently known, the amounts ultimately repayable to government agencies are not determinable. In addition, revenues include $2,290,000 of government grants (1995 - $693,000, 1994 - $2,406,000).

Investment in film and television programs includes a reduction of $10,291,000 (1996 - $10,810,000, 1995 - $10,209,000) with respect to government assistance for distribution of certain programs. In addition, revenues include $859,000 (1996 - $1,023,000, 1995 - $1,492,000) of government grants. Government assistance may be repayable in whole or in part depending upon future revenues generated by certain individual film and television programs. The potential amounts repayable are not determinable.

16. RELATED PARTY TRANSACTIONS

Included in accounts receivable is $218,000 (1996 - $nil) due from officers of the Company.

17. COMMITMENTS AND CONTINGENCIES

a) The Company is committed with respect to operating leases for office premises and equipment expiring at various dates to May 2007. The future minimum payments under the terms of such leases are as follows:

(In thousands of Canadian dollars)	
1998	$ 2,982
1999	1,679
2000	1,366
2001	1,423
2002	959
Thereafter	3,007
	$ 11,416

Rent expense for 1997 is $2,053,000 (1996 - $1,525,000, 1995 - $1,418,000).

b) The Company is involved in various legal actions. In the opinion of management, any resulting liability is not expected to have a material adverse effect on the Company's financial position.

c) The Company has a letter of credit of US$2,500,000 outstanding at March 31, 1997 (1996 - US$2,500,000, 1995 - US$2,500,000).

18. SEGMENTED INFORMATION

The Company is vertically integrated and operates exclusively in the production, distribution and structured production financing of television programs and motion pictures, broadcasting and music publishing industries, which are considered the dominant industry segments.

Revenues include $113,216,000 (1996 - $100,902,000, 1995 - $105,588,000) derived from foreign sources.

19. FINANCIAL INSTRUMENTS

Fair Value of Financial Instruments

The estimated fair values of financial instruments as at March 31, 1997 and March 31, 1996 are based on relevant market prices and information available at the time. The carrying value of cash and short-term investments, accounts receivable, loans receivable, long-term investments, operating loan and bank indebtedness, accounts payable and accrued liabilities, distribution revenues payable, loans payable, and convertible debenture approximates the fair value of these financial instruments. Financial instruments with a carrying value different from their fair value include:

(In thousands of Canadian dollars)	1997		1996	
	Carrying Value	Fair Value	Carrying Value	Fair Value
Financial Assets:				
Assets for which fair value approximates carrying value	$ 105,932	$ 105,932	$ 59,780	$ 59,780
Distribution contracts receivable	76,272	74,066	64,948	63,283
Financial Liabilities:				
Liabilities for which fair value approximates carrying value	$ 129,352	$ 129,352	$ 97,878	$ 97,878

NOTES TO THE FINANCIAL STATEMENTS
ALLIANCE COMMUNICATIONS CORPORATION

The fair value of distribution contracts receivable is based on discounting future cash flows using rates currently available for similar instruments. The Company has not written these receivables down as it expects to recover their carrying amounts fully by holding them to maturity.

Concentration of Credit Risk
Accounts receivable from the federal government and a government agency in connection with production financing represents 41% of total accounts receivable at March 31, 1997. The Company believes that there is minimal risk associated with the collection of these amounts. The balance of accounts receivable and distribution contracts receivable is widely distributed amongst customers. Loans receivable include amounts due from a relatively small number of customers. The Company maintains an allowance for credit losses in an amount considered adequate to absorb estimated credit-related losses.

20. RECONCILIATION TO UNITED STATES GAAP
The consolidated financial statements of the Company have been prepared in accordance with Canadian GAAP. The following adjustments and/or additional disclosures, would be required in order to present the financial statements in accordance with U.S. GAAP, as required by the United States Securities and Exchange Commission.

Under U.S. GAAP, the net earnings and earnings per common share figures and shareholders' equity for the years ended March 31, 1997, 1996 and 1995 would be adjusted as follows:

(In thousands of Canadian dollars)

	Net Earnings			Shareholders' Equity	
	1997	1996	1995	1997	1996
Canadian GAAP	$ 18,188	$ 10,365	$ 12,975	$ 150,424	$ 95,380
Adjustment to development costs and investment in scripts net of income taxes of $92 (1996 - $648, 1995 - $447)(a)	115	808	(562)	(401)	(516)
Adjustment to operating expenses with respect to stock options (b)	(77)	90	(457)	(799)	(722)
Adjustment to revenue with respect to television license agreements net of income taxes of $662 (1996 - $90, 1995 - $243)(c)	(2,062)	(2,501)	(125)	(5,718)	(3,656)
Adjustment to income tax provision excluding cumulative effect adjustment noted below (d)	-	-	166	193	193
Adjustment to retained earnings with respect to stock options.	-	-	-	799	722
U.S. GAAP excluding cumulative effect adjustment	16,164	8,762	11,997	144,498	91,401
Cumulative effect of income tax adjustment for years prior to April 1, 1993 (d)	-	-	-	(285)	(285)
U.S. GAAP	$ 16,164	$ 8,762	$ 11,997	$ 144,213	$ 91,116
Earnings Per Common Share Based on U.S. GAAP(e)					
Primary	$ 1.35	$ 0.88	$ 1.23		
Fully Diluted	$ 1.30	$ 0.86	$ 1.17		

a) Accounting for Development Costs and Investment in Scripts
Under Statement of Financial Accounting Standards No. 53 "Financial Reporting by Producers and Distributors of Motion Picture Films" (SFAS 53), expenditures associated with the development of stories and scenarios are expensed as incurred while expenditures for properties such as film rights to books, stage plays, original screenplays, etc. are expensed if the property has been held for three years and has not been set for production. Under Canadian GAAP, development costs and investment in scripts is amortized over three years commencing in the year following the year such costs are incurred. The net difference of the two adjustments is disclosed as a U.S. GAAP reconciling item.

b) Accounting for Stock Options and Share Issuances
During fiscal 1997, the Company adopted the disclosure-only provisions of Statement of Financial Accounting Standards No. 123 "Accounting for Stock-Based Compensation" (SFAS 123) but, as permitted, continues to apply Accounting Principles Board Opinion No. 25 "Accounting for Stock Issued to Employees" (APB 25) in accounting for its employee stock option plan for U.S. GAAP reconciliation purposes.

For the year ended March 31, 1996, compensatory employee stock options were issued and vested in the year. In accordance with APB 25, the difference between the quoted market price and the option price is recorded as compensation expense over the vesting period.

For the years ended March 31, 1997 and 1995, no compensatory employee stock options were issued which resulted in a compensation expense, however, a compensatory expense was recognized for options issued in prior years as they vested in the year.

Under SFAS 123, the Company's pro forma net earnings for U.S. GAAP would be $15,123,000 (1996 - $8,459,000) and primary earnings per common share would be $1.26 (1996 - $0.85).

As the provisions of SFAS 123 have not been applied to options granted prior to January 1, 1995, the resulting pro forma compensation cost may not be representative of that to be expected in future years.

For disclosure purposes the fair value of each stock option grant is estimated on the date of grant using the Black-Scholes option pricing model with the following weighted average assumptions used for stock options granted in 1997 and 1996, respectively: expected dividend yields of 0.0% for both years, expected volatility of 41.4% and 39.9%, risk-free interest rate of 5.9% and 6.5% and expected life of 3 years for all grants. The weighted average fair value of the stock options granted in 1997 and 1996 was $4.77 and $5.30, respectively.

c) Revenue Recognition From Television License Agreements
Under Canadian GAAP, revenues from license agreements for television programs are recognized as earned when the television program is completed and delivered, when amounts are due from exhibitor or when a contract is executed that irrevocably transfers distribution rights to a licensee, and there is reasonable assurance of collectability of proceeds. Under SFAS 53, revenues from license agreements for television programs are recognized at the time the license periods commence instead of at the time the license agreements are executed.

d) Accounting for Income Taxes
Effective April 1, 1993, the Company adopted Statement of Financial Accounting Standards No. 109 "Accounting for Income Taxes" (SFAS 109) for U.S. GAAP reconciliation purposes. The adoption of SFAS 109 changes the Company's method of accounting for income taxes from the deferral method to the asset and liability method. SFAS 109 requires recognition of deferred tax liabilities and assets for the expected future tax consequences of assets and liabilities that have been recognized in the financial statements.

As a result of the adoption of SFAS 109, the Company recognized an additional expense of $285,000, representing the cumulative effect of the change on results for year prior to April 1, 1993.

Under U.S. GAAP, the provision for income taxes for the year ended March 31, 1997 would be $9,218,000 (1996 - $2,493,000, 1995 - $2,802,000).

The application of SFAS 109 would increase broadcasting licences and income taxes by approximately $5,850,000 at March 31, 1997 (1996 - $nil).

e) Earnings per Common Share
Under Accounting Principles Board Opinion No. 15 "Earnings per Share" (APB 15), earnings per share is based on the weighted average number of common shares issued and outstanding and common stock equivalents, including stock options and warrants.

Certain stock options and shares are considered to have been outstanding from the beginning of the year for the earnings per common share calculations at March 31, 1997, 1996 and 1995. The treasury stock method was applied in the earnings per common share calculations.

Primary earnings per common share is calculated on the basis of 11,985,000 (1996 - 9,922,000, 1995 - 9,719,000) weighted average shares outstanding.

For U.S. GAAP disclosure purposes, the Company will adopt the new U.S. GAAP standard for computing earnings per share, Statement of Financial Accounting Standards No. 128 "Earnings Per Share" (SFAS 128) for the year ended March 31, 1998. The effect of applying SFAS 128 to years prior to March 31, 1998 does not produce a materially different earnings per share as computed under APB 15.

f) Consolidated Statements of Cash Flows
The Company's cash flows determined in accordance with U.S. GAAP would be as follows:

(In thousands of Canadian dollars)

	1997	1996	1995
Operating activities	$ 238,383	$ 174,282	$ 166,992
Investing activities	(252,676)	(195,037)	(198,479)
Financing activities	19,867	7,732	18,193
Effect of exchange rates on cash	113	(747)	218
Increase (decrease) in cash and cash equivalents	$ 5,687	($13,770)	$ (13,076)

21. SUBSEQUENT EVENT

On June 17, 1997, the Company sold a portion of its investment in Mainframe Entertainment Inc. in connection with Mainframe's initial public offering for net proceeds of $4,594,000 and realized a pre-tax gain on sale of $4,535,000. The Company retained a 7% ownership interest in Mainframe.

ATLANTIS
20TH ANNIVERSARY
1978–1998

Contents

1 1997 Highlights
2 Message to Shareholders
25 Management's Discussion and Analysis
32 Management's and Auditor's Reports
33 Consolidated Financial Statements

Financial Highlights

For the years ended December 31 (in millions of dollars, except per share information)	1997	1996	Change
Operating Results			
Revenue	$ 178	$ 138	29 %
Net earnings before unusual items	$ 5.6	$ 3.4	65 %
Net earnings	$ 5.6	$ 6.9(1)	(19)%
Financial Position			
Completed programs	$ 46.9	$ 44.7	5 %
Cash, net of loans payable	$ 19.8	$ 3.1	539 %
Interim financing	$ 67.1	$ 27.2	147 %
Shareholders' equity	$ 97.1	$ 68.8	41 %
Per Share Information			
Net earnings before unusual items	$ 0.55	$ 0.35	57 %
Net earnings	$ 0.55	$ 0.72(1)	(24)%
Book value	$ 7.82	$ 7.16	9 %
Shares Outstanding *(millions)*			
Average for the year	10.1	9.6	5 %
At year end	12.4(2)	9.6	29 %

Note (1): 1996 Net earnings include the gain on sale of the Company's interest in YTV of $3.5 million or $0.37 per share.
(2): Includes the conversion into common shares of 2.3 million Special Warrants issued in December 1997.

Net earnings before unusual items
($ millions)

Net earnings per share before unusual items
($)

1997 Highlights

★ ATLANTIS delivered 104 hours of original television drama, up 18 per cent from 1996, representing the renewal of four existing series, two new series and two television movies.

★ ATLANTIS' series *Gene Roddenberry's Earth: Final Conflict®* was the highest-rated original one-hour series to have entered U.S. syndication in the past two years.

★ ATLANTIS' television movie *Borrowed Hearts: A Holiday Romance* was the highest-rated program on all of American television for the last week of November 1997, garnering 30 million viewers in the U.S. and Canada.

★ ATLANTIS acquired 50 per cent of Calibre Digital Pictures, a leading animation and digital effects company, and reached an agreement to acquire Ironstar Communications, a Canadian distributor with a library of 300 hours.

★ ATLANTIS successfully launched Home & Garden Television (HGTV) Canada and imported the Food Network into over four million homes on October 17, 1997.

★ ATLANTIS applied to the CRTC (Canadian Radio-television and Telecommunications Commission) for five new Canadian cable channels: Food Network Canada, National Geographic Channel Canada, FIT TV Canada, Canada's Health Network and People Channel and is a minority partner in the CHAOS TV application.

★ ATLANTIS completed a successful $20 million equity offering in December 1997.

★ ATLANTIS' stock price closed the year at $10.50, a 50 per cent increase over the prior year.

Message to Shareholders

Nineteen ninety-seven was a year of operational, financial and strategic success for Atlantis Communications Inc. We achieved significant growth in revenues and net income and we did so in a manner that achieved our primary goal – to increase the ongoing sustainability and reliability of the growth in our operating results. The strategies we employed to achieve this primary goal in 1997 will be continued going forward.

Michael MacMillan, Chairman and Chief Executive Officer *(right)*, **Lewis Rose,** President *(left)*, on the set of *Traders*

Our first key strategy, given that the largest segment of our business is the production and distribution of original prime time television drama, was to increase the production of series that were renewable from year to year (as opposed to stand alone television movies). We wanted series that provide ongoing opportunities for future exploitation once a critical mass of episodes has been produced. We wanted series where Atlantis controlled major distribution rights.

All four of our one-hour series were renewed in 1997 – *Traders, PSI FACTOR®: Chronicles of the Paranormal, The Outer Limits* and *The Adventures of Sinbad;* as well, we launched two new series – *Cold Squad* and *Gene Roddenberry's Earth: Final Conflict®*. Importantly, the newer series – *Cold Squad, Gene Roddenberry's Earth: Final Conflict®* and *PSI FACTOR®: Chronicles of the Paranormal* – are all series where the Canadian and major international distribution rights are controlled by Atlantis.

Already, five of our series from 1997 have been renewed for 1998 and our two new series announced to date – *The World of Peter Cottontail* and *Sixth Grade Alien* – are also series to which Atlantis controls Canadian and all international distribution rights.

Reliable and sustainable earnings are also created through "output" or "package" deals, whereby customers commit to acquire a certain volume of programming prior to the programs being produced or even identified. Atlantis recently entered into a major "package" deal with the leading European entertainment company, Endemol Entertainment of The Netherlands. Endemol agreed to license European, African and Middle Eastern rights to a number of television series and movies produced by Atlantis in 1998 and each of the next two years, as well as a selection of Atlantis' library catalogue. This arrangement will continue to increase the predictability of our growth and provide revenue to Atlantis of $115 million over the three years.

The second key strategy we employed last year was to leverage the strength of our distribution infrastructure to take advantage of Atlantis' knowledge of and relationships within the Canadian and international television marketplace. We sought to add additional product lines to be exploited by our distribution company, Atlantis Releasing, so that we could grow our sales with only modest incremental costs.

This is why we were pleased to be named the exclusive Canadian distributor of CBS television programming. The CBS appointment began in 1997 and has an initial three-year term. This means that Atlantis is the distributor in Canada of such shows as *Touched By An Angel, 60 Minutes* and *Brooklyn South,* among others.

Likewise, our recent purchase of Canadian distributor Ironstar Communications gives Atlantis access to Ironstar's program library for both Canadian and international exploitation.

It was for similar distribution leverage purposes that we decided to increase the children's program component of our catalogue. By adding animation and more live action children's series to our production activity we feed our established distribution strength while complementing our core prime time drama catalogue. Thus, in 1997, we acquired 50 per cent of Calibre Digital Pictures, a successful Canadian animation company which creates all types of animation including leading edge computer generated animation. Calibre continues to grow under the leadership of its founder, Neil Williamson, and we intend to purchase the remainder of Calibre within two years.

In 1998 we are growing our animation and live action children's initiatives with success. We recently licensed two new series to YTV Canada, which we are currently placing with other buyers internationally. These are the live action series *Sixth Grade Alien,* based on new books by best selling children's author Bruce Coville and the animated series *The World of Peter Cottontail,* based on the celebrated books by author Thornton W. Burgess. We are fortunate to mark our entry into animation with a property as well known and popular as *The World of Peter Cottontail.*

The final key strategy for 1997 was to continue aggressively to develop our broadcasting activities. Last year we secured national analogue carriage of our new specialty channel Home & Garden Television (HGTV) Canada, which launched on October 17, 1997. Already, HGTV Canada is attracting a positive viewer and advertiser response and we are optimistic for its continued growth and financial success.

On September 30, 1997 Atlantis applied to the CRTC for permission to launch five new specialty channels, controlled by Atlantis – People Channel, National Geographic Channel Canada, Food Network Canada, FIT TV Canada and Canada's Health Network. We believe that each of these concepts will, if approved by the CRTC, be an excellent complement to our two existing channels, Life Network and HGTV Canada.

As an interim measure, Atlantis is the exclusive agent for Food Network (U.S.), which we are currently importing into four million Canadian cable homes. Our agreement with the owners of Food Network (U.S.), E.W. Scripps Co. (the owner of HGTV in the U.S. and our partner in HGTV Canada), is that when the CRTC approves our Food Network Canada application, Food Network (U.S.) will voluntarily withdraw from Canada. Then, Food Network Canada, which Atlantis will control and manage, will replace it.

E.W. Scripps Co. will become a 29 per cent shareholder in the Canadian channel, and Shaw Communications will own 20 per cent.

In recognition of the importance of our broadcasting activities, in 1997 we created a new business unit called Atlantis Broadcasting, incorporating Life Network, HGTV Canada, Food Network and the pending applications. Juris Silkans, who has played a key role in the development of Life Network and HGTV Canada, now has an expanded leadership role as President of Atlantis Broadcasting.

The North American television marketplace continues to change substantially and quickly; viewers clearly enjoy having an increased choice of channels to watch. As well, they obviously enjoy watching "themed" channels where they reliably know the type of programming to be presented.

In Canada and the U.S., viewing of specialty and pay channels has now risen to approximately 30 per cent of total television viewing. This is astounding growth, particularly in the last few years. Television advertising revenue in North America has not yet caught up to reflect this fundamental shift in how viewers are using television. We believe that advertising spending will shift to reflect the trends in actual viewing; as such, specialty channels like ours have an exciting and substantial growth opportunity.

In 1998 our broadcasting focus will be to grow HGTV Canada through its first full year, while we prepare for the CRTC hearings on the new channel applications, anticipated to be in the first quarter of 1999. Meanwhile, we are pursuing other possibilities of expanding the "brand" value of our existing channels both within Canada and through international opportunities.

I am particularly pleased that the strategies and initiatives described here have also been reflected in increased shareholder value. The Atlantis stock price began 1997 at $7.00 and finished the year at $10.50 – an increase of exactly 50 per cent. In the first months of 1998 the price has continued to strengthen. We completed a successful equity issue in December 1997, raising approximately $20 million of equity at $9.00/share. That equity issue combined with the increase in share price has materially increased the size of our market capitalization.

This year marks the 20th anniversary of Atlantis and the theme of this year's annual report celebrates these two decades. We are very proud of what we have accomplished and created. The growth and success of Atlantis over these 20 years reflects the growth of our industry worldwide. When we started Atlantis there was no meaningful use of VCRs in homes; there was no significant pay television or specialty television; there was limited private ownership of television networks outside of North America. Atlantis' growth was possible, in part, because of the new methods of delivering filmed entertainment to viewers. Looking ahead, the methods of delivering entertainment and information will continue to diversify and evolve with the advent of the Internet, digital signals and other, still unknown, opportunities. As these new technologies become real, we will again be reminded that, as in the past, it is the content, not the hardware, which ultimately matters the most. That is where we come in.

To ensure that we participate fully in this exciting future we will need to continue to attract and retain the best and the brightest to our management team and attract the best creative talent to all of our productions. That, I believe, is how we arrived at our position today. Over the past few years we have significantly strengthened our management, both corporately and within each of our operating companies. Included in those positive moves was the 1997 appointment of Lewis Rose as President of Atlantis Communications Inc.

Looking forward to the next two decades I am particularly thankful for the continuing friendship and business partnership with Seaton McLean. Seaton co-founded Atlantis with Janice Platt and me, amongst others, in 1978. Seaton has provided Atlantis its inspiration and leadership every step of the way for each of those 20 years.

Similarly, I look forward to the ongoing and vital contributions and friendships with Ted Riley and Peter Sussman who have shared most of the past 20 years with us and who initiated and led our expansion internationally and into the U.S.

Atlantis has extremely talented and dedicated employees. The achievements of 20 years and the prospect for future growth would, clearly, never have been possible without our terrific team, both past and present.

I also offer a heartfelt thank you to our casts, crews, writers, directors and all those who participate in the production of our programs, including producers, suppliers, broadcast customers and financiers, as well as to our shareholders and our Board of Directors whose advice is always appreciated.

Atlantis begins its third decade with a clear sense of opportunity, excitement and growth. The best is yet to come.

Michael I.M. MacMillan
Chairman and
Chief Executive Officer

Management's Discussion and Analysis

The following discussion and analysis for the years ended December 31, 1997 and 1996 should be read in conjunction with the consolidated financial statements and the notes to the consolidated financial statements included in this annual report.

Atlantis Communications Inc. is a leading international producer, distributor and broadcaster of popular high-quality television programming for audiences worldwide. Television Production includes the production of television programs, as well as ownership and management of studios and post-production facilities. Television Distribution includes the licensing of both proprietary Atlantis-produced and third-party acquired television programming. Atlantis' Broadcasting interests include 100% of the specialty channel Life Network, and a controlling 67% interest in the specialty channel Home & Garden Television (HGTV) Canada. Atlantis Broadcasting also is the exclusive agent in Canada for Food Network, FiT TV and America's Health Network.

The impact of the two broad business areas, Television Production/Distribution and Broadcasting, on the Company's results and financial position is discussed below.

Operating Results

Revenue

The Company's total revenue of $178.0 million increased by $40.0 million (29%) in 1997. Revenue from the Production/Distribution business increased by $35.8 million (32%) to $149.4 million, while revenue from the Broadcasting business increased by $4.1 million (19%) to $26.0 million, and Other Revenue, primarily from investments, increased by $0.1 million to $2.6 million.

Production/Distribution Revenue

Production/Distribution revenue consists of program licence revenue, other program revenue, and post-production revenue. The results of the Production/Distribution operations may vary significantly in any period depending on the number of hours of television programs delivered in that period. As a result, the Company's earnings for any one period are not necessarily indicative of results for future periods.

Program Licence Revenue

Program licence revenue is comprised of pre-sale licencing revenue (licensing of Atlantis-produced programs prior to the delivery of the program) as well as after-sale licencing revenue (licensing of completed Atlantis-produced programs or completed programs acquired from third parties). Program licence revenue is recognized when a program is delivered, the licence period begins and the collectability of proceeds is reasonably assured. In the case of a television series, revenue is recognized on a pro-rata episodic basis.

Program licence revenue increased $45.8 million (50%) to $137.4 million, largely as a result of increased revenue from pre-sale licencing and after-sales of *Gene Rodden-*

Revenue Analysis

(millions)	1997		1996	
Production/Distribution Revenue				
Program Licence	**$ 137.4**	**77%**	$ 91.6	66%
Other Program	**$ 10.9**	**6%**	$ 20.8	15%
Post-Production	**$ 1.1**	**1%**	$ 1.2	1%
	$ 149.4	**84%**	$ 113.6	82%
Broadcast Revenue	**$ 26.0**	**15%**	$ 21.9	16%
Other Revenue	**$ 2.6**	**1%**	$ 2.5	2%
Total Revenue	**$ 178.0**	**100%**	$ 138.0	100%

berry's Earth: Final Conflict® and *Cold Squad*, two new series added to the Atlantis slate during 1997. An increase in the number of episodes delivered of both *PSI FACTOR®: Chronicles of the Paranormal* and *The Adventures of Sinbad* also contributed to the significant year over year increase in program licence revenue. The 1997 library revenues increased by $5.6 million (52%) to $16.3 million and included the sale of all 65 episodes of the family drama *Neon Rider* to Pax Net, the new Paxson Communications Network in the U.S.

Atlantis continues to generate the majority (89%) of its program licence revenues from outside Canada, with 47% (46% – 1996) from the United States and 42% (43% – 1996) from other markets around the world (see chart). This reflects the global appeal of Atlantis' programming.

Other Program Revenue

Other program revenue is comprised of revenue raised by the Company from third-party sources to fund production costs. This revenue includes non-recourse investments in programs by government agencies and broadcasters and financing from the Canada Television and Cable Production Fund in both years. During 1996, other program revenue also included interest income from limited partnership syndications and proceeds from the sale of copyright to limited partnership syndications. Other program revenue is recognized when a program is delivered and the collectability of proceeds is reasonably assured. In the case of a television series, revenue is recognized on a pro-rata episodic basis.

Other program revenue declined by $9.9 million (48%) to $10.9 million. The decrease was due to the fact that 1996 was the final year in which the Company recognized revenue related to interest income and proceeds from sales of copyright to limited partnership syndications. The revenue recognized on these limited partnership syndications in 1996 was $11.9 million and related to purchase agreements entered into prior to December 31, 1995. During 1995, amendments to the Income Tax Act arising from the February 1995 Federal Budget were implemented to eliminate new limited partnership syndications of Canadian certified film and television productions effective December 31, 1995.

Other program revenue of $10.9 million in 1997, primarily represents financing from government incentive and regulatory programs, up from $8.9 million in 1996. In early 1998, the Federal government announced a three-year commitment for the CTCPF (Canada Television Cable Production Fund), but there is no assurance as to the eligibility criteria for programs, the funding caps, or the availability of funds for Atlantis programs given the first come first served nature of the Licence Fee Program.

Program Licence Revenue – Geographic Analysis

(millions)	1997		1996	
Canada	**$ 15.5**	**11%**	$ 10.1	11%
United States	**$ 64.1**	**47%**	$ 42.3	46%
Other Markets	**$ 57.8**	**42%**	$ 39.2	43%
Total Program Licence Revenue	**$ 137.4**	**100%**	$ 91.6	100%

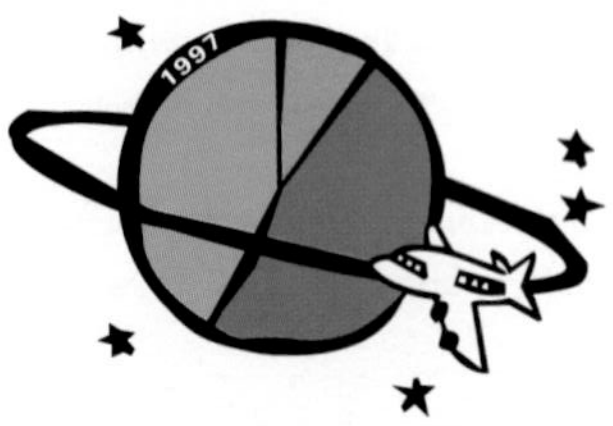

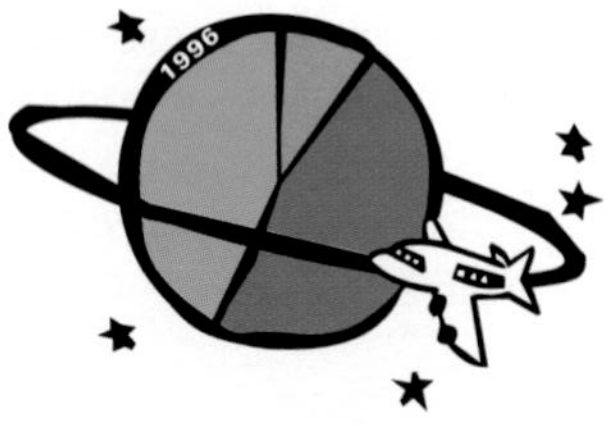

The Company continues to emphasize the creation of more commercial, market-driven programming which can be increasingly financed by pre-sale licences from the international market, with reduced reliance on the domestic market and related government incentives.

Post-Production Revenue

Post-production revenue is comprised of revenue from sound mixing, picture editing, and sound editing services for both television and theatrical films provided by a wholly-owned subsidiary, Casablanca Sound & Picture Inc., and is recognized as services are performed. In 1997, post-production revenue was $1.1 million ($1.2 million – 1996) after elimination of $4.0 million ($2.8 million – 1996) in respect of services performed for production companies in the associated Atlantis group of companies.

Broadcast Revenue

Broadcast revenue in 1997 is derived from the operation of the Company's specialty television channels: Life Network and HGTV Canada. Broadcasting revenue is comprised of two principal sources: cable subscriber revenue and advertising revenue. Cable subscriber revenue increased by $0.4 million (3%) to $13.8 million as the number of households that receive Life Network increased by 300,000 to 5.7 million at December 31, 1997. The HGTV Canada signal was received by over 4.0 million households at December 31, 1997 and was still in the free preview period at that date.

Advertising, ancillary and other revenue increased by $3.7 million (44%) to $12.2 million in 1997. This increase was due to continued advertiser confidence in Life Network's ability to deliver significant ratings from a desirable audience demographic, together with the launch of HGTV Canada on October 17, 1997 which provided synergies for the sales effort. The results have been a continued increase in sales of commercial time at more favourable rates during 1997.

Amortization

Amortization of $150.1 million in 1997 ($116.1 million – 1996) was comprised of amortization of completed programs, costs of distributing programs, amortization of broadcast rights and development costs.

Amortization of Atlantis-produced programs as a percentage of Production/Distribution revenue was 88% in 1997, which compares to 87% in 1996.

The Company's completed program asset represents the original cost of completed programs, net of accumulated amortization. The completed program inventory contains 745 hours of Atlantis-produced programming, including 104 hours delivered in 1997.

1997 Production Activity

Production Initiated in 1997	Episode Length (hours)	Total Series/ Movie Budget ($ millions)	Number of Hours Delivered Q1	Q2	Q3	Q4	1997	1998	Key Broadcasters
T.V. Series									
Gene Roddenberry's Earth: Final Conflict® I	1.0	37	—	—	3.0	10.0	**13.0**	9.0	Tribune Entertainment – U.S. Syndication, CTV/Baton Broadcasting System
Cold Squad I	1.0	11	—	—	—	6.0	**6.0**	5.0	CTV/Baton Broadcasting System
Outer Limits IIIB	1.0	41	—	—	—	2.0	**2.0**	20.0	Showtime, MGM – U.S. Syndication, Global
PSI FACTOR®: Chronicles of the Paranormal II	1.0	23	—	1.0	6.0	9.0	**16.0**	6.0	EYEMARK Entertainment (CBS) – U.S. Syndication, Global
The Adventures of Sinbad II	1.0	31	—	—	5.0	8.0	**13.0**	9.0	All American – U.S. Syndication, Global
Traders III	1.0	18	—	—	4.0	10.0	**14.0**	8.0	Global, CBC
T.V. Movies									
Borrowed Hearts: A Holiday Romance	2.0	6	—	—	2.0	—	**2.0**	—	CBS, CTV/Baton Broadcasting System
The Return of Alex Kelly	2.0	7	—	—	—	2.0	**2.0**	—	CBS, CTV/Baton Broadcasting System
			—	1.0	20.0	47.0	**68.0**	57.0	

Production Initiated in 1996 and delivered in 1997	Episode Length (hours)	Total Series/ Movie Budget ($ millions)	Number of Hours Delivered 1996	Q1	Q2	Q3	Q4	1997	1998	Key Broadcasters
T.V. Series										
Flash Forward II	0.5	8	8.0	3.0	—	—	—	**3.0**	—	ABC, Disney Channel, Family Channel (Canada), Global
Outer Limits IIIA	1.0	41	5.0	7.0	8.0	2.0	—	**17.0**	—	Showtime, MGM – U.S. Syndication, Global, TMN, Superchannel
PSI FACTOR®: Chronicles of the Paranormal I	1.0	22	16.0	5.0	1.0	—	—	**6.0**	—	EYEMARK Entertainment (CBS) – U.S. Syndication, Global
The Adventures of Sinbad	1.0	32	12.0	7.0	3.0	—	—	**10.0**	—	All American – U.S. Syndication, Global
			41.0	22.0	12.0	2.0	—	**36.0**	—	
Total number of hours delivered				22.0	13.0	22.0	47.0	**104.0**	57.0	

In addition, the Atlantis library contains 362 hours of acquired programs (including 300 hours obtained in the Ironstar acquisition which closed in early 1998). Atlantis also represents other third-party programs such as the CBS catalogue.

The Company utilizes the individual film forecast computation method in amortizing its completed programs. Capitalized production and/or acquisition costs, together with the estimated total cost of any residual payments, or other participations related to a particular program, are amortized in the ratio that revenue generated by the program in a particular period bears to management's estimate of total gross revenue, to be realized from that program over the next four years. Although the value of the completed programs at December 31, 1997, is expected to be fully amortized by December 31, 2001, management is confident that the library will continue to generate revenue well beyond the amortization period.

At December 31, 1997, the Company had amortized 92% of the original cost of its completed programs. The Company anticipates that these programs will be fully amortized after four years.

Amortization is based on management's estimates of future revenues, and as such, any significant negative variation between the estimated revenue and the actual revenue realized over time in respect of a program may require a write-down of that program. Management controls this risk by periodically reviewing and updating the estimates and assumptions involved in the calculations used to amortize the program inventory in the context of a continually changing marketplace.

The Company has applied for tax credits under federal and provincial tax credit programs. This funding, along with government grants, has been reflected as a reduction to the cost of completed programs in the amount of $16.5 million ($9.9 million – 1996), and a reduction of $2.6 million ($2.5 million – 1996) to the cost of programs in process.

Amortization of Broadcast rights in 1997 was 60% of total Broadcast revenue, compared with 75% in 1996. The Company's Broadcast rights asset represents the original cost of broadcast programming net of accumulated amortization. The Broadcast rights are amortized over the exclusivity period of the contract, if applicable, or otherwise over one-half of the duration of the contract.

The decrease in the ratio of Broadcast rights amortization to total Broadcast revenue can be attributed to the change in the required level of spending on Canadian content as required by condition of licence between Life Network's first and second year of operation. In 1997, Life Network's conditions of licence required it to maintain Canadian program expenditures at a level equal to 65% of the previous year's revenue from regulated broadcast activities less a 5% allowable variance. In its first full year of operation, ended August 31, 1996, Life Network expended $15.2 million on Canadian program expenditures, which was within the 5% allowable variance of the initial year requirement of $16.0 million in Canadian program expenditures.

HGTV Canada's conditions of licence will require it to maintain Canadian program expenditures at a level equal to 50% of the previous year's revenue from regulated broadcast activities within a 5% allowable variance. For its first year of operation, an expenditure level was not established as part of the licence conditions. Management expects that both Life Network and HGTV Canada will continue to meet this condition of licence at future fiscal year ends.

Operating Expense

Operating expense, net of capitalized operating expenses which relate directly to programs and development projects, increased by $0.3 million (2%) to $14.1 million in 1997. Gross operating expenses increased by $3.3 million (17%) to $22.9 million.

The entire increase in gross operating expenses is attributable to the Broadcasting group where additional costs were incurred for the start-up of the HGTV Canada channel and to accommodate growth at Life Network. The Company capitalized $2.1 million of pre-operating expenses for HGTV Canada, which represented $3.0 million of operating expenses net of advertising and ancillary revenue of $0.9 million. These capitalized operating costs will be amortized over five years from the commencement of commercial operations.

While gross operating expenses of $13.0 million did not increase in the Television Production/Distribution area, additional operating costs were capitalized to reflect the increased level of production activity for television programming during 1997.

Depreciation

Depreciation includes depreciation expense for fixed assets and the amortization expense related to goodwill, deferred start-up costs and other assets.

Depreciation expense increased by $1.3 million to $3.0 million in 1997. The increase relates to the goodwill associated with the Life Network acquisition, amortization of deferred start-up costs associated with Life Network and additional depreciation on capital expenditures made during 1997. The majority of the capital expenditures of $5.7 million were for broadcasting equipment associated with the start-up of HGTV Canada ($3.6 million) and information technology and financial systems investment throughout the Company ($0.8 million).

Gain on Sale of Investment
On August 30, 1996, the Company sold its 28% interest in YTV for net proceeds of approximately $25 million. The Company accounted for its share of equity earnings from YTV, as well as for amortization of related goodwill incurred in connection with the acquisition of its interest in YTV, up until the date of disposition. The gain on the sale of this investment was $5.3 million before taxes ($3.5 million or $0.37 cents per share, on an after-tax basis). The proceeds of disposition were retained by the Company in general cash reserves and contributed to the increase in the Company's cash and marketable securities at December 31, 1996 and the reduction in the Company's interest expense in 1996.

Interest Expense
Interest expense decreased by approximately $0.4 million (29%) in 1997. This decrease was primarily due to an increase in the average cash position of the Company throughout 1997. Interest expense attributable to interim financing is included in the production costs of the particular program to which it relates, and therefore does not appear as interest expense on the Company's Consolidated Statement of Earnings.

Income Taxes
The Company's effective income tax rate for 1997 was 43.7% of earnings before taxes (1996 – 34.7%). This effective tax rate reflects a 15.8% reduction in the effective income tax rate due to the utilization of loss carry-forwards, an increase in the income tax rate due to non-deductible expenses (5.8%), an accrual for income tax contingencies (8.4%) and other adjustments (0.7%).

The Company is currently undergoing audits of the taxation years ended 1992 to 1994 by Revenue Canada and the taxation years ended 1993 to 1995 by the Ontario Ministry of Revenue. The Company has not been reassessed by either body, and as such, any reassessment may result in additional tax liability not currently reflected in the Company's financial statements.

EBITDA (Earnings before interest, taxes, depreciation and amortization)
EBITDA for 1997 increased by $5.7 million (71%) to $13.7 million. The improvement in EBITDA results from increased margin from the production, distribution and broadcast of television programs, partially offset by a slight increase in net operating expenses.

Net Earnings
Net earnings for 1997 were $5.6 million, compared with net earnings before unusual items of $3.4 million for 1996. The total 1996 net earnings of $6.9 million included an after-tax gain of $3.5 million, or $0.37 per share, on the sale of the Company's interest in YTV (see Gain on Sale of Investment).

Net earnings per share in 1997, before unusual items, increased by $0.20 or 57% to $0.55 from $0.35 in 1996. Total net earnings per share in 1997 were $0.55 compared with $0.72 in 1996, which included the $0.37 per share after-tax gain described above.

The 1997 per share calculation is based on a weighted average of 10,067,074 shares outstanding (1996 – 9,603,294 shares). There were 10,119,244 shares outstanding at December 31, 1997.

Earnings before income taxes, before unusual items, were $9.8 million in 1997 compared with $4.9 million in 1996. The increase in earnings before income taxes, before unusual items, is a result of the increased margin from the production, distribution and broadcast of television programs ($6.0 million), plus a reduction in interest expense ($0.4 million). The increase in earnings was partially offset by increases in operating expenses ($0.2 million) and depreciation ($1.3 million).

Liquidity and Capital Resources

Cash and Cash Equivalents
During 1997, the Company's cash and cash equivalents increased by $15.6 million to $29.7 million at December 31, 1997. Net cash (cash and cash equivalents less loans payable) increased by $16.7 million to $19.8 million at December 31, 1997. In addition to these cash reserves, the Company has unused operating lines of credit of $22.4 million with Canadian chartered banks, and separate interim financing arrangements for productions.

The Company also has financing commitments, from a Canadian chartered bank for $29.4 million, which support the applications for five new specialty channels. The financing will be available to fund the Company's investment and operating debts in the specialty channels, should licence(s) be awarded.

The Company is generally required to make significant initial expenditures either to produce its own television programs or to acquire programs from third parties. As the revenues from these programs are received by the Company over an extended period of time, the Company has traditionally financed its working capital requirements in this initial period through cash generated by operations and its lines of credit. In the case of television series, where cash flow requirements are more substantial, the Company uses self-liquidating interim financing loans, primarily from Canadian chartered banks.

Cash used in Operating Activities
During 1997, the Company had a net cash inflow of $133 million compared with $137 million in 1996. The net use of cash was to primarily finance accounts receivable associated with the increased production activity and interim funding of applications for federal and provincial tax credit programs for both the 1996 and 1997 programs. This use of cash was partially offset by an increase in gross margin from television production, distribution and broadcasting activity.

Cash used in Investing Activities
During 1997, the Company had a cash outflow from investing activity of $181 million compared with $128 million in 1996. The 1997 cash outflow included increased investments in programs in process and completed programs due to the increased production activity ($30 million), increased expenditures for capital and other assets mainly associated with the start-up of HGTV Canada ($4 million) and the investment in Calibre Digital Pictures ($2 million).

The remaining variance results from activities in 1996, where the Company received proceeds of $25 million on the sale of its interest in YTV, partially offset by the purchase of the remaining 43% interest in the Life Network for $9 million.

Cash provided from Financing Activities
During 1997, the Company funded its operating and investment activities mainly through the use of interim financing and a private placement of Special Warrants that took place in December 1997. The cash provided from financing activities was $64 million for 1997 ($1 million – 1996).

Interim Financing
During 1997, the Company received $40 million of interim financing ($5 million – 1996) to support the increased production activity and the applications for tax credits under federal and provincial tax credit programs.

Interim financing on programs is debt which the Company raises in respect of a specific program in order to bridge the cash flow requirements of that program during its production. Interim financing is generally 100% secured by assigned accounts receivable of the program to which it relates. As such, the debt is self-liquidating. Interest expense attributable to interim financing is included in the production costs of the particular program to which it relates, and therefore does not appear as interest expense on the Company's Consolidated Statement of Earnings.

During 1997, the Company actively financed its programs through the use of an interim $45 million Production Revolver Facility with the Royal Bank of Canada. During 1997, the Company re-negotiated the terms of this facility, in conjunction with its lines of credit to obtain a more favourable overall credit package which provides lower borrowing costs and more efficient administration. The overall average interest rate for interim financing during 1997 was 4.7%, compared with 7.3% during 1996. The lower rate for 1997 is a result of the improved borrowing terms of the Production Revolver Facility and a lower average Canadian prime borrowing rate during 1997.

Private Placement of Special Warrants
On December 23, 1997, the Company issued 2,292,400 Special Warrants for cash consideration of $20.6 million ($9 per share). The Company's share issue costs including the underwriters' fees and expenses totaled $1.9 million ($1.0 million after taxes). On February 9, 1998, all of the Special Warrants were converted into subordinate voting shares on a one-for-one basis. As at April 2, 1998, there were 8,180,645 subordinated voting shares outstanding (12,418,144 total shares).

Year 2000
The year 2000 poses a challenge to businesses that are reliant on computer systems or other equipment that use the last two digits to represent a year. The Company has performed an analysis of the risks and uncertainties arising from the year 2000 issue and developed a plan to address the risks and uncertainties. The plan is reviewed on an ongoing basis by executive management and the Board of Directors. The scope of the analysis includes all computer hardware products, computer software products, broadcasting, production, post-production, animation equipment, and general office equipment. This analysis will be expanded to include the systems of the Company's key suppliers, customers and bankers during 1998.

The Company's inventory of software includes mainly third-party products and some custom-developed applications. The custom-developed applications, which have been implemented recently, were designed with four digit date processing and are fully year 2000 compliant.

An inventory of substantially all third-party hardware and software products has been taken and the state of year 2000 readiness evaluated. A significant number of products are already year 2000 compliant and supplier certifications from other third-party vendors have been obtained or are being pursued as part of the implementation plan. The Year 2000 plan includes some limited testing of major systems to ensure year 2000 compliance, in addition to relying on supplier certifications and the experience of their clients who conduct tests on these products. Contingency plans will be developed for any product where supplier certification has not been provided during fiscal 1998.

The costs associated with the Year 2000 plan are mainly administrative costs and will be incurred by existing in-house staff from 1997 through the year 1999. These costs will be expensed as incurred and are not expected to be material. The Company's existing budget for information technology includes the replacement of desktop technology and key financial operating systems during fiscal 1998. The replacement products that have been selected for implementation during 1998 are year 2000 compliant.

The Company presently believes that through testing and upgrading its systems and working with third-party vendors, it will ensure a smooth transition for the Company and its customers.

Outlook

The Company is committed to growth through excellence in television programming.

For 1998, five of the Company's six 1997 television series have been re-ordered for a further season of production, along with orders for two new children's television series, two series' pilots and one network movie. This totals over 125 hours of television production that is already committed and is expected to be delivered during 1998.

In an increasing global market for television programs, a significant amount of pre-sale revenue is required to create programs that are of a high quality and meet the necessary commercial appeal in the marketplace. In order to secure substantial pre-sale revenue for many projects, the Company has entered into program package/output arrangements with key customers including Endemol Entertainment for Europe, Africa and the Middle East and TV3 for New Zealand. The Endemol arrangement, signed in April 1998, also included a significant sale of the available rights for Endemol's territories of a variety of Atlantis' drama programs from its library.

The television production and distribution industry is experiencing consolidation both within Canada and North America and on a global basis, which may limit the number of customers and suppliers in the marketplace. In order to ensure that the Company remains competitive, it may from time to time pursue investment opportunities in the industry which expand its scale and scope in order to maximize its future growth and profit potential. During 1997, the Company acquired an interest in Calibre Digital Pictures to expand its capability in the area of animation and special effects. The investment opportunities will be carefully evaluated in terms of their overall strategic and financial value to the Company.

In 1997, the Company's broadcasting operation filed applications with the Canadian Radio-television and Telecommunications Commission ("CRTC") for five new specialty broadcasting services which Atlantis controls. They are: Food Network Canada, Canada's Health Network, People Channel, National Geographic Channel Canada and FIT TV Canada.
In addition, the Company participated as a 20% shareholder in Shaw Communications Inc.'s application for CHAOS TV. Over the next fiscal year, no decisions from the CRTC are expected with regard to the specialty broadcasting applications. The Company expects that the CRTC will hold hearings regarding the applications during the first quarter of 1999 and is optimistic that it will be successful in expanding its broadcasting operation beyond its current two channels, Life Network and HGTV Canada. Management believes that the addition of new broadcasting services to its existing operation will create synergies and improve overall operating results.

Management believes that the key events of 1997: continued development of a growing television program slate with international appeal; the significant growth in Life Network and the launch of HGTV Canada; the Company's entry into the animation and special effects business through the acquisition of Calibre Digital Pictures; coupled with the addition of new product lines such as the CBS representation agreement; and the application for five new specialty broadcast services, which Atlantis controls, are consistent with the Company's growth strategy to enhance shareholder value.

Management's Report

The accompanying financial statements and all information contained in this annual report of Atlantis Communications Inc. are the responsibility of Management and have been approved by the Board of Directors. Financial and operating data elsewhere in the annual report is consistent with the information contained in the financial statements. The financial statements and all other information have been prepared by Management in accordance with generally accepted accounting principles. The financial statements include some figures and assumptions based on Management's best estimates which have been derived with careful judgement.

In fulfilling its responsibilities, Management of the Company has developed and maintains a system of internal accounting controls. These controls ensure that the financial records are reliable for preparing the financial statements. The Board of Directors of the Company carries out its responsibility for the financial statements through its Audit Committee. The Audit Committee reviews the Company's annual consolidated financial statements and recommends their approval by the Board of Directors. The auditors have full access to the Audit Committee with and without Management present.

The financial statements have been audited by Deloitte & Touche Chartered Accountants, whose findings are contained in this annual report.

Michael I.M. MacMillan Chairman and Chief Executive Officer	Lewis N. Rose President	Kerri Golden Chief Financial Officer

Auditors' Report

To the Shareholders of Atlantis Communications Inc.

We have audited the consolidated balance sheets of Atlantis Communications Inc. as at December 31, 1997 and 1996 and the consolidated statements of earnings and retained earnings and changes in financial position for the years then ended. These financial statements are the responsibility of the Company's management. Our responsibility is to express an opinion on these financial statements based on our audits.

We conducted our audits in accordance with generally accepted auditing standards. Those standards require that we plan and perform an audit to obtain reasonable assurance whether the financial statements are free of material misstatement. An audit includes examining, on a test basis, evidence supporting the amounts and disclosures in the financial statements. An audit also includes assessing the accounting principles used and significant estimates made by management, as well as evaluating the overall financial statement presentation.

In our opinion, these consolidated financial statements present fairly, in all material respects, the financial position of the Company as at December 31, 1997 and 1996 and the results of its operations and the changes in its financial position for the years then ended in accordance with generally accepted accounting principles.

Deloitte & Touche
Chartered Accountants

Toronto, Ontario
April 02, 1998

Consolidated Balance Sheets

As at December 31 (in thousands of Canadian dollars, except for per share information)	**1997**	1996
Assets		
Cash and cash equivalents *(Note 2)*	**$ 29,669**	$ 14,099
Accounts receivable *(Note 3)*	**145,611**	75,645
Development costs	**4,147**	4,561
Programs in process	**40,308**	22,829
Completed programs *(Note 4)*	**46,932**	44,698
Broadcast rights *(Note 5)*	**13,517**	11,260
Notes receivable *(Note 6)*	**20,526**	140,673
Investments *(Note 7)*	**3,513**	1,500
Fixed assets *(Note 8)*	**12,537**	8,937
Deferred income taxes	**4,284**	—
Other assets *(Note 9)*	**12,503**	10,624
	$ 333,547	$ 334,826
Liabilities		
Accounts payable and accrued liabilities	**$ 42,592**	$ 24,591
Broadcast rights payable	**4,457**	5,043
Distribution revenue payable	**10,996**	9,419
Interim financing on programs *(Note 10)*	**67,055**	27,230
Loans payable *(Note 11)*	**9,847**	10,952
Deferred revenue	**78,842**	45,904
Notes payable *(Note 6)*	**20,526**	140,673
Deferred income taxes	**—**	2,186
Non-controlling interest	**2,145**	—
	236,460	265,998
Shareholders' Equity		
Capital stock *(Note 12)*	**76,705**	52,961
Retained earnings	**20,382**	15,867
	97,087	68,828
	$ 333,547	$ 334,826
Book value per share *(Note 13)*	**$ 7.82**	$ 7.16

See accompanying notes

On behalf of the Board:

Michael I.M. MacMillan
Director

Donald W. Paterson
Director

ATLANTIS

Consolidated Statements of Earnings and Retained Earnings

For the years ended December 31 (in thousands of Canadian dollars, except for per share information)	**1997**	1996
Revenue	**$ 177,960**	$ 137,984
Expenses		
Amortization	**150,101**	116,134
Operating	**14,129**	13,856
Depreciation	**3,029**	1,694
	167,259	131,684
Earnings before undernoted	**10,701**	6,300
Gain on sale of investment *(Note 9)*	**—**	5,272
Earnings before interest and income taxes	**10,701**	11,572
Interest	**947**	1,339
Earnings before income taxes	**9,754**	10,233
Provision for (recovery of) income taxes *(Note 14)*		
Current	**9,887**	2,954
Deferred	**(5,625)**	593
	4,262	3,547
Earnings before equity earnings and non-controlling interest	**5,492**	6,686
Equity earnings from investment	**73**	318
Non-controlling interest	**—**	(138)
Net earnings for the year	**5,565**	6,866
Retained earnings, beginning of year	**15,867**	9,001
Share issue costs *(Note 12)*	**(1,050)**	—
Retained earnings, end of year	**$ 20,382**	$ 15,867
Earnings per share *(Note 15)*	**$ 0.55**	$ 0.72

See accompanying notes

Consolidated Statements of Changes in Financial Position

For the years ended December 31 (in thousands of Canadian dollars)	**1997**	1996
Cash provided by (used in):		
Operating activities		
Net earnings for the year	**$ 5,565**	$ 6,866
Items not affecting cash		
Amortization and depreciation	**153,130**	117,828
Gain on disposition of an investment	**—**	(5,272)
Deferred income taxes	**(5,625)**	593
Non-controlling interest and equity earnings	**(73)**	(180)
	152,997	119,835
Changes in other non-cash balances	**(19,842)**	17,067
	133,155	136,902
Investing activities		
Development costs	**(2,565)**	(2,219)
Programs in process	**(19,749)**	(5,478)
Completed programs	**(129,945)**	(112,166)
Broadcast rights	**(18,436)**	(19,038)
Investments	**(1,940)**	(400)
Proceeds on sale of investment	**—**	25,145
Net additions to fixed assets	**(5,755)**	(1,831)
Acquisition of Life Network	**—**	(9,473)
Other assets	**(2,754)**	(2,899)
	(181,144)	(128,359)
Financing activities		
Notes receivable	**120,148**	(256)
Interim financing	**39,825**	5,097
Loans payable	**(1,105)**	(4,331)
Notes payable	**(120,148)**	256
Non-controlling interest	**2,145**	—
Capital stock issued	**23,744**	50
Share issue costs	**(1,050)**	—
	63,559	816
Increase in cash and cash equivalents	**15,570**	9,359
Cash and cash equivalents, beginning of year	**14,099**	4,740
Cash and cash equivalents, end of year	**$ 29,669**	$ 14,099

See accompanying notes

Notes to Consolidated Financial Statements

December 31, 1997 and 1996 (in thousands of Canadian dollars, except for per share information)

ATLANTIS COMMUNICATIONS INC., together with its subsidiaries (the "Company") is an international producer, distributor and broadcaster of television programs.

1. Summary of Significant Accounting Policies

Generally accepted accounting principles

These consolidated financial statements have been prepared in accordance with generally accepted accounting principles.

The Company has adopted United States Financial Accounting Standards Board Statement No. 53 for revenue recognition and amortization of program costs, as there are no Canadian accounting standards specific to the television industry.

Principles of consolidation

These consolidated financial statements include the financial statements of the Company, its subsidiaries, an equity ownership in Calibre Digital Design Inc. ("Calibre"), and a 50% joint venture interest in Cinevillage Inc. ("Cinevillage"). Calibre is accounted for using the equity method. Cinevillage is accounted for using the proportionate consolidation method to reflect the Company's share of assets, liabilities, revenues and expenses in the joint venture.

Revenue recognition

The Company's primary sources of revenue are derived from the production and distribution of television programs, and revenue derived from broadcast activities. Production and distribution revenue is comprised of program licence revenue, other program revenue, and post-production revenue.

Program licence revenue is derived from licensing distribution rights to broadcasters and syndicators. The Company recognizes program licence revenue when the program is delivered, the licence period begins, and the collectability of the revenue is reasonably assured. In the case of a television series, revenue is recognized on a pro-rata episodic basis.

Other program revenue is comprised of non-recourse investments in programs by government agencies and broadcasters and financing from the Canada Television and Cable Production Fund. The Company recognizes other program revenue when a program is delivered and the collectability of the revenue is reasonably assured. In the case of a television series, revenue is recognized on a pro-rata episodic basis.

Broadcast revenue is derived from the operations of the Company's specialty cable television channel, Life Network Inc. ("Life Network"), and is comprised of two principal sources: cable subscriber revenue, and advertising revenue. Cable subscriber revenue is recognized as the services are provided. Advertising revenue is recognized when the commercials are aired. Revenue of Home & Garden Television Canada Inc. ("HGTV") has been deferred as the channel is in the pre-operating stage.

Development costs

The Company capitalizes costs, including related overhead, incurred with respect to literary works and other underlying rights it intends to adapt for production. Non-recourse development financing received by the Company has been offset against the related development costs. Development costs are assessed periodically on a project by project basis, and are written off when determined not to be recoverable.

Programs in process

Programs in process represent the costs incurred by the Company in the production of television programs where principal photography has commenced, but where the programs were not delivered at year end. These costs include production expenditures, interest and overhead, net of federal and provincial tax credits and grants. Programs in process are not amortized as no revenue has been recognized.

Completed programs

Completed programs represent the costs incurred by the Company in the production of television programs which have been produced and delivered, or for which the Company has acquired distribution rights from third parties. These costs include production expenditures, acquisition costs, interest, overhead, third-party participation and print and advertising costs, net of federal and provincial tax credits and grants.

Completed programs are stated at the lower of cost, net of amortization, and net realizable value. The net realizable value of a completed program is the Company's share of the estimated future revenue to be earned from the program, net of the estimated future costs.

The individual film forecast method is used to amortize the cost of completed programs. Amortization for each completed program is based on the ratio that current revenue earned from that program bears to estimated future revenue, including subsequent licensing periods.

Broadcast rights

Broadcast subsidiaries are committed, under various contracts, to pay for the rights to broadcast programming. Broadcast rights and corresponding liabilities are recorded when the licence period begins and the program becomes available for use. Broadcast rights are stated at the lower of cost, net of amortization, and net realizable value. The cost of each contract is amortized over the exclusivity period, if applicable, and otherwise over one-half of the duration of the contract.

Investments

Investments in shares of associated companies over which the Company has significant influence, are accounted for by the equity method. Other investments are carried at cost.

Fixed assets

Fixed assets are carried at cost less accumulated depreciation. Depreciation is provided using the following rates and methods:

Building	5% declining balance
Broadcast and production equipment	20 – 30% declining balance
Furniture and other equipment	20 – 30% declining balance
Leasehold improvements	20% straight-line
Vehicles	30% declining balance

Other assets

Other assets include pre-operating costs and goodwill. Pre-operating costs primarily relate to HGTV and Life Network. HGTV is currently in the pre-operating stage. All start-up costs incurred during the pre-operating stage are being capitalized and will be amortized over five years from commencement of commercial operations.

Life Network was in the pre-operating stage to December 31, 1994. All start-up costs related to the pre-operating stage are being amortized from the commencement of operations on January 1, 1995 over 56 months.

Goodwill represents the excess of the cost of investments over the assigned values of assets and liabilities acquired, and is amortized using the straight-line method over periods not exceeding 40 years. The balance is reviewed on an annual basis and, in the event of a permanent impairment to goodwill, such as material change in the business practices or significant operating losses, the Company will record a reduction in the unamortized portion of goodwill.

Distribution revenue payable

Distribution revenue payable represents amounts owing to investors, co-producers and other third-party participants.

Deferred revenue

Completed program revenue is deferred until the program is delivered. Program licence revenue is also deferred until the licence meets the revenue recognition criteria as described in this note.

Government financing, tax credits and grants

The Company has access to government financing that is designed to assist television production and distribution in Canada. Financing from government agencies is considered revenue, and is recognized in accordance with the Company's revenue recognition policy. Federal and provincial tax credits and grants related to programs in process and completed programs are recorded as a reduction in the cost of the respective program.

Use of estimates

The preparation of financial statements in conformity with generally accepted accounting principles requires management to make estimates and assumptions that affect the amounts reported in the financial statements. Actual results could differ from these estimates.

Amortization of completed programs is based on management's estimates of future revenue. Accordingly, any significant negative variation between the estimated revenue and the actual revenue realized over time in respect of a program, may require a write-down of that program. Due to a continually changing marketplace, management controls this risk by periodically reviewing and updating these estimates and assumptions.

The Company is currently undergoing audits by Revenue Canada and the Ontario Ministry of Revenue. As the result of these audits is unknown and as no reassessments have been made to date, a reassessment may result in additional tax liability not currently reflected in the Company's financial statements.

Income taxes

The Company accounts for income taxes using the deferral method.

2. Cash and Cash Equivalents

Bank demand loans have been netted against cash and marketable securities. The Company has unused operating lines of credit of $22,400 with Canadian chartered banks, secured by general security agreements over the Company and a first floating charge over the assets of certain subsidiaries. Outstanding borrowings of $1,350 ($Nil – 1996), are due upon demand and bear interest at prime.

3. Accounts Receivable

Accounts receivable includes $39,818 ($8,934 – 1996) of receivables which are non interest bearing and are due subsequent to December 31, 1998.

4. Completed Programs

	1997		1996	
	value	**%**	value	%
Original cost of completed programs	**$ 596,786**	**100 %**	$ 477,056	100 %
Less: accumulated amortization	**(549,854)**	**(92)**	(432,358)	(91)
Completed programs, net of accumulated amortization	**$ 46,932**	**8 %**	$ 44,698	9 %

As at December 31, 1997, the Company anticipates that approximately 99% of these original program costs will be amortized after three years and 100% after four years.

5. Broadcast Rights

	1997		1996	
	value	**%**	value	%
Original cost of broadcast rights	**$ 28,789**	**100 %**	$ 21,462	100 %
Less: accumulated amortization	**(15,272)**	**(53)**	(10,202)	(48)
Broadcast rights, net of accumulated amortization	**$ 13,517**	**47 %**	$ 11,260	52 %

6. Notes Receivable and Notes Payable

Notes receivable from limited partnerships become due on various dates up to January 15, 1999 and are exactly matched by dates and amounts of the Notes payable. These Notes receivable are secured by assignments of promissory notes from a financial corporation which are in turn secured by financial instruments and the promissory notes of the private investors in the limited partnerships.

7. Investments

	1997	1996
Calibre Digital Design Inc. – equity basis	$ 2,435	$ —
Other investments – at cost	1,078	1,500
	$ 3,513	$ 1,500

The Company's share of the difference between the replacement cost and the net book value of Calibre's assets at the date of purchase was $1,304. This difference is being amortized over a period of 60 months, beginning on June 1, 1997.

8. Fixed Assets

	1997		1996	
	Cost	Accumulated Depreciation	Cost	Accumulated Depreciation
Building (including land of $363)	$ 3,592	$ 1,266	$ 3,582	$ 1,171
Broadcast and production equipment	10,671	4,213	5,691	1,654
Furniture and other equipment	4,863	2,307	3,305	1,743
Leasehold improvements	2,193	1,062	1,738	835
Vehicles	82	16	29	5
	$ 21,401	$ 8,864	$ 14,345	$ 5,408
Net Book Value		$ 12,537		$ 8,937

As at December 31, 1997, $3,219 ($3,620 – 1996) of the equipment described above, less accumulated depreciation of $1,275 ($1,202 – 1996), was subject to capital leases.

9. Acquisitions and Divestiture

Investment in Calibre Digital Design Inc.

On May 31, 1997, the Company acquired 50% of the voting shares (60% equity) of Calibre for $2,545, including $1,045 relating to restructuring and integration costs. This acquisition has been accounted for using the equity method.

Acquisition of 43% of Life Network

In 1996, the Company increased its ownership in Life Network from 57% to 100%. The Company acquired the remaining interest for aggregate consideration of $9,473 comprised of cash, rights and 474,981 treasury shares of the Company. Also included in this amount is approximately $2,000 relating to restructuring and integration costs. Part of the consideration, including the treasury shares, was paid subsequent to December 31, 1996 (see Note 12). The 43% interest in Life Network was acquired from related parties, including management and a significant shareholder of the Company.

The increase in ownership of Life Network was accounted for as a purchase. As a result of the acquisition, goodwill, included in other assets, increased by $6,466, and non-controlling interest decreased by $3,007.

Divestiture of 28% of YTV Canada, Inc.

In 1996, the Company sold its 28% interest in YTV Canada, Inc. for net proceeds of $25,145. The pre-tax gain on the sale of YTV amounted to $5,272, or $3,532 ($0.37 per share) on an after-tax basis.

10. Interim Financing on Programs

Interim financing on programs at December 31, 1997 bears interest at various rates up to U.S. prime rate plus 1.0% (U.S. prime rate plus 1.0% – 1996). Of the outstanding balance, $2,537 represents U.S. dollar borrowings. The loans are fully secured by direct assignments of accounts receivable.

The Company has available $45,000 under an interim production credit facility, secured by direct assignments of accounts receivable. Outstanding borrowings of $35,018 at December 31,1997 ($Nil – 1996) bear interest at prime plus 5/8%.

11. Loans Payable

	1997	1996
Mortgages payable		
Bear interest from a fixed rate of 9.99% to 3.0% above average cost of funds to the mortgagee, secured by land and building, maturing at the latest October 2005	**$ 3,421**	$ 3,576
Bank term loans		
Bear interest at rates up to prime rate plus 1.5%, secured by various assets and distribution licencing agreements or territories, maturing at the latest November 2001	**3,244**	2,790
Other debt	**1,581**	2,580
Obligation under capital leases	**1,601**	2,006
	$ 9,847	$ 10,952

Principal payments are due as follows:

1998	$ 4,438
1999	1,548
2000	1,107
2001	244
2002	255
Thereafter	2,255
	$ 9,847

12. Capital Stock

	1997		1996	
	# of Shares	**Value**	# of Shares	Value
Authorized				
Multiple Voting Shares (MVS)	**4,237,499**		4,237,499	
Subordinate Voting Shares (SVS)	**Unlimited**		Unlimited	
Preference Shares	**Unlimited**		Unlimited	
Share Purchase Warrants (SPW)	**2,292,400**		—	
Issued and Outstanding				
Share Purchase Warrants	**2,292,400**	**$ 20,631**	—	$ —
Multiple Voting Shares (ten dollars book value)	**4,237,499**	**—**	4,237,499	—
Subordinate Voting Shares	**5,881,745**	**56,074**	5,371,550	52,961
Total Voting Shares	**10,119,244**	**56,074**	9,609,049	52,961
Total Capital Stock		**$ 76,705**		$ 52,961

The MVS carry 10 votes per share and SVS carry one vote per share. MVS are convertible into SVS on a one-for-one basis. The MVS and SVS rank equally with respect to dividends and capital distributions, however, there are restrictions on ownership and transfer of the MVS. The MVS and SVS are currently constrained to limit non-Canadian ownership to levels which will not adversely affect the Company in carrying on any regulated business. Currently the CRTC limits non-Canadian ownership to 33 1/3% of the Company's voting shares. The SVS are entitled to specific rights, including coattail provisions, in the event of a take-over bid.

On December 23, 1997, the Company issued 2,292,400 Special Warrants for cash consideration of $20,631 ($9 per share). The Company's share of issue costs including underwriters' fees and expenses totalled $1,895 ($1,050 net of related taxes). On February 9, 1998, all of the Special Warrants were converted into subordinate voting shares on a one-for-one basis. During 1997, the Company issued 13,414 SVS to the Directors as consideration for services in the amount of $99, and 15,600 SVS, with an ascribed value of $94, were issued in connection with 1996 bonuses payable. In addition, 6,200 options with a total value of $37 were exercised by option holders.

In 1997, the Company paid the consideration which was accrued at December 31, 1996 in conjunction with the acquisition of the remaining interest in Life Network (Note 9). In conjunction with this acquisition, the Company issued 474,981 SVS on January 20, 1997, with a total value of $2,850.

During 1996, the Company issued 7,405 SVS to the Directors as consideration for services in the amount of $50.

Options

As at December 31, 1997, there were 1,453,964 options (960,164 – 1996) authorized to purchase SVS, and 1,014,323 options (884,469 – 1996) to purchase SVS were outstanding at prices ranging from $5.95 to $14.50 per share with a weighted average price of $8.72 ($10.08 – 1996). These options vest over time and will expire, at the latest, by May 2002.

Subsequent to December 31, 1997, 76,500 options were issued at $10.25. These options vest over time and will expire, at the latest, by February 2003. Subsequent to December 31, 1997, 20,934 options were cancelled or expired, and 6,500 options were exercised.

13. Book Value Per Share

Book value per share represents the total of shareholders' equity divided by the number of shares and Special Warrants outstanding at year end.

14. Income Taxes

(a) The effective rates of income taxes provided in the statements of earnings vary from the rates specified in the tax statutes as follows:

	1997	1996
Combined basic federal and provincial income tax rate	**44.6 %**	44.6 %
Non-deductible expenses	**5.8**	—
Reduction due to income taxed in other jurisdictions	**—**	(4.6)
Gain on sale of investment taxed at capital gains rate	**—**	(5.7)
Use of loss carry-forwards	**(15.8)**	(3.5)
Increase in income tax accrual	**8.4**	—
Other	**0.7**	3.9
	43.7 %	34.7 %

During the year the Company accrued an additional amount for income tax contingencies.

(b) Loss carry-forwards of certain of the Company's subsidiaries, for which no benefit has been recognized, amount to $133 as at December 31, 1997 ($4,083 – 1996) and are available for utilization against future taxable income. As at December 31, 1997, the loss carry-forwards expire as follows:

2002	$ 35
2003	98
	$ 133

15. Earnings Per Share

	1997		1996	
	Basic	**Fully Diluted**	Basic	Fully Diluted
Operating earnings per share	**$ 0.55**	**$ 0.52**	$ 0.35	$ 0.34
Earnings per share from unusual items	**—**	**—**	0.37	0.33
Total earnings per share	**$ 0.55**	**$ 0.52**	$ 0.72	$ 0.67
Weighted average number of shares	**10,067,074**	**11,195,706**	9,603,294	10,844,792
Number of shares outstanding at December 31	**10,119,244**	**13,425,967**	9,609,049	10,493,518

Earnings per share from unusual items in 1996 represents the after-tax earnings per share from the gain on sale of YTV (see Note 9).

16. Government Financing, Tax Credits and Grants

Revenue includes $10,589 of government program financing for the year ended December 31, 1997 ($8,947 – 1996). A portion of this amount is repayable depending on the future revenue of the individual program, and therefore has been reflected in the determination of the net realizable value of the program as a future cost. Completed program costs for the year ended December 31, 1997 are net of $16,471 of federal and provincial tax credits and grants ($9,877 – 1996). Programs in process costs for the year ended December 31, 1997 are net of $2,591 of federal and provincial tax credits and grants ($2,493 – 1996).

17. Financial Instruments

Fair values

The estimated fair values of financial instruments as at December 31, 1997 and December 31, 1996 are based on the relevant market prices and information available at that time. The fair value estimates are not indicative of the amounts that the Company might receive or incur in actual market transactions.

	1997		1996	
	Book Value	**Fair Value**	Book Value	Fair Value
Financial assets				
Assets for which fair value approximates book value	**$ 29,669**	**$ 29,669**	$ 14,099	$ 14,099
Accounts receivable	**145,611**	**142,843**	78,448	78,061
Notes receivable	**20,526**	**19,650**	140,673	139,813
Financial liabilities				
Liabilities for which fair value approximates book value	**$ 133,846**	**$ 133,846**	$ 77,128	$ 77,128
Obligations under capital lease	**1,601**	**1,549**	—	—
Notes payable	**20,526**	**19,650**	140,673	139,813

Cash and marketable securities, accounts payable and accrued liabilities, broadcast rights payable, distribution revenue payable, loans payable and interim financing on programs are all short-term in nature and as such, their carrying value approximates fair value.

The fair value of accounts receivable on balances due subsequent to December 31, 1998, was estimated using discount rates based on an average of market interest rates.

The fair value of notes receivable and notes payable was estimated based on quoted market prices or discounted cash flows, using discount rates based on market interest rates. Amounts recorded as fair value relating to notes receivable and payable are based on amounts due and receivable subsequent to December 31, 1998. The terms of these instruments require the notes receivable to be matched with the notes payable.

Forward contracts

The Company has committed to the sale of 800 million Italian Lira on February 27,1998, at an exchange rate of U.S. $0.00647.

The Company has committed to the sale of U.S. $31,786 under forward exchange contracts. The contracts are at rates of exchange ranging from Cdn. $1.3592 to $1.4205, and maturing at various dates to August 15, 2000.

The unrealized loss on forward exchange contracts at December 31, 1997 is $821. This loss has not been recorded as the contracts are considered to be hedges.

Concentration of credit risk

Accounts receivable from one customer, excluding receivables from government programs, represents 14% (24% – 1996) of total accounts receivable at December 31, 1997. The Company believes that there is no risk associated with the collection of this amount. The balance of accounts receivable are widely disbursed amongst customers.

18. Contingent Liabilities and Commitments

(a) In addition to the mortgage payable obligation (Note 11), the Company has jointly and severally guaranteed an additional $3,500 to a mortgagee of Cinevillage.

(b) The Company has entered into agreements with program investors on a number of projects under which the Company has guaranteed payments to such investors in aggregate of $297 as at December 31, 1997 ($2,357 – 1996). The Company anticipates that revenues from each of the programs in connection with which guarantees were given will meet or exceed obligations to respective program investors.

(c) The Company is committed to further payments totaling $1,500 related to marketing the launch of HGTV. These payments will be made during the current year.

(d) As at December 31, 1997 the Company is committed to future minimum operating lease payments as follows:

1998	$ 2,442
1999	2,215
2000	1,515
2001	492
2002	492
Thereafter	—
	$ 7,156

19. Segmented Information

(a) The Company's only significant activity is the production, distribution and broadcasting of television programs and ancillary rights.

(b) Revenue for the year ended December 31, 1997 includes $121,925 ($81,405 – 1996) derived from non-Canadian sources.

20. Supplementary Information

The Company has a 50% investment in Cinevillage. The Company's proportionate share in the assets, liabilities and net earnings from operations of Cinevillage is as follows:

	1997	1996
Assets, including fixed assets, at cost less accumulated depreciation of $1,398 ($1,275 – 1996)	**$ 2,423**	$ 2,548
Liabilities	**3,532**	3,708
Net income (loss)	**$ 52**	$ (258)

21. Comparative Figures

Certain comparative figures have been reclassified to conform with the current year's presentation.

Present and Future Values

APPENDIX II

Learning Objectives

LO1 Describe the earning of interest and the concepts of present and future values.

LO2 Apply present value concepts to a single amount by using interest tables.

LO3 Apply future value concepts to a single amount by using interest tables.

LO4 Apply present value concepts to an annuity by using interest tables.

LO5 Apply future value concepts to an annuity by using interest tables.

Appendix Outline

- **Present and Future Value Concepts**
- **Present Value of a Single Amount**
- **Future Value of a Single Amount**
- **Present Value of an Annuity**
- **Future Value of an Annuity**

APPENDIX PREVIEW

The concepts of present value are described and applied in Chapter 17. This appendix helps to supplement that discussion with added explanations, illustrations, computations, present value tables, and additional assignments. We also give attention to illustrations, definitions, and computations of future values.

Present and Future Value Concepts

LO1 Describe the earning of interest and the concepts of present and future values.

There's an old saying, *time is money.* This saying reflects the notion that as time passes, the assets and liabilities we hold are changing. This change is due to interest. *Interest* is the payment to the owner of an asset for its use by a borrower. The most common example of this type of asset is a savings account. As we keep a balance of cash in our accounts, it earns interest that is paid to us by the financial institution. An example of a liability is a car loan. As we carry the balance of the loan, we accumulate interest costs on this debt. We must ultimately repay this loan with interest.

Present and future value computations are a way for us to estimate the interest component of holding assets or liabilities over time. The present value of an amount applies when we either lend or borrow an asset that must be repaid in full at some future date, and we want to know its worth today. The future value of an amount applies when we either lend or borrow an asset that must be repaid in full at some future date, and we want to know its worth at a future date.

The first section focuses on the present value of a single amount. Later sections focus on the future value of a single amount, and then both present and future values of a series of amounts (or annuity).

Present Value of a Single Amount

We graphically express the present value (p) of a single future amount (f) received or paid at a future date in Exhibit II.1.

Exhibit II.1

Present Value of a Single Amount

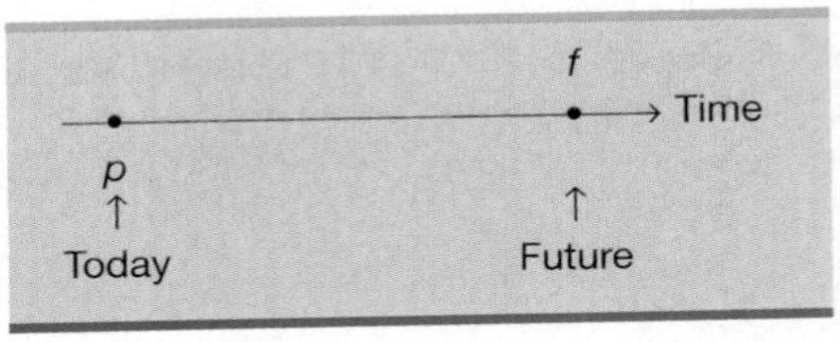

LO2 Apply present value concepts to a single amount by using interest tables.

The formula to compute the present value of this single amount is shown in Exhibit II.2 where: p = present value; f = future value; i = rate of interest per period; and n = number of periods.

Exhibit II.2

Present Value of a Single Amount Formula

$$p = \frac{f}{(1 + i)^n}$$

To illustrate the application of this formula, let's assume we need $220 one period from today. We want to know how much must be invested now, for one period, at an interest rate of 10% to provide for this $220.[1] For this illustration the p, or present value, is the unknown amount. In particular, the present and future values, along with the interest rate, are shown graphically as:

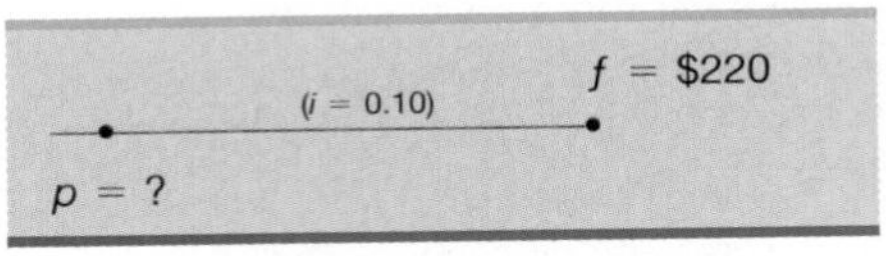

Conceptually, we know p must be less than $220. This is obvious from the answer to the question: Would we rather have $220 today or $220 at some future date? If we had $220 today, we could invest it and see it grow to something more than $220 in the future. Therefore, if we were promised $220 in the future, we would take less than $220 today. But how much less?

[1] Interest is also called a *discount*, and an interest rate is also called a *discount rate*.

To answer that question we can compute an estimate of the present value of the $220 to be received one period from now using the formula in Exhibit II.2 as:

$$p = \frac{f}{(1 + i)^n} = \frac{\$242}{(1 + .10)^1} = \$200$$

This means we are indifferent between $200 today or $220 at the end of one period.

We can also use this formula to compute the present value for *any number of periods.* To illustrate this computation, we consider a payment of $242 at the end of two periods at 10% interest. The present value of this $242 to be received two periods from now is computed as:

$$p = \frac{f}{(1 + i)^n} = \frac{\$242}{(1 + .10)^2} = \$200$$

These results tells us we are indifferent between $200 today, or $220 one period from today, or $242 two periods from today.

The number of periods (n) in the present value formula does not have to be expressed in years. Any period of time such as a day, a month, a quarter, or a year can be used. But, whatever period is used, the interest rate (i) must be compounded for the same period. This means if a situation expresses n in months, and i equals 12% per year, then we can assume 1% of an amount invested at the beginning of each month is earned in interest per month and added to the investment. In this case, interest is said to be compounded monthly.

A present value table helps us with present value computations. It gives us present values for a variety of interest rates (i) and a variety of periods (n). Each present value in a present value table assumes the future value (f) is 1. When the future value (f) is different than 1, we can simply multiply present value (p) by that future amount to give us our estimate.

The formula used to construct a table of present values of a single future amount of 1 is shown in Exhibit II.3.

Exhibit II.3

Present Value of 1 Formula

$$p = \frac{1}{(1 + i)^n}$$

This formula is identical to that in Exhibit II.2 except that f equals 1. Table II.1 at the end of this appendix is a present value table for a single future amount. It is often called a **present value of 1 table.** A present value table involves three factors: p, i, and n.[2] Knowing two of these three factors allows us to compute the third. To illustrate, consider the three possible cases.

Case 1 (solve for p when knowing i and n). Our example above is a case in which we need to solve for p when knowing i and n. To illustrate how we use a present value table, let's again look at how we estimate the present value of $220 ($f$) at the end of one period (n) where the interest rate (i) is 10%. To answer this we go to the present value table (Table II.1) and look in the row for 1 period and in the column for 10% interest. Here we find a present value (p) of 0.9091 based on a future value of 1. This means, for instance, that $1 to be received 1 period from today at 10% interest is worth $0.9091 today. Since the future value is not $1, but is $220, we multiply the 0.9091 by $220 to get an answer of $200.

[2] A fourth is f, but as we already explained, we need only multiple the "1" used in the formula by f.

Case 2 (solve for n when knowing p and i). This is a case in which we have, say, a \$100,000 future value (f) valued at \$13,000 today (p) with an interest rate of 12% (i). In this case we want to know how many periods (n) there are between the present value and the future value. A case example is when we want to retire with \$100,000, but have only \$13,000 earning a 12% return. How long will it be before we can retire? To answer this we go to Table II.1 and look in the 12% interest column. Here we find a column of present values (p) based on a future value of 1. To use the present value table for this solution, we must divide \$13,000 (p) by \$100,000 (f), which equals 0.1300. This is necessary because a present value table defines f equal to 1, and p as a fraction of 1. We look for a value nearest to 0.1300 (p), which we find in the row for 18 periods (n). This means the present value of \$100,000 at the end of 18 periods at 12% interest is \$13,000 or, alternatively stated, we must work 18 more years.

Case 3 (solve for i when knowing p and n). This is a case where we have, say, a \$120,000 future value (f) valued at \$60,000 (p) today when there are nine periods (n) between the present and future values. Here we want to know what rate of interest is being used. As an example, suppose we want to retire with \$120,000, but we only have \$60,000 and hope to retire in nine years. What interest rate must we earn to retire with \$120,000 in nine years? To answer this we go to the present value table (Table II.1) and look in the row for nine periods. To again use the present value table we must divide \$60,000 (p) by \$120,000 (f), which equals 0.5000. Recall this is necessary because a present value table defines f equal to 1, and p as a fraction of 1. We look for a value in the row for nine periods that is nearest to 0.5000 (p), which we find in the column for 8% interest (i). This means the present value of \$120,000 at the end of nine periods at 8% interest is \$60,000 or, in our example, we must earn 8% annual interest to retire in nine years.

Flash back

1. A company is considering an investment expected to yield \$70,000 after six years. If this company demands an 8% return, how much is it willing to pay for this investment?

Answer—p. II-9

Future Value of a Single Amount

We use the formula for the present value of a single amount and modify it to obtain the formula for the future value of a single amount. To illustrate, we multiply both sides of the equation in Exhibit II.2 by $(1 + i)^n$. The result is shown in Exhibit II.4.

Exhibit II.4

Future Value of a Single Amount Formula

$$f = p \times (1 + i)^n$$

Future value (f) is defined in terms of p, i, and n. We can use this formula to determine that \$200 invested for 1 period at an interest rate of 10% increases to a future value of \$220 as follows:

LO3 Apply future value concepts to a single amount by using interest tables.

$$\begin{aligned} f &= p \times (1 + i)^n \\ &= \$200 \times (1 + .10)^1 \\ &= \$220 \end{aligned}$$

This formula can also be used to compute the future value of an amount for *any number of periods* into the future. As an example, assume $200 is invested for three periods at 10%. The future value of this $200 is $266.20 and is computed as:

$$f = p \times (1 + i)^n$$
$$= \$200 \times (1 + .10)^3$$
$$= \$266.20$$

It is also possible to use a future value table to compute future values (f) for many combinations of interest rates (i) and time periods (n). Each future value in a future value table assumes the present value (p) is 1. As with a present value table, if the future amount is something other than 1, we simply multiply our answer by that amount. The formula used to construct a table of future values of a single amount of 1 is shown in Exhibit II.5.

Exhibit II.5

Future Value of 1 Formula

$$f = (1 + i)^n$$

Table II.2 at the end of this appendix shows a table of future values of a single amount of 1. This type of table is called a **future value of 1 table.**

It is interesting to point out some items in Tables II.1 and II.2. Note in Table II.2 for the row where $n = 0$, that the future value is 1 for every interest rate. This is because no interest is earned when time does not pass. Also notice that Tables II.1 and II.2 report the same information in a different manner. In particular, one table is simply the inverse of the other.

To illustrate this inverse relation let's say we invest $100 annually for a period of five years at 12% per year. How much do we expect to have after five years? We can answer this question using Table II.2 by finding the future value (f) of 1, for five periods from now, compounded at 12%. From the table we find $f = 1.7623$. If we start with $100, the amount it accumulates to after five years is $176.23 ($100 × 1.7623).

We can alternatively use Table II.1. Here we find the present value (p) of 1, discounted five periods at 12%, is 0.5674. Recall the inverse relation between present value and future value. This means $p = 1/f$ (or equivalently $f = 1/p$).[3] Knowing this we can compute the future value of $100 invested for five periods at 12% as:

$$f = \$100 \times (1\ /\ 0.5674) = \$176.24$$

A future value table involves three factors: f, i, and n. Knowing two of these three factors allows us to compute the third. To illustrate, consider the three possible cases.

Case 1 (solve for f when knowing i and n). Our example above is a case in which we need to solve for f when knowing i and n. We found that $100 invested for five periods at 12% interest accumulates to $176.24.

Case 2 (solve for n when knowing f and i). This is a case where we have, say, $2,000 ($p$) and we want to know how many periods (n) it will take to accumulate to $3,000 ($f$) at 7% ($i$) interest. To answer this, we go to the future value table (Table II.2) and look in the 7% interest column. Here we find a column of future values (f) based on a present value of 1. To use a future value table, we must divide $3,000 ($f$) by $2,000 ($p$), which equals 1.500. This is necessary because a future value table defines p equal to 1, and f as a multiple of 1. We

[3] Proof of this relation is left for advanced courses.

look for a value nearest to 1.50 (*f*), which we find in the row for six periods (*n*). This means $2,000 invested for six periods at 7% interest accumulates to $3,000.

Case 3 (solve for *i* when knowing *f* and *n*). This is a case where we have, say, $2,001 (*p*) and in nine years (*n*) we want to have $4,000 (*f*). What rate of interest must we earn to accomplish this? To answer this, we go to Table II.2 and search in the row for nine periods. To use a future value table, we must divide $4,000 (*f*) by $2,001 (*p*), which equals 1.9990. Recall this is necessary because a future value table defines *p* equal to 1, and *f* as a multiple of 1. We look for a value nearest to 1.9990 (*f*), which we find in the column for 8% interest (*i*). This means $2,001 invested for nine periods at 8% interest accumulates to $4,000.

Flash back

2. Assume you are a winner in a $150,000 cash sweepstakes. You decide to deposit this cash in an account earning 8% annual interest and you plan to quit your job when the account equals $555,000. How many years will it be before you can quit working?

Answers—p. II-9

Present Value of an Annuity

An annuity is a series of equal payments occurring at equal intervals. One example is a series of three annual payments of $100 each. The present value of an ordinary annuity is defined as the present value of equal payments at equal intervals as of one period before the first payment. An ordinary annuity of $100 and its present value (*p*) is illustrated in Exhibit II.6.

Exhibit II.6

Present Value of an Ordinary Annuity

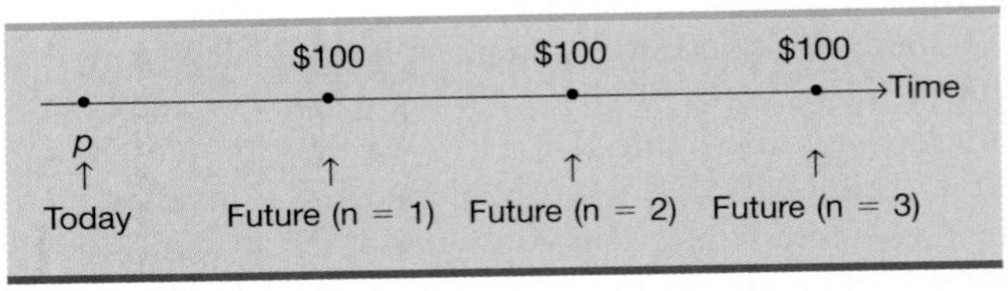

LO4 Apply present value concepts to an annuity by using interest tables.

One way for us to compute the present value of an ordinary annuity is to find the present value of each payment using our present value formula from Exhibit II.3. We then would add up each of the three present values. To illustrate, let's look at three, $100 payments at the end of each of the next three periods with an interest rate of 15%. Our present value computations are:

$$p = \frac{\$100}{(1 + .15)^1} + \frac{\$100}{(1 + .15)^2} + \frac{\$100}{(1 + .15)^3} = \$228.32$$

This computation also is identical to computing the present value of each payment (from Table II.1) and taking their sum or, alternatively, adding the values from Table II.1 for each of the three payments and multiplying their sum by the $100 annuity payment.

A more direct way is to use a present value of annuity table. Table II.3 at the end of this appendix is one such table. This table is called a **present value of an annuity of 1 table.** If we look at Table II.3 where $n = 3$ and $i = 15\%$, we see the present value is 2.2832. This means the present value of an annuity of 1 for 3 periods, with a 15% interest rate, is 2.2832.

A present value of annuity formula is used to construct Table II.3. It can also be constructed by adding the amounts in a present value of 1 table.[4] To illustrate, we use Tables II.1 and II.3 to confirm this relation for the prior example: We can also use business calculators or spreadsheet computer programs to find the present value of an annuity.

From Table II.1		From Table II.3	
i = 15%, n = 1	0.8696		
i = 15%, n = 2	0.7561		
i = 15%, n = 3	0.6575		
Total	2.2832	i = 15%, n = 3	2.2832

Flashback

3. A company is considering an investment paying $10,000 every six months for three years. The first payment would be received in six months. If this company requires an annual return of 8%, what is the maximum amount they are willing to invest?

Answer—p. II-9

Future Value of an Annuity

We can also compute the future value of an annuity. The future value of an *ordinary annuity* is the accumulated value of each annuity payment with interest as of the date of the final payment. To illustrate, let's consider the earlier annuity of three annual payments of $100. Exhibit II.7 shows the point in time for the future value (f). The first payment is made two periods prior to the point where future value is determined, and the final payment occurs on the future value date.

Exhibit II.7

Future Value of an Ordinary Annuity

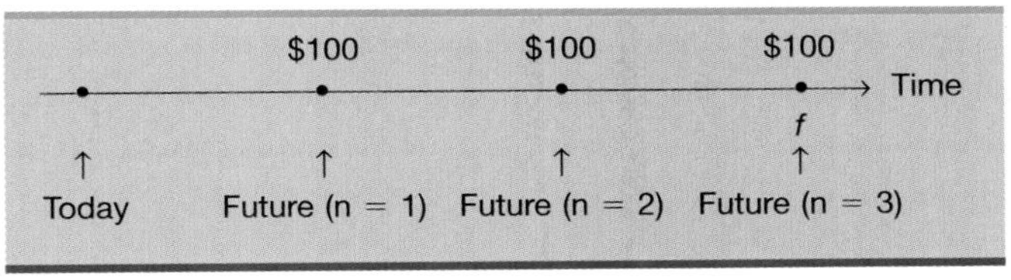

LO5 Apply future value concepts to an annuity by using interest tables.

One way to compute the future value of an annuity is to use the formula to find the future value of *each* payment and add them together. If we assume an interest rate of 15%, our calculation is:

$$f = \$100 \times (1 + .15)^2 + \$100 \times (1 + .15)^1 + \$100 \times (1 + .15)^0 = \$347.25$$

[4] The formula for the present value of an annuity of 1 is: $p = \dfrac{1 - \dfrac{1}{(1 + i)^n}}{i}$

This is identical to using Table II.2 and finding the sum of the future values of each payment, or adding the future values of the three payments of 1 and multiplying the sum by $100.

A more direct way is to use a table showing future values of annuities. Such a table is called a future value of an annuity of 1 table. Table II.4 at the end of this appendix is one such table. We should note in Table II.4 that when $n = 1$, the future values are equal to 1 ($f = 1$) for all rates of interest. That is because the annuity consists of only one payment and the future value is determined on the date of that payment — no time passes between the payment and its future value.

A formula is used to construct Table II.4.[5] We can also construct it by adding the amounts from a future value of 1 table. To illustrate, we use Tables II.2 and II.4 to confirm this relation for the prior example:

From Table II.2		From Table II.4	
i = 15%, n = 0	1.0000		
i = 15%, n = 1	1.1500		
i = 15%, n = 2	1.3225		
Total	3.4725	i = 15%, n = 3	3.4725

Note the future value in Table II.2 is 1.0000 when $n = 0$, but the future value in Table II.4 is 1.0000 when $n = 1$. Is this a contradiction? No. When $n = 0$ in Table II.2, the future value is determined on the date where a single payment occurs. This means no interest is earned, since no time has passed, and the future value equals the payment. Table II.4 describes annuities with equal payments occurring at the end of each period. When $n = 1$, the annuity has one payment, and its future value equals 1 on the date of its final and only payment. Again, no time passes from the payment and its future value date.

Flash back

4. A company invests $45,000 per year for five years at 12% annual interest. Compute the value of this annuity investment at the end of five years.

Answers—p. II-9

[5] The formula for the future value of an annuity of 1 is: $f = \dfrac{(1 + i)^n - 1}{i}$

Summary

LO1 Describe the earning of interest and the concepts of present and future values. Interest is payment to the owner of an asset for its use by a borrower. Present and future value computations are a way for us to estimate the interest component of holding assets or liabilities over a period of time.

LO2 Apply present value concepts to a single amount by using interest tables. The present value of a single amount to be received at a future date is the amount that can be invested now at the specified interest rate to yield that future value.

LO3 Apply future value concepts to a single amount by using interest tables. The future value of a single amount invested at a specified rate of interest is the amount that would accumulate at a future date.

LO4 Apply present value concepts to an annuity by using interest tables. The present value of an annuity is the amount that can be invested now at the specified interest rate to yield that series of equal periodic payments.

LO5 Apply future value concepts to an annuity by using interest tables. The future value of an annuity to be invested at a specific rate of interest is the amount that would accumulate at the date of the final equal periodic payment.

Guidance Answers to Flashbacks

1. \$70,000 × 0.6302 = \$44,114 (using Table II.1, $i = 8\%$, $n = 6$).
2. \$555,000/\$150,000 = 3.7000; Table II.2 shows this value is not achieved until after 17 years at 8% interest.
3. \$10,000 × 5.2421 = \$52,421 (using Table II.3, $i = 4\%$, $n = 6$).
4. \$45,000 × 6.3528 = \$285,876 (using Table II.4, $i = 12\%$, $n = 5$).

Quick Study

QS II-1 Identifying interest rates in tables LO1

You are asked to make future value estimates using the future value of 1 table (Table II.2). Which interest rate column do you use when working with the following rates?

a. 8% compounded quarterly
b. 12% compounded annually
c. 6% compounded semiannually
d. 12% compounded monthly

QS II-2 Present value of an amount LO2

Flaherty is considering an investment which, if paid for immediately, is expected to return \$140,000 five years hence. If Flaherty demands a 9% return, how much is she willing to pay for this investment?

QS II-3 Future value of an amount LO3

CII, Inc., invested \$630,000 in a project expected to earn a 12% annual rate of return. The earnings will be reinvested in the project each year until the entire investment is liquidated 10 years hence. What will the cash proceeds be when the project is liquidated?

QS II-4 Present value of an annuity LO4

Beene Distributing is considering a contract that will return \$150,000 annually at the end of each year for six years. If Beene demands an annual return of 7% and pays for the investment immediately, how much should it be willing to pay?

QS II-5
Future value of an annuity
LO5

Claire Fitch is planning to begin an individual retirement program in which she will invest $1,500 annually at the end of each year. Fitch plans to retire after making 30 annual investments in a program that earns a return of 10%. What will be the value of the program on the date of the last investment?

QS II-6
Interest rate on an investment
LO2

Ken Francis has been offered the possibility of investing $2,745 for 15 years, after which he will be paid $10,000. What annual rate of interest will Francis earn? (Use Table II.1.)

QS II-7
Number of periods of an investment
LO2

Megan Brink has been offered the possibility of investing $6,651. The investment will earn 6% per year and will return Brink $10,000 at the end of the investment. How many years must Brink wait to receive the $10,000? (Use Table II.1.)

Exercises

Exercise II-1
Using present and future value tables
LO1

For each of the following situations identify (1) it as either (a) present or future value and (b) single amount or annuity case, (2) the table you would use in your computations (but do not solve the problem), and (3) the interest rate and time periods you would use.

a. You need to accumulate $10,000 for a trip you wish to take in four years. You are able to earn 8% compounded semiannually on your savings. You only plan on making one deposit and letting the money accumulate for four years. How would you determine the amount of the one-time deposit?

b. Assume the same facts as in (a), except you will make semiannual deposits to your savings account.

c. You hope to retire after working 40 years with savings in excess of $1,000,000. You expect to save $4,000 a year for 40 years and earn an annual rate of interest of 8%. Will you be able to retire with more than $1,000,000 in 40 years?

d. A sweepstakes agency names you a grand prize winner. You can take $225,000 immediately or elect to receive annual installments of $30,000 for 20 years. You can earn 10% annually on investments you make. Which prize do you choose to receive?

Exercise II-2
Number of periods of an investment
LO2

Bill Thompson expects to invest $10,000 at 12% and, at the end of the investment, receive $96,463. How many years will elapse before Thompson receives the payment? (Use Table II.2.)

Exercise II-3
Interest rate on an investment
LO2

Ed Summers expects to invest $10,000 for 25 years, after which he will receive $108,347. What rate of interest will Summers earn? (Use Table II.2.)

Exercise II-4
Interest rate on an investment
LO4

Betsey Jones expects an immediate investment of $57,466 to return $10,000 annually for eight years, with the first payment to be received in one year. What rate of interest will Jones earn? (Use Table II.3.)

Exercise II-5
Number of periods of an investment
LO4

Keith Riggins expects an investment of $82,014 to return $10,000 annually for several years. If Riggins is to earn a return of 10%, how many annual payments must he receive? (Use Table II.3.)

Exercise II-6
Interest rate on an investment
LO5

Steve Algoe expects to invest $1,000 annually for 40 years and have an accumulated value of $154,762 on the date of the last investment. If this occurs, what rate of interest will Algoe earn? (Use Table II.4.)

Exercise II-7
Number of periods of an investment
LO5

Katherine Beckwith expects to invest $10,000 annually that will earn 8%. How many annual investments must Beckwith make to accumulate $303,243 on the date of the last investment? (Use Table II.4.)

Exercise II-8
Present value of an annuity
LO4

Sam Weber financed a new automobile by paying $6,500 cash and agreeing to make 40 monthly payments of $500 each, the first payment to be made one month after the purchase. The loan bears interest at an annual rate of 12%. What was the cost of the automobile?

Exercise II-9
Future value of an amount
LO3

Mark Welsch deposited $7,200 in a savings account that earns interest at an annual rate of 8%, compounded quarterly. The $7,200 plus earned interest must remain in the account 10 years before it can be withdrawn. How much money will be in the account at the end of the 10 years?

Exercise II-10
Future value of an annuity
LO4

Kelly Malone plans to have $50 withheld from her monthly paycheque and deposited in a savings account that earns 12% annually, compounded monthly. If Malone continues with her plan for 2 1/2 years, how much will be accumulated in the account on the date of the last deposit?

Exercise II-11
Present value of bonds
LO2, 3

Spiller Corp. plans to issue 10%, 15-year, $500,000 par value bonds payable that pay interest semiannually on June 30 and December 31. The bonds are dated December 31, 1999, and are to be issued on that date. If the market rate of interest for the bonds is 8% on the date of issue, what will be the cash proceeds from the bond issue?

Exercise II-12
Future value of an amount plus an annuity
LO3,5

Starr Company has decided to establish a fund that will be used 10 years hence to replace an aging productive facility. The company will make an initial contribution of $100,000 to the fund and plans to make quarterly contributions of $50,000 beginning in three months. The fund is expected to earn 12%, compounded quarterly. What will be the value of the fund 10 years hence?

Exercise II-13
Present value of an amount
LO3

McAdams Company expects to earn 10% per year on an investment that will pay $606,773 six years hence. Use Table II.1 to compute the present value of the investment.

Exercise II-14
Future value of an amount
L03

Catten, Inc., invests $163,170 at 7% per year for nine years. Use Table II.2 to compute the future value of the investment nine years hence.

Exercise II-15
Present value of an amount and annuity
L02, 4

Compute the amount that can be borrowed under each of the following circumstances:

a. A promise to pay $90,000 in seven years at an interest rate of 6%.

b. An agreement made on February 1, 2000, to make three payments of $20,000 on February 1 of 2001, 2002, and 2003. The annual interest rate is 10%.

Exercise II-16
Present value of an amount
L02

On January 1, 2000, a company agrees to pay $20,000 in three years. If the annual interest rate is 10%, determine how much cash the company can borrow with this promise.

Exercise II-17
Present value of an amount
L02

Find the amount of money that can be borrowed with each of the following promises:

Case	Single Future Payment	Number of Years	Interest Rate
a.	$ 40,000	3	4%
b.	75,000	7	8%
c.	52,000	9	10%
d.	18,000	2	4%
e.	63,000	8	6%
f.	89,000	5	2%

Exercise II-18
Present values of annuities
L04

C&H Ski Club recently borrowed money and agreed to pay it back with a series of six annual payments of $5,000 each. C&H subsequently borrowed more money and agreed to pay it back with a series of four annual payments of $7,500 each. The annual interest rate for both loans is 6%.

a. Use Table II.1 to find the present value of these two annuities. (Round amounts to the nearest dollar.)

b. Use Table II.3 to find the present value of these two annuities.

Exercise II-19
Present value with semiannual compounding
L01, 4

Otto Co. borrowed cash on April 30, 2000, by promising to make four payments of $13,000 each on November 1, 2000, May 1, 2001, November 1, 2001, and May 1, 2002.

a. How much cash is Otto able to borrow if the interest rate is 8%, compounded semiannually?

b. How much cash is Otto able to borrow if the interest rate is 12%, compounded semiannually?

c. How much cash is Otto able to borrow if the interest rate is 16%, compounded semiannually?

Table II.1

Present Value of 1 Due in *n* Periods

Periods	Rate 1%	2%	3%	4%	5%	6%	7%	8%	9%	10%	12%	15%
1	0.9901	0.9804	0.9709	0.9615	0.9524	0.9434	0.9346	0.9259	0.9174	0.9091	0.8929	0.8696
2	0.9803	0.9612	0.9426	0.9246	0.9070	0.8900	0.8734	0.8573	0.8417	0.8264	0.7972	0.7561
3	0.9706	0.9423	0.9151	0.8890	0.8638	0.8396	0.8163	0.7938	0.7722	0.7513	0.7118	0.6575
4	0.9610	0.9238	0.8885	0.8548	0.8227	0.7921	0.7629	0.7350	0.7084	0.6830	0.6355	0.5718
5	0.9515	0.9057	0.8626	0.8219	0.7835	0.7473	0.7130	0.6806	0.6499	0.6209	0.5674	0.4972
6	0.9420	0.8880	0.8375	0.7903	0.7462	0.7050	0.6663	0.6302	0.5963	0.5645	0.5066	0.4323
7	0.9327	0.8706	0.8131	0.7599	0.7107	0.6651	0.6227	0.5835	0.5470	0.5132	0.4523	0.3759
8	0.9235	0.8535	0.7894	0.7307	0.6768	0.6274	0.5820	0.5403	0.5019	0.4665	0.4039	0.3269
9	0.9143	0.8368	0.7664	0.7026	0.6446	0.5919	0.5439	0.5002	0.4604	0.4241	0.3606	0.2843
10	0.9053	0.8203	0.7441	0.6756	0.6139	0.5584	0.5083	0.4632	0.4224	0.3855	0.3220	0.2472
11	0.8963	0.8043	0.7224	0.6496	0.5847	0.5268	0.4751	0.4289	0.3875	0.3505	0.2875	0.2149
12	0.8874	0.7885	0.7014	0.6246	0.5568	0.4970	0.4440	0.3971	0.3555	0.3186	0.2567	0.1869
13	0.8787	0.7730	0.6810	0.6006	0.5303	0.4688	0.4150	0.3677	0.3262	0.2897	0.2292	0.1625
14	0.8700	0.7579	0.6611	0.5775	0.5051	0.4423	0.3878	0.3405	0.2992	0.2633	0.2046	0.1413
15	0.8613	0.7430	0.6419	0.5553	0.4810	0.4173	0.3624	0.3152	0.2745	0.2394	0.1827	0.1229
16	0.8528	0.7284	0.6232	0.5339	0.4581	0.3936	0.3387	0.2919	0.2519	0.2176	0.1631	0.1069
17	0.8444	0.7142	0.6050	0.5134	0.4363	0.3714	0.3166	0.2703	0.2311	0.1978	0.1456	0.0929
18	0.8360	0.7002	0.5874	0.4936	0.4155	0.3503	0.2959	0.2502	0.2120	0.1799	0.1300	0.0808
19	0.8277	0.6864	0.5703	0.4746	0.3957	0.3305	0.2765	0.2317	0.1945	0.1635	0.1161	0.0703
20	0.8195	0.6730	0.5537	0.4564	0.3769	0.3118	0.2584	0.2145	0.1784	0.1486	0.1037	0.0611
25	0.7798	0.6095	0.4776	0.3751	0.2953	0.2330	0.1842	0.1460	0.1160	0.0923	0.0588	0.0304
30	0.7419	0.5521	0.4120	0.3083	0.2314	0.1741	0.1314	0.0994	0.0754	0.0573	0.0334	0.0151
35	0.7059	0.5000	0.3554	0.2534	0.1813	0.1301	0.0937	0.0676	0.0490	0.0356	0.0189	0.0075
40	0.6717	0.4529	0.3066	0.2083	0.1420	0.0972	0.0668	0.0460	0.0318	0.0221	0.0107	0.0037

Table II.2

Future Value of 1 Due in *n* Periods

Periods	Rate 1%	2%	3%	4%	5%	6%	7%	8%	9%	10%	12%	15%
0	1.0000	1.0000	1.0000	1.0000	1.0000	1.0000	1.0000	1.0000	1.0000	1.0000	1.0000	1.0000
1	1.0100	1.0200	1.0300	1.0400	1.0500	1.0600	1.0700	1.0800	1.0900	1.1000	1.1200	1.1500
2	1.0201	1.0404	1.0609	1.0816	1.1025	1.1236	1.1449	1.1664	1.1811	1.2100	1.2544	1.3225
3	1.0303	1.0612	1.0927	1.1249	1.1576	1.1910	1.2250	1.2597	1.2950	1.3310	1.4049	1.5209
4	1.0406	1.0824	1.1255	1.1699	1.2155	1.2625	1.3108	1.3605	1.4116	1.4641	1.5735	1.7490
5	1.0510	1.1041	1.1593	1.2167	1.2763	1.3382	1.4026	1.4693	1.5386	1.6105	1.7623	2.0114
6	1.0615	1.1262	1.1941	1.2653	1.3401	1.4185	1.5007	1.5869	1.6771	1.7116	1.9738	2.3131
7	1.0721	1.1487	1.2299	1.3159	1.4071	1.5036	1.6058	1.7138	1.8280	1.9487	2.2107	2.6600
8	1.0829	1.1717	1.2668	1.3686	1.4775	1.5938	1.7182	1.8509	1.9926	2.1436	2.4760	3.0590
9	1.0937	1.1951	1.3048	1.4233	1.5513	1.6895	1.8385	1.9990	2.1719	2.3579	2.7731	3.5179
10	1.1046	1.2190	1.3439	1.4802	1.6289	1.7908	1.9672	2.1589	2.3674	2.5937	3.1058	4.0456
11	1.1157	1.2434	1.3842	1.5395	1.7103	1.8983	2.1049	2.3316	2.5804	2.8531	3.4785	4.6524
12	1.1268	1.2682	1.4258	1.6010	1.7959	2.0122	2.2522	2.5182	2.8127	3.1384	3.8960	5.3503
13	1.1381	1.2936	1.4685	1.6651	1.8856	2.1329	2.4098	2.7196	3.0658	3.4523	4.3635	6.1528
14	1.1495	1.3195	1.5126	1.7317	1.9799	2.2609	2.5785	2.9372	3.3417	3.7975	4.8871	7.0757
15	1.1610	1.3459	1.5580	1.8009	2.0789	2.3966	2.7590	3.1722	3.6425	4.1772	5.4736	8.1371
16	1.1726	1.3728	1.6047	1.8730	2.1829	2.5404	2.9522	3.4259	3.9703	4.5950	6.1304	9.3576
17	1.1843	1.4002	1.6528	1.9479	2.2920	2.6928	3.1588	3.7000	4.3276	5.0545	6.8660	10.7613
18	1.1961	1.4282	1.7024	2.0258	2.4066	2.8543	3.3799	3.9960	4.7171	5.5599	7.6900	12.3755
19	1.2081	1.4568	1.7535	2.1068	2.5270	3.0256	3.6165	4.3157	5.1417	6.1159	8.6128	14.2318
20	1.2202	1.4859	1.8061	2.1911	2.6533	3.2071	3.8697	4.6610	5.6044	6.7275	9.6463	16.3665
25	1.2824	1.6406	2.0938	2.6658	3.3864	4.2919	5.4274	6.8485	8.6231	10.8347	17.0001	32.9190
30	1.3478	1.8114	2.4273	3.2434	4.3219	5.7435	7.6123	10.0627	13.2677	17.4494	29.9599	66.2118
35	1.4166	1.9999	2.8139	3.9461	5.5160	7.6861	10.6766	14.7853	20.4140	28.1024	52.7996	133.176
40	1.4889	2.2080	3.2620	4.8010	7.0400	10.2857	14.9745	21.7245	31.4094	45.2593	93.0510	267.864

Table II.3

Present Value of an Annuity of 1 per Period

	Rate											
Periods	**1%**	**2%**	**3%**	**4%**	**5%**	**6%**	**7%**	**8%**	**9%**	**10%**	**12%**	**15%**
1	0.9901	0.9804	0.9709	0.9615	0.9524	0.9434	0.9346	0.9259	0.9174	0.9091	0.8929	0.8696
2	1.9704	1.9416	1.9135	1.8861	1.8594	1.8334	1.8080	1.7833	1.7591	1.7355	1.6901	1.6257
3	2.9410	2.8839	2.8286	2.7751	2.7232	2.6730	2.6243	2.5771	2.5313	2.4869	2.4018	2.2832
4	3.9020	3.8077	3.7171	3.6299	3.5460	3.4651	3.3872	3.3121	3.2397	3.1699	3.0373	2.8550
5	4.8534	4.7135	4.5797	4.4518	4.3295	4.2124	4.1002	3.9927	3.8897	3.7908	3.6048	3.3522
6	5.7955	5.6014	5.4172	5.2421	5.0757	4.9173	4.7665	4.6229	4.4859	4.3553	4.1114	3.7845
7	6.7282	6.4720	6.2303	6.0021	5.7864	5.5824	5.3893	5.2064	5.0330	4.8684	4.5638	4.1604
8	7.6517	7.3255	7.0197	6.7327	6.4632	6.2098	5.9713	5.7466	5.5348	5.3349	4.9676	4.4873
9	8.5660	8.1622	7.7861	7.4353	7.1078	6.8017	6.5152	6.2469	5.9952	5.7950	5.3282	4.7716
10	9.4713	8.9826	8.5302	8.1109	7.7217	7.3601	7.0236	6.7101	6.4177	6.1446	5.6502	5.0188
11	10.3676	9.7868	9.2526	8.7605	8.3064	7.8869	7.4987	7.1390	6.8052	6.4951	5.9377	5.2337
12	11.2551	10.5753	9.9540	9.3851	8.8633	8.3838	7.9427	7.5361	7.1607	6.8137	6.1944	5.4206
13	12.1337	11.3484	10.6350	9.9856	9.3936	8.8527	8.3577	7.9038	7.4869	7.1034	6.4235	5.5831
14	13.0037	12.1062	11.2961	10.5631	9.8986	9.2950	8.7455	8.2442	7.7862	7.3667	6.6282	5.7245
15	13.8651	12.8493	11.9379	11.1184	10.3797	9.7122	9.1079	8.5595	8.0607	7.6061	6.8109	5.8474
16	14.7179	13.5777	12.5611	11.6523	10.8378	10.1059	9.4466	8.8514	8.3126	7.8237	6.9740	5.9542
17	15.5623	14.2919	13.1661	12.1657	11.2741	10.4773	9.7632	9.1216	8.5436	8.0216	7.1196	6.0472
18	16.3983	14.9920	13.7535	12.6593	11.6896	10.8276	10.0591	9.3719	8.7556	8.2014	7.2497	6.1280
19	17.2260	15.6785	14.3238	13.1339	12.0853	11.1581	10.3356	9.6036	8.9501	8.3649	7.3658	6.1982
20	18.0456	16.3514	14.8775	13.5903	12.4622	11.4699	10.5940	9.8181	9.1285	8.5136	7.4694	6.2593
25	22.0232	19.5235	17.4131	15.6221	14.0939	12.7834	11.6536	10.6748	9.8226	9.0770	7.8431	6.4641
30	25.8077	22.3965	19.6004	17.2920	15.3725	13.7648	12.4090	11.2578	10.2737	9.4269	8.0552	6.5660
35	29.4086	24.9986	21.4872	18.6646	16.3742	14.4982	12.9477	11.6546	10.5668	9.6442	8.1755	6.6166
40	32.8347	27.3555	23.1148	19.7928	17.1591	15.0463	13.3317	11.9246	10.7574	9.7791	8.2438	6.6418

Table II.4

Future Value of an Annuity of 1 per Period

	Rate											
Periods	**1%**	**2%**	**3%**	**4%**	**5%**	**6%**	**7%**	**8%**	**9%**	**10%**	**12%**	**15%**
1	1.0000	1.0000	1.0000	1.0000	1.0000	1.0000	1.0000	1.0000	1.0000	1.0000	1.0000	1.0000
2	2.0100	2.0200	2.0300	2.0400	2.0500	2.0600	2.0700	2.0800	2.0900	2.1000	2.1200	2.1500
3	3.0301	3.0604	3.0909	3.1216	3.1525	3.1836	3.2149	3.2464	3.2781	3.3100	3.3744	3.4725
4	4.0604	4.1216	4.1836	4.2465	4.3101	4.3746	4.4399	4.5061	4.5731	4.6410	4.7793	4.9934
5	5.1010	5.2040	5.3091	5.4163	5.5256	5.6371	5.7507	5.8666	5.9847	6.1051	6.3528	6.7424
6	6.1520	6.3081	6.4684	6.6330	6.8019	6.9753	7.1533	7.3359	7.5233	7.7156	8.1152	8.7537
7	7.2135	7.4343	7.6625	7.8983	8.1420	8.3938	8.6540	8.9228	9.2004	9.4872	10.0890	11.0668
8	8.2857	8.5830	8.8923	9.2142	9.5491	9.8975	10.2598	10.6366	11.0285	11.4359	12.2997	13.7268
9	9.3685	9.7546	10.1591	10.5828	11.0266	11.4913	11.9780	12.4876	13.0210	13.5795	14.7757	16.7858
10	10.4622	10.9497	11.4639	12.0061	12.5779	13.1808	13.8164	14.4866	15.1929	15.9374	17.5487	20.3037
11	11.5668	12.1687	12.8078	13.4864	14.2068	14.9716	15.7835	16.6455	17.5603	18.5312	20.6546	24.3493
12	12.6825	13.4121	14.1920	15.0258	15.9171	16.8699	17.8885	18.9771	20.1407	21.3843	24.1331	29.0017
13	13.8093	14.6803	15.6178	16.6268	17.7130	18.8821	20.1406	21.4953	22.9534	24.5227	28.0291	34.3519
14	14.9474	15.9739	17.0863	18.2919	19.5986	21.0151	22.5505	24.2149	26.0192	27.9750	32.3926	40.5047
15	16.0969	17.2934	18.5989	20.0236	21.5786	23.2760	25.1290	27.1521	29.3609	31.7725	37.2797	47.5804
16	17.2579	18.6393	20.1569	21.8245	23.6575	25.6725	27.8881	30.3243	33.0034	35.9497	42.7533	55.7175
17	18.4304	20.012	21.7616	23.6975	25.8404	28.2129	30.8402	33.7502	36.9737	40.5447	48.8837	65.0751
18	19.6147	21.4123	23.4144	25.6454	28.1324	30.9057	33.9990	37.4502	41.3013	45.5992	55.7497	75.8364
19	20.8109	22.8406	25.1169	27.6712	30.5390	33.7600	37.3790	41.4463	46.0185	41.1591	63.4397	88.2118
20	22.0190	24.2974	26.8704	29.7781	33.0660	36.7856	40.9955	45.7620	51.1601	57.2750	72.0524	102.444
25	28.2432	32.0303	36.4593	41.6459	47.7271	54.8645	63.2490	73.1059	84.7009	98.3471	133.334	212.793
30	34.7849	40.5681	47.5754	56.0849	66.4388	79.0582	94.4608	113.283	136.308	164.494	241.333	434.745
35	41.6603	49.9945	60.4621	73.6522	90.3203	111.435	138.237	172.317	215.711	271.024	431.663	881.170
40	48.8864	60.4020	75.4013	95.0255	120.800	154.762	199.635	259.057	337.882	442.593	767.091	1,779.09

Accounting Concepts and Alternative Valuations

III

APPENDIX

Chapter Outine

Section 1— Accounting Concepts

- **Accounting Concepts and Principles**
- **Descriptive and Prescriptive Concepts**
- **Financial Statement Concepts**
  - Objectives of Financial Reporting
  - Qualities of Useful Information
  - Elements of Financial Statements
  - Recognition and Measurement

Section 2—Alternative Accounting Valuations

- **Historical Cost Accounting and Price Changes**
  - Impact of Price Changes on the Balance Sheet
  - Impact of Price Changes on the Income Statement
- **Valuation Alternatives to Historical Cost**
  - Constant Dollar Accounting
  - Current Cost Accounting
  - Mark to Market Accounting

A Look At This Appendix

This appendix describes accounting concepts, how they are developed, and the conceptual framework in accounting. It also discusses alternative valuations to historical cost accounting.

Learning Objectives

LO 1 Explain both descriptive and prescriptive concepts and their development.

LO 2 Describe the financial statement concepts for accounting.

LO 3 Explain how price changes impact conventional financial statements.

LO 4 Discuss valuation alternatives to historical cost.

APPENDIX PREVIEW

Accounting concepts are not laws of nature. They are broad ideas developed as a way of *describing* current accounting practices and *prescribing* new and improved practices. In this Appendix we explain the accounting concepts the CICA developed in an effort to guide future changes and improvements in accounting. We also discuss alternatives to the historical cost measurements reported in financial statements. Understanding these alternatives helps us with interpreting information in these statements.

SECTION 1 ACCOUNTING CONCEPTS

Accounting Concepts and Principles

LO1 Explain both descriptive and prescriptive concepts and their development.

Accounting *concepts* serve two main purposes. First, they provide descriptions of existing accounting practices. They act as guidelines that help us understand and use accounting information. Knowing how concepts are applied enables us to effectively use accounting information in different situations, and understanding accounting concepts is easier and more useful than memorizing a long list of procedures. Second, accounting concepts are important for the Accounting Standards Board (AcSB), which is charged with developing acceptable practices for financial reporting in Canada and with improving the quality of such reporting.

We defined and illustrated several important accounting *principles* in this book. Several of these major principles are listed in Exhibit III.1. Accounting principles describe in general terms the practices as currently applied.

We first explained these principles in Chapter 2, but we referred to them frequently in the book. The term *concepts* include both these principles as well as other general rules. The AcSB also uses the word *concepts* in this same way.

Exhibit III.1

Partial List of Accounting Principles

- **Business entity principle**
- **Conservatism principle**
- **Consistency principle**
- **Cost principle**
- **Full-disclosure principle**
- **Going-concern principle**
- **Matching principle**
- **Materiality principle**
- **Objectivity principle**
- **Revenue recognition principle**
- **Time period principle**

As business practices evolved in recent years, accounting concepts were sometimes difficult to apply in dealing with new and different types of transactions. This occurs because they are intended as general descriptions of current accounting practices. They do not necessarily describe what should be done. Since concepts do not identify weaknesses in accounting practices, they do not lead to major changes or improvements in accounting practices.

The AcSB, however, is charged with improving financial reporting. It was generally agreed that a new set of concepts needed to be developed for this purpose. They also decided this new set of concepts should not merely *describe* what is being done in current practice. Instead, the new concepts should *prescribe* (or guide) what ought to be done to improve things. Before we describe the concepts developed by the AcSB, we look more closely at the differences between descriptive and prescriptive uses of accounting concepts.

Descriptive and Prescriptive Concepts

Concepts differ in how they are developed and used. Generally, when concepts are intended to describe current practice, they are developed by looking at accepted practices and then making rules to encompass them. This bottom-up, or *descriptive*, approach is shown in Exhibit III.2.

Exhibit III.2

"Bottom-Up" Development of Descriptive Concepts

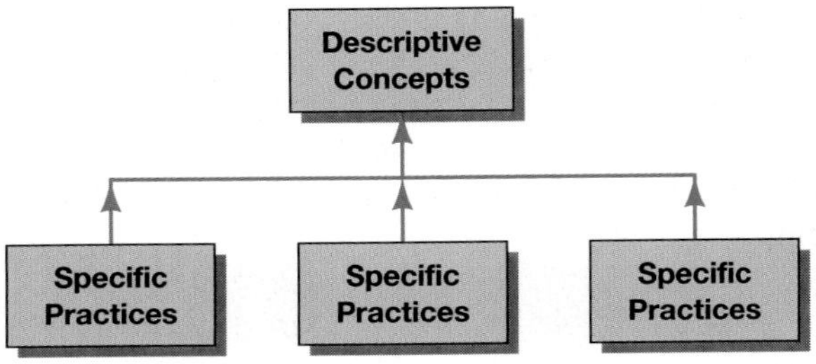

It shows arrows going from specific practices to concepts. The outcome of this process is a set of concepts that summarize practice. This process, for instance, leads us to the concept that asset purchases are recorded at cost.

But these concepts often fail to show how new problems might be solved. For example, the concept that assets are recorded at cost doesn't provide direct guidance for situations where assets have no cost because they are donated to a company by a local government. The bottom-up approach is based on the presumption that current practices are adequate. They don't lead to development of new and improved accounting methods. The concept that assets are initially recorded at cost doesn't encourage asking the question of whether they should always be carried at that amount.

Exhibit III.3

"Top-Down" Development of Prescriptive Concepts

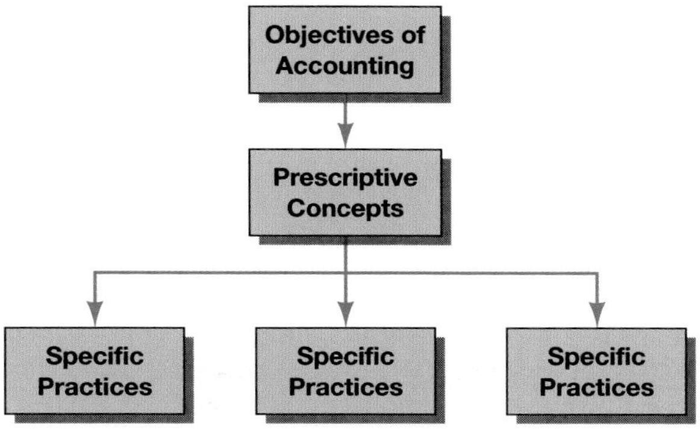

Alternatively, when concepts are intended to *prescribe* (or guide) improvements in accounting practice, they are likely to be designed by a top-down approach as shown in Exhibit III.3.

The top-down approach starts with broad accounting objectives. The process then generates broad concepts about the types of information that should be reported. These concepts lead to specific practices that ought to be used. The advantage of this approach is that these concepts are good for solving new problems and evaluating old answers. Its disadvantage is the concepts may not be very descriptive of current practice. The suggested practices may not even be in current use.

Since the AcSB uses accounting concepts to prescribe accounting practices, the Board used a top-down approach. The Board's concepts are not necessarily more correct than others. But new concepts are intended to provide better guidelines for developing new and improved accounting practices. The AcSB continues to use them as a basis for future actions and already has used them to justify many important changes in financial reporting.

It is crucial in setting accounting standards that the issues be properly identified and described. Section 1000, "Financial Statement Concepts" of the *CICA Handbook* helps the AcSB do this by providing common objectives and terms. Section 1000 also helps the Board focus on the important factors in accounting standard setting and, hopefully, reduces some of the political aspects of policy making.

Flashback

III-1. What is the starting point in a top-down approach to developing accounting concepts?

III-2. What is the starting point in a bottom-up approach to developing accounting concepts?

Answers—p. III-9

Financial Statement Concepts

LO2 Describe the financial statement concepts for accounting.

During the 1970s the accounting profession in both Canada and the United States turned its attention to the apparent need for improvement in financial reporting. In 1980 *Corporate Reporting: Its Future Evolution,* a research study, was published by the Canadian Institute of Chartered Accountants, and in 1989 "Financial Statement Concepts," section 1000 of the *CICA Handbook,* was approved. In the United States the Financial Accounting Standards Board (FASB) published, in the 1978–85 period, six statements regarded as the most comprehensive pronouncement of the conceptual framework of accounting. FASB (SFAC 1) and Accounting Standards Board (*CICA Handbook,* section 1000) identified the broad objectives of financial reporting.

The Financial Accounting Standard Board's approach to developing a conceptual framework is diagrammed in Exhibit III.4. The Board has issued six

Statements of Financial Accounting Concepts (SFAC). These concepts statements are not the same as the FASB's *Statements of Financial Accounting Standards (SFAS)*. The *SFASs* are authoritative statements of generally accepted accounting principles, whereas the *SFACs* are guidelines the Board uses in developing new standards. Accounting professionals are not required to follow the *SFACs* in practice.

Exhibit III.4

Conceptual Framework

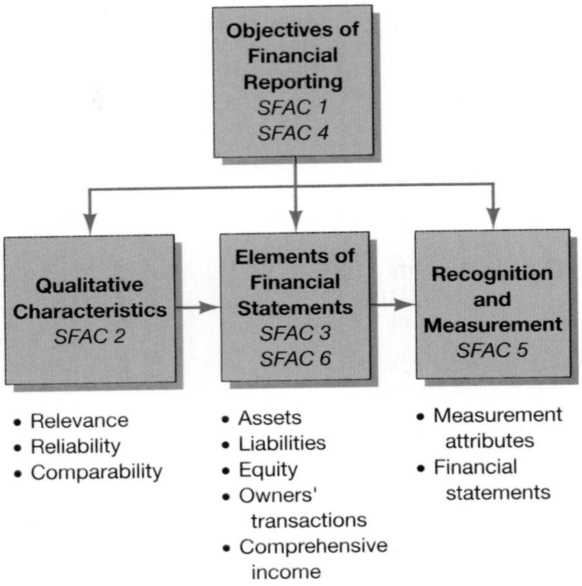

Objectives of Financial Reporting

"Financial Statement Concepts" identified the broad objectives of financial reporting. The most general objective stated in the *CICA Handbook,* par. 1000.12, is to "communicate information that is useful to investors, creditors, and other users in making resource allocation decisions and/or assessing management stewardship." From this beginning point the Accounting Standards Board (AcSB) expressed other, more specific objectives. These objectives recognize that (1) financial reporting should help users predict future cash flow and (2) in making such predictions, information about a company's resources and obligations is useful if it possesses certain qualities. All of the concepts in the "Financial Statement Concepts" are intended to be consistent with these general objectives. Of course, present accounting practice already provides information about a company's resources and obligations. Thus, although the conceptual framework is intended to be prescriptive of new and improved practices, the concepts in the framework are also descriptive of many current practices.

Did You Know?

On-Line Concepts
The CICA has a Web site [www.cica.ca] where we can access exposure drafts and the latest news from the Accounting Standards Board. This site also provides access to many current standards and happenings in accounting.

Qualities of Useful Information

Exhibit III.4 shows the next step in the conceptual framework was to identify the qualities (or qualitative characteristics) that financial information should have if it is to be useful in decision making. The Board discussed the fact that information is useful only if it is understandable to users. But the Board assumed users have the training, experience, and motivation to analyze financial reports. With this decision, the Board indicated financial reporting should not try to meet the needs of unsophisticated or casual users.

In *Section 1000*, the Board stated information is useful if it is (1) relevant, (2) reliable, and (3) comparable. Information is *relevant* if it can make a difference in a decision. Information has this quality when it helps users predict the future or evaluate the past and is received in time to affect their decisions.

Information is *reliable* if users can depend on it to be free from bias and error. Reliable information is verifiable and faithfully represents what is intended to be described. Users can depend on information only if it is neutral. This means the rules used to produce information are not designed to lead users to accept or reject any specific decision.

Information is *comparable* if users can use it to identify differences and similarities between companies. Complete comparability is possible only if companies follow uniform practices. But even if all companies uniformly follow the same practices, comparable reports do not result if the practices are inappropriate. For example, comparable information is not provided if all companies ignored the useful lives of their assets and depreciate them over two years.

Comparability also requires consistency (see Chapter 7). This means a company should not change its accounting practices unless the change is justified as a reporting improvement. Another important concept discussed in *Section 1000* is materiality (see Chapter 10). An item is material if it affects decisions of users. Items not material are often accounted for in the easiest way possible using cost-benefit criteria.

Elements of Financial Statements

Exhibit III.4 shows an important part of the conceptual framework is the elements of financial statements. This includes defining the categories of information that are contained in financial statements. The Board's discussion of financial statement elements included defining important items such as assets, liabilities, equity, revenues, expenses, gains and losses. In earlier chapters, we drew on many of these definitions. Recently, the Board has issued recommendations for not-for-profit accounting entities.[1]

Recognition and Measurement

The Board has established concepts for deciding (1) when items should be presented (or recognized) in financial statements and (2) how to assign numbers to (or measure) those items. The Board generally concluded that items should be recognized in financial statements if they meet the following criteria:

Defined.	Item meets the definition of an element of financial statements.
Measurable.	Has a relevant attribute measurable with sufficient reliability.
Relevant.	Information about it is capable of making a difference in user decisions.
Reliable.	Information is representationally faithful, verifiable, and neutral.

The question of how an item is measured raises a fundamental question of whether financial statements should be based on cost or on current value. The Board's discussion of this issue is more descriptive of current practice than it is prescriptive of new measurement methods.

Paragraph 1000.04 of the *CICA Handbook* states that a full set of financial statements should show:

1. Balance Sheet (financial position at the end of the period.)
2. Income Statement (earnings for the period.)
3. Statement of Retained Earnings
4. Statement of Cash Flows (cash flows during the period.)
5. Notes to financial statements and supporting schedules to which the financial statements are cross-referenced are an integral part of such statements.

[1] *CICA Handbook,* sections 4400ff, "Not-for-Profit Organizations."

Flashback

III-3. The AcSB's financial statement concepts are intended to:
- a. Provide a historical analysis of accounting practice.
- b. Describe current accounting practice.
- c. Provide concepts that are prescriptive of what should be done in accounting practice.

III-4. The notion that accounting practices should be consistent from year to year most directly relates to the AcSB's concept that information reported in financial statements should be (a) relevant, (b) material, (c) reliable, or (d) comparable.

III-5. What characteristics of accounting information make it reliable?

III-6. What do the elements of financial statements refer to?

Answers—p. III-9

SECTION 2 ALTERNATIVE ACCOUNTING VALUATIONS

Historical Cost Accounting and Price Changes

Most agree that conventional (historical cost based) financial statements provide useful information to users. But many also believe conventional financial statements inadequately account for the impact of changing prices. When prices changes, users often look for alternative valuations along with the conventional statements when making decisions.

LO 3 Explain how price changes impact conventional financial statements.

Impact of Price Changes on the Balance Sheet

Conventional financial statements reflect transactions recorded using historical costs. Amounts in statements are usually not adjusted even though subsequent price changes alter their values.[2] As an example, consider Company X who purchases 10 acres of land for $25,000. At the end of each accounting period, Company X reports a balance sheet showing "Land ... $25,000." Several years later, after sharp price increases, Company Y purchases 10 acres of land next to and nearly identical to Company X's land. But Company Y paid $60,000 for its land. Exhibit III.5 shows the conventional balance sheet disclosures for these two companies for the land account.

Exhibit III.5
Conventional Balance Sheet Comparison

	Company X	Company Y
Land	$25,000	$60,000

Absent the details, a user is likely to conclude that either Company Y has more land than Company X or that Company Y's land is more valuable. In reality, both companies own 10 acres that are identical. The difference is due to price changes.

[2] One exception to this is with the reporting of certain investments in debt and equity securities at their market values. We explained this exception in Chapters 10 and 17.

Impact of Price Changes on the Income Statement

The inability of a conventional balance sheet to reflect price changes also shows up in the income statement. As an example, consider two companies that purchase identical machines but at different times. Company A purchases the machine for $10,000 in 1998, while Company Z purchases the machine in 2000 when its price is $18,000. Both machines are depreciated on a straight-line basis over a 10-year period with no salvage value. Exhibit III.6 shows amortization expense in the conventional annual income statements for these two companies.

Exhibit III.6
Conventional Income Statement Comparison

	Company A	Company Z
Amortization expense, machinery	$1,000	$1,800

Although identical assets are being amortized, the income statements show a sharply higher amortization expense for Company Z.

Valuation Alternatives to Historical Cost

LO 4 Discuss valuation alternatives to historical cost.

This section discusses three alternatives to historical cost valuation for financial statements.

Constant Dollar Accounting

One alternative to conventional financial statements is to restate dollar amounts of cost incurred in earlier years for changes in the general price level. This means a specific dollar amount of cost in a previous year is restated as the number of dollars spent if the cost is paid with dollars having the current amount of purchasing power. Restating accounting numbers into dollars of equal purchasing power yields *constant dollar* financial statements. Constant dollar accounting changes the unit of measurement, but it is still based on historical cost.

Current Cost Accounting

All prices do not change at the same rate. When the general price level is rising, some specific prices may be falling. *Current cost* accounting measures financial statement elements at current values. It is not based on historical cost. The result of measuring expenses in current costs is that revenue is matched with current (at the time of the sale) costs of the resources used to earn the revenue. This means operating profit is not positive unless revenues are large enough to replace all of the resources consumed in the process of producing those revenues. Those who argue for current costs believe that operating profit measured in this fashion provides an improved basis for evaluating the effectiveness of operating activities. On the balance sheet, current cost accounting reports assets at amounts needed to purchase them as of the balance sheet date. Liabilities are reported at amounts needed to satisfy the liabilities as of the balance sheet date.

Mark-to-Market Accounting

We can also report assets (and liabilities) at current selling prices. On the balance sheet, this means assets are reported at amounts received if the assets were sold. Liabilities are reported at amounts needed to settle the liabilities. This method of valuation is called the current selling price method or, more commonly, *mark-to-market* accounting.

One argument supporting current selling prices of assets is that the alternative to owning an asset is to sell it. This means the sacrifice a business makes to hold an asset is the amount it would receive if the asset were sold. Also, the benefit derived from holding a liability is the amount the business avoids paying by not settling it. Shareholders' equity in this case represents the net amount of cash from liquidating the company. This net liquidation value is the amount that can be invested in other projects if the company were liquidated. It is a relevant basis for evaluating whether the income the company earns is enough to justify remaining in business.

Some proponents of current selling price believe it should be applied to assets but not liabilities. Others argue it applies equally well to both. Still others believe it should be applied only to assets held for sale. As Chapters 10 and 16 explain, companies use the current selling price approach to value some investments. Investments in trading securities are reported at their fair (market) values, with the related changes in fair values reported on the income statement. Investments in securities available for sale are also reported at their fair values, but the related changes in fair values are not reported on the conventional income statement. Instead, they are reported as part of shareholders' equity.

Summary

LO 1 Explain both descriptive and prescriptive concepts and their development. Descriptive accounting concepts provide general descriptions of current accounting practices and are most useful in learning about accounting. Prescriptive accounting concepts guide us in the practices that should be followed. These prescriptive concepts are most useful in developing accounting procedures for new types of transactions and making improvements in accounting practice. A bottom-up approach to developing concepts begins by examining the practices currently in use. Then, concepts are developed that provide general descriptions of those practices. A top-down approach begins by stating the objectives of accounting. From these objectives, concepts are developed that guide us in identifying the types of accounting practices one should follow.

LO 2 Describe the financial statement concepts for accounting. The CICA's Financial Statement Concepts begins by stating the broad objectives of financial reporting. Next, it identifies the qualitative characteristics accounting information should possess. The elements contained in financial reports are then defined, followed by recognition and measurement criteria.

LO 3 Explain how price changes impact conventional financial statements. Conventional financial statements report transactions in terms of historical dollars received or paid. The statements usually are not adjusted to reflect general price level changes or changes in the specific prices of the items reported. This can impact the statements with items not reflecting current values, which can lead to errors in judgment by users.

LO 4 Discuss valuation alternatives to historical cost. Constant dollar accounting involves multiplying cost by a factor reflecting the change in the general price level since the cost was incurred. Current cost accounting involves reporting on the balance sheet the dollar amounts needed to purchase the assets at the balance sheet date, and on the income statement the amounts needed to acquire operating assets on the date they are used. Mark-to-market accounting involves reporting current selling prices of assets and liabilities.

Guidance Answers to Flashbacks

III-1. A top-down approach to developing accounting concepts begins by identifying appropriate objectives of accounting reports.

III-2. A bottom-up approach to developing accounting concepts starts by examining existing accounting practices and determining the general features that characterize those procedures.

III-3. *c*

III-4. *d*

III-5. To have the qualitative characteristic of being reliable, accounting information should be free from bias and error, should be verifiable, should faithfully represent what is supposed to be described, and should be neutral.

III-6. The elements of financial statements are the objects and events that financial statements should describe; for example, assets, liabilities, revenues, and expenses.

Questions

1. Can a concept be used descriptively and prescriptively?
2. Which three qualitative characteristics of accounting information did the CICA identify as being necessary if the information is to be useful?
3. What is implied by saying that financial information should have the qualitative characteristic of relevance?
4. What are the four criteria an item should satisfy to be recognized in the financial statements?
5. Some people argue that conventional financial statements fail to adequately account for inflation. What general problem with conventional financial statements generates this argument?
6. What is the fundamental difference in the adjustments made under current cost accounting and under historical cost/constant dollar accounting?
7. What are three alternatives to historical cost valuation for financial statements?

Quick Study

QS III-1
Accounting concepts

LO 1, 2

Identify the following statements as true or false:

_____ **1.** Accounting concepts are good examples of laws of nature.
_____ **2.** There are really no viable alternatives to historical cost measurements for financial statement reporting.
_____ **3.** Practices suggested by applying CICA's Financial Statement Concepts must be in current use in practice.
_____ **4.** Accounting professionals are not required to follow the Financial Statement Concepts in practice.
_____ **5.** Only the Financial Statement Concepts describe authoritative generally accepted accounting principles.
_____ **6.** Relevance, as an important quality of financial information, is placed above reliability in the conceptual framework hierarchy.
_____ **7.** When concepts are intended to prescribe improvements in accounting practice, they are likely to be designed by a top-down approach.

QS III-2
Qualities of accounting information

LO 2

Match the desired qualities of financial information to the proper descriptions of the qualities. Use the following codes:

A. Relevant
B. Reliable
C. Comparable

_____ **1.** Timely
_____ **2.** Neutral
_____ **3.** Verifiable
_____ **4.** Requires consistency
_____ **5.** Makes a difference in decision making
_____ **6.** Useful in identifying differences between companies
_____ **7.** Faithful representation
_____ **8.** Free from bias and error
_____ **9.** Predictive

QS III-3
Impact of price changes on the balance sheet

LO 3

Identify *four* accounts from the following list that you feel are most susceptible to changing prices.

a. Accounts receivable
b. Inventories
c. Land
d. Equipment
e. Accounts payable

f. Cash
g. Long-term equity investments
h. Prepaid expenses
i. Income taxes payable

Exercises

Exercise III-1
Review of accounting principles

LO 1

Match the principle to its proper description

Principle

_____ **1.** Business Entity principle
_____ **2.** Going-concern principle
_____ **3.** Objectivity principle
_____ **4.** Revenue recognition principle
_____ **5.** Matching principle
_____ **6.** Time period principle

Decription

A. Requires that financial statement information be supported by something other than someone's opinion or imagination.
B. Requires that revenue be recognized at the same time that it is earned.
C. Assumes that the business will continue operating instead of being closed or sold.
D. Requires expenses to be reported in the same period as the revenues that were earned as the result of the expenses.
E. Requires every business to be accounted for separately and distinctly from its owners.
F. Requires identifying the activities of a business with specific time periods such as quarters or years.

Exercise III-2

LO 1, 2

Write a brief report explaining the difference between descriptive and prescriptive concepts. Indicate why the CICA's Financial Statement Concepts is designed to be prescriptive, and discuss the issue of whether specific concepts can be both descriptive and prescriptive.

Exercise III-3
Mark-to-market valuation

LO 4

Review Alliance's balance sheet in Appendix I. Identify three account balances that would likely change if its balance sheet were prepared on a mark-to-market basis rather than using generally accepted accounting principles.

Exercise III-4
Mark-to-market valuation

LO 4

Assume that your employer has asked you to prepare the company's balance sheet using mark-to-market accounting. You realize that some accounts have valuations that don't differ from the historical cost basis, such as cash, accounts receivable, accounts payable, and prepaid expenses. However, there are four accounts that you need to locate market values for. These accounts are inventory, land, equipment, and temporary investments. Identify possible sources you may need to consult for these market values.

Codes of Professional Conduct

Selections from the ICAO Rules of Professional Conduct[1]

Principles

- A member or student shall conduct himself or herself at all times in a manner which will maintain the good reputation of the profession and its ability to serve the public interest.
- A member or student shall perform his or her professional services with integrity and care and accept an obligation to sustain his or her professional competence by keeping himself or herself informed of, and complying with, developments in professional standards.
- A member who is engaged in an attest function such as an audit or review of financial statements shall hold himself or herself free of any influence, interest or relationship, in respect of his or her client's affairs, which impairs his or her professional judgement or objectivity or which, in the view of a reasonable observer, would impair the member's professional judgement or objectivity.
- A member or student has a duty of confidence in respect of the affairs of any client and shall not disclose, without proper cause, any information obtained in the course of his or her duties, nor shall he or she in any way exploit such information to his or her advantage.
- The development of a member's practice shall be founded upon a reputation for professional excellence. The use of methods of advertising which do not uphold professional good taste, which could be characterized as self-promotion, and which solicit, rather than inform, is not in keeping with this principle.
- A member shall act in relation to any member with the courtesy and consideration due between professional colleagues and which, in turn, he or she would wish to be accorded by the other member.

Standards of Conduct Affecting the Public Interest

201 Maintenance of reputation of profession
202 Integrity and due care
203 Professional competence

[1] ICAO, *Rules of Professional Conduct* (Toronto: Institute of Chartered Accountants of Ontario). Other provincial institutes have similar provisions.

204 Objectivity
205 False or misleading documents and oral representations
206 Compliance with professional standards
207 Informing clients and associates of possible conflicts of interest
208 Unauthorized benefits
209 Improper use of confidential information
210 Confidentiality of information
211 Duty to report breach of rules of professional conduct
212 Handling of trust funds and other property
213 Unlawful activity
214 Fee quotations
215 Contingency fees and services without fees
216 Payment or receipt of commissions
217 General advertising
218 Retention of documentation and working papers

Compliance with the ICAO Rules of Professional Conduct depends primarily on a member's understanding and voluntary actions. However, there are provisions for reinforcement by peers and the public through public opinion, and ultimately by disciplinary proceedings, where necessary. Adherence to the Rules helps ensure individual and collective ethical behaviour by CAs.

Selections from the Code of Professional Ethics for Management Accountants[2]

Introduction

- Professional Ethics is the behaviour of a professional toward peers, other professionals and members of the public. They concern the performance of professional duties in accordance with recognized standards of accounting and professional integrity.
- The codes of professional ethics vary from province to province in certain details in order to comply with provincial legislation and the by-laws of the provincial societies. The following discussion covers the elements common to these codes. Reference should be made to the relevant code of ethics for specific information.
- Every member of the Society is duty bound to uphold and increase the competence and prestige of the accounting profession. In keeping with high standards of ethical conduct, members will conduct their professional work with honesty, impartially, courtesy, and personal honour. Any breach of the principles of professional ethics will constitute discreditable conduct. The offending member will be liable to disciplinary measures the by-laws of the Society consider appropriate.
- A professional approach to resolving a problem of ethics requires that the rules of behaviour establish minimum, not maximum standards. Where the rules are silent, an even greater burden of responsibility falls upon the member to ensure that the course of action followed is consistent with general standards established by the Society.

General

- Members shall, in exercising their professional responsibilities, subordinate personal interest to those of the public, the employer, the Society and the profession.

[2] The Society of Management Accountants of Ontario, *Management Accountants Handbook.* (Toronto: SMAC).

- Any member convicted of any criminal offence or who has been a party to any fraud or improper business practice may be charged with professional misconduct and be required to appear before a Society disciplinary tribunal. If found quilty of such charges by the tribunal, the member may be subject to dismissal from membership in the Society and to forfeiture of the right to use the CMA designation, or to other penalties provided in the by-laws.
- A certificate of conviction in any court in Canada shall be sufficient evidence of a criminal conviction.
- No member shall report any false or misleading fact in a financial statement, or knowingly misrepresent any statement.

Relations with the Public

- Subject to provincial legislation, a Certified Management Accountant may offer services to the public as a management or cost accountant or consultant with the status of proprietor, partner, director, officer, or shareholder of an incorporated company and may associate with non-members for this purpose. A member associated with any company must abide by the rules of professional conduct of the Society. Certified members may use the initials CMA on the letterhead, professional cards or announcement in any public forum of the businesses with which they are associated.
- The right of Certified Management Accountants to sign an audit certificate or perform a review engagement varies from jurisdiction to jurisdiction across Canada. Members of the Society must comply with local legislation.
- No person except a Certified member, shall on letterhead, nameplates, professional cards or announcements claim membership in the Society.
- When practising as a management accountant in preparing or expressing an opinion on financial statements intended to inform the public or management, a member shall disclose all material facts, require all and sufficient information to warrant expression of opinion, and will report all material misstatements or departures from generally accepted accounting principles.
- Improper use by a member of a client's or employer's confidential information or affairs is discreditable conduct.
- The member will treat as confident any information obtained concerning a client's affairs. The member also has a duty to inform the client of any member interest, affiliation or other matter of which the client ought reasonably to be informed, or which might influence the member's judgement.

Relations with Employers

- No member shall use an employer's confidential information or business affairs to acquire any personal interest, property or benefit.
- A member shall treat as confidential any information, or documents concerning the employer's business affairs and shall not disclose or release such information or documents without the consent of the employer, or the order of lawful authority.
- A member shall inform the employer of any business connections, affiliations or interests of which the employer might reasonably expect to be informed.
- No member shall knowingly be a party to any unlawful act of the employer.

Relations with Professional Accountants

- No member shall criticize the professional work of another professional accountant except with the knowledge of that accountant unless the member reviews the work of others as a normal responsibility.
- Members will uphold the principle of appropriate and adequate compensation for work and will endeavour to provide opportunities for professional development and advancement for accountants employed by them or under their supervision.

Chart of Accounts

Assets

Current Assets

101 Cash
102 Petty Cash
103 Cash equivalents
104 Temporary investments
105 Allowance to reduce temporary investments to market
106 Accounts receivable
107 Allowance for doubtful accounts
108 Legal fees receivable
109 Interest receivable
110 Rent receivable
111 Notes receivable
115 Subscription receivable, common shares
116 Subscription receivable, preferred shares
119 Merchandise inventory
120 __________ inventory
121 __________ inventory
124 Office supplies
125 Store supplies
126 ______ supplies
128 Prepaid insurance
129 Prepaid interest
131 Prepaid rent
132 Raw materials inventory
133 Goods in process inventory, ______
134 Goods in process inventory, ______
135 Finished goods inventory

Long-Term Investments

141 Investment in ______ shares
142 Investment in ______ bonds
144 Investment in ______
145 Bond sinking fund

Capital Assets

151 Automobiles
152 Accumulated amortization, automobiles
153 Trucks
154 Accumulated amortization, trucks
155 Boats
156 Accumulated amortization, boats
157 Professional library
158 Accumulated amortization, professional library
159 Law library
160 Accumulated amortization, law library
161 Furniture
162 Accumulated amortization, Furniture
163 Office equipment
164 Accumulated amortization, office equipment
165 Store equipment
166 Accumulated amortization, store equipment
167 ______ equipment
168 Accumulated amortization, ______ equipment
169 Machinery
170 Accumulated amortization, machinery
173 Building ______
174 Accumulated amortization, building ______
175 Building ______
176 Accumulated amortization, building ______
179 Land improvements, ______
180 Accumulated amortization, land improvements ______
181 Land improvements ______
182 Accumulated amortization, land improvements ______
183 Land

Natural Resources

185 Mineral deposit
186 Accumulated depletion, mineral deposit

Intangible Assets

191 Patents
192 Leasehold
193 Franchise
194 Copyright
195 Leasehold improvements
196 Organization costs
197 Deferred income tax debits

Liabilities

Current Liabilities

201 Accounts payable
202 Insurance payable
203 Interest payable
204 Legal fees payable
205 Short-term notes payable
206 Discount on short notes payable
207 Office salaries payable
208 Rent payable
209 Salaries payable
210 Wages payable
211 Accrued payroll payable
214 Estimated warranty liability

215 Income taxes payable
216 Common dividends payable
217 Preferred dividends payable
218 UI payable
219 CPP payable
221 Employees' medical insurance payable
222 Employees' retirement program payable
223 Employees' union dues payable
224 PST payable
225 GST payable
226 Estimated vacation pay liability

Unearned Revenues

230 Unearned consulting fees
231 Unearned legal fees
232 Unearned property management fees
233 Unearned _______ fees
234 Unearned _______
235 Unearned janitorial revenue
236 Unearned _______ revenue
238 Unearned rent _______

Long-Term Liabilities

251 Long-term notes payable
252 Discount on notes payable
253 Long-term lease liability
254 Discount on lease liability
255 Bonds payable
256 Discount on bonds payable
257 Premium on bonds payable
258 Deferred income tax credit

Equity

Owners' Equity

301 _______, capital
302 _______, withdrawals
303 _______, capital
304 _______, withdrawals
305 _______, capital
305 _______, withdrawals

Corporate Contributed Capital

307 Common shares
309 Common shares subscribed
310 Common stock dividends distributable
313 Contributed capital from the retirement of common shares
315 Preferred shares
317 Preferred shares subscribed

Retained Earnings

318 Retained earnings
319 Cash dividends declared
320 Stock dividends declared

Revenues

401 _______ fees earned
402 _______ fees earned
403 _______ services revenue
404 _______ services revenue
405 Commission earned
406 Rent earned
407 Dividends earned
408 Earnings from investment in _______
409 Interest earned
410 Sinking fund earnings
413 Sales
414 Sales returns and allowances
415 Sales discounts

Cost of Sales

501 Amortization of patents
502 Cost of goods sold
503 Depletion of mine deposit
505 Purchases
506 Purchases returns and allowances
507 Purchases discounts
508 Transportation-in

Manufacturing Accounts

520 Raw materials purchases
521 Freight-in on raw materials
530 Factory payroll
531 Direct labour
540 Factory overhead
541 Indirect materials
542 Indirect labour
543 Factory insurance expired
544 Factory supervision
545 Factory supplies used
546 Factory utilities
547 Miscellaneous production costs
548 Property taxes on factory building
550 Rent on factory building
551 Repairs, factory equipment
552 Small tools written off
560 Amortization of factory equipment
561 Amortization of factory building

Standard Cost Variance Accounts

580 Direct material quantity variance
581 Direct material price variance
582 Direct labour quantity variance
583 Direct labour price variance
584 Factory overhead volume variance
585 Factory overhead controllable variance

Expenses

Amortization (Depreciation and Depletion Expenses)

601 Amortization expense, _______
602 Amortization expense, copyrights
603 Depletion expense, _______
604 Amortization expense, boats
605 Amortization expense, automobiles
606 Amortization expense, building _______
607 Amortization expense, building _______
608 Amortization expense, land improvements _______
609 Amortization expense, land improvements _______
610 Amortization expense, law library
611 Amortization expense, trucks
612 Amortization expense, _______ equipment
613 Amortization expense, _______ equipment
614 Amortization expense, _______
615 Amortization expense, _______

Employee Related Expense

620 Office salaries expense
621 Sales salaries expense
622 Salaries expense
623 _______ wages expense
624 Employees' benefits expense
625 Payroll taxes expense

Financial Expenses

630 Cash over and short
631 Discounts lost
633 Interest expense

Insurance Expenses

635 Insurance expense, delivery equipment
636 Insurance expense, office equipment
637 Insurance expense, _______

Rental Expenses

640 Rent expense
641 Rent expense, office space
642 Rent expense, selling space

643 Press rental expense
644 Truck rental expense
645 _______ rental expense

Supplies Expense

650 Office supplies expense
651 Store supplies expense
652 __________ supplies expense
653 __________ supplies expense

Miscellaneous Expenses

655 Advertising expense
656 Bad debts expense
657 Blueprinting expense
658 Boat expense
659 Collection expense
661 Concessions expense
662 Credit card expense
663 Delivery expense
664 Dumping expense
667 Equipment expense
668 Food and drinks expense
669 Gas, oil, and repairs expense
671 Gas and oil expense
672 General and administrative expense
673 Janitorial expense
674 Legal fees expense
676 Mileage expense
677 Miscellaneous expenses
678 Mower and tools expense
679 Operating expenses
681 Permits expense
682 Postage expense
683 Property taxes expense
684 Repairs expense, _______
685 Repairs expense, _______
687 Selling expenses
688 Telephone expense
689 Travel and entertaining expense
690 Utilities expense
691 Warranty expense
695 Income taxes expense

Gains and Losses

701 Gain on retirement of bonds
702 Gain on sale of machinery
703 Gain on sale of temporary investments
704 Gain on sale of trucks
705 Gain on _______
801 Loss on disposal of machinery
802 Loss on exchange of equipment
803 Loss on exchange of _________
804 Loss on market decline of temporary investments
805 Loss on retirement of bonds
806 Loss on sale of investments
807 Loss on sale of Machinery
808 Loss on sale of _________
809 Loss on __________
810 Loss or gain from liquidation

Clearing Accounts

901 Income summary
902 Manufacturing summary

Credits

Chapter 12, page 557, photo © Christopher Bissell/Tony Stone Images

Chapter 13, page 615, photo © Canapress Photo Service (Alexander Zemlianichenco)

Chapter 14, page 661, photo © Dick Hemingway: Photography

Chapter 15, page 693, photo courtesy the Toronto Stock Exchange

Chapter 16, page 731, photo © Dick Hemingway: Photography

Chapter 17, page 779, photo © David Young Wolff/Tony Stone Images

Chapter 18, page 831, photo © Terry Vine/Tony Stone Images

Chapter 19, page 875, photo © Jamieson Laboratories Ltd.

Chapter 20, page 939, photo © Walter Hodges/Tony Stone Images

Index

Abitibi Consolidated, 582
Accelerated amortization, 596
Account analysis, 888
Accounting changes, 746–747
Accounts payable, 618
Accounts receivable turnover, 958–959
Accrued interest expense, 794–795
Accumulated depletion, 582
Acid-test ratio, 958
Adidas, 564
Air Canada, 782, 783
Alcan Aluminium, 560, 617, 842, 843
Alliance Communications Corporation, 588, 700, 705, 944
Amortization, 596
  accelerated, 566–567
  accumulated, 571
  balance sheet, on, 570–571
  change in accounting estimate, 570
  cost, 562
  declining-balance method for, 566–567
  ethics, 572
  installment notes, of, 804
  intangible assets, of, 583–587
  methods, 563–564
  nature of, 562
  partial years, for, 569
  revising rates for, 569–570
  straight-line method for, 564–565
  technology, 569
  units-of-production amortization, 565–566
Analysis, financial statement. See Financial statement analysis
Annuity, 633, **645, 816**
  future value, II–7
  present value, 814–815, II–6
Antidilutive securities, 750
Appropriated retained earnings, 752, **760**
Asset turnover, 957
Atlantis, 942, 967
Authorized shares, 715

Balance sheet
  common-size comparative statements, 949
  comparative financial statements, 945, 946
  expenditures, 572
  stock dividends on, 735–736
Bank borrowing, 620–621
Bank of Montreal, 700, 742
Barrick Gold Corporation, 582, 617
Base amount, 949
Basic earnings per share, 748, **760**
Basket purchase, 561
Bay, The, 661
Bear market, 962
Bearer bonds, 782, **816**
Bell Canada Enterprises, 782
Betterment, 573, **596**
Blue chips, 941
Board of directors, 698
Bombardier, 565, 584, 587, 782, 842
Bond certificate, 783, **816**
Bond indenture, 783
Bond market values, 783
Bond rater, 786
Bonds, 630, **816**
  See also Discounting bonds
  accrued interest expense, 794–795
  advantages in issuing, 780–782
  allocating and amortizing premium, 790–793
  bearer, 782, 816
  book value, 786
  call premium, 797
  callable, 782, 797–798, 816
  carrying value, 786
  certificate, 783
  characteristics of, 781–782
  convertible, 782, 798
  coupon, 782
  disadvantages, 781
  discounted, 786–790
  face amount, 780
  face value, 780
  financial leverage, 780
  floating an issue, 783
  indenture, 783
  interest rates on, 785–786
  issue at par, 784
  issuing, 780, 783–784
  market rate, 785
  maturity date, 780
  mortgage security, as, 806–807
  par value, 780
  premium, 785
  present value, 795, 812–815
  pricing, 795
  quote, 795
  rater, 786
  rating, 784
  redeemable, 782
  registered, 782
  retiring bonds payable, 797–798
  secured, 781
  selling between interest dates, 793–794
  serial, 782
  sinking fund, 782
  sold at premium, 790–793
  term, 782
  transactions, 902, 904–905
  unregistered, 782
  unsecured, 781
  yield, 795
  zero-coupon, 785
Bonnie Piper, 731
Book value, 564, **596**
  bonds, 786
Book value of a share, 710, **715**
Book value per common share, 710, **715**
Book value per preferred share, 710, 715
Brokers, 941
Brunswick Corp., 802
Buildings, 560
Bull market, 962

CAE Electronics, 842
Call premium on bonds, 797
Call price, 708, **715**
Callable bonds, 782, 797–798, **816**
Callable preferred shares, 708, **715**
Canada Business Corporations Act, 696–697, 698, 700–703, 737
  retirement of share capital, on, 739
Canadian Tire, 744, 751, 782, 793, 794, 878
Capital accumulation, corporate, 695
Capital assets, 558–560, **596**
  cash flow and, 588
  cost principle, 559
  costs of, 559–560
  current assets compared to, 559
  discarding, 575–576
  exchanging, 577–579
  inventory compared to, 558
  low costs, with, 574
  nonmonetary exchanges, 579–581
  resource extraction, 583
  salvage value of, 562
  selling, 576–577
  service life of, 563
  transactions, 902
Capital Cost Allowance (CCA), 568, **596**
Capital expenditure, 572, **596**
  revenue and, 572
Capital lease, 637, **645**
Capital stock, 700, **715**
Capital structure, 961
Capitalized earnings, 735
Carrying amount, 786, **816**
Carrying value of bonds, 786
Cash equivalent, 877, 878

Cash flows, 876–880
analysis, 907–909
applying information about, 916–919
importance of, 876–877
sources and uses, 907
statement of, 876
total assets, 908
Cash transactions, 878
cash neutral items, 896–897
changes in current assets and liabilities, 898
changes in noncash items, 884
financing activities, 904
investing items, 901–903
nonoperating items, 897
operating activities and, 878
Changes in accounting estimates, 570, **596,** 753, **760**
amortization, 570
Changes in accounting policy, 760
Chief executive officer (CEO), 698
Chief operating officer (COO), 698
CIBC, 754
CICA Handbook
cash equivalents, 878
cash flow statement, 877
convertible bonds, 798
equity securities with significant influence, 836
financial instruments, 709
income statements items and, 745
investing transactions, 880–881
Classic Winery, 844
Coca-Cola, 574, 587, 942
CompCAN, 744, 746–747, 753
Common shares, 715
transactions, 905
versus bonds, 780
Common Shares Subscribed, 704, **716**
Common-size comparative statements, 949–950, **971**
balance sheet, 949
income statement, 949–950
Common-size statements, 971
Comparative financial statements, 943, **971**
analyzing and comparing, 945–946
balance sheet, 945, 946
income statement, 946
percentage increases and decreases, 944
trend percentages, 947–949
Comparative statements, 971
common-size, 949–950, 971
Complex capital structure, 750, **760**
Compounding interest, 631
periods shorter than one year, for, 634
Consistency principle, 746
Consolidated balance sheet
parent corporation, 851–857
subsidiary, 851–857
Consolidated financial statements, 839, **858**
foreign subsidiaries, with, 844
Consumer Research, 557
Contingent liability, 618–620, **645**
Contract rate, 785, **816**
Contributed capital, 702, **715**
Converse, 564
Convertible bonds, 782, 798, **816**
Convertible preferred shares, 707–708, **715**
Copyright, 585, **596**
Corporate taxes, 625–626, 696
Corporations
accounting, 699
advantages of, 694–696
characteristics of, 694–696
disadvantages of, 696
management of, 698
organization costs, 697
organizing, 696–697
privately held, 694
publicly held, 694
Cost, 559, **596**
amortization, 562
Cost principle, capital assets, 559
Coupon bonds, 782, **816**
Coupon rate, 785
Cumulative preferred shares, 706, **715**
Current assets, 559, 898, 957
compared to capital assets, 559
Current liability, 616, **645,** 898
Current portion of long-term debt, 645
Current ratio, 956–957

Date of declaration, 732, **760**
Date of payment, 732, **760**
Date of record, 732, **760**
Days' sales in inventory, 960
Days' sales uncollected, 959–960
Days' stock on hand, 960
Debentures, 781, 806
subordinated, 782
Debt guarantees, 628
Debt securities, 833–836
Debt/equity ratio, 961–962
Declining-balance amortization, 566–567, **596**
Deferred income tax liability, 645
Deficit, 732, **760**
Depletion, 562, 582, **596**
Depreciation, 562, **596**
Diluted earnings per share, 750, **760**
Dilutive securities, 750
Direct method, 919
Discount, II–2
Discount on bonds payable, 787, **816**
allocating discount, 787
Discount on note payable, 620, **645**
Discount rate, II–2
Discounting bonds, 786–790
allocating/amortizing discount, 787
interest method, 788–789
straight-line allocation, 787–788
Dividend yield, 754–755, **760,** 965
Dividends, 732–734
date of declaration, 732
date of payment, 732
date of record, 732
deficit, 733–734
liquidating, 734
stock, 734–737
Dividends in arrears, 706, **715**
disclosure in financial statements, 707
Dominion Bond Rating Service, 784
Double taxation, 696
Double-declining-balance method, 567
Dun & Bradstreet's, 846n, 940, 942

E-cash, 885
E.B. Eddy Paper, 838
Earnings per share, 748, **760**
complex capital structures, with, 750–751
simple capital structure, with, 748–750
stock splits and stock dividends, with, 749
Eaton's, 661
Effective interest method, 816
Efficiency, 941, 956, **971**
Equipment, 559
Equity method, 837–839, **858**
Equity ratio, 961, **971**
Equity securities, 836
Equity securities with controlling interest, 858
Equity securities with significant influence, 858
Ernst & Young, 663
Estimated liability, 624–627, **645**
Ethics, 572
Extraordinary gain or loss, 745, **760**

Face value of notes, 620–624
Fidelity, 835
Financial leverage, 708, **715,** 961
bonds, 780
Financial reporting, 942, **971**
Financial statement analysis, 971
accounts receivable turnover, 958–959
acid-test ratio, 958
common size, 949–950
comparative statements, 943–946
current ratio, 956–957
days' sales uncollected, 959–960
days' stock on hand, 960
debt/equity ratio, 961–962
dividend yield, 965
elements of, 941
information for, 941–943
merchandise inventory turnover, 959
pledged assets to secured liabilities, 962
price earnings ratio, 964
profit margin, 963
purpose of, 940
report, 966–967
return on common shareholders' equity, 964
return on total assets, 963
standards for comparison, 942–943
table of ratios, 965–966
time fixed interest charges earned, 962
tools of, 943
total asset turnover, 963
trend analysis, 947–949
Financial statements of partnership, 668–669
Financing activities, 879, **919**
full disclosure principle, 880
Fixed assets, 558, **596**
Foreign currency, 842–844
Foreign exchange rate, 842, **858**
Fox (corporation), 838
Free cash flow, 909
Full-disclosure principle
amortization and, 571
contingent liabilities and, 627–628
dividends in arrears and, 707
financing activities, 880
noncash investing, 880
warranties and, 624–625
Fully diluted earnings per share, 750, **760**
Future value, II–2
annuity, II–7
of one, II–5
single amount, of, II–5
table, II–13, II–14

GAAP (generally accepted accounting principles), 709
deferred income tax liabilities, 626–627
tax liabilities and, 625–626
Garner v. Murray, 675
General partner, 664, **679**
General partnership, 664, **679**
General purpose financial statements, 941, **971**
George Weston Limited, 589, 838
Get Real!, 779
Glaxo Canada Inc., 663
Globe and Mail, 701
Going concern principle, 571
Goods and Services Tax (GST), 618–620
contingent, 618–620

Goodwill, 586–587, **596**
Governmental regulation of corporations, 695
Group purchase, 561
Growth shares, 754
Gulfstream Resources, 750

Harley-Davidson, 738
Harmonized sales taxes (HST), 619n
Home Depot, 751
Honda, 587
Horizontal analysis, 943
Hydro Quebec, 790, 794

IBM Canada, 744
Imperial Oil, 563, 566, 701
Improvements, **596**
See also Betterment
Inadequacy, 563, **596**
Income shares, 754
Income statement
accounting changes and, 746–747
common-size comparative statements, 949–950
comparative financial statements, 946
discontinued operations, 744–745
earnings per share on, 755
extraordinary items on, 745
prior period adjustments, 753
Income statement expenditures. *See* Revenue expenditures
Income Tax Act, 568
Index numbers, 947
Indirect method, **919**
Industry Norms and Key Ratios, 846n
Infrequent gain or loss, 745, **760**
Installment notes, 801, **816**
Installment notes payables, 801
accrued interest, with, 802–803
calculating period payments on, 804–805
equal payments, with, 804–805
Intangible assets, 558, 583, **596**
accounting for, 583–584
amortization, 583–587
copyrights, 585
goodwill, 586–587
patents, 584
trademarks/trade names, 587
Intech, 557
Intel, 587
Interest, II–2
Interest method (interest allocation), 788–789, 791–792, **816**
versus interest method, 788–789
Interest-bearing note, 635
International House of Pancakes (IHOP), 624
Inventory, capital assets compared to, 558
Investing activities, 879, 901–903, **919**
Investments. See Long-term investments; Securities

JVT, 837

Known liability, **645**

L.A. Gear, 564
Land, 559, 560
Land improvements, 560, **596**
Largay, James, 877n
Large stock dividend, 735, **760**
Lease, 585, **596**
Leasehold, 585, **596**
Leasehold improvements, 586, **596**
Leasing liabilities, 637–638
Legal claims, potential, 694
Lessee, 585, **596,** 637
Lessor, 585, **596,** 637
Liabilities
accounting for, 619–620
corporate income taxes and, 625–626
current and long-term, 616–617
deferred income tax, 626–627
defining and classifying, 616–617
environmental, 629
estimated, 624–627
Goods and Services Tax, 618–620
known, 618–624
leasing, from, 637–638
legal claims, 628
long-term contingent, 638
long-term, estimated, 638
sales taxes and, 618–620
short-term notes payable, 619–622
uncertainty of, 617–618
Life expectancy, capital asset, 563
Limited liability partnership, **664**
Limited partners, 664, **679**
Limited partnership, 664, **679**
Liquidating cash dividend, 734, **760**
Liquidating dividends, 734, **760**
Liquidity, 941, 956, **971**
Loblaw, 838
Long-term debt, current portion, 638
Long-term investments, 559, 832, **858**
classes of, 832–833
debt securities, in, 833–836
equity method of accounting for, 837–839
equity securities, in, 836
international operations, in, 842–844
reporting, 836
requiring consolidated financial statements, 833–836
securities, in, 833–839
Long-term liability, 617, 630, **645**
Long-term notes, 634–637
Long-term notes payable, 798
interest-bearing, 799
non-interest bearing, 799–800
Long-term risk-capital analysis, 961–962
Lump-sum asset purchase, 561

Machinery and equipment, 561
Maclean's, 637
Magna International Inc., 746, 751, 782, 842
Magnum Skates, 780
Management Discussion and Analysis, 942
Manitoba Telecom Services Inc., 701
Market rate, 785–786, **816**
Market value of shares, 701, 711
Market value per share, 701, **715**
Matching principle
notes payable and, 622
warranties and, 624–625
Materiality principle, 574
disposals and, 574–576
organization costs and, 697
McCain Foods, 842
McDonald's, 661, 909
Merchandise inventory turnover, 959
Microcell Telecommunications Inc., 734
Micron Company, 837
Minority interest, 854, **858**
Molson's, 842
Moody's, 940, 942
Mortgage, 805, **816**
Multinational business, **858**
Multinational corporations, 842
Mutual agency, 663, **679,** 695

National Bank of Canada, 700
National Grocer, 838
Natural resources, 558, 582–583, **596**
Neilsen/Cadbury, 838
Neptune Theatre, 800
Net cash provided (or used) by operating activities
direct method of calculating, 885–886
indirect method of calculating, 886
Net change in cash, 906
Net profit margin, 589n
Net working capital, 956
Netscape, 697
NIKE, 587, 846, 909
No-par shares, 702, **715**
Nominal rate, 785
Noncash current assets, 896–897
Noncash investing and financing, 880–881
Noncumulative preferred shares, 706, **715**
Non-interest-bearing note, 620, 635–637, **645**
Nonmonetary asset exchanges, 579–581
Nonparticipating preferred shares, **715**
Noranda Inc., 706, 754
Notes payable, 622
bonds, versus, 780
long-term, 634–637
mortgage security, as, 806–807
present value, 812–815
short-term, 619–622
Nova Scotia Power, 754
Novicourt, 706

Obsolescence, 563, **596**
Ontario Corporations Act, 737
Operating activities, 878, **919**
Operating efficiency and profitability analysis, 963–964
Operating lease, 637, **645**
Organization costs, 697, **716**
Oshawa Group, 589

Par value, 703, **716**
Par value of a bond, 780, **816**
Parent company, 838, **858**
Parent corporation, 851–857
consolidated balance sheet, 851–857
Participating preferred shares, **716**
Partnerships, 662, **679**
accounting for, 664–668
admission of partner, 669
agreement for, 662, 675, 679
asset investment in, 669–670
assets sold at gain, 673–674
assets sold at loss, 674–675
bonus to new partner, 671
bonus to old partner, 670
change in partners, 669
co-ownership of property, 664
contract, 662, **679**
death of partner, 672–673
division of earnings, 665–667
financial statements for, 668–669
liability of partners, 664
limited life of, 662
liquidation of, 673–675, **679**
mutual agency of, 663
organizing, 665
salaries and interest, 666–667
sale of interest in, 669–670
taxation, 663
unlimited liability, 664
voluntary association and, 662
withdrawal of partner, 671–672

Patent, 584–585, **596**
PepsiCo, 909, 942
Plant and equipment. See Property, plant and equipment
Plant assets, 558
Pledged assets to secured liabilities, 807, **816,** 961, 962
Poison pill, 707
Polyair, 750
Power Corporation of Canada, 707
Preemptive right, 699, **716**
Preferred dividends, 706
Preferred shares, 701, 704–706, **716**
convertible, 707–708
cumulative/noncumulative, 706
dividends, 705
issuing, 705
nonparticipating, 707
participating, 707
reasons for issuing, 708–709
Premium, 785
Premium on bonds payable, 816
Prepaid expenses, 559
Present value, 630–631, **645,** 812–815, II–2
annuities, of, 633–634, 814–815, II–6
bonds, 812–815
discounted bonds and, 786–790
long-term notes and, 634–637
notes payable, 812–815
of one, II–3
tables, 631–633, **645,** 813, II–13, II– 14
Price-earnings ratio, 760, 964
using, 755–756
Principle of conservatism, asset exchanges, 577
Prior period adjustment, 753, **760**
Profit margin, 963
Profitability, 941, 962, **971**
Property, plant and equipment, 558, 582, **596**
Provigo, 750
Provincial sales taxes (PST), 618–620
Proxy, 698, **716**

Quick ratio, 958

Ratio analysis, 943, 955–966
Ratio and statistical analysis. *See also* Financial statement analysis
statement, 965–966
Redeemable bonds, 782, **817**
Redemption value, 708
Reebok, 564, 845, 846
Registered bonds, 782, **817**
Registrar, 700
Relative market values, 561
Rent expense, 585
Repairs, 573, **596**
revenue expenditures, 573
Reporting currency, 842
Residual value, 562, **596**
Restricted retained earnings, 752, **760**
Retained earnings, 702, **716,** 732–734
appropriated, 752
capitalizing, 735
contractual restrictions, 752
restricted, 752
statutory restrictions, 752
transactions, 905–906
Return on common shareholders' equity, 964
Return on total assets, 845–846, **858,** 963
Revenue, capital expenditures and, 572
Revenue expenditure, 572, **596**
repairs, 573
Reverse stock split, 738, **760**
Rogers Communications, 584
Royal Bank, 700, 711, 739
Rules of thumb, 942

Salvage value, 562, **596**
SCFP. See Statement of Changes in Financial Position
Scotia MacLeod, 700
Scrap value, 562, **596**
Second Cup, 587
Secured bonds, 781, **817**
Securities
debt securities held to maturity, 833–836
equity securities, 836
Segment of business, 744, **760**
Semi-Tech Corporation, 570
Serial bonds, 782, **817**
Service life, 563, **596**
Share capital, 700, **716**
See also Shares, corporate
Share capital retirement, 739–742
Shareholders, 694
equity accounts versus partnership accounts, 702
liability of, 694
mutual agency and, 695
rights of, 698
Shareholders' equity, 702, **716**
Shares, corporate, 698–700
authorized shares, 700
classes of, 701
issuance for cash, 702
market value, 701
noncash exchanges of, 703
organization costs, 703
subscription sales, 704
transfers of, 700
value of, 701
Shaw Communications, 744
Shaw Industries Ltd., 738
Short selling, 967
Short-term liabilities, 616
Short-term liquidity analysis, 956–960
Short-term notes payable, 619, **645**
adjusting entries for, 622–624
bank borrowings and, 620–621
extending credit period with, 620
face value of, 620–624
Simple capital structure, 760
Sinking fund bonds, 782, **817**
Small stock dividend, 735, **760**
Solvency, 941, **971**
Sony, 561
Speedy Muffler, 587
St. Laurent Paperboard, 783
Standard & Poor's, 940, 942
Starbucks, 751
Stated rate, 785
Statement of cash flows, 876, **919**
direct method of calculating, 885
direct method of reporting, 888–893
format of, 882
indirect method of calculating, 885–887
preparing, 882–883
spreadsheet, 916–919
Statement of changes in financial position, 877
analyzing cash account and, 883–884
cash/cash equivalents, 877–878
direct method for cash flows, 885–886
indirect method for cash flows, 886
noncash account analysis and, 884–885
preparation of, 82–883
working paper approach to, 916–919
Statement of changes in partners' equity, 668, **679**
Statement of changes in shareholders' equity, 754, **760**
Statement of changes in stockholders' equity, 754
Statement of partners' capital, 668
Stickney, Clyde, 877n
Stock dividend, 734, **760**
balance sheet, on, 735–736
reason for, 735
Stock option, 751, **760**
Stock split, 738, **760**
Stockholders. *See* Shareholders
Straight-line amortization, 564, **596**
Straight-line method (interest allocation), 787–788, 791, **817**
versus interest method, 788–789
Subordinated debentures, 782
Subscription, 704, **716**
Subsidiary, 838, 851, **858**
consolidated balance sheet, 851–857
foreign, 844
Suncor Energy, 563
Suncor Inc., 629

Taco Bell, 799
Taxation
double, 696
partnership, 663
Technology and amortization, 569
Term bonds, 782, **817**
Ticker prices, 943
Tim Hortons, 587
Times interest earned, 638–640, **645,** 962
Toronto Stock Exchange, 700
Total asset turnover, 588–589, **596,** 960, 963
net profit margin, 589n
Total assets, cash flow, 908
Trade name, 587, **596**
Trademark, 587, **596**
Transfer agent, 700
Treasury shares, 739, **760**
purchasing, 740–742
reissuing, 741–742
Trend percentages, 947–949
Trustee, 783

Underwriter, 783
Unearned revenues, 619
Units-of-production amortization, 565–566, **596**
Universal Studios, 838
Unlimited liability of partners, 679
Unregistered bonds, 782
Unsecured bonds, 781, **817**
Unusual gain or loss, 760
Useful life. *See* Service life

Vertical analysis, 943, 949, **971**
Viceroy Home, 754

W.T. Grant Co., 877
Waggonfabrik, 587
Wal-Mart, 577, 909
Warranty, 624, **645**
Washington Post, 835
Wasting assets, 582, **596**
Wendy's, 909
Woolworth, 577
Working capital, 956, **971**

X-Quest, 735

Zehrmart, 838
Zeller's, 661
Zero-coupon bonds, 785